THE GOTHIC REVIVAL

THE VICTORIAN LIBRARY

A HISTORY OF
THE GOTHIC REVIVAL

CHARLES L. EASTLAKE

EDITED WITH AN INTRODUCTION BY
J. MORDAUNT CROOK

LEICESTER UNIVERSITY PRESS
NEW YORK : HUMANITIES PRESS
1978

First published in 1872
Victorian Library edition published in 1970 by
Leicester University Press

Second edition 1978

Distributed in North America by
Humanities Press Inc., New York

Introduction, Appendix, Bibliography and Index
copyright © Leicester University Press

Printed in Great Britain by
Unwin Brothers Limited, Old Woking, Surrey

ISBN 0 7185 5033 1

THE VICTORIAN LIBRARY

There is a growing demand for the classics of Victorian literature in many fields, in history, in literature, in sociology and economics, in the natural sciences. Hitherto this demand has been met, in the main, from the second-hand market. But the prices of second-hand books are rising sharply, and the supply of them is very uncertain. It is the object of this series, THE VICTORIAN LIBRARY, to make some of these classics available again, at a reasonable cost. Since most of the volumes in it are reprinted photographically from the first edition, or another chosen because it has some special value, an accurate text is ensured. Each work carries a substantial introduction, written specially for this series by a well-known authority on the author or his subject, and a bibliographical note on the text.

The volumes necessarily vary in size. In planning the newly-set pages the designer, Arthur Lockwood, has maintained a consistent style for the principal features. The uniform design of binding and jackets provides for ready recognition of the various books in the series when shelved under different subject classifications.

Recommendation of titles for THE VICTORIAN LIBRARY and of scholars to contribute the introductions is made by a joint committee of the Board of the University Press and the Victorian Studies Centre of the University of Leicester.

CONTENTS

ADDITIONAL PLATES

Following page ⟨168⟩

1. C. L. Eastlake: Library book case (1868) (*Hints on Household Taste*, 1872 ed., pl. xi)
2. St John's College, Cambridge: Oriel window in the library (1624) (R. Willis and J. W. Clark, *Cambridge* ii, 1886, p. 269)
3. Sir Christopher Wren: Unexecuted scheme for completing Westminster Abbey (1713) (C. and S. Wren, *Parentalia*, 1750, p. 259)
4. Robert Smythson: Wollaton Hall, Nottinghamshire (1580–88) (J. Britton, *Architectural Antiquities* ii, 1809, p. 109)
5. Roger Morris: Inverary Castle, Argyllshire (begun 1745) (*Vitruvius Scoticus*, 1720–40, pl. 73)
6. Edward Woodward, John Phillips and George Shakespear: Alscot Park, Warwickshire (1750–52; 1762–9) (J. P. Neale, *Seats*, 1st series, iii, 1820)
7. Strawberry Hill: North Front (begun 1749) (*Description of . . . Strawberry Hill*, 1784, p. i)
8. Sanderson Miller: Gothick Ruin, Wimpole, Cambridgeshire (1750) (B. M. King's Top. Colln. viii, 83c, 1777: reproduced by courtesy of the Trustees of the British Museum)
9. Batty Langley: Gothick Chimneypiece (B. and T. Langley, *Gothic Architecture Improved*, 1742, pl. xlviii)
10. William Kent: Court of King's Bench, Westminster Hall (1739) (J. Vardy, *Designs of Inigo Jones and William Kent*, 1744, p. 48)
11. J. H. Muntz: The Gothick Cathedral, Kew (*c.* 1758) (Sir W. Chambers, *Gardens and Buildings at Kew*, 1763, pl. 29)
12. Downton Castle, Herefordshire (1772–8) (Neale, *Seats*, 2nd series, iii, 1826)
13. Robert Adam: Airthrey Castle, Perthshire (1790) (Neale, *Seats*, 1st series, iv, 1821)
14. James Wyatt: Fonthill Abbey, the Octagon (1796–1807) (J. Britton, *Fonthill*, 1823)
15. James Wyatt: Ashridge, Hertfordshire, the Great Hall (1808–17) (Neale, *Seats*, 2nd series, v, 1829)
16. Canterbury Cathedral: "Section of south transept and part of tower; elevation of north transept and part of tower" (J. Britton, *Cathedral Antiquities: Canterbury*, 1821, pl. iv)
17. A. W. Pugin: "The Present Revival of Christian Architecture" (A. W. Pugin, *An Apology for the Revival of Christian Architecture in England*, 1843, frontispiece)
18. William Butterfield: All Saints, Margaret Street, London (1850–59) (*Building News* v, 1859, p. 778)

19. William Burges: The Sabrina Fountain, Gloucester; unexecuted design (1858) (*Builder* xvi, 1858, 375)
20. William Burges: Warehouse, Upper Thames Street, London (1866) (*Builder* xxiv, 1866, 851)
21. Philip Webb: Houses and shops, 91–101 Worship Street, Finsbury, London (1862–3) (*Builder* xxi, 1863, 620)
22. Thomas Harris: Terrace at Harrow, Middlesex, in 'the Victorian style' (1860–61) (*Builder* xviii, 1860, 673)
23. S. S. Teulon: Elvetham Hall, Hampshire (1859–60) (*Building News* vi, 1860, 419)
24. E. Buckton Lamb: St Martin, Vicars Road, St Pancras, London (1866) (*Builder* xxiv, 1866, 779)
25. Sir T. N. Deane and B. Woodward: The Oxford Museum (1855–68) (*Building News* vi, 1860, 271)
26. Alfred Waterhouse: Manchester Town Hall (1868–77) (*Building News* xv, 1868, 315)

EDITOR'S FOREWORD

This volume was prepared for the press during the summer of 1968. Its purpose is twofold: to "bring Eastlake up to date" in the light of recent research; and to present the results in a way suitable for university teaching. The original edition has long been a collector's trophy. But with no index, few illustrations, and fewer references, it was a quarry rather than a guide to two centuries of architectural history. In a way it was both indispensable and unusable. This new edition has been designed primarily as a work of reference. The main body of Eastlake's text has been photographically reproduced; the limits of his appendix have been retained but its content has been wholly recast, incorporating corrections and references; a comprehensive bibliography and index have been inserted, together with twenty-six extra illustrations; and a new introduction has been added, giving details of Eastlake's career and summarizing the findings of recent research into the origins of the Gothic Revival in this country. My own educational experience of the Gothic Revival has been mostly indirect: a Vanbrughian kindergarten, a school by S. S. Teulon and an Oxford college by "Anglo" Jackson. My general debt to the man who belatedly taught me architectural history, Mr Howard Colvin, is therefore proportionately greater. As regards this particular project, I am grateful to Professor Jack Simmons for first talking over the idea during a memorable train journey to York; to my colleagues at Bedford College, London, for tangible encouragement in the shape of a sabbatical term; to Mr Roger Dixon, Mr John Harris, Mr Clive Wainwright, Mr Peter Howell and Mr David Walker, for many helpful suggestions; to Dr Alastair Rowan, who generously allowed me to use material from his Cambridge thesis on the Castle Style; to Mr Charles Handley-Read, who lavishly placed his learning – and his library – at my disposal; and to my wife for magically turning manuscript into typescript.   J.M.C.

A textbook is only as good as its latest edition. Ten years after preparation, this revised edition of Eastlake's classic work had itself become ripe for revision. Editor and publisher were faced with the old problem of fitting new material into a fixed typographical format. I am indeed grateful to Leicester University Press for allowing me to include so many alterations and additions: the bibliography, in particular, has been expanded almost to the point of reconstruction. A further study of the movement is now in progress.

J.M.C., 1978

INTRODUCTION

I Eastlake's *Gothic Revival*

Eastlake's *Gothic Revival* was finished late in 1870 and published early in 1872, at the zenith of the revivalist movement. It was an appropriate moment. The scaffolding had just been removed from the Albert Memorial, and its architect, George Gilbert Scott, was about to be knighted by the Queen at Osborne. The new hotel at St Pancras Station was almost ready to receive its first visitors, and G. E. Street's monumental Law Courts were slowly rising to completion in the Strand. But there were already signs of change. Architects and laymen alike had begun to question the whole revivalist ethic. Critics like James Fergusson and J. T. Emmett were attacking the very basis of the architectural profession. Pugin's gospel of structural "truth" had at last been separated from his religious obsessions, and Ruskin and Morris were already looking beyond the paraphernalia of medievalism towards the vision of a new society. The search for a new style — a recurrent nightmare for nineteenth-century architects — had entered a critical phase. Webb, Nesfield, Stephenson, Shaw, Robson and Champneys had begun to experiment with vernacular Renaissance forms. The "Queen Anne style" — that "vexatious disturber of the Gothic movement", as Scott called it — had arrived.[1] The Arts and Crafts phase, child of the Gothic Revival and ancestor of the Modern Movement, had already been born. It was a time for Gothic revivalists to take stock of their position, time to look back over the progress of the movement, time to evaluate its achievements, time to debate its future.

As a standard textbook on Victorian Gothic Eastlake has never been superseded, and never reprinted. When it first appeared the *Builder* was only mildly enthusiastic. The woodcuts by Orlando Jewitt were praised.[2] But the book's style was dismissed as "digressive and recapitulatory". Its judgments were said to be warped by the author's friendship with a number of architects discussed. And its lack of comprehension seemed to be underlined by the cursory treatment meted out to stone-carvers, smiths and other subsidiary craftsmen. At best, it was "smart and written with understanding".[3] The *Athenaeum* was kinder, emphasizing its range and factual content.[4] *The Times* reviewed it in time for Christmas

Notes are placed at the end of sections I and II.

1871 and named it "among the gift books of the season".[5] On one point, however, all the reviewers agreed: Eastlake's *Gothic Revival* was beautifully timed. The year 1870 has become a traditional watershed in the minds of architectural historians. The *Builder* called the new volume "a book of today for today". Yet it has turned out to be much more than an ephemeral manifesto. Nearly one hundred years later the current revival of interest in Victorian studies makes its republication particularly desirable. The author's approach was fundamentally archaeological. He set out to provide a detailed record of "one of the most remarkable revolutions in national art that this country has seen". He was determined "to chronicle facts rather than offer criticisms".[6] In a voluminous appendix he supplied details of no less than 343 neo-Gothic buildings erected between 1820 and 1870. In the main body of the text he dealt at length with the work of every major Gothicist from Walpole to Waterhouse. It was this factual approach which guaranteed the book's permanent validity as a work of reference. At the same time Eastlake's study merits reprinting as a barometer of contemporary taste, an aesthetic period piece.

Of course there were errors and omissions. This new edition sets out to correct a number of them. Eastlake was no historian, and his sections on sixteenth-, seventeenth- and eighteenth-century medievalism are undoubtedly thin. It is here that modern scholarship has most to add to his conclusions. So much so that the bulk of this introduction has had to be devoted to the earlier phases of the revivalist movement. Eastlake was however a first-class journalist. His judgments on contemporary architects have worn astonishingly well. The chief weakness in his treatment of Victorian Gothic lay in its lack of documentation. In this edition his appendix of selected examples has therefore been expanded to include references to primary and secondary sources, mostly contemporary journals and recent surveys. Eastlake's methods of collecting evidence were business-like rather than scholarly. He relied very largely on information supplied by correspondents in the form of answers prompted by a printed questionnaire. The result was an irritating number of minor errors. Questionnaires had been frequently used as a supplement to personal investigation by topographers such as Lysons, Britton and Lewis. But when an architect like Philip Webb refused to make a satisfactory reply Eastlake was faced with a serious gap in both interpretation and documentation. Webb considered that his work lay outside the main-stream of the Gothic Revival.[7] In fact Red House (1859) was merely a logical development from the domestic work of A. W. Pugin and William Butterfield. As such it obviously cries out for inclusion. And where are the works of Edward Buckton Lamb? It is doubtful whether Eastlake ever despatched a questionnaire to Lamb. He disapproved of architectural eccentricity. S. S. Teulon appears less frequently than orthodox Goths like John Norton and Joseph Clarke. Both Clarke and Norton would seem to have filled in their questionnaires with some diligence. Eastlake's coverage is certainly uneven. The exotic medievalism of William Burges [plates 19, 20], for example, is less than adequately represented. Eastlake himself belonged to a later generation than R. C. Carpenter, Benjamin Ferrey and the founders of the *Ecclesiologist*. For him ecclesiology was not enough. Some of the most effective sections of his book therefore concern the Eclectic phase of the 1850s and 1860s, the application of Gothic to a multitude of secular purposes and the various attempts to break free from the tyranny of Decorated or Second Pointed. Yet he implicitly condemned all Goodhart-Rendel's "Rogue Architects" – men like S. S. Teulon, E. Buckton Lamb, E. Bassett Keeling, George Truefitt and Thomas ("Victorian") Harris. He presumably regarded their bold eclecticism as showmanship rather than revivalism. Yet even Scott admitted that the architecture of his roguish rivals, for all its occasional absurdity, included "much of the best, the most nervous, and the most original results of the revival".[8] It therefore seemed sensible to soften this particular bias by including among the illustrations a few examples of High Victorian "GO" [plates 22, 23, 24]; and by way of contrast to these architectural "acrobatics", to include an early example of the work of Philip Webb [plate 21]. It has not been possible, however, except in the bibliography, to expand the chronological limits of Eastlake's work. That would require a different sort of volume altogether. This new edition sets out to remedy Eastlake's deficiencies, not to re-write the history of the Gothic Revival.

In tackling the story of the Gothic Revival Eastlake made one fundamental mistake: he treated the movement as a continuous process. His critical apparatus was rather naïvely progressive. Had he been a political or constitutional historian he would by now have been labelled "Whig". In his eyes the early products of revivalism were significant only in so far as they led to something later and better. His book was therefore not only biased, it was unbalanced. Naturally enough time has had its revenge, and the architecture of Eastlake's contemporaries has in its turn been subjected to the same process of distortion. Some people still seem to regard certain aspects of Victorian architecture as no more than tiresome prolegomena to the Modern Movement. The microscope is a safer instrument for historians than the telescope. By splitting up the Gothic Revival into a series of phases we lose something of the movement's sense of purpose. But we gain a great deal in objectivity. The main body of the movement can be conveniently divided into four periods: the Rococo, the Picturesque, the Ecclesiological and the Eclectic. Of course all four phases overlap, but their most characteristic products are readily distinguishable. Provided we mentally add on at either end a prologue on Gothic Survival and Gothick Revival and an epilogue on the Arts and Crafts movement, the overall picture is reasonably clear. Eastlake would himself have recognized only two of these categories. "Rococo", as applied to neo-Gothic, is a posthumous label; and although he uses "picturesque" often enough, he seems to have avoided "Picturesque" as a generalized visual category. With the Ecclesiological and the Eclectic he was of course only too familiar. Both are fully treated in the main body of the text and amply documented in the revised version of the appendix. Introductory comment has therefore been largely limited to the earlier stages of the movement, the origins of the Gothic Revival.

Since the appearance of Eastlake's work only one general study has approached it in importance, Sir Kenneth Clark's *Gothic Revival* (1928). That pioneering essay reopened the whole subject of English Gothic revivalism, its premises and achievements. But a number of questions surrounding the movement still remain unanswered. B. F. L. Clarke's *Church Builders of the Nineteenth Century* (1938) is a storehouse of information rather than a reassessment of nineteenth-century Gothicism. The late H. S. Goodhart-Rendel never produced that reinterpretation of Victorian architecture which he was so well qualified to write. Instead we have his *English Architecture Since the Regency* (1953) plus a selection of *obiter dicta* scattered among the back numbers of periodicals and treasured in the memories of his friends. As late as 1963, Sir Nikolaus Pevsner could remark: "there are no twentieth-century biographies of Barry, of Scott, of Street, of Butterfield, of Burges, of Brooks, of Bodley, of Pearson. It is a disgrace".[9] Now at last the biographies are beginning to be written. Books on five of those eight giants are in active preparation. Soon we may even have a satisfactory biography of A. W. Pugin. Popular interest in Victorian architecture increases daily, an interest nourished by the enthusiasm of Sir John Betjeman and sustained by the energy of the Victorian Society. And the recent expansion of art history teaching in universities augurs well for the future of eighteenth- and nineteenth-century architectural history in this country. Meanwhile our debt to two transatlantic scholars is immense. The late Paul Frankl's *Gothic* (1960) synthesizes a huge quantity of bibliographical material relating to international revivalism; and Professor Henry-Russell Hitchcock's *Early Victorian Architecture* (1954) and *Architecture: 19th and 20th Centuries* (1958) constitute a massive contribution to our understanding of the movement's international significance. When Sir Kenneth Clark republished his *Gothic Revival* in 1949 he urged that the history of the movement should be re-written, "neither apologetically nor defiantly, neither ironically nor ecstatically, but in a true critical spirit".[10] A few years from now such a history may well be possible for the first time.

I   Notes

1. G. G. Scott, *Recollections* (1879), p. 372.
2. For his career cf. *Builder*, xxvii (1869), 461; H. Carter, *Orlando Jewitt* (1962).

3. *Builder*, xxx (1872), 4.
4. *Athenaeum*, 2 March 1872, 277–8. See also *Dublin Rev.* xviii [lxx] (1872), 440–51.
5. *The Times*, 19 Dec. 1871, p. 4. See also *Notes and Queries*, viii (1871), 493.
6. See below, p. iii.
7. J. Brandon-Jones, "Letters of Philip Webb and his Contemporaries", *Architectural History*, viii (1965), 65–6, 72
8. Scott, *Recollections*, p. 211.
9. N. Pevsner, "Victorian Prolegomena", in *Victorian Architecture* (ed. P. Ferriday, 1963), p. 21.
10. Sir K. Clark, *Gothic Revival* (1964 ed.), p. xvii. The problem of objectivity was recognised by E. W. Godwin when Eastlake's work first appeared. In an important review he concluded that, as regards his contemporaries, Eastlake had been so discreet as to be almost panglossian. As a result, "the *History* of the Gothic Revival has yet to be written" (*The Architect*, vi, 1871, 271–3).

II Eastlake's Career

Charles Locke Eastlake came from a talented and artistic family. He was born on 11 March 1836 at Plymouth, the son of George Eastlake, Admiralty Law Agent and Deputy Judge Advocate to the Fleet.[1] His uncle Sir Charles Lock Eastlake P.R.A. (1793–1865) took a personal interest in the boy's education. Indeed he virtually adopted his young namesake, placing him at Westminster School and coaching him each weekend at his house in Fitzroy Square. "Every Saturday till Monday", recalled Lady Eastlake, "the little fellow was welcomed by the kind uncle, who laid aside his cares and work, and devoted himself to . . . the juvenile student". With no children of his own, the great artist found the company of "this unsophisticated little fellow" like "a beam of sunshine".[2] Like his uncle, young Eastlake began as an architect, then turned to painting, and finally ended up as an administrator. After training first under Philip Hardwick R.A. and then at the Royal Academy Schools, he turned from architectural drawing to watercolour, and after marrying in 1856 he travelled abroad sketching in France, Italy and Germany.[3] Eastlake "never really entered into practice as an architect, or carried out any building".[4] He won the R.A. silver medal for architectural drawing in 1854, and during the next two years exhibited several designs. In 1855 he offered a "Design for a Renaissance Palace".[5] In 1856 he exhibited a drawing of Gothic street houses which the *Ecclesiologist* dismissed for "Puginic mannerism".[6] In the same year he submitted a "Design for a Proposed Town Hall at Rugby": the *Builder* merely commented on its lack of drain pipes.[7] For several years after this Eastlake fell back on freelance journalism. During his career he contributed to a variety of journals, including the *Nineteenth Century*, the *London Review*, *Punch* (as "Roving Correspondent"), *Fraser's Magazine*, the *Cornhill*, the *Queen* and the *Building News*. As a young man he "used to sit up half the night writing for the press".[8] In 1861 he almost secured the Curatorship of Sir John Soane's Museum: two of the Trustees resigned when both he and Wyatt Papworth were defeated by Joseph Bonomi.[9] Five years later he at last landed his first administrative job, the Assistant Secretaryship of the Institute of British Architects.[10]

Eastlake took up his post at a time when the future R.I.B.A. was torn from top to bottom by the Battle of the Styles.[11] Goths and Classics were leagued against each other at every level, and Eastlake's appointment turned out to be something of a triumph for the Gothic party. His position as paid assistant to a council of unpaid amateurs was a ticklish one. His promotion in 1871 from the post of Assistant Secretary to that of the R.I.B.A.'s first permanent, salaried Secretary was secured only by riding roughshod over the feelings of that much-respected classicist, ex-President T. L. Donaldson.[12] A year later came the *History of the Gothic Revival*. But Eastlake's Secretaryship was marred by administrative friction as well as stylistic disputes. He seems to have been a smooth committee man, with an administrator's partiality for the *status quo*. His "industry, skill and courtesy" were not appreciated by dissident members who saw him as an obstacle to reform. One letter to the *Builder* was even headed: "Who puts the drag on the Institute?"[13] Still, he was certainly punctilious. When he resigned in February 1878 to take up the Keepership of the National Gallery, it was remembered to his credit that in all eleven years he had never missed a meeting.[14]

Before he left the R.I.B.A., Eastlake had published and thrice reprinted a book which in fact achieved far greater celebrity than his *Gothic Revival*. *Hints on Household Taste in Furniture, Upholstery and other Details* first appeared in 1868. Its effect in England was considerable. Its impact in America was dramatic: the author's name "became almost a household word, and a house furnished in improved taste was said to be 'Eastlaked' ".[15] Eastlake's "improved taste" in furniture design is best considered as part of that decorative revolution traditionally associated with the names of William Morris, Philip Webb, Eden Nesfield and Norman Shaw. During the 1860s a new furniture style evolved, ponderous, semi-Gothic and rectilinear, in contrast to the florid curves of the early Victorian period. Reacting against the decorative excesses of the 1851 exhibits, it rejected "shaped" forms, walnut veneers and buxom padding in favour of simplicity, rectangularity and honest craftsmanship. Decoration was limited to surface ornament: painted panels, tiles, inlaid wood, embossed leather, chased metal or embroidery. Eastlake's *Hints* helped to popularize that chunky, simplified carpentry first tried out by A. W. Pugin during the 1840s in reaction to his own spiky Gothickry of the previous decade.[16] In Eastlake's hands, Jacobethan forms were simplified almost to the point of "farmhouse revival". *Hints on Household Taste* contained little in the way of novelty. The flat, formal regularity of Eastlake's wallpapers, carpets and encaustic tiles, owed much to Owen Jones's *Grammar of Ornament* (1856). His square-cut furniture [plate 1] merely simplified for a popular market those *Gothic Forms* which Bruce Talbert had dedicated to G. E. Street in 1867. The *Hints* were indeed well timed: the market had already been tested by Robert Charles in the *Cabinet Maker* (1868) and, more significantly, by Messrs Gillow & Co. Only upholsterers disapproved. "If any 'upholsterer' murders Mr. Eastlake", wrote the *Athenaeum*, "he will die a martyr for Art".[17]

Eastlake's furniture set out to combine "a sense of the picturesque . . . with modern comfort and convenience", by adopting not "the absolute forms" but "the spirit and principles of early manufacture".[18] Compared with Viollet-le-Duc's exotic medieval furnishings, Eastlake's "Spartan designs" had all the familiarity of a trade circular.[19] His own house in London was stacked with furniture built to his own designs: "a velvet covered settle . . . copied from one in the long gallery at Knowle"; an oak hall table "with mouldings and incised carved work of a 16th century pattern"; a shelved sideboard laden with blue and white china, which unkind friends "compared to a kitchen dresser"; and a "substantial oaken settle", combining "modern comfort with the spirit of the 15th century", which in turn "reminded . . . critics . . . of a second class railway carriage". During the thirty years between the 1860s and 1890s Eastlake furniture became first fashionable, then commonplace. Some of his designs for dressers, wallpapers, curtains and wrought-ironwork sold only too well. By 1895 he could look back with some complacency on the changes he had helped to bring about since the 1850s, that "terrible time . . . when . . . our homes [were] at the mercy of the upholsterer. . . . Young housekeepers of the present age who sit in picturesque chimney corners, sipping tea out of Oriental china, or lounge on 17th century settles, in a parquetry-floored room filled with inlaid cabinets, Cromwell chairs, picturesque sideboards, hanging shelves and bookcases, can form no idea of the heavy and graceless objects with which an English house was filled some twenty years ago – the sprawling sofas, the gouty-legged dining tables, cut-glass chandeliers, lumbering ottomans, funereal buffets, horticultural carpets and zoological hearthrugs. Heaven save us from a return to that phase of ugly conventionalism, of life-less ornament, of dull propriety and inartistic gloom!"[20]

Eastlake's status as an interior designer proved to be ephemeral. True, we no longer regard his geometrical tiles, his Turkey carpets and square-cut oaken forms as pieces of calculated "hideousness".[21] But his austerely "picturesque" parlours seem today neither more nor less palatable, in their own way, than the padded drawing-rooms they replaced. Few "Eastlake" interiors remain unaltered. One fine example, at 18 Stafford Terrace, Kensington, illustrates the development of a richer version of the style during the 1870s, between Eastlake's *Hints* (1868) and R. W. Edis's *Decoration and Furniture of Town Houses* (1881). In the long run Eastlake's enthusiasm for overmantels, dressers, beaten metal and old china has made him the ancestor of countless suburban caricatures. Yet his prolific designs – from buckets to candlesticks, from bedsteads to decanters – did much to encourage a healthy reaction towards domestic simplicity and honest craftsmanship during the 1860s and 1870s. By catering for a mass market and yet refusing to dilute the puritanism of his aesthetic premises, he managed to work "a silent revolution in many a home in which he was never heard of".[22] Interior decoration and industrial design were the only aspects of his career for which Eastlake obtained popular recognition. His achievements as an administrator were less happily rewarded.

Eastlake's career as Keeper and Secretary of the National Gallery is a tale of disappointment and intrigue. Disappointment in his failure to obtain the coveted Directorship; intrigue in the persons of that formidable pair, his aunt Lady Eastlake and Sir Henry Layard the senior trustee. Scholar and *grande dame*, confidante and bluestocking, Elizabeth Rigby married Sir Charles Eastlake late in life after establishing an independent reputation as an art critic.[23] After the death of her "oracle" in 1865 she continued to press for the preferment of their favourite nephew. One of her closest contacts was her husband's old friend, Layard of Nineveh (1817–94).[24] And in the correspondence of that ageing *enfant terrible* – archaeologist, adventurer, politician, diplomat and man of action – we can trace the full story of young Eastlake's protracted frustration. In 1865 Lord John Russell almost appointed Layard to the Directorship in succession to Sir Charles Eastlake. Instead he made Layard a trustee and chose as Director a fashionable portrait painter, the future Sir William Boxall, R.A. (1800–79).[25] Boxall was already on the verge of retirement, and within a few years his old friend Frederick Burton was ready to take over. Backed by Richmond and G. F. Watts, Burton formally accepted Gladstone's offer early in 1874.[26] Four years later Disraeli appointed Eastlake as second-in-command, and the long-drawn intrigue began in earnest.

In 1868 Layard had received the R.I.B.A. Gold Medal. But in a letter to Lady Eastlake his reaction to the arrival of the Institute's ex-Secretary was characteristically astringent: "it is pleasant . . . to see the [Eastlake] name connected with the National Gallery: he is a good man of business, and he cannot but have hereditary taste. Has he any knowledge of pictures?"[27] He had, of course, but it was the random learning of a dilettante, not the professionalism of a connoisseur. Eastlake's extensive knowledge of Continental galleries was accumulated after his appointment rather than before.[28] Still, he worked laboriously at the reorganization, classification and publication of the National Gallery collections, and his efforts in this respect deserve to be better remembered. Unfortunately much of his work was obscured by a series of personal squabbles between Keeper and Director. Sir Frederick Burton (1816–1900) was "a thorough Irishman", a proud and reticent bachelor, a sensitive watercolourist who abandoned painting altogether after his succession to the Directorship. Layard was one of his very few friends. As Burton declined into senility, Eastlake waited with impatience. His uncle, "the Berenson of his day", had transformed the National Gallery "from a bad joke into one of the great treasure-houses of Europe".[29] Under

Boxall and Burton the collection continued to expand. "But it is useless to deny that Burton had his deficiencies. He was already 58 when he was appointed; he was never physically strong; and he would sooner lose a picture than depart from his established times, seasons and methods. . . . Again [he] was not a good valuer. . . . It is not surprising that the Treasury took fright" and cut down the gallery's allocation.[30] Layard thought the Eastlakes "somewhat hard upon Sir Frederick. With all his faults he is better fitted than any man I know for the post he occupies from his knowledge of art, and his taste". But Layard had to agree that what the gallery needed was "a little 'go' . . . the Trustees . . . are . . . a set of effete and useless old gentlemen".[31] Unlike his predecessor in the Keepership, R. N. Wornum, Eastlake tried hard to popularize the gallery and its facilities. Burton remained aloof. When Eastlake dared to answer criticisms of the gallery in *The Times*, all he received was a snub from the Director. "Like all permanent secretaries everywhere", wrote Burton to Layard, "Eastlake is inclined to take too much on himself".[32]

As an administrator rather than an artist, Eastlake's best hope of promotion lay in the possibility of reorganization. While Burton hovered on the brink of retirement, Lady Eastlake therefore pressed for the union of Keepership and Directorship in one man. Layard was not persuaded. During the 1880s and early 1890s, from Venice or Constantinople, he conducted a devious campaign on four fronts. To Lady Eastlake he returned a series of evasive answers.[33] To Eastlake's pleas for formal recognition he was polite but deaf.[34] With Sir Frederick Burton he continued to exchange letters which tactfully avoided all mention of retirement.[35] But by the summer of 1892 he had in fact already chosen his nominee, the future Sir Edward Poynter, P.R.A. (1836–1919), the art world's leading educationalist and a masterly painter of overblown historical scenes.[36] Son of the architect Ambrose Poynter, E. J. Poynter had known Layard well since the 1860s.[37] In the 1880s they were both involved with the Society for the Preservation of the Monuments of Ancient Egypt.[38] Backed by Layard, Millais and Burne-Jones, with Lord Carlisle, Lord Spencer and Sir William Harcourt putting pressure on Gladstone, Poynter eventually triumphed over the Eastlake faction and received the Directorship from Rosebery's hands in April 1894.[39] Three months later Layard was dead.

Poynter's appointment was a good one. But Eastlake never forgave the Trustees. The presentation on his retirement in 1898 must have been a chilly occasion. To his credit, however, he did not stoop to recrimination. Instead he turned to anecdote, and under the pseudonym "Jack Easel" published *Our Square and Circle* (1895), a nostalgic autobiographical sketch of considerable wit and charm. At his small house in Bayswater – 41 Leinster Square, nicknamed "terra cottage" on account of its colour – Eastlake lived out his declining years surrounded by mementoes and memories, books, paintings and furniture, "old china, Venetian glass and a hundred nicknacks". Jogging along on £1,000 a year, with his wife and cousin, enjoying good wine, plain food and the occasional Continental holiday, he drifted into "the age of old fogeydom", preferring domestic comfort to parties, concerts, private views and public dinners. On sunny days he would escape from "insufferable" omnibuses and "the bicycle plague", taking refuge in Kensington Gardens, "that . . . little sylvan paradise", where "thanks to a merciful fate, perambulators are scarce". Each evening he retired to his library to read and write. "The quaint colloquies in dear old Isaac Walton's 'Complete Angler', Carlyle's rugged eloquence – the rattling humour of Sheridan, Lamb's thoughtful essays, Longfellow's musical verse, Ruskin's delightful paradox, Nathaniel Hawthorne's charming prose and Mark Twain's laugh provoking fun. . . . Scarcely a night passes but I take some volume down, and presently a fragrant incense arises in its honour. It is from my pipe. . . ." The diversity of Eastlake's interests never flagged. He combined the instincts of a scholar with the talents of a born littérateur. On his own admission he was "a desultory reader . . . perhaps . . . a trifler. . . . People may say that I wear my beard too short, that I smoke too much, that I ought to rise earlier, that I am inclined to banter, that I am intolerant of long sermons, and what not. . . . There is, I fear, but little romance in my nature. It is certain that I have not much time for modern poetry. . . . But . . . in these solemn days of culture let us be thankful that we have some leisure left for small talk and frivolity".[40] He died, an unrepentant dilettante, in the year of the Liberal avalanche, 1906.

II Notes

1. An office held by the Eastlakes for several generations.
2. Lady Eastlake (ed.), *Contributions to the Literature of the Fine Arts* (2nd series, 1870), pp. 182–3. Young Eastlake was a Queen's Scholar at Westminster and later became a Governor.
3. For drawings see *Builder*, xvi (1858), 602–4; *R.I.B.A. Papers* 1872–3, 162 and 1874–5, appendix.
4. *Builder*, xci (1906), 607.
5. A. Graves, *R.A. Exhibitors, 1769–1904*, iii (1905), p. 9.
6. *Ecclesiologist*, xvii (1856), 33.
7. *Builder*, xiv (1856), 273. His address was given as 7 Caroline St, Bedford Square in 1855 and 7 Somerset Terrace in 1856. For Rugby Town Hall as built to designs by James Murray cf. *Builder*, xvi (1858), 293; *Rugby Advertiser*, 10 April 1858.
8. "Jack Easel" [C. L. Eastlake], *Our Square and Circle* (1895), p. 161.
9. *Builder*, xvii (1859), 369–70; xviii (1860), 402; xix (1861), 23, 165, 211–12; xx (1862), 165; *Building News*, vii (1861), 17, 26, 65, 85, 148, 211, 215, 230, 277, 293, 974.

10. Twenty-four candidates applied, including Dolman, Snell, Edward Hall, Tarbuck and Warren (*Builder*, xxiv, 1866, 947).

11. *Ibid.*, xxiii (1865), 230, 239–40, 263, 273, 298; xxvii (1869), 431, 452, 469. J. P. Seddon, the Gothicists' nominee as Hon. Sec. for Home Correspondence, even admitted: "I hold it for the purposes of my party, and so long as my party keep me in, so long I will remain."

12. *Ibid.*, xxix (1871), 180, 201, 300. The President, T. H. Wyatt, justified Eastlake's promotion on the grounds that he "*now practically* has the labour oar of the Institute, . . . edits our Transactions, prepares minutes, and . . . carries on the bulk of the correspondence . . . I know no one who could perform those duties more efficiently". See also J. A. Gotch (ed.), *Growth and Work of the R·I·B·A.* (1934), pp. 23–5. For Eastlake's "Historical Sketch of the Institute", cf. *R·I·B·A. Transactions*, xxvi (1875–6), 258–72.

13. *Ibid.*, xxxiv (1876), 151. "For some time past the Institute . . . has been one of the most unbusiness-like and unpunctual of societies. . . . Nothing can ever be done in time. . . . It is this dilatory, sleepy, procrastinating, slow-coach administration, which is tiring everyone out, and clogging the wheels of the machine."

14. *Ibid.*, xxxvi (1878), 187.

15. *Ibid.*, xci (1906), 607. "I find American tradesmen continually advertising what they are pleased to call 'Eastlake' furniture, with the production of which I have had nothing whatever to do, and for the taste of which I should be very sorry to be considered responsible" (*Hints on Household Taste*, 1878 ed., p. viii). The first American edition was published at Boston in 1872; the sixth (New York, 1881) has notes by C. C. Perkins. Gross distortions of the Eastlake style still survive in San Francisco; see W. D. Vail, *Victorians* (San Francisco, 1967). For Edward Eastlake, *Le Receuil de Meubles d'Art*, see *The House Furnisher and Decorator*, i (1872), 29.

16. "There was much to be learnt from the sensible construction of poor Pugin's woodwork" (M. Digby Wyatt, "Form in the Decorative Arts", *Lectures on the Results of the Great Exhibition*, 2nd series, 1853, p. 243). For changes in taste between 1851 and 1870 see T. S. R. Boase, *English Art, 1800–70* (1959), pp. 261 *et seq.*; N. Pevsner, *Matthew Digby Wyatt* (Cambridge, 1950), and *High Victorian Design* (1951); P. Thompson, *The Work of William Morris* (1967), p. 72; J. Steegman, *Consort of Taste* (1950), pp. 302–5; R. W. Symonds and B. B. Whinneray, *Victorian Furniture* (1962), pp. 45 *et seq.*

17. *Building News*, xv (1868), 206; *Athenaeum*, 28 Nov. 1868, 713–14. For favourable reviews see also the *Architect*, i (1869), 53–4 and viii (1872), 359. For criticisms cf. *Building News*, xvi (1869), 260–1, 281, 303, 321–2, 350. Parts of the book had already appeared in the *Queen* and *London Review*; and in *Cornhill Magazine*, ix (1864), 337–49.

18. *Hints* (1869 ed.), pp. vii, ix.

19. *Builder*, xxvi (1868), 853–5.

20. *Our Square and Circle*, pp. 13, 20. For Eastlake's Architectural Association paper on "Modern Furniture", 22 May 1868, cf. *Builder*, xxvi (1868), 390–1. He later published *Lectures on Decorative Art and Art-Workmanship* (delivered at the Social

Science Congress, Liverpool, 1876) and *The Present Condition of Industrial Art* (Spitalfields School of Design, 1877), and contributed to *Illustrations of Art Metal and Woodwork in the Byzantine, Medieval, Old English and Other Styles* (1877).

21. R. Dutton, *The English Interior* (1948), pp. 174–5 and *The Victorian Home* (1954), pp. 128–31.

22. The *Standard*, quoted in *Hints* (1878 ed.), supplement p. 2. Eastlake's theoretical debt to Jones and Morris is clear: "the moment a carved or sculptured surface begins to *shine*, it loses interest . . . machine-made ornament, invested with artificial lustre, is an artistic enormity. . . . Wood-carving . . . should be treated after a thoroughly *abstract* fashion, and made subservient to the general design. . . . The most commonplace objects of domestic use . . . are sure to be the most interesting in appearance. . . . I strongly advise my readers to refrain from buying any article of art-manufacture which is 'handsome', 'elegant' or 'graceful' in commercial slang: it is sure to be bad art. . . . The humblest article of manufacture, when honestly designed [has] a picturesque interest of its own. .'. ." (*Hints*, 1869 ed., pp. 53, 62, 76, 143, 150).

23. C. Eastlake Smith (ed.), *Journals and Correspondence of Lady Eastlake*, 2 vols. (1895).

24. Sir A. H. Layard, *Autobiography and Letters*, ed. W. N. Bruce, 2 vols. (1903); G. Waterfield, *Layard of Nineveh* (1963); F. Davis, *Victorian Patrons of the Arts* (1963), pp. 26–34.

25. Layard considered him "a portrait painter of great refinement, but of so scrupulous and sensitive a nature, that he was rarely satisfied with his own work, and left much which he undertook unfinished. . . . Although a man of nervous and anxious disposition, he had qualities which well fitted him for the post of Director – exquisite taste, literary requirements, a wide knowledge of art, and engaging manners – the latter very requisite in negociating for the purchase of pictures, especially with foreigners". (*Quarterly Rev.*, clxiii, 1886, 425).

26. Gladstone Papers, B.M. Add. MS. 44430 f. 1: 2 March 1871; and 44442 f. 302: 19 Feb. 1874.

27. Layard Papers, B.M. Add. MS. 38972 f. 63: 12 April 1878.

28. He published a series of four guides "intended for the ordinary amateur of pictorial art, when visiting the picture galleries of continental towns, during a holiday of limited length": *The Brera Gallery at Milan* (1883); *The Louvre Gallery at Paris* (1883); *The Old Pinakothek at Munich* (1884); *The Royal Gallery at Venice* (1888). The author admitted that "vexed questions of authenticity are . . . generally avoided", nor is there "any scientific analysis of principles, or technical dissertation on art".

29. J. Steegman, "Sir Charles Eastlake", *Architectural Rev.*, cxxxviii (1965), 364. For details of the National Gallery's history and administration, see Sir C. Holmes and C. H. Collins Baker, *The Making of the National Gallery, 1824–1924* (1924).

30. *The Times*, 17 March 1900, p. 10.

31. Layard Papers, B.M. Add. MS. 38972 f. 63: 12 April 1878; f. 67: 4 Nov. 1878 and ff. 85–6: 24 March 1892.

32. *The Times*, 2 April 1885, p. 7 and 8 April 1885, p. 10; Layard Papers, B.M. Add. MS. 39038 f. 130 [6 April 1885], f. 132: 9 April 1885 and f. 134: 12 April 1885. The next thing, he grumbled, "will probably be that the National Gallery should be

lighted up at night" (St Mark's Venice Committee Papers, B.M. Add. MS. 38831 f. 38: 6 Aug. 1880). Travelling scholarships he considered merely "a means of dissipating a young fellow's time and thoughts" (Layard Papers, B.M. Add. MS. 39040 f. 94: 12 April 1886).

33. "There is no one preeminently qualified to fill Sir Frederick's place" (*ibid.*, 38972 f. 86: 24 March 1892); "your nephew has discharged his duties . . . to the complete satisfaction of the Trustees and greatly to the advantage of the public. If the offices were to be united he would have a better claim than anyone. . . . But if the Treasury decides upon retaining the post of Director it would probably make the appointment without consulting the Trustees" (*ibid.*, f. 95: 12 Feb. 1893); "I have not heard anything as to Sir Frederick's resignation" (*ibid.*, f. 97: 20 April 1893).

34. "The duties of the Keeper and Secretary are double what they were in Mr Wornum's time, but . . . the improvements which I have effected . . . remain unknown to the Board and still more so to the Treasury" (*ibid.*, 39039 f. 163: 11 Dec. 1885); "I have undertaken these duties willingly . . . but I must frankly say that I should discharge them with greater pleasure if my participation were more directly recognised, and not regarded as a mere subordinate task, executed under orders" (*ibid.*, 39041 f. 9: 9 Nov. 1886).

35. *Ibid.*, 39037–40, *passim.*

36. *The Times*, 28 July 1919, p. 16. "Probably, with the exception of Alfred Stevens, the most versatile and accomplished draughtsman the English school has ever produced" (C. F. Bell, *D.N·B.*).

37. Layard Papers, B.M. Add. MSS. 38994–6, 39004, 39010, *passim.*

38. *Ibid.*, 39043–4, *passim.*

39. "Burne-Jones . . . tells me that you asked him to find out from me whether I should be disposed to undertake the Directorship. . . . I am bound to say . . . it is a place I should like to have" (*ibid.*, 39099 f. 48: 12 Aug. 1892); "in . . . a direct canvass, which would . . . be . . . repugnant to me, . . . I should be easily distanced by the J.C.R.s and Humphry Wards of the art-world, but I might perhaps . . . approach the other Trustees" (*ibid.*, f. 67: 26 Aug. 1892); "Lord Carlisle . . . has . . . had an interview with . . . Harcourt, in whose hands . . . the appointment will lie . . . [Perhaps] you can . . . [contact] any member of the Cabinet whose influence would be of value – as for instance Lord Spencer under whom I served at South Kensington. . . . Carlisle is very desirous of the post being filled by a painter . . . Millais and Burne-Jones have both strongly supported me with . . . Gladstone and . . . Harcourt" (*ibid.*, f. 259: 13 March 1893); "Lord Rosebery . . . has modified the . . . Directorship . . . so that . . . there will be no difficulties in the way of my accepting" (*ibid.*, 39100 f. 299: 24 April 1894).

40. *Our Square and Circle, passim.* Eastlake's will (Somerset House) shows that he left an estate valued at just over £15,000. Eastlake's occasional writings include: "Jack Easel on a Fashionable Neighbourhood" [Georgian Mayfair], *Building News*, xii (1865), 6: "The International Exhibition", *ibid.* 150–1; "Nuremburg", *ibid.* 387–9, 403–6; "St Paul's Cathedral", *Fraser's Mag.*, lxxxviii [N.S. viii] (1873), 284–97; "Picture-hanging at the National Gallery", *Nineteenth Century*, xxii (1887), 817–26; "The Poldi–Pezzoli Collection at Milan", *ibid.* xxxiii (1893), 981–93.

III   The Origins of the Gothic Revival*

a. Gothic Survival and Gothick Revival

Trying to track down a chronological watershed between the survival and revival of Gothic is like chasing a will-o'-the-wisp. For the Gothic style was resuscitated several times before it was dead, and it lingered unconscionably long in certain traditionalist areas. Survival and revival march side by side during the sixteenth and seventeenth centuries; and at times their paths overlap and merge with a third development, the introduction of Renaissance motifs. Long before the advent of Rococo Gothick in the 1720s, the Gothic style had been thrice revived. That is, it had been subject to three quasi-revivalist impulses: Elizabethan and Jacobean chivalry; Laudian Anglicanism; and the experimentalism of the age of Wren. None of these three phases is wholly revivalist. But each contains, to a greater or lesser degree, the seeds of genuine revivalism.

Now revivalism implies a self-conscious use of antique forms. It is this element of self-consciousness – the use of Gothic for non-functional reasons – which separates Revival from Survival. The first stages in this medievalizing process can be traced to the gloriously mongrel architecture of Elizabethan England, that strange Spenserian world, half Gothic half classic. It is here that the story of the Gothic Revival begins. The tournaments, the masques, the pageantry of the court and the cult of Gloriana, Sidney at Zutphen, Essex at Cadiz – the chivalry of Elizabeth's declining years naturally produced its appropriate architectural expression. Several of the "prodigy houses" of Elizabethan and Jacobean England employ forms which are posthumously Gothic: the window tracery at Wardour (1576–8), the tourelles of the central keep at Wollaton (1580–88) [plate 4], the battlements at Longford (c. 1580–91), Lulworth (1588–1609?) and Slingsby (c. 1630), the chapel windows at Hatfield (1608–12) and Temple Newsam (c. 1630), and – the culmination of this fashion – Bolsover Castle (1612) with its battlements and keep, vaulted hall and ogee-arched chimneypieces. All these can be labelled Revival. Bolsover's medieval format was now merely symbolic of

---

* The whole of this section is based on secondary material. Relevant books, articles and theses are listed in the bibliography.

martial strength, just as much an artificial echo of "olden time" as that eccentric piece of medievalism, the Hauteville monument at Chew Magna, Somerset, and the tomb of Sir Philip Carew (1589) in Exeter Cathedral. Longford Castle was actually built by patrons of Spenser; he may even have made it his model for the Castle of Temperance, "partly circular and part triangular", in the *Faerie Queene*. Robert Smythson, the leading architect of the period, drew heavily on Gothic precedents. At Wollaton, for example, he married a native plan deriving from Acton Burnell (1283), Hurstmonceaux (*c.* 1425) and Mount Edgecumbe (1546) to an imported design from Serlio's third book of Architecture (1540). Despite its overlay of Renaissance accretions — perhaps over-emphasized by historians — Elizabethan domestic architecture remained largely Gothic in inspiration. "Under Elizabeth", wrote John Aubrey in the mid-seventeenth century, "architecture made no progress but rather went backwards". Certainly the classicism of Longleat (1572–80) suffered a romantic set-back during the later years of the reign. Clear cases of Gothic Survival are not difficult to find: the rib-vaulting in the West front of Burghley House (1577), for instance. More important, the skeleton of the Elizabethan house — hall, grand staircase, great chamber and long gallery — as well as the basic ingredients of "the Elizabethan style" — great height, dramatic silhouette, bay windows, oriels, towers, turrets, gables, cupolas and battlements — can only be understood in a medieval context. The stylistic links between Burghley House and Richmond Palace (completed 1501), are very close. In secular circles, therefore, the Gothic style was practised in the sixteenth and early seventeenth centuries on two complementary levels: survival and revival. Traditional planning and traditional masonry techniques combined with a new-found nostalgia and the chivalry of neo-medievalism to produce the characteristic flavour of the period. Elizabethan architecture has justly been described by Dr Girouard as "pre-eminently a development from a living Gothic tradition . . . a magnificent late flowering of the Gothic age". The verdict would have surprised Eastlake.

In ecclesiastical buildings the situation was rather different. What Sir Nikolaus Pevsner has christened "the Elizabethan Settlement in architectural history" — the injection of Renaissance fashions into the Gothic bloodstream — was largely excluded from church architecture, at least until the Caroline period. The second half of the sixteenth century was not an age of church building. Examples of any sort are infrequent. When they do occur they are mostly humble cases of extension or reconstruction, as at Sutton Maddock, Shropshire (1579), and at Southwick (1566) and Droxford (1599) in Hampshire. This process — the survival of a Perpendicular, church-building vernacular — continued in country districts throughout the seventeenth century: Fulmer, Buckinghamshire (1610); Manningtree, Essex (1616); Wyke Champflower (1623–4) and Chapel Allerton

(1638) in Somerset; Godmanchester (1623) and Ramsey (1672) in Huntingdon-shire; Dauntsey (1630), Chippenham (1633) and Standlynch (1677) in Wiltshire; Foremark, Derbyshire (1662); Little Wenlock, Shropshire (1667); Llangad-waladr (1661) in Anglesey; Llanrwst (two chapels, 1633 and 1673) in Denbigh-shire; Stoneleigh (1665) and Compton Wynyates (1665) in Warwickshire; Monnington-on-Wye, Herefordshire (1679–80); Ashburnham (1665), Withy-ham (1663–80) and Stedham (1673) in Sussex; Dairsie Church, Fife (1621) and Michael Kirk, near Elgin, now Gordonstoun School chapel (1705). All these are instances of the survival of Gothic in rural areas, a pattern emerging with increas-ing clarity in the wake of that great topographical engine, *The Buildings of England*. In fact prior to the Restoration, seventeenth-century church building was entirely traditionalist. Before 1666 only two completely classical churches were built, both by Inigo Jones: St Paul's, Covent Garden, and the Queen's Chapel at St James's Palace.

Meanwhile in urban centres of architectural fashion, notably in London, Oxford and Cambridge, the Gothic style had again been given artificial respira-tion: during the Laudian phase of the 1620s and 1630s; and once more during the years after 1660. Archbishop Laud has long been absolved of any personal attempt to initiate a Gothic Revival. He did, however, preside over that religious renaissance stemming from the doctrines of Arminianism and tangibly expressed in what he himself termed "the beauty of holiness". Church and collegiate architecture received a new impetus and produced several remarkable buildings, Perpendicular structures with classical features veering between Mannerist and Baroque. In London St Katherine Cree (1628–31) boasts Perpendicular tracery and a shallow plaster rib vault resting on Tuscan arcades. Similar combinations occur at Great Stanmore, Middlesex (1632), at Shrivenham, Berkshire (1638) and later on at Holy Trinity, Berwick (1648–52) and Charles Church, Plymouth (finished 1665). Apart from Canterbury Quadrangle (1632–6) at St John's (not, as Eastlake assumed, by Inigo Jones), the Laudian spirit found memorable ex-pression at Oxford in the porch at St Mary's (1637), where barley-sugar columns and pedimental volutes disguise masonry fan vaulting of traditional excellence. Brasenose chapel (1666, incorporating earlier work, and not, as Eastlake believed, by Wren), forms a bizarre and belated conclusion to the same movement. But it was at Cambridge that the Laudian fashion produced its most significant results. In 1624 the rebuilding of the library at St John's [plate 2] supplied historians with a classic case of revivalism: Bishop Carey left it on record that "the old fashion of church windows" (curvilinear in this case) had been deliberately adopted, and Henry Man's design conveniently incorporated the date. Four years later Peter-house chapel was begun, a spectacular mixture of Perpendicular tracery and polygonal turrets, curly Flemish gables and niches with self-consciously ogee mouldings. At Peterhouse the work sponsored by Matthew Wren, Master of the college and uncle to Sir Christopher Wren, was continued by his successor Bishop Cosin. And it was thanks to Cosin's church-building zeal that the Laudian style was eventually transported as far north as County Durham. At Gateshead (1633–4) and Brancepeth (*c.* 1638) decorative Gothic motifs are combined with Jacobean strapwork; at Bishop Auckland (1660–72), Sedgefield (*c.* 1670) and Durham (*c.* 1663–5) the Classic-Gothic hybrid emerges full-blown, fusing elements of the Decorated, the Perpendicular and the Baroque. A similar synthesis occurs in the screen (*c.* 1620) at Cartmel Priory, Lancashire. Such eclecticism was the product of three sources: Survival, Revival and Renaissance. It was a transient mood, nicely caught at Stapleford Park in Leicestershire, when Lord and Lady Sherard added a new wing in 1633, strangely combining gables, mullions and niches. Not far away at Staunton Harold (1653–65) Sir Robert Shirley, who "did the best things in the worst times and hoped them in the most calamitous", defied the ethos of the Protectorate and built a church eloquent in its testimony to the strength of Laudian Anglicanism and the persistence of Gothic tradition. In the far North such traditionalism was less exceptional. The architectural career of Lady Anne Clifford, Countess of Pembroke, was distinguished by the number of castles and churches in Cumberland and Westmorland which she piously restored in consciously medieval style. Around the middle of the century architectural fashions were themselves confused, and in remote areas local craftsmen could produce vaguely Gothic work which almost defies classification: the strangely formalized tracery at Burford Priory Chapel, Oxfordshire, or at Kelmarsh church, Northamptonshire, for example; the columns and sub-medieval mouldings at Clegg Hall, Milnrow, Lancashire (*c.* 1660); or that freak of urban design, The Folly (1679) at Settle in Yorkshire.

Meanwhile a fresh revivalist impulse had begun to radiate from the central focus of architectural fashion, the Office of Works. For some time Court circles had been a centre of imported classicism. The legend, to which Eastlake subscribed, that the young Inigo Jones dabbled in Gothic, has long since been abandoned. His nearest approach to medievalism took a strictly ephemeral form: theatrical sets and designs for masques, such as *The House of Fame* (1609), *Oberon's Palace* (1610) or *The City of Sleep* (1638). His successors were less rigid. The architectural vocabulary of the age of Wren was wide enough to include Gothic forms. But it was Gothic for reasons which were neither sentimental, nor religious but environmental. Fergusson preferred to call this phase a "Gothic Renaissance" rather than a "Gothic Revival". Wren confessedly preferred "the better and *Roman* art of Architecture", on structural and aesthetic grounds. He was, however, prepared to design in Gothic according to circumstance; when "to deviate from the old Form, would be to run into a disagreeable Mixture, which no person of good Taste could relish". He might still talk of "Gothick rudeness"; of the unnecessary "Flutter of Archbuttresses"; of pinnacles which were "of no Use and as little Ornament"; and of "the Pride of a very high Roof" where "the Lead is apt to slip" because of its "indiscreet Form". But he was capable of cautious admiration for Henry VII's Chapel, Westminster: "nice embroidered Work . . . performed with tender *Caen*-stone"; and for Salisbury Cathedral: its creators "knew . . . that nothing could add Beauty to Light". Such an objective, un-romantic approach was shared by at least three of his followers: William Dickinson, Nicholas Hawksmoor and John James. The results of their efforts are still prominent in London, Warwick and Oxford.

Apart from an interesting scheme for the reconstruction of Old London Bridge, all Wren's Gothic work in the City was ecclesiastical. And at all four major churches where he or his assistants employed the style its choice was, to a greater or lesser extent, dictated by the environment. The survival of Gothic remains from before the Fire suggested the revival of Gothic forms after it: St Alban's, Wood Street (finished 1698); St Dunstan's-in-the-East (1698), its tower modelled on old St Mary-le-Bow; St Michael, Cornhill, with its sturdy tower (1721) by Hawksmoor; and St Mary Aldermary, its fan-vaulting (1682) elabo-rately echoing the work destroyed in the Great Fire and its remarkable tower (1702), probably by William Dickinson, anticipating the linear quality of eigh-teenth-century Gothick. Westminster Abbey saw the last and most celebrated display of Wrenean Gothic in the metropolis. In 1713 Wren had recommended the completion of the Western towers and the addition of a central spire [plate 3]. Between 1700 and 1725 Dickinson produced several schemes. And in 1735–45 the familiar twin towers were at last begun to Hawksmoor's designs and completed under the direction of John James. Despite occasional classic lapses, the overall effect is undeniably traditional; the spirit of Gothic had been revived, and the letter brilliantly re-interpreted.

The rebuilding of St Mary's Warwick after the fire of 1694 made possible a provincial variation on this metropolitan theme. As in London, Gothic was chosen on environmental grounds. Several preliminary designs were produced, possibly by Wren, more likely by Hawksmoor. The final, less exciting, result was designed by Sir William Wilson and completed in 1704 under the direction of a celebrated building family, the Smiths of Warwick. In its mixture of tracery and pediments, pinnacles and balusters, plaster vaults with Baroque cartouches and Perpendicular piers with acanthus mouldings, it hints at the freedom of the Laudian period. But the tower's precise Gothic details, handled in a basically un-Gothic manner, tie it firmly to the Wrenean phase. And inside, a remarkable neo-Gothic pastiche, the entrance to the Beauchamp chapel, added in 1704 by Samuel Dunkley, seems almost to herald the age of Pugin.

At Oxford environmental needs produced a parallel crop of Wrenean Gothic. Wren was a reluctant revivalist. But Tom Tower (1681–2) at Christ Church must surely rank as one of his happiest inventions. By a synthetic process of design he rationalized a variety of late Gothic precedents, manipulating them within a framework which is subconsciously classical. Tom Tower set the seal on this phase of revivalism. But perhaps its most remarkable product was still to come. Hawksmoor's extension to All Souls began in 1716; his familiar entrance "after ye Monastick Maner" was not finished until 1734. As the design developed it became more whimsical and less classic. Yet the sources of those fairy-tale twin towers – Beverley Minster and the octagon at Ely – have been so pulverized by Hawksmoor's classical intellect that the energizing qualities of Gothic design have been wholly eliminated. At All Souls we are already on the verge of a new epoch, on the brink of a new mood, the Rococo. But that is to anticipate a little. In 1708 Talman was preparing visionary designs for All Souls in North Italian Gothic. A few years later, just across the High Street at University College, masons were putting up scaffolding for the fan-vaulting in Radcliffe Quadrangle (1716–19). The masonry tradition which had culminated gloriously in the Great Staircase at Christ Church (c. 1640) was still a living force. At the close of the seventeenth century, Oxford was itself a microcosm of contemporary fashion. The eclecticism of the Laudian phase had disappeared. But the work of local masons and London architects, Survival and Revival, rose side by side. And Oxford was the heart of another movement, at first only indirectly architectural but in the long run crucial to the future of the Gothic Revival: antiquarianism.

The period between the Civil War and the arrival of the Hanoverians deserves to be remembered as the heroic age of English scholarship. The English topographical tradition already numbered men like Saxton, Norden and Camden among its pioneers. Selden, Prynne and Usher were scholars of remarkable range. But in the 1650s and 1660s a new-found specialism begins to emerge, prompted by political and religious motives, yet increasingly objective in its techniques. William Dugdale, our "first medievalist", building on Dodsworth's work, set new standards with his formidable *Monasticon* (1655–73), and then redoubled his reputation with volumes on *Warwickshire* (1656), *St Paul's* (1658) and the *Baronage* (1675–6). Equally monumental were Madox's *Formulare Anglicanum* (1702) and *Exchequer* (1711); Rymer's *Foedera* (1702–11); Wake and Wilkins's *Concilia* (1737); and Henry Wharton's *Anglia Sacra* (1691), the work of a strange, warped genius who burnt himself out at the age of thirty. Anglo-Saxon studies underwent a rare florescence at the hands of Humphrey Wanley, George Hickes and Elizabeth Elstob, "the Saxon nymph". Patrons such as Somers and Harley found the pleasure of scholarship, in Halifax's words, "like that of Wrestling with a fine Woman". As Gibbon put it, this was indeed an "age of Herculean diligence which could devour and digest whole libraries". At Oxford the antiquarian movement continued well into the eighteenth century. Dugdale's *Warwickshire* transformed into "a perfect Elysium" the life of the future author of *Athenae Oxonienses* (1691), young Anthony Wood. And thanks to Wood the antiquities of medieval Oxford are perhaps uniquely documented. But with Thomas Hearne, that archetype of the malicious Oxford scholar, "of sober Face with learned Dust besprent", it is hard to resist the conclusion that the antiquarian movement had reached something of an anticlimax. Pope found an easy target in Bodley's crusty bookworms, savouring "the Sacred Rust of twice two hundred years". Still, the scholars had worked well. Stylistic analysis of Gothic buildings was scarcely in its infancy. One needs only to look at that curious collection, Thomas Dingley's *History from Marble* (*c.* 1650–80). But the groundwork of documentation had been begun. By a nice paradox, Dugdale's "unspeakable energy" made possible the frivolity of Strawberry Hill, and engravings by Hollar and King supplied models for the age of Rococo.

The survivalist stream of English Gothic petered out during the early eighteenth century. The spurt of building which followed the Great Fire helped to break down the conservatism of masons in the metropolitan area, a tendency underlined by new economic trends. In Mr Colvin's words, "Gothic is essentially a mason's architecture", and "in eighteenth century London the mason was in retreat before the surveyor . . . and the builder"; Gothic "retreated with the mason to the stone districts of the Midlands, the West and the North". In the Cotswolds this rustic tradition held out long enough to merge with the revivalist impulse of the Rococo. The church towers at Dursley (1708–09), Berkeley (1747–53) and Great Witcombe (1750) in Gloucestershire, and at Sherston (1730–33) in Wiltshire show just how long traditional techniques survived in the hands of local masons like Thomas Sumsion and William Clark. But it was a survival with little hope of development. The future lay not with masons' Gothic but with architects' Gothick. One man's career, that of Edward Woodward, a mason from Chipping Camden, illustrates the transition. His father's work at Blockley church, Worcestershire (1725–7) had been wholly traditional. The work of father and son at St Swithun, Worcester (1734–6) combines survivalist and revivalist elements. The younger Woodward's own work at Alcester church, Warwickshire (1730–33) already hints at the purely decorative qualities of Rococo Gothick. And at Preston-on-Stour (1753–7) the revolution is complete. Here we have Colvin's "church of the Revival by a mason of the Survival"; a church designed moreover for just the sort of patron who eventually turned the Gothic Revival from a series of sporadic impulses into a national movement – James West, Esq. of Alscot Park, an antiquary. Preston-on-Stour deserves to become a textbook classic. But by the time it was completed, Rococo Gothick had already been established in fashionable circles for the best part of a generation. It is time, therefore, to turn from questions of Survival and Revival to the problem of Romanticism, from the prolegomena of the movement to the Gothic Revival proper.

b. Rococo Gothick

Romanticism idealizes the remote, it glorifies the distant, both in time and place. All revivals are romantic, and the Gothic Revival quintessentially so. As Geoffrey Scott put it, "to pass from Roman architecture and that of the Renaissance to the fantastic and bewildered energy of Gothic, is to leave humanism for magic, the study of the congruous for the cult of the strange". The literature of Romanticism is enormous. In 1936 F. L. Lucas claimed to have read 11,396 books on the subject. Its origins have been pushed further and further back, beyond Rousseau and Kant, to Bacon, even to St Paul. Grierson nominated Plato as the "first great romantic". Whibley suggested that Romanticism was "born in the Garden of Eden" and that "the Serpent was the first romantic". Since 1924, when Lovejoy attempted to untangle the typology of Romanticism, the situation has become a little clearer. The stock antithesis between Romanticism and Classicism has been exposed as a false dichotomy, a polarity which ignores the common ground between reason and imagination. The idea of a coherent Romantic Movement has been abandoned, and critics now tend to talk in terms of different aspects and phases of Romanticism considered as a permanent psychological condition. Of these aspects or phases English architecture in the eighteenth century was subject to two: the Rococo and the Picturesque. It is often hard to see a clear-cut division between them, but the effort is worth making. Both are to a certain extent complementary. The Rococo was principally expressed in decoration, the Picturesque in composition. The origins of Rococo Gothick were at least partly literary, the origins of Picturesque Gothick were pictorial. But whereas the Rococo was a Continental exotic, imported and absorbed, the Picturesque was a visual philosophy of entirely native origins. Each contained something of the other, and together they constitute the first two major phases of the Gothic Revival in this country.

Philologists derive "Rococo" from *rocaille* (rockwork) and *coquille* (shell), French words used to describe the irregular shell or scroll forms found in the encrusted decoration of grottoes. Such broken, naturalistic patterns were thought to symbolize an escape from logical order. In Hogarth's words, they lead the eye "a wanton kind of chase". It was a fashion born in France during the second decade of the eighteenth century, in reaction to the Baroque autocracy of Louis

XIV. In England it represented a similar rebellion, against the ordered world of orthodox Palladianism. The Rococo spirit permeated each of the visual arts in turn: landscape, furniture, sculpture, painting, architecture. Christopher Hussey, who first identified and explained the Rococo mood in English architecture, saw the new fashion drawing strength from this country's "underlying natural sentiment and empiricism", and finding comparable expression in the "mental stirrings" of the second quarter of the eighteenth century – that "renaissance of imagination and perceptiveness" variously displayed in the careers of Pitt and Wesley, Priestley and Hume, Hogarth and Gainsborough. Certainly Rococo art was but one aspect of Romanticism. Within the Palladian framework the serpentine forms of Rococo were directly and indirectly expressed: directly in intricate stucco decoration and indirectly in a new trend towards linearity, angularity, variation of outline and flexibility of plan. The revolution associated with the name of Robert Adam might therefore be described as Rococo in origin. Outside the Palladian canon the new fashion found easier expression via a novel interest in vernacular and exotic modes, such as Tudor and Oriental. Thus Palladianism in England came to be permeated by three new styles: French Rococo (*Rocaille*), Chinese Rococo (*Chinoiserie*) and Rococo Gothic (*Gothick*). And both inside and outside the Palladian system the arrival of Rococo forms encouraged the subordination of house to landscape, just as Baroque had postulated the reverse. Two houses sum up the multiple influence of the new vogue in all its various guises: Claydon House, Buckinghamshire (1760s) and Hagley Park, Worcestershire (1754–60). Of the movement's various forms the Gothick proved the least ephemeral. *Rocaille* stuccowork went under in the age of Adam. *Chinoiserie* was, almost by its very nature, peculiarly transient: Roger Morris described its "principals" as "a good choice of chains and bells, and different colours of paint". Although Sir William Chambers published *Designs of Chinese Buildings* (1757), he never regarded it as a serious architectural medium. But Rococo Gothick was a style with a future from the moment it first appeared in the 1720s. The reason was simple. Unlike its exotic rivals it had something to build on. It was grafted on to the nascent revivalism of the previous century.

Dr Girouard has traced this progressive emancipation of design to a group of artists loosely associated with the St Martin's Lane Academy in London and patronized by opponents of Sir Robert Walpole. The engraver Gravelot, Yeo the medallist, Moser the enamellist and the painters Hayman and Hudson were all of this circle. So were Hogarth, Gainsborough and Roubiliac, and the furniture makers John Linnell, Thomas Chippendale and William Hallett. On the periphery were other craftsmen like the silversmith Paul de Lamerie. All these helped to introduce Rococo forms from across the Channel. The leading architects of this fraternity, Isaac Ware and James Paine, might at first sight be identified as orthodox Palladians. But at Chesterfield House, London (1748–9) and perhaps also at Woodcote, Surrey (1745–52) and Belvedere near Erith (c. 1750), Ware demonstrated his mastery of French *rocaille* before he turned against this "crooked" foreign fashion. As for Paine, the plasterwork which he supervised at Nostell Priory, Yorkshire (1740) and the Doncaster Mansion House (1744) bears comparison with that Rococo *tour de force*, the great staircase (1755) at Powderham Castle, Devon. And at Stockeld Park, Yorkshire (1758–63), he showed just how far Palladian tradition could be broken up by the eccentric rhythms of the new fashion. For it was a fashion which was all pervasive. It was also synthetic. Paul Decker's *Chinese Architecture, Civil and Ornamental* and *Gothic Architecture, Decorated* (1759) contain patterns which are fundamentally similar. The "C" and "S" scrolls of *Rocaille* could be easily translated into Chinese fretwork or ogee arches. By 1754 the *World* was rejoicing at the "happy mixture" of Gothick and Chinese – "Anglo-Chinois". Two years later John Shebbeare was complaining that "almost everywhere, all is Chinese or Gothic. Every chair in an apartment, the frames of glasses and tables, must be Chinese: the walls covered with Chinese paper fill'd with figures which resemble nothing in God's creation, and which a prudent nation would prohibit for the sake of pregnant women . . . [As for] Gothic . . . you see a hundred houses built with porches . . . [and] rooms stuccoed . . . with all the minute unmeaning carvings, which are found in the most Gothic chapels of a thousand years standing". By the 1740s Gothick and Chinese could be savoured side by side in such a centre of fashion and folly as Vauxhall Gardens, London.

The champions of this new syncretic mode were Thomas Lightoler, William and John Halfpenny and Thomas and Batty Langley. Carpenters by training and publishers by chance, their popular handbooks turned "Carpenters' Gothick" into a household word. Like Chippendale's *Director*, Batty Langley's *Ancient Architecture Restored* (1742) and *Gothic Architecture Improved* (1747) supplied models for a multitude of provincial workmen. Like all writers of pattern books he set out to simplify and to rationalize. The Rococo did not take kindly to such an experiment. Its origins lay in a rebellion against logic, and its essence was complexity. By attempting to classify Gothic according to a spurious set of "orders", Batty Langley earned the contempt of every pundit from Horace Walpole onwards. But he also won the gratitude of village craftsmen and local builders trained in classical ways, unequal to the philosophy of Rococo, and incapable of Gothic masonry. Anyway, the result has an almost irresistible charm. What Gray called "the Batty Langley manner" was the product of Palladian. proportions and sinuous Rococo forms: sober sash windows and canted bays decked out with labels and battlements; classical saloons enlivened with four-centred chimneys and ogee-arched doorcases; plaster friezes composed of trefoils, quatrefoils, anthemions and palmettes; Chinese frets of doubtful parentage; walls decorated with wire-drawn arcading and clustered columns of delicious slenderness [plate 9]. It was a heady mixture of ancient, medieval and oriental motifs, sometimes flimsy and slap-dash, as with the "umbrello" at Painshill, Surrey (*c.* 1740); occasionally distilled with exquisite care as in the garden pavilion at Frampton Court, Gloucestershire (*c.* 1745) or at Stout's Hill, near Uley, Gloucestershire (*c.* 1750). Adam's decorative work at Alnwick (*c.* 1760–70) shows the synthesis at its subtlest. Among provincial masters, the work of T. F. ("Ironbridge") Pritchard of Shrewsbury is outstanding. He has recently been credited with the Rococo delights of both Croft Castle, Herefordshire (*c.* 1765) and Tong Castle, Shropshire (*c.* 1765). Perhaps one day he will be shown to have had some connection with the creation of that Rococo gem, Shobdon church, Herefordshire (1750–56). Disciplined in its proportions and undisciplined in its details, Rococo Gothick was capable of a very high degree of sophistication – one has only to instance Keene's Hartwell church, Buckinghamshire (1753–6) or Hobcraft's miniature chapel at Audley End, Essex (1768).

Eastlake's lack of interest in Rococo Gothick is summed up by the fact that he fails even to mention the name of its creator, William Kent. His scorn for this whole phase of architectural history – culminating in his abuse of Batty Langley's ghost – stemmed from a basic misconception. He failed to realize that the premises from which Rococo Gothick sprang were not so much revivalist as associational. Like Picturesque Gothick, Rococo Gothick was not concerned with archaeology. The blithe inaccuracy of both earlier periods separates them clearly from the two later phases, the Ecclesiological and the Eclectic. And this basic distinction between romanticism and archaeology, ignorance and scholarship, is traditionally expressed by a piece of typographical shorthand: *Gothick* for the earlier phases, *Gothic* for the later. Kent's Gothick made no attempt at archaeology; its inaccuracy is irrelevant. It was not merely the result of ignorance but a type of calculated whimsy. Eastlake's teleology turned early Georgian Goths into unregenerate ancestors of the Victorians, when he should really have judged them as innocent Romantics. At Waynflete's Tower (Esher Place) in Surrey (1729–33), Kentian Gothick was displayed for the first time: crenellated pediments and canted bays; slim machicolations and cupolas; pointed arches with labels but without imposts; ogee-arched doorways and quatrefoiled windows; and clustered columns with key-patterned capitals. Esher's descendants have been legion. Today Waynflete's Tower stands forlorn amid a mass of Stockbroker's Tudor. "The parent", notes Mr John Harris, "is doomed to brood upon its ugly progeny". Esher was a Romantic miscellany, not a consistent revivalist vocabulary. Kent's gateway at Hampton Court (1732) similarly combines Early English fenestration with Jacobean plasterwork. His illustrations to Spenser's *Faerie Queene* (1751) boast battlements supported on Ionic columns. Thornhill was producing much the same sort of fantasy as early as 1719 with his stage scenery for *Signor Van der Goth's in Lapland*. Kent's pulpit at York Minster (1741), his law courts at Westminster Hall (1739) [plate 10] and his choir screen at Gloucester Cathedral (1741) display his characteristic eclecticism in concentrated and elaborate form, articulated as usual within a classical framework. The vocabulary itself is unchanged, as it is again in his work at Rousham, Oxfordshire (1738–41) and in his unexecuted scheme for Honingham Hall, Norfolk (1737). But at Rousham the many facets of Kent's protean genius were simultaneously displayed. At Rousham, as Horace Walpole said of Esher, Kent is Kentissime: Palladian and Gothick side by side; furniture as well as decorative painting; plus that crucial ingredient in any Rococo conception, a naturalistic landscape.

Walpole thought Kent was the first who "leaped the fences and saw that all nature was a garden". Most modern writers would probably look beyond Kent to Charles Bridgeman, and beyond Bridgeman to Sir John Vanbrugh. As early as 1624 Sir Henry Wotton recommended that "Gardens should bee irregular, or at least cast into a very wilde Regularitie". In 1685 Sir William Temple put in a tentative plea for informality along Chinese lines. Milton's Garden of Eden had been quite unlike Versailles. And when he visited Italy in 1690 the Earl of Shaftesbury discovered that landscapes by Claude and the Poussins happily suited his conception of the original state of nature. Addison in the *Spectator* of 1712, Pope in the *Guardian* of 1713, mounted pungent attacks on the formal conventions of Dutch and French gardening. And these new ideas were first explained in detail in Stephen Switzer's *Ichnographica Rustica* (1718). But it was Vanbrugh and Bridgeman who turned theory into practice. During the second and third decades of the eighteenth century at Blenheim and Stowe, Eastbury and Claremont, they initiated that search for a romantic, ideal landscape which was to dominate aesthetic theory for several generations. Bridgeman is usually credited with being the first Englishman to make use of the ha-ha. In fact Beaumont's "Bastion" at Levens dates from *c*. 1700; the Vanbrughian ha-ha at Duncombe (1718–24) antedates Bridgeman's at Stowe; and the name itself had already been popularized by John James in his 1712 translation of d'Argenville's treatise of 1709. But it was certainly Bridgeman who made Hyde Park a permanent memorial to the Rococo revolution: it was he who created the Serpentine (1726–38) not far from the last flourish of formalism, Wise and London's sunken garden at Kensington. "At that moment", wrote Walpole, "appeared Kent, painter enough to taste the charms of landscape, bold and opinionated enough to dare and to dictate, and born with a genius to strike out a great system from a twilight of imperfect essays". The conquest of the landscape by the garden had already been accomplished in France. England's contribution was the conquest of the garden by the landscape. The search for an ideal form of nature had begun in earnest. First it was to be Rococo, then Picturesque. And in both stages Gothick buildings had a key part to play. The parkland at Stowe is a veritable palimpsest of landscape theory: first Vanbrugh, then Bridgeman, then Kent, then Capability Brown. At each stage architectural features were constructed to give point and focus to the design. Focal buildings were particularly important in the earliest types of landscape garden. Between seventeenth-century geometry and eighteenth-century naturalism, the English garden passed through a transitional stage which has been labelled Poetic or Sentimental. Its sources of inspiration were primarily literary. Pope was thinking of descriptions in Vergil, Pliny and Ovid when he wrote that "the taste of the ancients in their gardens" was for "the amiable simplicity of unadorned nature". Later on the Picturesque landscape was to translate into three dimensions the two-dimensional visions of Italian landscape painters. Meanwhile the Poetic or Sentimental landscape was based on the literary principles of association and recognition. In conjuring up memories of classical mythology or medieval romance, landscape architecture was invaluable. The avenues of Cirencester Park, the Rococo sinuosities of Pope's garden at Twickenham or Kent's miniature landscape at Chiswick, depended at least partly for their effect on architectural devices. There was no mistaking the message of a temple, strategically placed, especially if the memory was jogged by an appropriate lapidary quotation. And when it came to ruins, Gothick was unbeatable. The poetic cult of Melancholy, that *mal romantique*, certainly helped to make Rococo Gothick all the rage. So in a different way did the philosophical cult of Nature, the Noble Savage and the Chinese Sage. It is no coincidence that the early eighteenth-century revolution in garden design is associated with the names of poets like Addison, Pope and Shenstone. Nor was it accidental that Vanbrugh, Kent and Brown, leaders in the development of landscape design, were also key figures in the history of the Gothic Revival.

Vanbrugh's medievalism properly belongs to the pre-history of the Picturesque. The long-term significance of his castle at Greenwich (1717) was compositional rather than stylistic. His antique details have nothing to do with Rococo Gothick: he never employed a pointed arch. But his fondness for antiquities – the Holbein Gate at Whitehall or the old manor of Woodstock – puts him at the head of a long line of Rococo sentimentalists. Capability Brown became the leading practitioner of abstract Picturesque landscape. But his own architectural designs in the medieval manner – the garden buildings at Burghley House, Northamptonshire (1756–8) or at Corsham Court, Wiltshire (1761–4), for example – are Rococo in form and Poetic in inspiration. That is, they belong to that portion of the Gothic Revival which concerned itself with literary rather than pictorial images. This is the phase described by Sir Kenneth Clark under the heading

"Ruins and Rococo". It was the age of the Graveyard Poets, a time of "crepuscular romanticism". And the ruins fit for pondering poets were often partly genuine, symbols of romance and melancholy, rescued and re-erected: the Ruins (c. 1730) at Cranbury Park, Hampshire, retrieved from Netley Abbey; the Priory (c. 1755) at the Leasowes, Worcestershire, containing fragments from Halesowen Abbey; the Bristol Cross re-erected (c. 1760) at Stourhead, Wiltshire; Madingley Hall Archway (c. 1770), retrieved from the Cambridge University Schools. The climax of such operations was reached in Yorkshire in the 1750s and 1760s, when Fountains Abbey and Rievaulx were strikingly incorporated in landscapes at Studley Royal and Duncombe Park. As for artificial antiquities, the most typical products of this period are stylistically haphazard and historically vague, dedicated perhaps to

> Cadwaladr and Arthur, ancient kings,
> Full famous in Romantic tale.

In his *Architectural Remembrancer* (1751), Roger Morris even offers designs "in the Muscovite manner" and others "partly *Persian* and partly Gothic". At Cirencester Park a castellated wood-shed grew under the direction of Pope and Bathurst into a creeper-covered folly variously known as King Alfred's Hall or King Arthur's Castle, its style as uncertain as its title. It was begun in 1721, and by 1732 Mrs Pendarves was able to tell Swift "it is now a venerable castle and has been taken by an antiquarian as one of King Arthur's". Incorporating some genuine late medieval work, it is still "as jumbled as Jervaux", and manages, in Miss Barbara Jones's words, to recapture "the amorphous squalor of medievalism". In 1772 an Alfred's Tower was added to the Stourhead landscape from designs by Flitcroft, supposedly on the site overlooking Salisbury Plain where in 878 the Saxon hero set up his standard against the Danes. Another tower at Meanwood near Leeds was erected in 1787 "to the memory of Alfred the Great, the Wise, the Pious and Magnanimous, the friend of Science, Virtue, Law and Liberty". James Gibbs's Gothick Temple of Liberty (c. 1740–44) at Stowe boasts a traceried dome painted with the heraldry of the Saxon Heptarchy. Sanderson Miller designed a memorial in honour of Caractacus for Wroxton Park, Oxfordshire. After all this, one might be excused for supposing that Keene's Vandalian Tower (1774) at Uppark commemorated the barbarian conquerors of North Africa. In fact it recalls "Vandalia", an abortive colonial settlement in the New World. Perhaps the choicest specimen of this genre was Miller's tower at Edgehill, Warwickshire (1747–50). It was designed to enshrine a statue of Caractacus on the spot where Charles I raised his standard against the Roundheads, and was ceremonially opened on the anniversary of Cromwell's death. But that celebrated monument ushers in a new phase, the Picturesque; and introduces us at last to

Horace Walpole.

Horace Walpole is usually regarded as the prince of Rococo Goths. In fact Strawberry Hill was only begun after the style had been disseminated by men like Lightoler, Langley, Decker and Halfpenny. And more than anyone Walpole killed the freedom of Rococo by popularizing the cult of archaeology. His own passion for Gothick was perhaps born out of reaction to the solemn splendours of his father's Palladian seat at Houghton. It was a passion easily communicated to his friends. Walpole soon became the centre of a talented circle, and his influence extended even to his enemies. A new generation appeared, antiquaries as well as poets, "the founders of the Gothic Revival": Thomas Gray, John Chute, James West, Sir Roger Newdigate, Ivory Talbot, Richard Bentley, Thomas Barrett, Sanderson Miller, James Essex, Thomas Pitt – "those primal pseudo-Gothics", as Avray Tipping unhappily called them. Like Walpole they grew up under the shadow of Palladianism, but in the heretical corner of their hearts they adored Gothick and looked back fondly to a time when

> Art and Palladio had not reached the land,
> Nor methodised the Vandal Builder's hand.

Strawberry Hill saw Gray, Chute, Bentley, Barrett and Essex all in league with Walpole. At Radway Grange, Warwickshire (1744–6), Sanderson Miller cautiously Gothicized his own seventeenth-century home. At Belhus in Essex (1745–7) Thomas Barrett, later Lord Dacre, combined forces with Miller to medievalize a genuine Tudor house. Apart from an occasional "miscarriage into total Ionic", Walpole approved of the results as "good King James the First Gothic". Talbot once told Miller: "the Beauty of Gothick Architecture . . . consists, like that of a Pindarick Ode, in the Boldness and Irregularity of its Members". At lovely Lacock Abbey in Wiltshire (1754–5), with help from Miller and Keene, he put his beliefs into practice. At Donnington Grove, Berkshire (c. 1760–70), John Chute justified Walpole's description of him as that "oracle of taste", by building for J. P. Andrews, F.S.A., a Gothick retreat ("Chaucer's Grove") sufficiently elegant to satisfy even the young Beau Brummell who grew up there during holidays from Eton. And at Alscot Park (1750–52; 1762–9) [plate 6] and Arbury (c. 1748–95), both in Warwickshire, the ideals of this group came nearer to fruition than anywhere except Strawberry Hill. West's work at Alscot has already been noticed in connection with the transition from survivalist masonry to "Carpenters' Gothick". It also contains some superb plasterwork by the same stuccoist, Robert Moor, who worked at Radway and Arbury. At Arbury "a half-converted Jacobite", Sir Roger Newdigate – that "learned Knight of Taste" – spent half a century creating a masterpiece of Rococo Gothick. Hiorn, Miller, Keene and Couchman were the architects involved, plus Miller's mason Hitchcox, King the carver, Bromwich the decorator and Moor and Hanwell, plasterers. The result lives on as George Eliot's Cheverell Manor in *Scenes from Clerical Life* and as Mallinger Abbey in *Daniel Deronda*. All these patrons were antiquaries, as were other peripheral members of the Walpole-Miller circle: William Mason, Sir Edward Lyttelton and Bishop Hurd, author of *Letters on Chivalry and Romance* (1762). As decoration at Arbury neared completion it became more and more archaeological, with motifs from the Oxford Divinity School or the Great Staircase at Christ Church recalling Newdigate's patronage of his old university. It was a process brought to maturity at Strawberry Hill.

By comparison with the achievements of the seventeenth century, early eighteenth-century antiquarianism appears a dilettante occupation. Still, the Society of Antiquaries was founded in 1707 and re-formed in 1717, to be quickly followed by the Gentlemen's Society at Spalding in Lincolnshire and by others at Peterborough, Stamford, Doncaster, Wisbech, Lincoln, Worcester and Dublin. An affection for medieval antiquities lingered below the surface of fashionable classicism. Connoisseurs bought views by Buck as well as *Vitruvius Britannicus*. Ned Ward's *London Spy* (1699) had spoken of Henry VII's Chapel, Westminster, as worthy of "the admiration of the whole universe . . . knit together by the fingers of angels, pursuant to the directions of Omnipotence". E. Hatton's *New View of London* (1708) called it an "unparallelled edifice" with an "incomparable roof". Defoe's *Tour* (1724–7) contains a eulogy of Lichfield. Thomas Gent's *York* (1730) and *Ripon* (1733) burn with admiration: he found the "awful ruins" of Kirkstall Abbey produced a feeling of "inward veneration . . . enough to strike the most hardened heart into the softest and most serious reflection". By 1745 Joseph Warton's *Enthusiast* and Thomas Warton's *Pleasures of Melancholy* were really preaching to the converted. Protests against destruction or "restoration" were already beginning to be heard from men like Sir John Clerk (Roslyn Chapel) or the Earl of Scarborough (Roche Abbey). The career of William Stukeley sums up the gradual acceptance of Gothick by antiquarians. As a young man, a founder-member of the Society of Antiquaries, he wished only "to extirpate Gothicism". He regarded Hawksmoor's All Souls as "an anachronism of the Gothic degenerate taste", and even disliked the survivalist work at University College: "uniformity . . . is no sufficient reason for using the old style of building". But by about 1740 he could think of a visit to the ruins of Croyland Abbey as "a religious pilgrimage", and described York Minster as "superior . . . to any building upon earth", even preferring its Chapter House to the Pantheon. He ended by himself designing a Gothick bridge (1744) and mausoleum for the Duke of Montagu, and actually installed a Gothick grotto (1738) for potted plants in his garden at Stamford, admitting "the building is theatrical". By 1750

Burke's "sacred awe" in Westminster Abbey was a very conventional emotion. "In truth", Sprague Allen concludes, "Walpole was no more the 'father' of Gothicism than Shakespeare . . . was the 'father' of English drama. Strawberry Hill was the outgrowth of a taste that had long been maturing and represented merely a stage in its evolution . . . Walpole brought to a focus artistic and anti-quarian interests that he found already current".

Walpole was himself convinced that Strawberry Hill marked a great step forward. So it did, but not quite in the way that he expected. Details borrowed directly from his plasterwork reappear in places as far apart as Raby Castle, Co. Durham; Drumtochty Castle, Kincardineshire; and Castleward, Co. Down. Indirect influence was, however, still more pervasive, and much more permanent. Walpole's restless urge to alter and improve – in his own words he was "always piddling about alterations and improvements" – accidentally gave his "small capricious house" an organic plan formation of considerable influence in the development of Picturesque Gothick. And the romantic gusto with which he approached the task found incidental expression in *The Castle of Otranto* (1765), a portent of much Gothickry to come. Advised by his "Strawberry Hill Com-mittee", he consciously set himself up as Gothick arbiter in chief. Kent's library at Rousham he dismissed as "a half-kind of Gothic", although the architect had at least "stuck as close as *he* could" to the true style. In Gray's words, Kent "had not read the Gothic classics with taste or attention". Walpole thought Belhus "not up to the perfection of the Committee". Sanderson Miller's Picturesque ruins were agreed worthy to win him "the freedom of Strawberry". But an *imprimatur* could hardly have been awarded to that insouciant piece of Gothickry, Miller's Billiard Room at Enville, Staffordshire (1750), its Batty Langley manners garnished with busts of Homer and Cicero. Walpole was aiming at something different, something more precise than "the true rust of the Baron's wars". He found it in archaeology, in the simulation of antique fragments.

Strawberry Hill became a treasure-house of Gothick souvenirs. The chimney-piece in the China Room derived its upper part from a window at Bradfield Hall and its lower part from a chimney at Hurstmonceaux. One of his bedroom chimneypieces was based on the tomb at Westminster of William Dudley, Bishop of Durham. The adjoining tomb of another Bishop of Durham, Thomas Ruthall, supplied a model for another chimney in the parlour. Bentley's Holbein Chamber derived its ceiling from the Queen's Dressing Room at Windsor, its chimney from the Warham tomb at Canterbury and its pierced screens from the choir gates at Rouen. Gray thought it the best room in Strawberry Hill. He was less happy about the Gallery, designed by Chute and Pitt. Although the door came from the north portal of St Albans, the stucco ceiling from the fan-vaulting in the side aisles of Henry VII's Chapel, and the recesses from the Bourchier tomb at

Canterbury, he felt that the general effect "had degenerated into finery . . . all Gothicism and gold, and crimson and looking glass". The Cabinet or Tribune was perhaps Walpole's favourite – his "Star Chamber". With its roof recalling the chapter house at York, its niches from St Albans, its "altar" from the tomb of Edward III's children at Westminster, lit from above "in all the glory of Popery" by a star of yellow glass, it seemed indeed to have "all the air of a Catholic chapel – bar consecration". In the Library Chute's bookcases came from the side doors to the choir in old St Paul's, and the chimneypiece echoed the tombs of John of Eltham at Westminster and the Duke of Clarence at Canterbury. In the garden Gayfere's Chapel echoed Bishop Audley's tomb at Salisbury; Essex's gatepiers were modelled in Coade stone with details taken from the tomb of Bishop William de Luda at Ely, and even the stepped brick wall was copied from that at Aston Hall near Birmingham. Of course there was a good deal of romance about it all. The staircase was decorated with wallpaper modelled on Prince Arthur's tomb at Worcester. But it was lit by a Gothick lantern designed by Bentley to cast "the most venerable gloom . . . that was ever seen since the days of Abelard". And Essex's Beauclerk Tower was the prettiest bauble of all: "my little hexagon . . . so small, so perfect, so respectable; you would swear it came out of Havering in the Bower, and that Catherine de Valois used to retire in it to write to Owen Tudor. . . . It is one of those tall thin Flemish towers with a roof like an extinguisher, and puts me in mind of that at Thornbury called Buckingham's Plotting Closet".

Yet Walpole's "little Gothic castle" did embody a new element in the history of the Gothic Revival: the archaeological principle. His models were engravings in Dugdale's *St Paul's* (1658), Dart's *Westminster* (1723), Dugdale's *Warwickshire* (1656), Thomas's *Worcester* (1737) and Sandford's *Genealogical History of the Kings of England* (1677). When Robert Adam began work in the Round Room, Walpole personally sent him copies of Dugdale and Dart. Even those he trusted most – Chute, "the genius that presided over poor Strawberry", or J. H. Muntz – creator of the Gothick Cathedral at Kew (1753) [plate 11], "a painter . . . an engraver . . . a mechanic . . . everything" – were subject to a careful and constant supervision. "I do not love to trust a hammer or a brush," he wrote, "without my own supervisal." Before long he found his own earliest efforts lacking in accuracy and precision. In 1788 he admitted the "imperfections and bad excesses of my attempts; for neither Mr Bentley nor my workmen had *studied* the science". By 1794 he confessed that "every true Goth must perceive" that his first operations had been "more the works of fancy than of imitation". At the very start in 1749 he had even relied on a man who was almost completely ignorant of Gothic, the government architect, William Robinson. By the 1780s, however, Strawberry Hill had been placed in the hands of a scholarly designer of very different stamp, James Essex – "our only architect", as Mason called him. And towards the end of his life Walpole was looking to the rising star of a wholly new generation, James Wyatt. It was a generation identified not with the Rococo, but with the next stage in the history of the movement, the Picturesque.

c. Picturesque Gothick

The word "picturesque" derives from the Italian *pittoresco* meaning "after the manner of painters". The formation of the word is itself an explanation. A group of seventeenth-century French and Italian masters, chiefly Claude Lorraine, Salvator Rosa and Gaspar and Nicholas Poussin, so impressed the susceptibilities of early eighteenth-century Grand Tourists that they conditioned the English-man's way of seeing for more than one hundred years. By the time "Picturesque" assumed its capital letter in the second half of the eighteenth century this way of looking at nature as though it were a series of pictures had been elevated into a visual philosophy, and its product – "le jardin anglais" – had begun a triumphal progress around the world.

As early as 1709 Vanbrugh had suggested that the ruins of Woodstock Manor, set in the landscape at Blenheim, "would make one of the most Agreeable Objects that the best of Landskip Painters can invent". Indeed he is reported to have said, "you must send for a landscape painter". Pope approached the same point of view with his dictum, "all gardening is painting". But it was Kent who first taught the English how to "plant pictures". And it was not until the 1730s and 1740s that this pictorial mode of vision was popularized through the medium of landscape poetry by "that Claude of Poets", James Thomson. Capability Brown produced innumerable pictorial landscapes but no textbooks. For some time the principles of the Picturesque varied with the sensibility of the individual. The very term "Picturesque Beauty" was only coined by the Reverend William Gilpin in 1768. But as the eighteenth century progressed English aesthetic theory experienced a gradual hardening of the categories. Brown's tentative naturalism was found to lack intellectual stuffing: from being "immortal Brown" in 1767 he had become by 1794 that "thin meagre genius of the bare and bald". Rigorous analysis of the new vision began with Burke's *Inquiry into the Origin of our Ideas of the Sublime and the Beautiful* (1756). And in 1794–5 the conjunction of philosophy and practice was belatedly accomplished with the simultaneous publication of Sir Uvedale Price's *Essays on the Picturesque*, Humphry Repton's *Sketches and Hints on Landscape Gardening* and Richard Payne Knight's poem, *The Landscape*, a prelude to his *Analytical Inquiry into the Principles of Taste* (1805). From the

1790s onwards the Picturesque was supreme, dominating the architecture and landscape of the Regency. Both the architecture and town-planning of John Nash are quintessentially Picturesque. Ruysdael and Hobbema had replaced Claude and Poussin as ideal models; but "savage Rosa" was still a fruitful source of inspiration.

As a significant factor in design the Picturesque remained influential until well into the High Victorian period. J. C. Loudon inherited and elaborated Repton's theories, turning the Picturesque into the Gardenesque. Barry, Burn and Salvin long enjoyed what Goodhart-Rendel christened "the empiric hedonism of Picturesque indiscipline". And as late as the 1870s Professor Kerr was combating the Rev. J. L. Petit's penchant for Picturesqueness with his own derivative philosophy of the Architecturesque. Yet Eastlake omits the whole protracted controversy, thus ignoring a key factor in Gothic revivalism from Vanbrugh to Norman Shaw. Perhaps like Ruskin he privately dismissed the Picturesque as "parasitical sublimity". The generation after Eastlake's was even less concerned. Interest in the movement only revived when it could be regarded less as a recipe for design than as a subject for academic discussion. It was not until the 1920s that Christopher Hussey looked out at the view from Scotney Castle and saw that it was Picturesque.

From the start the Picturesque included Gothick elements. Ruined buildings and antique fortifications could usually be found in

> What e'er *Lorrain* light-touched with softening Hue,
> Or savage *Rosa* dashed, or learned *Poussin* drew.

When the Italian landscape was anglicized such buildings were mentally translated into ruins of vaguely medieval provenance. By the end of the eighteenth century, when the qualities assumed to be Sublime, Beautiful or Picturesque had been argued over for the best part of fifty years, Gothick was seen to be seldom Beautiful, frequently Sublime and always Picturesque. The qualities of smoothness and gentleness which Burke identified in Beauty were scarcely attributes of medievalism. But the vastness, infinity and terror of the Sublime, the ruggedness and variety of the Picturesque, were recognized as eminently Gothick. In the minds of the Gothick architect, or the Gothick novelist, sublimity and picturesqueness frequently merged in an attempt to recapture that elusive medieval haze. And since sublimity was more easily recaptured in words than in bricks and mortar, the Gothick buildings of George III's reign are best categorized by the single label "Picturesque". In practice this means above all two things: irregularity and pictorial impact. Walpole considered "Kent's ruling principle was that Nature abhors a straight line". Certainly irregularity became one of the hallmarks of Romantic taste, the link between Rococo and the Picturesque. It was soon regarded as something of a cliché, as Garrick and Colman pointed out in *The*

Clandestine Marriage (1766): ". . . none of your strait lines here – but all taste – zig-zag – crinkum-crankum – in and out – right and left – so and again – twisting and turning like a worm". The naturalistic landscapes of Brown or Repton proceeded from the same Romantic impulse which produced a long line of asymmetrical buildings stretching from Vanbrugh to Nash, and beyond. In each case the landscape was more than a suitable setting. Uvedale Price recommended that an architect "accommodate his building to the scenery, not make that give way to the building". The Rococo began, and the Picturesque completed, the conjunction of architecture with nature. Architectural composition became a matter of overall conception, based on the principle of points of vision, linking up a series of scenic entities and aiming first and foremost at pictorial effect. Picturesque Gothick may therefore be most frequently recognized by its calculated irregularity. And whenever it appears it can only be fairly judged by its degree of pictorial impact. Such judgments came hard to Eastlake: he was too close to Pugin to understand what he called the "pre-Puginesque" period.

The habit of regarding buildings as scenery, with or without the help of a "Claude glass" or "camera obscura", encouraged not only irregular skylines and asymmetrical plans, but triangular, hexagonal and octagonal features, eyecatchers, and all manner of follies. The "prospect tower" already had a history going back to medieval hunting parties. Its Gothick successor reversed the original purpose: it was designed not to look from, but to be looked at. Horton Tower, Dorset (*c.* 1700), is early enough to look both ways. After that the triangular Gothick Tower is a basic landscape feature: the tower at Whitton Park, Middlesex (*c.* 1725), by Gibbs or Roger Morris; Shrub Hill (later Fort Belvedere), Windsor (*c.* 1750); Paty's Blaise Castle (1776) near Bristol; Hiorn's Tower at Arundel (*c.* 1787); the Racton Tower, Sussex (1772); the Belvederes of 1773 and 1788 at Powderham and Haldon in Devon; Jupp's Sevendroog Castle on Shooter's Hill (1784); and Paxton's Tower, Carmarthenshire (1805), designed by S. P. Cockerell – to name only a few. Robert Adam discovered that the Picturesque triangle embodied his own criteria of "movement" and adopted jt in castellated form at Airthrey (1790) and elsewhere. Triangular also were Carter's Midford Castle, Somerset (*c.* 1775), Carr's Grimston Garth, Yorkshire (1781–6), Harrison's Hawkestone Citadel, Shropshire (*c.* 1824), and the castle at Aberystwyth designed by John Nash in the early 1790s for no less a pundit than Uvedale Price. All these are triply Picturesque. But James Wyatt went one, or rather several stages better with his tower "in the Saxon [i.e. Neo-Norman] style" on Spring Hill above Broadway in Worcestershire (1794). It has three round turrets and three canted sides: six corners in all. The Culloden Tower at Richmond, Yorkshire (1746), follows the same principle, this time in octagonal form – and its Kentian interior serves to underline the continuity between Rococo forms and

Picturesque theory. Eyecatchers like King John's Hunting Lodge (*c.* 1730), overlooking Dogmersfield Park, Hampshire, or the "Gothick Object" designed *c.* 1755 by Sanderson Miller as a focal feature visible from Ralph Allen's house in Bath, demonstrate the scenic properties of Gothick in the simplest possible way. Sanderson Miller, *maestro ruinante*, achieved his greatest successes in this particular genre with those celebrated scenic ruins of 1747–8 and 1750 at Hagley Park, Worcestershire and Wimpole, Cambridgeshire [plate 8]. Commenting on Hagley in 1748, Shenstone remarked that "there is no great art or variety in ye Ruin, but the situation gives it a charming effect". Such effects were often novel and dramatic, and sometimes beautiful. At Arnos Court near Bristol in 1760–65, a prosperous copper smelter built himself a Gothick seat complete with fantastic stables ribbed with slag. Even Walpole was shaken to find it "coal black and striped with white; I took it for the devil's cathedral". At Ottershaw Park in Surrey, *c.* 1800, James Wyatt constructed a Gothick dairy fitted out in the shape of a cruciform church, with central tower, apse and Perpendicular tracery. And at Croome D'Abitot, Worcestershire (1761–6), Capability Brown and Robert Adam together produced a Rococo Gothick church which managed to be eminently Picturesque without being in the least meretricious. Still, most eyecatchers were flimsy creations, making no pretence of functionalism: their function was effect. In domestic architecture, however, this pursuit of optical devices occasionally produced bizarre results. Castle Goring, Sussex (*c.* 1790) and Castleward, Co. Down (*c.* 1762) both boast two independent façades, one classical in style, the other medieval. Smirke's Lowther Castle, Westmorland (1806–11), was only slightly more subtle in combining complementary images, one Gothick, one castellated. Wordsworth thoroughly approved, praising its

> Cathedral pomp and grace in apt accord
> With the baronial castle's sterner mien.

But such deceits were sitting targets for the ethical aestheticians of a later generation.

So medieval styles were exploited in Picturesque contexts because of their optical effects. They were also of course powerfully evocative. And in this respect two factors contributed greatly to the popularity of Picturesque Gothick: the cult of wild scenery and the craze for "horrid" novels. Seventeenth-century travellers were not amused by rugged landscapes. Three soldiers wandering in Westmorland in 1624 found the Lake District "nothing but hideous hanging hills and great Pooles". Twenty years later John Evelyn dismissed the Alps as "the rubbish of the earth . . . strange, horrid . . . fearful . . . and . . . very dangerous". But by 1738 the Picturesque had begun its conditioning process. Dr Thomas Herring discovered that he actually enjoyed wild Wales: "the rubbish of creation" made him "agreeably terrified"; as for rocks, cataracts, woods, herds and peasants, "all these images together put me in mind of Poussin's drawings, and made me fancy myself in Savoy, at least, if not nearer Rome". In the following year Horace Walpole visited the Grand Chartreuse and gasped: "Precipices, mountains, torrents, wolves, rumblings, Salvator Rosa! . . ." By 1778 Lakeside excursions were regarded as "the *ton* of the present hour", and wondering visitors were instructed to look out for "the delicate touches of *Claude* . . . on *Coniston* Lake, . . . the noble scenes of *Poussin* . . . on *Windermere*-water, and . . . the stupendous romantic ideas of *Salvator Rosa* realised in the Lake of *Derwent*". In a series of lyrical tours Gilpin opened up the beauties of the Wye valley for general consumption. As for Scotland, Gray simply reported: "the mountains are ecstatic". Thinking pictorially, Walpole summed up the new attitude with his remark: "mountains are very good frames to a prospect". Amid such surroundings Gothick buildings fitted happily, and the more, "ruinated" the better. In 1770 Gilpin even dared to suggest that Tintern Abbey might be scenically improved by "a mallet judiciously used (but who durst use it?)".

Fiction, however, permitted the use of mallets and indeed of many fiercer weapons. *The Castle of Otranto* spawned a whole brood of Gothick romances. Novels like Clara ·Reeve's *Old English Baron* (1777), Mrs Ann Radcliffe's *Mysteries of Udolpho* (1794), and C. R. Maturin's *Melmoth the Wanderer* (1820) employed a veritable armoury of Gothick properties: dungeons and battlements, clanking chains, windy ramparts and cloud-capped towers. Titles like *Manfrone, or The One-Handed Monk, Horrid Mysteries* and *The Castle of Wolfenbach* speak for themselves. "The public . . . rushed upon" *Udolpho*, wrote Scott; "the volumes flew, and were sometimes torn from hand to hand". M. G. Lewis carried the cult of the horrid to an unwholesome climax with his scabrous saga of *The Monk* (1796). Gray remarked that *Otranto* kept people awake at nights. Coleridge denounced *The Monk* as a positive incentive to sin. Mary Shelley's *Frankenstein* (1818) could hardly do more. It was a fashion based partly on English and partly on foreign sources. It was heralded by a revival of interest in old English literature and brought to maturity by the influence of German romanticism. Macpherson's *Ossian* (1760–63), Percy's *Reliques* (1765), Chatterton's *Rowley Poems* (1777), run parallel to a remarkable upsurge of interest in Spenser and Shakespeare. By the 1760s translations from Goethe and Schiller were also very much in vogue. In 1798 Lady Holland noted in her journal: "the rage for German plays still continues". Southey announced in the same year: "Coleridge's ballad 'The Ancient Mariner' is . . . the clumsiest attempt at German sublimity I ever saw". But twelve months later he admitted that the spate of translations had made him "hunger and thirst after German poetry". The stupendous Neo-Norman chambers of Thomas Hopper's Penrhyn

Castle (*c.* 1827–47) belong to the same school of Gothick fantasy as Schinkel's medieval stage sets (*c.* 1817) and "Monk" Lewis's translations from E. T. A. Hoffmann. The far East was another source of inspiration. But despite its oriental setting, *Vathek* (1786) belongs firmly in the Gothick mould. And its author, William Beckford, joined forces with James Wyatt to create that apotheosis of the Sublime and the Picturesque, Fonthill Abbey (1796–1807) [plate 14]. The worst excesses of the horrid novel were over when Sir Walter Scott began to produce the Waverley Novels (1814–32). But the Gothick properties are still there, only used with far greater facility and discretion. Shelley himself wrote Gothick novels like *The Assassins* (1814); Byron's epic tales are suffused with Gothick imagery; and the stained glass of Hopper's Gothick chapel at Stansted, Sussex (1819) lives on in Keats's *Eve of St Agnes* and *Eve of St Mark*. The popularity of medievalism was immense. After all, as Walpole remarked, though taste is required to appreciate Greek, one only needs passions to like Gothic. The passions associated with Gothickry had always been the mainstay of revivalism. Mad monks and mountains followed naturally from ruins and rococo. Both the Rococo and the Picturesque emphasized the allusive, associational aspects of architectural design. And in 1790 associationalism was at last made philosophically respectable by Archibald Alison's *Essays on the Nature and Principles of Taste.*

The classic Picturesque building type was of course the Gothick castle, or rather the country house "in the castle style". The German poet Novalis defined Romanticism as an attempt "to give sense to the vulgar, mysteriousness to the common, dignity of the unknown to the obvious, and a trace of infinity to the temporal". The Gothick castle satisfied most of these criteria. It could express the pride of ancient lineage; and it could turn a grocer's residence into a fairy-tale palace. The Victorians admired medieval architecture for both its intrinsic and ethical qualities. But the qualities admired in the eighteenth century were primarily evocative. The fascination of horror played a big part in the popularity of the Picturesque. Even scholars like the topographer Captain Grose held a curiously over-dramatic view of life in a medieval fortress: "dreary mansions . . . where the enjoyment of light and air was sacrificed to the consideration of strength . . . times when this unhappy kingdom was torn by intestine wars; when son was armed against father, and brother slaughtered brother; when the lives, honour and properties of the wretched inhabitants depended on the nod of an arbitrary King, or were subject to the more tyrannical and capricious wills of lawless and foreign barons". Such ideas about feudal castles were eventually translated into fortifications appropriate to the age of gunpowder. In Dr Rowan's words, most of the early revivalists saw "among the mists of antiquity an insistent haze of cannon smoke". As early as 1699 castellated additions had been made to Hampton Court in Herefordshire, perhaps by William Talman; a few years later Stukeley was entertained there by Lord Coningsby in medieval fashion with an "ancient bard" playing the harp. But it is only with the work of Captain Vanbrugh at Blackheath (1717), Stowe (Bourbon Tower, *c.* 1720) and Castle Howard (fortified walls in the Chester manner) that the castle style really begins. And it was not until the arrival of another architect bred in the traditions of the Ordnance Office – Robert Adam – and an amateur pundit of almost equal prestige – Richard Payne Knight – that the Picturesque castle was truly launched.

Gothick castles can be sorted, according to their layout, into three groups: those with courtyard plans; those with centralized plans; and those with irregular plans. Enmore Castle, Somerset, was built during the early 1750s around an immense quadrangle, and boasted moat, drawbridge, watch-towers, and a gatehouse modelled on Hurstmonceaux. It was designed by an eccentric Earl of Egmont, "whose hobby horse was the feudal system". Not surprisingly, it had few successors. The centralized plan form, however, was widely adopted. In fact its combination of central keep, rectangular ramparts and four corner turrets, endlessly mimicked in pantomime or nursery, eventually entered the Englishman's subconscious as the prototype fairy-tale castle. Inveraray Castle, Argyllshire (begun 1745) [plate 5] is the classic example. Designed by Roger Morris, an architect and officer in the Board of Ordnance, on the lines of a scheme by Vanbrugh; executed by William, John and Robert Adam, completed by Robert Mylne and altered by Joseph Bonomi, its greenish bulk stands four-square in the centre of a romantic tradition. It looks back via Clearwell (*c.* 1735) and Mount Edgecumbe to Wollaton, Lulworth, Bodiam and Beaumaris. It looks forward to James Wyatt's Kew Palace (1802–11) and Ashridge, Hertfordshire (1808–13 and 1813–17), to Smirke's Lowther Castle, Westmorland and Eastnor Castle, Herefordshire (1812–15), to Taymouth Castle, Perthshire (1806), by James and Archibald Elliot, and The Lee, Lanarkshire (1820), by James Gillespie Graham, and so on to a host of lesser imitations. It was a tradition which joined the convenience of Palladian planning to a simple, massed silhouette, instantly, naïvely medieval. The Gothick castles of Robert and James Adam may perhaps be counted as a subdivision of this group: their plans are regular, or at least geometrical, without being centralized. After experimenting with Rococo Gothick at Strawberry Hill, Croome, Alnwick and Ford, the brothers developed a transitional style classical in conception, medieval in detail, as at Ugbrooke (1762), Mellerstain (1770–8) and Wedderburn (1771). Later Adam castles, notably Culzean (1777–87), Airthrey (1790) [plate 13] and Seton (1789–91), are less concerned with medieval souvenirs and more with compositional effects. Such translations of Adam's doctrine of movement into castellated terms – the three-dimensional massing at Seton for example – make orthodox "centralized" castles look somewhat pedestrian. As regards detail, moreover, the later Adam castles constitute a marvellous synthesis of ancient, Renaissance and vernacular sources. The towers at Maudslie, Lanarkshire (1792), were borrowed from Falkland and Holyroodhouse; the Auchincruive Tower, Ayrshire (1778), derives from Theodoric's Mausoleum at Ravenna; and the parapet, cornice and fenestration at Seton have been traced to Diocletian's palace at Split. Such hybrid creations, suitably placed, were often highly Picturesque. Culzean's dour hulk, looming high on a rocky outcrop, must surely rank as one of Robert Adam's most dramatic works. But the Adams never really shook off the habits of their classical training. Their Gothick castles wear medieval clothes a little self-consciously. By 1806 J. C. Loudon was dismissing the imposture as "ridiculous". "It was", Dr Rowan concludes, "as if the brothers had rewritten in Church Latin the classical text of Vitruvius; the immediate impression was medieval, yet underneath the logic of classicism remained." It was the third group of Gothick castles, those with irregular form, which best satisfied the tenets of the Picturesque and held the key to the future development of the Gothic Revival.

Three milestones mark the progress of the irregular Gothick castle: Blackheath (1717 onwards); Strawberry Hill (1749–76) [plate 7] and Downton Castle, Herefordshire (1772–8) [plate 12]. All three are only accidentally irregular; each was the product of a spasmodic building programme. Visually and ideologically, Payne Knight's Downton occupies a key position, the link between Walpole and Nash. Its organic plan and irregular silhouette were accentuated in later additions by Nash. And it was Nash who carried this particular genre to a brilliant conclusion with such Irish triumphs of Picturesque design as Killymoon, Co. Tyrone (1803), Lough Coutra, Co. Galway (c. 1817) and Shanbally, Co. Tipperary (c. 1812) – not to mention exquisite Luscombe Castle (c. 1800) in Devon and his own country seat, East Cowes Castle (c. 1798) in the Isle of Wight. Nash certainly adopted Payne Knight's allusive approach to style. His Gothick castles are boldly unarchaeological. Repton's comment on Downton could be applied with equal force to East Cowes Castle: "its outline was directed by the eye of a painter, rather than that of an antiquary". Nash's details seldom repay a second look. They mostly consist of castellated fragments misapplied in a domestic medium. James Wyatt's technique, on the other hand, made a habit of secularizing ecclesiastical sources. The result was a synthetic style, frequently handled with considerable panache. Lee Priory, Kent (1783–90), that "child of Strawberry, prettier than the parent", made Walpole sigh for William of Wykeham's misfortune in being born too early. By the same analogy Belvoir Castle, Leicestershire (1801–13; additions by Thoroton 1816–30), must surely have electrified the ghosts of both Henry III and Edward I. It was Repton who first identified Wyatt's eclecticism as "the mixed Gothic style". Of Ashridge, Herts. (1808–17) [plate 15], he wrote: "It may perhaps be asked by the fastidious antiquary, whether the whole most resembles a castle, an abbey or a collegiate pile. To which may be given this simple answer: it is a modern house, on a large scale." Payne Knight himself could have said no more. Individual details at Ashridge or Belvoir are often surprisingly accurate – usually adaptations of well-known Perpendicular sources. It is their combination and scale which is irregular, and the materials which are false. But as Goodhart-Rendel pointed out, "it is arguable that Wyatt's careless eclecticism was an advantage to him as a creative artist. His strength was very great in that most architectural of processes, the composition of masses, in which he may be considered almost a second Vanbrugh". From the Picturesque point of view, Wyatt's most significant castellated houses were perhaps Norris Castle, Isle of Wight (1799), Pennsylvania Castle, Isle of Portland (1800), and a design for Shoebury Castle, Essex (1797). All three show the architect moving towards a truly Picturesque conception, independent of historicist detailing. It was, however, his "mixed" Gothick, "the architecture of olden time", which found the greatest number of imitators. And in the hands of lesser men, like H. E. Kendall or William Atkinson, Picturesque Gothick degenerated into a spurious asymmetry, what Dr Rowan acutely calls "the concatenation of symmetrical parts" – castles like Panshanger, Hertfordshire (1806–22), or Chiddingstone, Kent (c. 1810), "at their best . . . fortuitously pretty, at their worst . . . the nadir of the castle style". Byron's *Don Juan* found an easy target in

> . . . Norman Abbey . . .
> An old, old monastery once, and now
> Still older mansion, – of a rich and rare
> Mixed Gothic . . .

It was against such buildings as these that Pugin directed some of his fiercest salvoes.

The degeneration of the Picturesque during the Regency period applied to landscape as well as to architecture. What began as the pursuit of a pictorial ideal ended as an obsession with "irregular effects". Compare the Arcadian simplicity of Stourhead with the calculated clutter of Alton Towers, mostly laid out by the fifteenth Earl of Shrewsbury between 1814 and 1827. "Such a labyrinth of terraces," wrote Loudon, "curious architectural walls, trellis-work arbours, vases, statues, stone stairs, wooden stairs, turf stairs, pavements, gravel and grass walks, ornamental buildings, bridges, porticoes, temples, pagodas, gates, iron railings, parterres, jets, ponds, streams, seats, fountains, caves, flower baskets, waterfalls, rocks, cottages, trees, shrubs, beds of flowers, ivied walls, rock-work, shell-work, root-work, moss houses, old trunks of trees, entire dead trees, etc., that it is utterly impossible for words to give any idea of the effect." Disraeli immortalized Alton as Muriel Towers in *Lothair*:

After luncheon they visited the gardens . . . formed in a sylvan valley enclosed with gilded gates. . . .

"Perhaps too many temples," said Lothair, "but this ancestor of mine had some imagination."

"I hope I shall see the wild cattle," said Lady Corisande. . . .

The *Official Guide* used to assure spectators that "the scene is like a piece of superb theatrical scene-painting. Here Boccacio might have wooed, and Watteau painted". At the entrance a replica of the Lysicrates monument remembers the fifteenth Earl: "he made the desert smile". Generations of visitors have replied with the old quip: "and a very polite desert it was not to laugh outright". When Pugin was eventually called in by the sixteenth Earl, he was certainly not amused.

In its effect on architecture, therefore, the Picturesque encouraged pictorial qualities at the expense of architectural qualities: movement, irregularity, contrast, mystery, romance and texture rather than Wotton's Vitruvian trio, "commoditie, firmness and delighte". One picture sums it all up: Turner's visionary painting (*c.* 1807) of Hafod in Cardiganshire, designed in several stages by Thomas Baldwin and John Nash for an eccentric collector, Thomas Johnes M.P. With later additions by Wyatt and Salvin, the building history of the estate stretched over a period of seventy years between the 1780s and the 1850s, incorporating a multiplicity of styles and scenic devices. Its description in Borrow's *Wild Wales* (1854), effusive and pardonably inaccurate, serves almost as an epitaph on the whole Picturesque movement: "A truly fair place it looked, beautiful but fantastic. . . . At the South end was a Gothic tower; at the Northern an Indian pagoda; the middle part had the appearance of a Grecian villa. The walls were of resplendent whiteness, and the windows which were numerous shone with a beautiful gilding." Borrow gazed at it bemused for fifteen minutes, "sometimes with admiration, sometimes with a strong disposition to laugh". Carried to extremes, the purely aesthetic criteria of Picturesque Gothick were just as fallacious as later obsessions with moral and ethical criteria. As Gothicists, Nash, Wyatt and their lesser followers were basically "great picture-makers". In Goodhart-Rendel's words, "they exploited the emotional associations of Gothic forms without reference to their constructional significance. Theirs is not a very high form of architecture; but to condemn it utterly shows a Ruskinian lack of humour or an unwholesomely small love of adventure". A sense of humour, however, was something which the next generation of Goths conspicuously lacked. Anyway, by the 1830s the time was ripe for a return to first principles. The Picturesque retreated to the Celtic fringe. Its last full-blown examples, careless of precedent and wildly dramatic, are in Wales: Gwyrch, Denbighshire (C. A. Busby, 1814) and Bodelwyddan, Flintshire (Hansom and Welch, *c.* 1830?); Cyfartha, Glamorganshire (*c.* 1825) and Maesllwch, Radnorshire (1828–39) by Robert Lugar. When realism replaced romanticism the Gothick castle disappeared. Sir Jeffry Wyatville's Windsor (1824–40) was perhaps the last. Hopper's Penrhyn (*c.* 1827–47), Salvin's Peckforton, Cheshire (1844–50) and Blore's Goodrich Court, Herefordshire (1828) are all in their different ways fanatically historicist, and therefore no longer truly Gothick. The Picturesque has survived in vestigial form even into the twentieth century. But it was never the same again after Pugin had translated into Gothic terms the French rationalists' gospel of "truth".

The first step in this quest for architectural verities arose out of an increasing concern for archaeology. To devotees of the Picturesque, accuracy of detail was irrelevant to "modern Gothick". Starting from the premise that "there is no pure Gothic", Payne Knight ended by advocating the use of "mixed Gothic" or Tudoresque. After all, there were plenty of variegated precedents in "that mixed style which characterises the buildings of Claude and the Poussins". Besides, copyism was only the first step towards fraud: "a house may be adorned with towers and battlements, or pinnacles and flying buttresses; but it should still maintain the character of a house of the age and country in which it was erected; and not pretend to be a fortress or monastery of a remote period or distant country". As late as 1827 G. L. Meason's *Italian Landscape Architecture* was still offering amorphous, hybrid buildings culled from Raphael, Titian or Solimena as suitable models for imitation. Inevitably, however, those antiquaries who were really the backbone of the revivalist movement gradually encouraged a greater concern for authenticity. But it was not until the 1830s that the publication of Gothic source material matched the classical publications of the eighteenth century in either quality or quantity.

Before the arrival of Dugdale's works, illustrations of Gothic buildings were rare and wholly inadequate – the indistinct woodcuts in Lambard's *Perambulations of Kent* (1570), for example, or the marginal engravings in Speed's *Theatre of the Empire of Great Britain* (1611). But even Dugdale – like Aubrey and Thoroton after him – concentrated on literary rather than pictorial evidence. Kip, Knyff and Buck were likewise limited by the conventions of their bird's-eye surveys. Stukeley's *Itinerarium Curiosum* (1725) was the first to incorporate plans rather than views, and Price's *Salisbury* (1753) first made use of sectional drawings to explain the structural premises of Gothic design. Unlike Browne Willis, "old wrinkle-boots" as he was called, Francis Price was concerned with the fabric of a building rather than its history, with stones rather than records. From the 1760s onwards there are signs of a growing wish to get beyond the generalized enthusiasm of Gray and Walpole to a genuine understanding of Gothic based on detailed membrological and ichnographical study. Price's influence is reflected in Bentham's

Ely (1771), Halfpenny's *York* (1795) and Milner's *Winchester* (1798). But the impact of these topographical classics was limited. Murphy's *Batalha* (1795) was rather more influential. Twenty-seven architects subscribed; and certain details of Fonthill Abbey confirm the debt which Wyatt's Gothick owed to an Irishman's impressions of a Portuguese monastery. It was only with the arrival of John Carter, John Britton and A. C. Pugin, however, that the English Gothic Revival at last gave up romanticism for archaeology. *Gothick* became *Gothic*. The careers of all three men are dealt with at some length by Eastlake, and there is little point in duplicating his details here. From the 1830s onwards Eastlake's account can stand on its own feet. The point to remember is that between them Carter, Britton and A. C. Pugin destroyed the stylistic *laissez-faire* of the Picturesque, just as A. W. Pugin later exposed its ethical bankruptcy. The *Gentleman's Magazine* christened this formidable trio "the Wycliffe . . . Tyndale and Cranmer . . . of our Architectural Reformation". Carter supplied the fire, and A. C. Pugin the artistic technique, but it was Britton's talent for publicity which carried through that bibliographical revolution which separates the Picturesque and Ecclesiological phases of the Gothic Revival. Britton's *Architectural Antiquities* (5 vols., 1807–26), his *Cathedral Antiquities* (14 vols., 1814–35) [plate 16], and his sponsoring of A. C. Pugin and E. J. Willson's *Specimens* (2 vols., 1821–3), radically transformed the progress of the whole movement. Plans, cross-sections, geometrical elevations, measured examples, these replaced the Picturesque views of Gilpin or Grose in the libraries of patrons and on the drawing boards of fashionable draughtsmen.

By the 1830s a new tradition of Gothic craftsmanship was beginning. When Browne Willis rebuilt the chapel at Fenny Stratford (1724–30), he had to Gothicize the master-builder's elevation himself. When in 1751 the Bishop of Durham first began to medievalize he had to ask Sanderson Miller to send him a competent workman from the Midlands, "as our People at Durham do not understand the kind of Antique Work". For the first three-quarters of the eighteenth century progress was very slow. Compare those Leicestershire milestones of revivalism: the elder Wing's church tower at Gaulby (1741), and the younger Wing's nearby church at King's Norton (1760–75). The first is a curiosity, with top-heavy pinnacles of almost Chinese complexity. The second is a suave and sophisticated piece of work, but still happily unaware of structural precedents. Its linear, papery forms reappear at Hiorn's Tetbury church, Gloucestershire (1777–81). Commissioners' churches like Goodwin's Holy Trinity, Birmingham (1820–23), or Rickman's nearby St George's (1819–21) show some progress in the handling of Perpendicular detail, but none at all in matters of authentic structure and liturgical planning. When James Savage's masonry vault at last appeared at St Luke's, Chelsea (1819–25), the congregation was understandably nervous: the apparent lack of support was said to give them "roof on the brain". Eastlake chose that strangely unimpressive building as the origin of the true Gothic Revival in this country. And his claim that St Luke's was the first stone-vaulted church of the Gothic Revival has yet to be disproved. Professor Hitchcock has nominated a church by John Pinch, St Mary's, Bathwick, Bath (1814–20). But Pinch's vault is made of plaster. It was not, however, a church by Savage, nor even one by Rickman, which marked the real breakthrough in matters of style, but Edward Garbett's Holy Trinity, Theale, Berkshire (1820–25). Still, Eastlake's principle of demarcation was a valid one. With the arrival of structural Gothicism, strictly based on archaeological precedents, a new era in British architecture had begun.

Gothic details had now been made available in quantity, to be assimilated into the bloodstream of British architecture. Well might one critic label Britton and his indefatigable partner E. W. Brayley, "the Castor and Pollux of topographers". Accuracy was about to become the very touchstone of architectural orthodoxy. Even the terminology of medieval styles had apparently been reduced to an acceptable formula – Thomas Rickman, the "Quaker quack" as Britton unkindly called him, had produced his magically simple classification just as those age-old controversies regarding the origin and typology of Gothic were beginning to settle. Churches were no longer built "in the modern Gothick manner" but as "Early English", "Decorated" or "Perpendicular" – or perhaps as "first", "second" or "third Pointed". The precision of such nomenclature was more apparent than real: the stylistic labels in Eastlake's appendix (mostly chosen by the architects themselves) are often irritatingly vague. But the triumph of historicism was clear enough. Victorian Gothic had now become a possibility. The Anglican and Catholic revivals added a new and crucial ingredient, liturgical enthusiasm. And in the hands of A. W. Pugin, Carpenter and Butterfield, liturgy and archaeology were transmuted into architecture. In this way the Gothic Revival, which began as a domestic fashion, emerged almost as an ecclesiastical dogma. After the 1830s the Gothic Revival was no longer a cult. It had become a crusade.

J. Mordaunt Crook

BIBLIOGRAPHICAL NOTE

A History of the Gothic Revival: An Attempt to Show how the Taste for Mediæval Architecture which Lingered in England during the Two Last Centuries has since been Encouraged and Developed, by Charles L. Eastlake, was published in London by Longmans, Green and Co. in 1872. The work has never been reprinted.

The present volume reprints photographically Eastlake's Preface and narrative text. The concluding section of the work, comprising pages 373–427 of the original edition, was a chronological survey in tabulated form of "Selected examples of Gothic buildings erected between 1820 and 1870". Entries were listed across facing pages. The verso of each opening contained information about the date, name, situation, architect and style of each building. The recto facing included additional remarks and, where appropriate, references to the text. In the present edition the 343 examples selected by Eastlake are retained but the list has been corrected and additional details and references have been incorporated. A bibliography and index have also been added to increase the reference value of the work. The illustrations included in the original edition have been supplemented by additional plates.

J. L. Madden

The earlier sections of Eastlake's work – up to the death of Pugin in 1852 – first appeared in serial form as "Materials for a History of the Gothic Revival", *Building News*, xi (1864), 607–8, 623–4, 639–40, 656–7, 720–2, 760–1, 780–2, 815–17, 868–9, 917–18, 938–9, 956–7.

J.M.C.

THE GOTHIC REVIVAL

Ave Maria: gratia dilecta: Dominus atecum: benedicta tu inter mulieres: et ecce concipies in utero et paries filium: et vocabis nomen ejus Jesum:

The Annunciation: part of a mural painting by Henry Holiday in the Chancel of All Saints' Church: Notting Hill: William White: FSA: Architect:

A HISTORY

OF

THE GOTHIC REVIVAL

AN ATTEMPT TO SHOW HOW
THE TASTE FOR MEDIÆVAL ARCHITECTURE
WHICH LINGERED IN ENGLAND DURING THE TWO LAST CENTURIES
HAS SINCE BEEN ENCOURAGED AND DEVELOPED

BY

CHARLES L. EASTLAKE

F.R.I.B.A., ARCHITECT

AUTHOR OF 'HINTS ON HOUSEHOLD TASTE'

' *Sic volvenda ætas commutat tempora rerum,*
Quod fuit in pretio, fit nullo denique honore:
Porro aliud succedit, et e contemtibus exit,
Inque dies magis appetitur, floretque repertum
Laudibus, et miro est mortaleis inter honore '

LUCRETIUS

LONDON
LONGMANS, GREEN, AND CO.
1872

PREFACE.

IF ANY PREFACE to this book be needed, it should perhaps take the form of an ample apology for the time which has elapsed between its original announcement and its publication. During that interval, and in such leisure as more urgent duties left at my disposal, I gradually realised the difficulties of the task which I had undertaken.

It has been said of contemporary history that its events are less easy to ascertain with accuracy than those of past time. For my own part, and in reference to this work, I can testify to the fact that much information which I imagined might be obtained for the asking has cost me more trouble to procure than that which required literary research.

As it is, I fear that the following pages will be found deficient in many details, the omission of which I regret, not because it affects in any material degree the thread of my narrative, but because in describing works of equal merit or importance I had hoped to bestow an equal attention on each, and this, in the absence of necessary particulars respecting some of them, has not always been possible.

If I have not ventured to dwell at any length on the present prospects of the Revival, or attempted to enter into details respecting the application of Mediæval design to the specific requirements of domestic and ecclesiastical architecture, it is from a conviction that I could add little or nothing to what has been already said on these points. Mr. G. G. Scott's 'Remarks on Secular and Domestic Architecture,' and Mr. Beresford-Hope's 'English Cathedral of the Nineteenth Century,' are works so exhaustive in their nature, and so practical in their aim, that they leave scarcely a plea to urge or a suggestion to advance in the interest of modern Gothic.

My own object, as will be seen, is of a different kind.

For some years past it has seemed to me that the causes which brought about, and the events which attended, one of the most remarkable revolutions in national art that this country has seen were worthy of some record, if only to serve as a link between the past and future history of English Architecture. In attempting to supply this record, it was my intention from the first to chronicle facts rather than offer criticisms, and where I have departed from this rule it has been for the most part in the case of works which illustrate some marked change in the progress of the Revival.

I felt, as my book advanced, that technical descriptions

of even noteworthy buildings would, if frequently repeated, become tedious to the unprofessional reader. For this reason I have in the majority of instances confined such descriptions to the Tabulated List appended to this volume, in which will be found a selection from the most remarkable structures of a Mediæval character erected by various architects during the last fifty years, chronologically arranged.

In the choice of these examples I have been guided by various considerations ; the date of a building, its local influence on public taste, or the novel character of its design frequently rendering it, in relation to my purpose, an object of greater interest than many others of more intrinsic importance. This explanation will, I trust, be sufficient to account for the absence of many works of acknowledged excellence from my List, which, as it is, has reached a length far beyond what I had anticipated when I began to compile it.

Little or no mention has been made of ‘ Restorations ’— partly because it would have been difficult to draw a definite line between those which have been a simple repair of old buildings, and others which have required archæological skill in execution, but chiefly because in either case such works cannot be said to represent, except indirectly, the genuine progress of modern architecture.

The large proportion of engravings which illustrate buildings erected between 1860 and 1870 as compared with those of former years has prevented their even distribution over the volume. This is hardly satisfactory, but it will probably be considered a less evil than the only possible alternative, viz. their separation from the text to which they relate. I may here observe that the size of these woodcuts does not permit them, though very fairly executed, to convey more than a general idea of the designs represented, and that, like photographic portraits, they never flatter the original. If my readers will kindly remember this, I make no doubt that the architects concerned will be equally indulgent.

To the Editor of the 'Building News' I am indebted for permission to incorporate with this volume a small portion of its contents, which originally appeared in that journal. To many friends, who have kindly helped me with information and suggestions, my best acknowledgments are due for their assistance and advice.

CHARLES L. EASTLAKE.

6 UPPER BERKELEY STREET WEST,
HYDE PARK, W.

CONTENTS.

—◦—

CHAPTER I.

CHAPTER II.

CHAPTER III.

CHAPTER IV.

CHAPTER V.

CHAPTER VI.

CHAPTER VII.

CHAPTER VIII.

CHAPTER IX.

CHAPTER XIV.

CHAPTER XV.

CHAPTER XVI.

CHAPTER XVII.

CHAPTER XVIII.

CHAPTER XIX.

CHAPTER XX.

Errata.

Page 102, line 22, *for* mezzo-relievo *read* mezzo-rilievo.
  „ 191,   „ 26, *for* had *read* had been.
  „ 243,   „   4, *for* latter *read* former.
  „ 270,   „   7, *for* has *read* have.

ILLUSTRATIONS.

———◆◇◆———

Church of St. Andrew, Plaistow, Essex.

James Brooks, Architect, 1867.

HISTORY

OF

THE GOTHIC REVIVAL.

———◦———

CHAPTER I.

THE RENEWAL, in this country, of a taste for Mediæval architecture, and the reapplication of those principles which regulate its design, represent one of the most interesting and remarkable phases in the history of art. Unlike the Italian Renaissance, which was intimately associated with, and in a great measure dependent on, the study of ancient literature, our modern English Revival fails to exhibit, even in its earliest development, many of those external causes to which we are accustomed to attribute a revolution in public taste.

To the various influences which raised this school of art from the crumbling ruins of the Roman empire to its glory in Western Europe, and then permitted it to lapse into degradation in the sixteenth century, history points with an unerring hand. But for the stranger influence which slowly though surely has rescued it from that degradation, which has enlisted such universal sympathy in its behalf, and which bids fair, in spite of ignorant and idle prejudice, to adapt it, after two hundred years of neglect and contumely, to the requirements of a mercantile people and a practical age—for this influence, indeed, if we search at all, we must search in more than one direction.

At first it may seem strange that a style of design which is intimately associated with the romance of the world's history should now-a-days find favour in a country distinguished above all others for the plain business-like tenour of its daily life. But this presents a paradox more obvious in a moral than in an historical sense.

It is not because England has been stigmatised as a nation of shop-keepers that she is necessarily indifferent to the progress of architecture. The fairest palaces of Venice were raised at a time when her commercial prosperity stood at its zenith, but her art and her commerce had grown up together, and if the latter was genuine and healthy, the former was unsophisticated and pure. They had had a common origin in the welfare of the State. With the decay of the State they declined. Art in the thirteenth century was no mere hobby of the educated, nor a taste which depended on antiquarian research for its perfection. It belonged to the habits, to the necessities, one might almost say to the instincts, of civilised life. Men did not then theorise on the fitness of style, or the propriety of this or that mode of decoration. There was but one style at one time—adopted, no doubt, with more or less success, according to the ability of the designer, but adopted with perfect confidence and uniformity of purpose—untrammelled by the consideration of dates or mouldings, or any of the fussiness of archæology, and maintaining its integrity, not by the authority of private judgment, but by the free will and common acceptation of a people.

The difference of condition between ancient and modern art has a direct analogy with that which exists between ancient and modern poetry, and which has been ably illustrated by one of the greatest of our modern writers. ' In a rude state of society,' says Macaulay, ' men are children with a greater variety of ideas. It is, therefore, in such a state of society that we may expect to find the poetical temperament in its highest perfection. In an enlightened age there will be much intelligence, much science, much philosophy, abundance of just classification and subtle analysis, abundance of wit and eloquence, abundance of verses, and even of good ones; but little poetry. Men will judge and compare; but they will not create.'

If this reasoning be just in regard to the poetry of language, it is equally so with respect to the poetry of art. As a nation, we have grown too sophisticated to enjoy either intuitively. But there is another kind of admiration which we, in common with all modern Europe, may hope to feel for both, and which is derived from and dependent on the cultivation of the human intellect. The graceful action of a child at play is mainly due to its utter artlessness. It may skip and jump and roll upon the greensward in a manner which defies our artificial sense of decorum. Yet every movement associated with that age of innocence has a charm for us. It may be free and unconventional, but never clumsy. It may be quaint or even boisterous, but never vulgar. Such is the comeliness of nature, which by-and-by is handed over to the mercies of the dancing-master, who, with fiddle in hand and toes turned outwards, proceeds to teach our little ones deportment. From that moment ensues a dreary interval of primness and awkwardness. Who has not noticed the semi-prudish *gaucherie* of little ladies from the age of (say) twelve to sixteen? As a rule they stand, sit, walk, and converse with a painful air of restraint, in which all natural grace is lost in an overwhelming sense of propriety, nor is it until they ripen into womanhood that they acquire that easy confidence of manner which is at once characteristic of the most perfect breeding and the purest heart.

It is precisely such an interval as this—an interval between youthful grace and mature beauty—which must fall to the fate of every art during the progress of civilisation. But, instead of years, we need centuries of teaching to re-establish principles which were once independent of education, but which have lapsed away before the sophistry of theoretic science, or have been obliterated by the influence of a false economy. It has now come to be an universally accepted fact that the arts of design attain their greatest perfection under two conditions. We must either have theories of the most refined and cultivated order, or we must have no theories at all. In the present age, when theory is everything—when volume after volume issues from the press replete with the most subtle analysis of principles which are to guide us in our estimate of the beautiful, it is hopeless to expect that men will work by the light of nature alone, and forego the influence of precedent. If the ' Dark Ages ' had continued dark in the ordinary sense of the epithet, what might we not have expected from the beauties of the Pointed style ? Even if literature had kept pace with art, they might have gradually emerged together with the dawn of Western civilisation. But the change, though gradual, was too thorough for such a result, and when at length the dazzling light of the Renaissance burst in upon our monasteries and cathedrals, the spirit of their magnificence faded away before the unexpected meteor. The tree of knowledge had been tasted, and it was vain to expect sustenance from the tree of life. Thenceforth, the art whose seed had been sown in the earliest period of European history—which had developed with the prosperity of nations, and borne good fruit in abundance after its kind—was doomed to wither away, neglected, into a sapless trunk—to be hedged round, indeed, by careful antiquaries, and pointed at as a curiosity, but never, as it once seemed, likely to flourish again on English soil.

And here, if it were not time to drop the metaphor, one might extend its significance yet further. For there are two theories respecting the revival of Gothic architecture in this country. One is, that it appears among us as a new exotic plant, requiring different culture from its ancient prototype, which is supposed to have become utterly extinct. But there are those who love to think that the old parent stem never altogether lost its vitality, and that the Mediæval tendencies which crop up among us now in this latter half of the nineteenth century may be compared to the fresh green sprouts which owe their existence to the life still lingering in some venerable forest oak.

The supporters of this latter theory have a great deal to urge on

Old House on Pride Hill, Shrewsbury.

From a Sketch by C. L. Eastlake.

their side of the question. In the first place the Renaissance school, from which we are accustomed to date the extinction of Gothic art, although it appeared in Italy with Brunelleschi at its head during the early part of the fifteenth century, was scarcely recognised in England until a hundred years later, and long after that period, even when the works of Lomazzo and Philibert de l'Orme had been translated into English, and John Shute, an architect of Queen Elizabeth's time, had returned from Italy (whither he had been sent by his patron Dudley, Duke of Northumberland), no doubt full of conceits for, and admiration of, the new style, there was little to be seen of that style, save the incongruous details with which it became the fashion to decorate the palatial houses of the aristocracy. But though Italian stringcourses and keystones, quoins, and cornices, were introduced abundantly in the bay-windows and porticoes of the day, the main outline of the buildings to which those features belonged remained in accordance with the ancient type. This was especially the case in rural districts. The counties of Shropshire, Chester, and Stafford, bear evidence to this day, in many an old timber house which dates from the Elizabethan period, of the tenacity with which the old style held its own in regard to general arrangement, long after it had been grafted with the details of a foreign school. Even down to the reign of James I., the domestic architecture of England, as exemplified in the country houses of the nobility, was Gothic in spirit, and frequently contained more real elements of a Mediæval character than many which have been built in modern times by the light of archæological orthodoxy. Inigo Jones himself required a second visit to Italy before he could thoroughly abandon the use of the Pointed arch. But its days were now numbered, and when in 1633 the first stone was laid for a Roman portico to one of the finest cathedrals of the Middle Ages, the tide of national taste may be said to have completely turned, and Gothic architecture, as a practicable art, received what was then no doubt supposed to be its death-blow.

By a strange and fortunate coincidence of events, however, it happened that at this very time, when architects of the period had learned to despise the buildings of their ancestors, a spirit of veneration for the past was springing up among a class of men who may be said to have founded our modern school of antiquaries. Sometimes, indeed, their researches were not those of a character from which much advantage was to be expected. James I. spent a great deal of his own and his architect's time in speculating on the origin of Stonehenge, and no doubt many ingenious theorists were content to follow the royal example. But luckily for posterity, the attention of others was drawn in a more serviceable direction. Up to this time no work of any importance had been published on the Architectural Antiquities of England. A period had arrived when it was thought necessary, if only on historical grounds, that some record of ecclesiastical establishments should be compiled. The promoters of the scheme were probably little influenced by the love of Gothic as a style. But an old building was necessarily a Gothic building, and thus it happened that, in spite of the prejudices of the age, and probably their own æsthetic predilections, the antiquarians of the day became the means of keeping alive some interest in a school of architecture which had ceased to be practically employed.

Early in the reign of Charles I., Mr. Roger Dodsworth, who appears to have belonged to a good family in Yorkshire, inspired by that love of archæology which distinguished many gentlemen of the time, began to collect materials for a history of his native county. In the course of his research, he necessarily acquired much interesting information concerning the origin and endowments of those religious houses of the North which had been established previous to the Reformation. While Dodsworth—a man somewhat advanced in years—was engaged in this pursuit, a younger antiquarian than himself, Mr. William Dugdale, of Blythe, was similarly occupied in compiling a history of Warwickshire. Sir Henry Spelman, who knew both, and appreciated the value of their labours, perceived that, by uniting the labours of these gentlemen, a valuable result might be obtained. He therefore did his best to bring them together, and we have reason to be thankful that he succeeded in doing so, for a literary partnership ensued, and the produce of their joint authorship was the ' Monasticon Anglicanum.'

Opinions are much divided concerning Dugdale's share in the earlier portions of this work. Mr. Gough, in his ' British Topography,' contends that the two first volumes were compiled entirely by Dods-worth. This opinion has since been refuted, with what success need not here be discussed. It suffices to state that Dodsworth, who was indubitably the original projector of the undertaking, died a year before the publication of the first volume, which occurred in 1655. This volume appeared without dedication, and, indeed, it would have been difficult to find, in those stormy times, and among the Puritan leaders of the Commonwealth, a patron who was sufficiently interested in the object of the work to lend his name to the title-page. Nor were the interests of literature likely to be better supported by the Royalists themselves, who had just been iniquitously deprived of one-tenth of their estates under the military despotism which then obtained in England. The book, in short, met with a miserable sale, so much so that it was not until seven years later, after the Restoration, that the second volume appeared—this time accompanied by a dedication to his gracious Majesty King Charles II., who no doubt was much edified by its perusal. The third volume came out in 1673—the memorable year of the Test Act—and, by an entry in Dugdale's diary, it seems that he received fifty pounds for it. In this concluding portion of his labour he had been assisted by Sir Thomas Herbert and Mr. Anthony à Wood.

In 1682 a new and improved edition of the first volume was published (*Editio secunda auctior et emendatior ; cum alterâ ac elucidiori indice*), and of this edition many copies exist. It has a double title page, the first containing a sort of genealogical tree, on the branches of which are represented, in a kneeling attitude, little groups of figures emblematical

of various religious and monastic orders.   At the foot of the tree stand
St. Benedict, St. Dunstan, St. Gregory, St. Augustine, and St. Cuth-
bert.   The engraving opposite this is remarkable for two facts connected
with it.   Although the work to which it introduces the reader treats of
none but Mediæval buildings, the design of this page is essentially Italian
in character, and in fact represents a kind of Roman triumphal arch, so
indifferent were its authors to the interests of Gothic art.   But their
sympathy with the fate of many an ecclesiastical institution which had
perished under the rule of Henry VIII. is indicated by two vignettes
which appear at the bottom of the plate.   In one of these a king is seen
kneeling before an altar and dedicating some grant ' *Deo et ecclesiæ* ' in
behalf of an abbey which appears delineated in the distance.   In the
second compartment the abbey is in ruins, and 'bluff King Hal,'
straddling in the foreground, and *apart from his Royal predecessors*,
points with his stick to the dismantled walls, exclaiming ' *Sic volo.*'

It is impossible to mistake the spirit which found vent in these
symbols.   The engravings which were published with the original
editions of the 'Monasticon' were executed by Hollar and King, two
artists, of whose names one would certainly not otherwise have reached
posterity.   Those by Hollar are the best, and are chiefly illustrative
of the various costumes worn by ancient religious orders in England.
King undertook the architectural views, which are for the most part
of a rude and unsatisfactory description.   They are frequently out of
perspective, and are neither faithful in matters of detail nor drawn
with any artistic spirit.   They are, however, not uninteresting to the
modern student, as they include many records of buildings, or portions
of buildings, which have long since perished under the hand of time.
Among Hollar's may be mentioned a view of Lincoln Cathedral, showing the spire previous to its destruction in 1547, and the views of
Salisbury with its detached belfry (on the north side), since removed.

The descriptive text is written in Latin, after a fashion common with
such works of that date.   From an allusion in his diary in 1658,

Dugdale seems to have feared that 'Mr. King' (probably a clerk in his employ) was about to publish a translation of the 'Monasticon.' That such a work was prepared to the extent of the first volume is evident from the fact that Dugdale himself alludes to its being 'erroneously Englished' in many places. The abridged translation, however, which was subsequently published, did not appear until 1692, six years after Sir William Dugdale's death, and being signed 'J. W.' was ascribed to Mr. James Wright, a barrister of the Middle Temple, who, in 1684, published the 'History and Antiquities of the County of Rutland.' Other abridgments and extracts from the original work followed, many of which were inaccurate.

The modern edition is well known. It was the result of the joint labours of three gentlemen eminently qualified for the task which they undertook :—The Rev. Bulkeley Bandinell, D.D., keeper of the Bodleian Library ; Mr. John Caley, keeper of the Records of the Augmentation Office (who, at a later period, held a similar post at Westminster) ; and Mr. (afterwards Sir Henry) Ellis, keeper of the MSS. in the British Museum. It is needless to say that the amount of erudition thus brought to bear upon the subject materially increased the historical value of the work. Hundreds of Religious Houses of which Dugdale knew little or nothing were added to the list. Most of Hollar's prints were re-engraved. Those by King were rejected as worthless. But, in order to supply their place, the authors availed themselves of an artist's assistance, whose work, though it may appear indifferent when judged by a more recent standard of merit, is by no means deficient in artistic quality, and was no doubt among the best of his time. The engravings from Mr. John Coney's drawings will scarcely satisfy those who look for minute attention to the detail of Gothic ornament. But in breadth of effect, and in treatment of chiaroscuro, they will bear comparison with Piranesi. It is to be regretted that the initial letters and a few other characteristics of the early text were not reproduced. But taken as a whole, and considering the period at which it was brought out, the modern edition of the 'Monasticon' is a work which does credit to its authors and the spirit which induced its publication.

In examining the condition of what is commonly known as Pointed architecture during the seventeenth century, the student will be not a little puzzled who attempts to ascribe, with anything like chronological accuracy, its various characteristics to such a sequence of events as influenced it before, or have prevailed upon it since, that period. In the present day, when a few hours' journey enables us to pass from one end of England to another, and even into the heart of the Continent—when the increased facilities and cheapness of publication have rendered the public familiar with all sorts and conditions of ancient and modern art, it is difficult to estimate the importance which once attached to the merit and capabilities of individual example. Every builder's clerk who can now get away for a month's holiday may spend his time profitably among the churches of Normandy, or fill his portfolio with sketches in Rhineland. But, two hundred years ago a travelled archi-tect was a great man, entitled to an amount of respect which quickly secured for him the highest patronage, and enabled him to form a school of which he became the acknowledged leader. The development of such a school, however, was often necessarily limited to that portion of the country where he found a field for the display of his talents. Meantime, many a rural practitioner was content to imitate the work of his forefathers; and thus, while the influence of the new Italian school was brought to bear upon public and important works, a large propor-tion of minor and domestic buildings still continued to be designed in that style which, though debased in character, may be fairly described as Mediæval.

It is well known that the earliest works of Inigo Jones himself were Gothic; and even after his return from Italy, where he had studied the works of Palladio, he could not entirely forsake the groove in which his youthful efforts had been exercised. The north and south sides of the quadrangle at St. John's College, Oxford, still bear witness of his genius in a design which, though it has with justice been described as bastard in its details, is nevertheless an eminently picturesque composition, and shows, moreover, how fondly the elder university still adhered to those ancient traditions of art which had shed a glory on her most venerable foundations. That work was undertaken at the cost of Archbishop Laud, whose tastes, so far as we can now infer, had but little in common with the then rising school of architecture. Indeed, it is not difficult to imagine that a prelate so zealous for the constitution and privileges of his order, so conservative in his notions of matters ecclesiastic, so attached to ceremonial and that form of worship which had most sympathy with Rome and least with Geneva, must have looked with some jealousy on a style of art which England owed to the Revival of Literature and to the Reformation.

It is a remarkable fact that, during Laud's episcopate, and some years after the new art-doctrines had been promulgated, more than one Gothic church was consecrated by him and probably reared at his expense. Among these may be mentioned St. Catharine Cree, in Leadenhall Street, and the parish church at Hammersmith, of which the first stone was laid in 1629. Bishop Cosin, another patron and connoisseur of architecture, who was raised to the See of Durham in the reign of Charles I., unbeneficed during the Commonwealth, and who returned to his diocese after the Restoration, also sustained by his aid the now waning influence of Mediæval design. He partly rebuilt the palace and chapel of Bishop's Auckland, with far more reverence for ancient precedent than could be found in many a work of his contemporaries. The windows of the chapel are (at least in general conception) by no means bad imitations of geometrical tracery. The stalls, the pulpit and reading-desk, the reredos and roofs, though belonging to a class of art which we should not like to see reproduced in our own day, have nevertheless a certain dignity about their form which is worthy of a better age.

The design of the stalls and font-cover of Durham Cathedral may be referred to the same date, and probably to the same influence. The chancel of Brancepeth Church, near Durham, is supposed to have been fitted up after the Reformation, and is on that account remarkable for its chancel-screen. There is another of similar design at Ledgefield, and indeed the retention of this feature, until a late period, in the parish churches of Durham is a peculiar characteristic of that county. The general proportions of the Brancepeth screen are excellent: the stalls are evidently copied from earlier work, and the whole of the woodwork, though naturally deficient in purity of detail, is thoroughly Gothic in motive.

Such examples become the more interesting when we remember that they were probably executed long after the dilettanti of the day had been imbued with a taste for Italian art. So early as 1624, Sir Henry Wotton, one of the most accomplished authorities of the day, had published his ' Elements of Architecture ' a lengthy essay, which if we except the work of John Shute,* is perhaps the most important that had then appeared on the subject. In the introduction he says, ' I shall not neede (like the most part of Writers) to celebrate the subject which I deliver. In that point I am at ease. For Architecture can want no commendation where there are Noble Men or Noble Mindes; I will therefore spend this Preface rather about those from whom I have gathered my knowledge; For I am but a gatherer and disposer of other men's Stuffe at my best value.' He then goes on to describe Vitruvius as ' our principall Master,' and alludes to the works of Leon-Battista Alberti, whom he reputes ' the first learned architect beyond the Alpes.' The metaphysical character of his theories, as well as the analogies

---

* The title of Shute's book (probably the earliest work of the kind published in England) was, ' The first and chiefe Grounds of Architecture used in all the ancient and famous Monyments, with a farther and more ample Discourse uppon the same than has hitherto been set forthe by any other.' By John Shute, paynter and architecte. Printed by John Marshe, fol., 1563. There is no copy of it either in the British Museum or in Sir John Soane's Library.

which he draws between Nature and Art, remind us of modern writers, and especially of one who has so ably espoused a very different cause— Mr. Ruskin.

Wotton begins his dissertation by stating that 'building hath three conditions; Commoditie, Firmenes, and Delight.' It is curious to compare this division of qualities with the 'Seven Lamps of Architecture,' by which the present generation has been illumined, and to note how the old author puts in a plea for circular plans on the ground that 'birds doe build their nests spherically.' This is precisely the sort of argument which Mr. Ruskin uses when he recommends the pointed arch because it is the shape of leaves which are shaken in the summer breeze. The admirer of Mediæval art will probably consider that in the main object of their teaching, Mr. Ruskin is perfectly right, and Sir Henry Wotton was perfectly wrong, but when they base their opinions on such facts as these, they might change places without much damage to either cause.

Sir Henry quotes largely from Vitruvius, and enters upon those wonderful comparisons between the Orders and the human race which have been so often reproduced in Handbooks of Architecture, and have been the delight of Pecksniffs from time immemorial.

But what after all is the real value of such fanciful derivations of style? What artistic principle do they illustrate? What information do they convey? Is there any rational critic who actually believes that he can detect the slightest resemblance between the Tuscan pillar and a 'sturdy well-limbed labourer,' between the fluting of an Ionic column and the folds of a woman's dress, or discover in a capital of acanthus leaves any of that meretricious *abandon* which is supposed to have characterised the ladies of Corinth? These are fables which may have pleased the pedants of King James's day, but it is time to forget them now.

The subject of Gothic architecture Wotton passes over in this essay with silence, and it is only in discussing the shape of arches that he is betrayed into expressing his contempt for what we now call the 'Tudor style.'

As semicircular arches (says he) or Hemisphericall vaults being raised upon the totall diameter, bee of all other the roundest and consequently the securest . . . . so those are the gracefullest which, keeping precisely the same height, shall yet bee distended one fourteenth part longer than the sayd entire diameter, which addition of distent will conferre much to their Beauty, and detract but little from their Strength . . . . As for those arches which our artizans call of the third and fourth point; and the Tuscan writers *di terzo* and *di quarto acuto*, because they alwayes concurre in an acute Angle and doe springe from division of the Diameter into three, foure, or more parts at pleasure; I say such as these, both for the natural imbecility of the sharpe angle it selfe, and likewise for their very Vncomelinesse, ought to bee exiled from judicious eyes, and left to their first inventors, *the Gothes* or Lumbards, amongst other Reliques of that barbarous Age.

In spite of the contumely thus heaped upon Gothic, and the neglect with which it was treated by the followers of Palladio, it met with respect in some quarters and especially among the antiquaries. We have already seen that an interval of seven years elapsed between the publication of the first and second volumes of the 'Monasticon.' But in that interval a work was produced by the same author which could not fail to draw attention to the beauties of what was once one of the finest cathedrals in the world, and the memory of which has been thus happily transmitted to our own time in the form of a well written and well illustrated record. Dugdale's 'History of St. Paul's Cathedral' has passed through several editions. It has been enlarged by Maynard, continued and further amplified by Sir Henry Ellis, and decorated with new engravings by Finden and Heath. But to the antiquary no copy of it possesses half the interest of that dear old time-stained volume, 'printed,' as the title-page sets forth in red and black type, in London 'by Tho. Warren in the year of our Lord God MDCLVIII.'

It was a memorable epoch in the annals of English history. The man who had sacrificed his king to the interests of his country, who had redeemed the honour of the British flag where it had long been insulted, who had begun life as an earnest enthusiast for civil and religious liberty, and ended it as a tyrant—Cromwell, the greatest prince of his age and the most miserable regicide, covered with military glory only to be filled by-and-by with abject remorse, the hero of Marston Moor and Naseby, who could not sleep for fear of assassination, died of fever on September 3, in the same year which saw the publication of Dugdale's book.   Discontent had long been gathering in the country, and a time had now arrived when the rising influence of the Royalist party no doubt encouraged the efforts of many a man who, like Dugdale, was a staunch supporter of the Church.   It may be doubted whether the volume appeared before or after Cromwell's death, but it is certain that it must have been published within a few months of that event, and therefore to this original edition, printed as it was before the plague and fire of London, and perhaps conned over in turn by Roundhead and Cavalier, something more than ordinary interest is attached.

The etchings which accompany this valuable work are by Hollar, and in many respects superior to those which appear with the ' Monasticon.' Facing the title-page there is a portrait of Dugdale himself at the age of fifty, wearing the broad-brimmed hat, buttoned coat, and Geneva bands with which we are accustomed to associate Master Izaak Walton and many other worthies of his time.   The dedicatory epistle is to the Right Honourable Christopher Lord Hatton, Comptroller of the Household to the late King Charles, and one of his Majesty's most Honourable Privy Council.   In it the writer cautiously but plainly deplores the late aspect of affairs, and quotes the almost prophetic words of Sir Walter Raleigh, who forty years before, ' discerning even then the increase and growth of sectaries in the realm,' observed, ' that all cost and care bestowed and had of the Church wherein God is to be served and worshipped was accounted by those people a kinde of Popery ; so that time would soon bring it to passe, if it were not resisted, that God would be turned out of Churches into Barnes, and from thence again into the Feilds and Mountains and under Hedges; and the office of the Ministry (robbed of all dignity and respect) be as contemptible as those places; all order, discipline, and Church-government left to newness of opinion and men's fancies; yea, and soone after, as many kindes of religion spring up as there are parish churches within England; every contentious and ignorant person cloathing his fancie with the Spirit of God and his imagination with the gift of Revelation,' &c.

This letter is dated from the author's residence in Blythe Hall, Warwickshire, July 7, 1657, from which we may, perhaps, infer that the volume issued from the press early in the following year, and before that event occurred which brought about a very different state of things.

An interesting account of the foundation and various endowments of the old cathedral then follows, assigning dates to the completion of different portions of the structure. After this is a description of the monumental epitaphs accompanied by illustrations (many of which are executed with great care) of the tombs and brasses, &c. Most of them are Italian, and though of a most objectionable design, are interesting in the evidence which they afford of early Renaissance conceits.

A series of general views is then added. A perspective of the cloisters from the south shows the chapter-house then standing in the quadrangle which they enclosed. Another perspective of the south front of the cathedral includes a view of the spire after its 'restoration' in 1553, and previous to its final destruction by lightning in 1561. On this last occasion the fire spread over the roof of the nave and aisles, burning the rafters and all that was combustible within the space of four hours; 'Whereupon the Queen (Elizabeth) out of a deep apprehension of this lamentable accident, forthwith directed her Letters to the Lord Mayor of London, requiring him to take some speedy order for its repair; and, to further the work, gave out of her own purse a thousand marks in gold, as also warrant for a thousand loads of timber, to be taken in her woods or elsewhere.'

The work of repair was prosecuted 'with such dilligence' (!) that before April, 1566, all the roofs were finished and covered with lead. The larger trusses had been framed in Yorkshire, and brought to town by sea. Various models were made for restoring the steeple, but neither in Queen Elizabeth's reign, nor subsequently, were any of these plans carried out.

In the eighteenth year of the reign of King James I., that monarch having been repeatedly solicited by one Master Henry Farley, a gentleman who appears to have taken great interest in the cathedral, at length turned his attention to its dilapidated condition, and Dugdale records that ' his princely heart was moved with Such Compassion to this decayed fabrick that, for prevention of its neer approaching ruine (by the corroding quality of the coale smoake, especially in moist weather, whereunto it had long been subject), considering with himself how vast the charge would be ; as, also, that without very great and publick helps it could not be born ; to beget the more venerable regard towards so worthy an enterprize, and more effectually to put it forwards, he came in great state thither on Horseback upon Sunday, 26th of March 1620.'

An appropriate sermon was preached on this occasion by the Bishop of London (Dr. King), to whom his Majesty had himself supplied the text (Psalm 102, v. 13 and 14). After which the royal party adjourned to the bishop's palace, where, it appears, the hospitable prelate entertained them with ' severall set Banquets.'

The result of this visit became manifest in a Royal Commission, which was appointed in November of the same year. It included many eminent noblemen and ecclesiastics, but of all the names on the list the one which bears most on our present subject is that of Inigo Jones, ' Esquire,' then surveyor to his Majesty's works. The Commission bore, in some respects, a resemblance to many such Commissions of our own day. It wasted a great deal of time in talking. Months and years slipped away. The Bishop of London, who had subscribed liberally to the undertaking, died. His royal master did not long survive him. Still nothing important in the way of restoration had been begun. Meantime the taste for classic art was rapidly gaining ground. In the fourth year of King Charles's reign (1628) another Royal Commission was appointed, but it was not until 1633 that the first stone of the work was laid. Inigo Jones had been formally appointed to superintend it. The then Bishop of London was his old patron Laud, at whose cost the eastern wing of St. John's College, Oxford, had just been erected. In that instance some respect had been felt for the original style of the building, and the new wing was at least Gothic in its general outline.

It would not have been surprising if similar deference had been paid to the original design of so grand a specimen of Mediæval architecture as old St. Paul's. It might have been hoped, too, that the bishop would have recommended an adherence to ancient precedent, if only on the score of congruity. But Jones had not travelled to Italy for nothing. Here was an opportunity of displaying his skill in a field which seemed not only magnificent in itself, but had all the additional attraction of novelty. He went to work without the slightest scruple. The walls of the nave were remodelled. Round-headed lights, with cherubim for key-stones, supplanted the delicate tracery of the old windows. Buttresses were replaced by pilasters, and battlements by balustrading. The façades were scored all over with ugly lines of exhibited masonry, obelisks stood in the place of pinnacles, and heavy cornices were introduced where formerly a modest drip-stone or string-course had done good and all-sufficient service. Finally, at the west end was placed a Corinthian portico, which, however magnificent a feature in itself, must have been a hideous deformity where it stood. It was not fated to stand there long. A quarter of a century had scarcely elapsed before the whole fabric was in ruins. It has been said that the present building—confessedly a noble work in its way—rose like a Phœnix from the ashes of the Great Fire. But, if we are to indulge at all in such a poetical conception, let us rather say that the good genius of old St. Paul's survived the catastrophe, in a less substantial form, indeed, but invested with a more congenial spirit—that spirit which has induced us to reverence and imitate elsewhere, after centuries of time, the elements of design which constituted its ancient glory.

CHAPTER II.

WE have seen that a considerable interest in the ancient architecture of Britain was sustained during the seventeenth
century by antiquarian research. Among men of the day to
whom posterity is most deeply indebted for labours in that direction
was one who has been already mentioned in connection with the third
volume of the 'Monasticon' (which he had assisted Dugdale to
prepare), but whose name is better known as the sole author of an
equally important work, the 'Athenæ Oxonienses.'

Anthony, son of Thomas Awood, or, as it is usually written, *à
Wood*, Bachelor of Arts and of Civil Law, was born in the year 1631,
opposite Merton College, Oxford, where in due time he matriculated
and took his M.A. degree. He appears to have been inclined from
early youth to the study of English history and archæological lore.
Oxford was a field which naturally presented every attraction for the
exercise of his tastes as an antiquarian. It was his native town. It
was his place of education. It supplied him at once with a rich mine
of historical interest, and with the means of working it. While he was
still a young man he wrote a treatise on the antiquities of Oxford,
which was esteemed so highly by the heads of the various colleges that
they ordered a Latin translation of it, which appeared in 1674, under
the title of '*Historia et Antiquitates Universitatis Oxoniensis, duobus
voll. comprehensæ*,' fol. It was prepared with immense pains, and the
author intended to have added to the English copy some account of the
city as well as of the colleges. But he was hindered by his labours for
another work, the famous 'Athenæ,' or 'An exact History of all the

Writers and Bishops who have had their education in the most ancient and famous University of Oxford, from the fifteenth year of King Henry VII. Dom. 1500, to the end of the year 1690. To which are added the Fasti, or Annals of the University for the same time.' On this book, as the dates in the title show, he was engaged during the greater part of his life, and it is impossible to overrate the extraordinary patience and research involved in its production. Public and private libraries were ransacked, wills at the Prerogative Office examined, church windows inspected, and parish registers consulted, to attain his object. It might with reason be supposed that such untiring industry, coupled with so excellent a result, would have gained him favour and credit at Oxford. But in those days a mere scholar had little to hope for in the way of patronage. Wood's manners were not of that polished kind which will always command a certain order of popularity. His habits were simple. He was careless in his dress. It was rumoured that he had joined the Romish faith. It is certain that he received more support from Roman Catholics than from members of the Established Church. Among all the Dons of the University it seems that Mr. Andrew Allam, Vice-Principal of St. Edmund's Hall, was the only one who aided his exertions. Unfortunately, in the 'Athenæ,' he had alluded to Lord Clarendon in somewhat uncomplimentary terms. This was at the time sufficient to bring the work into ill-odour, and Wood had the mortification of finding it expelled from the University. He was now advanced in years, and his health succumbed to the trials which he had undergone. He died in his sixty-fifth year. In the east corner of the north side of St. John's Church, adjoining Merton College, is a small tablet to his memory :—

H. S. E.

ANTONIUS WOOD: ANTIQUARIUS.

OB. 28 Nov. A°. 1695. ÆT. 64.

A century had nearly elapsed when John Gutch, chaplain of All Souls' and Corpus Christi Colleges, republished the ' History and Antiquities of Oxford,' in the popular edition which bears his name.

The origin of the Gothic Revival presents so many complicated features, and so difficult is it to distinguish the latest efforts of the old school from the earliest attempts towards its resuscitation, that it would be almost impossible to draw any line which should definitely divide the two periods. The date of the Great Fire of London presents, no doubt, an important boundary between the one and the other. Yet neither to Wren nor to Inigo Jones can be ascribed the first introduction of Italian art. So early as the reign of Henry VIII., Hans Holbein had designed the porch of Lord Pembroke's house at Wilton, and some portions of Windsor Castle, in a style which testified the influence of a foreign school. John Thynne, who built old Somerset House in 1567 ; Robert Adams, superintendent of royal buildings to Queen Elizabeth ; Theodore Havens, who erected Caius College in the same reign ; and one Stickles, who practised in England about 1596, had all adopted this mongrel species of architecture, which it would be incorrect to describe as Gothic. On the other hand, Wren, who had reached a point of excellence in classic design which we have not since seen surpassed, himself not only restored Mediæval buildings, but raised new ones in imitation of them.

This extraordinary man was born on October 20, 1632 (one year after the birth of Anthony à Wood). He was the son of a clergyman, and the nephew of Dr. Matthew Wren, whose name is prominent in the ecclesiastical history of his times.* He received an excellent education, and no one was better fitted to profit by it. It is recorded that at the age of thirteen he had invented an astronomical machine, and a few

* Dr Matthew Wren was impeached by order of the House of Commons in 1641, and altogether suffered imprisonment for twenty years. Sir Christopher, as a young man, became intimate with Claypole, who had married Cromwell's daughter, and there is an interesting anecdote that '*Mr.* Wren' once met the Protector at the house of his son-in-law, and received from his own lips the remission of Dr. Wren's punishment, which he immediately conveyed to his uncle.

years later made discoveries in astronomy and gnomonics. It is certain that, at twenty-five, he was made Astronomical Professor at Gresham College, which office he resigned in 1660, for the Savilian professorship at Oxford. His life was a long one, but most actively employed, and it is wonderful to think how, in the midst of his professional labours, and while he was in the height of his practice, he could find leisure for the scientific pursuits which then constituted his chief amusement. At one time, we find him lecturing before the Royal Society (of which he became president) on the nature of ice and the polarity of sapphires, at another discussing the properties of phosphorus : now his opinion is asked regarding the horns of a moose-deer found in some Irish quarry ; then he turns his attention to the art of mezzotint engraving ; presently he reappears engaged in experiments relating to artificial incubation, or writes a report on some phenomenon of medical science. In short, he was a man of most versatile talents, and the various details of his useful life afford material for a digression which might be interesting but which would be redundant in these pages. With the Gothic Revival, indeed, Wren's career may seem at first sight to have little in common. Yet it would be a pity to omit any link which joins them, and there is more than one point of contact with that subject, both in his writings and his practice.

Up to the age of thirty-one, he had received no public commissions as an architect. In 1663, he was employed by Charles II. to prepare designs for a royal palace at Greenwich, and about the same time the erection of the Sheldonian theatre at Oxford was begun under his superintendence. But an event was at hand which soon afforded more ample scope for his abilities. The Great Fire of London, whose ruins covered no less than 436 acres ; which extended from the Tower to the Temple Church, and from the north-east gate to Holborn-bridge ; which destroyed in the space of four days eighty-nine churches (including St. Paul's), the City gates, the Royal Exchange, the Custom House, Guildhall, Sion College, and many other public buildings, besides

13,200 houses, and laid waste 400 streets, opened a field for practice which no Government architect had ever found before, or will probably ever find again.

Within a few days after the fire, Wren began his plan for rebuilding the City, to which Mr. Oldenburg, secretary of the Royal Society, alludes in a letter to the Hon. Robert Boyle, dated September 18, 1666. 'Dr. Wren has, since my last, drawn a model for a new city, and presented it to the king, who produced it before his council, and manifested much approbation of it. I was yesterday morning with the Doctor, and saw the model, which, methinks, does so well provide for security, convenience, and beauty.'

It would appear from this fact that Wren was at that time acting as the Government architect, and, indeed, the Parentalia fix his appointment as surveyor-general before that period ; but, according to Mr. Elmes (whose life of Wren was published in 1823), that event did not occur till 1669, when he succeeded to the office in place of Sir John Denham, who had previously held it.

In 1668 he was employed to survey Salisbury Cathedral. In his report thereon he speaks of the whole pile as magnificent, and 'one of the best patterns of architecture in the age wherein it was built.' He finds fault, however, with the foundations and 'poise' of the building, and his remarks on that subject are curious and interesting :—

Almost all the cathedrals of the Gothic form (he writes) are weak and defective in the poise of the vault of the aisles ; as for the vaults of the nave they are on both sides equally supported and propped up from spreading by the bows of flying buttresses, which rise from the outward walls of the aisles ; but for the vaults of the aisles they are, indeed, supported on the outside by buttresses, but inwardly they have no other stay but the pillars themselves, which, as they are usually proportioned, if they stood alone without the weight above, could not resist the spreading of the aisles one minute ; true, indeed, the great load above of the walls and vaults of the *navis* should seem to confirm the pillars in their perpendicular station, that there should be no need of buttresses inward. But experience hath shown the contrary ; and there is scarce any Gothic cathedral that I have seen, at home or abroad, wherein I have not observed the pillar to yield and bend inwards from the weight of the vault of the aisle ; but this defect is most conspicuous upon the angular pillars of the cross, for there not only the vault wants butment, but also the angular arches that rest upon that pillar ; and, therefore, both conspire to thrust it inward towards the centre of the cross, and this is very apparent in the fabric we treat of. For this reason, this form of churches has been rejected by modern architects abroad, who use the better and Roman art of architecture.

In 1673 Wren was made a member of the Royal Commission for the rebuilding of St. Paul's, and at the same period received his appointment as architect to the new structure. From that date up to within a few years before his death his time was actively employed in works of great importance, but which, being of a definitely Italian character, need not here be enumerated. His attempts at Mediæval design in London were among the later works of his life, and will be presently described. His earlier efforts in that direction appear in a field itself remarkable for the continuity of examples which it affords in illustration of Gothic architecture, from the Middle Ages down to the eighteenth century.

A tendency to conservatism, a respect for ancient traditions, a jealousy of changes which it has had no share in originating, are characteristics which have long been associated with the University of Oxford. That this feeling extended to questions beyond those of doctrine or politics—that it exercised an influence in retaining the old Tudor style of building for colleges at Oxford long after the followers of Palladio had introduced a new fashion of art, no one can reasonably doubt. Nor is it strange that the members of such an ancient and splendid institution should have been unwilling to reject that venerable type of architecture which already existed in so many local examples, and which prevailed at a period whence its wealth and magnificence were derived.

An early specimen of seventeenth century Gothic at Oxford is that of Wadham College, built on the site of the monastery of Austin Friars during the years 1610–13, the first stone having been laid on July 31 in the former year, and the first warden, Dr. Wright, admitted on April 20, 1613. The entrance gateway, groined with fan tracery, is a curious and interesting example of the respect shown for local traditions of design, even when national taste in architecture had undergone a complete change.

So excellent in character are the style and construction of the chapel windows that they have been referred to an earlier period, but the college books contain an account of the expenses incurred during their erection, and thus leave little doubt on the subject.* The interior of the hall contains a good timber roof and oak screen, Gothic in general form, but with Italianised detail. The great south and oriel windows are very fine and remarkable examples of this period.

The eastern wing of the Bodleian Library was also completed in 1613, and is a very creditable work, in keeping with the older building to which it was then added. Three years later Sir John Acland built the hall at Exeter College, one of the best specimens of a refectory in Oxford. It was restored and refitted in the early part of this century by Nash. But the general design is still what it was, and it may be questioned whether the former details were not superior to those which replaced them. The late chapel of the same college was erected in 1624. Its interior was divided into two aisles. The windows were considered very good for their date.† It is supposed that no part of the quadrangle is older than the time of James I.

Another instance of Jacobean Gothic may be recognised in the hall of Trinity College, which, although it has undergone some alteration since, was originally erected, with the apartments above it, about 1619.

The buildings of Oriel College come under the same class. The

---

* The late Mr. O. Jewitt, in a careful and ably written essay, read before the Archæological Institute at Oxford in 1850, described with great accuracy the tracery of the windows in the chapel and ante-chapel, which, though differing considerably in motive of design and apparently in date, appear to have been executed at one and the same time.

† This building was removed some years ago. The present chapel, which will be described in due course, was erected in 1857–58, from a design by Mr. G. G. Scott, R.A.

south and west sides of the outer quadrangle were rebuilt about 1620; the northern side, together with the hall and chapel, finished in 1637. They are unpretentious in character, but picturesque in their way, and exceedingly interesting as links in the chain of our present history.

Immediately opposite the front of Exeter is that of Jesus College, originally founded by Queen Elizabeth, but a great portion of the present structure is due to the munificence of Sir Eubule Thelwall, Knt., who held the office of principal in 1621. He built the principal's lodgings at his own expense, as well as the kitchen, buttery, with chambers over them, and one half of the south side of the first quadrangle. The chapel, which stands on the north side, was consecrated on May 28, 1621. The east window, by no means a bad specimen of its kind, was added in 1636. The hall was completed by Sir Eubule Thelwall, of whom it is recorded that he 'left nothing undone which might conduce to the good of the college.' It contains an elaborately carved screen (Jacobean in its details), and is lighted by a large bay window which forms a conspicuous feature in the quadrangle. The roof, though now hidden by a plaster ceiling, was originally of solid oak, and ornamented with pendents.*

In 1624 died Thomas Holt, an architect of York, to whose design many of the University buildings of this period are attributed, and who certainly seems to have respected the ancient traditions of his art in resisting the influence of a foreign taste. According to Parker's 'Handbook' the groined vault of the passage under the eastern wing of the Bodleian Library (usually called the 'Pig market') is a specimen of his skill, as well as many college gateways of the same date and character. He also designed the 'Schools' which had been founded by Sir Thomas Bodley, but who unfortunately did not live to see them

---

* The buildings facing the Turl and Market Street were refronted in 1856 under the superintendence of Messrs. Buckler. The chapel was restored and refitted by Mr. G. E. Street in 1864, when the old oak wainscoting which formerly lined its walls was removed.

begun. Holt was buried at Oxford in Holywell churchyard. His name is little known to posterity; but admirers of that architecture which he strove to sustain against the tide of popular caprice will cherish his memory with a feeling akin to gratitude.

Among the buildings at Oxford erected during Holt's lifetime, if not designed by himself, is the chapel of Lincoln College, which was built at the expense of Lord Keeper Williams (successively Bishop of Lincoln and Archbishop of York), and consecrated on September 15, 1631. The interior is sixty-two feet long by twenty-six feet in width, and is handsomely furnished with a screen and wainscoting of cedar. It contains some rich and brilliantly coloured glass, some of which is said to have been brought from Italy in 1629.* The south quadrangle of the same college is earlier, having been begun about the year 1612, when Sir Thomas Rotheram, formerly a fellow, gave 300*l.* towards the expense of its erection.

Another specimen of the same school—more important in point of size, but hardly equal to it in merit—is University College. Although this is one of the oldest foundations in Oxford, and claims King Alfred for its earliest patron, no portion of the present structure existed before the time of Charles I. In 1634 the first stone of the west side was laid, and in the following year the hall and chapel front, as well as the High Street front, were begun. The east side is much later, and was not finished until 1674. One Mr. Greenwood, a fellow of the college, is said to have suggested the design, and to have contributed 1,500*l.* towards the work.

The quadrangle is one hundred feet square, and is entered by a vault, groined over with fan tracery, and supporting a superstructure which rises a storey higher than the adjacent buildings. The following particulars are added from Parker's 'Handbook to Oxford':—

---

* The glass of the east window, which bears the date 1631, is very curious as indicating a well-defined transition of style from ancient to modern art. The figures are small and represent incidents in the Old and New Testaments, Mediæval in general design, but evidently influenced by the growing taste for *realistic* treatment.

Over the gate on the north side is a statue of Queen Anne, whilst the niche in the interior is filled with one of James II., given to the college by Obadiah Walker, master, in 1687, who afterwards lost his headship for his adherence to the Church of Rome. The lesser quadrangle measures about 80 ft. square, and is open to the south. The north and east sides, the latter of which is occupied by the master's lodgings, were built about the year 1719. . . . The interior of the chapel—notwithstanding, as Dr. Ingram remarks, the incongruity of Corinthian ornaments in a Gothic room—is admired for the elegance of its general appearance, which is much assisted by the groined ceiling and the carving in the style of Gibbons in the oak screen and cedar wainscot which encloses the altar.

The present hall was completed about 1657, but the interior entirely refitted in 1766 at the expense of members of the college whose armorial bearings are represented on the wainscot panels. The fireplace bears some resemblance to the canopy of an altar tomb in the Decorated period. It was the gift of Sir Roger Newdigate, founder of the well-known university prize for English verse which bears his name. The hall is paved with slabs of Swedish and Danish marble. A library, built over the kitchen and at right angles with the hall, was added in 1669.

In 1640 Dr. Saunders, principal of St. Mary Hall, erected, on the site of an older edifice, the hall and refectory of that foundation, with the chapel above. The windows of the latter building are enclosed by flat-pointed—almost semicircular—arches ; the mullions do not run up straight to the arch head, but branch off in tracery, which intersects at regular intervals and terminates without mitre at the intrados—a form frequently adopted in work of this period. There is a church at Plymouth, commonly called Charles' Church—probably because it was erected in the time of the Stuarts—which has tracery of this description, and is a very curious example of seventeenth century Gothic.*

---

* ' A petition was ordered to be prepared from the Corporation, setting forth the state of the parish, and praying the king to grant permission for the building of a new church " upon a piece or parcel of land called or known by the name of the Coney Yard, now Gayer's Yard, lately given us by John Hele, of Wembury, Esquire, to that use." The

Coeval with St. Mary Hall is the staircase entrance to the hall of Christchurch. It is vaulted over with fan tracery of a very chaste and beautiful description. The stairs were altered to their present form by Wyatt, but the groining and central pillar date from 1640, or even earlier. The celebrated Tom Tower, of the same college, was designed by Wren, and, from the prominent position which it occupies, presents one of the most remarkable features in the university. It rises from the great entrance, commonly called the Tom Gate, which formed part of Wolsey's splendid scheme. It is octagonal in form, and introduced to the square substructure by that species of huge chamfer or splay which may be observed in other designs by this master, and an intervening panelled storey, on one face of which the clock is placed. On this the upper portion of the tower is raised, its eight sides being pierced to full two-thirds of its height by pointed windows, canopied by an ogival hood-moulding. These windows are divided into two lights, the space above the springing being filled in with tracery, the style of which is copied from late Perpendicular work. Between the windows, and at each angle of the octagon, buttresses occur, terminating below the panelled storey in a corbel and upwards in a crocketted pinnacle. The whole is surmounted by a dome-shaped roof similar in character to those which crown the turrets on either side of the entrance. It was completed in 1682.

Act for dividing the parishes passed in 1640, and the church appears to have been commenced forthwith; but troublous times were in store for Plymouth; the civil war broke out; the town sided with the Parliament, and during its three years' siege had little time or inclination to proceed with the church to be dedicated to the king. In 1645, active steps were taken for completing the building, but it was a long and tiresome job for architect, builder, and employers; and not until 1658 was the church finished, and then *minus* the spire, which appears not to have been built before 1707. Shortly after the Restoration, the church was consecrated, and ever after went by the name of Charles' Church.

'For its time, Charles' Church—which consists of a nave with aisles, and a chancel not very deeply recessed—is a remarkably good building. . . The *outline* of the tower and spire is almost perfect. The east window of the chancel is a fine specimen of geometric tracery. Elsewhere, however, there is a contradiction of styles, and a jumble of Perpendicular, Elizabethan, and classic details.'—Extract from Mr. J. Hine's published paper on 'The Ancient Buildings of Plymouth.'

The Tom Tower, Christ Church, Oxford.

Sir Christopher Wren, Architect, 1682.

This example is cited as one of the most important of Wren's Gothic designs at Oxford. He had, however, made other essays there in the same direction at a much earlier period. The library and chapel of Brasenose College, which were finished in 1663, are ascribed to him. They consist in a curious mixture of the two styles, composite pilasters between two pointed windows, and Mediæval pinnacles surmounting an Italian cornice. The east window is, however, a very fair imitation of Mediæval art, and the roof, adorned with fan tracery, shows at least that the example of earlier times was not without influence upon the designer.

In addition to those already mentioned, there are several instances in and near Oxford of buildings which illustrate an attempted revival of Gothic architecture after the accession of Charles II. Among these may be named Islip Church, where the chancel was rebuilt by Dr. Robert South on an ancient model and with tolerable success in 1680.*

We must now, however, revert to Wren's work in London, of which there are one or two examples which bear directly on our subject. The first of these in chronological order was his so-called restoration of the north side of Westminster Abbey and the erection of its towers. Previous to this, however, he had drawn up a report on the state of the building. It was addressed to the Bishop of Rochester, and contains some remarkable observations, not only on the abbey itself but upon Gothic architecture in general. Wren had no doubt a greater constructive genius than Inigo Jones, and his comments on the structural mistakes committed by Mediæval builders are often to the point. But it must be remembered that the conditions of the art in which he proved himself so efficient a master, were, and ever will be, utterly dissimilar from those which directed the aim of Mediæval builders. With an abundant supply of material we may always raise a strong edifice ; but when the external appearance of that edifice is not required to convey

---

* This church has since been much altered, and under the plea of restoration the curious and historically interesting chancel raised by Dr. South has been destroyed.

an accurate notion of the size or shape of its interior there is absolutely no limit to the stability which it may assume. Supposing, for instance, St. Paul's had been hewn out of the solid rock, the proportions would have remained unaltered; but there would have been no human science in its strength. This is, of course, a *reductio ad absurdum*, but it may serve to illustrate a principle. If the superficial area of old St. Paul's be contrasted with that of Wren's building; if the cubical contents of the one be measured with those of the other; if the proportion of solid masonry employed in each structure be compared with the available space which it contains; it may be questioned whether the science displayed in the original building was not of a higher order than that which distinguishes the present edifice. For the former cathedral was in practical reality what it seemed to be, and as it possessed no one constructive feature which did not serve a purpose, so also no portion of its external appearance belied its internal capacity. Wren's dome, on the contrary, with its elaborate complication of conical walls, pendentives, iron chains, paraboloid and hyperboloid curves, may be a triumph of mathematical and engineering skill, but, as architecture, is nothing more than a grand and magnificent sham; and few of those who admire the graceful contour of its outline, towering high above the smoke and dust of busy London, recollect, or were ever aware, that it is a simply ornamental feature, which not only has little connection with the dome they have admired while standing in the choir or nave of St. Paul's, but which, if really executed as it seems to be, would look ugly and disproportionate from within.

But Sir Christopher, who did not hesitate to expend thousands of pounds on a gigantic artifice, and who, for the mere sake of effect, reared this grand but useless portion of his building hundreds of feet into the air, could not forgive the employment of those features of Gothic architecture which he blindly deemed unserviceable in regard both to its construction and embellishment. 'Pinnacles,' says he, in his report on Westminster Abbey, ' are of no use and little ornament.

The pride of a very high roof raised above reasonable pitch is not of duration, for the lead is apt to slip, but we are tied to this indiscreet form, and must be content with original faults in the first design.' He then goes on to lament, with some reason, that oak was not more used instead of chestnut in Westminster Hall and other places, and proceeds to describe the steps he had taken towards the ' restoration ' :—

First, in repair of the stone work, what is done shows itself. Beginning from the east window, we have cut out all the ragged ashlar, and invested it with better stone out of Oxfordshire, down the river from the quarries about Burford . . . . We have amended and secured the buttresses in the cloister garden, as to the greatest part, and we proceed to finish that side. The chapels on the south are done, and most of the arch buttresses all along as we proceeded. We have not done much on the north side, for these reasons : the houses on the north side * are so close that there is not room left for the raising of scaffolds and ladders, nor for passage for bringing materials ; besides the tenants taking every inch, to the very walls of the church, to be in their leases, this ground, already too narrow, is divided, as the backsides to houses, with wash-houses, chimnies, privies, cellars, the vaults of which if indiscreetly dug against the foot of a but-tress may inevitably ruin the vaults of the chapels (and, indeed, I perceive such mischief is already done by the opening of the vaults of the octagonal chapel on that side), and unless effectual means will be taken to prevent all nuisances of this sort, the works cannot proceed ; and if finished may soon be destroyed . . . . The angles of pyramids (!) in the Gothic architecture were usually en-riched with the flower the botanists call *calceolus*, which is a proper form to help workmen to ascend on the outside to amend any defects, without raising large scaffolds upon every slight occasion.

He then alludes to the state in which he found the old western towers. ' It is evident,' he writes, ' that they (the towers) were left

* The appearance of Westminster Abbey in those days must have been very similar to that presented by many Continental cathedrals in our own time. It seems to have been crowded and built round with tenements of a humble description. Happily these have been long since cleared away ; but so little respect was paid to the building, even down to the beginning of this century, that a thoroughfare was permitted right through the nave, and porters lounged there with their loads.

D

imperfect, and have continued so since the dissolution of the monastery, one being much higher than the other, though still too low for bells, which are stifled by the height of the roof above them ; they ought certainly to be carried to an equal height, one storey above the ridge of the roof, still continuing the Gothic manner in the stone-work and tracery.'   He fully recognises the use of the steeple in giving superincumbent weight, and therefore stability to the piers below, and attributes to the absence of that feature over the crux a deviation from the perpendicular, noticeable in the shafts which occur at the intersection of nave and transepts.   He proposes that the central tower should be carried up as much above the roof as it is wide, and adds, that if a spire were added to it, it would give a grace to the whole fabric, and the west end of the city, ' which seems to want it.'   ' I have made a design,' he adds, with reference to this scheme, ' which will not be very expensive, but light, and still in the Gothic form, and of a style with the rest of the structure, *which I would strictly adhere to throughout the whole intention.*   To deviate from the whole form would be to run into a disagreeable mixture, which no person of a good taste could relish.'

How far Sir Christopher maintained this resolution—or rather, let us say, how far he understood the characteristics of that noble building which he thus undertook to restore and even to improve upon—those who examine his work at Westminster with a critical eye will soon determine.   The best that can be urged in his favour is that he worked according to the light which was in him, and that the stone which he employed in his repairs was of more durable kind than that of which most of the original masonry was composed.   But there are few, perhaps, among us who would not have preferred even the crumbling relics of the ancient building to the cold and uninteresting patchwork which now defaces the north transept.   We find heavy circular discs replacing boss-work of the most delicate description, and huge acorn-shaped lumps of stone where formerly many a chastely profiled corbel was in service.   The old arch mouldings are, indeed, copied with tolerable accuracy here and there, but the rich and crisp leafage of the Early English capitals is feebly imitated in that lifeless carving which forms its present substitute. As for the western towers, they are too well known to need much comment here. But when we examine their heavy horizontal lines of cornice and string-course, their circular panels crowned by hideous pediments (which, to use Wren's own words, can be 'of no use and little ornament'); when we raise our eyes to the ugly, uncusped tracery of their upper windows, and that bungling ogival hood-mould which surrounds them, or still higher to the clumsy truss-work which supports the topmost pinnacles—we can but lament that a man whose fame has been transmitted to posterity as the greatest architect whom England has produced should have been thus associated with the degradation of one of her fairest monuments.

Crude and unsatisfactory as Wren's attempts at design in Pointed architecture undoubtedly were, it is impossible not to regard them with interest when we remember that they formed exceptions not only to the popular taste of their day, but to the unparalleled successes of their author himself. That Sir Christopher ever adopted a style in which he saw few merits, and such merits as certainly are not pre-eminently characteristic of that style, must always appear strange. It is difficult to imagine that a mind which could conceive such an edifice as St. Paul's could have much sympathy with the spirit of Mediæval buildings. But it is stranger still, if he admired them at all—and Wren certainly professed to do so—that he should have been so utterly incapable of recognising or imitating the most essential elements of their grace. Yet it was better that such churches as St. Mary Aldermary and St. Dunstan's-in-the-East should be erected than that the use of the Pointed arch should be clean forgotten in our metropolis. They are, indeed, melancholy examples of Gothic art, but any examples which date from such a period become valuable links in the history of its revival.

The year in which St. Mary Aldermary was completed is quoted by

Elmes as 1711. His authority is doubtless from the 'Parentalia, or Memoirs of the Wren Family,' published by Sir Christopher's grandson, in 1750. But the 'Parentalia,' as Elmes himself points out, contain many chronological errors, and probably this is one of them. According to a tablet on its walls, St. Mary Aldermary was opened for public service in 1682.* The original church had been burnt down in the Great Fire. It was rebuilt at the cost of one Henry Rogers, on the same plan as the old building, which will to some extent account for the style, and for the fact that the east wall of the chancel is not at right angles with the nave, an accident which we may be sure Wren's love of *eurythmia* would not have permitted had he not been compelled to adhere to the ancient boundary by some stringent conditions. It consists of a nave and two aisles, each roofed over inside by plaster groining. That over the nave (which is lighted by clerestory windows) is divided into circular panels decorated with cusping and filled in the centre with floral enrichment. The panels which occur over the aisles are oval in plan, and some are pierced as skylights.† They are surrounded at their outer edge by leaf ornament. These panels are met and intersected by groining, which springs from slender attached shafts, over each pier in the nave, and from small corbels in the aisles. Below the base line of these shafts, and in the spandrels of the nave arches, is introduced stonework carved with shields, scrolls, and cherubim. The latter are no doubt intended to be grotesque, for they wear grimaces seldom seen in this ordinary type of plethoric celestiality. They are, however, very far removed from that school of conventional art which Ruskin has called ' noble grotesque,' and, indeed, the whole

---

* The inscription runs thus :—'This church was pav'd and wainscoted at ye charge of both parishes, namely, St. Mary Aldermary and St. Tho. ye Apostle, and also opened in ye year of our Lord God, 1682. Ralph Smith, &c. Churchwardens.'

† The north aisle wall is decorated internally by blank windows, in imitation of those on the opposite side. They never were constructed to admit light: in fact, when the church was rebuilt, this wall abutted on some adjoining buildings (now removed). Hence the necessity of skylights.

of the carving, though clever in its way, is anything but Gothic in character.

The east window consists of five lights, divided by a heavy transom of peculiar section. Each light has a cinquefoil head. The chancel is roofed by a segmental vault, of which the central compartment is oval, and the rest is divided into little oblong panels, with ogival trefoiled heads, such as are common in late Perpendicular work. By this arrangement, the obliquity of the east gable-wall, which has been already mentioned, is made less apparent. This ceiling is also executed in plaster. The arches of the nave are flat-pointed, and appear to have been struck from four centres, though the contour of their intrados is such as almost to justify the belief that it is elliptical in parts. A string-course, which runs down the nave, just above the apex of each arch divides them from the clerestory windows. The piers are similar in plan to those of many Tudor churches in the west of England, and consist of three-quarter shafts stopping against a plain face, and separated by a hollow, which is carried round the arch. The bases occur about four feet from the ground, the rest of the pier being boxed in by wainscoting. The base moulding is very peculiar, and unlike any example of even late *genuine* Gothic. In section it resembles the profile of an Early English cap inverted. Three-light windows occur in the clerestory and south aisle.

Neither the font, pulpit, nor altarpiece can be said to have any pretensions to a Gothic form. The first bears date 1682. The last is a composite design, not inelegant of its kind, and distinguished by some good carving which has been attributed to Grinlin Gibbons. An incised slab in the pavement describes it as the gift of Dame Jane Smith, relict of a worthy knight of that name. The old tower, which escaped destruction during the Fire, is still standing, and bears evidence of Wren's repair in its upper windows and other portions of the detail. The organ and organ gallery are later in date, and belong to that class of design which is ignominiously known as ' carpenter's Gothic.'

In the year 1699 Wren finished the spire of St. Dunstan's-in-the-East. The body of the church had only been repaired by him. This latter portion of the structure was taken down early in the present century and rebuilt by Mr. Laing, then architect to the Custom House,* so that the tower is all that remains there of Wren's work, and therefore all that it is now necessary to describe.

Including the spire, which occupies about one-third of its height, it stands 167 ft. from the ground. The tower itself is divided into three storeys, of which the lower are strengthened by buttresses placed anglewise at each corner. Above the second storey these become octagonal turrets, surmounted by pinnacles above the parapet. From the base of these pinnacles spring flying buttresses in an elliptical curve, and the latter meeting together form the base of a spire, pierced with lights at its lower end, but terminating in solid masonry above. The union of the buttresses with the spire is ingeniously managed by carrying up the stonework in stepped courses over the last voussoir of each arch, and thus forming a firm foundation for the superstructure. It is remarkable that these steps are not 'weathered' after the manner of ordinary buttresses, yet so excellent is the quality of the stone employed that it does not seem to have suffered the slightest decay, and indeed the whole of the masonry of this portion appears as sound as if it had been just executed.

The spire itself is octagonal in plan and crowned at the top by a flat-headed finial, gilt ball, and weathercock. Small pinnacles occur in the centre of the parapet on each side of the tower, after a fashion very prevalent in Somersetshire churches. The base of the tower, which is at the west end of the building, forms a porch roofed over inside with a spherical vault panelled *à la Renaissance*. The south and west doorways are spanned by a pointed arch, of which the tympanum is of panelled stonework pierced for light in the centre, and supported by a

---

* With the assistance of Mr. (now Sir William) Tite, who supplied the design and superintended its execution.

lower segmental arch which forms the door-head. The central storey of the tower contains on the east and west sides a circular window, foiled with eight cusps, and enclosed by a square moulded panel. A similar space on the north and south sides is allotted to a clock, which is marked with the date 1681. These circular windows, and the tracery of those in the upper storey, are among the best features of the tower. The spire itself, though lamentably deficient in purity of detail, has a certain picturesque character of its own, which the sound and straight-forward principles on which it was built could not fail to impart. Mr. Elmes, in his 'Life of Wren,' alludes to it in terms of unmeasured praise. 'Of this masterpiece of construction,' says he, 'it is not too much to say that it stands unrivalled for elegance, beauty, and science. When Sir Christopher designed this steeple, *the noblest monument of geometrical and constructive skill in existence* (!), and unequalled also for lightness and elegance, he had doubtless those of St. Nicholas, at Newcastle-on-Tyne, and of the High Church, Edinburgh, in his mind, but he has surpassed them in every essential quality.'

There is an anecdote, unauthenticated by any data, concerning this tower, that Wren, though convinced of the accuracy of his calculations for its stability, and of the theories which had guided him in its design, felt some apprehension as the time drew near for the practical test of his skill. He is said to have watched the removal of the framework which had supported the spire during its construction, through a telescope from London Bridge, and to have felt great relief when a rocket announced that all was safe. Failure at such a moment might, indeed, have damaged his professional reputation, great as it then was, to say nothing of the terrible consequences which must have attended an accident; but we may question whether a man of such profound mathematical attainments, and of so vast a practical experience as Sir Christopher, could have so far underrated his capabilities as to doubt on such a point at all. Indeed, it is well known that on one occasion when he was informed that there had been a hurricane on the previous night which had damaged all the steeples in London, he replied at once, ' Not St. Dunstan's, I am sure.'

St. Alban's, Wood Street, may be mentioned as another of Wren's attempts at Gothic, but it is hardly worth description. It was finished in 1685.

St. Michael's, in Cornhill, was a more important work. The tower appears to have been completed from Wren's design in 1722. It bears some resemblance to that of Magdalen College, and is divided into four storeys, of which the second and third are lighted by semicircular headed windows, exhibiting a huge hollow jamb in their external reveal. They are divided by mullions into two lights. The upper windows are much longer and narrower than the others, and are separated by a buttress which stops upon a string-course below. The lights are labelled with the same ugly type of ogival drip-stone, which may be recognised in most of Wren's Gothic designs. Octagonal turrets, round which the horizontal string-courses break, and which are decorated with corbel heads, occur at each angle of the tower, and are carried up to some height above its main walls, terminating in four heavy-looking ogival finials. The intermediate buttress is also carried up, and finishes with a pinnacle above the parapet, which is battlemented in two awkward-looking courses, evidently parodied from the Magdalen tower.*

It was almost the last work which Wren lived to see carried out. He had now reached a great age, and it is sad to think that his last days had been embittered by the disgraceful cabals of ungenerous rivalry. The commissioners for conducting the rebuilding of St. Paul's intrigued against him. Wren petitioned the Queen that he might be freed from their interference. Had her Majesty lived, it is probable that he might have defied his enemies to the last. But Anne died in 1714, and when the Elector succeeded to the throne he was surrounded by his countrymen, with whom Benson, an architect of mean pretensions

* The modern restorations of this church were executed from the designs of Mr. G. G. Scott, R.A.

and unscrupulous effrontery, managed to become a favourite. The old Commission at length expired, and in 1715 a new one was issued. The king was prevailed on to supersede Wren's patent as surveyor-general. His consent must have mortified Wren, but it certainly disgraced himself. In his eighty-sixth year, this good and faithful servant of the crown was dismissed from an office which he had held during four reigns, and for a period of nearly half a century. Benson was installed in his place, only to lose it on the first occasion, when his gross incapacity became manifest. Wren retired to his residence at Hampton Court, coming up to town, however, from time to time for the purpose of inspecting the repairs of Westminster Abbey, and other works which were being still carried out under his superintendence. In one of these excursions he caught a cold, which possibly may have hastened his end. But he died at last peacefully, after falling asleep in his arm-chair, on the 25th of February, 1723.

CHAPTER III.

I F in the history of British art there is one period more distinguished than another for its neglect of Gothic, it was certainly the middle of the eighteenth century. In a previous age architects had not been wanting who endeavoured to perpetuate the style whenever occasion offered, and when the taste of their clients raised no obstacle. Wren had himself condescended to imitate in practice those principles of design which he despised in theory. But these were exceptional cases, and, as time advanced, and the new doctrine spread more widely, they became still rarer. Nor did the lovers of archæology much help the waning cause. The old antiquarians were dead, or had ceased from their labours. Their successors had not yet begun to write. An interval occurred between the works of Dugdale and Dodsworth, of Herbert and Wood, on the one side, and those of Grose, Bentham, Hearn, and Gough, on the other— between the men who recorded the history of Mediæval buildings in England, and the men who attempted to illustrate them. In this interval an author appeared who did neither, but to whose writings and to whose influence as an admirer of Gothic art we believe may be ascribed one of the chief causes which induced its present revival.

Horace Walpole, third son of the Minister, Sir Robert Walpole, first Earl of Orford, was born in 1718. At the age of twenty his fortune was secured by some valuable sinecures, and he thus found himself enabled at an early period of his life to indulge in those tastes and pursuits which to him seemed of much more importance than his Parliamentary duties, and which have combined to render his name so famous.

It is impossible to peruse either the letters or the romances of this remarkable man without being struck by the unmistakable evidence which they contain of his Mediæval predilections. His 'Castle of Otranto' was perhaps the first modern work of fiction which depended for its interest on the incidents of a chivalrous age, and it thus became the prototype of that class of novel which was afterwards imitated by Mrs. Ratcliffe and perfected by Sir Walter Scott. The feudal tyrant, the venerable ecclesiastic, the forlorn but virtuous damsel, the castle itself, with its moats and drawbridge, its gloomy dungeons and solemn corridors, are all derived from a mine of interest which has since been worked more efficiently and to better profit. But to Walpole must be awarded the credit of its discovery and first employment.

The position which he occupies with regard to art resembles in many respects that in which he stands as a man of letters. His labours were not profound in either field. But their result was presented to the public in a form which gained him rapid popularity both as an author and a *dilettante*. As a collector of curiosities he was probably influenced more by a love of old world associations than by any sound appreciation of artistic design. In this spirit he haunted the auction rooms, and picked up a vast quantity of objects that were destined by-and-by to crowd his villa at Twickenham. Nothing to which the faintest semblance of a legend attached was too insignificant for his notice. Queen Mary's comb, King William's spur, the pipe which Van Tromp smoked in his last naval engagement, or the scarlet hat of Cardinal Wolsey, possessed for him an extraordinary interest. But among these relics he acquired much that was really valuable in the way of old china and stained glass, and thus formed the nucleus of what at one time promised to become an important Mediæval museum. The acquisition of these treasures could not but influence his taste, which has been ably defined by an eminent writer of our own day. 'He had,' says Lord Macaulay, 'a strange ingenuity peculiarly his own, an ingenuity which appeared in all that he did, in his building, in his gardening, in his upholstery, in the matter and in the manner of his writings. If we were to adopt the classification—not a very accurate classification—which Akenside has given of the pleasures of the imagination, we should say that with the Sublime and the Beautiful Walpole had nothing to do, but that the third province, the Odd, was his peculiar domain.' It was probably this eccentricity of taste, combined with his fondness of Mediæval lore, which induced him to imitate, in the design of his own dwelling, a style of architecture which by this time had fallen into almost universal contempt.

On the grounds now known as Strawberry Hill, there existed, towards the middle of the last century, a small cottage, built by a person who had been coachman to the Earl of Bradford. It was originally intended for a lodging house, but the Fates had decreed for it a more honourable use. Even before the occupancy of the owner with whose name it will be for ever associated, it had become the residence of some notable people. The famous Colley Cibber once lived there. Dr. Talbot, then Bishop of Durham, and the Marquis of Caernarvon (afterwards Duke of Chandos), had been its tenants. It was afterwards hired by Mrs. Chenevix, a dealer in toys, at that time well known in London. It does not appear that there was anything of a Gothic character in the original structure, but it struck Walpole's fancy. He first purchased the lease of Mrs. Chenevix, and the following year bought the fee simple of the estate. In a letter to Mr. (afterwards Marshal) Conway, dated June 8th, 1747, Walpole announced that he had taken possession. 'You perceive by my date,' he writes, 'that I am got into a new camp, and have left my tub at Windsor. It is a little plaything house that I got out of Mrs. Chenevix's shop, and is the prettiest bauble you ever saw.'

This small and whimsical abode Walpole enlarged at various times between the years 1753 and 1776. He did not take down the old work, but altered it to suit his taste, and added to it bit by bit, so that the whole at length became a straggling but not unpicturesque mass of buildings. 'It was,' says an old writer, 'the amusement of his leisure;

and, circumscribed in its dimensions as it is now seen, it enabled him to perform with sufficient success his original intention, which was that of adapting the more beautiful portions of English or Gothic castellated and ecclesiastical architecture to the purposes of a modern villa. A wide and somewhat novel field was here opened for the exercise of taste. The task was precisely suited to the talent of the designer; and this choice specimen of the picturesque effect which may be produced by a combination of the graces of ancient English style, even when those beauties are unaided by the ivyed mellowness of time, has greatly assisted in introducing a passion for the Gothic.'

Just as the little cottage of Mrs. Chenevix grew into a villa under Walpole's care, so the villa which Walpole designed has since developed into a mansion. Within the last few years a new wing has been added by its present owner, the Countess Waldegrave, and the old work has been so completely renovated that it is not at first easy to trace the original form of old Strawberry Hill amid the various embellishments which surround it. The principal entrance was formerly by the road-side—an arrangement which may have answered very well in Walpole's time, but in these days of busy traffic would hardly have ensured sufficient privacy to the inmates. A piece of ground, therefore, which now forms a portion of the garden, was reclaimed from the highway, and a new road formed round it in exchange. The old entrance was by a low pointed arch from which a narrow corridor led on the left hand to an inner door. This passage is decorated with mural arcuation, consisting of slender attached shafts, and tracery in low relief, the bays being separated by canopied niches, enriched internally with carved work in imitation of groining. The crockets employed in this work are of that feeble type which characterised the latest and most debased Jacobean Gothic, and the little corbels are executed in the acorn pattern which Wren so extensively used.

The main walls are of brick or rubble masonry, rough cast with plaster. Many of the doors and windows on the north side are spanned by a pointed arch. On the first floor are several oriel and bay windows, constructed of wood, of which the upper portions are filled with stained glass. They are surmounted by a light cornice crested with wooden tracery. The west wing, in which Walpole set up his printing-press, is a battlemented building two storeys in height. It is lighted by square windows, divided by what seem to be modern casement frames into two and three compartments, and labelled above with an imitation of a Tudor drip-stone. The portion of the building nearest the Thames is evidently the oldest part, and is said to have been the actual cottage purchased of Mrs. Chenevix. It presents two fronts, one facing the west and the other the south. A semi-octagonal porch projects from each side. The pointed windows of this wing are remarkable as bearing more resemblance to Venetian Gothic than to any English example. Their arches are cusped once on either side and terminate in that abrupt ogival curve, of which so many examples may be seen from the Grand Canal. The likeness is the more striking because the plaster is carried up to the edge of the intrados, and thus leaves the arch with no apparent voussoir. There are two storeys of these windows, the upper floor being lighted by simple quatrefoil openings about three feet across. A battlemented parapet crowns the whole. The latter feature is probably executed in lath and plaster. It is certain that the coping of both merlons and embrasures is of wood, and that wooden pinnacles occur at the angles and at regular intervals along the front. The porches on the south and east sides (also battlemented) are carried up two storeys in height. Over the east porch a stepped gable rises, lighted by an oriel window and ornamented at its upper end by a wooden cross let in flush with the plaster. At the apex of the roof is another (Maltese) cross by way of finial. The east corner of the south front is occupied by an apartment now used as a study, but which was formerly the dining-room, or, as Walpole would have it, the '*refectory*.' It is lighted by a bay window rectangular in plan and surmounted by a wooden cresting. In the storey immediately above this is the library window, divided into three lights by slender wooden columns. The arch over this window differs from the rest in having a flat double cusp on either side, but terminates like the others in an ogival curve. It is filled with rich stained glass. On either side above it, and lighting the same chamber, are two quatrefoil openings similar to those we have described. A chimney shaft projects on the east side and is carried up straight to about three-fourths of its height, where it is splayed back in the usual manner. The window heads of the south porch are flatter than the rest, but preserve the same general outline.

The picture gallery runs from east to west, connecting the original tenement with the round central tower and attached staircase-turret, which Walpole built, and which have been lately carried up an additional storey in height. The west front of the gallery (standing about thirty feet from the ground) is divided into bays by buttresses, and contains two storeys, whereof the lower is occupied by servants' offices. The windows of each floor are spanned by four-centred Tudor arches. The voussoirs and quoins appear to be of stone—at all events in some portions of the work; but the whole has been so plastered over in successive renovations that it is difficult to distinguish the solid masonry from rubble-work. The upper windows are labelled with late drip-stone mouldings. The round central tower, which forms an important feature in the group, has a battlemented parapet running round the wall over a corbelled string-course.

The interior, or rather that portion of it which Walpole designed, is just what one might expect from a man who possessed a vague admiration for Gothic without the knowledge necessary for a proper adaptation of its features. Ceilings, screens, niches, &c., are all copied, or rather parodied, from existing examples, but with utter disregard for the original purpose of the design. To Lord Orford, Gothic was Gothic, and that sufficed. He would have turned an altar-slab into a hall table, or made a cupboard of a piscina, with the greatest complacency if it only served his purpose. Thus we find that in the north bed-chamber, when he wanted a model for his chimney-piece, he thought he could not do better than adopt the form of Bishop Dudley's tomb in Westminster Abbey. He found a pattern for the piers of his garden-gate in the choir of Ely Cathedral. It is to be feared that his lordship's enthusiasm not only led him to copy such portions of ancient work, but sometimes to appropriate fragments of an original structure. Unfortunately his example has been imitated by collectors even in our own time.

The picture gallery was supposed to be Walpole's *chef-d'œuvre*. It is fifty-six feet long, seventeen feet high, and thirteen feet wide. The design of the ceiling was borrowed from an aisle in Henry the Seventh's chapel, and is rich in pendants and panelled work. The principal entrance to this apartment is copied from the north door of St. Alban's, and the two smaller doors are parts of the same design. The most richly decorated side of the room is to some extent in imitation of Archbishop Bouchier's tomb at Canterbury. It has five canopied recesses, and is elaborately enriched throughout.*

There is a small building in the garden still called the 'chapel,' though whether that name should be retained for a room which a congregation of six people would inconveniently crowd may be doubted. Its greatest length, including the porch, is not more than fifteen feet. Internally it is about eight feet wide. The inner portion is on a sort of quatrefoil plan, of which three sides are roofed with

---

* The completion of Walpole's villa caused a great deal of sensation at the time, and its merits were freely discussed by the press. Some doggerel rhymes concerning it appeared in a paper called the 'Craftsman.' The first stanza is as follows:—

> 'Some cry up Gunnersbury,
>   For Sion some declare:
> And some say that with Chiswick House
>   No villa can compare:
> But ask the beaux of Middlesex
>   Who know the country well,
> If Strawb'ry Hill—if Strawb'ry Hill
>   Don't bear away the bell?'

plaster groining, and the fourth is left open to the porch.   Ribs spring
from each angle towards a quadrilateral space above, from which a pendant hangs.   Each side forms a recess, of three faces, separated by a
slender attached column.

The front of the porch is executed in Portland stone, and is really a
very creditable performance if we consider the time at which it was
erected.   The upper portion is principally occupied by a three-light
window spanned by a flat four-centred arch.   The sill of this window
is formed by a heavy stone transom, which separates it from a doorway
and little window below.   Three small niches occur on either side,
moulded and canopied with some delicacy of workmanship.   The extreme corners of the front are decorated with octagonal shafts panelled
in their upper portions.

The whole of the carving, and, indeed, the general design of the
chapel, has been executed with great care and more attention to detail
than one might expect from such a period.   Walpole's Gothic, in
short, though far from reflecting the beauties of a former age, or anticipating those which were destined to proceed from a redevelopment
of the style, still holds a position in the history of English art which
commands our respect, for it served to sustain a cause which had otherwise been well-nigh forsaken.

In tracing the history of any particular branch of art or science it is
often needful, if only for the sake of continuity, to take cognisance of
facts which in themselves seem unimportant, and of personages whose
names, but for the object of research, might remain in the oblivion to
which they have long been consigned.   It is trusted that this will be
deemed a sufficient excuse for a reference to the works of an architect
whose connection with the subject before us is interesting only because
it is curious.

The age in which Batty Langley lived was an age in which it was
customary to refer all matters of taste to rule and method.   There
was one standard of excellence in poetry—a standard that had its

E

origin in the smooth distichs of heroic verse which Pope was the first
to perfect, and which hundreds of later rhymers who lacked his nobler
powers soon learned to imitate.   In pictorial art, it was the grand school
which exercised despotic sway over the efforts of genius, and limited
the painter's inventions to the field of Pagan mythology.   In architecture, Vitruvius was the great authority.   The graceful majesty of the
Parthenon—the noble proportions of the Temple of Theseus—the
chaste enrichment which adorns the Choragic monument of Lysicrates,
were ascribed less to the fertile imagination and refined perceptions of
the ancient Greek, than to the dry and formal precepts which were
invented centuries after their erection.   Little was said of the magnificent sculpture which filled the metopes of the Temple of Minerva;
but the exact height and breadth of the triglyphs between them were
considered of the greatest importance.   The exquisite drapery of
Caryatids and Canephorœ no English artist a hundred years ago thought
fit to imitate; but the cornices which they supported were measured
inch by inch with the utmost nicety.

Ingenious devices were invented for enabling the artificer to reproduce, by a series of complicated curves, the profile of a Doric capital,
which probably owed its form to the steady hand and uncontrolled
taste of the designer.   To put faith in many of the theories propounded by architectural authorities in the last century would be
to believe that some of the grandest monuments which the world has
ever seen raised owe their chief beauty to an accurate knowledge of
arithmetic.   The diameter of the column was divided into modules;
the modules were divided into minutes; the minutes into fractions of
themselves.   A certain height was allotted to the shaft, another to the
entablature.   These proportions might vary certainly, but such
variation entirely depended upon whether the 'order' was mutular or
denticular (in other words, whether the cornice was ornamented with a
few large projecting blocks or a great number of little ones), and
whether the capital was simply moulded, or carved into the form of

acanthus leaves. Sometimes the learned discussed how far apart the columns of a portico might be. To the ordinary mind this would soon resolve itself into a question of light and facility of access. But in the days to which we allude they called things by grand names, and the *eustyle* and *diastyle* each had their supporters.

Batty Langley, who had no doubt well read his Vitruvius and knew to a decimal point the orthodox height and projection of every feature in the five orders, possessed, with all his classical predilections, an undercurrent of admiration for Mediæval art. It was an admiration, however, not untempered by disdain, and, perhaps, when he gazed on the mysterious grandeur of our English cathedrals, he felt what he conceived to be a generous pity that such large and important works should have been undertaken in ages which appeared to him so dark and barbarous in their notions of design. The style had some merit certainly. It was pretty and fanciful. It would do very well for a porch in the country or for a summer-house ; but if it was ever contemplated to employ it again in buildings of any importance, something must be done to modify the style—that was certain. The question remained how this could be managed. Here was a crude and unmethodical order of architecture which resembled neither Doric nor Corinthian, whose columns were sometimes two diameters high and sometimes twenty, and might be, as far as rules were concerned, two hundred. All sorts of foliage were used in the capitals. The cornice profiles were eternally varying, and, worse than all, those ignorant Goths had directly violated the most obvious principles of eurythmia. Could nothing be done to improve the style and rescue it from utter degradation ? Mr. Batty Langley thought that he would try.

It was perhaps a somewhat ambitious venture ; but, after all, what advantages had Boyden and de Bek, Thomas of Canterbury, and William of Wykeham, compared with the erudition of the eighteenth century ? Our reformer was, as we have said, well versed in those mysterious relations of shaft and capital, column and entablature, which characterised the designs of Palladio. It occurred to him that some such system might be applied with advantage to Gothic architecture. He actually imagined that by assimilating the proportions of Mediæval features to those of the Classic school or by grafting Gothic mouldings on an Italian façade, he should be able to produce a style which would rival, if not surpass, any building which had been raised during the Middle Ages; that because the folly of the late Renaissance designers had attached a false importance to modules and minutes, a like system of measurement would ennoble and purify an art which included among its examples the choir of Ely Cathedral and the chapter-house of York Minster.

Accordingly, in the year of grace 1742, a work appeared in the form of a neat folio volume with this astounding title:—

'Gothic Architecture, improved by Rules and Proportions in many Grand Designs of Columns, Doors, Windows, Chimney-peices, Arcades, Colonades, Porticos, Umbrellos (!), Temples and Pavillions, &c., with Plans, Elevations, and Profiles; geometrically explained by B. and T. Langley.'

These gentlemen, whose book appears to have been subsequently accompanied by text which few have had the good fortune to peruse,* begin by announcing the discovery of five new orders of columns, plain and enriched; and then proceed to show their application to the various features of a dwelling 'in the Gothick manner.' The entire height of the first order they divide into eleven parts, whereof one is given to the subplinth, half to the base of the column, seven to the shaft, another half to the capital, and the remaining two to the entablature, which, by the way, is in its turn subdivided into architrave, frieze, and cornice, after the Roman fashion. The upper members of the cornice are the ordinary cyma, fillets, and corona of Italian design, but, in place of the bed-mouldings, a huge cavetto succeeds, enriched with

---

* The British Museum copy contains illustrations only; the letter-press probably appeared in a later edition.

a sort of trefoil panelling and separated from the frieze below by a bird's beak and reversed cyma moulding. The rest of the features are parodied in a most preposterous manner from the Classic school. The metopes become quatrefoil panels; the triglyphs are grooves with cusped and pointed heads. The plan of the shaft itself is quatrefoil, and a careful diagram shows how it may be fluted with advantage. The base-mouldings are of that type which may be occasionally seen at the foot of an iron column in a monster railway-station. A page or so farther on we have the same order with more elaborate enrichments : the corona bears lozenge-shaped dies, raised upon a sunk ground; the cyma, torus, and minor mouldings are decorated after a manner peculiar to Mr. Langley, and which, if not very graceful in itself, has at least the merit of originality. Acanthus leaves crop up in the cavetto, the triglyphs are hung with strings of beads, and the whole presents an appearance of incongruity which it would be hardly possible to match elsewhere. The most extraordinary feature of these designs is the great trouble the author has given himself to work out every detail employed. The elevations are projected from plans with the nicest accuracy; each feature is set out with unerring care, and the engravings themselves are remarkably good and carefully executed.

Of the other so-called ' orders ' in this curious book it will be sufficient to say that each surpasses the last in absurdity. Now and then one finds a crude attempt to embody the characteristics of Pointed Art in the way of decoration, but, as a rule, the ornament introduced is at once feeble and vulgar, and reflects about as much of the spirit of classic or Gothic design as may be recognised in the proportions of a modern bed-post.

Batty Langley's ideas of pointed doors and windows were not a whit better. It is singular that they should be conspicuous for that fault which Mr. Ruskin deftly pointed out as one of the chiefest signs of debased Gothic. The *impost* of the arch is almost always omitted, and where it does occur it is rarely moulded, and never enriched with

carving.   Langley has, moreover, with that fatuity which marked all
the Mediæval revivalists, insisted on inventing a new species of crocket,
which has precisely missed the spirit, and reversed the principle, of that
useful feature in genuine work.   It does not seem to bud from, but
rather to *creep up*, the hood-moulding or pinnacle to which it is attached.
Sometimes a battlemented cornice is introduced over a porch.   But
merlons and embrasures are all numbered, and the height and width of
each bear a certain proportion to some unit which forms the basis of the
whole design.

As for the ' porticos ' and ' umbrellos,' the arcades and colonnades,
which are included in the work, they are simply Italian in general
outline, with a bastard detail, which one can only call Gothic because it
can be called nothing else.   Any carpenter's foreman could now use his
pencil to better purpose.   The chimney-pieces have as much affinity with
the art of the Middle Ages as the monuments which may be bought of
a New Road statuary.   The ' temples ' are Mediæval in the same sense
as similar structures at Cremorne or Rosherville.   Posterity may
wonder whether any of these remarkable works were ever executed—
whether men in whose hearts was still cherished a lingering love of Old
English architecture put any faith in this eccentric, vain enthusiast—
what his contemporaries thought of him—whether he shared the contempt which fell upon Ripley, or forgave Lord Pembroke for recommending his rival Labelye's designs for Westminster Bridge in preference to his own.   Certain it is that Batty Langley's commissions
were not numerous, nor do those which he undertook reflect much
credit on their author.   His name is chiefly remembered in association
with the singular but now worthless volume on whose title-page it is
inscribed.   Gothic architecture has had it vicissitudes in this country.
There was a time when its principles were universally recognised ; there
was a time when they were neglected or forgotten.   But in the days of
its lowest degradation, it may be questioned whether it would not have
been better that the cause should have remained unespoused than have
been sustained by such a champion as Batty Langley.

CHAPTER IV.

ALTHOUGH the eighteenth century was, on the whole, more distinguished for its neglect of Mediæval architecture than the age which preceded or the age which followed that period, still many examples of the style exist, which were certainly erected during the reigns of the first Georges. Among these is the gateway on the east side of the second quadrangle at Hampton Court. A reference to early plans of the palace will show that a considerable portion of that façade was remodelled later than the reign of Queen Anne; and, indeed, a stone tablet inserted in the wall immediately above the apex of the arch contains the initials G^{II}. R., and the date 1732. This work derives especial interest from two remarkable facts. In the first place, it was executed *after* Wren's classic additions to Hampton Court, and midway between the stately quadrangle and the Ionic colonnade which contributed no little to his fame, and which, in his own day, no doubt commanded universal admiration. That an architect within a few years after Sir Christopher's death, and while the taste for Italian art which he had so ably encouraged was at its height, should have ventured on a design whose principles were diametrically opposed to those held and taught by so great a master, is notable in itself. But this is not all. The building thus altered had been originally Gothic, it is true, but Gothic of a very different kind from that which was subsequently engrafted on it. Every one familiar with that example of the Tudor style will remember the low four-centred arches which span the older gateways of Hampton Court. If any form of Mediæval architecture found favour in the last century, it was certainly that which had prevailed during the reign of Henry VII.

The most obvious course for an architect to pursue under the circumstances would have been to adopt, in any alterations of the palace, the style in which it had been originally conceived. That, however, was not done in the instance mentioned. The entrance archway is not a four-centred, but an Early Pointed arch. The windows above it belong more to the Transition, or to the Decorated, than to the Perpendicular period, while the whole design bears the impress of an originality in design which is unusual in work of this date, and seems to indicate that it was undertaken by some one who possessed something more than the mere skill of a copyist.

The gateway is enclosed by two semi-octagonal turrets (decorated with string-courses and medallion heads) which rise above the battlemented parapet, and are surmounted by stone cupolas, octagonal in plan and ogival in profile, terminating in finials of the same character. The wall space between these turrets is divided into three storeys, in the uppermost of which is a window partitioned by mullions into four lights, whereof the two central ones rise higher than the others, and are included in an ogival arch round which a drip-stone is carried. The lower window also consists of four lights with cinquefoil heads, under a four-centred arch, the spandrils between being filled in with tracery. This window has no label of the ordinary kind, but is surmounted by a stone canopy of a peculiar design, and slender shafts, with caps and bases, are used in place of the principal mullions. Each window has a moulded sill, which projects from the face of the wall.

The mouldings of the archway below are particularly good of their kind, and the attached columns which decorate the jamb on either side are well-proportioned. Their capitals are, however, without foliage, nor is there any carving in the usual sense of the word, throughout the whole design.

It is almost impossible to cite any instance of Pointed architecture of this date in which groining, where introduced, is not altogether a sham, or set out on a wrong principle. In this case the vault under the passage is executed in plaster, and on such a plan as to make it at once apparent that no constructive element is involved in the design. From each corner of the vault springs a quadrant of fan tracery. The rest is simply a flat roof, panelled after a manner which might represent the *plan* of a groined vault, but which itself is, in reality, nothing more than a ceiling.

In addition to this example, which may be classed under the head of public works, a great many mansions for the nobility and landed gentry of this country were either restored or rebuilt some years later, in a style which humbly imitated, if it could not rival, the art of former days. Among these may be mentioned Belhus, the seat of Lord Dacre, in Essex, which was remodelled towards the latter half of the last century. Lord Dacre was an accomplished amateur in architecture, and a learned antiquarian. His researches had been of a kind which well qualified him for the task, and his appreciation of Mediæval art was, for the age in which he lived, very considerable.

Adlestrop Park, in Gloucester, the property of Lord Leigh, was the field of another Gothic restoration. The old house dated from a good period, and care was taken in the alterations to preserve its original character. Llanerchydol, in Montgomeryshire, a stone mansion in the 'castellated' style (as it was then called), appears to have been built in 1776, and is by no means a bad example of the school.

Beeston Hall, Norfolk, which was built in 1786 for Mr. Jacob Preston, is another specimen of the Revival. It presents, or rather presented at the time of its erection, a simple elevation, two storeys in height. At each angle of the façade are slender octagonal turrets, terminating in pinnacles, ornamented in the usual way with crockets and finials. The three divisions into which the front is divided are surmounted by battlements, with blank shields introduced on the merlons, above which rises a somewhat high-pitched roof with clustered chimneys. Canopied niches occur on either side of a large central window in the upper storey.

Costessy, or Cossey Hall, the seat of Lord Stafford, in the same county, may be said to have presented in its earlier state and subsequent improvement, two distinct and interesting links in the history before us. The original building was erected in 1564, and the purity of its general conception is a pleasing evidence of the respect which still obtained for the old style. But the chapel, which was designed by Mr. Edward Jerningham,* in the last century, is equally remarkable as one of the best and earliest designs in modern Gothic. The Mediæval spirit almost seems to have been an heirloom with the owners, or at least to have been part and parcel of the estate. The last rays of a declining art illumined the founders, and the earliest dawn of the Revival enlightened the restorers of Cossey Hall.

In Scotland the old baronial type of residence was long preserved, and it would not be difficult to cite instances of its adoption in successive ages from feudal days down to our own time. For present purposes, however, it will be sufficient to mention one which belongs to the period now reached by our history. Inverary Castle, near Loch Fyne, was begun by Archibald, Duke of Argyle, in 1745, and completed a few years afterwards. It is a large square building, flanked at each angle by a round tower, the centre block rising to a height sufficient to give light from above to a large hall. Pointed windows occur in the principal façade and in the towers at each angle. The main body of the building is two floors in height, but the towers are carried up a storey higher. The parapet wall is battlemented throughout. On the western side is the chief entrance leading into the grand hall, which is hung round with old Highland weapons and armour. This hall corresponds in design with the general character of the building, but the rest of the interior is modern.

---

* This gentleman, an amateur of great taste, was a younger brother of Sir George Jerningham, the owner of the mansion. He also supplied the designs and superintended the restoration of Stafford Castle, which had been demolished by order of Cromwell to within fifteen feet of the basement.

It is easy to conceive that in a country like Scotland, where the tales and traditions of Border chivalry still lingered, and which had hardly yet succumbed to the modernising influences induced by a union with this nation, there should have existed a romantic but genuine love for an architecture so intimately associated with its early and martial history. But in England the case was different. Events had occurred which tended to dissipate that species of nationality which finds an echo in national art. The character of our literature, our intercourse with France, and the vulgar superstition which then and long afterwards identified the Pointed arch with the tenets of Rome, had all helped to efface anything like a popular feeling in favour of Gothic. Where it existed with individuals it generally assumed the form of a false and eccentric sentiment based on a cockney notion of old ecclesiastical life, but which had no more in common with real monastic seclusion than Byron's affected misanthropy had with the doctrines of Apemantus. The novels of Walpole and the pseudo-Mediæval whims which he cherished did much to encourage this feeling in the clique to which he belonged. Among those who imbibed it earliest was Thomas Barrett, a gentleman who had been elected as the representative of Dover in 1773, but who retired into private life on the dissolution of Parliament which followed soon afterwards, and devoted himself to rural pursuits at his country house in Kent. There Lord Orford, his friend and correspondent, visited him, and no doubt found some pleasure in examining and criticising the queer old mansion of his host, which, originally built in the time of James I., had since undergone numerous alterations. One room especially struck his lordship's fancy. He compared it to an abbot's study, and Mr. Barrett, who had long thought of remodelling the house, caught at the notion, Gothicised his dwelling in 1782, and, though it neither was nor ever had been connected with any conventual establishment, insisted on calling it 'Lee Priory.' The elder Wyatt, then a young man rising into notice, was the architect employed in the design, which has been reckoned among the most successful efforts of his youth.

The principal entrance front of the ' Priory' is on the north side, where the centre is occupied by a square embattled tower with pinnacles at the angles.   At the extremities of this front are octagonal turrets. The chief feature of the west front is a large mullioned window, above which rises the large eight-sided tower containing the library.   It is surmounted by a parapet of stone designed in tracery and probably copied from some old example.   It terminates in a well-proportioned spire, conspicuous in the more distant views above the mass of foliage by which the house is surrounded.   The south elevation is flanked by a square tower.   Although the greater part of the building is only two storeys in height, its outline is sufficiently varied to redeem it to some extent from the cold formality which characterises this period of the Revival.

Of a still earlier date (1771) was Milton Abbas, in Dorsetshire, built for the Earl of Dorchester by Sir William Chambers, on the site of an old abbey house, of which the refectory was allowed to remain and became incorporated in the new design.   The latter presents a symmetrical façade.   The central block, which contains the principal entrance, is a three-storeyed building, ornamented at each angle by an octagonal turret and cupola.   Right and left of this block are minor buildings two floors high, connecting it with side wings which again rise to a height of three storeys and project some feet beyond the rest.

Arundel Castle, Sussex, the seat of the Duke of Norfolk, was in a ruinous condition, until it was ' restored' by his Grace in 1771. The Gothic element is certainly present in this structure, but it is of that kind which we are more accustomed to associate with the scenes of a theatre than with the masonry of the Middle Ages.   The most important elevation contains the anomaly of a Norman doorway surrounded by perpendicular windows.

Ashburnham Place, in Sussex, is another building of the same class, and of no higher pretensions to art. The chief façade is divided into compartments by octagonal solid turrets, which occupy the place of buttresses. It is crowned by a heavily-machicolated cornice. The windows are square-headed, and labelled with a Tudor drip-stone. A carriage-porch in the centre presents a lofty archway (without impost) on three sides. It was designed by George Dance.

In Swinton Park, Yorkshire, stood an old mansion, which, towards the end of the last century, was enlarged and improved (?) by James Wyatt, architect. He built the drawing-room, assisted by Mr. John Foss, of Richmond, and made other additions to the house, in what was then called the castellated style. Early in this century, Mr. Danby, who then resided there, built a massive, tower-like wing at the east end of the same residence, from the designs of Robert Lugar.

Instances of the application of Gothic in church restoration, between 1700 and 1800, are by no means rare, but inasmuch as they were for the most part mere reproductions of old work, due rather to a respect for the integrity of the building than to a love of the style, it is hardly worth while to quote them here.

The central tower of Beverley Minster may, however, be mentioned as a meagre specimen of Perpendicular work, which dates from this period. In Manchester, the Church of St. Mary and Salford Chapel have Gothic belfry-storeys in their towers—the rest of the buildings in each case being Italian, and about the time of Queen Anne. A chapel in Windsor Park—Mediæval at least in motive—was designed early in the reign of George III.

The close of the last century was remarkable for the erection of a building which, for its size, eccentricity of character, and bold adaptation of Gothic form, is unequalled in importance by any which had preceded it, and indeed caused no small sensation among the critics and general public of the day. The fashion which once prevailed of investing, either by name or other means, any modern residence which happened to include a pointed arch in its composition with something of an ecclesiastical character has been already mentioned. In no case was this foible more conspicuous than in the once celebrated Fonthill Abbey.

The history of this strange place presents so many features for consideration, and is so inseparably associated with that of its still more extraordinary owner, that they form together a subject which calls for special comment.

William Beckford, son of the famous alderman of that name, and author of 'Vathek,' a wild Oriental romance which has been long forgotten, was born at Fonthill-Giffard, near Salisbury, on September 29, 1759. His father had acquired great wealth in the West Indies, and was celebrated for his munificence, both in the office of Lord Mayor (to which he was twice elected, in the years 1763 and 1770) and as an encourager of the fine arts. When the young heir came of age, he succeeded to a fortune of a million of money, and an income of 100,000*l.* a year. An early predilection for the study of heraldry, and the opportunities which he enjoyed of foreign travel, no doubt combined to form in him a taste for Gothic architecture, which in later life he gratified by raising for himself, in that style, one of the most remarkable mansions of the day.

He had previously made himself notorious by encircling the greater portion of his estate at Fonthill with a wall twelve feet high, and protected by a *chevaux de frise*. It was about seven miles in length, and was finished by the contractor in little more than a year. It was built to prevent the intrusion of sportsmen on the planted and arable portion of the grounds, Mr. Beckford having a great dislike to the pursuits of hunting and shooting. The erection of this wall had the effect of cutting off the general public from any chance of inspecting the new residence which, in accordance with the whim of its owner, was called Fonthill Abbey, and which, in fact, assumed to a great extent the appearance of an ecclesiastical building. It was cruciform in plan, its length from north to south being 312 feet, while the transverse portion extended to 250 feet, from east to west. The principal feature was an octagonal tower, which rose from the centre to a height of 278 feet. To give an idea of the mystery which attended its construction, we may mention that in a number of the 'Gentleman's Magazine' it was seriously announced that the lantern at the top would command a view of the surrounding country to an extent of eighty miles, and that, notwithstanding the enormous height of the tower, a coach and six might be driven with convenience from the base to the summit, and down again.

During the progress of the works, which were conducted from the designs and under the superintendence of James Wyatt, architect, this tower accidentally caught fire, and Beckford, who possessed, or perhaps affected, through life, a philosophical indifference to misfortune of all kinds, is said to have enjoyed from his garden the magnificent spectacle of its conflagration. The erection of Fonthill Abbey was begun in 1796, and extended over a period of many years. During part of this time the number of artificers engaged on it, in various capacities, was extraordinary. On one occasion all the available labour of the neighbourhood was monopolised for it, and even the agricultural industry in the district was sensibly affected. On another, the royal works at St. George's Chapel, Windsor, stood still for the same reason. No less than 460 men were then employed on the building. They worked night and day, relieving each other in gangs. The expenses thus entailed must have been enormous. Beckford himself stated that the entire cost of Fonthill Abbey was over 273,000*l*. The former family seat, inhabited by Alderman Beckford, was an Italian structure. After the completion of the 'Abbey' it was pulled down, and the building materials alone sold for 10,000*l*.

South of the central abbey tower was a wing, then known as St. Michael's Gallery. On the west side was a covered cloister, which connected the hall with a block of buildings at the end of the south wing, buttressed and flanked by two octagonal turrets. Between this cloister and the south wing of the Abbey was a *cortile*, in the centre of which a fountain played.   The east wing was carried up rather higher than the rest, and included in its design two turrets, copied from those in the entrance gateway of St. Augustine's Monastery, at Canterbury, and features of the same kind, but of a smaller size, were repeated at the end nearest the central block.   The south side of this wing was lighted by three large pointed windows, filled with tracery.

The principal entrance was on the west side, and consisted of a lofty doorway, thirty-one feet high.   It was spanned by a richly moulded pointed arch, the drip-stone of which bore crockets and terminated its ogival curve in a finial.   In the wall above was a small window, and above this the gable was decorated at its apex by a niche containing a statue of St. Anthony of Padua.

The oratory was richly ornamented throughout.   The ceiling was of oak, gilded and divided into pendental compartments.   To ensure a dim and mellow light, the windows of this room were inserted in a hollow or double wall, of which the outer fenestration was not immediately opposite the inner openings.   The latter were filled with stained glass.

The hall, one of the chief internal features of the Abbey, was of important dimensions, being sixty-eight by twenty-eight feet on plan, and seventy-eight feet high.   Thence, under a lofty arch, the grand staircase led to the floor of the saloon above.   This central apartment, which formed what we may call the first floor of the octagonal tower, was connected with the several wings of the building by four lobbies. In the space between them were deep recesses about fifty feet high and lighted by windows which had been copied from some in the Royal Monastery at Batalha ; over the apex of the arches thus used was a gallery which ran round the tower.   Attached columns were corbelled out in the spandrels, and from these sprang the groining which carried the lantern above.   Both the east postern tower and that at the south-east were strengthened with buttresses, and their parapets, in common with those throughout the building, were battlemented.

A staircase which led to the gallery and upper portion of the tower was entered through a lobby on the left of the western vestibule. The dining-room and library were both elegantly fitted up with oak. Indeed, the arrangements of the interior, though far from compatible with comfort (owing to the nature of the plan and a constant sacrifice to external effect), were of a most costly and magnificent character. Pictures, objects of art and *virtù*, and every luxury which wealth could command were assembled there in profusion. Some idea of their value may be formed when we state that in 1819, at the sale of the Abbey and its contents to Mr. Farquhar, 7,200 catalogues at a guinea each were sold in a few days.

It was only when the building had passed out of Beckford's hands that he became fully aware of its instability and how shamefully Wyatt (who, by the way, died before its completion) had been deceived by those to whom the construction of the Abbey had been entrusted. A few years after the sale, Mr. Beckford was summoned to the death-bed of a man who had been clerk of works at Fonthill. He confessed that, though a large sum of money had been paid for sound foundations under the central tower, the inverted arches described in the specification had never been provided. The whole fabric, or at least this portion of it, might fall down at any time. The only wonder was how it had kept so long together. Beckford lost no time in communicating with Mr. Farquhar on the subject; but that gentleman remarked with coolness that he had no doubt it would last his lifetime. He was, however, mistaken. Not long afterwards the tower fell in a heap of ruins. Fonthill Abbey has since undergone various repairs and alterations. A new mansion has been erected near its site; but little or no vestige remains of that strange ambitious building which was once the wonder of the western counties, and which formed so important a feature in the Gothic Revival.

We have already seen how materially literature and the labours of the antiquary helped to sustain the traditions of Mediæval art. Let us now take a rapid survey of those books which were published during the eighteenth century in connection with this subject.

So early as 1683 Lord Clarendon had begun his 'History and Antiquities of Winchester Cathedral.' The work was continued by Mr. Samuel Gale, who in 1715 published the result of their joint labours. The volume contained a full description of the tombs and monuments in the church, together with an account of all its bishops, deans, and prebendaries, to which was added the history and antiquities of Hyde Abbey. A later edition appeared in 1723.

Thomas Pownall, Fellow of the Royal Society and of the Society of Antiquaries, a gentleman of considerable learning and political knowledge, was born at Lincoln in 1722, and died in 1805. He wrote on the 'Origin of Gothic Architecture.' The treatise is little known, and there is no copy of it in the British Museum.

In 1722–3 two additional volumes to Dugdale's 'Monasticon' were added by Mr. John Stevens.

In 1762 appeared Perry's 'Series of English Medals,' in which the author attempted to illustrate and classify Gothic tracery from the Conquest downwards. The descriptive text was written by Mr. John Aubrey.

A more important work was published in 1771 by James Bentham, M.A., Fellow of the Society of Antiquaries and rector of Feltwell St. Nicholas, Norfolk. It was entitled 'The History and Antiquities of the Conventual Church of Ely, from the Foundation of the Monastery, A.D. 673, to the year 1771.' It was printed at the Cambridge University Press, and was illustrated with engravings on copper of interior views, plans, monuments, &c., by P. S. Lamborn, from the drawings of Mr. Heins. Some of the architectural examples are selected with little discrimination, but they are, on the whole, very finely etched.

'The Carpenter's Treasure, a collection of designs for temples, with their plans, gates, doors, rails, &c., in the Gothic taste,' is a curious little book by one Wallis, which made its appearance in 1774, and may perhaps be still met with at old bookstalls.

Grose's ' Antiquities of England and Wales'—one of the most comprehensive works of the kind which had appeared since Dugdale's ' Monasticon'—was published in four folio volumes, to which were afterwards added two supplementary volumes, between the years 1773 and 1787. It is amply illustrated with careful engravings. In a lengthy preface the author gives a useful essay on Gothic Architecture, including a general history of ancient British castles, explaining the terms relative to the construction of their garrisons, and the old machines used for attack and defence. To this information is added a useful account of British monastic institutions, compiled from the (then) best existing authorities, including Domesday Book, which is frequently quoted. The architectural drawings which accompany this work vary in merit. Ornamental sculpture, when given in detail, is feebly drawn, but the general views are useful, and doubly interesting when we remember that many of the buildings which they illustrate have since perished. Fonts, brasses, and other objects of ecclesiastical service are represented, and the second volume of the supplement includes some etchings and descriptive text of Druidical remains in the Channel Islands. In treating the English and Welsh antiquities, each county is separately considered and accompanied by a small map, with a list of the places most worthy of notice. Mr. Grose was assisted in this work by various antiquarians, clergymen, and artists of his time. He makes especial mention of Mr. Gough, Thomas Sandly, then professor of architecture to the Royal Academy, and several noble-men and gentlemen who furnished descriptions or histories of their seats.

In 1789 the same author produced his ' Antiquities of Scotland' in two folio volumes, a useful work of its kind, prefaced by an introduc-tion, in which the history and leading characteristics of Mediæval Scotland are described. The engravings, most of which were executed by a Mr. Sparrow, are inferior to those of the England and Wales series.

In 1795 Mr. Grose undertook the same sort of work for Ireland, on this occasion in two *quarto* volumes—also prefaced by a description of Irish architecture. It is remarkable that, in almost all illustrations of sculptured ornament which were produced at this time, there is one unvaried and conventional treatment noticeable. If a knot of foliage or a carved head is to be represented on a cornice or in a capital, it is drawn in outline or with the faintest indication of half-tone, while the ground on which it is supposed to be relieved is shaded flat, without any attempt to show cast shadows. The result of this is an extraordinary meanness of effect, much at variance with the bold and artistic manner in which general views were often treated by the same draughtsman.

This fault was to some extent avoided by Mr. Carter, an architect, who in 1786 published his 'Specimens of ancient Sculpture and Painting,' which he dedicated to Horace Walpole. It contained numerous illustrations and letter-press descriptive of monuments, brasses, encaustic tiles, wall-painting, and mural sculpture, &c., and was a most valuable contribution to the art literature of his time. In 1795 the same gentleman brought out his 'Ancient Architecture of England.' It was divided into two parts, the first being entitled ' The *Orders* * of Architecture during the British, Roman, Saxon, and Norman eras.' The second part was called ' The Orders of Architecture during the reigns of Henry III., Edward III., Richard II., Henry VII., and Henry VIII.' The engravings in this book, though somewhat coarse, are boldly and skilfully executed, the author's professional skill, no doubt, enabling him to render the illustrations of a more useful and practical kind than many which had preceded them;

* It was long before the use of this foolish word was abandoned. It had been unsatisfactory in its application to Greek and Roman art, but it became ridiculous in connection with Mediæval architecture.

details were now given, with plans and sections of mouldings, and the examples were selected with taste and judgment. In the delineation of carved foliage, the spirit of ancient art was still misinterpreted, and many of the early English capitals in Carter's book remind one more of the Renaissance school than of the period to which they belong. But, taken as a whole, the work was a decided advance on what had hitherto appeared. It was dedicated to the Duke of York, who had been a patron of Carter, and had employed him to carry out some designs at Oatlands in accordance with the style which, it appears, His Royal Highness, as well as our author, affected.

Hearne's 'Antiquities of Great Britain,' illustrated by views of monasteries, castles, and churches, many of which were then existing in a ruined state, was printed by James Phillips, in George Yard, Lombard Street, and published jointly by T. Hearne and W. Byrne, the former of whom drew and the latter engraved the illustrations, in 1786. The architectural views, like many others of the same class and date, were executed with reference rather to general and picturesque effect, than to any accuracy of detail. Short descriptions, written in French and English, accompany each plate in the volume, which is of an oblong quarto size.

In the same year (1786) Gough published his 'Sepulchral Monuments of Great Britain,' a large and important work of five folio volumes, which gave not only excellent illustrations of tombs, mural monuments, brasses, costumes, armour, &c., of the Middle Ages, but descriptive text of great value to the antiquary.

Although the merits of Pointed architecture were now becoming gradually acknowledged, its decorative features had still been little studied. The publication, therefore, of a work devoted almost exclusively to the illustration of Mediæval sculpture was an event of some importance. In 1795 Mr. Joseph Halfpenny brought out a book of this description entitled 'Gothic Ornaments in the Cathedral Church of York.' The illustrations were drawn and etched by himself. They are exceedingly careful and delicate in execution, but wanting in spirit, and, in fact, are far too smooth and neat to be characteristic of ancient art. The carved work is coldly drawn, and wherever two sides of a capital are identical in motive, the foliage is reproduced line by line at each corner without the slightest deviation of curve. The result is of course an absence of vitality for which no refinement can atone. Again, the leaves themselves are frequently bounded by a hard outline or mass of shadow gradated evenly from their edges to the ground behind. This gave them a sharp metallic appearance which is absolutely false in effect. But the most curious and inexcusable fault of all was the manner in which the sculpture of human features was delineated. Almost all the grotesque heads in Halfpenny's engravings are leering at each other with *pupilled* eyes. Such representations fail to convey the notion of sculpture altogether, and become vulgar caricatures. This foolish conceit has, happily, long been abandoned.

In 1798 James Bentham and Brown Willis published a 'History of Gothic and Saxon Architecture in England, exemplified by descriptions of the Cathedrals, &c.' It appeared in a thin folio volume, containing large engravings of perspective exteriors, not devoid of grace, but wanting in appreciation of detail. In this treatise Bentham defends Mediæval architecture from the stigma of 'barbarism' with which modern ignorance had associated it. He was, however, but a cautious champion of the style, and evidently laboured under the impression, which has been entertained even in our own day, that King's College Chapel represented the culminating glory of the Middle Ages.

Indeed, it seems to be only within the last decade of years that we have learned to reverse that theory, and to admire the period of Mediæval art which was distinguished, not for the cunning intricacy of its ornament, but for graceful simplicity of design and for sound principles of construction.

It would be ungrateful, however, to ignore the services rendered to the cause of the Gothic Revival by many an antiquary and many an author of the last century, because their opinions and their books fail to suggest or illustrate those principles of taste which have since been enlightened by later research and more practised skill.

It was something, at least, to draw attention to the noble works of our ancestors, which had long been neglected and despised: to record with the pencil or the pen some testimony, however inadequate, of their goodly forms and worthy purpose: to invest with artistic and historical interest the perishing monuments of an age when art was pure and genuine.

And if, at the present day, we flatter ourselves that the buildings which we raise have at length realised the spirit of old English architecture, and reproduced its most essential merits, let us remember that these works have been aided by the past, and will be judged by a future generation, and as the former strove to teach, the latter will not fail to criticise.

CHAPTER V.

IN reviewing the various phases through which the fine arts have passed from their earliest development down to the present time, it has long been the custom to indicate such phases chronologically by the names of successive centuries. This has been especially the case with English architecture of the Middle Ages, because it would be hardly possible by any different system to distinguish schools which followed, or rather grew out of, each other so gradually and imperceptibly, and in which the change from style to style must be attributed to the inevitable progression of national taste rather than to that influence of individual skill or genius which marks the history of pictorial art.

It is, however, but an approximately correct method of classification, and if imperfect as an index to the varieties of ancient architecture, will be found doubly so in dealing with the works of modern days. The present age, from numerous causes upon which it is not now necessary to dilate, presents a greater diversity of opinion on matters æsthetical than probably ever before existed in one country at the same time. Yet in this nineteenth century, or rather that portion of it included within the last thirty years, the glimmering sparks of enthusiasm for Mediæval art first quickened into a flame, which though it is still exposed to the fitful gusts of private bias and public caprice, promises one day to burn long and steadily.

It would, of course, be impossible to give anything like a detailed description of even the prominent examples of the Revival during that period. As they increase in number they necessarily diminish in, at least, historical interest, and it will therefore be desirable that the more modern section of this history should be devoted to the characteristics of each architect, as typified in his most important works, rather than to the endless task of describing every building which in this generation, by pinnacle or pointed arch, puts in an appearance as Gothic.

The instances, however, of that style which belong to what we may be allowed to call the *præ-Puginesque* era are entitled to our respect as resulting from a spirit that stemmed the current of popular prejudice before the genius and ingenuity of later minds had been brought to bear on the subject, or the maturer study of ancient models had taught experience in design.

Among the architects who at the dawn of the present century contributed by their works to the Revival were Wyatt and Nash. The former has been already mentioned in connection with Fonthill Abbey, which he did not live to see completed. He was employed on many other large works in Wiltshire, including the restoration of Salisbury Cathedral.

Nash's alterations and additions to Windsor Castle—especially the Waterloo Gallery, though far from embodying the spirit of the ancient structure—were nevertheless good of their kind. His country houses, especially in Ireland, were chiefly of the pseudo-baronial sort, which, for want of better definition, received the general name of ' castellated.' Among them the mansions of Lord Lorton and Lord Gort may be mentioned. Ravensworth Castle, at Gateshead, is another example of his skill. Luscombe, near Dawlish in Devonshire, was begun for Mr. Charles Hoare, from designs by Nash, in 1800, and finished in 1804. The south or garden front * consists of a large octagonal tower in the centre, united by three of its sides to the main building, which extends east and west of it. At the east end is a cloister of Tudor arches with an embattled parapet. The piers of each bay are strengthened by

---

* In this and other cases it must be remembered that the description given is of the *original* design. Many houses of this date have, of course, since undergone alteration, and some have been pulled down.

buttresses which terminate in pinnacles above. On the west side is a porch of the same character, with a mullioned window deeply recessed. The first floor of the tower is lighted by two large pointed windows filled with stained glass. The dining-room is at the east end. The west is occupied by offices, and on the north is a square tower, the lower part of which forms an opened porch, with a pointed arch on three sides. The whole is a bold and vigorous composition.

Belvoir Castle, in Leicestershire, is an old building which was entirely remodelled in the early part of this century by the Duke of Rutland, under the direction of James Wyatt, at an expense of, at least, 200,000*l.* Its principal feature is a circular tower, four storeys in height, crowned by a machicolated parapet. The windows of this tower are flat-pointed, or nearly round-headed. They are divided into two lights, each head being filled with tracery. The rest of the building presents a straggling but not unpicturesque assemblage of features, including two octagonal turrets with pinnacles at each angle, and three square towers of various dimensions, also machicolated. Some of the windows here and there are pointed, but as a rule they have square heads with Tudor labels— a species of decoration which once passed for good Gothic. The lower part of the principal tower forms a colonnade from which stone brackets project to carry a verandah above. The buttresses used here, and throughout Wyatt's work, are generally of a thin and wiry description. They are, for the most part, divided, whatever their height may be, into two pretty equal portions by one set-off. On October 26, 1816, while the works were in progress, a most calamitous fire broke out, which destroyed a considerable portion of this building. Among the rest, a valuable picture gallery was consumed, and many paintings of Sir Joshua Reynolds, including the celebrated ' Nativity,' perished in the flames.

During the works recently carried out at Combe Abbey, the Earl of Craven's seat, an old room was taken down which had long been supposed to belong to the Elizabethan age. Before its demolition, however, certain facts were brought to light with regard to constructive detail which leave little doubt that it was erected at a much later period. The ceiling had been decorated with papier-mâché ornament, and the panel lining of the wall proved, on examination, to be composed of deal strips glued in their places, instead of being worked in solid wood. A transomed window by which the room had been lighted was executed in *cast iron*. The fireplace alone was genuine old work. It had evidently been refixed when the room was 'remodelled,' which is supposed to have happened in 1803.

The foundation-stone of Lord Bridgewater's seat, Ashridge, in Buckinghamshire, was laid in 1808. It was a large and important mansion of a Mediæval character, built on the site of an old edifice, of which portions were allowed to remain and become incorporated in the new work which was carried out by Wyatt. The style is Tudor. Its principal façade is decorated with turrets, and with a porch which reminds us of the 'Lords' entrance' in the present Houses of Parliament. The design exhibits no obtrusive faults, but is remarkable for great coldness of treatment.

Elvaston Hall, near Derby, was an old mansion belonging to Lord Harrington, but the principal portion was rebuilt early in this century by Mr. Walker, an architect who, however, only carried out Wyatt's plans. It contains the usual complement of turrets and battlements, but has also a very fair oriel window. Nash built Garnstone House in Herefordshire, and a house for Colonel Scudamore, at Kentchurch Park, both of which may be considered examples of the Revival. Childwall Hall, Lancashire, was another of his efforts in the same direction. It is a two-storeyed building, flanked by square and octagonal towers, and heavily machicolated. His designs for Magdalen College, Oxford, were much admired at the time—they were, however, never executed. In his own residence, East Cowes Castle, he had an opportunity of indulging a taste which was more distinguished for its appreciation of Gothic than that which characterised most of his contemporaries.

Donnington Hall, in Leicestershire, the property of Lord Hastings, was erected between 1790 and 1800, by Mr. W. Wilkins, architect. In composition it presents a rectangular mass, with a porch, tower, and turrets. Coleorton Hall, in the same county, once the country seat of the generous art patron, Sir George Beaumont, was one of the few attempts in the way of Pointed architecture which were made by G. Dance.* Stanley Hall, in Shropshire, was built early in the present century by Mr. Smalman, an architect of Quatford, near Bridgnorth, and is not a bad specimen of provincial work. Armitage Park, about six miles from Lichfield, in Staffordshire, and Rindlesham Hall, near Woodbridge, Suffolk, are interesting as early specimens of nineteenth-century Gothic.

Hawarden Castle was built by Sir John Glynne in 1752. There had formerly existed on the same spot an old mansion of wood and plaster belonging to the Ravenscroft family, called Broadlane House. The new residence was an unpretending but substantially constructed house, which retained its original name until 1809, when Sir Stephen Glynne, assisted by the professional advice of Mr. Thomas Cundy, caused the brick exterior to be cased with stone in the 'castellated' style.

Lord Montagu's seat at Ditton Park, Somersetshire, was designed by Mr. Atkinson, architect, about 1811. It is in part a three-storeyed building, while the rest consists of only two floors. In general plan it is nearly quadrangular. The central feature is a square tower, to which a turret is added at one corner. The windows are square-headed and protected by an ordinary Tudor drip-stone. About the same time Lord De la Warr's old country mansion, Bourn House in Cambridgeshire, was restored by Mr. John Adey Repton, who introduced new features, such as bay-windows, chimney-shafts, &c. Cobham Hall, Kent, then the residence of Lord Darnley, was another old building on which the elder Repton and his two sons, besides Wyatt, were employed at various times for additions and restoration.

* A new storey was added to this building (Coleorton Hall) in 1862, from the designs of Mr. F P. Cockerell.

Eaton Hall, Cheshire (before alteration in 1870)—the Seat of the Marquis of Westminster.

One of the most important attempts at Pointed architecture of this date is Eaton Hall, Cheshire, the seat of the Marquis of Westminster. In design it is a mixture of Early and Late Gothic. It was built on the site of an old mansion, erected by Sir Thomas Grosvenor in the reign of King William. The later structure was designed by Mr. Porden, an architect whose name has been long forgotten, but who, no doubt, had considerable practice in his day. It was probably finished quite early in this century, for a full account of it is given in the 'Monthly Magazine' for September 1814.

The south-east view presents a large quadrangular block of buildings irregularly divided into bays by buttresses and turrets. It is three storeys in height, with a battlemented parapet running round the main walls. The windows were filled with tracery, but the latter was executed in cast iron, moulded on both sides, and grooved to receive the glass. The walls, balustrades, battlements, and pinnacles, are of a light-coloured stone. The principal entrance to the house is in the middle of the west front, under a vaulted portico, which admits a carriage to the steps leading to the hall, a spacious and lofty apartment occupying the height of two storeys, and roofed by a vaulted ceiling. The pavement is of coloured marble arranged in geometrical patterns. 'At the end of the hall a screen of five arches supports a gallery that connects the bed-chambers on the north side of the house with those on the south. Under this gallery two open arches to the right and left conduct to the grand staircase, and opposite to the door of the hall is the entrance to the saloon.' The grand staircase itself is enriched with canopied niches, and with groining under the landings and sky-light. The second staircase was constructed of cast iron, after a design which no doubt was then considered very appropriate. The saloon forms a square on plan about thirty feet each way. Fan tracery, executed in plaster (but now removed), sprang from attached columns at the angles and sides of the room to receive the vault, which in plan was nearly octagonal. On the right and left are little vestibules which must be passed to reach the drawing-room and dining-room. The windows of these rooms are traceried and filled with painted glass. The dining-room at the north extremity of the east front is about fifty feet long. The ceiling was panelled, and a central pendant was constructed to carry a chandelier. The drawing-room occupies the south extremity of the east front, and is of the same form and general dimensions as the dining-room, with the addition of a large window (now blocked up) which had a southern aspect.* The library is in the centre of the south front; its ceiling and large bow window being decorated in character with the other features above mentioned. It is fitted up with oak. In the principal façades, the windows are pointed, and many have ogival hood-mouldings. The middle window of the saloon opens on a vaulted cloister, occupying the space between the dining-room and drawing-room, and from the cloister a flight of steps leads to a spacious terrace. The size of this building alone would make it imposing, but the distribution of parts, as in many efforts of that day, is more suited to the outline of an Italian composition than that of a Gothic design, while the character of the details is of a pseudo-ecclesiastical kind. Indeed, here as in many other contemporary examples of the Revival, it is evident that the architect sought his inspiration in the churches rather than in the domestic architecture of the Middle Ages. The noble mansions of old England had still to be studied.

Seldon House, near Croydon, had for its garden front a sort of arcade, divided into five bays, each spanned by a pointed arch with buttresses between. This arcade was flanked on either side by turrets which rose above the parapet of the building. It was completed early in this century.

At the same period Lord Derby's residence at Knowsley Park was

---

* Since this description was written, Mr. A. Waterhouse has been employed by the present Marquis of Westminster to remodel the building, which will thus undergo considerable alteration and improvement. The internal decorations will be of an exceedingly rich and beautiful description.

rebuilt, 'in the style of a baronial mansion,' under the superintendence of Mr. Foster of Liverpool, while Mrs. Bulwer Lytton adopted the now rapidly developed taste in erecting Knebworth House, in Hertfordshire, about fifty years ago.

Warleigh House, a two-storeyed building, was raised in 1814 for Mr. Henry Skrine by Mr. Webb, a Staffordshire architect.

After Wyatt and Nash perhaps Smirke may be next reckoned in importance. He built Eastnor Castle, in Herefordshire, for Lord Somers. It is a massive and gloomy-looking building, flanked by watch-towers, and enclosing a keep. To preserve the character at which it aimed, the windows were made exceedingly small and narrow. This must have resulted in much inconvenience within. Indeed all the admirers of Pointed architecture fell at this time into the grievous error of supposing that its merits lay in the quaint uncouthness of early necessity rather than in those immutable but ever applicable principles which should really hold as good now as they did five hundred years ago, and accommodate themselves to every new requirement and modern invention. The building in question might have made a tolerable fort before the invention of gunpowder, but as a residence it was a picturesque mistake.

Wilton Castle, in Yorkshire, was built by Smirke, on the site and out of the ruins of an ancient edifice. Offley Place, in Hertfordshire, a Tudor mansion, also designed by him, is a large building three storeys high, having in the centre of its block a tower 20 feet square which contains the staircase, and is lighted by painted windows. The library is nearly 40 feet long.

In Scotland, Gillespie was the great revivalist of his day. Lord Macdonald's seat at Armidale, in Inverness, was built from his designs. He enlarged Wishaw, in Lanarkshire, for Lord Belhaven, and also erected Culdees Castle, once the residence of General Drummond. The latter is in the oft-quoted 'castellated' style and includes in its composition a square tower, which, like the one at Offley Place, is used for a hall and staircase.   It has a large pointed window on one side enriched with tracery.

Crichton was another Scotch architect of some note.   He prepared plans for Abercairny Abbey, in Perthshire, which his successors, Messrs. Dickson, of Edinburgh, afterwards carried out.

In Ireland, the reintroduction of Pointed architecture was mainly due to the skill and ingenuity of the Messrs. Morrison (Richard and William), two architects who lived at Walcot, near Bray, and were extensively employed in works of a Mediæval character.   They restored Kilcuddy Hall, and executed façades of Shelton Abbey for Lord Wicklow.   They also built Ballyleigh Castle, Kerry, the seat of Colonel James Crosbie, M.P.   The latter was a very creditable performance, and the beauty of the scenery by which it is surrounded contributed no little to its effect.

Having briefly examined some of the chief examples of Pointed architecture which were designed in the early part of this century, under the patronage or direction of those from whom the Revival received especial encouragement, let us now turn to another source of impulse which helped the same cause, viz., the archæological literature of the day.   In the consideration of this subject, one name stands pre-eminently forward, the name of an extraordinarily prolific writer, who, if he did not possess a high order of genius, was distinguished for his indomitable industry, and for the zeal which enabled him, year after year, to contribute to the press the results of his research during a period which extended far beyond the limits of ordinary authorship—a name which, in the history of art, connects at least four generations, for it belonged to one who was a young man when Sir Joshua Reynolds still wielded his brush, but who lived to see Eastlake president of the Royal Academy.

John Britton was born at Kingtown, near Sodbury, in 1771, and died in London exactly fourteen years ago.   In addition to a list of nearly seventy works, of more or less importance, whose titles may be read in the British Museum catalogue, he has left behind him an auto-biography, which he did not live to complete, but which was published after his death. What length that memoir would have assumed, in a finished state, may be inferred from a perusal of its present contents. It is impossible to read the first few pages without coming to a conclusion that the author had kept a diary since he had learned to write, and intended to publish the whole of it up to the time of his death. Indeed, though this intention, if it ever existed, was never carried out, a more diffuse and erratic narrative never issued from the press. Amidst his numerous good qualities, it cannot be denied that the author had one failing—vanity, and to this fact we may attribute the unnecessary care with which he chronicles the details of his early life. He begins with a description of his native village, which alone occupies some pages— gives us the character of his father, the caprices of his uncle—relates how he fell out of a bedroom window, and was raked out of the squire's fishpond—tells us what he drew on his slate at school, and what became of all his schoolfellows—gravely reports that he once made a large snowball, which rolled down hill and made a breach in some garden wall. The most trivial and unimportant incidents, in short, which help to vary the monotony of schoolboy life, he records with something like schoolboy pride ; but these may be at once passed over.

On October 25, 1785, he set out with his uncle for London, where young Britton was at length apprenticed to Mr. Mendham, a wine merchant, by whom he was initiated into the mysteries of the trade. His time was chiefly employed in bottling and corking, an occupation which he soon began to feel was beneath his abilities, and which led him to regard even the occasional visits of excisemen as a pleasant relief. The house of business where he laboured in this humble capacity was known as the Jerusalem Chambers, Clerkenwell. He appears to have been in the habit of rising early, and taking walks into the suburbs before the hours of work. In one of these excursions, he fell in with a man named Essex, who painted figures on watch faces, and having struck up an acquaintance with him, was introduced to Brayley, who at that time was also an enamel painter, but who afterwards became associated with Britton in the publication of several topographical works. They composed and published between them a song called ' The Guinea-pig '—intended as a satire on the powder tax. It was Britton's first published work, and years afterwards he flattered himself that a time might come when it would be regarded with curiosity.

In the course of time a love adventure with Mrs. Mendham's lady's maid caused him to run away from his employer, and follow the object of his affections into Devonshire, where, however, he became disenchanted, and after vainly endeavouring to get employment at Bath, he returned to town on foot. Here fortune so far smiled on him as to permit his filling the post of cellarman at the London Tavern, and he afterwards obtained a similar situation with a hop-merchant's widow, who allowed him 40*l.* a year and his breakfast. About this time his ambition led him to frequent the third-rate debating societies and spouting clubs with which the metropolis then abounded, and this helped him to form new acquaintances, by whose assistance he at length became engaged as a lawyer's clerk to Mr. Simpson, an attorney, at a salary of fifteen shillings a week. On the death of his master, he entered the service of Messrs. Parker and Wix, solicitors, whose practice was not so extensive as to prevent Britton from finding time to read—an opportunity of which he was only too ready to avail himself.

In 1799 he was hired by a Mr. Chapman to write, sing, and recite for him at a theatre in Panton Street, Haymarket, where he received three guineas a week. This led to an acquaintance with Lonsdale, manager of Sadler's Wells, at whose house he met Dibdin, Grimaldi, and the famous Egyptian traveller and antiquary, Belzoni, who, strange to say, was at that time performing as an acrobat in London theatres.*

* Belzoni was six feet six inches high and proportionably muscular. He was a native of Italy, and had received an education for the priesthood. Having saved some money, he sailed for Egypt, where he so pleased the Pasha by some mechanical invention that he obtained permission to open the pyramid of Gizeh and several tombs at Thebes. We are indebted to his zeal for many valuable relics of antiquity now in the British Museum.

Britton's first literary efforts were of the humblest description. He was tempted by the great success of one of Sheridan's plays (translated and altered from the German of Kotzebue) to write a romance, entitled 'The enterprising Adventures of Pizarro.' For this performance he received ten pounds. The most valuable of his early friends and patrons was Wheble, who induced him to begin those topographical researches of which the world first saw a result in his 'Beauties of Wiltshire.'

His first expedition is thus described :—

With maps, a pocket-compass, a small camera obscura (for the more portable and simple camera *lucida* was not then known), two or three portable volumes, an umbrella, and a scanty packet of body linen, &c., I commenced a walk from London, on June 20, and returned again to it on September 30. During that excursion, I visited Oxford, Woodstock, Stratford-upon-Avon, Warwick, Kenilworth, Birmingham, Hagley, 'the Leasowes,' and Church Stretton. Thence I made diverging excursions to Shrewsbury, Welsh Pool, and several other places within twenty miles of my residence, and returned through Ludlow, Leominster, Hereford, Ross, down the Wye to Chepstow, to Bristol, and Bath ; thence to several parts of Wiltshire, and back to London. This long and toilsome, but eminently interesting and attractive journey, cost me only 11*l.* 16*s.* 9*d.* I was compelled to practise economy, for my finances were low, and I knew not how or where to recruit them. My sister kindly presented me with 5*l.*, and her good husband lent me ten more, which seemed to me a fortune.

'The Beauties of Wiltshire' met with such commercial success, that Britton, in conjunction with his friend and fellow-worker Brayley, was employed on the more extensive work which followed or rather developed from it. 'The Beauties of England and Wales' formed a series of eighteen volumes, which were published between 1800 and 1816, and contained 'original delineations, topographical, historical, and descriptive of each county.' They included about 700 engravings of mansions, views, &c. Some of the woodcuts were by Bewick, and worthy of that master ; but, as a rule, the illustrations were poor, and of a kind which will not bear comparison with those given in Britton's later works. Britton himself when he began his literary career knew little of architecture, and thus in 'The Beauties of Wiltshire,' while the tombs and painted glass in the churches which he visited are fully described, the buildings themselves inspire him only with that vague admiration which results from uneducated taste.

But Britton was not a man to be easily discouraged. He soon began to qualify himself for the pursuit which he had chosen. In 1803 he had attained sufficient skill with the pencil to produce his 'Drawings of Stonehenge,' and in 1805 he began a more important work, 'The Architectural Antiquities of Great Britain,' which appeared in forty parts, and made four quarto volumes, the last bearing date 1814, and a fifth being added in 1818. They were illustrated with nearly three hundred plates, after drawings by various artists, among whom were Turner, Cattermole, and Westall, but by far the best are those which were engraved by Le Keux from drawings by Mackenzie, and which will be easily recognised by the care and delicacy of their execution.*

The work included many examples of ancient domestic, as well as ecclesiastical English architecture. Abbeys, priories, castles, with an occasional view of a cathedral, or the details of some remarkable building—such as Crosby Hall—were delineated for the first time with something like accuracy, as well as artistic power, and in many cases the ichnography of buildings—so essential to the student—was added.

In 1813 Britton published a description of St. Mary Redcliffe Church, at Bristol, to which he appended an essay on the life and writings of Chatterton, and in 1814 he began his most important work, 'The Cathedral Antiquities of Great Britain.' The letterpress which accompanies this series bears evidence of great research on the part of its author, who spared neither time nor pains to collect material. Besides a description of the buildings themselves, which he was by this

* Portions of the text in this, and some other publications by Britton, were from the pen of Mr. E. J. Willson, F.S.A., of Lincoln.

time fully competent to give, he adds a vast quantity of information regarding their history and foundations, with anecdotes and brief memoirs of the principal dignitaries of the Church who were from time to time associated with them.   As may be supposed, the 'Monasticon Anglicanum' is constantly quoted by him, but, in addition to this work, he consulted Sumner, Batteley, Godwin's Catalogue of English Bishops, and a host of other authorities.

The original edition appeared in fourteen parts, the illustrations of the earlier numbers being executed by Britton's old fellow-workers Mackenzie and Le Keux, who had now attained a perfection in their peculiar branch of art which had not hitherto been reached, and has since been scarcely surpassed.   It is indeed to be regretted that all the plates were not entrusted to their hands.   It will be no detraction from the merit of Cattermole to say that his acknowledged excellence as a water-colour artist unfitted him for the less dignified labour, but nicer accuracy, of an architectural draughtsman.   He could throw an effect upon the view of a ruin with perhaps greater skill than Mackenzie, but for refinement, perspicuity, and attention to detail, especially in outline views, Mackenzie distanced every one.

Perhaps the least satisfactory of the cathedral series, in regard to illustration, is the one on Bristol, in which a great falling off is noticeable in the execution of the plates.   The careful hand of Le Keux redeemed some from the charge of slovenliness, but in many those qualities are wanting which should render such works of value to the architectural student.*

* The cathedral series appeared in the following order :—

Salisbury	.	. 1814	Bath Abbey	.	. 1825
Norwich	.	. 1816	Exeter	.	. 1826
Winchester	.	. 1817	Peterborough	.	. 1828
York	.	. 1819	Gloucester	.	. 1829
Lichfield	.	. 1820	Bristol	.	. 1830
Canterbury	.	. 1821	Hereford	.	. 1831
Oxford	.	. 1821	Worcester	.	. 1835
Wells	.	. 1824			

In 1827, Pugin and Le Keux brought out their 'Specimens of the Architectural Antiquities of Normandy,' for which Britton, who acted as their publisher, supplied the descriptive text. This work is in one quarto volume, and contains illustrations of the Caen churches, of Bayeux Cathedral, the Hôtel de Bourgtheroulde, and Abbey of St. Amand, Rouen, with views of various churches at Caudebeck, Caen, Vancelles, and Dieppe. The original drawings were either executed by the elder Pugin himself, or prepared under his immediate superintendence. They were exceedingly careful, and have been admirably engraved by Le Keux. The letterpress is very useful in its way, and, as Britton takes care to tell us, was printed and published as a separate work.

Meanwhile our author did not confine his labours to the production of these volumes. His 'Fine Arts of the English School, with Biographical and Critical Descriptions, illustrated by engravings after Reynolds, Flaxman, Westall, Romney, Nollekens, Northcote, West, etc.,' appeared in 1812. In 1830 he brought out his 'Picturesque Views of English Cities,' a quarto volume copiously illustrated. 'A Dictionary of the Architecture and Archæology of the Middle Ages' was compiled by him, and published in 1838, with illustrations by Le Keux.

It will be unnecessary to mention a host of minor works, of which he was either joint author, editor, or publisher. For the space of half a century his pen was continually active, and it may be safely said that he did more to promote the due appreciation of Mediæval Art than any contemporary writer.

His long association with architecture, and with men who adopted its profession, prompted him more than once in his life to try his hand at design. His sketch for a monument to Chatterton, of which an illustration is given in his life, might provoke the ridicule of our modern architects ; but the plans which he submitted in competition for the Nelson cenotaph, though by no means realising our present notions of Gothic, are far from contemptible ; and, if we remember the time when they were prepared (1839), probably represented the average ability of his day. It is, however, but fair to state that in the latter work he availed himself of the services of Mr. W. Hosking, to whose care, if the design had been successful, its execution would have been committed. Neither in this case, however, nor in that of the Chatterton memorial, were Britton's suggestions adopted.

The materials of his autobiography are diffuse and scattered. He seems to have followed no regular plan in its compilation. It is wanting in chronological sequence. If he is describing a town as he saw it in 1814, he is reminded of some circumstance which occurred there when he revisited it in 1840, and forthwith the two epochs are jumbled together. In his youth he made many acquaintances, of whom he writes at full length. He saw many other people whose life and characters he finds it necessary to touch upon. Those he only heard of are still more numerous; yet, about these, too, he has something to say. Meanwhile, though he is prolix on the subject of his infancy, he gives us little or no information of his life as a man. We know, however, that his services in the cause of art became gradually and steadily appreciated. He who began his London career as a humble cellarman, lived to be fêted and honoured by those who had themselves grown famous in the world.*

The rapidity with which Britton wrote, the occasional inaccuracy of his pen, and perhaps, too, the very success which he achieved, have laid him open to the charge which is often brought against men who, without aspiring to the higher departments of literature, accept author-ship as a business and means of livelihood, and cater for public enter-

---

* The last proof-sheets of his autobiography were sent to the printer on December 2, 1856, with an intimation that Mr. Britton would rest for a day or two before he resumed his work. He was destined never to resume it. On the 4th of the same month, he was taken ill with bronchitis, a disorder to which he was subject, and from which he now felt that he should not recover. He sent for his old friend Le Keux, and gave him some last instructions about certain prints and drawings which he desired should be sold. He died at last, we are told, peacefully and with resignation.

tainment or information as 'book-makers.' But granting that Britton belonged to this class of writers, it may safely be urged that he did more service to the cause of the Gothic Revival in such a capacity than he could have rendered in any other. Before a national taste can be made effective it must be instructed, and before it is instructed it must be created. Britton himself was of course no designer. He did not even attempt to teach what good design ought to be. But for many years he supplied the public with illustrations and descriptions of ancient English architecture which had previously been familiar to the antiquary alone. He helped, and successfully helped, to secure for Mediæval remains that kind of interest which a sense of the picturesque and a respect for historical associations are most likely to create.

While Britton was thus enlisting the sympathies of the amateur world, two architects were engaged in preparing a practical and valuable work for the use of professional students. The examples of Gothic architecture which had hitherto been selected for publication, were chiefly those which either served to illustrate a principle in the history of the style, or possessed some picturesque attractions in the way of general effect. But neither of these were of real service to the practical architect, who required geometrical and carefully measured drawings of ancient roofs, doors, and windows to guide him in his designs, and to help him in reviving a style the details of which had been as yet most imperfectly studied. Pugin and Willson's 'Specimens of Gothic Architecture' supplied this want. It was a happy accident which brought these men together—the one eminently qualified as a draughtsman for the task, the other equally fitted to undertake its literary labour.

For the first time the structural glories of Westminster Hall were revealed with mathematical nicety ; the graceful mouldings of York and Lincoln were accurately profiled on a large and intelligible scale ; the towers and gateways of Oxford were measured with scrupulous care. Many an oriel window and groined porch, many a canopied tomb and flying buttress, the proportions of which had been simply guessed at by those who endeavoured to imitate its design, was now transferred to paper, line for line, with every dimension clearly figured, with every feature separately dissected and explained.

Instead of the vague and frequently inaccurate sketches of ancient tracery and groining which had previously been published, we find in this work plans and sections of stone vaulting and elevations of windows drawn out with the utmost care, the radius and centre of every seg-mental curve ascertained, and the 'mitering' of every junction clearly shown. The individual character of 'cusping,' once considered, if we may judge from early illustrations, a matter of little moment, is here rendered with singular fidelity. The same may be said of crockets, finials, and decorative panelling.

The advantage of all this to the professional designer was immense. The time had not yet arrived when architects, engaged in any impor-tant practice, thought it worth while to measure and study for them-selves the relics of Mediæval architecture; still less had they reached that sort of skill which would have enabled them to design in the spirit of ancient art without absolutely reproducing its details. In this dilemma they had copied after a rough and ready fashion, and their copies were contemptible. But now, by simply turning over the leaves of a convenient volume, they were enabled for the first time to enrich their designs, and perhaps in some instances to work them out as a whole, from 'Specimens' which were unimpeachably correct in style.

The consequence may be easily imagined. An age of ignorance was succeeded by an age of plagiarism. If an architect wanted a spire for his new church, there was that of St. Mary's at Oxford drawn to scale and ready for imitation. If a Gothic monument was to be raised in the same edifice, the altar tombs of Westminster Abbey, engraved in Pugin and Willson's book, supplied a series of examples for selection. The details of Crosby Hall, of Hampton Court, and of

Eton College were adapted for many a modern country mansion. The oriels of Lincoln Palace were revived in St. John's Wood.

This was by no means a satisfactory state of things, but it was better than that by which it had been preceded. Faithful copies of old work were at least more tolerable than bungling attempts at original design. And it was simply impossible for modern architects to originate successful designs in Gothic, until they had learned to appreciate the value of proportion, and had mastered the grammar of detail in ancient examples. ' The Specimens of Gothic Architecture' helped their studies in an eminent degree, and perhaps not less by the carefully written and well-arranged text than by the illustrations which formed the bulk of the volume. It is to be feared that Mr. Willson's share in the preparation of this work has never been thoroughly appreciated. But it must be evident to all who read his descriptions of the plates, and the introductory essays which preface each volume, that he was thoroughly master of his subject, both in its antiquarian and artistic aspect. Pugin's own reputation was considerable, but it was destined to be far eclipsed by that of his son, whose career and works will be described in due course.

CHAPTER VI.

THE publication of practical and accurately illustrated books in Gothic Architecture may be considered as the main turning-point in the progress of the Revival, and for obvious reasons it is necessary to measure by a very different standard the artistic merits of work executed before and after this great assistance had been afforded to professional designers. We must also bear in mind the important influence brought to bear upon the movement by a gradually increasing conviction that our churches and other national relics of the Middle Ages ought not only to be kept in a state of repair, but also to be 'restored' or 'improved' as occasion might warrant.

To realise what this then meant, and what it afterwards came to mean, it may be advisable to turn back a little in our History.

If, in the last century, an architect, led by any rare instinct of individual taste or by any accidental circumstances, devoted his attention to Mediæval Art with a view to its adaptation for a modern work, he was obliged to rely almost entirely on the advice and assistance of the antiquaries. James Essex, who was born at Cambridge and was brought up with a boyish admiration for King's College Chapel, may perhaps have been an exception to the rule. But it is probable that his friendship with Bentham, who had employed him, as a young man, to prepare illustrations for the famous 'History of Ely' (already mentioned), exercised no small influence on his early predilections.

In those days there was little or no scope for an architect with mediæval tendencies except in the way of restoration. The choir of Ely Cathedral was altered under his direction in 1770, and during a period of some twenty years he superintended very extensive repairs in the same building. He was afterwards employed on similar work at Lincoln Minster, where he erected a stone reredos, and at King's College Chapel, for the east end of which he designed a stone screen. The Memorial Cross at Ampthill may be mentioned as another of his works. He also enlarged and repaired the ancient mansion of Madingley, which is well known to Cambridge men of our own time as the residence selected for the Prince of Wales while he remained at the University. He repaired the Tower of Winchester Cathedral, and carried out what were then called 'improvements' at Merton and Balliol Colleges, Oxford. Some of these were important works in their way, and, no doubt, led to many others which were subsequently undertaken under the plea of 'restoration.' Essex may be fairly described as the first professional architect of the last century who made a study of Gothic. But he was far from a thorough appreciation of its merits.*

At the time that Essex died (1784), James Wyatt had, in the opinion of contemporary critics, just established his reputation as a Gothic architect by the remodelling of Mr. Barrett's house at Lee, which has been already mentioned, and which won the admiration of Horace Walpole. In one of Lord Orford's letters (1782) he says :—

I have seen, over and over again, Mr. Barrett's plans, and approve them exceedingly. The Gothic parts are classic : you must consider the whole as Gothic, modernised in parts—not as what it is, the reverse. Mr. Wyatt, if more employed in that style, will show as much taste and imagination as he does in Grecian.

And again, in a letter to Mr. Barrett himself, he admits the defects of Strawberry Hill, and adds, 'My house was but a sketch by beginners : yours is finished by a great master.'

---

* It is stated that, while professionally engaged on the works at Ely Cathedral, Essex advised the destruction of the Galilee and South-west transept, as being 'neither useful nor ornamental' and 'not worth preserving.'

Posterity, judging from Wyatt's later works, as for instance the Military Academy at Woolwich, his alterations of Windsor Castle, and his design for the (old) House of Lords, will scarcely feel inclined to confirm this opinion, or indeed to regard him in the light of a *master* at all. But the lapse of a century has brought about a great revolution in public taste, and with it a deeper study of Mediæval Art.

No English architect has perhaps been so much overrated by his friends, or so unfairly abused by his enemies, as James Wyatt. It is probable that both praise and blame were honestly given, but neither his admirers nor his maligners have done him thorough justice. Raised by private interest and the caprice of public taste to be the fashionable architect of his day—loaded with commissions from every quarter, patronised by Bagot and flattered by Walpole—it is no wonder that this highly favoured and fortunate gentleman not only believed himself to be a great architect, but induced the world to think so too. The country squires who sent for him to embellish their family seats, the Oxford dons who allowed him to pull down and rebuild the ancient colleges of their University, the Deans and Chapters who committed our noble cathedrals to his notions of improvement and restoration, never stopped to inquire what qualifications he had for the several tasks which he only too readily undertook, or what amount of personal supervision he could afford to allot to each. It was sufficient for these illustrious patrons and reverend *dilettanti* to know that Mr. Wyatt was the 'eminent' architect of their day. Artistic reputation has a rapidly accumulative quality. Everybody had employed him, and therefore everybody continued to do so. It would almost have been bad *ton* to seek for assistance elsewhere. Other practitioners might have his ability, but who had heard of them? In consulting a person of Mr. Wyatt's reputation, the world of fashion thought it was quite safe.

At first sight this seems reasonable enough. The most distinguished physician of his day will always command, and has a right to command, the most extensive practice. The most noted counsel will get the most briefs. The most popular preacher will attract the largest congregations. But it must be remembered that in the consulting room, in the law court, and the pulpit we can at least secure the personal presence and individual talent of our favourite doctor, lawyer, or divine.

In the field of architectural practice it is different. The mere name of an architect goes a great way. The rest is a matter of conscience. A man may throw his whole energy into the work on which he happens to be employed, or he may satisfy himself and his employers by occasional visits. He may bring all his inventive power and skill to bear upon the design, or he may simply hand over a slight sketch to be worked out entirely by his assistants. In short, he may make an art of his calling, or he may make it a mere business; and in proportion as he inclines to one or the other of these two extremes, he will generally achieve present profit or posthumous renown.

If Wyatt did not make a fortune by his profession, it was certainly from no undue prominence of artistic feeling. His practice was large and lucrative. His designs do not seem to have given him any very great trouble to prepare. It is recorded that many of them were improvised and even executed in his travelling carriage as he rolled along the road to his country clients. He was a great man in his way, and no doubt a pencil sketch by Mr. Wyatt was thought more valuable than a whole set of working drawings prepared by an inferior hand. Can we blame him if, when commissions poured in upon him from every side, he accepted them all, dashed off his notions upon paper, left them to be realised by his subordinates, and took no pains to consider and revise them, lest he should meanwhile be losing another job? If this sort of practice is to be condemned, let us call it the fault, not of the overworked architect, but of the public who insist on giving him more than he can possibly manage, with credit to himself, to undertake. The very extent of Wyatt's professional employment must have left him little or no leisure for the study of ancient examples; and the consequence was that, in instances where he ought to have led, or at least to have tempered and corrected the vitiated taste of his day, he simply pandered to it. So long as this was confined to the design of modern mansions, no great harm was done. The present inheritors of many a country house erected under his instructions may indeed deplore the ignorance of their grandsires in adopting a style of architecture which is 'Gothic' only in the original and contemptuous sense of the word. It may have brought discredit on the cause of the Revival, and to some extent retarded its progress. Still, it involved no national loss; it inflicted no positive injury on the nobler and purer works of a previous age. But when our fair English churches and venerable colleges were committed, one after another, to Wyatt's care, when he was invested with full power not only to restore but to alter and 'improve' these ancient structures, the result was melancholy indeed. Durham, Winchester, Salisbury, and too many other cathedrals bore for a long while, and in some cases still bear, painful evidence of his presumption or ignorance. And even in cases where a later and more educated taste has removed his ill-devised additions, and replaced features which he was permitted to destroy, one cannot help feeling that such repairs, however well-intentioned and skilfully executed, can never make the building what it was, or satisfactorily realise the spirit of its original design.

The Revival of the Pointed style, for ecclesiastical and other build-ings in this country, has led in our own day to a question on which the mediævalists are divided against themselves. Happily for their cause England is still rich in examples of a school of art which, after three centuries of neglect and contumely, has been hailed as one eminently fitted by grace, convenience, and national characteristics for modern readoption. But though these venerable monuments have survived, as it were, to plead their cause, most of them have suffered terribly from the ravages of time, fanaticism, or wilful negligence. Cathedrals

in which the thurible once swang its incense high up into roof and
vault, churches which needed no further warmth than that which
they received from the flame of votive candles and the constant presence of worshippers who thronged to Mass, have long grown damp
and mouldy from disuse.   Those old baronial halls, which once echoed
with the clank of armour and noise of revelry, are silent and deserted
now ; those ample fireplaces, once piled high with oak and pinewood,
are cold and empty ; and rain and wind beat in through mullioned
windows, which once cast a gay and chequered light upon the rush-
strewn floor.

Of course, one's first impulse would be, if only for association's sake,
to rescue these fast-decaying relics of a by-gone age—to replace the
rotten timbers with sound wood—to fill in with newly-moulded voussoirs
those cruel gaps in arch and groin—to pull out the aged, crumbling
imposts and corbels and set fresh stone-carving in their places—to
exchange the battered old casements for modern painted glass—to
reconstruct, on what we consider the original model, every part which
we think fit to pull down.   This is what the parson or the country
squire—maybe the architect himself—does, and calls it ' restoration.'
It is generally a well-intentioned work, but unfortunately, in nine
cases out of ten, it defeats its own purpose.   These good people fancy
they are perpetuating the design of their forefathers.   In reality they
are falsifying it.   Let us take a case in point.   The jamb mouldings
of an ancient doorway need repair.   They are chipped and rubbed
away in some places more than in others.   The mason who is employed on the job selects one stone which appears to him less damaged
than the rest, and moulds his new quoins as nearly as he can in imitation of this example.   The probability is that he will not be very
careful ; so, when the jamb is set up, to prevent any trifling inaccura-
cies, the old work is ' tooled ' over, and the whole is rubbed down
together.   When the ' restoration ' is complete, will any one undertake
to say how much of this doorway is new and how much old, or how far

it may be reckoned upon as a transcript of that which once stood in its place, when we remember that the depth of a quarter of an inch may make all the difference in the contour of a moulding? But this is not the worst to be apprehended. If the reproduction of the mouldings be attended with difficulty, what can we say of wood and stone carving in its wider sense? Every one who has studied the principles of Mediæval art knows how much its character and vitality depend upon the essential element of decorative sculpture—on the spirit of what Mr. Ruskin has called 'noble grotesque,' in its nervous types of animal life and vigorous conventionalism of vegetable form. The capitals, the corbels, the bosses, the enriched spandrils of Pointed Architecture, are the jewels—and more than the jewels, the very blossom and fruit—of that prolific style. To copy these line for line, even when sound and fresh from the chisel, and yet preserve the spirit of the original, would have been a difficulty in the best ages of art. The Mediæval sculptors never—to use an artistic phrase—repeated themselves. If the conditions of their work required a certain degree of uniformity in design, they took care to aim at the spirit, but not the letter, of symmetry. Part might balance part in a general way, but not with that slavish precision which could be tested with the rule and compass. Indeed, common sense points to the fact that no noble work can be thus transcribed without losing in effect. But modern carvers employed in 'restoration' are not unfrequently men who can only be trusted to copy in the most literal sense of the word. The fragments which serve them for a model are frequently mutilated, and afford to any but the most experienced eye a very incorrect notion of their original form. The consequence is that a copy is too frequently produced not only deficient in spirit, but with the same degree of accuracy which might be expected from a Chinese engraver who should undertake to imitate line for line and spot for spot a damaged print. Of course in large works, and where the supervision of an efficient architect is secured, these mistakes are avoided; but there remains the broad fact that many of our 'decorative' sculptors, modern carvers with quite as much mechanical skill and twice as good working tools as their Gothic ancestors, can do little more than tamely copy the inventions of others. Under these circumstances, we cannot hope that their work will be worthy to stand in place of that executed by men whose hands realised the inventions of their own fertile fancy—who took the birds of the air and the flowers of the field for their models, but who seemed to know instinctively the true secret of all decorative art, which lies in the suggestion and symbolism rather than the presumptuous illustration of natural form.

Does it follow from this that we are to suffer our cathedrals, our Tudor mansions, and other monuments of antiquity to perish for want of timely succour ? By no means. There is much useful work which can be done, and done honestly, towards preserving such buildings from decay. Any mason can square a stone and put it in its proper place, or secure the safety of a tottering wall. There is work for the carpenter, the plumber, the slater, and others whose handicraft is of a purely mechanical kind. But the *thought* of the old artist sculptor— his wit, his satire, his love of leaves and flowers, his gay or grim notions of life and death—these we must see fade away before our eyes and let them pass. We cannot reanimate the mouldering freestone, or realise with a sober modern chisel the wayward fancies of the Middle Ages. Before, therefore, we ' restore,' let us endeavour to preserve what still remains to us of our old national architecture—let us watch its very fragments with a jealous eye, propping them up when needed, shielding them so far as we can from the effects of weather and wanton destruction. If any portions are already past this care, and in absolute danger of falling, it is better to pull them down at once than falsify them with new work. A porch, a tower, or a window may frequently be rebuilt entirely with advantage ; but then it should be ostensibly the work of the nineteenth century, and not be so incorporated with the rest as to deceive the student of the next generation. A brass plate or a stone tablet let into the wall might record in legible characters the date and

circumstances of the re-erection. There can be no objection to perpetuating the style of the original buildings, but it is of far more
importance to adopt the spirit than to follow the letter of the design.

Thus, it may be presumed, would reason many of the rising school of
architects in our own time ; but in Wyatt's day, while the grammar of
Mediæval art had still to be re-acquired—while the sentiment which had
begun to recommend it to popular favour remained, as yet, but a weak
and misdirected sentiment, it was in vain to expect that restorations would
be conducted on any other principle than that which suggests a literal
reproduction of old work. In so far as Wyatt confined himself to this
principle, he was successful ; but when he presumed—and he frequently
presumed—to alter and, as he thought, to *improve* upon the architecture
of the Middle Ages, the result was a lamentable failure.

The most notable instance of his ability in the field of restoration
is certainly that of Henry VII.'s Chapel at Westminster. During the
last century the exterior of the building had been rapidly decaying,
and, in a period of about twenty years, a sum exceeding 28,000*l.* had
been spent on repairs. In the year 1803 a fire broke out in the roof
which involved an expense of several thousand pounds, and the Dean
(Dr. Vincent) and Chapter, feeling that the ' Fabric Fund ' which had
been set apart for repairs was no longer sufficient to meet the annual
outlay required, determined to apply to the Government for assistance.
Accordingly a memorial was drawn up and presented to the Treasury in
1806. That department referred the subject to a Committee of Taste,
who were good enough to promise their opinion on any plans for the
restoration which might be submitted to them, but did nothing further.

In the following year the Dean and Chapter, nothing daunted,
prepared another petition, this time to the House of Commons, stating
that ' the petitioners had long seen with extreme regret the decay and
ruinous appearance of King Henry VII.'s Chapel, the most beautiful
specimen of Gothic architecture in the kingdom, and perhaps in Europe.'
They added that it appeared from the survey of their architect (Mr.

Wyatt) that the decay had hitherto only affected the exterior of the building; that the interior was still in a fairly sound state; and that, if the exterior were repaired before the weather was suffered to make further ravages, the whole structure might be preserved. The petitioners concluded by asking for an annual grant of 1,000*l.* and an additional sum of 1,000*l.* 'extraordinary' for the first year. The House appointed a Committee, who, as a first step, examined Wyatt as to the probable cost of the restoration. He stated that it would be difficult to estimate it exactly, but he conceived that about 14,800*l.* would be required for 'necessary repairs,' and probably 10,400*l.* for ornamental work. He added that the works might be completed in three years. As is often the case in such undertakings, it turned out in due course that both the time and the amount of money required had been considerably underrated. The House of Commons voted 2,000*l.* as the first instalment towards the work, and at Dr. Vincent's request the general arrangements for the scheme were left in the hands of a body of gentlemen, then known as the 'Committee for the Inspection of Models for National Monuments.' This Committee included among its members the Marquis of Stafford, the Marquis of Buckingham, Lord Aberdeen, Sir George Beaumont, Mr. Thomas Hope, Mr. R. Payne Knight, and other distinguished amateurs. But the Government showed its good sense by adding several artists to the Committee. Among these were Flaxman, Banks and Westmacott, three of the most eminent sculptors of the day. Sir Charles Long acted as chairman.

Every care was taken to ensure the use of a good quality of stone for the restoration. Gayfere, the abbey mason, who appears to have played a far more prominent part in the work than would be allotted to any similar official in our own time, was examined and directed to report on this subject. He visited Bath and St. Albans Abbey, and at length decided in favour of Kentish stone and that of Coomb Down quarries. An incident occurred during Gayfere's examination which shows the tendency, even in those days, to cheapen the cost of artistic work at a sacrifice of its quality. Bernasconi's composition (a species of terra cotta) had then come into use, and Gayfere was asked what he thought of the durability of this material, if it were employed instead of stone for the external carvings. The document from which these particulars are gleaned records no answer to this enquiry. Whether it was actually answered does not now signify. But, as a matter of fact, Bernasconi's composition was *not* used, and we may be thankful for the decision.

Just as the works were to have been begun they were delayed by an untoward accident. A vessel bringing 150 tons of stone from Bristol was wrecked off the Isle of Portland. In 1809 the restoration was fairly begun, and though some slight misunderstandings appear to have at first arisen between the Dean and Chapter and the Parliamentary Committee, it was carried on gradually and successfully for many years, grants being made by Government even during the war with France, until it was finally completed (long after Wyatt's death) in 1821.

Restorations such as this, conducted with a careful reverence for ancient work and an accurate reproduction of its detail, would have won for Wyatt the respect of his antiquarian contemporaries, and saved him from the censure of later critics. But unfortunately he had had in the early days of his practice many cathedrals and other Mediæval buildings of importance committed to his care by those who placed the fullest confidence in his ability, and who had themselves but a scanty acquaintance with even the elementary principles of Gothic art. It is not exactly on record that the ecclesiastical authorities of the day declared him to be a greater architect than Bertram of Salisbury or Waynflete of Winchester, but it is not improbable that they believed it. How far Wyatt may have been morally responsible for the deeds of vandalism which were too frequently carried on in his name; whether his vanity or his ignorance led him to remodel architectural work of the Middle Ages, the excellence of which he could never hope to imitate, may be doubtful; but the plain fact remains, that on such occasions he far exceeded his professional duty, and that having been called on to repair, he did not hesitate to alter and even to destroy.

It was to be hoped that, at least, one stronghold of Mediæval art would have been proof against Wyatt's innovations. Oxford, as we have seen, had preserved, down to a late period, the traditions of a national style. In our own time it has distinguished itself by a strenuous and successful attempt to revive them. But a dark interval occurred between the two epochs, and though, during that interval, the University acquired many buildings which were creditable specimens of Italian architecture, the character of local Gothic sank to zero. So long as Hawksmoor's work at All Souls' College remains standing, it will probably retain the reputation of being the most debased travesty of Pointed Architecture in Oxford. Wyatt's designs did not exactly descend to this level, but they approached it. No one who has any reverence for Mediæval art can examine the, present condition of New College Chapel without a feeling of surprise that even in Wyatt's day such work as his plaster reredos, mean as it is in material, and vulgar in the extravagance of its detail, could have passed for *restoration*. Yet it is not improbable that, at the time when it was executed, the College dons considered it a finer specimen of art than that which had been doomed to destruction by Bishop Horne. Westmacott's sculptured panels, in mezzo-relievo, are at least of real marble, and exhibit some inventive skill; but the dramatic action of his figures is completely out of character with the architecture of the building which they were intended to decorate. Fragments of the old sculpture, removed to make place for this work, may still be seen in the adjoining cloister. Impartial critics, who compaie the Mediæval carving with its modern substitute, will, probably, consider the neat finish and anatomical correctness of Westmacott's groups a poor exchange for the earnest and vigorous, though somewhat rude, treatment of the old design.

If Wyatt's innovations had been confined to decorative detail, more excuse might be made for him at the present day. A style of art which has fallen into neglect for two or three centuries is not likely to be revived with much of its original spirit in the course of a few years. The natural tendency of modern uneducated taste is to set an undue value upon mere elaboration of ornament and on the literal imitation of natural forms. It is liable to mistake the noble abstractive treatment so well understood in past ages of art for ignorance or incapacity of hand. We may charitably suppose that Wyatt thought the fruit and foliage of his plaster reredos a real improvement on the crockets and finials of a Mediæval sculptor. But that an architect who was entrusted to restore buildings erected in the Middle Ages should have presumed to sacrifice important and constructive features in more than one cathedral for the sake of satisfying his own notions of proportion and effect, is an example of intolerable vanity and ignorance. He who had studied in Rome the principles of classic architecture would, probably, have been the first to resent an impertinent remodelling of the Pantheon. One might reasonably suppose that if he possessed half the respect for Gothic art with which he was accredited by his contemporaries, he would have seen the same necessity for preserving the integrity of its remains. Unfortunately Lichfield, Durham, and Salisbury bear evidence to the contrary.

It is possible that much of the vandalism committed at this time, under the plea of restoration, has been since unjustly attributed to Wyatt. But that he was in several well-known instances directly responsible for needless destruction and injudicious repairs is quite certain. How long such work would have been permitted to go on by those whose duty it was to watch with jealous care the venerable buildings entrusted to their charge, may be doubted. Luckily, remonstrance was at hand from an unexpected quarter. It was administered sharply, authoritatively, and persistently, and, in course of time, with excellent effect.

Mention has already been made of John Carter's 'Specimens of Ancient Sculpture and Painting,' published in 1786. But this and other works of the same class, and by the same hand, creditable as they are to their author, will reflect less permanent honour on his memory than the fact that, for a period of nearly twenty years, he employed his pen in a vigorous protest against the ruthless and ignorant 'innovations' of his day.

The history of this doughty champion of Gothic architecture may be sketched in a few lines. He was born in the middle of the last century. His father, who had carried on business which may be euphemistically described as that of a monumental sculptor, but which really included the manufacture of mantel-pieces, died in 1763, leaving his son at the early age of fifteen almost entirely dependent on his own exertions for a livelihood. The lad had been taken from school to assist his father in the preparation of the working drawings necessary to guide the workmen who executed his designs. This occupation taught him to use his pencil, which he soon employed to better purpose. In 1764 young Carter made a perspective view of the Herald's Tower, Windsor Castle—the first of a long series of similar productions, which at first brought him bread, and afterwards renown. Builders of the day, who seem to have frequently acted without the supervision of architects, gladly secured his artistic services. In 1786 he was engaged to prepare illustrations for the 'Builder's Magazine,' probably the first professional journal brought out in this country.

But a more important engagement dates from a few years previously, when the Society of Antiquaries, recognising his delineative skill and knowledge of architecture, employed him to etch many of the views of ancient buildings, published under their direction. The cathedrals of Exeter, Durham, Gloucester, and York; the abbeys of Bath and St. Albans, with a host of others, became, in turn, subjects for his pencil. Every ancient building which he visited was useful to him in a twofold sense. He made drawings and he made notes. The drawings were a source of immediate profit. By means of the notes he, by degrees, laid up a store of archæological information which, in course of time, placed him among the foremost antiquaries of the day. As an architect he seems to have had little or no practice. A small chapel at Sevenoaks, a few almshouses, and a monument or two, are the only works on record for which he was directly responsible; but it is well known that he was frequently consulted by other members of the profession, who were in the habit of submitting their designs to him for approval or correction. The study of Mediæval architecture had been almost an instinct with him from his earliest youth. His delight was to sketch, to measure, and to describe every ancient English building which he saw, and in such pursuits he passed the greater part of a long life. One other taste, indeed, he had, which occasionally beguiled him from his antiquarian researches. It was for that art which is allied to architecture by some mysterious link long imaged by poetical conception and not unfrequently confessed in the experience of ordinary life. He was passionately fond of music.*

It may easily be conceived that a man of Carter's accurate knowledge and ardent temperament saw with a feeling stronger than impatience our national relics of Mediæval architecture one by one perishing through neglect, injured by clumsy restoration, and in some cases being partially destroyed by ignorant attempts to improve upon their original design. In such instances, if we may believe his contemporary critics, he felt all the indignation which might be justified by a personal affront. If his private character had been attacked he could scarcely have been more inclined to resent the injury. The manner in which he did resent it was characteristic not only of the man but of the age in which he lived. Towards the middle of the year 1798 a letter was published in the 'Gentleman's Magazine,' calling attention to certain injudicious repairs and alterations which had been carried on in Peterborough Cathedral. The writer signed himself 'An Architect,' and if no further correspon-

---

* Carter's enthusiasm for music led him, as an amateur, not only to perform but to compose. He was the author of two operas, produced at one of the minor theatres, but long since forgotten—'The White Rose,' and 'The Cell of St. Oswald'—which were intended to illustrate dramatically English life in the Middle Ages. In each case the words, as well as the music, were his own. He also painted the scenery.

dence had ensued, it is possible that he would have preserved his *incognito*. But this letter was only the first of a long series which continued to appear, at intervals, in the same journal and under the same signature, for the extraordinarily long period of twenty years. In the year 1817 this remarkable correspondence was brought somewhat abruptly to a close, not, however, before the writer had begun to depart from his original theme, viz. the 'Pursuits of Architectural Innovation.' The 212th letter promised that the subject should be continued, but the Fates had ordered otherwise. The writer had laid down his pen for the last time.

The fact that Carter died in 1817 is scarcely required to prove the authenticity of these letters. During the time which elapsed since the first appeared, considerable advance was made in the study of Gothic architecture. As years rolled on, other men might have been found equal to the task of criticising modern 'improvements' as shrewdly, as learnedly, and as carefully as Carter. But it may safely be asserted that no one else would have sustained the task with such prolonged energy and perseverance.

It is true that the very nature of his ordinary occupation afforded peculiar facilities for this additional work. Every sketch which he made was, to his appreciative eye, a fresh lesson in architectural style. Every tour which he made gave him an opportunity, not only for artistic study, but for critical inspection. At Gloucester he laments the injury caused by turning it into a place for periodical music meetings, and notices the absence of heraldic propriety in the restoration of sculptured details. At Canterbury he calls attention to the modern disfigurement of Archbishop Wareham's monument and to the shameful condition of St. Augustine's Monastery.* At Lichfield the transept windows and the choir arches were walled up. At Salisbury the Beau-

---

* Now rescued from desecration, restored, and converted into St. Augustine's (Missionary) College, by the timely munificence of Mr. Beresford Hope, M.P., and the professional skill of Mr. W. Butterfield. This building will form the subject of some later remarks.

champ Chapel was destroyed. He found Winchester neglected and Howden Church half in ruins. He visited the Welsh castles, and was ashamed of their dilapidations and still more deplorable repairs. The condition of the ancient churches of Coventry excited his pity and his anger. He went to Oxford, and finding himself excluded from Divine service at Magdalen College Chapel, was indignant not only with the architectural innovations, but with the ecclesiastical polity of the Establishment. At Westminster he groaned over alterations which had been made, and deprecated others which were threatened in the Abbey. He waxed wroth at discovering that while the New Courts of Justice were accepted as examples of good modern Gothic, the beautiful Chapel of St. Stephen was condemned to desecration as a dining room.

These and a hundred other similar grievances formed the subject-matter for the letters of ' An Architect.' They declared war *à outrance* to modern innovation, by whatever hand or under whatever direction it was carried on. Sometimes this interference was resented by replies also published in the Magazine, and then a sharp controversy ensued, in which Carter generally came off victorious.* The style of his letters must not be judged by the literary standard of our own day. To the modern reader they will seem stilted and extravagant in language. But his remarks were always to the point, and when they were answered by an opponent, Carter returned again and again to the charge, bringing fresh arguments and new evidence in support of his original assertions.

The information which he supplied and the criticism which he offered must have been invaluable at the time. Thousands of readers who had previously regarded Gothic as a barbarous kind of architecture to which no recognised canon of taste would apply, learnt for the first

---

* Occasionally the correspondence took a serious turn. At the conclusion of one of his letters (January 1810), Carter, referring to the communications of ' An Amateur,' who had contradicted him flatly on a point of fact, replied as follows: ' The " Amateur " may be assured that I am ready to meet him on any ground, let his onset be what it may, question or answer, or *otherwise*!' It does not, however, appear that any hostile encounter was the result of this challenge.

time their mistake. Many a country parson who had allowed his parish church to fall into decay, must have been reminded that it was his duty to take an interest in its repair. Many a Dean and Chapter who had indulged in grand notions about cathedral 'improvements,' paused before they lent themselves to a work of destruction which was now so reasonably condemned. The sentiments of 'An Architect' found grateful response, not only in the pages of the 'Gentleman's Magazine,' but in other journals. Wyatt, for whose professional ability Carter appears to have entertained no small contempt, died in 1813, and thenceforth a new era began to dawn for the Gothic Revival.

Of course it was long before restorations were conducted with that careful attention to detail which can alone justify such repairs. The character of ancient mouldings and of sculpture ornament had still to be analysed and studied before the nineteenth-century architect could hope to approach the grace and refinement of the original forms which he professed to imitate. But the presumptuous folly of attempting to alter and improve upon work elevated by its excellence far beyond the aim of modern design and workmanship was now openly confessed and by degrees abandoned.

The generation of British architects whose professional career extended from the past to the present century includes many names which have long been forgotten, and many others which will soon follow them into oblivion, but which were in their time more or less associated with the Revival of Gothic.

In this list William Atkinson occupies an early and not undistinguished place. Born at Bishop Auckland about 1773, he began life as a carpenter, but through the patronage of Dr. Barrington, then Bishop of Durham, he became a pupil of James Wyatt, and in 1797 obtained the gold medal of the Royal Academy. In the course of his practice he designed Scone Palace, Perthshire, for the Earl of Mansfield (1803–6); Rossie Priory for Lord Kinnaird (1810–15); Abbotsford, Roxburghshire, for Sir Walter Scott, and many other country mansions in England and Scotland.*

Between the years 1814 and 1822 Mr. L. N. Cottingham did some service to the Revival by publishing several works in illustration of old English architecture. His plans, &c. of Westminster Hall appeared in 1822. Shortly afterwards he brought out a more voluminous work on Henry VII.'s Chapel. His working drawings of Gothic ornaments are ill-selected and coarse in execution, but curious as being perhaps the first full-size illustrations of Mediæval carving published in this form. He built Snelston Hall in Derbyshire, and in 1825 designed a new central tower for Rochester Cathedral, besides restoring other portions of the same building. In 1829 he was the successful competitor for the restorations (completed in 1833) of the interior of Magdalen College, Oxford. Under his superintendence repairs were also carried on at Hereford Cathedral, St. Albans Abbey, and the Church of St. James at Louth.

It is, however, as a collector of Mediæval antiquities rather than as an architect that his name has been chiefly associated with the Revival. In addition to a vast number of casts taken from capitals, bosses, and other examples of decorative sculpture in English and foreign cathedrals, he had acquired many specimens of original carved work in wood and stone—in some cases entire features of buildings which had been dismantled or pulled down. These, in addition to a host of other objects, including ancient furniture and metal-work, formed a most

---

* It is necessary to distinguish this architect from others of the same surname, and all born in the last century, viz.: Peter Atkinson (the son of a carpenter), who practised at York; Peter Atkinson, the son and partner of the last-mentioned, who was employed by the Duke of Devonshire, and who erected many churches for the Ecclesiastical Commissioners between 1821 and 1831; Thomas Atkinson, who made additions to the Archiepiscopal Palace, Bishopsthorpe, near York, in 1769; and T. W. Atkinson, a London architect, who published 'Gothic Ornaments Selected from the different Cathedrals and Churches of England,' in 1829.

valuable and interesting Mediæval museum long before public energy or national funds had been devoted to a similar purpose.*

Among Carter's friends and contemporaries was Mr. John Buckler, F.S.A., who published some fine 'Views of the Cathedral Churches of England and Wales, with Descriptions.' His son, Mr. John Chessell Buckler, designed in 1825 the modern portion of Costessey Hall, Norfolk, for Lord Stafford—one of the most important and successful instances of the Revival in Domestic Architecture. It is built of red and white brick, with stone dressings, and the style is Tudor, of the type adopted in Thornbury Castle.†

The general appearance of the building is that of an irregular but well grouped and interesting composition, in which stepped gables, angle turrets, and richly moulded chimney-shafts form picturesque features, and exhibit a knowledge of detail and proportion far in advance of contemporary work. In the centre of the block rises a solid square tower, crowned with machicolations and an embattled parapet.

Internally the rooms are fitted up with great care, the carved ceilings, stone mantel-pieces, and carved panel-work being all of rich design, and in character with the external architecture; which is more than can be said for many of the so-called Gothic mansions of the day.

The old mansion, erected in the reign of Queen Mary, still occupies the site of the intended hall and principal staircase. The chapel erected early in the present century has been already mentioned.

Mr. J. C. Buckler was largely employed at Oxford in the restorations of and additions to the various buildings of the University. St. Mary's Church, as well as Oriel, Brasenose, Magdalen, and Jesus Colleges, bear evidence of his professional handiwork. He also restored Oxburgh Hall, Norfolk, and Hengrave Hall, Suffolk. Among the

---

* Mr. Cottingham's collection was sold by public auction a few years after his death, which occurred in 1847.

† Erected in Henry VIII.'s reign by Edward Stafford, Duke of Buckingham, an ancestor of the present Baron.

country mansions which he was entrusted to design may be mentioned Dunston Hall, Norfolk, and Butleigh Court, in Somersetshire. In 1823 Buckler published a description of Magdalen College, adding to it an account of the 'innovations' then recently executed there, and a protest against others which were threatened. This little work, which for personal reasons existing at the time was published anonymously, did good service at Oxford. It argued well and earnestly for the preservation of the old colleges, which had been sadly maltreated under the guise of 'improvement.' Antiquaries, in short, no longer stood alone as champions of the Revival. The cause was espoused by many professional architects of ability and repute. This would not in itself have sufficed to secure the support of public taste. But public taste received a stimulus of its own, as we shall presently see.

CHAPTER VII.

ANIFOLD as the influences are to which the modern revival of Gothic Architecture have been referred, they may, if taken broadly, be classed under three heads, viz. literary, religious, and antiquarian. To the first may be assigned the taste for mediæ- valism, which was encouraged in this country by the writings of Sir Walter Scott, Bishop Percy, and Dr. Lingard ; in France by those of Chateaubriand ; and in Germany by those of Friedrich von Schlegel. It is impossible to read either the poems or the novels of Scott without perceiving how greatly their interest depends on that class of sentiment, half chivalrous and half romantic, which is centered in the social life and history, the faith, the arts, and the warfare of the Middle Ages. ' Ivanhoe,' ' The Abbot,' ' Woodstock,' ' The Fair Maid of Perth,' and ' The Monastery,' abound in allusions to the Architecture, either military or ecclesiastical, of a bygone age. It forms the background to some of the most stirring scenes which the author depicts. It invests with a substantial reality the romances which he weaves. It is often inti- mately associated with the very incidents of his plot.

We need not necessarily infer that Scott possessed anything more than a superficial knowledge of the art which he so enthusiastically ad- mired. On the contrary, the descriptions which he gives of Mediæval buildings not unfrequently betray an ignorance of what have since been called the true principles of Gothic design. The poetic but erroneous notion that the groined vault of a cathedral church had its prototype in the spreading branches of a tree—the comparison of clustered shafts to bundles of lances bound with garlands—may raise a smile from those who have studied with any attention the real and structural beauties of old

English Architecture. The truth is that the service which Scott rendered to the cause of the Revival was to awaken popular interest in a style which had hitherto been associated, except by the educated few, with ascetic gloom and vulgar superstition. With the aid of his magic pen, the Castle of Coningsburgh is filled as of yore with doughty warriors; Branksome Hall is restored to its feudal splendour; Kenilworth becomes once more the scene of human love, and strife, and tragedy; the aisles of Melrose echo again with a solemn requiem.

The Waverley novels and the poems which preceded them were read with an eager interest which we can only realize in this *blasé* generation when we remember the class of fiction, in prose or verse, with which our grandsires had been previously supplied. With the exception of Horace Walpole and Mrs. Radcliffe, no author of any note had sought for inspiration in the old-world lore; and though the ' Castle of Otranto ' and the ' Romance of the Forest' have had, no doubt, their admirers, the Mediæval element which they contain bears no nearer relation to ' Ivanhoe' and ' The Monastery ' than the Gothic of Batty Langley does to the designs of Butterfield.

The works of Fielding and Smollett—and, if we may compare small things with great, of Richardson—derived their chief interest from the delineation of character in scenes of contemporary life. Mr. Thomas Jones and Mr. Roderick Random are essentially *modern* heroes. Their respective adventures point a doubtful moral to a disreputable tale, not without redeeming points of sparkling wit, trenchant satire, and genuine philosophy. But we may search them, and many similar novels of the same age and class, in vain to find the least evidence of that order of sentiment which depends on national tradition or reverence for the past. Sir Walter Scott was the first *historical* novelist that England produced. Whether he gave a reliable picture of social life in the Middle Ages may be doubted. It is the province of such a writer to deal with his material after the manner of all artists. He must keep virtues for his hero and faults for those who cross his hero's path. He must fill in the lights and shades of his story as best befits its climax. He must keep probability subservient to effect. All this Sir Walter did to perfection, and he did more. He drew public attention to the romantic side of archæology. It had hitherto been regarded as a formal science. He charmed it into an attractive art. And this he accomplished without any parade of the special knowledge which he had acquired in the study of old English life and its picturesque accessories. We find in his romances none of that laboured accuracy in regard to detail which has characterised the writings of those who have endeavoured in a similar field to unite the taste of the *dilettante* with the imagination of the novelist. In reading such a work as the 'Last Days of Pompeii,' one is struck with the palpable effort which its author makes to describe and turn to dramatic account the latest facts and discoveries concerning the disinterred city. Scarcely an incident is recorded, scarcely a scene is described, which does not reveal the narrator's aim at correctness in his studies of what a painter would call ' still life.' It is as if he had invoked the shade of Sir William Hamilton instead of the Muse of Fiction to aid him in his task, and had composed his story after spending a week in the Museo Bourbonico.

With far more subtle skill and magic power, Scott entered on his work. The pictures which he sets before us of life in the Middle Ages are not encumbered with needless minutiæ of material fact. The aspect of the dwellings, the costume, the household gods of our ancestors, is not indeed forgotten, but they are not allowed to obtrude on the reader's attention, and they are always kept subordinate to the interest which is elicited by character and conversation. It is somewhat remarkable that the 'Antiquary,' a novel in which Scott might have found it easy to display his acquaintance with the relics of ancient art, should contain so little evidence of the author's taste in that direction. Mr. Oldbuck, who is familiar with the rare quarto of the Augsburg Confession, who is an authority in heraldic matters, whose wrath is kindled by the spurious poems of Ossian, and who quotes everything he has read from Virgil to a Border ballad, would have cut a poor figure in the Camden Society. He collects indeed Roman lamps, and Scottish thumbscrews, but for aught we can gather from his discourse, he knows no more of Jedburgh Abbey than of the Palace of the Cæsars.

The Mediæval sympathies which Scott aroused were enlisted less by reference to the relics of Pointed architecture than by the halo of romance which he contrived to throw around them. The fortunes of the Disinherited Knight, the ill-requited love of poor Rebecca, the very jokes of Wamba and the ditties of the Bare-footed Friar, did more for the Gothic Revival than all the labours of Carter and Rickman. The description of the desecrated church in the ' Abbot' excites our interest not merely because its niches have been emptied and its altar despoiled, but because it forms a background to the figures of Magdalen and Roland. The castles of the Rhine appear to every modern tourist picturesque monuments of antiquity, but they acquire a double charm in association with the story of 'Anne of Geierstein.'

It would be difficult to overrate the influence which Scott's poetry has had on both sides of the Tweed, in encouraging a national taste for Mediæval architecture. Every line in the ' Lay of the Last Minstrel,' every incident in ' Marmion,' is pregnant with that spirit of romance which is the essence of traditional art. The time may perhaps have now arrived when the popular mind can dispense with the spell of association, and learn to admire Gothic for its intrinsic beauty. But in the early part of this century, England could boast of no such author as Mr. Ruskin, to teach, discriminate, and criticise, in matters of taste. Guided by his advice and influence, we may succeed in kindling the Lamps of Life and Power. But fifty years ago, in the darkest period which British art has seen, we were illumined by one solitary and flickering flame, which Scott contrived to keep alive. It was the Lamp of Memory.

Strange as it may appear to us in these days of advanced ritualism, the earliest instances of the application of Gothic as a definite style at that period were to be found, not in the churches, but in the mansions of modern England.   In our own time, the most bigoted opponents of the style are generally found to admit that if unsuitable for a dwelling, it may with propriety be employed—to use their own language—for a ' place of worship.'   But when Scott was in the zenith of his fame, the reverse of this opinion would appear, at first sight, to have prevailed. While many country houses of the nobility and gentry were designed, or rebuilt, in what was then known as the Castellated style, almost every modern church that was erected aped the general arrangement of a Greek temple, or the pseudo-classic type of the Renaissance.

The explanation of this apparent anomaly becomes obvious when we remember the condition of things under which it occurred.   In the first place, the revived taste for Mediæval Architecture was as yet caviare to the multitude.   It seemed but natural that the landed proprietors—the heads of ancient families, the source of whose lineage was intimately associated with the early welfare of this country—should feel some interest in a style which kept alive the memories of the past, and symbolised at once the romance of history and the pride of name.   But the majority of parsons and churchwardens, the committee-men and vestrymen, of a town parish, could scarcely be expected to participate in these sentiments.   Their notions of grand architecture were linked to the Five Orders, or based on a glimpse of Stuart's Athens; their ideas of devotion were centered in the family pew.   And it was only in town parishes that the church architect then found exercise for his ability.   The expediency of providing additional churches for the increasing population of rural districts was a problem which had not as yet presented itself to the parochial mind.   And it must be confessed that if it had, the necessity of acting on it would have been doubtful.   A large parish does not always, and certainly did not in those days, mean a large congregation.   In plain language, it would have been absurd to build new churches while the old ones remained half filled.   How far the clergy, and how far the people themselves, were responsible for this state of things, it is difficult to estimate. But of one fact we may be quite sure, that at this period the Church of England had lost its hold on popular favour, and ecclesiastical sentiment was almost unknown. No doubt much of the apathy which then prevailed was due to the uninteresting character of the service and all that pertained to it. To the zealous artist or devotee of the present day, the interior of a church fitted up at that period would have presented indeed a melancholy spectacle. We must tax the recollections of our childhood, if we would realise to some extent the cold and vapid nature of the ceremonies which passed for public devotion in the days of our grandfathers.

Who does not remember the air of grim respectability which pervaded, and in some cases still pervades, the modern town church of a certain type, with its big bleak portico, its portentous beadle, and muffin-capped charity boys? Enter and notice the tall neatly grained witness-boxes and jury-boxes in which the faithful are impanelled; the 'three-decker' pulpit placed in the centre of the building; the lumbering gallery which is carried round three sides of the interior on iron columns; the wizen-faced pew-opener eager for stray shillings; the earnest penitent who is inspecting the inside of his hat; the patent warming apparatus; the velvet cushions which profane the altar; the hassocks which no one kneels on; the poor-box which is always empty. Hear how the clerk drones out the responses for a congregation too genteel to respond for themselves. Listen to the complicated discord in which the words of the Psalmist strike the ear, after copious revision by Tate and Brady. Mark the prompt, if misdirected zeal, with which old ladies insist on testing the accuracy of the preacher's memory by turning out the text. Observe the length, the unimpeachable propriety, the overwhelming dulness of his sermon!

Such was the Church, and such the form of worship which prevailed in England while this century was still in its teens. It may have been, and probably was, well suited to the religious feeling of the day.

The reaction which has since ensued may have its errors and its dangers. But one fact is certain, that that art, with the history of which we have alone to deal in these pages, had sunk at this period to its lowest level, and required the services of more than one doughty champion to rescue it from oblivion.

It is a common error to suppose that the Church of Rome has encouraged to any great extent, or for any special purpose, the Revival of Gothic Architecture. Those who have witnessed the gorgeous ceremonial with which her rites are celebrated in Italy, will be aware how utterly independent they have become of any association with Mediæval usage, so far as outward appearance and ecclesiastical appointments are concerned. It is, however, remarkable that two of the first, and in their time unquestionably the most eminent, apologists for the revival of the style in this country were Roman Catholics, viz. Milner and Pugin. Beyond the fact that their creeds and their architectural tastes were in common, no parallel can be drawn between them. Both, indeed, contributed to the literature of art, but under different conditions, at a different time, and in a very different vein. Dr. Milner was a priest and a bishop of his Church. Pugin was a layman and a professed architect. Dr. Milner wrote with the sober judgment of an antiquary; Pugin with the fiery enthusiasm of a religious convert. Finally, Milner, who was born in 1752, preceded Pugin by nearly half a century.

It was in the year 1792 that Dr. Milner resolved to build a new chapel at Winchester, in place of one which, erected in the seventeenth century, had fallen into a ruinous state. Of this work he says (in his 'History of Winchester') :—

Instead of following the modern style of building churches and chapels, which are in general square chambers with small sash windows and fashionable decorations hardly to be distinguished, when the altars and benches are removed, from common assembly rooms, it was concluded upon to imitate the models in this kind which have been left to us by our religious ancestors, who applied themselves to the cultivation and perfection of ecclesiastical architecture.

Although competent to give general instructions for the execution of this work, Dr. Milner had the good sense to seek the professional assistance of Mr. John Carter, of whose talents he always had a very high opinion.

'I know one man, indeed,' he writes in one of his essays, 'who is eminently qualified to direct any work of this nature, and who, without either an original or a copy to look at, could sit down and make pure and perfect drawings for any kind of building in the Pointed Style, from a monument to a cathedral, according to any one of its different periods. But this architect . . . . . is so inflexibly strict in adhering to ancient rules and practice, that he would not build for a prince who should require the slightest deviation from them.'

This was high praise in 1800. In some respects, perhaps, it would be higher praise at the present day.

The chapel is described by Dr. Milner himself as 'a light Gothic building, coated with stucco resembling freestone, with mullioned windows, shelving buttresses, a parapet with open quatrefoils, and crocketed pinnacles terminating in gilt crowns.' This description is not very suggestive of the glories of Gothic art in its modern Revival. But if we remember the benighted period at which it was written, we may be thankful for this link, however humble, in the chain of our history.

Dr. Milner's 'Survey of the Antiquities of Winchester,' a carefully written and, for its time, an erudite work, was chiefly remarkable for the short, but now famous essay which it contained, 'On the Rise and Progress of the Pointed Arch.' This essay, together with three others by Professor Warton, the Rev. J. Bentham, and Capt. Grose, all bearing on the subject of Gothic Architecture, were published by Taylor in 1800, with an introductory letter by Milner. To dilate on the various opinions expressed by these gentlemen would probably be tedious, and would certainly not be edifying to the reader of these pages. Dr. Milner himself seems inclined to lose patience with two of the learned antiquaries, who, differing in their nomenclature, are at variance on the question, whether Salisbury Cathedral is or is not a Gothic structure. In his own Essay and Introduction, which form the most interesting part of the volume, he uses for the first time an expression which has since been universally accepted as a generic term for the Architecture of the Middle Ages, viz. the *Pointed Style.*

The origin of the Pointed Arch has proved a subject of as much fruitless discussion as the authorship of Junius, or the identification of the Man in the Iron Mask. In Britton's Architectural Antiquities alone no fewer than sixty-six different theories appear on the subject. Milner's had at least the merit of simplicity. But the origin of the Pointed Arch, as Mr. Fergusson has justly observed, is after all far less important than the history of its use, and the light which the last-mentioned work has thrown upon that history is worth all the countless conjectures regarding a structural feature whose form was probably defined by expedience rather than by sentimental or æsthetic considerations.

In 1810, Milner was invited by Dr. Rees to furnish an article on Gothic Architecture for his Encyclopædia. The research necessary for this purpose led to the publication of a ' Treatise on the Ecclesiastical Architecture of England during the Middle Ages,' which appeared in the following year—a scholar-like and interesting work, which it is impossible to peruse without feeling how far its author was in advance of his time, not only as an antiquary, but as a man of taste. To him we are indebted for one of the earliest protests against the injudicious restoration, or rather remodelling, of our ancient cathedrals. The works carried out under Wyatt's professional direction at Durham and at Salisbury had given, as we have seen, great dissatisfaction among the antiquaries of the day. Dr. Milner became their spokesman in a pamphlet entitled ' A Dissertation on the Modern Style of altering Ancient Cathedrals, as exemplified in the Cathedral of Salisbury.' His charges against Wyatt were thus summed up: 'the loss of several valuable monuments of antiquity; the violation of the ashes and the memorials of many illustrious personages of former times, and the destruction of the proportions, and of the due relation of the different parts of the Cathedral.'

These were serious charges, and that they were made with some acrimony may be inferred from the fact that the Essay, which was to have been read before the Society of Antiquaries, had to be withdrawn. It was, however, printed in 1798 with the well-known lines from Horace, ' Humano capiti,' &c., significantly prefixed as a motto on the title-page. Whatever opinion we may now form of the justice of Milner's strictures upon Wyatt, it is impossible to help admiring the shrewdness with which they are supported by arguments the very essence of which proves the writer's thorough acquaintance with the leading principles of Mediæval design. Thus, in referring to the so-called ' uniformity,' then wrongly considered to be an essential element of Ecclesiastical Architecture, he says :—

This I have proved to be contrary to the original nature and design of Cathedrals, and likewise to the form in which they are everywhere built. For when the Lady Chapel is let into the Choir of Salisbury Church, does it form one and the same room in conjunction with it ? No more than a small chamber does with an adjoining spacious hall when the door of it is left open. And when the transepts are swept clean of their chapels and monuments, and nothing is seen in them but the naked high whitewashed walls, do they assimilate and become uniform with the lengthened halls which these gentlemen are so fond of? By no means. On the contrary, it is plain that they would destroy them also if it were in their power to do so.

Milner was well pleased to find that Horace Walpole (then Lord Orford) entirely agreed with him on this point, and had so expressed himself in a letter to Gough, which the author took care to print at the end of his Essay.

Midway in point of time between Milner and Pugin, and possessing, though in a minor degree, the talents of both, Thomas Rickman, as an architect and author, plays no unimportant part in the history of the Revival. His churches are perhaps the first of that period in which the details of old work were reproduced with accuracy of form. Up to this time antiquaries had studied the principles of Mediæval architecture, and to some extent classified the phases through which it had passed, while architects had indirectly profited by their labours when endeavouring to imitate in practice the works of the Middle Ages. Rickman united both functions in one man. He had examined the best examples of Gothic with the advantage of technical information. He did his best to design it after the advantage of personal study. In the science of his art he will not, of course, bear comparison with Willis. In the analysis of its general principles he must yield to Whewell. In capability of invention he ranks, even for his time, far below Pugin. But it may be fairly questioned whether; if we consider him in the twofold capacity of a theorist and a practitioner, he did not do greater service to the cause than either his learned contemporaries or his enthusiastic disciple.

It is probable that what may be called the *grammar* of Mediæval architecture interested him more than its constructive problems or its religious associations. With the latter indeed he could have had but little sympathy. As a member of the Society of Friends he must, in the course of his studies, have investigated with mixed feelings the iconography and symbolism of a faith so intimately allied with his beloved Gothic—so distantly removed from the simplicity of his early creed. Whether he laid aside his scruples so far as to bow down (with æsthetic reverence at least) in the House of Rimmon—or whether he sensibly considered that his conscience was not committed by his taste, we need not stop to enquire. Certain it is that Rickman was largely employed by the clergy for ecclesiastical and other works in various parts of England. In Bristol, Birmingham, Leeds, Preston, Liverpool, Carlisle, and Canterbury, to say nothing of smaller towns and villages, he erected churches. In Northumberland he designed a mansion for

Sir E. Blackett; in Staffordshire another for Miss Herickes. Barfield Lodge, near Bristol, Brunstock House, near Carlisle, and two residences (one for Colin Campbell) in the neighbourhood of Liverpool, were either executed or rebuilt under his instructions. To measure such works as these by the standard of modern taste in Gothic would be obviously unfair. To enter on any detailed account of their design, to attempt to fix their precise position as links in the chain of the Gothic Revival, would be tedious. It suffices to know that Rickman worked according to the light which was in him. It was indeed a light of no great brilliancy, but he turned it to good account, and it served in his day as a beacon to many, who without it would have groped in utter darkness.

St. George's Church at Birmingham, built in 1822, may be accepted as a fair specimen of Rickman's ability in design. Its style may be described as late Middle Pointed. It consists of a lofty nave, with clerestory, north and south aisles, a square tower at the west, and flanked by porches, and a sort of parvise at the east, connected with the main body of the church by flying buttresses. The window tracery is remarkably good in motive, but, sad to say, is all executed in cast iron. For this unfortunate solecism various reasons might be assigned, the most probable one being that it was a cheap means of obtaining an effective fenestration. Yet it is remarkable that no other structural meanness is observable in other parts of the building. The walls are of fair thickness, stouter indeed than those in some of Pugin's churches. The tower, especially its upper part, is well designed; and but for the rigidly formal arrangement of its subordinate features, the west end would have been an effective composition. Internally, the nave arches have a bolder span, and the aisle windows are splayed more deeply than was usual in contemporary work. The roofs of both nave and aisles are flat, and divided by ribs into square panels. It was only in later years that the high pitched and open timber roof was recognised as an essential feature both for internal and external effect.

The reredos, though of a design which we should now call common-place, is unobjectionable in proportion, and really refined in detail. The introduction of galleries in the aisles was an inevitable concession to the utilitarian spirit of the age. In dealing with them it is, however, only fair to state that Rickman left them independent of the nave arcade, and not as now intruding on it.*

It would be curious to compare the cost of such a church as this with that of one—one of many hundreds—which has been erected in our own time for a congregation of similar number. If experience has taught the modern architect anything, it ought to have taught him this, that when there is but little money to spare, it should be devoted to stability of construction, to sturdy walls, stout rafters, and efficient workmanship. Judicious proportion and a picturesque distribution of parts will always atone, and more than atone, for the absence of merely decorative features. Fifty years ago this principle was not understood. Walls were reduced to a minimum of thickness, buttresses were pared down to mere pilasters, roof timbers were starved of their just proportions, while the cost saved by this miserable economy was wasted on the loveless carving of empty niches, and redundant pinnacles, with bosses and crockets, multiplied *ad nauseam*.

The study of ancient examples was the best remedy for such an egregious error of judgment—an error which Rickman, by his researches rather than by his executed works, contrived to amend.

In 1819 he published at Liverpool his 'Attempt to Discriminate the Styles of English Architecture'—a little book which undoubtedly did great service both in educating popular taste and in supplying to professional architects, who had by this time begun to try their 'prentice

---

* In the churchyard of St. George, and under the shadow of the building which he designed, Rickman himself lies buried. A canopied monument of a simple Gothic character, raised by some of his friends and admirers, marks the site of his grave, and a modest inscription, briefly referring to his aim in life, informs us that he died in 1841, aged sixty-four.

hands at Gothic, a recognised standard by which they could test to some extent the correctness of their designs. In the compilation of its contents Rickman was probably indebted in some measure to the labours of his predecessors, but he was the first to turn them to practical advantage. Much had already been written on the subject of Gothic. Endless theories had been propounded as to the origin and development of style. It was reserved for Rickman to reduce the result of these researches to a systematic and compendious form, and in place of ponderous volumes and foggy speculation, to provide his readers with a cheap and useful handbook.

It is a remarkable evidence of the inferior place which Mediæval Art still occupied in public estimation, and of the caution necessary in any departure from the much revered canons of classic taste, that Rickman should have prefaced his book with a formal description of the Five Orders. What possible connection they can have had with 'English Architecture from the Conquest to the Reformation' it is difficult to conceive, and one can only suppose that this first portion of the volume was introduced as a peace-offering to the shade of Vitruvius.

The main division of periods adopted, if not originated, by Rickman remains unaltered at the present day. The nomenclature of the various parts of a church has been but little modified. The popular error by which Norman work was still supposed to be the work of Saxon architects he pointed out and refuted. In a clear and methodical manner every feature of a Mediæval building is taken in turn and described under the head of that period with which the author deals in chronological order. The peculiar characteristics of style are thus brought prominently forward and impressed upon the reader's mind. In matters of detail there are, no doubt, many points on which additional light has since been thrown. But a better system of instruction than that which Rickman employed could scarcely have been devised. The engravings which illustrate the text are few and coldly executed, but they serve their purpose. The notes appended to the volume 'On Ancient

Examples of Gothic Architecture in England,' must have been most useful at that time as an itinerary to the Architectural student. The work has since passed through several editions, enlarged and revised.

The fruits of Rickman's labours were gradually manifested in an improvement not only of public taste but also of professional skill. It is probable that many of the then young and rising architects of the day were at least stimulated by his example, even if they did not profit by his research, in the study of Mediæval art. Among these may be mentioned Shaw, Scoles, Salvin, and Poynter, each of whom played a part, more or less conspicuous, in the history of the Revival.

Before the first quarter of the present century expired Mr. John Shaw had made some important additions to Christ's Hospital, which, if they did not exactly revive the ancient glory of 'Grey Friars,' were by no means contemptible specimens of modern Gothic. He was subsequently employed to design the present hall, which is erected partly on the foundations of the ancient refectory and partly on the site of the old city wall. According to the original scheme, it had been proposed to convert the old hall into dormitories, but upon examination it proved to be in such a dilapidated state, that it was condemned to destruction, and indeed a portion of it fell during the progress of the modern building, the foundation-stone of which was laid with much ceremony on April 28, 1825. The interior is of ample dimensions, being 187 feet long by 52 in width and 48 feet high. It has a ceiled roof, of which the main timbers are moulded and decorated with pendants, while the panels are rendered in plaster, coloured in imitation of oak. The hall is lighted on the south side by nine lofty mullioned windows, divided by transoms in the centre. It is remarkable that, although these windows are crowned with four centred arches, the minor lights between the mullions are lancet-pointed. They are filled with stained glass, chiefly heraldic in decoration. The opposite wall is panelled to a height of some twelve feet in deal, grained to look like oak. A wood screen and organ-loft at the east end, and the visitors' gallery at the west, form picturesque features, and give a certain character to the interior, which, though sadly deficient in refinement of detail, is on the whole effective. The hall is vaulted underneath with flat brick arches, which, where necessary—as in the kitchen—are carried on monolith blocks of Dartmoor granite. Neither in the basement nor in any part of the building which is out of public sight were any pains taken to preserve a structural consistency of design. The Gothic of that day was, it must be confessed, little better than a respectable deception. It put a good face on its principal elevations, but left underground offices and back premises to take care of themselves. The superficial qualities of the style were imitated with more or less success, but the practical advantages of its adaptation had still to be learned and appreciated.

The front towards Newgate Street may, in its general proportions, lay claim to architectural effect. Its open cloister, its staircase turrets, its traceried windows, and its battlemented parapet may be described as *well-intentioned* features in the design, which fails, as many a Gothic design of this period failed, not from a positive misuse of detail either constructive or ornamental, but from the coarse and clumsy character of its execution. Thus the subdivision of buttresses into two *equal* parts by a splayed weathering introduced exactly in the centre of their height, the exaggerated projection and deep undercutting of string course mouldings, the employment of large and uniformly sized blocks of stone in the masonry of its walls, are all quite opposed to the spirit of ancient work. Considered separately these mistakes may seem of small importance to the unprofessional critic, who would, perhaps, fail to recognise them as mistakes at all. It is, nevertheless, such points as these which constitute the difference between poor and genuine work. Many an amateur has examined a modern church or group of school buildings, feeling generally dissatisfied with a result which seems—he knows not exactly why—to have missed the spirit of ancient art, while professedly aiming at its conditions. In the majority of such cases it is the details which are at fault, and these are precisely what the uninitiated know nothing about. To this ignorance may be attributed much of the ill-deserved praise and unjust censure which is occasionally bestowed on the designs of modern architects by the public press. The specious attractions of a building remarkable for its size or the profusion of its ornament are loudly recognised, while thoughtful and scholarlike work, if it present itself in a modest form, is passed over as commonplace, or if it be displayed in features which are unfamiliar to a conventional taste, is voted eccentric and even ugly.

In 1826 St. Katharine's Hospital was begun from the designs of Mr. A. Poynter. The original institution was of great antiquity, and had occupied quarters in the East of London, on a site now occupied by St. Katharine's Docks. When those works were undertaken, it became necessary to remove the Hospital elsewhere, and the present group of buildings was erected in Regent's Park. In plan they are symmetrically disposed round three sides of a small quadrangle. The chapel with its large west window flanked by two lofty octagonal turrets occupies a central position, and is connected with the domestic buildings right and left of it by open screens with Tudor arches. Internally the chapel has a flat ceiled roof of oak and its walls are panelled to a height of some ten feet with the same material. According to the fashion of the day, part of the west end of the chapel is screened off to form an entrance porch. The domestic buildings have ordinary low-pitched roofs, mullioned windows and obtuse gabled dormers. The walls are of white brick with stone dressings, the chapel being faced entirely with stone. As a design this work must be judged by the standard of its day, when rigid formality of composition was an inevitable condition of all plans, from a cottage to a palace, and when architects made a little Gothic go very far. The details of St. Katharine's Hospital were very fair for their time, and the carving, especially in some of the decorative panels, exhibits no small advance in design and workmanship.

Mr. A. Salvin, another architect whose career was destined to be one of great success, and who, throughout his life, took a conspicuous part in the Revival, came into public notice about this time. He built Moreby Hall, in Yorkshire, for Mr. Henry Preston—a house presenting no remarkable characteristics beyond the evidence which it affords of a gradual return to the manorial Gothic of old English mansions. The windows are square-headed, and are provided with double transoms as well as mullions of stone. The roofs are raised—not, indeed, to the high pitch which should properly belong to the style—but at an angle of about 45°. Chimney shafts, instead of being kept out of sight or arranged in symmetrical stacks at each end of the building, are allowed to rise where they are most needed, and being designed in accordance with the rest of the work, become picturesque features in the composition. Servants' offices, instead of being crowded at the back of the house (an almost inevitable condition in the Palladian villa), are planned so as to extend to the right or left in buildings of lesser height, and thus give scale to the principal front.

The facility with which this kind of domestic Gothic could be adapted to the requirements of any sort of plan, or any size of house which the owner might require, was probably a strong plea in its favour. Even those country squires and landed gentlemen who had affected a taste for classic architecture, began to ask themselves whether the dignity of a Greek portico or an Italian façade was worth the inconvenience which such features were sure to entail on the house at their rear ; whether there was not some greater advantage to be derived from the employment of a style which was not only thoroughly English in character but also permitted every possible caprice regarding the distribution of rooms to be freely indulged without detriment to the design.

Salvin soon found ample employment for his talents, and it is but fair to add that every work executed under his superintendence shows a steady advance in his knowledge of the style which he had made his special study. Mamhead, the seat of Robert Newman, near Exeter, was begun in 1828, and occupied some years in erection. The size and importance of this mansion, no less than the skill with which, for that day, it was designed, make it an interesting specimen of revived domestic Gothic. Scotney Castle, in Sussex, was erected some years later, for Mr. Edward Hussey, a gentleman of great taste as an amateur. The building derives its name from an exquisite relic of Mediæval fortified architecture still standing in the grounds. The modern mansion, for obvious reasons, did not aim at the reproduction of a fourteenth-century stronghold, but it realises many of the picturesque features of a Tudor manor-house. The internal fittings are remarkably good, and reflect great credit on the skill and ingenuity of the designer.

Scoles was a pupil of Ireland, who, as a Roman Catholic architect, was patronised by Dr. Milner—at that time vicar-apostolic of the Midland District. Ireland built several Roman Catholic Churches, one of the earliest of which was that at Hinckley, in Nottinghamshire. It is probable that for the details of these designs he was indebted to Carter's supervision. Scoles himself designed a church at St. John's Wood, which was afterwards copied at Edgbaston, near Birmingham. The churches of St. Ignatius, at Preston, and St. Peter, at Great Yarmouth, are also specimens—and by no means bad ones—of his Gothic. But his best works were executed at a later period, which our History has not yet reached.

In 1832, Rickman, accompanied by his friend Whewell (afterwards the famous master of Trinity), who had already contributed out of his vast and comprehensive store of information some valuable 'notes' on German Gothic, spent some time in the north of France, and visited the chief cathedral towns in Picardy and Normandy for the purpose of architectural study. On his return, he addressed to the Society of Antiquaries a series of letters descriptive of his tour. These were afterwards published in the 'Archæologia' of the Society. It is interesting to think of the simple Quaker and his clever, shrewd-headed companion linked together by a bond of common admiration for Mediæval Art, and with the same purpose exploring the magnificent relics of ancient

Scotney Castle, Sussex—the Residence of Edward Hussey, Esq.

A. Salvin, Architect, 1837.

architecture at Rouen, Abbeville, and Amiens; sketching, noting, and measuring at Lisieux, Caen, and Coutances. Few objects out of the range of art could thus have brought into close association men of such opposite lives, ambitions, and temperaments.

The comparison which Rickman drew between the Mediæval remains in France and England have been most useful in determining the history of style and the various influences to which it has been subject. Whewell's notes on the same journey are well known, and afford a remarkable instance of the success with which an amateur, backed by generally scientific education and encouraged by enthusiasm, may investigate and speculate on a subject for the technical details of which he has had no special training. His comparison of French and English 'decorated' is all the more interesting because the study of continental Gothic has greatly increased of late years, and we have borrowed so much from our neighbours across the Channel, that there was at one time some fear of our losing all national characteristics in modern design.

Happily a reaction is already taking place. That it will be universal in its effects or exclusive in its tendency need not be feared. But thoughtful men are beginning to feel that the wholesale and sudden importation of a foreign style subject, as it must be, to perversions and misadaptations by the uneducated, will work no good for the national architecture of this country. The changes which mark the progress of that art in past ages have been always gradual, and were brought about not by the whims of individual caprice, but by a concourse of events of which they became a material and lasting record. We must learn to labour and to wait. It will be time enough to think of improving on the taste of our forefathers when we have learned to realise the period of its highest perfection, and when we have identified and rejected those errors which first led to its decline.

CHAPTER VIII.

THOSE disinterested outsiders who are content to survey the ' Battle of the Styles ' from neutral ground, would be not a little surprised to find, on closer scrutiny, how much of civil warfare exists on either side.   If it were merely a question of Goth against Greek, of arch against lintel, the issue might be dubious, but the cause of strife would be plain and intelligible.   As it is, the partisans of Mediæval art, at least, have been divided against themselves by constant faction.   We have been disputing for upwards of half a century as to what really constitutes the style which we desire to uphold.   Its very name is still a vexed question.   If, then, doubts prevail in our own day, with all the light which has been thrown on this much-discussed subject, it is not difficult to imagine the perplexities which arose in the minds of those who, fifty years ago, in turn assumed the championship of Gothic.   The theories then individually propounded, regarding the origin of the style, outnumbered in extent and diversity those which have arisen from time to time about the use of Stonehenge.   Some writers ascribed the form of the Pointed arch to the intersection of round arches ; some found a prototype in the interlacing branches of trees ; others recognised in its outline the sacred Vesica ; while a fourth and more romantic kind of speculator insisted that it was but a symbol of the human hands raised upwards in an attitude of prayer !

The introduction, or development of the style in this country, became a subject of endless controversy.   Evelyn, in a previous age, had not hesitated to express his opinion that ' the Goths and Vandals, having demolished the Greek and Roman architecture, *introduced* in its stead a certain fantastical and licentious manner of building, which we have since called modern, or Gothic.' Wren endorsed this opinion, and there the matter rested for a while, but in the beginning of this century, various arguments were again rife. The style was Gothic; it was Saracenic; it had been brought to England by the crusaders; it had been invented by the Moors in Spain; it was an adaptation of the designs of Dioti Salvi; it might be traced to the pyramids of Egypt. One ingenious theorist endeavoured to reconcile all opinions in his comprehensive hypothesis that ' the style of architecture which we call cathedral or monastic Gothic, was manifestly a corruption of the sacred architecture of the Greeks or Romans, by a mixture of the Moorish or Saracenesque, which is formed out of a combination of Egyptian, Persian, and Hindoo!'

The labours of Milner, of Rickman, and of Whewell, helped in their several ways to check the extravagance of these notions, and to dissipate the cloud of doubt and ignorance by which the history of Mediæval art had been hitherto enveloped. Before their time the taste for Gothic, such as it was, and so far as the general public were concerned, had been but a sentiment, chiefly based on the more romantic associations of our national history, and in a few rare instances on a lingering attachment to the faith of our forefathers. The material characteristics of the style had hitherto been examined neither in an artistic nor a practical sense. Even the antiquaries had blundered in their dates and definitions. Those who would form a just estimate of the popular taste for old English Architecture, in the latter part of the last century and in the beginning of the present, need only examine any of the so-called Gothic buildings of that period to perceive the utter want of discrimination which then existed, not only regarding what may be called the unities of the style, but also regarding the use and just proportion of its most accentuated features. In those days a pointed arch was a pointed arch. The position of the centres from which it was struck, the profile of the mouldings by which it was enriched, the depth of wall in which it was inserted, were matters of little moment. In like manner the buttress and the pinnacle were introduced here and there, with little reference to their structural service, and with certainly no regard for their artistic form. One of the chief glories of old northern buildings, as Mr. Ruskin has justly pointed out, had been the high pitched roof. This was a feature which especially suffered in treatment during the decline of Gothic in Tudor days, when its angle was allowed to become more and more obtuse. In the earliest days of the Revival it was held of no importance whatever, and was frequently so flat as to be concealed by the parapet of the building which it covered.

But in no particular was the Gothic of our grandfathers' time more singularly deficient than in the character of its carved work and ornamental detail. A general impression seemed to exist that although the decorative sculpture of the classic schools could be measured by some standard of taste, and was suggestive of graceful form either animate or conventional, Mediæval sculpture on the contrary could aim at no such ideal, but was expressly suited to embody the wildest conceptions of definite ugliness. There is no more melancholy page in the history of art than that which records the wretched attempts at Gothic carving which were executed fifty or sixty years ago. Ignorance itself affords no apology for such work. Incapacity can scarcely excuse it. The bosses, the corbels, the niched figures, the gargoyles which in a thousand varying forms testified in turn the sense of beauty, the veneration, the love of nature and the ready wit of our ancestors, were still in existence, and might have served as models but for the egregious vanity of the day. King George's loyal subjects thought they knew better than those of King Edward. So they went to work and left us specimens of their handicraft, the like of which civilised Christendom never saw before, and it is to be devoutly trusted will never behold again. Beautiful no one expected it to be. But it also was not clever; it was not interesting; it was not life-like; it was not humorous; it was not even ugly after a good honest fashion—it was deplorably and hopelessly *mean*.

The truth is, that up to this period no one had made a special study of the details of Gothic architecture because no one knew how to begin to study them. Professional architects, with a few exceptions, would have ridiculed the attempt. Amateurs who essayed found themselves perplexed by apparent incongruities in the style. After a careful perusal of the works of Chambers they could readily distinguish the Doric order from the Ionic order, the Ionic from the Corinthian, but when they explored our cathedrals, the gradual erection of which extended over centuries of time, an endless variety of types presented themselves in illustration of the same feature. Some columns were round; others were octagonal; others were moulded. Some arches were semicircular; others were acutely pointed; others were flat. The groined roofs and porches, the window tracery and door-mouldings, were continually differing in form, in character, and proportion. How much of this variety was due to caprice or individual taste, and how much to change of style? What rules of art could be applied to such architecture, and how was the student to trace its progress and development?

A solution to these questions was at length supplied by three men in utterly distinct positions of life, who, without acting in concert, and indeed without agreeing in points of detail, managed between them to lay the foundation for a methodical study of Mediæval buildings. One touch of nature makes the whole world kin. One aim in art had enlisted the contemporary services of a Roman Catholic bishop, a professional Quaker, and a Cambridge don.

The antiquaries and dilettanti of the day could perhaps learn but little new from their researches, but the architects and the general public could learn a great deal, and by degrees they learned it. For the vague and, originally, contemptuous name of 'Gothic,' the words

' Pointed Style' were occasionally substituted. Amateurs began to discriminate between early English, Decorated, and Tudor architecture; and the choir of Canterbury Cathedral, the nave of York, and Henry the Seventh's Chapel at Westminster, each had its admirers. Attention was for the first time called to the important and distinctive character maintained by mouldings. The design of windows was studied with more care, and it was ascertained by comparison how ' plate' tracery had developed into geometrical patterns; geometrical had been beguiled into ' flowing' lines, and how the last had degenerated into ' Perpendicular.'

The various parts of a church, and the several uses to which they were assigned, were recognised and explained. The tower, the porch, the buttress, and the parapet, all afforded evidence in their general form or decorative detail of the period when they had been designed. Internally the groined vault and timber roof, the choir screen and sculptured corbel, were examined not only for their artistic value, but as a means of proving the date of the building to which they belonged. It was gradually discovered that there was such a thing as a principle of design in Gothic, that the quaint or graceful features which distinguished it were invented or fashioned with a purpose and were not the mere picturesque inventions of a random fancy.

These researches and convictions soon led to a more scientific classification of style than had hitherto prevailed.

Milner had been brought up as all amateurs of architecture then were, with a faith in the Orders which he could not entirely abjure. He did not indeed attempt, like Batty Langley, to modify the details of Gothic architecture, so as to conform with this division, but he gave his readers distinctly to understand that if there were three separate types of classic column and entablature with their respective members, ornaments, and proportions, so there existed among the buildings of the Middle Ages a similar and easily recognisable division into first, second, and third Pointed Styles. This division, which has long since been universally adopted in the art nomenclature of this country, was of great service in helping designers at an early period of the Revival to avoid anachronisms in the imitation of ancient work. But like all results of antiquarian research, it has had its drawbacks as well as its advantages in the development of modern taste.

For years afterwards a sort of chronological propriety hampered the inventive faculties of men. As the study of ancient examples progressed, and architects became more and more accustomed to associate certain features with a certain epoch, they came to believe less in the spirit than in the letter of Gothic. They sat down to design a 'decorated' church, because, perhaps, the windows of that style admitted more light than the windows of an earlier period, but in doing so they felt compelled to adopt in their tracery the meretricious faults of the later style; they hesitated to exchange the complex mouldings and trivial foliage of the one for the bold arch-soffit and noble capitals of the other, lest their work should be called incongruous. The so-called Tudor style had many advantages for domestic buildings. It had also some artistic and constructive defects. But because architects in that age had adopted a weak form of arch, and an ugly type of dripstone, the architects of the Gothic Revival reproduced both in their new churches and manor-houses—out of pure respect for tradition. At last it seemed necessary to find a precedent for every detail, and, to quote the humorous hyperbole uttered by a well-known member of the profession, no one was safe from critics, who knew to a nicety the orthodox *coiffure* of a thirteenth-century angel, and who damned a moulding that was half an hour too late.

Pugin himself designed furniture which was intended to be *in keeping* with the later additions to Windsor Castle, but which he lived to pronounce a mistake. He was, however, like a true genius, always in advance of his age, and it may with truth be said, in spite of the disparagement which has since been passed on his works, that if he had lived to accomplish the reformation he so gallantly began, he would have been reckoned among the foremost architects of the present day.

There remains, however, a short period to consider before Pugin became known to fame. In that period, many men who were either his elders, or had better opportunities than himself to establish a practice, achieved a notoriety which, if less splendid, was more profitable than his own. Among these was Edward Blore, who was born towards the close of the last century. According to Britton, Mr. Blore might date his knowledge of architecture from the year 1816, when he made an elaborate section of the east end of Winchester Cathedral. He had, however, no regular education as an architect, and was about thirty years old before he began to practise. His father was an antiquary of some note, and probably encouraged the taste for drawing which young Blore, at an early age, began to evince. The sketches of monuments, etc., which he made as a boy were carefully outlined and shaded with Indian ink. In point of accuracy they have been compared to photographs. He was apprenticed to an engraver, and rapidly made progress in the art which he afterwards turned to such good account. For some time he was actively employed as a draughtsman, and an engraver of architectural drawings. About the year 1822 the Rev. T. F. Dibdin published his ' Ædes Althorpianæ,' for which Blore supplied the illustrations. It was probably this accident which brought him into connection with the Spencer family, and thus formed the basis of an acquaintance which proved eminently useful to him in after life.

In 1823 he made an excursion into the North of England, for the purpose of collecting materials for a work which he brought out in parts, the whole volume being completed in 1826. It was entitled the ' Monumental Remains of Noble and Eminent Persons,' comprising the sepulchral antiquities of Great Britain, with historical and biographical illustrations, by the Rev. Philip Bliss, D.C.L. Mr. Blore was by this time so well known as to be made a fellow of the Society of

Antiquaries. All the illustrations were drawn, and many of them engraved, by himself. Le Keux undertook the rest. In point of execution these engravings will bear comparison with any which have been published in England, before or since. They are thirty in number. The accompanying letterpress is, as the title set forth, rather a biographical sketch of the heroes whom the monuments commemorate, than a description of the monuments themselves. A flattering notice of the first number appeared in the ' Gentleman's Magazine ' for 1824, but the critic, evidently being under the impression that both letterpress and illustrations were Mr. Blore's work, finds fault with the memoir of the Black Prince, who is represented, by a common error, to have derived his *sobriquet* from the colour of his armour.

The ' Gentleman's Magazine ' spoke with authority on such points, for in those days it was almost the only periodical in which the arts were duly represented. It was the ' Art Journal ' —the ' Building News '—the ' Notes and Queries ' of its time. It registered all the metropolitan improvements—described the new churches—chronicled all the archæological discoveries—gave the latest literary gossip of the day, and, though it was not blind to the merits of Classic art, it steadily and faithfully recorded the progress of the Gothic Revival. The critiques on public buildings are spiritedly written, and though their phraseology betrays to modern ears an ignorance of technicalities, they are often just and discriminating in theory.

In 1826 Mr. Blore was appointed surveyor to Westminster Abbey, and shortly afterwards, in his professional capacity, discovered that the roof of the case in which the wax figures of Queen Anne, the Earl of Chatham, and the other effigies commonly known as the ' ragged regiment ' were then placed, bore marks of ancient decoration. He had it removed, and examined it carefully. It turned out to be one of the rarest and most valuable specimens of early painting extant. Blore had a double reason for protecting it. Westminster was not then, as now, guarded by circumspect vergers, who are stimulated to additional

vigilance by the sixpences of the faithful.   There was scarce a monument in the place which had not suffered from ruthless violence, for at
that time or not long before the choristers made a playground of the
venerable abbey, and the Westminster scholars played at hockey in the
cloisters.   In the following year Mr. Blore read a paper on the subject of
his discovery before the Society of Antiquaries.   About this time,
through some mistake, he got the credit of having executed the extensive repairs of Winchester Cathedral, which, however, were carried out
by Mr. Garbett, a local architect, who designed the episcopal throne
there among other fittings.   The design of the organ case had been
entrusted to Mr. Blore in 1824.   In 1827 we find the latter gentleman
alluded to as 'the eminent architect,' and engaged to furnish plans for
the chancel fittings of Peterborough.   Shortly afterwards he was employed to restore Lambeth Palace, then in a state of semi-ruin.   It had
been three times destroyed and rebuilt.   Mr. Blore found it necessary to
remove some of the walls, which had literally decayed from age, but
one of the principal roofs—that which now spans the dining-room—was
preserved.   The chamber known as Old Juxon's Hall was converted
into a library, the old library having been pulled down.   The 'new'
palace extends eastward from the tower, which joins the chapel, and is
for the most part on the site of the old building.   Near the hall (or
new library), and over a modern gateway, was constructed a fire-proof
room for the preservation of manuscripts and archives.

Among Mr. Blore's other works were an Elizabethan Town Hall at
Warminster ; Goodrich Court, on the Wye, for Mr. Samuel Meyrick ;
Crewe Hall ; Pull Court, Gloucestershire ; the Chapel of Marlborough
College, Wilts ; Worsley Hall, for Lord Ellesmere ; and Moreton
Hall.   He also designed churches at Stratford and Leytonstone, the
Pitt Press at Cambridge, and additions to Merton College, Oxford.
The repairs of Glasgow Cathedral were likewise carried out under his
superintendence, as well as certain improvements at Windsor Castle ;
and, before Sir Charles Barry was employed at Cauford (near Win-

bourne), the works there were entrusted to Mr. Blore. His restorations at Westminster Abbey, though wanting in life and vigour, abound in careful detail. This was, in short, his great *forte*. He had studied and drawn detail so long and zealously that its design came quite naturally to him, and in this respect he was incomparably superior to his contemporaries.

As a typical building of the præ-Puginesque period, St. Luke's Church at Chelsea, designed by Savage in 1824, must not be forgotten. Indeed, its cost, its size, and construction place it in the foremost rank of contemporary Gothic examples. It was raised at an outlay of 40,000*l*. to accommodate a congregation of 2,500 persons, and it was probably the only church of its time in which the main roof was groined throughout in stone. The plan, arranged with that rigid formality which was the fashion of the day, consists of a lofty nave with clerestory and triforium niches, north and south aisles, a western tower and narthex, and a low square vestry which projects from the east end. The general style of the design is Perpendicular, though the groining and certain details have an earlier character. The window heads are filled with tracery and enclosed within a four-centred arch of somewhat ungainly curve. The tower has octagonal turrets at each angle, which terminate in pinnacles of open stonework. The porch, which extends the whole width of the west front, is divided by piers and arches into five bays, of which two are on either side of the tower, while the fifth and central one is formed by the lowest story of the tower itself, vaulted over inside, and decorated externally by a cusped and crocketed canopy. Flying buttresses, to resist the thrust of the groining, span the aisles on either side, and divide them externally into a series of bays.

In examining such a structure as this, which includes in its design every feature necessary and usual for its purpose; which is ample in its dimensions and sound in its workmanship; on which an exceptionally large sum of money was expended, but which is, nevertheless, mean and uninteresting in its general effect, it is well to put oneself in the position of an intelligent amateur, who, feeling it to be a failure from an artistic point of view, desires to know what special faults have contributed to this result, and why, individually, they should be considered faults at all. To such an enquiry, it may be briefly answered that the prominent blunders in this design are an unfortunate lack of proportion, a culpable clumsiness of detail, and a foolish, overstrained balance of parts.

The want of proportion is eminently noticeable in the lanky arches of the west porch, with their abrupt ogival hood moulding; in the buttresses, which are divided by their 'set-offs' into two long and *equal* heights; in the windows, which are identical in general outline throughout the church; in the octagonal turrets of the tower, where the nine string courses occur at scrupulously regular intervals all the way up; and, finally, in the masonry of the walls, where large blocks of stone are used in uninterrupted courses, scarcely varying in height from base to parapet.

All these accidents combine not only to deprive the building of scale, but to give it a cold and *machine made* look. In a far different spirit the Mediæval designers worked. Their buttresses were stepped in unequal lengths, the set-offs becoming more frequent and more accentuated towards the foundation. Their string courses were introduced as leading lines in the design, and were not ruled in with the accuracy of an account book; their windows were large or small as best befitted the requirements of internal lighting; their walls were coursed irregularly, the smaller stones being used for broad surfaces, and the larger ones reserved for quoins and the jambs of doors and windows.

It is less easy to define in words the crude vulgarity of detail which pervades this church, but no one who examines with attention the character—if character it may be called—of the carved work, can fail to perceive the absence of vitality it exhibits in the crockets and finials which are supposed to adorn its walls. No educated stone carver employed on decorative features would care to reproduce the actual forms of natural vegetation for such a purpose, but in his conventional representation of such forms he would take pains to suggest the vigour and individuality of his model. Fifty years ago this principle was almost ignored. There was naturalistic carving, and there was ornamental carving; but the noble *abstractive* treatment which should find a middle place between them, and which was one of the glories of ancient art, had still to be revived.

The third and perhaps the most flagrant fault in this building—a fault which Savage as a designer shared with many of his contemporaries—is the cold formality of its arrangement. It seems astonishing that one of the essential graces of Mediæval architecture, that uneven distribution of parts which is at once necessary to convenience, and the cause of picturesque composition, should have been so studiously avoided at this time. Whether it resulted from mere want of inventive faculty in design, or from an unfortunate adherence to the grim proprieties of a pseudo-classic taste for which *eurythmia* is indispensable in places where

> each alley has a brother,
> And half the platform just reflects the other,

can scarcely be determined. But certain it is that nine-tenths of the so-called Gothic buildings raised before Pugin's days were designed on this plan, and that an architect would no more have thought of introducing a porch on the south aisle which had not its counterpart on the north, than he would have dared to wear a coat of which the right sleeve was longer than the left.

There are, however, some redeeming points about St. Luke's Church. The upper part of the tower, though foolishly over-panelled, is good in its general proportions. The same may be said of the octagonal turrets at the east end. The groining of the nave is really excellent, for its time, and is all the more remarkable, when we remember the wretched shams by which such work was then too frequently burlesqued. The reredos, though designed on a principle which would render it unsuitable for the present requirements of church architecture, is, for its date, by no means contemptible; and as for the galleries—fatal as they are to any attempt at internal effect—and redundant as everyone but the mere utilitarian will consider them—we must remember that many churches of later date, and far more pretentious in character, have maintained such features with far less excuse and under more enlightened conditions.

CHAPTER IX.

HOWEVER much we may be indebted to those ancient supporters of Pointed Architecture who, faithfully adhering to its traditions at a period when the style fell into general disuse, strove earnestly, and in some instances ably, to preserve its character ; whatever value in the cause we may attach to the crude and isolated examples of Gothic which belong to the eighteenth century, or to the efforts of such men as Nash and Wyatt, there can be little doubt that the revival of Mediæval design received its chief impulse in our own day from the energy and talents of one architect whose name marks an epoch in the history of British art, which, while art exists at all, can never be forgotten.

Augustus Northmore Welby Pugin was born on March 1, 1812, at a house in Store Street, Bedford Square. His father, as is well known, had been a French refugee, who, during the horrors of the revolution in his own country, escaped to England, and obtained employment in the office of Mr. Nash, then one of the most celebrated and successful architects of his day. Nash was not slow to perceive the bent of his assistant's talents, and advised the young Frenchman to begin a series of studies illustrative of English Gothic—with a view to publication. Some of these sketches were picturesquely treated, and of sufficient merit to cause Pugin's election as a member of the old Water Colour Society, in 1808. But it was by his later and more strictly professional works that the elder Pugin first established a reputation. His ' Specimens of Gothic Architecture ' in England and his ' Antiquities of Normandy ' have been already mentioned. In addition to these, he published 'The Edifices of London,' in two volumes; 'Examples of Gothic Architecture,' quarto, 1831 ; 'Ornamental Timber Gables,' &c.

Of professional practice the elder Pugin had very little, and it is remarkable that, of his many pupils, but few have followed the profession for which they were intended.   There were, however, some exceptions, among whom may be mentioned Sir James Pennethorne, late Surveyor to the Office of Works, Talbot Bury, and B. Ferrey, who was destined to become the biographer of the younger and more famous Pugin.   The latter was educated at Christ's Hospital, where he showed at an early age great aptitude for learning.   Even as a child, we are told, he was quick in all that he attempted, and expressed his opinions with a confidence which certainly did not abate in later life.   After leaving school, young Pugin entered his father's office, where the natural facility of his hand for sketching soon declared itself. He passed through the usual elementary course of study in his profession, learnt perspective, and at once began to make drawings in Westminster Abbey.

About the year 1825, the elder Pugin went with some of his pupils to Paris, for the purpose of preparing a series of views illustrative of that city.   His son, then a mere boy, accompanied him, and made such good use of his pencil that he was of real service to his father.   In July, 1826, young Pugin and Mr. B. Ferrey visited Rochester, where they made many sketches of the Castle—the former carrying his researches so far as to take an accurate survey of the foundations.   In the prosecution of this work he was more ardent than discreet, and twice narrowly escaped with life the consequences of his temerity.

In 1827, he again accompanied his father on a professional tour in France, and gratified his now rapidly developing taste for Mediæval art by visiting the splendid Churches of Normandy.   Up to this time his dislike to sedentary pursuits, and the dry routine of an architect's office, had prevented his entering on any practical work.   The first employment which he received independent of his father appears to have been from Messrs. Rundell and Bridge, the well-known gold-smiths. A member of that firm, while engaged in examining some ancient designs for plate in the British Museum, had observed young Pugin copying a print from Albert Dürer, and soon became aware of his taste for Mediæval art. The lad's services were secured forthwith, and some clever designs resulted from the commission. Shortly after-wards Messrs. Morel and Seddon, the King's upholsterers, applied to Mr. Pugin for his professional assistance in preparing drawings for the new furniture at Windsor Castle, which had been entrusted to their care, and which it was determined should partake of the ancient cha-racter of that building. This was an excellent opportunity for the display of young Pugin's abilities, and, though he afterwards frankly admitted the errors of his youthful effort, it is probable that at the time the designs were made, no better could have been procured.

During the progress of the works at Windsor, Pugin formed the acquaintance of Mr. George Dayes, a son of the artist of that name. This man occupied a humble position in the management of the scenery at Covent Garden Theatre. To a boy of fifteen who had never yet seen a play, the description of stage effects and scenery offered great attractions. At last his curiosity was gratified. He was introduced to the mysterious little world beyond the footlights—learned the art of distemper painting, and when the new opera of 'Kenilworth' was produced in 1831, and it was required to produce something like a faithful representation of Mediæval architecture, young Pugin designed the scenes. During the period of this connection, and partly to aid him in his study of effect, he fitted up a model theatre at his father's house, where all the tricks and appliances of the real stage were in-geniously mimicked.

His tastes in this direction were but transient, and he was next possessed by an extraordinary passion for a maritime life. To the great distress of his father he actually commanded for a short while a small merchant schooner which traded between this country and Holland. In addition to the little freight, for the convoy of which Pugin was responsible, he managed to bring over some interesting specimens of old furniture and carving from Flanders, which afterwards helped to fill his museum at Ramsgate. In one of these cruises he was wrecked on the Scotch coast near Leith—a temporary misfortune, which he had no reason to regret, for it brought him into contact with Mr. Gillespie Graham, an Edinburgh architect of some repute, who, doubtless knowing his father's name, and perceiving the ability of young Pugin, recommended him to give up his seafaring hobby and stick to his profession—a piece of sound advice, which the young man had good sense enough to follow.

At this time, though many architects had adopted Mediæval architecture in their designs, few were acquainted with Gothic detail, and young Pugin's studies in that direction thus rendered him extremely useful to many who were glad to avail themselves of his services. Not content, however, with this secondhand employment, he embarked in sundry speculations by which he undertook to supply carved work in stone and wood to those who required it for the ornamental portion of their works. But his inexperience in the varying price of labour and material soon brought him into pecuniary difficulties, and, but for the assistance of his relations, he would have been imprisoned for debt. This failure showed him the importance of adhering exclusively to the profession for which he had been educated, and to which thenceforth he turned his serious attention. That he must have realised some money by its practice is pretty evident from the fact that, while still a minor, he married in 1831 Miss Garnet, a grand niece of Dayes, the artist, who has been already mentioned. His first wife (for he married three times) unfortunately died in childbirth, and a few years afterwards Pugin built himself a house near Salisbury, in the style to which he was so much attached. It was, however, far inferior to his later works, and he had not yet learned the art of combining a picturesque exterior with the ordinary comforts of an English home.

It was during his residence at St. Marie's Grange that he began to inveigh so bitterly against the barbarisms which were still practised by the introduction of hideous pagan monuments into our noble cathedrals and churches, and which he afterwards exposed more systematically in his published works. He made a tour for the purpose of inspecting the principal examples of Mediæval architecture in the west, and improved his taste by constant study. In the meantime he had married again. His second wife does not appear to have been pleased with his residence. At all events, Pugin, who had expended upwards of 2,000*l.* on the house, made up his mind to sell it at a great sacrifice. It only fetched 500*l.* He had now a gradually increasing practice, his principal work at the time being Scarisbrick Hall, Lancashire, an interesting example of domestic Gothic, in which the lofty clock-tower forms a graceful and picturesque feature.

Pugin's father and mother died in 1832–3, and by their death he succeeded to some property which had belonged to his aunt, Miss Welby. His secession from the Church of England had meanwhile been an important event in his life. The causes which led to a change of his religious convictions, and the controversies which then arose, not only between members of the Anglican and Roman branches of the Church Catholic, but among those who belonged to the communion he embraced, have been amply discussed elsewhere. That he was sincere in his change of faith, and that it was the result of more serious considerations than those associated with the art which he practised, no one can, charitably, doubt. On the other hand, it must be admitted that the importance then attached to certain proprieties of ecclesiastical furniture and decorations has been vastly overrated on both sides.

In 1836 Pugin published his celebrated ' Contrasts,' a pungent satire on modern architecture as compared with that of the Middle Ages. The illustrations which accompanied it were drawn and etched by himself, and afford evidence not only of great artistic power, but of a keen sense of humour. To the circulation of this work—coloured though it may be by a strong theological bias—we may attribute the care and jealousy with which our ancient churches and cathedrals have since been protected and kept in repair. For such a result, who would not overlook many faults, which, after all, had no worse origin than in the earnest zeal of a convert?

In 1832, Pugin had the good fortune to make the acquaintance of the Earl of Shrewsbury, who, not only from his high rank, but from his attachment to the Church of Rome, and to Pugin's own views regarding art, proved to him a most valuable patron. This nobleman at once employed him in the alterations and additions to his residence—Alton Towers, which subsequently led to many other commissions.

The success attending Pugin's publication of the ' Contrasts ' induced him, in 1841, to bring out his ' True Principles of Gothic Architecture,' the title of which has since passed almost into a proverb among the friends of that style. ' An Apology for the Revival of Christian Architecture in England,' followed in 1843, and in 1844 appeared ' The Glossary of Ecclesiastical Ornament and Costume,' compiled and illustrated from ancient authorities and examples. The influence of this work, as Mr. Ferrey truly remarks, upon polychromatic decoration in our churches has been immense. Among Pugin's other literary productions are ' The present state of Ecclesiastical Architecture in England,' reprinted from the ' Dublin Review,' 1843 ; ' Floriated Ornament, a series of thirty-one designs,' 1849 ; 'Some Remarks on the Articles which have recently appeared in the " Rambler," relative to Ecclesiastical Architecture and Decoration,' 1850. In the same year he published ' The Present State of Public Worship among the Roman Catholics,' by a Roman Catholic ; and in 1851 appeared his ' Treatise on Chancel Screens and Rood Lofts, their antiquity, use, and symbolic signification,' a work in which certain theories were advanced that called forth much warm discussion among ecclesiologists.

In 1841 Pugin left Salisbury and came to London, where he resided

for some time at Cheyne Walk, Chelsea; but having previously purchased ground at the West Cliff, Ramsgate, he not only built for
himself a large and commodious house on that site, but began at his own
expense a church, which advanced from time to time, as he could
best spare the means from his yearly income.   In 1844 he became
again a widower.   His wife was buried at St. Chad's, Birmingham, a
church which he had himself designed.   Lord Shrewsbury showed his
respect and affection for Pugin by attending the funeral.   This severe
loss was all the more to be deplored, because Pugin had at this time
reached the zenith of his professional fame.   After remaining a widower
for five years, he married lastly Miss Knill, a lady of good family.

In 1847 he made a tour in Italy, and his antipathy to Italian Architecture was in nowise lessened by his visit to Rome, from which place
he wrote home in utter disgust with St. Peter's—with the Sistine
Chapel—with the Scala Regia, and most of the architectural 'lions'
which the ordinary traveller feels bound to admire.   The Mediæval
art of North Italy, however, filled him with admiration, and confirms
the general opinion that, had he lived to see the present aspect of the
Gothic Revival, he would have gone with the stream in regard to
the character of his design.

In estimating the effect which Pugin's efforts, both as an artist and
an author, produced on the Gothic Revival, the only danger lies in the
possibility of overrating their worth.   The man whose name was for at
least a quarter of a century a household word in every house where
ancient art was loved and appreciated—who fanned into a flame the
smouldering fire of ecclesiastical sentiment which had been slowly
kindled in this country—whose very faith was pledged to Mediæval
tradition—such a writer and such an architect will not easily be forgotten,
so long as the æsthetic principles which he advocated are recognised
and maintained.

But it must not be overlooked that the tone of his literary work is
biassed throughout, and to some extent weakened, first by an absolute

assumption on the part of its author that the moral and social condition of England was infinitely superior in the Middle Ages to that of
the present, and secondly that a good architect ought to inaugurate his
professional career by adopting the faith of the Roman Catholic
Church. Such convictions as these are excusable in the mind of a
zealous convert, but they have no legitimate place in the polemics
of art.

Again, as a practical architect, it can scarcely be said that Pugin
always followed in the spirit of his work the principles which he was
never tired of reiterating in print. If there is one characteristic more
apparent than another in the buildings of our ancestors it is the ample
and generous manner in which they dealt with constructive materials.
But Pugin's church walls are often miserably slight, his roof timbers
thin, his mouldings poor and wiry. It may be urged—and, indeed,
was more than once urged by himself—that the restriction of cost had
often affected to considerable disadvantage the execution of his design.

To this it must be answered that stability of workmanship is a
primary condition of architectural excellence, and that in the same
churches which exhibit these defects there is an unnecessary and even
profuse display of ornament. The money lavished on elaborate carving
in wood and stone, on painting and gilding work which had better
in many instances have been left without this adventitious mode of
enrichment, would often have been more advantageously spent in adding a
foot to the thickness of his walls and doubling the width of his rafters.
The fact is, that the very nature of Pugin's chief ability tended to
lead him into many errors. Of constructive science he probably knew
but little. His strength as an artist lay in the design of ornamental
detail. The facility with which he invented patterns for mural diapers,
and every kind of surface decoration, was extraordinary. Those decorative features which with many an architect are the result of thoughtful
study were conceived and drawn by him with a rapidity which astonished his professional friends. During the erection of the Houses of

Parliament, and while his services were engaged to assist Mr. Barry, he dashed off, with a ready fancy and dexterous pencil, hundreds of sketches which were frequently wanted on the spot, and at a short notice, for the guidance of workmen. Indeed, even his more important designs were remarkable for their hasty execution, and were rarely finished after the fashion of an ordinary 'working drawing.' To record on paper his notion of a church tower, or the plan of a new convent, was with him—if a labour at all—a labour of love.* But the production of ornament he treated as mere child's play.

It is, therefore, no wonder that his artistic genius should have been often beguiled into an elaboration of details of which his memory supplied an inexhaustible store, and which his hand was ever ready to delineate. The carver, the cabinet maker, the silversmith who sought his assistance, or whose work he was called on to superintend, might reckon with safety on the rich fertility of his inventive power, and in truth Pugin's influence on the progress of art manufacture may be described as more remarkable than his skill as an architect. For the revival of Mediæval taste in stained glass and metal work we are indebted to his association with Messrs. Hardman. The attention which he bestowed on ecclesiastical furniture has been the means of reviving the arts of wood-carving and embroidery—of improving the public taste in the choice of carpets and paper-hangings. Those establishments which are known in London as 'ecclesiastical warehouses' owe their existence and their source of profit to Pugin's exertions in the cause of rubrical propriety.

His labours in that cause, and the strictures which he ventured to utter in connection with the subject, were not confined to the Anglican community. He found much that was irregular and contrary to tradition in the appointment and ceremonies of the Church which he had

---

* Many of the etchings which he prepared for the illustration of his books were executed when he was afloat on some yachting expedition. He was very fond of the sea, and would certainly have been a sailor if he had not been an architect.

entered, and he did his best to reform what he considered to be a degeneracy from ancient custom, and from the true principles of design. In his essay on the ' Present State of Ecclesiastical Architecture in England,' he lays down, with great care and minute attention to detail, the orthodox plan and internal arrangements of a Roman Catholic church. He describes the proper position and purpose of the chancel screen, rood and rood loft; the plan and number of the sedilia ; the use of the sacrarium and revestry ; the shape and furniture of the altar. These are matters upon which at the present time the clergy of neither Church would require much information; but it must be remembered that before Pugin began to write, ecclesiastical sentiment was rare, and artistic taste was rarer. The Roman Catholics had perverted the forms and ceremonies which pertained to the ancient faith. The Anglicans had almost forgotten them.

But a change was at hand : a new impulse was received from an unexpected quarter, which turned the tide of popular interest towards these matters. Whether the cause of religion has gained or lost by this movement need not here be discussed, but that it has been advantageous on the whole to national art there can be no question.

One of the most successful of Pugin's churches was that of St. Giles, at Cheadle. The arrangement of its short compact plan, the proportions of its tower and spire, and the elaborate fittings and decoration of the interior, make it as attractive an example of Pugin's skill as could be quoted. Its chancel will certainly bear a favourable comparison with that of St. Mary at Uttoxeter, or that of St. Alban, Macclesfield. Indeed, in the latter church the flat pitch of the chancel roof, and the *reedy*, attenuated look of the nave piers are very unsatisfactory, nor does the introduction of a clerestory (a feature which, from either choice or necessity, was omitted from many of Pugin's churches) help in any great degree to give scale and proportion to the interior.

In London, the most important work which Pugin executed was the pro-cathedral in St. George's Fields, Westminster. The fact that the upper portion of the tower and spire of this church has never been completed, and the subsequent addition of buildings at the east end, not contemplated in the original design, make it difficult to judge of the exterior as a composition. But it may fairly be doubted whether, under any conditions, it would convey to the eye that sense of grandeur and dignity which one might reasonably expect from a structure of such size. In the first place, the common yellow brick used for the walls is the meanest and most uninteresting of building materials, and in London, where it is chiefly used, speedily acquires a dingy appearance. But independently of this drawback, there is a want of vitality about the building. The pinnacles which crown the buttresses are cold and heavy. The carved work, though executed with care and even delicacy here and there, is spiritless, except in the treatment of animal form. Crockets and ball-flower ornaments are needlessly multiplied. The tracery of the windows is correct and aims at variety ; and the doorways are arched with orthodox mouldings, but there is scarcely a single feature in the exterior which arrests attention by the beauty of its form or the aptness of its place.

Internally the nave is divided into eight bays, with an aisle on either side, carried to nearly the same height as the nave. There is, consequently, no clerestory. The nave arches reach at their apex to within a few feet of the roof, and the great height thus given to the thinly moulded piers (unintersected as they are by any horizontal string courses, which at once lend scale and apparent strength to a shaft) is a defect which becomes apparent at first sight. The aisle walls are singularly slight for so large a church, and one looks in vain for the bold splay and deep reveal which are characteristic of old fenestration.

Still there are features in the interior which reflect no small credit on the architect when one remembers the date of its erection (1843). The double chancel screen, with its graceful arches and light tracery, though suggestive of wood-work rather than stone in design, is picturesque, and is effectively relieved against the dimly-lighted chancel behind.   The chancel itself was said to have been well studied from ancient models.   Architects of the present day may smile at the simplicity of its reredos, a row of ten narrow niches be-pinnacled, and canopied, and crocketed, each containing a small figure, flanked by two broader and higher niches of the same design, each containing a larger figure.   But here again one must bear in mind that these details were designed and executed at a time when such design and such execution rose to the level of high artistic excellence beside contemporary work. Pugin had with the greatest patience trained the artisans whom he employed, and whatever may be said of the aim of their efforts, no one can doubt its refinement.   We have far more accomplished architects in 1871 than we had thirty years ago, but it may be doubted whether we have more skilful workmen.

The church of St. Chad, at Birmingham, may fairly be ranked among Pugin's most important works.   In plan it presents no great peculiarity, but the sloping line of the ground on which it stands, the lofty height of its nave, the towers which flank its western front, and the sculpture with which it is enriched, combine to give a character to its exterior which is wanting in many of Pugin's churches.   The general effect indicates some tendency on the part of the designer to a taste for German Gothic, without, however, any careful reproduction of its noblest features.   Indeed, a glance at the details reveals at once the period of its erection—that period in which after long disuse the traditions of Mediæval art were revived in the letter rather than the spirit. Its slate-roofed spires are 'broached' at an abrupt and ungraceful angle.   Its buttresses are long and lean, with 'set-offs' at rare intervals, and coarsely accentuated.   Its walls of brick—once red, but now toned down by time and the noxious smoke of Birmingham to dingy brown— have a mean impoverished look about them, which is scarcely redeemed by the freestone tracery of its windows, or the canopied and really cleverly-carved figures which adorn its western portal.

Internally the building displays evidence of Pugin's strength and weakness in an eminent degree. The chancel fittings, the rood screen with its sacred burden, the altar tombs—in a word, the *furniture* of the church—are, if we accept the motive of the style in which they are designed, as correct in form as any antiquary could wish, and are wrought with marvellous refinement. But in general effect the interior is far from satisfactory. The attenuated and lanky nave piers rise to such a disproportionate height as scarcely to leave room for the arches which surmount them. The walls are thin and poor, the roof timbers slight and weak looking. There is no clerestory, and the aisle roofs follow that of the nave in one continuous slope. The aisles are more-over extraordinarily high in proportion to their width. An English poet has described to us the beauties of the 'long-drawn aisle,' but here the aisles appear to have been drawn out the wrong way. The chancel is of far better proportions, and with its elaborate rood screen richly gilt and painted, its oak fittings and bishop's throne, its canopied reredos and mural decoration, is decidedly *the* feature *par excellence* of this church.* The rest of the interior is plain, and depends for its effect on the stained glass used in the windows. Much of this glass is well designed so far as the drawing of figures and character of ornament are concerned, but it has the all-important defect which distinguished most of the glass of this period, viz.—a crude and inharmonious association of colour. This is especially noticeable in the windows of a chapel in the north aisle, where the tints used are peculiarly harsh and offensive.

In no department of decorative art have the works of the Middle Ages been until recently so hopelessly misunderstood and so cruelly burlesqued as in the design of stained glass. In the last century the inventions of Reynolds, of West, and others plainly indicate the pre-vailing belief that a painted window should be a transparent picture;

* In the north aisle is an altar tomb of Caen stone with an elaborately carved ogival canopy in the style of late decorated examples. It is cleverly designed, and executed with great refinement of detail and astonishing delicacy of workmanship. This tomb was erected in 1852. It had been previously sent to the Great Exhibition of 1851.

and when Sir Joshua filled the west end of New College Chapel at Oxford with work of this description, he probably conceived that it was a great advance on the style of old glass—fifteenth-century glass— specimens of which may still be seen by its side.   How far this notion was correct may be judged by any intelligent amateur who will compare the two works.   The effect of Sir Joshua's window, with its simpering nymphs who have stepped on pedestals in order to personate the Virtues, is cold and lifeless, while the old glass, quaint and conventional though it may be in its *abstractive* treatment of natural form, glows with generous colour, which acquires double value from the fact that it is broken up into a thousand various shapes by the intersecting lines of lead as it crosses the glass at every conceivable angle.

The glass stainers of Pugin's time did not indeed fall into the error of supposing that they could treat the design of windows after the same fashion as an easel picture.   But it is evident that they and their suc- cessors for years after gave less attention to the question of colour than to the drawing and grouping of their figures.   The saints and angels of old glass are, it must be admitted, neither very saintly nor angelic in their action, if we are to regard them in the light of pictorial represen- tations.   But we may be sure that neither the most profound hagio- logist, nor the sincerest devotee, nor the most enlightened amateur who has visited the cathedrals of York and Exeter, has regretted this fact in the very slightest degree. As well might a connoisseur of ' six mark ' China deplore the want of probability in every incident portrayed on a Nankin vase, or an admirer of old textile art object to the nondescript forms which pass for leaves and flowers on a Turkey carpet !

The truth is that in the apparent imperfections of some arts lies the real secret of their excellence. The superior *quality* of colour which long distinguished old glass from new was due in a great measure to its streakyness and irregularity of tint.   In the early days of the Revival this was regarded as a defect, while the quaint and angular forms by which, in old work, the human figure was typified or suggested, rather than represented, were deemed barbarous and ungraceful.

So our enlightened art reformers of the nineteenth century set to work to remedy these faults. They produced a glass without blemish; their figures were drawn and shaded with academical propriety. But this was not all. It occurred to them that by using larger pieces of glass they might dispense with half the dull heavy lines of lead which meandered over the old windows. Finally, they determined that the odd-looking patches of white or slightly tinted glass which they found in ancient work should be replaced in their designs by glass as brilliant as the rest.

Whatever may have been the contemporary opinion of these supposed 'improvements,'* the modern critic can scarcely fail to regard them as thorough blunders.

Every one now admits that the conditions of design in a painted window belong to decorative, not to imitative art. It was with a wise purpose—or at least with a sound instinct, that the old craftsman shaped those awkward heroes and graceless saints in his window— crossed their forms with abrupt black lines of lead, and left broad spaces of delicate *grisaille* to relieve the more positive colours of their robes. The advantage of such treatment will be best measured by those who take the trouble to compare it with the blaze of ill-associated colour and dull propriety of outline which distinguish the glass manufactured some forty years ago. In our own time, indeed, accomplished designers like Mr. Burne Jones and Mr. Holiday have aimed at combining a certain abstract grace of form with beauty of colour, but the instances of such success are rare, and even when they occur it may be doubted whether such designs would not have been doubly admirable if employed for mural decoration.

The Church of St. Wilfrid, in Manchester (built externally of red

---

* In a letter signed 'Philotechnicos,' which appears in the 'Civil Engineers' Journal' for 1837, the following passage occurs :—

'Many persons have an extraordinary idea that the art of painting on glass is lost. Lost forsooth! why the idea is the most fallacious that ever existed; and so far is it from the fact, that the present state of excellence *was never before equalled.*' (!)

brick), exhibits in the design of its nave arcade a more refined sense of proportion than is observable in many of Pugin's larger works. Here the piers are (comparatively) short, and the arches which they support are acutely pointed. The aisle windows are narrow, and, indeed, would, no doubt, have been insufficient for light, but for those of the clerestory with which the church is provided. The rood screen—that indispensable feature in Pugin's churches, and one which subsequently became the subject of much controversy, is richly painted. The treatment of the altar and reredos is extremely simple, but far more dignified than the fussy elaboration of those objects in some examples of later work. One of the most interesting features in the church is the stone pulpit, which does not stand isolated, but is corbelled out from the wall on the south side of the chancel arch.

One of the main objections which were raised against the revival of Gothic for Church Architecture at this time was the additional expense which it involved when compared with the *soi-disant* classic style which had been so long in vogue. Pugin determined that St. Wilfrid's, which was erected in 1842, should prove, both in its design and execution, the fallacy of this notion. How far he succeeded in this endeavour may be inferred from the fact that the entire cost of the church (which will hold a congregation of about 800 persons) and of the priest's house attached to it, did not exceed 5,000*l.* Although Pugin was thus not unwilling to enter the lists with utilitarians in a financial sense, he strongly objected to be led by their arguments in matters which affected his artistic views. The chancel of St. Wilfrid's was found to be very dark, and some time after its erection enquiry was made of him, as the architect of the church, whether there would be any objection to introduce a small skylight in its roof, just behind the chancel arch, where it would be serviceable without obtruding on the design. Pugin sternly refused to sanction—even on these conciliatory terms—the adoption of any such plan, which he declared would have the effect of reducing his sanctuary to the level of a Manchester warehouse.

St. Marie's Church, Liverpool, is an early and interesting example of Pugin's skill. It is built of local red sandstone, and displays in the mouldings of its door jambs and fashion of its window tracery considerable refinement of detail. It has no chancel in the proper sense of the word, but the easternmost part of the nave serves for that purpose. The nave arches are acutely pointed, and their mouldings die into an octagonal block just above the impost moulding of the pier. The peculiarity of this treatment is the more remarkable when we remember the stereotyped appearance which a nave arcade of this date (1838) usually presented, and the narrow license which was then accorded to inventive taste in the design of such features.

St. Marie's, in its plan as well as in the general character of its composition, is essentially a *town* church. It is now, and probably always was, surrounded by lofty warehouses of gaunt and dismal exterior, but stored inside, no doubt, with ample fruits of human labour and commercial industry. It is curious to turn aside from the narrow, dirty, bustling streets in which these buildings stand, and find oneself at once so suddenly and so thoroughly removed from the noise and turmoil of the outside world in this fair, quiet, modest house of prayer. It has no claim to architectural grandeur. It was built at a melancholy period of British art. Its structural features just do their duty and nothing more. The nave, which is of great length, has been left plain and undecorated. But on the 'wall-veil' and altar fittings at the east end of the church both architect and workman have lavished their utmost skill. The reredos of the high altar is extremely simple in general form but exhibits great refinement of detail. That of the Lady Chapel is most elaborate in design and workmanship. Figures, niches, canopies, pinnacles, crockets, and finials crowd into a sumptuous group—worthy of the best workmanship in the latter part of the fourteenth century. Modern critics urge with reason that that period affords by no means the best type of Mediæval art for our imitation. The revived taste for Gothic, which in our own day at first manifested itself in a reproduction of Tudor mansions and churches of the Perpendicular style, has been gradually attracted towards earlier—and still earlier—types. But we must remember that in Pugin's time late Decorated work was still admired as the most perfect development of Pointed Architecture, and he certainly did his best to maintain its popularity. The altar and reredos in the Lady Chapel of St. Marie are real gems in their way, and may be cited as specimens not only of Pugin's thorough knowledge of detail, but also of the success with which in a very few years he had managed to educate up to a standard of excellence, not realised during many previous generations, the art-workmen whom he entrusted to execute his designs.

Whether such excessive elaboration was judicious in a town church so dimly lighted as St. Marie's—whether it was even justifiable in a building whose structural features are certainly on no generous scale of stability, may be questioned. It has frequently been affirmed, and with some show of reason, that Pugin enriched his churches at a sacrifice of their strength—that he starved his roof-tree to gild his altar. It is only fair, however, to point out that in many instances where this apparent inconsistency has been observed, although the buildings were commenced with but slender funds, subscriptions or bequests were added just as the works approached completion, and that the architect was thus called upon to spend in mere decoration money which, if it had been available earlier, he would gladly have devoted to a worthier purpose.

It is certain that in the one work which he carried out completely to his own satisfaction, because he was in this case—to use his own words —'paymaster, architect, and builder,' there is no stint of solidity in construction. For that reason the church of St. Augustine, which he founded at Ramsgate, may be regarded as one of his most successful achievements. Its plan, which is singularly ingenious and unconventional in arrangement, consists of a chancel about thirty-five feet long, and divided into two bays, with a Lady Chapel on its south side, a central tower and *south* transept only, a nave and south aisle. The outer bay of

JEWITT & CO. SC.

Church of St. Augustine, Ramsgate.

The late A. W. Pugin, Architect, 1842.

the south transept is divided from the rest of the church by a richly-carved oak screen, and forms the 'Pugin Chantry Chapel.' The annexed view is taken from under the tower looking south. It shows the screen of the Pugin Chantry, the arch in front of the Lady Chapel, and a portion of the rood screen.

The whole church is lined internally with ashlar stone of a warm grey colour, the woodwork of the screen, stalls, &c., being of dark oak. The general *tone* of the interior, lighted as it is by stained glass windows (executed by Hardman, and very fair for their time), is most agreeable and wonderfully suggestive of old work. The roofs of the chancel, Lady Chapel, and transept are panelled; those of the nave and aisles are open timbered, but all are executed in oak. The altars and font are of Caen stone, richly sculptured. On them, as well as on the rood screen and choir stalls, Pugin has bestowed that careful study of detail for which, in his time, he stood unrivalled.* The exterior of the church is simple but picturesque in outline. As a composition it can scarcely be considered complete in its present state, seeing that Pugin intended to carry up the tower a storey higher than it is at present, and to roof it with a slate spire.† The walls are of cut flint, with string-courses and dressings of dark yellow stone. No student or lover of old English Architecture can examine this interesting little church without perceiving the thoughtful, earnest care with which it has been designed and executed, down to the minutest detail. It is evident that Pugin strove to invest the building with *local* traditions of style. This is shown in its general arrangement, the single transept and other peculiarities of plan being characteristic of Kent.

* A lofty wooden canopy over the font was exhibited in the Mediæval Court of the Crystal Palace in 1851 and attracted much attention.

† It seems a great pity that this feature, which would add so much to the external appearance of the church, should be left unfinished nearly twenty years after Pugin's death. Surely some of the numerous art manufacturers who profited so largely by Pugin's genius might now subscribe between them the small sum (probably about 500*l.*) required for this purpose, and thus do honour to his memory by completing his favourite work.

Close to the west end of St. Augustine's Church is Pugin's house, externally a very simple and unpretending brick building with a square embattled tower of no great height, a steep roof, and mullioned windows. The internal plan is one which no doubt was convenient and pleasing to Pugin himself, but which would hardly meet the modern requirements of an ordinary home. The principal entrance (from a paved courtyard at the back of the house) opens at once on a hall which is carried up to the entire height of the building. Two sides of this hall are occupied by a staircase ; the other two, wooden galleries are bracketed out, and give access to the bedrooms above. This is a picturesque arrangement, but open to objection, inasmuch as it would appear impossible for inmates to pass from one reception room to another, or to reach the rooms above, without coming within sight of the entrance door. The drawing rooms (on the right of the hall) are fitted with carved stone mantel-pieces and panelled ceilings of mahogany—a wood which Pugin seems to have liked very much—the centre of each panel being painted with some conventional ornament.

The dining room, which is opposite the entrance doorway, is a well proportioned apartment, depending chiefly on panelled work for its decoration. Here may be seen some of the quaint furniture which Pugin so cleverly and readily designed. The walls are papered with the armorial bearings of the Pugin family—a black martlet with the motto ' *En avant.*' The windows throughout the house are fitted with casements, the modern *sash* being among the owner's peculiar aversions. Plate glass was permitted in those windows which command a sea view, but small ' quarried ' glazing is chiefly adopted for the others.*

Attached to the house is a small but well-proportioned private chapel, the interior of which is very effective in design.

---

* In Scarisbrick Hall, when Pugin was employed as architect, the leadwork of the windows in front of the house was *gilded*. The effect, as may be supposed, is very rich and beautiful.

The list of Pugin's works is a long one, including churches, besides those already mentioned, at Derby, Kenilworth, Cambridge, Stockton-on-Tees, Newcastle-on-Tyne, Preston, Rugby, Northampton, Pontefract, Nottingham, Woolwich, and a host of other places. Bilton Grange, erected for Captain W. Hibbert, Warwick; Lord Dunraven's seat at Adare, in Ireland (since remodelled by Mr. P. C. Hardwick), Scarisbrick Hall, St. John's Hospital, Alton, and the restoration at Chirk Castle, Denbighshire, may be mentioned among his works in domestic architecture. But notwithstanding the size and importance of some of these buildings, it must be confessed that in his house and the church at Ramsgate one recognises more thorough and genuine examples of Pugin's genius and strongly marked predilections for Mediæval architecture than elsewhere. With one great national undertaking, indeed, his name has been intimately associated. But this marks so important a stage in the history of the Gothic Revival, that it must be reserved for another chapter.

CHAPTER X.

THE development of modern art in most countries may be generally assigned to one and sometimes in succession to each of three causes : individual genius, public sentiment, and State patronage. We have seen that the two first were not wanting in England to promote the cause of Gothic architecture. An event was now at hand which helped to secure for it the last, and in its day the most important impetus. The incidents which attended the selection of Mr. Charles Barry's design for the Houses of Parliament are among the most interesting in the history of the Revival. His earliest efforts in the direction of Mediæval design were creditable for their time, but by no means extraordinary. As a student he had given little or no attention to the style. In his first Continental tour he had turned aside from the magnificent west front of Rouen Cathedral to sketch a modern classic church. In Paris, Notre-Dame and the Sainte Chapelle had but small attractions for him. But the Italian palaces filled him with genuine admiration and afforded models for his imitation in many a London club-house and private English mansion, whose merits having been fully acknowledged and described elsewhere it will be unnecessary to mention in these pages, further than by remarking that they contributed for some years, and indeed still tend, to divide public taste on the question of national style—at least so far as the modern buildings of this metropolis are concerned.

It is curious, however, that the first works of any importance entrusted to him were two churches—one at Prestwich and the other at Campfield, Manchester. They were designed in a style which no doubt at the time (1822) passed for very satisfactory Gothic, though in after life he looked back with no small amusement at these early efforts. St. Peter's Church, Brighton—the commission for which he gained in competition soon after—was a more important building, and though far from realising the genuine spirit of Mediæval architecture was probably not surpassed by any contemporary architect—Rickman alone excepted. In 1826 he was employed by the Rev. D. Wilson, Rector of Islington,* to design three churches: one at Holloway, another at Ball's Pond, and another in Cloudesley Square. It would be fruitless to enter upon any description of these and many other similar structures which, under the general name of Gothic, were erected in England about this time. In spite of the large sums which in many instances were spent on their execution, it can scarcely be denied that they fail to realise in any important degree even the general forms—still less the decorative details of ancient work. The cause of this deficiency must not be ascribed to mere ignorance. It is true that up to this time the buildings of the Middle Ages had been but imperfectly studied. But a man of Barry's zeal and artistic ability might soon have overcome this obstacle. The venerable parish churches of England were open to his inspection, and would have served him for models as excellent in their way as the palaces of Florence and of Venice, which, by the aid of his dexterous pencil, as with a magic wand, he had summoned to Pall Mall. The truth is he did not imitate the ancient types of Ecclesiastical Architecture, partly because he had not studied them, but chiefly because he did not care to do so. In the interesting Life of Sir Charles which has recently been published, his opinions on this point are clearly and definitely expressed :—

He himself felt strongly that the forms of Mediæval art, beautiful as they are, do not always adapt themselves thoroughly to the needs of a service which is

* Afterwards Bishop of Calcutta.

essentially one of ' Common Prayer.' Deep chancels, high rood screens, and (in less degree) pillared aisles, seemed to him to belong to the worship and institutions of the past rather than the present. Time-honoured as they were, he would have in some degree put them aside, and accepting Gothic as the style for Church Architecture he would have preferred those forms of it which secured uninterrupted space, and gave a perfect sense of unity in the congregation, even at the cost of sacrificing features beautiful in themselves, and perhaps of interfering with the ' dim religious light ' of impressiveness and solemnity.

It is probable that these views would find but little favour among professional admirers of Gothic at the present day, and by some indeed they would be accounted as flat heresy. But when Barry was a young man ecclesiastical sentiment was at a discount. Those extreme forms of ceremonial in public worship, which, whether rightly or wrongly, are described as a revival of ancient Anglican usage, were almost unknown and were certainly unadopted. Forty years ago a cross on the gable of a church or on the back of a prayer-book would have seemed like rank popery in the eyes of many honest folks who have lived to see the English Communion Service gradually assimilated to the Roman Mass.

But if Barry had little sympathy with the revival of Church Architecture modelled on Mediæval plans, he certainly deserves credit for the attention which, in spite of his Italian proclivities, he gave to the study of domestic Gothic. His design for King Edward VI.'s School at Birmingham exhibits a remarkable advance in the knowledge of that late development of the style which is generally described as 'Perpendicular' work, and it may safely be assumed that at the time the building was commenced (1833) no contemporary architect could have achieved a more satisfactory result. Those who examine the *façade* towards High Street (and the conditions of the site were such as to admit only of a street front) cannot fail to recognise many peculiarities of detail which were afterwards reproduced in the Houses of Parliament. And this fact may be especially recommended to the attention of critics who have ventured to question the authorship of the latter design with which his name has been chiefly associated.

It was on the night of October 16, 1834, that Mr. Barry, as we are informed by his biographer, was returning to London on the Brighton coach, when a red glare of light illumining the horizon warned him of that memorable fire which caused the destruction of the old Palace of Westminster, and was the indirect means of raising him to fame and fortune. The history of the professional competition in which this able and industrious architect won the great prize of his life, has been in one form or another frequently narrated, and is probably familiar to all who take an interest in the fact itself or in the various circumstances by which it is surrounded. That the rapidly developing taste for ancient English architecture had by this time assumed a national and definite character may be assumed from the fact that a Parliamentary Committee, in drawing up the terms of the competition, stipulated that the design for the new buildings should be either Gothic or Elizabethan. This condition, indeed, left a wide range of choice open to the competitors. Pointed architecture had passed through many distinct phases of style from the time of the Plantagenets to that of the Tudor line. There was the Early English type, with its dignified simplicity of outline, its noble conventionalism of sculptured forms, its stout, bold buttresses, and pure arch contour. There was the Fourteenth Century type, with its maturer development of decorative features, its foliated window tracery, its enriched mouldings, its elaborate niches and canopies. And, thirdly, there was the Perpendicular type which, deficient in many of the characteristic graces of its predecessors, debased in general form, vulgarised in ornamental detail, and degenerate in constructive principles, still retained enough of the old traditional element of design to justify its title to nationality. But whatever may have been the standard of taste in days when King's College Chapel was regarded as the crowning glory of Gothic, it requires no great discernment on the part of modern critics to perceive both in the Tudor and in the Elizabethan styles abundant evidences of a fallen art. Roman Doric is not more essentially inferior to Greek Doric : the age of Valerian does not exhibit a greater decline from the age of Augustus : the school of Carlo Dolce is not further removed from the School of Mantegna : than English architecture in the days of the last Henry ranks below that in the reign of the first Edward.

It is perhaps not surprising that in the earliest period of the Revival, professional designers should have sought their inspiration among those examples of Pointed work which were—so to speak—freshest from the hands of the mason, and therefore more complete and more numerous than earlier specimens. To take up the thread of traditional art where it had been dropped was, if not the wisest, at least the most obvious and the most natural course. But the clue, if it was to lead to excellence, could only lead in one direction, and that was backwards. Unfortunately this fact was not at first perceived. With a few rare exceptions, all architects interested in the Revival devoted themselves to the study of Perpendicular work, and there their devotion ended. The designs of Reginald Bray and John Hylmer were preferred to those of Bertram of Salisbury and Eversolt of St. Albans. Bath Abbey and St. George's Chapel, Windsor, were considered finer things in their way than Lincoln Cathedral or the choir of Canterbury.

It was while public taste in England remained under such delusions as these that the competition for the New Houses of Parliament was announced. Into that competition ninety-seven candidates entered. The total number of drawings prepared was fourteen hundred. The Committee of the House of Lords had previously decided that not more than five designs, and not less than three, should be submitted to the King for approval. The author of the first in order of merit was to receive an award of 1,500*l.*, and unless there were grave reasons to the contrary, was to be appointed architect to the new buildings. The rest were to be recompensed by a prize of 500*l.* each. The

Commissioners selected four designs : first, that of Mr. Charles Barry ; second, that of Mr. John Chessel Buckler ; third, that of Mr. David Hamilton (of Glasgow); and, fourth, that of Mr. E. Kempthorne. That this decision was followed by some dissatisfaction among the out-siders may be, as a matter of course, assumed. The time and labour required for the preparation of the drawings were considerable, and could scarcely have been spent to no purpose without creating a strong disposition to chagrin among the unsuccessful. But, on the whole, a good feeling prevailed. A meeting of the competitors was held at the ' Thatched House Tavern,' and a resolution was passed declaring that, in the opinion of those present, the competition had been ' alike honourable and beneficial to the architects of this country,' and expressing a belief that the Commissioners had made their selection with ' ability, judgment, and impartiality.' The resolution concluded by recommending a public exhibition of all the designs submitted.

In course of time this suggestion was carried out, and was attended by a very good result. Hundreds of amateurs, who had had no patience to wade through antiquarian discourses on the origin of the Pointed arch, and to weigh the merits of Mediæval art, saw for the first time, side by side, the designs of men who had made that art, with more or less success, their study. They heard them compared, criticised, and in turn lauded or condemned. And the criticism of that day was certainly more in advance of professional skill than is the criticism of the present day. We have indeed more accomplished designers now than then, but public opinion on such subjects is neither so readily offered nor comparatively so valuable as it once was.

To those who had thought seriously on the terms of the competition, the words ' Gothic or Elizabethan ' seemed somewhat unsatisfactory. Britton, in a paper read before the Institute of British Architects (then just established), protested against them as undefined. ' Elizabethan,' he urged, might mean anything from Tudor to Renaissance. His objections, as it turned out, were not without foundation. Some of the competitors actually submitted Italian designs. The majority of them, however, complied with the spirit as well as the letter of their instructions, and prepared designs which were at least in aim either Gothic or Elizabethan.

As might have been anticipated, the knowledge of either style displayed was in many cases not profound. One candidate proposed as the central feature of his design an enormous octagonal dome, apparently magnified from one of the turrets of Henry VII.'s Chapel, which was to be supported by flying buttresses of gigantic size. Another described his invention as ' an example of the pure English of Edward III.'s time.' In reality it was an exaggerated medley of features, almost exclusively ecclesiastical in character, and borrowed from the cathedrals of England. The west front of York Minster was (after decapitation) introduced in the group. Exeter, Lincoln, and Canterbury, were laid under contribution. St. Stephen's Chapel was not only preserved, but reproduced in duplicate at the opposite angle of Westminster Hall, in order to give uniformity to the composition.

A third design was likened at the time to a union workhouse, and was only redeemed from the charge of being commonplace by bringing Westminster Abbey into the perspective view, and raising over its *crux* a central spire, to which the chief objection was that it could never have been erected. A fourth was described as a sort of Brobdignag church, with a transept in the centre, and octagonal towers at the extremities. But perhaps the most original idea was that of a gentleman who had devised as the leading feature in his design a colossal circular tower, on which ' statues of monarchs and patriots, flying buttresses, pinnacles, and pierced windows, raise up in regular gradations a vast and ornamental object, distinguishable from all parts of the metropolis, about the size of the Castel St. Angelo in Rome.'

Extravagances of this kind were, it is needless to say, avoided by those who took the foremost rank in the award. The especial merit of Buckler's design—second only to that of Barry in the opinion of the judges—was that it avoided the multiplication of detail and of those features which are more rightly employed in ecclesiastical than in domestic or palatial types of Gothic. He adopted what was then familiarly known as a pyramidal line for the general effect of his composition, the central feature of which was a lofty tower with angle turrets. In this design, St. Stephen's Chapel, restored, formed a conspicuous object. The plan in general arrangement was considered picturesque, and, so far as the relative position of the two Houses was concerned, convenient. Mr. Buckler obtained credit for the purity of his ornamental details, which, if they exhibited no striking originality of design, were at least well selected. Among the outsiders whose plans found favour may be mentioned Rhind, who had apparently borrowed his details from the architecture of Hatfield; and Salvin, whose towers were suggestive of Heriot's Hospital. Opinions were divided as to what proportion of the ancient buildings should be preserved. Many of the competitors desired to retain St. Stephen's Chapel. Cottingham exhibited a model for its restoration. Wyatt and Goodridge were for lengthening it. Some considered that the Painted Chamber might still be kept intact; while a few still more conservative admirers of Mediæval art proposed that every vestige of the old Palace which was not absolutely in a ruinous state should be repaired and incorporated with the new structure.

Barry, as a practical man, took a middle course. He had found St. Stephen's Chapel not exactly in ruins, but in such a condition that its preservation was impossible, while to restore it with anything like accuracy would have been a hazardous undertaking. Such, at least, was the opinion of Sir R. Smirke, of Wilkins, of Laing, and other contemporary architects of repute, who were consulted on the subject. From this opinion Cottingham and Savage differed. But those gentlemen had been competitors, and no doubt felt pledged to the views which, in that capacity, they had maintained. The idea of restoring the chapel was abandoned, but the crypt, part of which had been degraded to the uses of a scullery, was preserved.*

The case of Westminster Hall was different. Any scheme which had failed to provide for the retention of this venerable structure—intimately associated as it is with many an incident in our national history—would have been at once rejected, not only by the Government, but by public opinion. Even the common rabble of the town, when they assembled on the banks of the Thames to watch the progress of the fire which destroyed the old buildings, had raised a cry of genuine dismay when for a short while the roof of the Hall appeared in danger. To save it from the flames was perhaps an easier task than to settle how to deal with it afterwards. Left in its original condition, it would have been an interesting relic of antiquity, but it would have been useless and even inconvenient in its relation to the plan of the new buildings. On the other hand, to disturb its integrity for the sake of modern improvements and mere notions of convenience seemed little short of sacrilege. It was reserved for Barry's ingenuity to devise a plan which satisfied—as far as they could be reasonably satisfied—these opposite considerations of utility and antiquarian conservatism.

He determined to make Westminster Hall the main public entrance to the New Palace, and for this purpose he recommended ' that a handsome porch with a flight of steps should be added to the south end of the Hall, from which the approach should be continued' through St. Stephen's Hall (proposed to be erected on the site of St. Stephen's Chapel) into a central lobby of great size, and lighted by an octagonal lantern midway between the two Houses, and in immediate connection with the public lobbies attached to each, and with the Committee Rooms. The practical effect of this arrangement was to add some twenty or thirty feet to the length of the Hall. It has been argued that this interfered

* The restoration of this interesting relic of Mediæval art was subsequently carried out by Mr. E. M. Barry, R.A., the well-known architect, and a son of Sir Charles.

with the proportions of the interior as originally designed, and it may have been on that ground that Barry at one time proposed to raise to a greater height the roof itself. This suggestion was, however, never carried out, and indeed the present aspect of the Hall is such as may well satisfy the most fastidious critic, when it is remembered with what practical difficulties and conflicting opinions the scheme for its alteration was beset.

The site itself was by no means an easy one to deal with, and many a plea might have been raised on artistic grounds for erecting the New Palace in a more elevated and commanding site in the metropolis. But historical associations presented an overwhelming argument in favour of that part of Westminster which was in the immediate neighbourhood of the great Hall and the Abbey, and it was an argument which happily prevailed. If anything could reconcile to this decision those who considered mere architectural effect of paramount importance, it was the opportunity given for a noble river front to the New Palace. Barry at once saw the necessity of securing this feature in his design. He recommended that the building should be kept close to the Thames, and only separated from it by a terrace, the line of which was to be as nearly as possible at right angles to Westminster Bridge. Such a *façade*, it was true, would not be exactly parallel to Westminster Hall, and this must affect the position of the grand corridor which led from the south end of the Hall to the central vestibule. But by making the latter octagonal in plan, and by altering the line of embankment, this discrepancy was reduced to a minimum, and in execution is scarcely noticeable.* The result was an elevation which, if we accept the aim of its design, is eminently successful in effect. Many a critic, in pointing out the faults of the building as a whole, has admitted the excellence of its river front.

* A reference to the plan of the new Houses of Parliament, published in the interesting Life of Sir Charles Barry by his son, Dr. Barry, will best explain the ingenuity of this arrangement.

Before the building was actually begun, Barry had to encounter two distinct kinds of opposition to his scheme. There were those who objected on various grounds to the employment of Gothic altogether. There were those who objected on antiquarian grounds to the particular type of Gothic which he selected, and to his mode of dealing with the old buildings. The best answer which could be given to the latter class of opponents was simply this, that whatever defects might be perceived, whether in the nature of his scheme or the quality of his art, no one, in an open competition, had on the whole surpassed him. It was easy to talk of restoring St. Stephen's Chapel and the Painted Chamber, of leaving Westminster Hall absolutely intact and of preserving every relic of the ancient palace. The question really came to be how far these proposals were compatible with the main object in view, viz. the design of the New Houses of Parliament, in which convenience of plan was a first necessity. That there might have been found among the competitors men whose knowledge of Gothic detail was more advanced than his own is probable. But no one had so successfully united that knowledge with the practical requirements of the case.

The arguments which were brought to bear against the adoption of Gothic altogether as the style of the new buildings seemed plausible to the ignorant or prejudiced, but were to a great extent founded in error, and were certainly ill-timed. Protests of such a kind should have been made—not after the result of the competition, but when its conditions were first announced. That which attracted most notice at the time was embodied in letters addressed by Mr. W. R. Hamilton to the Earl of Elgin in 1836–37. Hamilton was a scholar and a *dilettante*, but his literary tastes and his antiquarian researches had been turned in one direction only. He saw in classic art an expression of intellectual refinement and of ideal beauty, compared with which the science and the exuberant fancy of the Mediæval architect and sculptor were as things of nought. He regarded the temples of Greece and Rome as the noblest achievements of human invention. He associated the monuments of the Middle Ages with ideas of gloom, of superstition and barbarous extravagance. Whole volumes might be written to prove that he was right and to prove that he was wrong. To the end of time men will probably be divided in opinion as to whether the Parthenon or Chartres Cathedral represents the more exalted phase of architectural taste, or gratifies the purer sense of mental pleasure. The real question at issue was whether Gothic should or should not be adopted for the New Houses of Parliament. Hamilton brought the whole force of his scholarship and literary ability to prove that the adoption of Gothic would be a mistake. His letters developed into essays, which would have been more interesting if they had been less prolix in matter and less diffuse in style. He quoted Pindar, he quoted Cicero, he quoted Aristotle, he quoted Plutarch, he quoted Plato. He quoted Bacon, Hume, Winckelman, Hallam, Coleridge, Fresnoy, and Sir James Mackintosh. That the sentiments of each and all of these eminent authors, in their several ways, and at different periods of the world's history, have been a source of pleasure or instruction to mankind no one will deny, but that their opinions could have much influence in determining the style of the New Palace of Westminster may be doubted.

Mr. Hamilton's arguments, like those of many an able pleader, occasionally proved too much. Thus, in his first letter he says:

It is notorious to all who have attended to the history of Architecture, that every age and every country have progressively formed to themselves each its own peculiar style and character, and, excluding from the question those cases where there may have been a self-evident decline from good to bad, from the beautiful to the deformed, from simplicity to meretricious ornament, from cultivated to barbarous periods, it seems right that each age and each country ought to hold fast to that style which, whether foreign or indigenous, circumstances and improved knowledge have introduced into general practice.

It is difficult to see how the force of this reasoning can be admitted without coming to a conclusion that Italian architecture ought never to have been introduced into this country at all; that Englishmen ought to have held fast to their Tudor, which, in the fifteenth century, was a thoroughly national style, and certainly superior to that by which it was at first replaced.

Mr. Hamilton pointed out with truth that, at the time he wrote, the larger portion of public buildings erected in Great Britain during the past half century had been of a classic character; but when he went on to say that this was due to 'the good sense of the British public,' which 'could not be borne down by the fancies of individuals,' he must have been laughing in his sleeve. It would be curious to speculate to what depth of absurdity and degradation the condition of national art might in course of time descend in this country but for the influence of private taste and individual genius. A fair evidence of the architectural effects which have been secured by the good sense of the British public, when completely unfettered, may be noticed in Gower Street and in Russell Square.

It seems to have been assumed by Mr. Hamilton and other anti-Gothic critics of his day, that because pictorial art had made but little advance in England during the Middle Ages, the efforts of modern painters would have been incompatible with the conditions of Mediæval Architecture. If this were really so, the best hope to express would have been, not for the extinction of Gothic, but for the rise of better painters. The Padua Chapel sufficed for Giotto; the Orvieto Cathedral for Luca Signorelli; the Gothic palaces at Siena and Venice for Spinello and Tintoret. It might well have been urged that if the artists who were to be employed on the decoration of the Houses of Parliament approached the old Italian masters in excellence there would be no great reason for complaint.

The arguments which Mr. Hamilton endeavoured to base upon a quasi-religious ground, were such as could scarcely impose upon the most bigoted Puritan of his time. It is of course open to any writer to comment on the licentious vagaries and irreverent shapes of Mediæval sculpture, but when he proceeds to remark that our ancient churches and cathedrals were built to give the mass of the people a false impression of religious awe, and to instil a respect and terror for those who presided in them, he ought to remember that both charges cannot be well maintained side by side. It is impossible to inspire respect by licentiousness, or religious awe by irreverence. No one can be openly profane and pretend to piety at one and the same time. The truth is that these Mediæval folks were neither quite so bad nor quite so good as modern critics by turn would have us believe. The ecclesiastic of the Dark Ages has been frequently portrayed as an ill-favoured fanatic, with a countenance in which evil passions are scarcely masked by hypocrisy, and with a pocketful of indulgences, which he is ready to grant for the commission of any crime that is well paid for. Or he is described as an angel in sackcloth—a model of wisdom, of self-denial, of benevolence, and of purity. The knight-errant of romance is either a lawless marauder, eager for spoil and reckless of every principle of morality ; or he is a gallant gentleman, who derives his sole means of livelihood from the pleasant, but scarcely profitable, occupation of rescuing damsels in distress.

Fallacies of a like kind are promulgated by those who have endeavoured to prove on the one hand that art in the Middle Ages was wilfully turned to superstitious and even vicious purposes, and on the other that every missal painter and sculptor of saintly effigies was himself a saint.

The bigotry of the first presumption is only equalled by the folly of the second. It would be manifestly unfair to measure by a modern standard of refinement the rude expression of humour, or the coarse symbolisms of vice and its punishments, which found embodiment in Mediæval Art. Every one knows that many a joke which passed current in polite society three centuries ago, would scarcely bear repetition among modern schoolboys ; yet it by no means follows that the dames and cavaliers of Queen Elizabeth's Court were less virtuous than our modern world of fashion.

On the other hand, to presume that what may be called the religious aspect of ancient art resulted from the specially religious life of those who practised it, is a piece of sentimentalism which is founded neither in philosophy nor in fact.   If experience teaches us anything on such a point, it teaches us that constant familiarity with the material adjuncts of an outward form of faith is likely to beget, not an increase, but rather a diminution of reverence for such objects.   It is probable that, except in a few rare instances, the monks who sat down to illuminate a breviary, and the sculptors who were engaged in the carving of a reredos, regarded their work with the interest of skilful craftsmen rather than with the enthusiasm of earnest devotees.   In modern days we have unconsciously drawn a distinction between religious art and popular art.   In the Middle Ages they were thoroughly blended, so that while the incidents of sacred history frequently found illustration in the decorative features of domestic architecture, the details of carved work in many a church and cathedral exhibit a mere expression of humour, and humour of not always the most elevated kind.

A considerable portion of Mr. Hamilton's letters is occupied by the utterance of sentiments in the truth of which the world has been long agreed.   That Greek Architecture is grand and simple in its general character ; that the invention of printing opened the mind of man ; that we have not yet succeeded in rivalling the sculpture of Phidias ; that genius may be occasionally led astray by public taste ; and that the principles of good art, when more understood, will present a more enlightened standard, are as true as that Shakespeare was a great poet, or that gunpowder was unknown to the ancient Britons.   But the assertion of such abstract propositions, even expressed as they were in unexceptionable English, and amplified by endless illustrations from the classics, did not throw much new light on the question as to what style of design was best suited for the Houses of Parliament.   Stripped of rhetoric, of dissertations on the age of Pericles, and prejudiced denunciations of Mediævalism, Mr. Hamilton's arguments merely went to prove this : that he had an artistic taste of his own, and that the Government as well as the nation were bound to follow it. On the score of convenience he adduced scarcely a single reason for the rejection of Gothic which might not have been applied with equal force to the rejection of Greek architecture, presuming that the latter had been adopted in all the primitive severity of its present type.* The fact is that neither style could be adopted without considerable departure from ancient precedent, and, if both must undergo the modification necessary for modern requirements, it was surely more reasonable to modify and accept a style, once at least eminently national in its characteristics, than to revert to one which belonged neither to the age nor to the country for which it was proposed.

It was one of Hamilton's arguments that the revival of Gothic for the New Houses of Parliament would confound time and usages. On this point Colonel Jackson, who published a pamphlet in reply, very sensibly expressed himself :

I think time is less confounded by constructing an edifice in a style of nearly similar date with the institution of the assembly for whose purpose it is intended, than by building it in any other style. At all events, it must be allowed that, adapting to a British House of Parliament, under the Christian reign of William IV., the style of architecture adopted in heathen Greece in the time of Pericles, some twenty-three centuries before, is a much greater confounding of time than any which can result from the employment of Gothic. As to usages that will be confounded by a Gothic House of Parliament, I am not aware that any precise usage has ever obtained in these matters : they have generally depended upon the fashion of the times or the taste of the reigning prince. If, however, anything like constancy has ever prevailed in this country, it has unquestionably been in favour of Gothic Architecture.

It would be fruitless to review the countless arguments which were put forward, on both sides of this much-vexed question, in pamphlets, maga-

---

* That this was what Mr. Hamilton really desired is apparent from his second letter. The adoption of Italian Architecture was a compromise which he might have tolerated, but would never have approved.

zine articles, and letters to the public press, before the Houses of Parliament were actually begun.   Those arguments have been since renewed from time to time, under different circumstances, and in a variety of forms, with more or less enthusiasm.   For upwards of a quarter of century, the Battle of the Styles was carried on, and, if it has ceased at the present day to rage with its old violence, it is probably because the weapons used in that prolonged warfare have become blunted and worn out. Everything that could be said in favour or disparagement of Gothic has been said.   Mutual concessions have since been made ; old prejudices have disappeared ; misunderstandings have been cleared up ; but the event which first raised the controversy into national importance was undoubtedly the decision that Gothic should be adopted for the Palace of Westminster.

The first stone of the new building (after the river-wall and foundation had been completed) was laid, without ceremony, on April 27, 1840.*   The practical and constructive difficulties which Barry had to encounter at the outset of his work were great, but they sank into insignificance compared with the annoyances to which, in his professional capacity, he was subjected from a variety of causes—some no doubt inseparable from the external management of so great an undertaking, but others that might well have been avoided.   These, however, were in time met, and in a great measure dispelled, by the tact and ability which formed part of Barry's character, and which contributed so largely to his success.

From the original design as submitted in competition, several important alterations were made.   The Victoria Tower was reduced in the dimensions of its plan, but carried to a far greater height than had at first been intended.   The roof of the House of Lords was raised. The Central Hall—in consequence of the conditions proposed by

---

* Such is the date given in the ‘ Life of Sir Charles Barry.’ But according to the ‘ Civil Engineers’ and Architects’ Journal ’ the first stone was laid on March 5, 1839. Possibly this was for some portion of the substructure.

Dr. Reid, for a scheme of ventilation (afterwards abandoned)—was lowered. The House of Commons was again and again remodelled in the endeavour to effect a compromise between requirements based in turn upon considerations of convenience, acoustic principles, and architectural effect. The extraordinary increase which, during the progress of the building, occurred in the business of Parliamentary Committees, necessitated considerable modifications. All these facts ought to be remembered in estimating the effect of a design whose execution extended over a far longer period of time than was originally contemplated, and must have been subject to a number of internal influences, of which the public take small account, but which no architect would find it possible to disregard.

Much of the artistic criticism which was passed on Barry's design at first, and during the progress of the building, was undoubtedly just.

The strong tendency to long unbroken horizontal lines in composition, was the natural fault of an architect the bent of whose taste was confessedly in favour of the Italian School. ' Tudor details on a classic body !' Pugin is said to have exclaimed to a friend as they passed down the river in a steamboat. And unfortunately the Tudor details were needlessly multiplied. There are general principles of taste which may be safely accepted independently of the question of style, and among these is that one which requires for elaborate ornament a proportionate area of blank wall-space. Barry utterly ignored, and possibly disputed, this principle. As the eye wanders over every compartment of every front in this building, it seeks in vain for a quiet resting-place. Panels moulded and cusped—carved work in high and low relief—niches statued and canopied—pinnacles bossed and crocketed— spandrelled window-heads—battlemented parapets—fretted turrets, and enriched string-courses—succeed each other with the endless iteration of a recurring decimal. It is hardly too much to say that, if half the decorative features of this building had been omitted, its general effect would have been enhanced in a twofold degree. One of the peculiar failings exhibited by Gothic architects of the day seems to have been the incapacity to regulate the character of design by the scale on which it was to be applied. The extraordinary size of the Victoria Tower required in its general outline and surface decoration a very different treatment from that of the building which lay at its base. In this case, Barry contented himself with magnifying small features into large ones. The result has proved to be that while the tower individually loses in apparent grandeur by reason of its elaborated detail, when seen in connection with the main body of the building, it has the unfortunate effect of dwarfing the proportions of the latter by reason of its own overwhelming bulk.

In spite of these and other defects which critics have not failed to point out (without considering the long lapse of time that ensued between the first conception of Barry's design and the completion of his work), it must be admitted that, taken as a whole, the Palace of Westminster was eminently creditable to its author, and probably equal, if not superior, to any structure which might have been devised and carried out in the same style and under similar conditions by the most skilful of his competitors. Thirty years have made a vast difference in the professional study of Mediæval Architecture, and in public appreciation of its merits. Qualities of design which were once considered essential to artistic grace are now ignored and even condemned, while the so-called faults which the last generation of architects strove to avoid have risen to the level of confessed excellence.

It is easy to say that if these Houses of Parliament had been begun in 1865 instead of 1835, a nobler type of Gothic would have been adopted in the design. Who knows how far the taste for Mediæval Art might have been developed at all but for this timely patronage of the State? Is it not rather true that the decision of the Government as to the style of the new buildings gave an impulse to the Revival which could have been created in no other way—an impulse that has kept this country advanced before others in the earnestness with which ancient types of national Architecture are studied and imitated by professional men ? *

In the department of Art Manufacture it would be impossible to overrate the influence brought to bear upon decorative sculpture, upon ceramic decoration, ornamental metal-work, and glass staining, by the encouragement given to those arts during the progress of the works at Westminster.　In the design of such details Pugin's aid was, at the time, invaluable.　It was frankly sought and freely rendered. Hardman's painted windows and brass fittings, Minton's encaustic tiles, and Crace's mural decoration, bear evidence of his skill and industry.† They may be rivalled and surpassed in design and execution at the present day ; but to Pugin, and to the architect who had the good sense to secure his services, we shall ever be indebted for the rapid advance made in these several departments of Art during the first half of the present century.

Nor must we overlook the important step gained in connection with this work by the appointment of a Fine Arts Commission in 1841. To assert that the statues and paintings which now decorate the Houses of Parliament are all that could be desired in point of style or ex- ecution, would be very far from the truth.　But before they were undertaken, no public encouragement worth mentioning had for some time past been given either to painters or sculptors.　They were now associated in the completion of a grand national work.　The Pictorial Art Competition, and display of prize cartoons in Westminster Hall, had the effect of bringing under public notice the talents of many an artist who might otherwise have long remained in obscurity.　The technical details of fresco painting, which for centuries had been for-

* In the literature of the Gothic Revival we are, however, far behind the French.　No work has been produced in England which can compare, in amount of research and use- fulness, with M. Viollet le Duc's admirable ' Dictionnaire Raisonnée.'

† For the execution of the decorative sculpture, Mr. Thomas (acting of course under the direction of Sir Charles Barry) was alone responsible, and probably at the time no one was better qualified to undertake it.

gotten in this country, received scientific attention ; and if the issue has not been altogether satisfactory, it is from no want of pains or extent of research.

If it be argued that these results could have been equally attained by the adoption of any other style of architecture for the Houses of Parliament, the answer is that no other style would have served so well to preserve—at least in aim—the unities of a *School* of Art. Before the commencement of this work, many public buildings were erected in the pseudo-Greek and revived Italian fashion of the day, but the accessories with which they were invested had by long sufferance been allowed to remain deficient in the character and consonance of design.

The Classic Renaissance, even in its palmy days, had failed to inspire that sort of uniformity which should mark the return to a former style of art. Fashionable portrait-painters who in the seventeenth century had depicted their royal patron as a Roman warrior in a full-bottomed wig, were not more inconsistent than many a contemporary architect, who suffered the most incongruous modernisms to intrude in the interior and fittings of a palace which was professedly classic in taste.

In the Houses of Parliament it was Barry's endeavour to maintain, down to the minutest article of furniture, the proprieties of that style which the voice of the nation had selected for his design. How carefully and thoroughly he did this, the work itself testifies in every detail. It may not belong to the highest class of art. But, of its kind, it is genuine, well studied, and complete.

CHAPTER XI.

WHILE the adoption of Mediæval design for civic, and thus indirectly for domestic, buildings was encouraged by the decision of Government that the New Houses of Parliament should be Gothic, the revival of ancient Church Architecture received a fresh and no less powerful impetus from the rapidly increasing taste for ecclesiology, which had by this time begun to develop itself in England. The origin of this taste may be traced to two causes. First to the necessity of providing additional churches of some kind—a necessity which had been already recognised by the State—and, secondly, to that remarkable change which was gradually taking place in the religious convictions of English Churchmen, and which resulted in a movement known under various names at different periods of its progress, but really representing a tendency to invest the Church with higher spiritual functions, and to secure for it a more symbolical and imposing form of worship than had for many generations past been claimed or maintained.

So early as 1818 an Act of Parliament had been passed for building and promoting the building of additional churches, and a Royal Commission had been appointed for carrying the Act into execution. The Reports issued by this Commission during some twenty or thirty years after their appointment afford curious statistics as to the gradual change in architectural taste. In the tabulated statement of the first Report (1821), it was not even considered necessary to name the style of the new churches in course of erection. In later Reports this deficiency is supplied, and 'Gothic with Tower and Spire' is found alternately with 'Roman of the Tuscan Order,' or 'Grecian Doric with Cupola.' The

western and northern counties seem to have been the first to return to
the ancient type, but in London and the east of England the classic
element still predominated.   For some years York and Lancashire distanced other provinces in the number of their new churches, and for
their steady adhesion to a style of design which can only be called
' Mediæval ' because it can be called nothing else.   With a few
notable exceptions, some of which have been mentioned, these buildings were erected at small expense, and therefore were not designed
with any aim at architectural effect.   The walls were as slight as structural safety would permit.   The roofs were of low pitch and ceiled
internally.   The porches were small and meagre.   As for the chancel
—a feature now considered almost indispensable to every village church
—it was either omitted altogether or reduced to the condition of a
shallow recess, just large enough to contain the communion table.   The
great object was to secure as many sittings as possible, consistently
with the maintenance of that thoroughly modern institution, the family
pew.   And here religious zeal clashed with notions of personal comfort.
For the high-backed, luxuriously cushioned and carpeted pew occupied
of necessity a great deal of room, and, on the other hand, to sit on
uncovered wooden benches as congregations do now in half the modern
churches of London—to make, in short, no distinction between the rich
and poor assembled in common worship—would have been considered
something altogether incompatible with the requirements of a genteel
congregation.   In this dilemma it was obvious that the only expedient
by which a certain number of sittings could be obtained without
doubling the size and cost of the church was the erection of galleries,
and these were freely adopted, without the slightest reference either to
ancient precedent or to architectural effect.

The suggestions published about this time of the Incorporated
Society for Promoting the Enlargement, Building, and Repairing of
Churches and Chapels, plainly indicate the spirit in which such works
were then undertaken.   Durability and convenience were the qualities

mainly insisted on. The site was to be central, dry, and sufficiently distant from factories and noisy thoroughfares; a paved open area was to be made round the church. If vaulted underneath, the crypt was to be made available for the reception of coals or the parish fire-engine. Every care was to be taken to render chimneys safe from fire, but side by side with this excellent counsel was a suggestion that they might be *concealed in pinnacles !* The windows, it was naïvely remarked, 'ought not to resemble modern sashes; but whether Grecian or Gothic the glass should be in small panes and not costly.' The most favourable position for the 'minister' was stated to be 'near an end wall, or in a semicircular recess under a half-dome.' It was indeed stipulated that the pulpit should not intercept a view of the altar, but the *sine quâ non* was that all the seats should be placed so as to face the preacher. Pillars of cast iron were recommended for supporting the gallery of a chapel, though it was hinted that ' in large churches they *might* want grandeur.' Ornament was to be ' neat and simple,' yet '*venerable'* in character. The Society even went so far as to recommend Gothic ; but in order to satisfy another class of taste, it was added that 'the Grecian Doric is also eligible.'

Such were the structures which, under the half contemptuous name of ' Commissioners' Churches,' began to spring up in various districts throughout England in the second and third decades of the present century. Within a dozen years after the Act had been passed, one hundred and thirty-four had been completed, and fifty more were in course of erection. In Birmingham, Liverpool, Manchester, and Leeds, in Stockport, Sheffield, Leicester, Bolton, and Huddersfield, besides a host of smaller towns, may still be found examples—and, in some cases, many examples—of this phase of the Revival. They possess, as a rule, little or no merit in the way of architectural design, having been chiefly built for the sole purpose of providing as speedily and as cheaply as possible church accommodation for manufacturing districts, which of late years were rapidly increasing in population. Had the church building movement been confined to this object and to such districts, spiritual instruction of a certain kind might indeed have been secured where it was obviously necessary, but much of the zeal and interest which has since been awakened among laymen would have been lost, while Architecture as an art would have suffered to an incalculable extent.

Concurrently, however, with this public and praiseworthy endeavour to build what may at least be called houses of prayer, a strong desire began to manifest itself in this country for a return not only to the ancient type of national church, but to a more decent and attractive form of service. The tendency of religious thought in England, after combatting the scepticism of the seventeenth century, and rallying from the indolence of the Hanoverian period, had drifted almost unconsciously into that condition of doctrine which is commonly named, or as some think misnamed, 'Evangelical.'

That in their time and in their own way the followers of this school did excellent work in the Church has since been admitted by all who are not prejudiced to the extent of bigotry. But whatever may have been their claim to Evangelical functions in a spiritual sense, they certainly brought no good message to the cause of Art. The symbolism, the ceremonies, the sacred imagery, the decorative adjuncts of a material church, they regarded not only with indifference, but with pious horror. No service could be too simple, no chapel could be too plain, no priest too unsacerdotal for the exigencies of their creed. To what purpose, they asked, had the Reformers worked and suffered if we were to revive in the nineteenth century the ecclesiastical architecture, the idolatrous gewgaws, the superstitious forms and ceremonies which had prevailed in the Middle Ages? Whether a congregation of Christians assembled for public worship in a cathedral or a barn their prayers would be equally acceptable. The best form for a church, they reasoned, was surely that which was the simplest—in which all could see the preacher and hear his words. For the plan, a mere parallelogram would suffice. The chancel, with its Popish rood screen, its credence table and sedilia, was but a relic of the Dark Ages, and totally unsuited to the requirements of a Protestant community. Crosses, whether on the reredos or the gable-top, were to be avoided as objects of superstitious reverence. Ornamental carved work, decorative painting, encaustic tiles, and stained glass were foolish vanities which lead the heart astray. The very name of the altar was a scandal and a stumbling-block to the right-minded.

Such were some of the objections raised against a revival of Ancient Church Architecture by those who conceived that they recognised in it a source of immediate danger to the Reformed faith. But there were others whose arguments took a more practical form. In their opinion, a refined type of structure and ecclesiastical decoration was to be avoided, not so much because it might be spiritually dangerous, but because it was decidedly expensive. For the cost of one stone church with a groined roof, or even an open timbered roof, two might be built in brick with plaster ceilings; and who could dare to say that worship in the plainer building would be less devout or sincere than that which was offered in the other?

Apologists were not wanting for this economical scheme of church extension—a scheme which combined in its purpose the distinct but not opposed virtues of benevolence and frugality, and which thus awakened the consciences while it guarded the pockets of the faithful. A notable little book was published for the express purpose of showing for what small sums of money some modern churches had, and others might be, built. The designs were indeed not of that order of taste which would have commended itself to the Wykehams and the Waynfletes of past ages, or to the Streets and Butterfields of our own day. But, on the other hand, the most jealous critic would have frankly pronounced them free from any semblance of superstitious symbolism—from those artistic attractions in which one section at least of the religious public saw at that time a pitfall and a snare. They were, in short, very Protestant, and what was then equally important, they were very cheap. The ingenious author took a pride in carrying his suggestions into matters of detail. He narrated how in one church a neat portable font had been purchased for the sum of 14*s.* This did not indeed include the price of a pedestal, but when required for use it might be placed on the communion table, in which position he (a clergyman in the Church of England) recommended that it might be used for the service of baptism. Again it was sheer extravagance to employ gold or silver for the sacramental plate, when a perfectly serviceable chalice, salver, and flagon (of Britannia metal) could be bought in Sheffield for 3*l.* 19*s.*

The economy thus suggested was, no doubt, a well-purposed economy. Money saved in such a manner might have been applied to many excellent purposes, and among others to that of parochial relief. But it is impossible to contemplate the intention without calling to mind another instance of benevolent thrift, proposed and authoritatively rebuked in the earliest history of Christianity—when, to do honour to her Master, the woman of Bethany broke her box of precious ointment, and the people murmured at its cost.

There is a sanguine maxim in physics, as in every-day philosophy, that when things are at their worst we may hope for amendment. To what contemptible level the utilitarian spirit which prevailed some forty years ago might have dragged the Church of England it is difficult to say, if a strong and steady influence had not been exercised in an opposite direction. English antiquarians, as we have seen, had laboured to maintain the traditions of Mediæval Art at a time when popular taste had declared for an exotic style of Architecture. The time had now come when that taste was on the wane. The most important public building yet raised in modern England was being erected, at the suggestion of Government, after a Gothic fashion, at least in details. The revival of a still earlier style of design for our churches was due to the ecclesiological interest and researches which were the result of a reaction from previous apathy and ignorant prejudice.

Just as the decision of the Synod of Dort had, in the seventeenth century, indirectly helped to encourage Arminian doctrines under the Stuarts, so the intolerant Puritanism that prevailed in this country half a century ago by degrees engendered an ecclesiastical sentiment, the character of which was half artistic and half doctrinal.

Of course there was a large body of ' outsiders ' to whom points of taste and points of doctrine were matters of equal indifference. Against them the chief charge which could be brought—and it is a sufficiently grave one—was this : that they had allowed church fabrics to fall into decay, and church services to lapse into slovenliness. The modern generation, with its trim village churches carefully repaired, decently appointed, and bedecked with flowers on festivals ; or its town churches, rich in marble, in tapestries and decorative painting, with a daily service all the year round, and a full choir every Sunday—the orthodox modern church-building generation can form but little notion of the carelessness, the irreverence and ignorance which prevailed in regard to matters ecclesiastical half a century ago. Children were allowed to grow up utterly uninformed as to the nature and significance of the English Liturgy and the Sacraments. Baptism was a mere ceremony frequently performed—in polite life—under the parental roof. Confirmation was in most cases dispensed with altogether. Many an undergraduate learnt for the first time at his University the difference between Lent and Advent. The observance of Saints' Days was confined to the denizens of the Cathedral close and to a few fanatics beyond it.

In country districts a bad road or a rainy day sufficed to keep half the congregation away, even from Sunday services. Of those who attended, two-thirds left the responses to the parish clerk. The rest carefully repeated the Exhortation and Absolution after the clergyman. Cracked fiddles and grunting violoncellos frequently supplied the place of the church organ. The village choir—of male and female performers—assembled in the western gallery. When they began to sing, the whole congregation faced about to look at them; but to turn towards the east during the recitation of the Creed, or to rise when the clergy entered the church, would have been considered an instance of abject superstition. No one thought of kneeling during the longer prayers. Sometimes the Litany was interrupted by thwacks from the beadle's cane, as it descended on the shoulders of parish schoolboys, who devoted themselves to clandestine amusement during that portion of the service. When the sermon began, all, except the very devout, settled themselves comfortably to sleep. The parson preached in a black gown, and not unfrequently read the Communion Service from his pulpit.

Cathedral services were celebrated with a little more decorum, but with scarcely less apathy. The buildings themselves, from being neglected altogether, were now preserved by shutting out the people. The author of 'The Broad Stone of Honour,' writing in 1824, thus speaks of their condition:

What would have been the feelings of Johnson if he had lived to see a cathedral in England closed upon Sundays, with the exception of a small part of the choir; the nave and the great body of the building converted to all intents and purposes into a museum, to afford amusement to the curious and emolument to the vergers; and an order recognised and established which decreed that they should never be entered as a place of worship and for the purpose of devotion? Yet such is the regulation which now exists in the interior of the most celebrated of our ecclesiastical structures.

It is melancholy to think that many of the abuses thus recognised and deplored should still linger in our system of Cathedral economy; that the elements of beadledom and vergerism should yet remain to be eradicated from the ecclesiastical polity of many a Chapter in the United Kingdom. But, on the other hand, a great change has since taken place in the mode and management of ordinary Church services. The study of ecclesiology, of Mediæval Architecture, of sacred music, and of rubrical usages, has by degrees transformed a conventional and sometimes scarcely reverent ceremony into a picturesque and interesting rite. Various influences combined to originate this change. It is not, however, too much to say that they would have been practically valueless but for the exertions and combined action of certain Churchmen, who, when the cause which they had at heart was still unpopular and misunderstood, strove zealously and disinterestedly to teach and maintain its fundamental principles.

For some years previous to the period which our History has now reached, there existed an ' Architectural Society ' at the University of Oxford, and an ' Antiquarian Society ' at Cambridge ; but the former only timidly and the latter only incidentally engaged in those researches which were afterwards called *ecclesiological*. In 1839 two undergraduates of Trinity College at the latter University conceived the idea of founding a Society for the Study of Church Architecture in connection with ritual arrangements. One of these young men was Mr. (afterwards the Rev.) J. M. Neale, now dead, whose name as an author is well known. The other, Mr. Benjamin Webb, is the present incumbent of St. Andrew's Church, Wells Street. They communicated their proposal to their college tutor, the Rev. T. Thorp (now Archdeacon of Bristol), who received it favourably, and after some discussion the Cambridge Camden Society was formed. Their corporate name was perhaps not very well chosen. It was intended to commemorate that of the famous antiquary, but it had already been adopted by a literary Society in London.

Mr. Thorp became the first president. Several senior members of the University gave the Society a condescending rather than zealous support ; but as time went on they cautiously withdrew their patronage, with one exception. This was Dr. Mill, the Regius Professor of Hebrew, who from first to last remained true to the cause. At first the Camden had naturally to depend on the exertions of young men—the undergraduates and B.A.'s of Cambridge. Among its earliest members were many who have been since distinguished in life. One (Mr. H. Goodwin) became Dean of Ely, and is now Bishop of Carlisle ; another (Mr. P. Freeman) is the present Archdeacon of Exeter ; a third (Mr. J. S. Howson) was in time preferred to the Deanery of Chester ; a fourth (Mr. E. Venables) obtained a stall at Lincoln.   To this list the names of F. A. Paley, a distinguished scholar, and S. N. Stokes, now an inspector of schools, must be added, and lastly, though by no means least, that of Mr. Beresford Hope, M.P., who, by his taste, his zeal, and his liberality, has perhaps done more to promote the revival of Mediæval Church Architecture than any layman in our time.

By degrees the Society systematised its efforts and fell into efficient working order.   It held general meetings : it delegated special committees.   It held periodical ' field days,' when the principal churches in the neighbourhood were visited, and every remarkable feature in their design became the subject of discussion and research.   It published a series of pamphlets, among which Neale's ' Few Words to Churchwardens' attracted much attention, and laid the foundation for a thorough reform, then sorely needed, in the care and management of ancient ecclesiastical structures.   This *brochure* went through several editions, enlarged and adapted to certain special requirements, and was followed by the ' History of Pews,' an ingenious, exhaustive, and scholarlike little treatise.   At length, in 1841, the Society founded a magazine of its own.   This was no other than the ' Ecclesiologist,' which has since taken its place in the art literature of its day, but the very name of which was at that time a novelty, and to some an enigma.

On May 9, 1840, the Committee of the Cambridge Camden Society issued their first annual Report—not without satisfaction to themselves, as may be inferred from the fact that within the space of twelve months the number of members enrolled had increased from eight to one hundred and eighty.   Four distinct methods were recommended, by which the aim of the Society might be fulfilled.   First, the restoration of mutilated architectural remains ; secondly, the description of all churches visited ; thirdly, the execution of drawings illustrative of ecclesiastical architecture; and, fourthly, the collection of brass-rubbings. Patience, zeal, and scrupulous care were insisted on as virtues indispensable to the antiquary, and while a modest 'balance in hand' testified the prudence of financial administration, promoters of the good cause were urged to contribute to its resources with a liberal hand.

A systematic plan was devised for obtaining necessary information as to the original design and modern condition of ancient churches throughout the kingdom. Blank forms were printed and issued to members of the Society, suggesting, under several heads, the details required for description. These forms were rapidly filled up and returned. In course of time they formed a stock of ecclesiological lore, which has since become most useful not only to amateurs, but to professed students of Mediæval Art.

Of course the objects which the Society kept in view and plainly announced could not long be dissociated from questions of doctrine among the clergy and congregations to whom it especially directed its appeal. In some quarters the movement in favour of church restoration and ancient rubrical usage excited distrust and even repugnance. It was the peculiar merit of Mr. Neale's pamphlets to unite, in the advice which they contained, the zeal of an enthusiastic Churchman, the knowledge of a skilled antiquary, and that cautious tact which was essential in an endeavour to enlist the sympathies of the general public, without offending prejudices rooted sometimes in religious principle and more frequently in sheer ignorance.

No one who attends church at all, and still less the churchwardens, on whom the care of the sacred building itself should devolve, can venture to dispute the proposition that it is as much the duty of a parish to preserve its church in decent condition as it is the duty of the civic authorities to keep a town hall in good order, or of a householder to maintain the stability and cleanliness of his dwelling. Yet it was a patent fact thirty years ago that many a church, both in town and country, had fallen into shameful and even dangerous neglect. This was the first point to which Mr. Neale drew urgent attention. Why, he asked, while private houses were kept clean and comfortable, should the House of God be suffered to decay or be patched up in a manner which would disgrace the poorest cottage whose inmates could afford its repair? With what conscience could the country squire leave his spruce and well-appointed mansion to attend Divine service in a building where the windows were broken or boarded over, the walls mouldy with damp, the rotting roof rudely plastered out of sight, the floor ill-paved, the ancient decorative features replaced by the meanest substitutes?

These are questions which, if needed at all in the present day, would find an obvious and ready answer. But there was a time, and within the memory of many Churchmen, when they seemed to take the general public by surprise. Many of Mr. Neale's suggestions towards a much-needed reform were of a practical kind. He detailed the best means of preserving churches from damp, of keeping them clean and well ventilated. But he also went on to describe what many of his readers must have learned from him for the first time, viz.: the plan and purpose of an ancient parish church, the uses of its several parts, the significance and symbolism of its internal arrangement. To this he added many excellent hints on the subject of restoration and refitting of naves and chancels. The subject of rubrical reform was cautiously approached, and the author endeavoured to give weight to his suggestions by appealing to the piety and good sense of intelligent laymen rather than by any direct reference to questions of doctrine.

The first number of the 'Ecclesiologist'* appeared in November 1841, and its publication was hailed as an important step in the revival of Church Architecture. Its primary object was to keep those members

---

* It is to be observed that the words 'Ecclesiology' and 'Ecclesiologist,' though now commonly adopted, were originally invented and first used by the Cambridge Camden Society.

of the Cambridge Camden Society who resided at a distance from the University regularly informed as to the Society's transactions. But it was also proposed to conduct the magazine in such a manner as to afford means of inter-communication on the subjects of church building, restorations, and antiquarian lore. Its pages were to be open to all enquirers on points of architectural taste, rubrical propriety, or disputed ecclesiastical usages. By these means it was hoped to establish a bond of union between the Cambridge Camden, and Oxford, and other Architectural Societies, and to maintain a common field of labour in which the clergy, professed architects, and zealous amateurs might work together with the advantage of mutual assistance.

The whole career of the Society at Cambridge was an eventful and exciting one. Inaugurated by a small coterie of college friends, it rapidly extended its relations in all parts of the kingdom. It received patronage and support from some of the highest dignitaries of the English Church. Beneficed clergy, University dons, distinguished laymen in every condition of life, wealthy amateurs, as well as many an architect and artist of note, were enrolled among its members. With many of these the principles of reform, whether æsthetic or ecclesiastical, which it advocated, were extremely popular. But by many outsiders they were regarded with suspicion and positive dislike. Among the latter, Mr. Close (the present Dean of Carlisle) proved a determined though not very formidable antagonist. His famous ' Fifth of November' sermon was confessedly an attack on the Society. It was preached in the parish church, Cheltenham, and was afterwards published under a preposterous title which, no doubt, the reverend author has long since wished to forget.*

Unanimity did not always prevail among members of the Society itself, especially when questions of doctrine were involved in the official censorship which its acting committee occasionally assumed. The first number of the ' Ecclesiologist' contained a somewhat severe criticism on a

* 'The Restoration of Churches is the Restoration of Popery,' &c.

church then recently erected at New Town, Cambridge. Some of the University dons took alarm at what no doubt they conceived to be a sacrifice of Protestant principles to antiquarian orthodoxy. They drew up and addressed to the committee a remonstrance, in which they expressed a fear that there existed ' in some quarters a desire to convert the Society into an engine of polemic theology instead of an instrument for promoting the study and practice of Ecclesiastical Architecture.' This remonstrance met with a conciliatory reply. The first number of the magazine was republished, and the article was remodelled in such a manner as to avoid cause of offence. As a rule the notices of new churches and of restorations published by the Society were doubly valuable, inasmuch as they not only conveyed intelligence of such works to the amateur, but by degrees established a standard of architectural taste and propriety in the planning and arrangement of churches to which even professional designers paid deference.

The restoration of the Temple Church, one of the first events chronicled in the pages of the ' Ecclesiologist,' was certainly an important one at this stage of the Revival. That pure and beautiful specimen of Early English Architecture, sharing a common fate with many other relics of mediæval art, had suffered severely from neglect and modern innovations. Its chancel was blocked out from the nave. The nave was filled with pews which rivalled a jury box in size. The walls were wainscoted. The floor was raised by an accumulation of rubbish to a height of some feet above its original level. A hideous altar screen rich in pagan symbols, and a pulpit such as Gulliver might have sat under if he had attended Divine Service in Brobdignag, had been erected. The mural decorations of the interior had been allowed to perish or were obscured by monumental tablets of execrable taste. How far the Templars themselves were individually or collectively responsible for this desecration it is impossible to say. But a day arrived when they awoke to a sense of shame and to a memory of those early architectural traditions which had once been associated with their Order. It was decided that the Temple Church should be restored. The work necessarily extended over many years, and more than one architect was employed in its supervision. It would of course be invidious to compare the earlier portion of the repairs executed with the later and more scholarlike renovations by Mr. St. Aubyn. At the present day when half the cathedrals of England are undergoing similar treatment after the advantage of a whole generation of ecclesiological study it would be surprising indeed if any obvious mistake were made in reproducing the original design. But considering that this work was begun thirty years ago, the world of art may be thankful for the general success with which it has been carried out.

It is to be noted that although the Cambridge Camden Society reckoned among its members many architects of high repute, whose advice and assistance were always available, and freely rendered, it selected its working committee entirely from amateurs. By this rule, which from first to last was strictly maintained, the infringement of professional etiquette was avoided.

The committee was for years charged with all the active functions of the Society; but as time went on and many of its members left the University, it became obvious that the local 'Camden' must either remove to London or be dissolved. Luckily the former course was adopted, and in 1846 it took the name of the 'Ecclesiological (late Cambridge Camden) Society.'* With this change its special connection with the University ceased, and it elected on its committee amateurs distinguished for their architectural and antiquarian taste, whether Cambridge men or not. Among those who took a prominent position in the Society during its second phase, and in addition to its earlier members, were Sir Stephen Glynne, Sir C. Anderson, Mr. F. H. Dickinson (late M.P.), Messrs. J. D. Chambers, J. F. France, T. Gambier Parry (whose name, as well as that of his colleague the late H. S. Le Strange, has been since most notably associated with the theory and practice of

---

* The words 'late Cambridge Camden' were afterwards dropped.

decorative art), the Rev. G. H. Hodson, the Rev. T. Helmore, and the Rev. G. Williams.

The meeting at which it was decided that the Society should change its name was held in the school-room of Dr. Chandler, the Dean of Chichester, who by this time had joined the Society, and was one of its most zealous supporters. The encouragement which this dignitary, a representative of the old school of English High Church clergy, gave to the Revival of Church Architecture deserves notice. By opening his cathedral—as no cathedral had been previously opened—to the erection of memorial windows, he created a new and valuable impulse to the art of glass-painting. The architectural restoration of the building he entrusted to the late Mr. R. C. Carpenter, whose name stands foremost among professional designers for his accurate knowledge of ancient work, his inventive power, and his refined treatment of decorative details. Through Dr. Chandler's exertions a new church (from Carpenter's design) was built at Chichester, and he afterwards became the founder of St. Andrew's, Wells Street—the first church erected under Peel's Act, and the earliest district church in London which was on completion fitted up in accordance with ancient and correct usage, as regards its chancel, stalls, &c.*

The appointment of Dr. Peacock to the Deanery of Ely, and the great works carried out in that cathedral under his authority, were coincident with the establishment and early history of the 'Cambridge Camden Society;' and although he never enrolled himself among its members, yet the interest which he felt in the Revival and the practical character of his efforts were of signal value to the cause.

After the Society had moved to London it became the custom to invite the attendance at its committee meetings of architects and decorative artists for the purpose of exhibiting and discussing their designs and productions, which by common consent were afterwards reviewed in the 'Ecclesiologist.' In the pages of that journal, and

* Further mention of this structure will be made in Chapter XIII.

during the second phase of its existence, the Society found a sufficient record of its opinions and transactions. But it also published a useful and matterful 'Handbook of English Ecclesiology,' based to some extent on a previously issued pamphlet, but now rewritten chiefly by Sir S. Glynne and Mr. Neale. In 1847 appeared the first series of ' Instrumenta Ecclesiastica,' a collection of designs for church fittings, &c., partly original and partly illustrative of old examples. This was compiled by an architect whose early ability had won for him a confidence which has since been well sustained. Among the host of modern churches which have been raised in England during the last twenty years there are none which bear the stamp of originality and thoughtful work in a more eminent degree than those designed by Mr. Butterfield.

Nearly contemporary in origin and almost identical in object with the ' Cambridge Camden ' was the ' Oxford Society for promoting the Study of Gothic Architecture,' established under the patronage of the Archbishop of Canterbury and the Bishop of the Diocese. Its first president was the President of Magdalen College. Among its earliest members were many eminent clergymen and others whose names have since become famous in the several departments of art, literature, and science.* By means of donations it soon formed the nucleus of a useful library and an interesting collection of drawings and casts from the details of mediæval remains.

If not quite so fervent as the Camden in its zeal for the revival of Gothic, the Oxford Society showed from the first a wise and discriminating judgment on the question of ' restorations,' which had the effect of tempering a policy that elsewhere might have sacrificed to considera-

---

* As, for instance, the late Dr. Buckland, afterwards Dean of Westminster, the Rev. S. J. Rigaud, afterwards Bishop of Antigua ; the Earl of Athlone, the Earl of Dunraven, Lord Courtenay, Lord Dungannon, Chevalier Bunsen, Sir Henry Ellis, Sir Francis Palgrave, and Mr. Ruskin, besides Messrs. E. Blore, B. Ferrey, J. Plowman, W. J. Underwood, A. Salvin, and other architects of note.

tions of style many a relic of past times deficient indeed in the highest qualities of architectural grace, but deserving on other grounds the interest and protection of posterity.   A paper read before the Society in 1841 by the Rev. H. G. Liddell (the present Dean of Christchurch) contains a remarkable passage bearing on this point.

Societies, no less than individuals, when much interested in one object, are apt to become either microscopic or one-sided in their views ; both these tendencies are a kind of pedantry, a fault to which all persons are liable who confine their views too much to one object, and against which it may be useful to warn this and other similar Societies.   We must remember how liable every man's mind is to be biassed and warped by systems of exclusive study, and that antiquarians are peculiarly open to this failing.   Let us therefore take warning, and not set our affections on one style only, or on absolute uniformity in each style. This is the pedantry of architecture ; this is the one-sidedness we must guard against.   Many people, who, to avoid offence, may be called not pedants but purists, seeing a fine old church disfigured, as they would say, by alterations, would begin sweeping all such disfigurements clean away, and restoring the church just as it stood when built.   But the alterations of old buildings are in great part their history, and however much you may restore, you cannot recover the original work ; and so you may be removing what is of the highest possible interest, to make room for work, correct indeed as a copy, but in itself of little or no value.

The practical value of these remarks is enhanced when we remember that they were uttered thirty years ago, when the Revival of Mediæval art had all the charm of novelty to amateurs, many of whom took up the cause with more enthusiasm than discretion, and who were inclined to make short work of any relics which did not exactly fulfil their notions of architectural propriety.

In 1841 the Oxford Society published a list of old English bridges for which pontage-charters had been granted, together with a set of printed queries as to the modern condition of these and other ancient structures.   By such means much useful information was acquired, and the Society learned by degrees in what direction their aid or interference might be made available.   In 1842 they purchased the entire collection of architectural sketches, nearly 2,000 in number, made by Rickman in England and on the Continent. They had evidently been intended to form a chronological series of examples, and though the author did not live to complete his project, the drawings, especially those which illustrated the progress of window tracery, were extremely useful for reference at a time when but few architects had troubled themselves to study with anything like accuracy the monuments of the Middle Ages. Ecclesiastical furniture and fittings received, in due course, special attention, at first from amateurs, and afterwards from architects and manufacturers. Monumental brasses were sedulously hunted up, and a collection of heel-ball rubbings was formed to record their design and inscriptions. Encaustic tiles were carefully reproduced from ancient models. Wood carvers were encouraged to imitate as closely as possible the bosses and bench-ends which, full of vigour in fancy and execution, had remained for centuries neglected in many a country church. The history and art of glass-painting were studied with enthusiasm. For practical attention to this subject, as well as to many others allied by association or æsthetic conditions with Mediæval architecture, the world of art was indebted during many years of the Revival to the labours of amateurs.

After making due allowance for the occasional over-fussiness of antiquarianism, and the excess of ecclesiastical sentiment which was inevitably imported into the movement by its connection with the Universities, there can be no doubt that the Architectural Societies at Oxford and Cambridge did immense service in popularising the Gothic cause among men of refinement and education, who were young enough to acquire a taste, and had leisure to cultivate it without seriously encroaching on the business hours or professional duties of life.

In no other way could the seeds of this taste have been scattered so widely throughout the land. Graduates who left their college rooms for curates' quarters in remote parishes, or to settle down as doctors and attorneys in many a country town, carried away with them a pleasant recollection of the friendly meetings at Hutts' and Wyatts', the cheerful field days and church explorations, the interesting papers and lively discussions by which they had profited as boys. By degrees the Mediæval *furore* began to localise itself in various parts of England. At Bristol, Exeter, York, Lichfield, and many other cathedral towns ' Diocesan' or Archæological Societies were formed for the definite purpose of encouraging the Revival, of elucidating the principles of Gothic design, and of applying them to the building and restoration of churches.

It is certain that these societies, besides doing much practical good by the direct intervention and agency of their members, became the means of eliciting and turning to advantage a great deal of literary ability. Thus Markland's well known and ably written little work on English Churches had its origin in a letter addressed to and published by the Oxford Society under the title of ' Remarks on the Sepulchral Memorials of Past and Present Times,' &c. Numerous papers descriptive of ancient churches were read both at Oxford and Cambridge, and were afterwards printed among the Transactions of each Society, and illustrated with careful woodcuts by Jewitt. In like manner some useful essays prepared for the various diocesan societies gained a popularity and exercised an influence which would have been wanting if they had appeared under the author's name alone.[*]

But results of a more immediate and practical kind soon ensued from these associations. It was while Mr. Beresford Hope was an undergraduate at Cambridge, and a member of the Cambridge Camden Society in 1840, that he determined to rescue from the ranks of the commonplace in modern ecclesiastical architecture the village church of

---

[*] Among these may be mentioned ' An Essay on Cathedral Worship,' by the Rev. H. Dudley Ryder ; ' Remarks upon Wayside Chapels,' by the Messrs. Buckler ; ' A Guide to the Architectural Antiquities in the neighbourhood of Oxford ; ' ' A Paper on Monuments,' by the Rev. John Armstrong ; and ' The Pue System,' by the Rev. W. Gillmor ; besides numerous descriptions of churches which stood in need of restoration.

Kilndown in Mid Kent, which had been commenced by his kinsman Viscount Beresford and other subscribers in the previous year. He began by instructing Mr. Salvin to design a solid stone altar copied from the (Third Pointed) altar tomb of William of Wykeham at Winchester, and raised by three steps above the floor of the church. Acting under the advice of Mr. Whewell, he ordered from the royal works at Munich stained glass for all the lancet windows. The eastern triplets were filled with the figures of the Virgin and Child, St. Peter and St. Paul. In the south aisle windows were St. Cyprian, St. Ambrose, St. Jerome, St. Augustine, and St. Gregory the Great. The north aisle was devoted to British saints, viz.: St. Alban, St. Augustine of Canterbury, St. David, the Venerable Bede, St. Edward the Confessor, and King Charles the Martyr. In quality and general treatment these windows are much superior to what is ordinarily known as Munich glass.

Mr. Hope's next work at Kilndown was to improve the fittings of the church, which had previously been of a very poor description. It had been planned without a chancel, but a space 15 feet in depth was now set apart at the east end of the nave to serve as a sanctuary. A handsome chancel screen designed by Carpenter (a young architect then rising into notice), and decorated by Willement, was erected. Stone sedilia and oak stalls were added, and a pulpit of the Beaulieu type corbelled out from the south wall of the nave formed a picturesque and at that time novel feature in the interior. A brass lectern and two coronæ designed by Butterfield were placed in the chancel.

Externally the low pitch of the roof was concealed by a stone parapet pierced with trefoils. In after years various other alterations and additions were made. A stone lych-gate gave access to the churchyard. An unsightly gallery was removed from the west end of the church, and a richly sculptured reredos was presented by Mr. Hope, in 1869. On the south side of the church the late Lord Beresford erected a handsome canopied monument * over the family vault, in which he

* In memory of his wife the Viscountess Beresford (Mr. Beresford Hope's mother).

himself was afterwards buried. The general form of this monument was borrowed by Mr. Carpenter, who designed it, from that of Archbishop Gray in York Cathedral, with certain modifications rendered necessary by the external site and double tomb.

Thus enriched and altered from time to time, Christ Church, Kilndown, without pretending to be a very complete or important specimen of modern Gothic, is interesting in the evidence which it affords of the gradual progress of the Revival during a quarter of a century. Built at a moderate cost to meet the spiritual requirements of a rural district, it will hereafter be associated with the memory of a family to whom it owes its origin and gradual improvement, and whose name has long been distinguished for their attachment to the English Church and to the interests of art.

When its foundations were first laid, Mr. Beresford Hope was a young but zealous member of a society pledged to the practical study of ecclesiology. Twenty years later he was elected its president. During that period great changes took place in the spirit of national art, and in the tendency of religious sentiment in England. Taste in architecture and painting reached a higher standard. Public worship assumed a more imposing form. And the efforts of those who first entered on the task of uniting the long dissevered elements of comeliness and devotion may well be remembered with gratitude.

CHAPTER XII.

THE year in which the foundation stone of the Parliament Houses was laid may be taken as a turning point in the History of the Revival.   In the decade of years preceding that event, viz.: from 1830 to 1840, the names of many architects had become more or less associated with the then modern efforts at Gothic design.   Of these the most notable (after Pugin, who was probably the youngest) were Shaw, Poynter and Blore, Salvin, Ferrey and Scoles. Others destined to be as intimately and in some instances more conspicuously identified with the movement, were already in practice; but it was not until after the year 1840 that they were employed in works of any importance, or indeed, that such works assumed the distinctive character of a school.   Previous to that period a great deal of Mediæval sentiment had been engendered in the public mind, but it was a sentiment easily satisfied; and though a vast amount of erudition had been brought to bear upon the examination of ancient buildings, upon the analysis of styles, and the elucidation of principles, it does not seem to have resulted in the erection of any structure which fulfilled the true conditions of Pointed Architecture without incurring the charge of direct plagiarism.

Between 1840 and 1850, however, though portions of old buildings continued to be copied, they were reproduced with more intelligence and with a better sense of adaptation.   The pioneers of the Revival began to design with greater confidence themselves, and were soon joined by others who, profiting by their labours, advanced upon their taste, and laid the foundation for a more scholarlike treatment of the style. Among the new-comers were the late R. C. Carpenter, whose career was destined to be a short but brilliant one; G. Gilbert Scott, the present R.A., whose works would need a volume to describe; M. E. Hadfield, of Sheffield, who for some years divided with Pugin the practice which fell to the share of Roman Catholic architects in this country: T. H. Wyatt, now President of the Royal Institute of British Architects, who, on his own account as well as in conjunction with his partner, Mr. D. Brandon, was largely employed in the restoration and erection of country mansions; J. L. Pearson, E. Christian, and R. Brandon, the most important of whose works were executed after 1850; J. C. Buckler, whose name has been already mentioned; and E. Sharpe, of Lancaster, who, as an antiquary and an author, as well as by his practice, aided in no small degree the progress of the Revival.

These gentlemen, with the exception of Messrs. Wyatt and D. Brandon, devoted themselves almost entirely during their professional career to the study and design of Gothic. But there were other contemporary architects who, without pledging themselves to that, or indeed, to any individual style of architecture, achieved success in that particular field. Among these was the late Philip Hardwick, R.A., whose son, Mr. P. C. Hardwick, superintended the design and execution of Lincoln's Inn Hall.

From the *bizarre* and feeble specimens of modern Gothic which were raised in England between 1840 and 1845, and while the writings of Pugin exercised their earliest influence, this building stands notably apart. The Revival of any extinct school of art must necessarily depend, in the first instance, on an imitation of the letter rather than on a realisation of the spirit of ancient work. But the new theorists had yet to learn what they should imitate. It is now generally admitted that the types of English and French Architecture which prevailed between the twelfth and fourteenth centuries are incomparably superior to those which followed them. But the early champions who fought for the Pointed Arch saw more beauty in King's College than in the Choir of Lincoln or the nave of Canterbury, and, what was worse, they could not in general distinguish between the merits and demerits of the later style.   The earlier portions of Hampton Court Palace, and Henry the Seventh's Chapel at Westminster, both belong to what is generally called the Tudor Period.   Tested by a modern standard of educated taste, neither the one nor the other seems to represent the real excellence of Gothic architecture.   But for a large public building of a secular character, there can be little doubt which of these two types is capable of being treated with the more becoming grandeur.   We are now enabled to compare their respective merits in modern work.   In an artistic point of view the selection of the style adopted for the Houses of Parliament has been long since pronounced a mistake.   Mr. Hardwick, with infinitely less scope for display, and at a comparatively small outlay, designed a building which will still bear comparison with many which have been raised a quarter of a century later, with all the advantages of additional study and maturer criticism.

In general arrangement the plan is exceedingly simple, but well considered both for effect and convenience.   It consists of two main blocks, viz.: the Great Hall, which extends from north to south, and the Library, which is at right angles to the Hall.   These are connected by an octagonal lobby, flanked by the Benchers' Room and Council Room, while the kitchen and servants' offices occupy the ground floor and basement stories.   All the external walls are faced with a fine red brick, chequered at intervals with black 'headers' distributed in ornamental patterns, as in old buildings of this character: the quoins, oriels, window dressings and arch mouldings, being of stone.   An octagonal turret at the north-west angle forms a picturesque and pretty feature in the main front, and the general proportions of the whole design are excellent.   As a rule, the constructive features of this building are honestly introduced when they are wanted; and there is a careful avoidance of those scenic and complicated shams which were unfortunately employed in many works of the same date for the mere sake of effect.   The south elevation is boldly and broadly treated.   It presents the gable end of the Great Hall, flanked by two square towers, of which that on the east side is used, on the first floor level, as a porch. Much of the effect of this front depends on the great simplicity of its masses : it is not cut up into meaningless detail, nor overloaded with a profusion of ornament. On the contrary, there is a good broad surface of wall for the eye to rest on, and therefore, where carving is introduced (as in the band of panels at the summit of each tower) its artistic value is considerably enhanced.

The character of the carved work is somewhat in advance of its day, but it lacks—especially in the treatment of animal form—the refinement, while it scarcely imitates the vigour, of old work. A notion once prevailed with the detractors, and even with some of the admirers of Gothic art, that the conception of those quaint and extravagant monsters which do duty for gurgoyles and corbels in many a Mediæval building was due to the old sculptors' utter disregard of anatomy. That such a notion is altogether erroneous, will, however, be admitted by all who have examined these grotesque examples with attention. On the contrary, many of them exhibit a strong suggestion of muscular power. It is certain that they possess a vitality of action which the modern artist finds it difficult to realise in such objects, especially when he has to work from a drawing by another hand. The old carver was his own designer, and it was his rude unsophisticated interpretation of Nature, not his wilful contempt of her pattern-book, which lent his handiwork its charm.

The interior of the Great Hall is undoubtedly very imposing, and is equal if not superior to anything of the kind which had then been attempted in modern Gothic. Its open timber roof, well framed, and of generous dimensions, is well suited, both in pitch and construction, to the proportions of the Hall itself. At the south end of the Hall there is a wooden gallery, picturesque in general arrangement, but open to criticism in points of detail, the figures with which it is decorated being somewhat large for their situation ; and the carved foliage—like all similar work of that date—being coldly though carefully executed. The Hall is panelled all round the other sides to a height of about twelve feet, the upper parts of the north end having been since decorated with the large and well-known fresco painting by Mr. G. F. Watts, R.A.

The general design of the Library roof was apparently suggested by that of Eltham Palace, but it is partially ceiled, and thus loses the character of the original. The octagonal lobby, which connects the Great Hall and Library, shares the fate of all vestibules designed on a similar plan : internally, it is too lofty for its width ; externally, the octagon, which scarcely rises above the roofs around it, is insignificant in height.

A terrace walk runs along the whole length of the building on the east side. This feature, in addition to the gardens by which it is surrounded, considerably enhances its effect ; and indeed, the situation, in itself favourable, has been altogether most judiciously and successfully treated. The entrance gate-way, lodges, &c., were all carefully designed in accordance with the character of the main block, and the isolation of the whole group from surrounding buildings is very advantageous to its appearance. Considering that Lincoln's Inn Hall was begun nearly thirty years ago, while the reproduction of Gothic was still marked by the most flagrant solecisms, and hampered by the grossest ignorance of those principles which are essential to the style, this building may fairly be ranked, for its time, as one of the best and most successful examples of the Revival.

The completion of any public structure in London or any populous town does more to educate architectural taste than whole libraries full of books and essays. But there was a large portion of provincial England which had yet to be converted by other means, and apostles willing to preach what they conceived to be a great artistic truth were not wanting.

In 1842, the Rev. W. Drake delivered a series of lectures upon Church Architecture in St. Mary's Hall, Coventry, which had considerable effect on the local encouragement of Gothic. The lecturer insisted upon the importance of adhering to ancient types of ecclesiastical art, and deprecated the erection of cheap buildings. He drew attention to the neglected state of many rural churches, gave some useful information as to their proper appointments, and added his testimony to the abuses of the pew system, which were now beginning to be generally acknowledged by all who cared to think on the subject.

In the same year Mr. A. Bartholomew published his essay ' On the Decline of Excellence in the Structure and Science of Modern English Buildings.' This did good service to the Revival by showing the close connection which existed between structural stability and architectural grace in mediæval designs. The authors of this time who wrote in defence of Gothic, had been generally content to base their recommendation of the style on considerations of taste, convenience, historical interest, or nationality. Its structural superiority from a scientific point of view seems as a rule to have escaped notice. Pugin, indeed, had in his ' Contrasts ' endeavoured to draw attention to the judicious skill displayed by the Mediæval builders as compared with those of a modern and degenerate age ; and Professor Willis, in his well-known essay on the Vaulting of the Middle Ages (published by the Royal Institute of British Architects, in 1842), had thrown considerable light on a subject concerning which in this country at least much ignorance still prevailed. But Pugin was too superficial, and Willis too deep, for the ordinary professional reader. The average architect of thirty years ago was neither an enthusiastic sentimentalist, nor a profound mathematician. He regarded the art mainly in a practical light ; and, if he was to be converted to theories respecting the advantage of one style over another, it was necessary that he should be approached in a matter-of-fact and practical manner. A handy book, or manual to assist architects in the preparation of specifications, was much needed at this time, and Bartholomew, himself a member of the profession, undertook to prepare one. This portion of his work, though since superseded by another more suited to the requirements of the present day,* was very useful in its time, but it was preceded by an essay which occupied nearly half the volume and with which the author's name will be more permanently associated. In this essay Bartholomew pointed out ' the decline of excellence in the structure and in the science of modern English buildings,' and added ' a Proposal of remedies for those defects.' Many of his comments and suggestions may seem superfluous to the modern critic, but at the time they were made, and coming as they did from a man of no narrow or bigoted views, their influence was widely felt. In a lucid and perfectly impartial manner he demonstrated the structural stability of the pointed arch, the scientific relations of vaults and their abutments, the origin of form in flying buttresses, and the use of pinnacles. He deplored the degeneracy, the flimsiness, the alternate stint and waste of material in modern architecture : condemned the improper use of stucco, abused the medley of styles which still found favour in his day, and was especially severe on ' the gross corruption of the kind of building called " Elizabethan." '

Bartholomew, moreover, was probably the first to enunciate a principle now generally accepted by writers on art, viz. : that the conditions of true taste in architecture have always been intimately associated with those of structural excellence, and that, whenever the latter have been disregarded, the former have suffered in consequence. His treatise abounds in sound and pertinent remarks on this and many other branches of the subject. Here and there it may be verbose —a fault which the literary style of the day no doubt helped to encourage—but it is always readable, and there was some excuse for saying a great deal on matters which had so long escaped attention. The essay is methodically divided into short chapters, which are subdivided into sections, illustrated (where necessary) by diagrams and woodcuts. Nothing can be clearer than his explanations : nothing more reasonable than his arguments. He wrote with no blind en-

* By Professor Donaldson, F.R.I.B.A., &c.

thusiasm for Gothic—and indeed seems equally in favour of Classic design—but he protests emphatically against the impositions, the faulty construction and the pedantry of modern architecture, and is never tired of repeating how widely it has departed from the principles of ancient art. Occasionally, it is true, in matters of detail he advanced opinions which the purist of our own day would condemn as heretical. An architect who proposes to divide a stone mullion into two halves, for the purpose of securing the advantage of a sash window in his Gothic house, may justify the proposal by considerations of expediency, but can scarcely defend it on practical grounds. It may be folly to reject a modern convenience for the sake of artistic effect. But if we adopt it, we must adopt with it the external conditions which belong to its use. A stone mullion shaped to receive a casement is an intelligible and perfectly legitimate feature; but two strips of stone shaped to look like a solid mullion, and really concealing a hollow sash frame, represent at best a clumsy compromise between traditional form and present requirements in architecture.

Notwithstanding a few minor errors of this kind—errors which may be the more readily excused when we remember that the study of the style was still in its infancy—Bartholomew's essay may be described on the whole as the work of a thoroughly practical man, who drew attention to the scientific side of mediæval architecture at a time when most of its supporters talked of nothing but its sentimental or artistic claims to adoption.

The antiquarian societies, however, on their part, did good service in continuing their efforts to preserve as samples for study many a relic of ancient art which had remained neglected in country districts where Mediæval sympathies were as yet unknown. Among these the British Archæological Association, formed 'for the encouragement and prosecution of researches into the Early and Middle Ages, particularly in England,' soon enrolled as its members some of the most eminent architects, artists, and *dilettanti* of the day. An acting committee was appointed, who put themselves in communication with similar societies in the provinces and on the Continent ; held frequent meetings ; promoted investigations with the aid of professional assistance ; interfered, when possible, to preserve ruinous monuments from destruction ; collected drawings illustrating such remains ; arranged for visits to the most remarkable Cathedral towns, &c., in England, and published reports of their proceedings for general information.

The choice of style of the Houses of Parliament was now a matter beyond dispute ; but the nature of its internal decoration remained to some extent an open question. For this reason, and with a view, no doubt, to test the public taste in such matters, Her Majesty's Commissioners of Fine Arts decided on holding an exhibition at Westminster of the designs, &c., which had been submitted for the fittings and furniture of the New Palace. It included specimens of woodcarving, stained glass, and metal work suggested for use in various parts of the building. Being destined for this purpose, they naturally aimed at a mediæval character ; and, though probably few approached the standard of excellence by which such objects were judged ten years later, the exhibition was of undoubted value, as an incentive to industrial art, and a means of educating public taste before the rage for International Exhibitions had developed itself.

Meanwhile Pugin continued to issue volume after volume and pamphlet after pamphlet, not only in support of the Revival, but in abuse of what he loved to call the Pagan styles, and not unfrequently in severe criticism of Gothic designs by his professional contemporaries. Among others, Mr. Scoles, himself a Catholic architect, who had essayed—not very successfully, it must be confessed—to build a Norman Church at Islington, was soundly rated by this merciless censor, who published a view of the old parish Church of St. Mary, Islington, which he declared (without sufficiently considering the conditions of site) should have formed a model for the new building.

On the other hand, Pugin constantly exposed himself to reproof in the public press by his violent attacks not only on the art, but on the faith of those who chanced to differ from his own convictions, as well as by the injudicious manner in which he insisted on measuring every modern institution and social custom by a Mediæval standard.   It required no great sagacity to perceive that requirements of life in the nineteenth century could never possibly be met by reverting to the habits of our ancestors four or five centuries ago ; and if this was to be a necessary condition of the Revival, no one could be blamed for declining to sacrifice the comforts of advanced civilization for the sake of architectural taste.

The most important Anglican Church erected about this time (1843) was undoubtedly that built, at Wilton, by the Hon. Sidney Herbert, then Secretary to the Admiralty, from the design of Messrs. T. H. Wyatt and D. Brandon.   The Lombardic character of this structure excludes it from the list of Gothic examples ; but the liberal munificence of its founder, who spent 20,000*l.* upon the building, and the sumptuous nature of its decoration, exercised in course of time a great and valuable influence on private patronage and public taste in architecture.

Among domestic buildings the Proprietary College at Cheltenham, erected from designs by Mr. J. Wilson of Bath, may be mentioned as a fair specimen of early modern Gothic.   Its oriel windows, battlemented turrets, flying buttresses, and crocketed pinnacles do not indeed realise the true spirit of Mediæval design, but associated in a façade some 250 feet in length, could scarcely fail to impress the unprofessional critic in favour of the style.

Up to this date architecture had no representative in the cheap periodical journals of the day.   The publication, therefore, of the ' Builder,' in 1843, brought for the first time within the reach of art workmen and students, an illustrated weekly record of professional news.   Without pretending to an exclusive devotion to Gothic, it became the means as time went on of familiarising the general public with many a relic of antiquity, which would otherwise have been known only to those who could afford to buy expensive works on architecture. It published views of churches and manor houses, with details drawn to a larger scale. These woodcuts, rudely as they at first were executed, became very serviceable for reference and information.

A curious evidence of the gradual extension of ecclesiastical sentiment in connection with the Revival—even to our school girls—may be noted in the appearance of a little book, entitled 'Aunt Elinor's Lectures on Architecture,' published nearly thirty years ago. Its object was to inform young ladies—and no doubt there were many who wished to be informed—of the general history of the Pointed Styles, the orthodox arrangement and fittings necessary in a church, the names and use of its various parts and furniture. All this was very skilfully and carefully explained by the authoress (now known to be Miss M. Holmes), who supplemented her architectural teaching by many hints and suggestions as to the manner in which her readers might best employ their energies in the service of the Church, viz., not by working slippers for their favourite curate, or by subscribing to present him with a piece of plate, but by employing their needles in the embroidery of altar-cloths, and by saving their pocket-money to pay for a fald-stool or lectern.

Meanwhile the effect of the Cambridge Camden Society's exertions had begun to manifest itself in various quarters throughout the United Kingdom. At Llangorwen in Cardiganshire, a church was erected about 1842, which was pronounced to be in point of style and internal arrangements one of the most complete and successful imitations of ancient models that had yet been produced. It had a stone altar, with an arcaded reredos, a rood screen, a lectern, a Litany desk, and open stalls of oak for the clergy and congregation. At Birmingham, Kingston-on-Thames, Woking, Hanwell, and Shaftesbury, churches were built about the same time from the designs of Mr. G. G. Scott, whose 'Martyrs' Memorial' at Oxford contributed in no small degree to establish his reputation as a Gothic architect. These structures were freely criticised by the Society, who naturally objected to every plan which departed in the least degree from ancient tradition in its arrangement.   The absence or curtailed proportions of the chancel constituted a *gravamen*, to which attention was frequently called, and at length with success.   At the present day an architect would as soon think of building a church without a chancel, as of building one without a roof.

Mr. Ferrey's design for the Holy Trinity Chapel at Roehampton was much admired at the time.   He was one of the earliest, ablest, and most zealous pioneers of the modern Gothic school.   His architectural taste was for years in steady advance of his generation, and as an authority on church planning and general proportions he had scarcely a rival.   His work possessed the rare charm of simplicity, without lacking interest.   By the use of carefully studied mouldings and a spare but judicious introduction of carved ornament, he managed to secure for his buildings a grace that was deficient in many contemporary designs, which had been executed with far more elaborate decoration and at greater cost.   His country churches are especially notable for this reticent quality of art, and in that respect recall in a great measure the excellence of old examples.   As a specimen of the class (though erected at a later period), that of Chetwynd in Shropshire may be cited: there is a picturesque and quiet dignity in its composition which is eminently suggestive of Old English Architecture.

In the neighbourhood of London no church of its time was considered in purer style or more orthodox in its arrangement than that of St. Giles, Camberwell, designed by Mr. Scott in 1841.   The nave is divided into five bays by piers alternately round and octagonal in plan, supporting acutely pointed arches, with plain chamfered edges and a dripstone.   The clerestory windows (of two lights each) are spanned by arches which spring from attached columns corbelled from the wall.   The chancel is probably one of the earliest which during the Revival was built of proper length; is lighted on either side by three

Church of S. Mary, Chetwynde, Shropshire.

B. Ferry, Architect, 1865.

windows, with a five-light window at the east end. The crux is groined under the tower, which externally, with canopied niches at its junction with the spire, presents a very picturesque feature. The nave, chancel, and transepts have open timber roofs of a plain and un-objectionable character, but the wood fittings generally are hardly worthy of the rest. It is curious to observe in this and other churches of the same date that the aisle galleries, in spite of archæological and antiquarian protests, continued to be retained as an indispensable feature. That it was a feature inconsistent with a faithful reproduction of ancient models could not, of course, be denied. But it was found difficult to answer the plea in its favour put forward by utilitarians, who argued that by means of a gallery a definite number of additional sittings could be secured. It does not seem to have occurred to these economists that their argument pushed to its limits would have reduced the plan of every church to a simple parallelogram, would have abolished the chancel, substituted iron columns for stone piers, and in short, converted their church into a meeting-room. Few persons as yet fully appreciated the absurdity of doubling the cost of a church by the erection of a tower and spire, while the expense of its superficial area was to be saved by piling the congregation on each other's heads. Happily in the present day sanitary considerations have had their weight in preventing the intrusion of galleries; for, it is obvious that unless the aisles of a church be heightened out of due proportion, the difficulties of ventilation are increased by every gallery which is introduced.

The decorative carving in the capitals, &c. of St. Giles's Church is better in design than execution, being coarsely cut in parts. Yet in these and other details the work showed a decided advance in operative skill. The stained window at the west end, though open to objection in the style of drawing, caught something of the tone of old glass. The metal work and gas fittings (if contemporary with the church) are very creditable for their date. Externally the building would have gained in effect if the masonry had been carried up in courses less uniform in depth, and if the roof had been covered with tiles or slates of the ordinary size.　Nevertheless, seen from the road, with its tower and spire rising from the centre of a compact plan, it forms an excellent and well-composed group invested with a certain charm of artistic proportion, which the ordinary church architect of that day seldom or never succeeded in realising.　To give even a brief description of the numerous works on which Mr. Scott at this early period of his life was engaged, would be simply impossible.　Even to catalogue those which he has since undertaken would be an arduous task.　Perhaps among the admirers of his early skill there may be those who regret that his practice should have been so extensive as to preclude that concentrated attention which every artist would gladly bestow on his work. But in any case it must be remembered, that for years he was in the van of the Revivalists : that for years he was *facile princeps* of designers : that for years he laboured with his pen as with his pencil to support the cause which he had at heart ; and that if the fashion of art has undergone a change since he was young, in the Middle Ages themselves it was subject to a like mutability.—

> Credette Cimabue, nella pittura,
> Tener lo campo, ed ora ha Giotto il grido.

Mr. R. C. Carpenter's name has been already mentioned among the group of English architects who between 1840 and 1850 distinguished themselves and advanced the Gothic cause by their ability in the field of design : and perhaps it is not too much to say that in that group his name should have pre-eminence—if not for the extent of his works —(though they were numerous for his unfortunately short life)—at least for their careful and scholarlike treatment.　No practitioner of his day understood so thoroughly as Carpenter the *grammar* of his art. From his earliest youth the study of Mediæval Architecture had been a passion with him ; and it is said that when only nineteen years of age he had prepared the design for a ' First Pointed ' Church of a large and sumptuous character, which but for an accidental circumstance might have been erected at Islington. As a pupil he appears to have given remarkable attention to the character and application of mouldings, and indeed the judicious use which he made of them and other details bears ample testimony to the fact. A knowledge of the laws of proportion, of the conditions of light and shade, and the effective employment of decorative features are arrived at by most architects gradually and after a series of tentative experiments. Carpenter seems to have acquired this knowledge very early in his career, so that even his first works possess an artistic quality far in advance of their date, while those which he executed in later years are regarded even now with admiration by all who have endeavoured to maintain the integrity of our old national styles. Whether, if Carpenter had lived, he would have been influenced by the growing taste for Continental Gothic, which for a while threatened to obliterate the traditions of English architecture, may be doubted. It is certain that up to the time of his death, which occurred in 1855, we find no trace of such an influence on his designs.

His first church was that of St. Stephen at Birmingham, probably commenced in 1841, about which time he became (through Pugin's introduction) a member of the Ecclesiological Society. St. Andrew's (also in Birmingham) was his next commission, for the execution of which he deservedly obtained great credit. It is built of red sandstone, and belongs in common with most of his works to the ' Middle Pointed ' period. The plan consists of a nave and rather short chancel, with an engaged tower of three stages at the north-west angle. The stone spire surmounting the tower is from a Rutlandshire model, and far less *élancée* in its proportions than the ordinary modern spire of its date (1844.) The interior is very plain, with a partially open roof over the nave, which is five bays in length. The chancel roof is ceiled and panelled. The window tracery partakes both of a geometrical and flowing character, and is well studied. The arch mouldings of the entrance porch and the weathering of the buttresses show a marked improvement in the treatment of detail.

In the following year Mr. Carpenter began the Church of St. Paul at Brighton, a well-known structure, remarkable not only for the great advance which it indicates in the study of decorative features, but for the peculiarities of plan which, owing to the conditions of its site, became a matter of necessity. This was probably one of the first modern country-town churches erected with a palpable recognition of those changes of ritual which were now openly encouraged by a certain section of the clergy and as certainly approved by a large body of laymen. Among others erected from Mr. Carpenter's designs were those of Cookham Dean ; St. James, Stubbing, in Berkshire ; St. Nicholas at Kemerton in Gloucestershire ; St. Andrew at Monckton Wyld in Dorsetshire ; St. Peter the Great at Chichester ; St. Mary Magdalene, in Munster Square, London (an excellent example of his skill) ; Christchurch at Milton-on-Thames ; and St. John the Baptist at Bovey Tracy in Devon. The restorations conducted under his superintendence were very numerous—as were also the schools and parsonages which he built in various parts of England. His most important works, the Colleges of St. John, Hurstpierpoint, and of St. Nicholas, Lancing, were designed at a later period, and unfortunately he did not live to see the latter building executed.

The progress of the Gothic Revival during Carpenter's lifetime, and —while the style of design with which its name is associated was as yet *caviare* to the multitude—received timely aid and encouragement from the taste and munificence of private patrons whose antiquarian researches and accurate connoisseurship raised them above the prejudices which still lingered to the disadvantage of Mediæval Art. Among these Mr. Beresford Hope may be reckoned one of the most active and enthusiastic. The instances in which this gentleman has exercised an influence, either directly, or by means of his public position, to effect not only the restoration and maintenance of Old English Architecture, but also the

College at Lancing, Sussex.

Begun by the late R. C. Carpenter, Architect, 1854. Continued by Messrs. W. Slater and R. H. Carpenter.

reproduction of its beauties in modern work—are too well known to need enumeration here. A notable example may, however, be mentioned in which he found a field for the twofold accomplishment of his wishes.

St. Augustine's Abbey at Canterbury was one of the numerous monastic buildings which were disestablished after the Reformation. It had been originally founded by St. Augustine as the burial-place of the Kings of Kent and of the Archbishops. The courts and buildings which were once included within its walls, are said to have covered sixteen acres of ground. Upon the dissolution of the Abbey its site and ruins became Crown property, and it was in a mansion partly remodelled and partly reconstructed on this spot that Charles I. first met his betrothed.

The venerable gateway, which once formed the entrance to the Abbey, and which dates from the fourteenth or early part of the fifteenth century, was standing in 1845, but had been preserved for an ignoble purpose. The room within its upper portion, once the state bed-chamber of the Abbey and Palace, had been converted into a brewer's vat, having previously been used as a cockpit. The sacred precincts of the Abbey itself were desecrated by the presence of a common beershop, raised on the site of the Guests' Hall. The Guests' Chapel and the Abbey Church were in ruins. The enclosure, which once echoed only the solemn tread of cloistered monks, or the peaceful ringing of the Angelus, had come to resound with the low brawling of skittle players, and a wall which stood under the shadow of the tower raised by Scoland (the first Norman Abbot) was given up to target practice.

Such was the condition of St. Augustine's Abbey at a period when the sympathies of English Churchmen were being roused in favour of Colonial Missions by the praiseworthy exertions of Edward Coleridge. The property was put up for auction, and luckily, both for antiquarian and ecclesiastical interests, it fell into good hands. Mr. Beresford Hope —then M.P. for Maidstone, recognised in the time as well as in the place, an excellent opportunity to serve at once the National Church and the National architecture of England. The want of a Training College for our Missionary Clergy had long been felt. If such an Institution was to be established, what better site could be found for it than the Archiepiscopal city of Canterbury; and on what foundation could it be more appropriately raised than on the ruins of a building rich in associations of ecclesiastical history, and dedicated to the first Apostle of England? Mr. Hope succeeded in purchasing—not without considerable expense and trouble—the site and remains of the Abbey, and placed them at the disposal of the Archbishop of Canterbury for this purpose; munificently supplementing his gift with funds towards its endowment. The good work and its purpose excited public interest. Friends of the Church came forward with donations in aid of the scheme. Mr. Butterfield—even then one of the most accomplished architects of his day—was engaged to restore such portions of the ancient structure as might be restored, to rebuild where necessary, and to unite the whole into a building worthy of its name. The result was St. Augustine's College.

The general appearance of this work—like most of Mr. Butterfield's domestic architecture—is remarkable for its extreme simplicity. On entering the College through the ancient gateway which has been already mentioned, the visitor finds himself in a spacious quadrangle, three sides of which are occupied by buildings. To the left are the students' quarters—a long range of rooms under one roof, raised on an open cloister, and reached by two turret staircases, which form effective features on the north side. The floor of these rooms is carried on stone ribs, which span the cloister and abut on piers between the windows. On the east side is the library, a noble and well-proportioned structure, lighted by six pointed windows, for the tracery of which the architect found an excellent and appropriate model in the ancient Archiepiscopal Palace of Mayfield. The basement story of this building, vaulted with brick groins and stone, forms an admirable work-room for the students, who there learn something of practical carpentry, and the details of such other handicraft as may be useful in the Colonies.

An ample porch and picturesque flight of steps lead to the library; which has an open timber roof, simply but ingeniously framed, and exhibiting a more thorough knowledge of construction than was common in Gothic wood-work of the time. The west side of the quadrangle is occupied by the chapel and refectory, standing at right angles to each other, the former having been recently rebuilt, and the latter partly restored from the old Guesten Hall. The chapel is fitted with stalls to the whole length of both sides, each stall having its 'miserere' seat carved after a different design. Every detail in this chapel, from the encaustic tiles with which the floor is paved to the braced roof overhead, exhibits evidence of careful study. The proportions of part to part are excellent, the mouldings graceful and refined in character, and the decorative features—which are but few—skilfully and effectively introduced.

The Warden's Lodge and other domestic buildings extend southwards from the chapel. Externally, the walls of the whole College are chiefly of flint, with stone dressings—the roofs being covered with tiles of light red. These simple materials lend an air of homely rural beauty to the architecture, which is in thorough unison with the dignified modesty of the design. The task which Mr. Butterfield had to execute was not an easy one. Of the ancient monastery there were not sufficient remains left standing to justify what, in an antiquarian sense, would have been a complete restoration. On the other hand, the venerable gateway, though much mutilated, and portions of the block of buildings on its right, were substantially sound, while the excavations on the site of the library disclosed evidence of foundations which it would have been vandalism to disregard. The architect had to steer a middle course between a reverence for the past and the necessities of the present age. How admirably he succeeded, no one who examines St. Augustine's College with attention can doubt. The entrance gateway was repaired just sufficiently to arrest its decay and no further. The ' under croft' of the old refectory was rebuilt, and served as a substructure for the new library. The chapel and hall were carefully restored, with such modifications in regard to plan as were deemed necessary. The cloister and students' rooms occupying the north side of the quadrangle are entirely modern, but the character of their design is in perfect harmony with those portions of the old building which served as a key-note for architectural style.

A quarter of a century has elapsed since St. Augustine's was begun. Mr. Butterfield's name has since been associated with larger and more important commissions. But though his later works exhibit evidence of maturer taste and a wider range of study, no architect of our time has deviated so little from the principles of design which he adopted at the outset of his professional career, and which, in this case, are abundantly manifest.

CHAPTER XIII.

AMONG the difficulties which beset the consistent re-adoption of Mediæval Architecture in England at a time when the expedience of its revival at all remained a vexed question, was the perplexity in which both architects and their employers were involved by the selection of style. For the generic term ' Gothic ' was itself but a vague appellation of several fashions of house-building and church-building which had succeeded each other with more or less continuity through four centuries. This left a wide range of choice, even if, by common consent, the advocates of Mediæval art had confined themselves to English types. But as the facilities for foreign travel increased, professional students and enthusiastic amateurs came back from the Continent with notes and sketches in Belgium, France, and Italy, which soon suggested a still wider field of taste.

The Rev. J. L. Petit, who died only recently, was a clergyman of the Church of England, who throughout a long life devoted himself to the study and illustration of architecture. He sketched with rapidity and cleverness, and though his drawings were always too rough and hastily executed to be useful for reference on matters of detail, they conveyed an excellent notion of the general design of a building judged simply as a picturesque composition. In 1841 he published two volumes entitled ' Remarks on Church Architecture,' profusely illustrated with sketches, chiefly made on the Continent. In the selection of subjects he allowed himself free range. Romanesque, Transitional, and Flamboyant types of Gothic, the churches of Normandy and the ruins of Rhineland, Lombardic belfries, Italian campanili, Swiss bridges and Welsh chapels, became in turn studies for his pencil, and texts for his discourse. His remarks on the development of style —on the analogies which exist between various types of architecture in Europe, and the features which are characteristic of each—show that he must have studied with close attention and with the advantage of an excellent memory. But his taste was of too cosmopolitan an order to be of practical service to the English Revival, and where it found decided expression might fairly be challenged as questionable. A critic who, after traversing Europe in search of architectural beauty, pronounces Milan Cathedral the finest Continental church which he has seen, and who considers that the introduction of the Perpendicular line *saved* English Gothic from debasement, affords a signal proof of the fact that even the most comprehensive study and the most accurate archæological information will not always suffice to educate an amateur in the principles of structural excellence.

Petit was not the only champion of the Tudor arch. Mr. E. A. Freeman, in a paper which he read before the Oxford Architectural Society, ' On the Development of Roman and Gothic Architecture, and their Moral and Symbolical Teaching,' plainly expressed his preference for both the earliest and latest types of Gothic to that which was then and indeed is still designated as ' Middle Pointed.' The author happened to add some remarks respecting the prevalent taste of the day, which seemed to be directed against the Cambridge Camden Society. This was noticed in a short review of his essay which appeared in the ' Ecclesiologist.' Mr. Freeman replied in a long and learned letter, defending his principles, condemning the commonly accepted nomenclature of the Pointed styles, and entering on a metaphysical dissertation as to the nature of Proto-symbolism, which must certainly have awakened some of the young architects of the day to a sense of the philosophy of their art. But the subject was not allowed to drop here. The next number of the ' Ecclesiologist ' contained an article, thirty-two pages in length, in which the principles of Mediæval architecture, the doctrines of the Christian faith, and the minutiæ of mystic symbolism, were considered in relation to each other. In following the lengthy arguments of this and many similar essays of the day, the modern reader will naturally feel surprised at the amount of time, of patience, and of learning which was bestowed on the discussion of theories advanced in the name of ecclesiology, but scarcely calculated to promote either the encouragement of art or the interests of religion. That the outward and visible form of Church Architecture was in the Middle Ages influenced by theological creed there can be little doubt, but that this influence extended to every detail of construction and ornament—that it inspired the designers or workmen with anything more than an ordinary respect for the traditions of their craft, or that as a rule they allowed the principle of symbolism to interfere with more practical considerations—it is impossible to believe, without rejecting the plainest evidence of common sense. Take, for instance, the occasional deviation of the chancel from the axial line of the nave, which has been supposed, and with some probability, to have indicated the inclination of Our Saviour's head on the Cross. Was such symbolism considered of value or worth perpetuation in Mediæval times? If it were, we, in this degenerate age, can only express our surprise that in ninety-nine cases out of a hundred it was rejected as superfluous. Assuming that the triplet window was intended to typify the doctrine of the Trinity, what do the theologians say to a window of two lights, or of five?

Again, we know that the arts of sculpture and of painting were frequently employed in honour of the Christian virtues, and to cast shame on every opposite vice. But there are instances of decorative detail in many a church which point no moral and proclaim no truth beyond the fact that art in any age may descend to obscenity. Are we to suppose that the authors of such work as this pursued it with a pure and reverential sense of duty to their faith? Is it not more likely that they wielded the brush and chisel—with a more skilful hand indeed, but with no higher or moral purpose than any workmen of our own time? The experience of modern life teaches us that great artistic refinement may be found occasionally associated with boorish manners and sensual indulgence.   And if this is possible in the nineteenth century, why may it not have been so in the thirteenth?   The fashion of taste may have changed, but not the morality of art.

Between the false sentiment and the redundant symbolism which have been associated with Mediæval architecture in turn by fanatical devotees and over-zealous antiquaries, it is no wonder that men who do not share the extreme views of either party should have become nauseated with the very name of Gothic.

In 1843 a translation of Durandus was published by two well-known members of the Cambridge Camden Society.   It is remarkable that this work, which may be considered the fountain-head of ecclesiastical symbolism, should contain so little evidence of these essentials in form and number which, in the clerical mind, some thirty years ago, constituted the chief grace of architectural design.   But there are other difficulties in the way.   An earnest Churchman, who believes with the Bishop of Mende, that 'a church consisteth of four walls,' because it is built on the doctrine of the Four Evangelists, cannot fairly complain that the plan of a Methodist chapel is too simple in form.   Durandus points to the weathercock on the summit of a church as the appropriate symbol of a watchful preacher.   The writer of an epigram in the 'Ecclesiologist' calls it the symbol of a wavering mind, and applauds its removal to make room for a cross.   According to Durandus, 'the chancel (that is the head of the church) being lower than its body, signifieth how great humility there should be in the clergy.'   It happens to be one of the peculiar points insisted on in the design of every orthodox modern church, that the chancel shall be *higher* than the nave.   These inconsistencies are merely mentioned here to show what little importance can be attached to the letter of symbolism when studied as a science.   Yet into defence of this symbolism the 'Ecclesiologist' earnestly entered, and in accordance with its principles, many an honest parson and clever architect, whose time might have been better employed, proceeded to ransack every church and rack his brains with the hope of discovering some mysterious significance in structural or decorative features of wood and stone, which owed their origin, in most cases, to simple expedience or ingenious fancy. Durandus was soon outdone. Every curate who meddled in such matters hit a fresh nail on the head as he examined the framing of his church door. A new light illumined him when he looked up at the west window. Enthusiastic amateurs took to counting the piers of the nave and measuring the chancel floor, involved themselves in wonderful calculations as to the ancient use of the mystic numbers 3 and 7, and, figuratively speaking, when they wanted an inch they not unfrequently took an ell.

Concurrently with the mania for symbolism, the vexed question as to the nomenclature of styles was maintained with extraordinary vigour. Into how many distinct periods Pointed Architecture could with propriety be divided; whether the first should receive the name of 'Lancet,' 'Early English,' or 'Complete'; whether the next should be called 'Second Pointed' or 'Decorated'; whether 'Decorated' could be subdivided into 'Geometrical' and 'Flowing'; whether 'Flowing' meant the same thing as 'Continuous'; whether there was a 'Discontinuous' style, and in what respect they all differed from 'Flamboyant,' were matters under eternal discussion. And the more they were discussed the more hopelessly confused the student became.

It required more than ordinary intelligence to remember off-hand what a writer meant by such a complicated expression as 'the early days of Late Middle Pointed,' and this was simple and perspicuous compared to some of the terms employed. The absurdity of attempting to form, except in the most general way, a system of terms which should at once imply the date and fashion of every architectural structure without reference to the effect produced by local traditions, material, and the accidents of individual caprice, or ability, can only be fully realised if we suppose the same system applied to the history of

any other art—that of Painting, for example.   At present, the school
of Raffaele, the school of Padua, and the Eclectic schools, are terms
frequently employed and easily recognisable, inasmuch as they suggest,
respectively, the influence of a person, a locality, or a class of painters.
But if art critics spoke of the paulo-post-Peruginesque, or the Late
Middle Francian manner, we should be led to suspect first their intelligence and then their accuracy.   No rational observer can suppose
that the Mediæval builders were guided in their modifications of style
by any but practical or æsthetic considerations, induced sometimes by
the requirements of the work in hand, sometimes by the force of
example, and more frequently perhaps by that instinctive love of
change which is a universal law in the progress of art.   One or more
of these causes was sure in course of time to affect the plan of a
window, the pitch of a roof, or the profile of a capital.   But to suppose that they evolved out of their inner architectural consciousness a
series of complete and irrefragable rules, which associated a certain form
of arch with a fixed character of moulding, and set apart a certain
pinnacle of a particular buttress, after the manner of Sir William
Chambers and the Five Orders, would be to rob genuine Gothic of half
its interest.

   While the antiquaries were disputing over dates and styles, and
ecclesiologists were divided as to whether symbolism should be alle-
gorical or anagogic, it is lucky that a few architects contributed by their
more practical studies many important additions to the Literature of the
Revival.   Among these, Sharpe's 'Architectural Parallels,' a work
illustrating the progress of Ecclesiastical Architecture through the twelfth
and thirteenth centuries, deserves especial mention.   Though Britton and
others had devoted pen and pencil to the history and delineation of our
Cathedrals, though Willson and Pugin had measured and described
the most notable 'Pointed' churches and examples of our old domestic
architecture, the ruins of those magnificent abbeys which are scattered
over Yorkshire and other parts of England were as yet little known to

the professional student. Mr. E. Sharpe, an architect who had already distinguished himself as a Cambridge graduate, set himself to repair this deficiency. He published two folio volumes, the one devoted to perspective views of the buildings as they stood, the other to geometrical elevation and plans accurately figured, as well as detail drawings of those parts which remained intact or could be safely 'restored' in illustration. A new mine of architectural interest was thus opened.

The simple grandeur of the remains at Fountains and Kirkstall, the graceful fenestration of Tintern, the elegant proportion of Whitby and Rievaulx, and the refined enrichment of Howden and Selby, were now delineated, not with the hasty touch of a pictorial artist, but with the careful accuracy of a draughtsman who understood the construction and *rationale* of every feature which he saw. The student who referred to the plates of detail found at a glance the section of every moulding in these venerable structures drawn to scale and ranged side by side. He could compare the piers of Furness nave with those of Jervaulx, the window jambs of Bridlington with those of Guisborough. Studies such as these are only appreciated by men who have made architecture a profession, and it is not too much to say that the publication of Mr. Sharpe's works exercised a great influence on professional taste, by drawing attention to older and purer examples of Gothic than had yet been imitated.

As a designer, Mr. Sharpe had already won his spurs by the erection of many churches in Lancashire, Yorkshire, and Cheshire, the largest of which was Trinity Church, Blackburn, planned to accommodate a congregation of 1500 persons, with a lofty tower and spire—and the best, perhaps, that of Knowsley, near Prescot, built for the late Lord Derby. The churches at Lever Bridge, Bolton, and that of Platt, near Manchester, by the same architect, were built completely of terra cotta. The former is a small church with a west tower and a traceried spire standing on an octagonal lantern. Here the whole of the window tracery, as well as the pinnacles, finials, and other decorative features employed, is of fire-clay. This was probably the first attempt to adapt that material to the construction and enrichment of every part of a Gothic Church, and it is satisfactory to know that for twenty years it has stood the effects of Lancashire smoke and atmospheric influences without being in the slightest degree injuriously affected.

The second example belongs, like the first, to that style which Mr. Sharpe would call 'Curvilinear.' It has a nave, aisles, and chancel, with a S.W. tower and spire, the latter being solid but crossed by bands of tracery. In both churches the moulded work is rich and varied.

In the neighbourhood of Burnley, Preston, Knutsford, and Settle, not to mention other places, are examples of Mr. Sharpe's design, executed for the most part between the years 1836 and 1846. He also erected a number of mansions, of which the most important were Capernwray Hall, near Burton, and Hornby Castle, in Lancashire. The instances are rare in which architects, at least of our own day, have found time for contributing to the literature of their art during a professional practice. But both by his books and his works, Mr. Sharpe has identified himself with the cause of Mediæval art, and we may be sure that in years to come his name will be inseparably associated with the Gothic Revival.

In 1845, Mr. F. A. Paley, then Honorary Secretary of the Cambridge Camden Society, published a practical little treatise on Gothic Mouldings, profusely illustrated with examples from the earliest to the latest types. This was followed by 'A Manual of Gothic Architecture,' from the pen of the same author. The latter has been superseded by larger and more important works, but to this day 'Paley's Mouldings' will be found among the books recommended for study. About the same time appeared 'Bloxam's Principles of Gothic Architecture,' a small but well-digested volume admirably adapted for the use of amateurs. Within a few years it went through nine editions, showing the rapidly increasing popularity of Gothic among the non-professional public.

Messrs. Bowman and Crowther's 'Churches of the Middle Ages,' was a large and sumptuous work illustrating well- selected specimens of the Early and Middle Pointed structures, together with a few of the purest Late Pointed examples. The art of lithography had by this time much improved, and was admirably adapted for illustrations of architecture on a large scale, especially when it was desired, as in this case, to publish perspective views of an artistic character in the same volume with plans, elevations, and studies of detail. The scrupulous care with which these plates were prepared rendered them invaluable for reference to many an architect who had had neither time nor opportunity to study the admirable churches of Lincolnshire and other counties whose treasures were now revealed for the first time, not by merely general views, but by accurate drawings on a large scale, of spires, porches, window tracery, sedilia, canopies, and all those decorative features which give life and character to the buildings of the middle ages. These features were drawn with far more knowledge and expression of architectural form than heretofore, and though the sketches of carved work were still coldly executed, they represented a considerable advance in delineative skill.

It is remarkable that neither in this case nor in that of Sharpe's 'Parallels,' any descriptive text should have been printed with the plates. Perhaps the authors thought that enough and more than enough had been said about Gothic in other quarters, and that the time had arrived when it was better to let the merits of Mediæval art speak for themselves.

Meanwhile a more popular work, both by reason of the subjects selected for illustration and the nature of the illustrations themselves, was reviving a taste for that old manorial style of domestic architecture which, subject to many modifications of detail, and varying considerably in qualities of design, had prevailed in this country from the fifteenth to the seventeenth centuries. Nash's ' Mansions of England in the Olden Time,' conveyed in its very title so much interest even to the most superficial critic that it is no wonder it attracted attention. But it was, moreover, the work of an accomplished artist who had at an early age, and in an extraordinary degree, acquired the knack of investing with a picturesque charm every object which he chose to portray. The facility of his pencil was as the facility of Sir Walter Scott's pen, and they were both devoted with equal success to recalling the romance of Mediæval life. It required no technical knowledge of architecture to appreciate the venerable aspect of Haddon Hall, with its panelled rooms, its ample fire-places, and tapestried walls. The air of dignified repose, of jovial hospitality, and lordly splendour, indicated throughout such apartments as those of Levens in Westmoreland, of Adlington, Bramhall, and Brereton in Cheshire, of Athelhampton in Dorsetshire, and of Hatfield in Herts, appeals at once to the taste and sympathies of many an amateur who may be unable to discriminate nicely between Tudor and Elizabethan work, but who feels instinctively that the country houses of our ancestors, for a century or more, realised every necessary comfort in their day, while they were a hundredfold more artistic and interesting than the cold formal mansions of the Georgian era.

Seen in their present state, some half modernised, some damaged by time and wilful neglect, others spoilt by injudicious restoration, many of these ancient mansions are but dimly suggestive of their former magnificence. It was Nash's aim to represent them as they were in the days when country life was enjoyed by their owners, not for a brief interval in the year, but all the year round, in days when there was feasting in the hall and tilting in the courtyard, when the yule log crackled on the hearth, and mummers beguiled the dulness of a winter's evening, when the bowling-green was filled with lusty youths, and gentle dames sat spinning in their boudoirs, when the deep window recesses were filled with family groups, and gallant cavaliers rode out a-hawking ; when, in short, all the adjuncts and incidents of social life, dress, pastimes, manners, and what-not, formed part of a picturesque whole of which we in these prosaic and lack-lustre days, except by the artist's aid, can form no conception.

When these delightful volumes were published a fresh impulse was given to the study of ancient architecture for domestic purposes. People began to see for themselves that the old national style of house-building was neither so gloomy nor uncomfortable as it had once been considered. They found that the rooms might be lofty, the windows wide, the chimney corners cosy, the staircases ample and convenient. They learned that a gabled roof was not inconsistent with grandeur, and that a walled porch afforded better shelter from the weather than an open portico, that chimney shafts, buttresses, and many another feature which the modern ' Italian ' architect makes a shift to hide, may become the ornaments of a Gothic house, that the style admits of every variety of plan, and may embrace every modern requirement, that it is as well adapted for a cottage as a palace, and above all that the preposterous notion of grafting on domestic buildings the distinctive features of a church or a convent, as had been the case at Fonthill and Eaton Hall, was altogether wrong, and without precedent in genuine examples.

It was an evil inseparable from the nature of Nash's work that he was guided in his selection of subjects solely by considerations of pictorial effect. In that respect his selection was excellent. But, unfortunately for the interests of art, pictorial effect may be, and indeed in architecture of the seventeenth century frequently was, allied with unsatisfactory design as far at least as details are concerned. He illustrated many specimens of the Elizabethan and Jacobean periods which possessed sufficient archi-tectural merit to satisfy a half-educated taste, but which, as models of decorative treatment, were models of all that should be avoided. Tares were thus sown with the wheat, and to this day it is difficult to teach some people how to distinguish between the two crops.

If the publication of Nash's ' Ancient Mansions ' did good service to the Revival in England, Mr. Robert W. Billings was hardly less suc-cessful in drawing the attention of his countrymen to Mediæval archi-tecture north of the Tweed. Until the appearance of his ' Baronial and Ecclesiastical Antiquities of Scotland,' no illustrations worthy of the name had recorded the characteristics of a style which, whatever its faults may be, is as thoroughly national both in its rise and its decline as any that prevailed in Europe during the middle ages.   The grand severity of Borthwick Castle, the picturesque ruins of Craigmillar and Dirleton, the graceful simplicity of Dryburgh Abbey, and the rich details of Melrose, represent each in their several ways pages in the history of ancient art well worth the professional student's examination ; and though he may turn with disappointment from the coarse and vitiated detail of Rosslyn Chapel, he must be a fastidious critic who fails to admire such noble work as that at Pluscardine, Iona, and Jedburgh.

The views in Billings' volumes are neither so large nor treated in such a pleasantly scenic manner as those by Nash, but Billings had the advantage of being an architect, and knew the value of correct delineation of detail.   Many of the studies of parts are engraved with much care and on so large a scale that they would be of practical value for reference without a plan or section.   The ichnography, indeed, of these examples the author did not supply ; probably because it would have greatly increased the cost of his work, without interesting the majority of his subscribers, among whom were hundreds of unprofessional men. On the other hand, each set of plates was accompanied by a short essay, in which the history and peculiarities of every building portrayed were fully described.

Notwithstanding the appearance of these and other similarly illustrated books, a work was still wanting by means of which the student might arrive at more technical knowledge of Mediæval design, and especially with regard to those details of wood-work and internal fittings which had hitherto escaped study, but which were becoming more and more in demand as the necessity for completeness and thorough consistency in the appointments of a modern Gothic building became apparent.

This deficiency was in course of time supplied by the Messrs. Brandon who, with infinite pains and considerable ability, both of an artistic and literary kind, produced in 1847 two quarto volumes entitled ' An

Analysis of Gothic Architecture,' illustrated by upwards of seven hundred specimens of architectural features carefully selected from the best periods of ancient work both ecclesiastical and domestic. These illustrations were accompanied by letter-press, in which the origin and development of window tracery, the distinctive character of mouldings, of piers, arches, and buttresses, and the treatment of wood-work and metal-work, were discussed. The comprehensive nature of the analysis, the skill with which the details, especially of carved work, are sketched, and the thoroughly practical nature of the information conveyed, soon rendered this work popular in the professional world, and indeed it may still be considered one of the most useful of its class which has issued from the press. Without a genuine knowledge of detail, the very alphabet of architectural design remains unlearned. An ill-spelt essay, an ungrammatical speech, would not present a greater anomaly than a building in which the individual parts indicate a want of study. It was Mr. Raphael Brandon's early and untiring researches in this direction which enabled him at a later period to raise one of the grandest and most effective modern churches which have marked the Revival,* and though his intimate acquaintance with the minutiæ as well as the proportions of old work may have here and there betrayed him into plagiarism, this was a venial fault at a time when an architect was expected to give his authority for every moulding that he used, and when the completely original designs which were produced did but little credit to the Gothic cause or to their respective authors.

A large proportion of the modern Pointed structures raised between 1840 and 1850 were copied either entirely or in part from old examples, and perhaps it was the best thing that could have happened. For with a few brilliant exceptions, which it would be invidious to name, no architects of that day could have been trusted to work, as many have since done, in the *spirit* of old art alone and without borrowing largely from their books and sketches.

* The 'Apostolic' Church in Gordon Square, London.

Among the instances of successful adaptations from old design, the church of St. John, Salford, Manchester, by Messrs. Hadfield and Weightman, may be mentioned. In this case the tower and spire of Newark, the nave of Howden, and the choir of Selby, were copied, not absolutely in proportion, but in detail. The nave, indeed, was one bay shorter than its original, and certainly did not gain in effect by the deduction; but on the whole the result was considered very satisfactory by contemporary critics, and especially elicited the admiration of Pugin. It was begun in 1844, and was opened in 1848. The interior, fitted up as it is for the service of the Roman Catholic Church, with its chantries and altar tombs, its stout piers and broad transepts, is very striking. The nave has a clerestory and open timbered roof, the chancel and chancel aisles being groined in wood.* The screens which divide the chancel from its aisle, as well as some of the altars and other fittings, were designed some years later by Mr. G. Goldie, who had then joined Messrs. Hadfield and Weightman in partnership. The decorative sculpture of this period, though refined and wrought with extraordinary delicacy, as may be seen here in an altar tomb in the north chantry, was treated in far too naturalistic a manner for the conditions of good art. For instance, the *Rosa Mystica*, carved on a church panel, is a sacred emblem, and should be an ideal abstraction of nature. Here the carver has literally copied the flower, leaf for leaf, with so unfortunately accurate an eye and so injudiciously sharp a chisel, that his work looks like a petrified rose. During the Revival, it took a decade of years to teach workmen to carve carefully. It took another to get them to carve simply. We may expect more than a third to elapse before they have learnt to carve nobly.

* Although this fact may fill the modern purist with æsthetic horror, it is not without precedent even in Mediæval times, and was certainly more excusable twenty-five years ago than now, when we are supposed to have mastered the true principles of Gothic design. But it is an expedient still practised; and if clients will insist on adopting it, what is the unfortunate architect to do? It is curious that the Roman Catholic clergy have been and still are responsible for much that has been perpetrated in this way.

St. John's (R.C.) Cathedral, Salford, Manchester.

Hadfield and Weightman, Architects, 1845

JEWITT & CO. SC.

Two other Roman Catholic churches were erected about this time by Messrs. Hadfield and Weightman, viz. at Sheffield, and at Burnley in Lancashire, each being dedicated to Saint Mary. The design of the latter was based on a study of Heckington Church, with certain modifications, the principal departure from the plan of the original being the addition of a chapel on the north side of the north aisle. The reredos of the high altar was entrusted to Pugin, whose work here, it must be confessed, suffers by comparison with that of the architects of the church. The reredos and side altar of the chapel, to the left of the high altar, are far more vigorously treated, and there are other examples of decorative sculpture in the interior which are excellent both in taste and execution. In the tracery of the windows a certain tendency towards the German and Belgian schools may be noticed. The west window, supplied by Messrs. Hardman & Co., from a design by Pugin, is very good for its date and indeed superior to those put up at a later period by the same firm. The masonry of this and other churches erected by Mr. Hadfield exhibits evidence of an appreciation of those 'true principles' of constructive detail which were then more preached than practised. The window arches, &c., instead of being turned in large blocks of stone, according to the prevailing custom, are executed in small and numerous voussoirs, which give scale and significance to the work. The wall courses, instead of being rubbed down to the smoothness of paper (a method of finish at once wasteful of labour and uninteresting in effect), are left simply dressed with the chisel. The mouldings are delicately and sharply cut, and the details of iron-work in the screens, &c., are handled with a vigour far in advance of the time.

In 1845, the church of St. Francis Xavier was begun at Liverpool from the designs of Mr. J. J. Scoles. In plan it includes a nave and aisles, a shallow chancel, and a finely-proportioned tower at the south-west angle. The nave arcade, of lancet-pointed arches, rests on iron columns which, from their shape and colour, might almost be mistaken for marble.   The propriety of using iron for such a purpose has been much questioned, and is still open to dispute; but of one fact there can be little doubt, viz. that if it is so used, the nature of the material should be at once revealed by the character of the design.   The roof of the nave is polygonal, and divided into panels decorated with colour. Without possessing any *ad captandum* excellence, this church is a very creditable work for its day, though the effect of the interior is greatly marred by the unfortunate glazing of the aisle windows.*

The Roman Catholic churches erected at this period had one decided advantage over those designed for the Establishment, viz. in the rich treatment of their interiors.   Ritualism, it is true, was gradually finding favour among the Anglican clergy, but as yet its principal effect had been to ensure a general orthodoxy of plan and proportion in the buildings erected.   A tamely-carved reredos, generally arranged in panels to hold the Commandments, a group of sedilia and a piscina, with perhaps a few empty niches in the clerestory, were, as a rule, all the internal features which distinguished an Anglican church from a meeting-house.   The sumptuously sculptured dossels, the marble altars inlaid with mosaic, the elaborate rood-screens and decorative painting, which private munificence has since provided for many of our national churches, with the approval of the clergy and to the delight of many a devout congregation, were then rare, and would, in nine cases out of ten, have created a scandal, even among the supporters of the Revival. But no scruples on this score prevented the introduction of such features in the Roman Church, where the worst innovation that could be feared was an exchange of good taste for bad.   The ritual of Rome had always aimed at effect, though her priests might be robed in copes of miserable design.   Her altars were meant to be attractive, though they were

---

* The designs for the altars, pulpit, and some other fittings of this church were commenced by Mr. S. J. Nicholl during the term of his pupilage with Mr. Scoles, and were at Mr. Scoles's request completed by him after that term had expired. The Chapel of the Sacred Heart, the last of these works, was finished in 1851. It is a very rich example, carefully designed in the style of the church, but with considerable originality.

decked with tawdry artificial flowers. Her shrines and niches were never empty, though they were too often filled with imagery from the toy-shop. Pugin raised his voice long and loudly against these artistic heresies, and in course of time his denunciations had their effect. For some years the Church of Rome went hand in hand with the Church of England in a new and goodly Reformation—a Reformation which caused no rivalry but that of devotion, which involved no loss but of what was worthless, which pursued no policy but that of truth, which effected no change but one from meanness to beauty, and from heartlessness to love.

CHAPTER XIV.

BEFORE the first half of this century was reached, a number of new churches had been erected in London, which, in their design and execution, far surpassed the productions of previous years, and at last seemed as if a standard of excellence had been reached beyond which it would be difficult to proceed. For up to this time the chief care of the modern Gothic architect had been to imitate with more or less precision, not only the plan and arrangement, but the proportions and decorative details of old work. If he succeeded in doing this satisfactorily, even in a literal copy, the critics found no fault with him. But any attempt at the introduction of an unusual feature—any departure from the several canons of style, which by dint of observation, sketches, and measurement had been arrived at by the antiquarian, and enunciated by the Camden Society, would have been regarded as heretical, and forthwith condemned.

And in truth, at that period the only safety from error lay in absolute respect for ancient precedent. Those luckless designers who tried to emancipate themselves from that authority, and to strike out in a new independent line of taste, only brought ridicule on their heads by the crudity and clumsiness of their work. It was easy to argue that old art was a dead letter : that the requirements of modern life, the conditions of modern religion, and the sentiment of modern taste, pointed one and all to the necessity for a change of style, or to the freest possible interpretation of old styles, both in our churches and our homes. But when our art-reformers consolidated their ideas in brick and stone, the question became no longer one of style, but of taste, and no educated

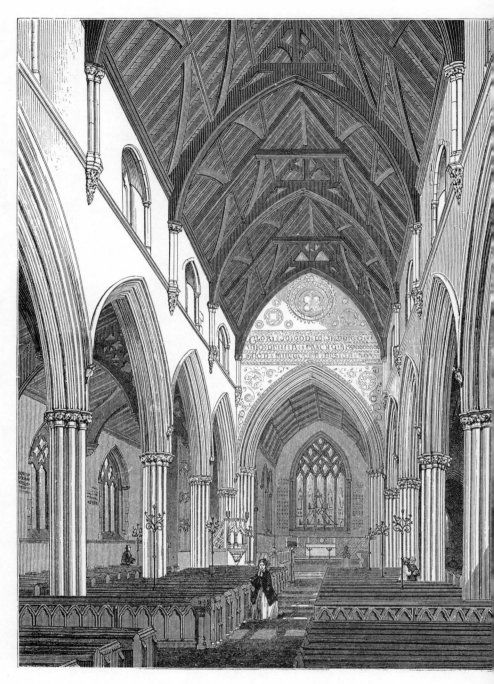

Church of S. Stephen, Westminster.

B. Ferry, F.S.A., Architect. 1846.

taste could have approved the result of their experiments. The last twenty years have seen more than one divergence in the progress of our National Architecture. Those who follow it as a profession are no longer content to make slavish copies of old work, but one fact must be admitted, viz. that whenever a good and decidedly original design has been executed, it has been by those who at some period of their lives studied closely from ancient examples, and whenever a mean or commonplace (though equally original) building has been planned, it has been by some one who never considered such study worth the trouble.

The Church of St. Andrew, in Wells Street, London, designed by Mr. Daukes, and consecrated in 1847, deserved and obtained great credit for the ingenuity with which the architect managed to deal with a very awkward site, irregular in shape, bounded on the north and south by houses, and on the east by a mews. The selection of so late a type of Gothic, was a mistake ; and the introduction of galleries an unfortunate necessity. But the west front, with its engaged tower, standing at an odd angle with the line of the street, is picturesque, and internally the arrangements of the chancel, with its stalls, sedilia, and raised sacrarium, gave great satisfaction to the High Church party, by whom the building was long regarded as a model of orthodoxy until its more famous rival All Saints' was raised in the adjoining street.*

Meanwhile, Miss Burdett Coutts, to whose well-directed liberality many an English Church is indebted, had commissioned Mr. B. Ferrey to design and erect the Church of St. Stephen, at Westminster, on a site where it was much needed, viz. at the corner of Rochester Row, surrounded by houses of the poorest description. The denizens of Tothill Fields, and the Westminster Scholars who came to play cricket in Vincent Square, saw, with mingled pleasure and surprise, a tower and stone spire rising to a prodigious height from the east end of the north aisle. The critics pronounced the spire too attenuated, even

---

* The interior of St. Andrew's Church has since undergone considerable additions, under the able direction of Mr. G. E. Street, R.A.

for its style (Middle Pointed), but approved the small courses of stone which were used for the masonry below, and confessed the knowledge of detail which the porches and window tracery exhibited.* By and by the church was opened, revealing treasures of carving in stone and wood, encaustic tiles, and stained glass—not indeed of that quality which would now be accepted as satisfactory, but certainly as good as could then be obtained. The walls are plastered internally, but the plaster is stopped, as it should be, at the window quoins. The pulpit is original in design, and the mouldings throughout the church delicate and refined. An open-timbered roof, very good in style, covers the lofty nave, while that of the chancel is polygonal and panelled. Here, then, we have two metropolitan churches, one Perpendicular and the other Decorated in design, representing a steady advance in the character of Modern Gothic. A third example may be mentioned in which the style adopted was Early English, and which from various causes has since attained a celebrity quite apart from its architectural merit, although that was not inconsiderable.

The Church, Parsonage, and Schools of St. Barnabas, Pimlico, designed by Mr. T. Cundy, were erected at a time when every step forward in the direction of Ritualism was persistently opposed by the ultra-Protestant party—when the furniture and fittings of a chancel were considered proof-positive of Popery, and when every clergyman who preached in a surplice was suspected of being a Jesuit in disguise. It was, therefore, with astonishment and dismay that certain good folks who had the curiosity to examine this church shortly after its completion, found a chancel separated from the rest of the building by a screen and parcloses, fitted with a stone altar and reredos, stalls and miserere-seats, sedilia and recessed credence, the floor rich in encaustic tiles, and the walls glowing with coloured diapers, while a *corona* of beaten metal and glass bosses depended from the panelled roof. They

---

* The schools attached to this church were opened before its completion, and are excellent examples of Domestic Pointed work.

turned from the brass lectern to the marble pulpit, from the stained glass windows to the Latin texts which ran round the arches in mysterious characters, and asked themselves whether in sober earnest the Church of England could have come to such a pass as this.

Externally, even the house and schools were viewed askance, for the windows were narrow and pointed, and to the uninitiated the whole building looked like a convent. Convents were popularly supposed to be dreadful places. Some young ladies, no doubt, were scandalised at the notion; and we may be sure that there were not a few in Pimlico for whom the life of a nun had no great attractions.

The architect who could regard the building without prejudice, and from a purely professional point of view, saw with some interest a type of Gothic hitherto neglected in the Revival (for the so-called Early English buildings had been but meagre travesties of that style) adapted not only to a church and parochial schools, but to a modern dwelling-house. The Domestic Architecture of the Revival has since passed through many phases, ranging from ancient Venetian to cockney vernacular; but the St. Barnabas Parsonage was probably the first instance in which a Victorian drawing-room received its light from a lancet window.

The church itself was destined to become, as time went on, the cause, if not the actual scene, of ecclesiastical strifes and disputes, which, though unfortunately associated with the history of the Revival, will find no record in these pages—strifes in which bigotry has sometimes been mistaken for zeal, and ignorant prejudice for conscientious scruple; disputes which, if prolonged till Doomsday, will never be settled except by the mutual concession that in spiritual, as well as worldly matters, there may be two ways of attaining the same end.

In 1849, the foundations of two more London churches were laid, which, apart from their merits considered respectively as works of art, are interesting as evidence of a decided change in the development of the Revival. Hitherto, Mr. Butterfield and the late Mr. Carpenter may be said in many respects to have occupied common ground in the field of design. Both had formed their taste by a careful study of old examples. Both exhibited an apparent preference for the 'Middle Pointed' period. Both had up to this time carefully avoided incongruities of style and that restless striving after effect, at the sacrifice of dignity, which has been the bane of Modern Gothic. The works of each, in short, were thoughtful, refined and scholarlike.

Of Mr. Carpenter's Church, St. Mary Magdalene, close to Munster Square, it is not too much to say that no contemporary structure raised in London, of its class and size, surpassed, or even approached, it in excellence. There is a simple grace in its proportions—a modest *reticence* (if one may use such an expression in architectural criticism) about the treatment of its decorative features that distinguishes it, on the one hand, from the cold expressionless Gothic which then passed for orthodox, and on the other from the rampant extravagance of treatment which has occasionally found favour in later days. This church was originally designed with two aisles, but that in the south side only was built. To this accident, and the fact that chairs instead of benches are used for the congregation, perhaps the unconventional aspect of the interior is due ; but an examination of the mouldings and other details will show how carefully every part was studied. There are few modern churches of which the interior may be called truly pictorial, but in this one twenty years have helped to mellow the local colour of its walls ; and under certain conditions of sunset, with the light streaming through the west windows, leaving the rest of the church in gloom, the effect is very fine.

St. Mary Magdalene's was perhaps the last church of any note erected in London before the Revival became sensibly, though by no means universally, affected by certain new doctrines of taste in architecture —doctrines which were proclaimed from an unexpected source, and which at one time bade fair to revolutionise and reform those very principles of design that Pugin had recently laid down with so much care.

It had long been a project of the Cambridge Camden Society to found a model church, which should realise in its design and internal arrangements a *beau ideal* of architectural beauty, and fulfil at the same time the requirements of orthodox ritual. Some years after the Society was transferred to London, an opportunity presented itself for the execution of this scheme. The late incumbent of Margaret Street Chapel, in the parish of All Souls (of which Dean Chandler was then rector), had conceived the idea of rebuilding the chapel in what (for that day) would have been a correct ecclesiastical style, and for this purpose a sum amounting to nearly 3,000*l.* had been collected. On Mr. Oakley's secession to the Church of Rome he was succeeded by the Rev. W. Upton Richards, by whom the undertaking was still fostered. In 1845 it occurred to Mr. Beresford Hope that the two schemes might be combined with advantage, both to the Margaret Chapel congregation and to the supporters of the Cambridge Camden Society. This proposal was well received both by the Dean and Mr. Richards, and, having been submitted to Bishop Blomfield, met with his ready approval. It was arranged that the architectural and ecclesiological control of the project should be vested entirely in the Cambridge Camden Society, by whom Sir Stephen Glynne and Mr. Beresford Hope were appointed as the executive. The avocations of the former gentleman, however, prevented him from taking an active part in the matter, and thus the main responsibility devolved on Mr. Hope. Mr. Butterfield was selected as the architect, and the next question considered was the choice of site.

In many parts of London this would have presented no difficulty, but the congregation of the old Chapel naturally showed their preference for Margaret Street, and there, after many obstacles in the way of negotiation, and not without reluctance on Mr. Hope's part, a piece of ground was purchased at a cost of 14,500*l.* It is to be regretted that feelings of sentiment were allowed to prevail over practical considerations in coming to this conclusion, for the site was confessedly disadvantageous in regard to light, a point which in a model town church should not have been disregarded. However, in 1849, the work was fairly begun, the foundation stone having been laid by Dr. Pusey, and the building dedicated to All Saints.

The generous liberality with which the scheme was supported shows the great interest felt in its development by modern Churchmen, and affords a striking contrast to the niggardly thrift which the previous generation had shown in matters ecclesiastical. Among the subscriptions placed at Mr. Beresford Hope's disposal in aid of the object was the munificent sum of 30,000*l*., contributed by Mr. H. Tritton; Mr. Lancaster gave 4,000*l*. The cost of the baptistery at All Saints was defrayed by the Marquis of Sligo, and many other instances of private generosity might be quoted. Altogether, the church, including the site and endowment, cost about 70,000*l*.

Whether Mr. Butterfield's design for All Saints' Church was or was not influenced by the theories enunciated in the 'Seven Lamps of Architecture,' it is certain that the building itself, as it was gradually raised, and still more when it came to be decorated, revealed a tendency to depart from ancient precedent in many important particulars. In the first place, the use of red brick for the external walls was a novelty, brick having been hitherto only used for the cheap churches, while in this case the very quality of the brick used made it more expensive than stone. Again, the tower and spire were of a shape and proportions which puzzled the antiquaries, scandalised the architects, and sent unprofessional critics to their wit's end with amazement. Passers-by gazed at the iron-work of the entrance gateway, at the gables and dormers of the parsonage, at the black brick voussoirs and stringcourses, and asked what manner of architecture this might be, which was neither Early English, Decorated, nor Tudor, and which could be properly referred to no century except the nineteenth.

Internally, it is true, they found much to admire in the beauty of the materials used ; in the marble, alabaster, and coloured brick, in the fresco paintings, delicate carving, and brilliant glass. But the treatment of all was so novel and eccentric, the proportions so unusual, the application of colour was so strange, that people of taste could not make up their minds whether they ought to like it or not; while with people who did not pretend to a taste it was decidedly out of favour. Undoubtedly the work is not without its faults, but they are precisely those faults which do not present themselves to an uneducated eye. The tendency of a superficial critic, as a rule, is to sneer at every specimen of modern art that departs in any marked degree from a conventional standard; to ignore the specific conditions which regulate design; to prefer obvious and commonplace prettiness to the nobler but more subtle beauties of proportion and refinement, and restless elaboration to sober dignity of effect. For instance, without necessarily approving the outline of the spire at All Saints', it is easy to perceive that much of the disparagement which it elicited was founded on an ignorance of its wooden construction. People involuntarily compared it with the ordinary type of stone spire which they had been accustomed to see in English churches, and could not understand why it was not broached in the usual way, or surrounded with a parapet at its base. Again, the interior of the church was pronounced too high for its width. There was no east window; and there were no windows in the north aisles. But all these peculiarities were the inevitable result of the site, for the choice of which the architect could not be held responsible. Objections were raised to the character of the carving and of the metal-work, but no better reason could be given for these objections than that nothing of precisely the same kind had been seen before.

The truth is that the design was a bold and magnificent endeavour to shake off the trammels of antiquarian precedent, which had long fettered the progress of the Revival, to create not a new style, but a development of previous styles; to carry the enrichment of ecclesiastical Gothic to an extent which even in the Middle Ages had been rare in England ; to add the colour of natural material to pictorial decoration ; to let marbles and mosaic take the place of stone and plaster ; to adorn the walls with surface ornament of an enduring kind ; to spare, in short, neither skill, nor pains, nor cost in making this church the model church of its day—such a building as should take a notable position in the history of modern architecture.

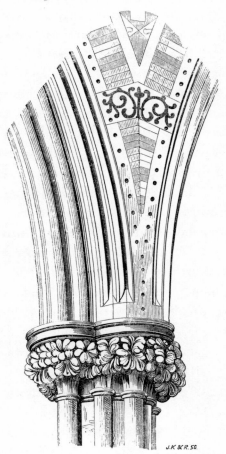

J.K & R. St.

If Mr. Butterfield had been a man of less cultivated taste, or if he had had more funds at his disposal for this purpose, the experiment might have proved a failure —in the former case, because the numerous instances which we have since seen of 'original' Gothic, prove how few are yet to be trusted with the license in design which he took ; and in the latter case, because there is evidence, even at All Saints', that the secret of knowing where to stop in decorative work had still to be acquired. The multiplicity of line patterns * on the walls of this church, and the elaboration of ornament, generally make it a matter of regret that there are no broad surfaces of wall on which the eye can rest unoccupied. Frescoes, marbles, geometrical patterns, carving, mosaics, stained glass, gilding, dazzle it by their close association, and even trench on each other's claim to attention. It seems a

* For the most part incised on the ashlar and filled in with coloured mastic.

commonplace truism now to say that veined marble should not be carved, yet this was permitted in the alabaster capitals. The work is excellent, the material lovely, but the sculptor's chisel and nature's colour-brush are ill-assorted. Again, the treatment of the nave arcade suggests an inlay of bricks in a marble arch, as if the more precious material were employed as a setting for the commoner one, which is unsatisfactory. How far the architect foresaw or was responsible for the effect of the stained glass windows may be doubtful, but as a simple question of polychromy, the flood of green and yellow light which streams in from the west window is *out of key* with the colour of the walls, and widely removed from the rich mellow tones of old glass, in which the brightest hues are employed so sparingly that they sparkle like jewels. These remarks are merely typical of objections raised at the time on the subject of this work, and would not be made here but as some qualification of the praise to which Mr. Butterfield is justly entitled for this otherwise magnificent work. None but those who have examined it with attention can appreciate the masterly skill with which every proportion has been studied, or the loving care which has been bestowed on the minutest detail. Ten years elapsed during its completion, and long before the church was consecrated a change had taken place in the current of public taste, as will presently be shown.

Meanwhile, Mr. Butterfield had accepted and in many instances executed other commissions. Among these was the rebuilding of the parish church of Yealmpton, in Devonshire, undertaken at the cost of the late Mr. Bastard, of Kitley.* This was probably the first rural structure of its class in which decoration was introduced by the employment of natural colour. The chancel screen (about four feet high) is

---

* This amiable and accomplished gentleman was a sincere admirer of Mediæval architecture, the principles of which he had well studied. Soon after the completion of the church, he joined the Romish communion, and built a chapel for the Roman Catholic poor of the neighbourhood. At his death, however, which followed soon after, it ceased to be supported, and is now used as a parish school.

of Devonshire marble. The nave piers are of the same material, arranged in alternate courses (light grey and dark veined). A narrow label of marble inlay is also carried round the aisle walls and over the windows in a trefoiled form with discs (intended for lettering) in the spandrils. This label and the treatment of the chancel arch are peculiar and not very satisfactory features in the church, which, however, in other respects is designed with a great sense of beauty both in proportions and detail. As an example of Domestic architecture in the same county and by the same architect, the Anglican Conventual Establishment of 'Abbey Mere,' near Plymouth, may be mentioned. This is an unfinished but picturesque pile of buildings. Seen from across the Stonehouse Lake, on rising ground, with its walls divided into heights of two or three stories as occasion required, breaking out occasionally into an octagonal bay, or sweeping round in an apselike curve, and surmounted by a high-pitched roof of slate, it forms an admirable group. The cold grey limestone, which is the building material of this district, is generally a dull and formal one for local masonry ; but Mr. Butterfield, by breaking it up into irregular courses, has given it life and interest. Internally, the plan, though probably added to from time to time, seems excellently adapted for its purpose, and possesses the rare quality in modern Gothic of being thoroughly practical and straightforward in its arrangement.

At Leeds, Huddersfield, Eton, Sheen, Wykeham, Milton (near Adderbury), and Braisfield in Hampshire, churches, and in some cases parsonages, were built by Mr. Butterfield. In London he reaped more laurels by the erection of St. Matthias, at Stoke Newington, where the 'saddle-back' roof of the square tower was a novelty in ecclesiastical design. The same feature was introduced over the belfry of St. Alban's, Holborn, one of the most perfect and interesting examples of the architect's skill, which, through the munificent liberality of Mr. Hubbard, was raised in one of the poorest metropolitan districts, where it was much wanted. It is especially characteristic of Mr. Butterfield's design

Belfry of S. Alban's Church, London.

W. Butterfield, Architect, 1858.

that he aims at originality not only in the form but in the relative pro-portion of parts. Thus in St. Alban's the first thing that strikes one on entering is the extreme width of the nave as compared with the aisles, and the great height of the nave as compared with its width. This indeed is the secret of the striking and picturesque character which dis-tinguishes his works from others which are less daring in conception and therefore less liable to mistakes. Mr. Butterfield has been the leader of a school, and it is necessary for a leader to be bold.

Over the chancel arch and in the space included between it and the roof above, the wall is enriched with ornamental brickwork arranged in diaper patterns which are intersected here and there by circular panels filled with the same material. These panels are disposed, apparently, without the slightest reference to the outline of the arch below, which indeed intersects them abruptly as if it had been cut through the wall at random. Here then is an excellent illustration of what some of Mr. Butterfield's critics called his culpable eccentricity of taste. How easy it would have been, they argued, to adapt this ornamental brickwork to the space for which it is intended—to map out the patterns so as to look as if they had been intended for this particular piece of wall and no other, and let the bounding lines of construction regulate and deter-mine the nature of the patterns within !

This is indeed precisely what an ordinary architect would have done. But does nature decorate after this fashion ? The ablest art-critic of our own day has deftly pointed out that the variegations of colour on the skins of beasts and the plumage of birds have little or no relation with the forms which they adorn. And if this be considered a far-fetched authority, we have only to remember the extraordinary success of Japanese decoration, where symmetry (as we moderns understand the word) and what may be called the *methodism* of ornament are utterly discarded, and with so admirable a result that the highest grace of European manufacture in an artistic sense sinks into insignificance beside it.

With a designer of such genius and originality as Mr. Butterfield, it is difficult to estimate how much of his departure from accepted conventionalities of form and arrangement is due to conviction and how much to accident. It is difficult to conceive how an architect with a keen sense of beauty and fitness could have tolerated so unfortunate a distribution of lines as that which occurs in the central portion of the reredos at St. Alban's, or have adopted such an unconstructive type of corbel as that which supports the engaged shafts of the clerestory.

Yet the mouldings of the nave arcade are modelled with singular felicity, and the mural arcuation of the aisles is treated with consummate skill.

In examining the character of this architect's work here and elsewhere one can scarcely avoid the conclusion that the guiding principle of his taste is rooted in a determination to be singular. And on this principle he acts at any sacrifice, whether of tradition, convenience, or grace. Architectural features which it is the fashion to elaborate he reduces to the severest and most archaic forms. On comparatively unimportant details he frequently lavishes his fondest care. He aims at grandeur and effect when most designers are content with simplicity. Yet he has nothing in common with that school whose chief aim is to make their buildings picturesque. In this respect he presents a marked contrast to Pugin, and a still greater contrast to those who, taking up Gothic Art where Pugin left it, have endeavoured to improve upon his design—not by a wider range of study but by a freer exercise of license.

Perhaps there is no matter of detail in the treatment of which Butterfield has displayed more originality than decorative iron-work. Thirty years ago one might have safely predicted the type of railing which would enclose the sacrarium of a new church. The lock-escutcheons and hinge-fronts which ornamented the entrance door were sure to be designed on one of a dozen patterns. The gas-standards, coronæ, and other metal fittings might be found portrayed in the Mediæval ironmongers' advertisements.

Butterfield's iron-work was almost from the first original. In All Saints' and afterwards in St. Alban's Church he adopted for his screens that strap-like treatment of foliation, which was then a novelty in the Revival, but which is not without precedent and is unquestionably justified by the nature of the material used.

It has been observed, and with some truth, that in the embellishment of his churches Mr. Butterfield has introduced but little sculpture and shows a decided preference for pictorial decoration. This is so far true that in both his principal London buildings, viz. All Saints' and St. Albans', we find little or no figure-carving while the chancels in each case are resplendent with colour. Without attempting to divine the precise cause of this peculiarity, it is not unreasonable to assume that it is due in some measure to the general difficulty which architects have found in getting decorative sculpture satisfactorily executed. There is no want of manipulative skill, or of imitative ability, but from some cause or another there is a great want of spirit,

in the present carver's work.   The Mediæval sculptor, with half the
care and less than half the finish now bestowed on such details, managed
to throw life and vigour into the capitals and panel subjects which grew
beneath his chisel.   The 'angel choir' at Lincoln is rudely executed
compared with many a modern bas-relief, but the features of the winged
minstrels are radiant with celestial happiness.   There are figures of
kings crumbling into dust in the niches of Exeter Cathedral which
retain even now a dignity of attitude and lordly grace which no
' restoration ' is likely to revive.   Our nineteenth century angels look
like demure Bible-readers, somewhat too conscious of their piety to
be interesting.   Our nineteenth century monarchs seem (in stone at
least) very well-to-do pleasant gentlemen, but are scarcely of an heroic
type.   The roses and lilies, the maple foliage and forked spleenwort,
with which we crown our pillars or deck our cornices, are cut with
wonderful precision and neatness, but somehow they miss the charm of
old-world handicraft.   And as we examine the corbels and *subsellæ* of
a subscription church—features which in days of yore revealed after a
grotesque fashion the sins and frailties of humanity, we shall now
find no uglier record than of art's decline, and if we blush it will not be
at the indelicacy of the subject but for the incapacity of the workman.
The frescoes executed by Mr. Dyce for the chancel of All Saints' differ
so essentially in motive and sentiment from the water-glass paintings
designed by Mr. Le Strange at St. Alban's that they can hardly be
compared.   The former were begun at a time when the German *heilige*
school was generally considered the best model of taste in decoration,
and though Mr. Dyce invested his figures with a grace of colour and
arrangement which was all his own, there is a certain tendency to acade-
micism and over-refinement of handling in his work that is somewhat
out of keeping with the architecture of the church.

Mr. Le Strange went into the opposite extreme.   He had on the
east wall of St. Alban's chancel to deal with ten large panels, separated
from each other by narrow slabs of alabaster.   This he filled with ten

Balliol College Chapel.

W. Butterfield, Architect, 1856.

paintings representing incidents in the life of Our Lord—treated, so far as the style of drawing is concerned, after a thoroughly archaic fashion—surrounding each with a broad border of colour, on which, however, the figures intrude so much as to leave the spectator in some doubt as to which is border and which is background. The effect was a little glaring at first, but time and London smoke have considerably toned down the hues, which at present are not inharmonious.

How much Mr. Butterfield values the aid of colour, even for the exterior of his buildings, may be noticed in the Chapel of Balliol College, Oxford, where the admixture of grey and purple tiles in the roof, and the introduction of bands of reddish stone in the main body of the walls, add singular grace to the design. The interior of this chapel is wonderfully effective, and rendered more so no doubt by the fact that some old stained glass of the former building has been re-inserted in windows on the north side. The design of the roof is simple to severity—plain rafters (with plaster between) being used over the body of the chapel, and the principals being only slightly decorated with colour at the east end. The voussoirs of the window arches are accentuated by the occasional use of a brownish stone, alternating, though by no means at regular intervals, with the white ashlar. The chancel is lined with alabaster scored over with incised lines so as to form diamond-shaped panels, at the intersection of which quatrefoils are sunk to the depth of an inch, giving them at a little distance the effect of black inlay. All this is of course foreign to English Pointed work, and is the more remarkable, because, in his mouldings and tracery, Mr. Butterfield's design as a rule is thoroughly national. The wood fittings of the chapel are very peculiar, and, though by no means wanting in refinement, partake of that dry formal character which distinguishes some of the quasi-Gothic carpentry of the last century.

But if criticism is invited by such oddities as these, it is openly defied by the design of Keble College, where this architect, in the immediate neighbourhood of buildings rendered venerable by association with the past, has recently ventured on a more emphatic departure from local traditions of style than Oxford has yet seen, either in the decadence or the Revival of Gothic, applied to buildings of a similar class. Perhaps it is hardly fair to judge of this building so soon after its erection, when the horizontal bands of stone, of black brick, and of white brick, oppose each other so crudely that in looking at the various fronts—east, west, north, or south—one can see nothing but stripes. Yet, even when time has toned down the colour of the materials, they will be always predominant in the design, and if such an innovation be tolerated at Oxford—once the head-quarters of Mediæval taste—we need not be surprised to find it imitated elsewhere. Indeed, this mode of surface decoration has been long practised in other works, though by no means with equal skill. In Keble College the main mass of the walls is executed in red brick, and the architect has cunningly broken up his black bands with white bricks and his white bands with black ones, in order to relieve each other from monotony and heaviness. The window dressings and mullions are of stone, and the general design—except in the particulars mentioned—is distinguished by intense simplicity.

It is a remarkable fact, and one which is keenly suggestive of this paradoxical age of art, that Mr. Butterfield's professional followers are the most conservative in their opinions, the most exclusive in their taste, and the stanchest admirers of traditional English Gothic among contemporary architects, and yet there is no one who in some respects has more deliberately discarded tradition than their leader. But then he has done so consistently. There is a sober earnestness of purpose in his work widely different from that of some designers, who seem to be tossed about on the sea of popular taste, unable, apparently, to decide what style they will adopt, and trying their hands in turn at French, at Italian, and what not, with no more reason than a love of change or a restless striving after effect. He does not care to produce *showy* buildings at a sacrifice—even a justifiable sacrifice—of constructive strength.   To the pretty superficial school of Gothic, busy with pinnacles, chamfers, and fussy carving, he has never condescended. He has his own (somewhat stern) notions of architectural beauty, and he holds to them whether he is planning a cottage or a cathedral. His work gives one the idea of a man who has designed it not so much to please his clients as to please himself.   In estimating the value of his skill, posterity may find something to smile at as eccentric, something to deplore as ill-judged, and much that will astonish as daring, but they will find nothing to despise as commonplace or mean.

CHAPTER XV.

T was suggested in the last chapter that during the ten years which elapsed between the commencement and the completion of All Saints' Church, the public taste in architecture underwent a decided change. It would perhaps have been more correct to say two or three changes, but undoubtedly the first and perhaps the most important one was expressed by that phase in the Gothic Revival which has since been distinguished—and in one sense honourably distinguished—by the name of Ruskinism.

If the author of ' Modern Painters ' had been content to limit his researches, his criticism, and the dissemination of his principles to the field of pictorial art alone, he would have won for himself a name not easily forgotten. No English amateur had measured so accurately the individual merits and deficiencies of the old schools of painting, or was so well qualified to test them by the light of reason. No critic had educated his eye more carefully by observation of Nature. No essayist enjoyed the faculty of expressing his ideas with greater force or in finer language. But Mr. Ruskin's taste for art was a comprehensive one. He learnt at an early age that painting, sculpture, and architecture are intimately associated, not merely in their history but in their practice, and in the fundamental principles which regulate their respective styles. His love of pictures was not that of a mere collector or dilettante, who buys them to hang up in gilt frames to furnish his drawing-room, but that of an artist who considers no noble building complete without storied walls and sculptured panels, and who believes that even in an ordinary dwelling-house there might, under a proper condition of things, be found scope for the carver's handiwork and limner's cunning.

Mr. Ruskin looked around him at the modern architecture of England and saw that it not only did not realise this ideal but was diametrically opposed to it. He found the majority of his countrymen either profoundly indifferent to the art or interested in it chiefly as antiquarians and pedants. He saw public buildings copied from those of a nobler age, but starved or vulgarised in the copying. He saw private houses— some modelled on what was supposed to be an Italian pattern, and others modelled on what was supposed to be a Mediæval pattern, and he found too often neither grandeur in the one nor grace in the other. He saw palaces which looked mean, and cottages which were tawdry. He saw masonry without interest, ornament without beauty, and sculpture without life. He walked through the streets of London and found that they consisted for the most part of flaunting shop fronts, stuccoed porticos, and plaster cornices. It is true there were fine clubs and theatres and public institutions scattered here and there ; but after making due allowance for their size, for the beauty of materials used, and for the neatness of the workmanship, how far could they be considered as genuine works of art ? Mr. Ruskin was by no means the first person who asked this question ; but he was the first who asked it boldly, and with a definite purpose.

Pugin for years had argued that it was the duty of modern Christians to Christianise their architecture—that is, as he explained it, to revive the style of building which prevailed in this country for some centuries before the Reformation ; but he made no secret of his hope that in readopting Gothic, Englishmen would gradually learn to readopt their ancient faith ; and this was what a large proportion of them did not exactly contemplate with satisfaction. The High Church party, too, were mainly anxious for the Revival, because they saw in it an opportunity of carrying out their notions of orthodox ritual, and of reviving ecclesiastical ceremonies which had long been obsolete. It would be hard indeed to blame either the author of 'The True Principles' or the followers of Dr. Pusey for viewing the matter in this light. The interests of religion are of higher importance than the interests of art, but art has more than once been the handmaid of religion, and the seeking to retain her in that service, from conscientious motives, was in both cases a most natural and obvious course.

Twenty years ago, however, the extreme Protestant party was still a strong one. They saw mischief lurking in every pointed niche, and heresy peeping from behind every Gothic pillar. They regarded the Mediævalists with suspicion, and identified their cause with Romish hierarchy, with the Inquisition and Smithfield. It would be a curious matter for speculation to ascertain how far the Revival has been encouraged, and how far it has been retarded, by ecclesiological zeal or idle bigotry.

When Mr. Ruskin first entered the lists as a champion of Gothic Architecture, it was certainly not as a Ritualist or as an apologist for the Church of Rome. His introduction to the 'Seven Lamps of Architecture' partook largely, as indeed much of his writing then did, of a religious tone, but he wrote rather as a moral philosopher than as a churchman, and though his theological views found here and there decided expression they could hardly be identified with any particular sect. His book, therefore, found favour with a large class of readers who had turned from Pugin's arguments with impatience, and to whom even the 'Ecclesiologist' had preached in vain. With regard to architecture as an art, he openly declared himself a reformer.

I have long felt (he wrote) convinced of the necessity, in order to its progress, of some determined effort to extricate from the confused mass of traditions and dogmata with which it has become encumbered during imperfect or restricted practice, those large principles of right which are applicable to every stage and style of it. Uniting the technical and imaginative elements as essentially as humanity does soul and body, it shows the same infirmly balanced liability to the prevalence of the lower part over the higher, to the interference of the constructive, with the purity and simplicity of the reflective, element. This tendency, like every other form of materialism, is increasing with the advance of the age ; and the only laws which resist it, based upon partial precedents, and already regarded with disrespect as decrepit, if not with defiance as tyrannical, are evidently inapplicable to the new forms and functions of the art which the necessities of the day demand.

This was enough to alarm that school of the Revivalists whose aim was to reproduce, line for line, the works of the Middle Ages in England, and their alarm was increased when they found that Mr. Ruskin's taste was of so comprehensive an order as to include Italian Gothic among his models of structural beauty. Up to this time English architects, whether of the Gothic or Classic school, had regarded such buildings as the Doge's Palace at Venice, or the Church of San Michele at Lucca, as curious examples of degenerate design— interesting indeed as links in the history of European art, but utterly unworthy of study or imitation. It was, therefore, with some surprise that they found features from those buildings engraved in the 'Seven Lamps' as instances of noble carving and judicious ornamentation, while the lantern of the Church of St. Ouen at Rouen, which the old school of Mediævalists had accepted as a miracle of grace, was described as one of the basest pieces of Gothic in Europe. But Mr. Ruskin did not confine his remarks to general praise or censure of existing works. Arranging the principles which he conceived had regulated or should regulate architectural design under several heads, he proceeded to show how far they had been developed in past ages, and to what extent they were liable to be missed or falsified in the present. In doing this he occasionally traversed old ground ; but he avoided as far as possible the footsteps of his predecessors, and even where he agreed with their conclusions, he generally led up to them with a different line of argument. There are sentiments expressed in 'The Lamps' of Sacrifice, of Truth, and of Memory, which had been frequently expressed before ; but they are founded on novel theories, identified with minutiæ of facts which had hitherto escaped attention, or so clothed in metaphysical language as to assume a different aspect. He showed, for example, more clearly and emphatically than any previous writer on art, the folly of wasting money on the meaningless and uninteresting fineries of a modern house, while a tenth part of the expense thus thrown away on so-called decoration, which no one cares for or enjoys, ' would, if collectively offered and wisely employed, build a marble church for every town in England.' But he carefully guarded himself against the imputation of advocating either meanness in domestic architecture, or ostentatious display of magnificence in ecclesiastical.

The most advanced practitioners of the day had long agreed that it was undesirable to employ iron for visible construction in a Gothic building. But many of them had not hesitated to use its where it could be concealed from view. On this point Mr. Ruskin found himself embarrassed by some doubt. He had propounded the dogma that there was no law based on past practice which might not be overthrown by the invention of a new material, and he could not avoid the conclusion that a fresh system of architectural laws might gradually be evolved from the modern use of iron. Besides, there were examples of its employment in good ages of art—as the Florence dome and the central tower at Salisbury—to say nothing of minor instances. On the other hand, all his artistic sympathies were opposed to the nature of metallic construction. After deliberating on this confliction of theory and practice, he came to the conclusion that iron might be used as a *cement*, but not as a support—or, as an architect would say, as a tie, but not as a strut. This was a distinction, though in arriving at it he forgot to notice the distinct qualities of strength in tension and compression respectively possessed by wrought and cast iron.

Professor Willis had already demonstrated that Gothic tracery had been gradually developed from the close association of pierced openings in the solid arch-heads of early windows. The prevalent opinion was that the full beauty of tracery had only been reached when this primitive type was forgotten, and the stone ribs themselves, rather than the spaces which they enclosed, were reduced by geometrical rule to definite form. Mr. Ruskin held, on the contrary, that in proportion as this stage had been approached, the true grace of tracery had diminished. He pointed out that the forms which the penetrations assumed were of primary importance, and that whereas in the early windows they were simple and severe in outline, in the late windows they became distorted and extravagant, while the flowing unstone-like character of the tracery itself gave rise to a foolish supposition among the ignorant, viz. that it originated in the imitation of vegetable form.

To this supposition Mr. Ruskin alluded in terms of well-deserved contempt, yet it is not a little remarkable that in defining the conditions of architectural beauty he himself endeavoured to trace its source in almost every instance to the example of nature. This was, in short, the foundation and elementary belief of his teaching. From this belief he derived, or thought that he derived, a fixed and lasting standard, by which the value of every structural feature, the quality of all ornament, and indeed the excellence of most designs as a whole, might be tested. In endeavouring to prove this theory he encountered endless difficulties, involved himself in many apparent contradictions and inconsistencies, and though it enlisted the sympathies of those whose opinions on art are based on sentiment rather than study, it was received with incredulity by a large proportion of his readers, while professional architects, as a rule, regarded him in the light of a vain and misinformed enthusiast.

There is nothing in the world easier than the expression of a simple opinion on matters of taste; but there is nothing more difficult than to succeed in justifying it, not only in one's own mind, but to the satisfaction of other people. It was of course open to Mr. Ruskin to declare the Greek triglyph and the Greek fret ugly things. So far many of his readers, and especially the Gothic architects of the day, agreed with him.   But when he attempted to prove that the triglyph was ugly because it suggested no organic form, and that the fret ornament was ugly because its natural type was only found in crystals of bismuth, even his admirers began to smile.   They felt that this mode of reasoning carried a little farther would tend to condemn many architectural features, the use of which has been long sanctioned by custom, and even authorised by expedience, but which has no semblance of a prototype in the book of Nature.

Assuming the application of Mr. Ruskin's theory to be correct in these instances, it would be difficult to assign any reason for retaining such distinctively Gothic details as the pinnacle, the battlemented parapet, the moulded arch, or that peculiar form of Venetian billet decoration, of which he himself says, in another work, that ' nothing could be ever invented fitter for its purpose.'   Indeed, they are all admirable in their place, but it must be a poetical order of mind which could detect in them any resemblance to natural form.

The truth is that Mr. Ruskin was continually advancing propositions, often excellent in themselves, which he as frequently failed to maintain—not for want of argument, but because his arguments proved too much.   Nothing, for instance, can be more rational than a great deal of what he says in the ' Lamp of Beauty ' on the subject of proportion.   That subtle quality of architectural grace was, he averred, not a science which could be taught, but the result of individual genius in the designer.

Proportions are infinite (and that in all kinds of things, as severally in colours, lines, shades, lights, and forms), as possible airs in music ; and it is just as rational an attempt to teach a young architect how to proportion truly and well by calculating for him proportions of fine works, as it would be to teach him to compose melodies by calculating the mathematical relations of the notes in Beethoven's ' Adelaïde ' or Mozart's ' Requiem.'   The man who has eye and intellect will invent beautiful proportions and cannot help it ; but he can no more tell us how to do it than Wordsworth could tell us how to write a sonnet or than Scott could have told us how to plan a romance.

This is all very well, but a few pages further on we find our author dissecting the flower stem of a water-plantain, and using arithmetical formulæ to show the subdivision of its branches, from which he implies that a lesson is to be learnt. Now it may or may not be true that the anatomy of water-plantains is suggestive of good proportion in architecture, and it may or may not be right that Mr. Ruskin should recommend us to examine it for that reason ; but if the secret of right proportion is, as he has said, not to be learnt, it follows that both the sermon and its text are thrown away. It was one of the same writer's early opinions that the scientific study of perspective was quite useless. In course of time he wrote a treatise himself on the subject, which is certainly not less complicated or obscure than many others which had previously been published.

These inconsistencies and prejudices are to be regretted, not only on their own account, but because they have from time to time exposed the author to criticism which is not only severe, but, up to a certain point, justifiable.

Many an architect who had no time to read through the 'Seven Lamps' with attention cast the book impatiently aside as he lighted on some passage which betrayed the author's inexperience in technical details. Many a journalist who knew nothing of technicalities was fully alive to irreconcilable dogmas and flaws of logic. Meanwhile, the great moral of his teaching was overlooked. His opinions were regarded by many of the profession as utterly absurd and irrational. The general press admired his eloquence, but questioned his arguments, and stood aghast at his conclusions. For Mr. Ruskin had even then hinted at certain social reforms, which he has since endeavoured to reduce to a system, but which have as much chance of being realised as the discovery of the philosopher's stone. To what extent morality and art were allied in the Middle Ages, or at any other period of the world's history, may be doubtful. What we do know is, that in the nineteenth century a bad artist is not unfrequently a very good

Christian, and that an indifferent Christian may be an excellent artist. The services of architects, sculptors, and painters have, it is true, been of late years secured for the Church; but it is probable that they undertook their work as they would have undertaken any other sort of work—zealously, but, except in a few rare instances, without extraordinary enthusiasm. It would, no doubt, be beneficial to the interests of society if every art-workman were to become a religious man; but the chances are that the progress of art would not be advanced by his conversion.

Mr. Ruskin is one of the most accomplished art critics, and perhaps the most eloquent writer on art that England has seen, in this or any other age. He is also, if any man ever was, a theoretical philanthropist. His views on the subject of art may in the main be sound; his philanthropical intentions are, we doubt not, sincere; but, considered in combination as they are usually associated, they present a scheme which is utterly impracticable.

On the Gothic Revival, as it was ordinarily understood, Mr. Ruskin himself did not look very hopefully. He had seen the fitful variations of taste to which modern architecture had already been exposed, and perhaps he foresaw other and more radical changes by which it was threatened. He was impatient of the tame and spiritless formality which distinguished too many specimens of contemporary design; but, on the other hand, he was sick of the cant which continually demanded novelty and freedom from precedent.

A day never passes without our hearing our English architects called upon to be original and to invent a new style : about as sensible and necessary an exhortation as to ask of a man who has never had rags enough on his back to keep out the cold to invent a new mode of cutting a coat. Give him a whole coat first and let him concern himself about the fashion of it afterwards. We want no new style of architecture. Who wants a new style of painting or of sculpture? But we want *some* style.

This is not exactly one of the happiest of Mr. Ruskin's similes, but it serves to illustrate his meaning. What he meant was that a style of national architecture should be definitely selected for adoption, and universally practised. The choice of a style he limited to four types : (1) Pisan Romanesque ; (2) Florentine of Giotto's time ; (3) Venetian Gothic; and (4) the earliest English Decorated. Of these he considered that the last would, on the whole, be the safest to choose; but it was to be 'well fenced' from the chance of degenerating again into Perpendicular, and might be enriched by the introduction of a French element.

To ensure conformity of taste to this standard when once settled, Mr. Ruskin proposed that an universal system of form and workmanship should be everywhere adopted *and enforced*. How it was to be enforced and by whom he did not venture to explain. Whether it was to become the law of the land; what provision was to be made for its fulfilment; what penalties were to be attached to its neglect or violation , whether the architect of a Jacobean mansion would be subject to a fine, or how far any decided tendency to Flamboyant design could be considered as a misdemeanour; all these were details of his scheme which he left others to determine. That the scheme presented a difficulty he was aware, but he did not consider that any difficulty could affect the value of his proposition.

It may be said that this is impossible. It may be so. I fear it is so. I have nothing to do with the possibility or impossibility of it. I simply know and assert the necessity of it. If it be impossible, English art is impossible. Give it up at once. You are wasting time and money and energy upon it, and though you exhaust centuries and treasuries, and break hearts for it, you will never raise it above the merest dilettanteism. Think not of it. It is a dangerous vanity, a mere gulf in which genius after genius will be swallowed up, and it will not close.

It was wild and impetuous reasoning such as this which broke the spell of Mr. Ruskin's authority and robbed his eloquence of half its charm. People began to ask themselves whether a man gifted,

T

even as they knew him to be gifted, with a keen appreciation of the beautiful in art and nature, with intellectual faculties of a high order, with a moral sense which revealed itself in the minutiæ of æsthetics— whether even such a guide as this was to be trusted when he allowed his theories to waft him into dreamland, or to culminate in plans which would have been considered unfeasible in Utopia.

In so far as the author of 'The Seven Lamps of Architecture' confined himself to strictures on all that was false or mean or meretricious in bad art, or pointed out the truth, the purity, and grace of noble art (and on the whole no one was better qualified to draw these distinctions), he did excellent service to national taste. In so far as he allowed his prejudices to get the better of his judgment, in so far as he attempted to form—what never will be formed—a perfect and universally acceptable test of architectural excellence, or pursued fanciful theories at the expense of common sense, he exposed himself to the obvious charges of unfairness and inconsistency, and damaged the cause which he had most at heart.*

Two years after the publication of 'The Seven Lamps,' Mr. Ruskin came before the world as the author of another and more important work, with which his name has been more permanently associated, and for which, if we regard collectively the character of its contents, the nature of its aim, or the beauty and vigour of its language, there is no parallel in the range of English literature.

The Mediæval architecture of Venice had hitherto been to most of our countrymen an unexplored mine of artistic interest, which probably few, if any, professional students in this country considered worth the working. Since the days of Joseph Woods, a man of education and refined taste, who came back from his Continental tour to tell the British public that he could find no beauty in St. Mark's, it is probable that our architects who went there to sketch and to measure

---

* It is but fair to state here that Mr. Ruskin has since expressed himself dissatisfied with the form in which many of his early opinions were recorded at this period of his life.

were content to fill their portfolios with drawings of the Libreria and the Renaissance palaces, and to leave the Byzantine and Gothic relics to their fate. Those who had not visited Venice itself could form no idea of such remains from the cold and lifeless engravings of Cicognara's work. Fontana gave (to the artist) even less information. But at last the merits of Venetian Gothic found an able and a doughty exponent. Mr. Ruskin for many years of his life had returned again and again to examine it, to admire it, to sketch its details with a loving hand, to note carefully and minutely its peculiar characteristics, and to lay up a stock of information respecting its origin, its development and decay, such as never had before been so copiously accumulated or turned to so excellent an account.

The same year which saw the first-fruits of this labour witnessed the realisation of a scheme of world-wide reputation, which had also for its object—or at least one of its main objects—the advancement of art; but it is impossible to conceive two modes devised for that end more thoroughly opposed to each other in sentiment, in purpose, and example, than the publication of ' The Stones of Venice ' and the opening of the Great Exhibition of 1851.

That ' The Stones of Venice ' expanded into three volumes is no matter of surprise when we remember that the author's aim was not only to give an historical and artistic description of Venetian architecture but to incorporate with that description his ideas of what modern architecture should be : not only to illustrate, but to moralise, expound, and advise. In entering on so bold and comprehensive an undertaking as this, it was of course necessary to proceed in a methodical manner, and if classification of subject could ensure this end Mr. Ruskin did his best to ensure it. Not only was each volume divided into chapters, not only was each chapter divided into sections, but further divisions and sub-divisions were made to such an extent that it became an effort to remember in what precise relation they stood to each other.

The ' virtues of architecture ' were declared to be three. The main duties of architecture were declared to be two. The divisions of architecture were declared to be six. The first of the two main duties of architecture were concerned with Walls, Roofs, and Apertures. The Wall was divided into the Foundation, the Body or Veil, and the Cornice. The roof was of two kinds—the Roof proper and the Roof mask. The Cornice was of two kinds—the Roof Cornice and the Wall Cornice. Roof cornices were, again, subdivided into the Eaved cornice and the Bracket. Eaved cornices were of several kinds, brackets were of several kinds, and, in short, to trace intelligibly the ramifications of each feature on Mr. Ruskin's plan would be to rival the intricacy of a genealogical tree.

In pursuing this system of classification Mr. Ruskin did not hesitate to coin names and employ phrases unknown in any architectural glossary and certainly unfamiliar to professional ears. The 'expressions' 'wall-veil,' 'arch-load,' 'linear and surface Gothic,' and 'ignoble grotesque,' though now intelligible enough to those who have read his works, were at the time, and simply because of their novelty, pronounced by many to be obscure and affected. For precisely the same reason many of his theories were condemned as untenable. The injustice of this inference is obvious. It was not affectation which led Mr. Ruskin to spend month after month in studying the capitals of the Ducal Palace ; in measuring the intercolumniations of the Fondaco de' Turchi ; in planning the churches of Torcello and Murano ; in delineating the rich inlay of the Palazzo Badoari. It was the work of no shallow reasoner to show step by step the development of the pointed arch with all its varieties of outline and tracery, to analyse and define the conditions of sculptured decoration, to draw nice distinctions between the profiles of base-mouldings and string-courses, to demonstrate the relations between archivolt and aperture. In these and a hundred other instances he showed that his appreciation of architecture was not that of a mere amateur, but based on an earnest study of its fundamental principles.

It is true that here and there he betrayed an imperfect acquaintance with the science of construction, but it was chiefly on points which did not affect his arguments; while in all that related to the philosophy of his favourite art or the elements of its beauty he generally proved his case whether he was answering Mr. Garbett or posing Mr. Fergusson.

Indeed Mr. Ruskin discoursed on art with advantages not often possessed by ordinary art critics. Before he ventured to write on the subject his curriculum of study had extended over a wide field. He had had a university education. He had looked into natural science. He was better acquainted than most men who have not devoted themselves specially to such pursuits with geology and botany. He was well read in classic literature. His taste and skill as an artist were remarkable, and his sketches of architecture and of decorative sculpture are even now second to none in refinement and delicacy of execution. A man who with such qualifications sets himself seriously to examine the principles of a particular branch of art has a right to be heard when he talks of it.

And, for all his errors and failings, Mr. Ruskin *was* heard.* Never, since the days of the English decadence—never, since the Pointed arch was depressed into Tudor ugliness—never, since tradition lost its sway in regulating the fashion of structural design—has the subject of Gothic

---

* A curious evidence of the extent to which ' Ruskinism ' was at this time recognised in English society may be mentioned. The Latin Epilogue to the ' Westminster Play ' is generally a reflex of some popular taste or current topic of sufficient notoriety to afford scope for good-humoured satire. In 1857 the *Epilogus ad Adelphos* contains the following dialogue :

Ctesipho. Græcia in hac ὕλη palmam fert semper. *Æschinus.* Ineptis !
Est cumulus nudæ simplicitatis iners.
Ars contrà mediæva haud lege aut limite iniquo
Contenta, huc, illuc, pullulat ad libitum.

     *   *   *   *   *

Ctesipho. An rectum atque fidem saxa laterque docent ?
Æschinus. Graiâ et Romanâ nihil immoralius usquam
Archi-est-tecturâ—(*turning to* ' *The Seven Lamps* ') pagina sexta—tene.
Sic ipsus dixit. *Ctesipho.* Vix hæc comprendere possum.
Æschinus. Scilicet Æsthesi tu, miserande, cares.

Architecture been rendered so popular in this country, as for a while it was rendered by the aid of his pen. All that had been argued—all that had been preached on the subject previously, was cast into the shade by the vigour of his protest. Previous apologists for the Revival had relied more or less on ecclesiastical sentiment, on historical interest, or on a vague sense of the picturesque for their plea in its favour. It was reserved for the author of ' The Stones of Venice ' to strike a chord of human sympathy that vibrated through all hearts, and to advocate, independently of considerations which had hitherto only enlisted the sympathy of a few, those principles of Mediæval Art whose application should be universal. There are passages in this work recording nobler truths concerning architecture than had ever before found expression in our mother tongue. The rich fertility of the author's language, his happy choice of illustrative parallels, the clear and forcible manner in which he states his case or points his moral, and, above all, the marvellous capacity of his descriptive power, are truly admirable. No finer English has been written in our time. It is poetry in prose.

That he made many converts, and found many disciples among the younger architects of the day, is not to be wondered. Students, who but a year or so previously had been content to regard Pugin as their leader, or who had modelled their notions of art on the precepts of the ' Ecclesiologist,' found a new field open to them, and hastened to occupy it. They prepared designs in which the elements of Italian Gothic were largely introduced : churches in which the ' lily capital ' of St. Mark's was found side by side with Byzantine bas-reliefs and mural inlay from Murano ; town halls wherein the arcuation and baseless columns of the Ducal Palace were reproduced ; mansions which borrowed their parapets from the Calle del Bagatin, and windows from the Ca' d'Oro. They astonished their masters by talking of the Savageness of Northern Gothic, of the Intemperance of Curves, and the Laws of Foliation ; and broke out into open heresy in their abuse of Renaissance detail. They went to Venice or Verona—not to study the works of Sansovino and San Michele—but to sketch the tomb of the Scaligers and to measure the front of the Hotel Danieli.   They made drawings in the Zoological Gardens, and conventionalised the forms of birds, beasts, and reptiles into examples of 'noble grotesque' for decorative sculpture. They read papers before Architectural Societies, embodying Mr. Ruskin's sentiments in language which rivalled the force, if it did not exactly match the refinement, of their model.   They made friends of the Pre-Raphaelite painters (then rising into fame), and promised themselves as radical a reform in national architecture as had been inaugurated in the field of pictorial art.   Nor was this all.   Not a few architects who had already established a practice began to think that there might be something worthy of attention in the new doctrine. Little by little they fell under its influence.   Discs of marble, billet-mouldings, and other details of Italian Gothic, crept into many a London street-front.   Then bands of coloured brick (chiefly red and yellow) were introduced, and the voussoirs of arches were treated after the same fashion.*

But the influence of Mr. Ruskin's teaching reached a higher level than this, and manifested itself in unexpected quarters.   Years afterwards, in the centre of the busiest part of our busy capital—the very last place one would have supposed likely to be illumined by the light of 'The Seven Lamps'—more than one palatial building was raised, which recalled in the leading features of its design and decoration the distinctive character of Venetian Gothic.

The literature of the Revival was sensibly affected by the same cause. It is impossible not to recognise even in the title of Mr. Street's charming volume, 'The Brick and Marble Architecture of North Italy,' a

---

* In the suburbs this mode of decoration rose rapidly into favour for cockney villas and public taverns, and laid the foundation of that peculiar order of Victorian Architecture which has since been distinguished by the familiar but not altogether inappropriate name of the Streaky Bacon Style

palpable echo from ' The Stones of Venice,' while in some of his theories
—as, for instance, that the undulation in the pavement of St. Mark's
was intended to typify the stormy seas of life—we find a reflex of
Mr. Ruskin's tendency to natural symbolism.

For a considerable time, indeed, the principles enunciated by this
accomplished author and critic gained ground even in spite of violent
opposition.   It was perhaps while they were most vigorously attacked
on one side that they received the staunchest support from the other.
But the current of public taste, even in the artistic world, is capricious
in its course, and is subject to constant deviation.   Of late years other
influences have been at work—for good or evil one can scarcely yet
say, but certainly to some purpose.   If the Gothic Revival has lost
Mr. Ruskin as a leader, it is to be trusted that he may still watch its
progress as a counseller and a friend.

CHAPTER XVI.

THE flourish of trumpets which announced to an admiring crowd that the Great Exhibition of 1851 was open to the world found many an echo outside that ingeniously-contrived building. Not content with prophecies of future peace and plenty for England—not content with proclaiming that the ambition of kings, international jealousies, and all other incentives to war would thenceforth yield to the beneficent influence of commercial intercourse—not content with inventing poetical names for the structure in Hyde Park which were widely remote from its purpose and material being—the enthusiastic public declared that a new order of architecture had at last been discovered that would soon supersede every kind of style which had hitherto been devised, and that it needed but time to ensure its universal adoption.

If more practical men did not precisely share these anticipations, it must be confessed that a few did their best to encourage them. One architect at least, whose acquaintance with the history of his art extends over all time, and compasses regions from the North Sea to the Arabian Gulf, from the Sierra d'Estrella to the Himalaya Mountains, did not hesitate to avow his conviction that Mr. Paxton, guided by the light of ' his own native sagacity ' had achieved a success which proved incontrovertibly how mistaken we had been in endeavouring to copy from ancient examples ; that the architecture of the future should be the architecture of common sense ; and that if the same principles which had inspired the designer of the Exhibition building had been applied to the Houses of Parliament, to the British Museum, and to the new churches then in course of erection, millions of money would have been saved and a better class of art secured.

Sanguine converts to the new faith began to talk as if glass and iron would form an admirable substitute for bricks and mortar, and wondrous changes were predicted as to the future aspect of our streets and squares. The failure of the professional competition invited by the Royal Commissioners of 1850 was pointed out with triumph, and architects were warned that if they still fondly clung to the traditions of the past they had better abandon their vocation altogether.

At length a climax of absurdity was reached. The intelligent gentleman whose professional occupation had previously been limited to the study and practice of horticulture, and to whom it had occurred that the objects collected for international display would be better lodged in an enormous greenhouse than anywhere else, was professionally consulted as an architect and employed on the restoration of a church!

It did not take many years to dissipate the dreams of universal philanthropy to which the Exhibition scheme had given rise, and with these dreams the charming visions of a glass-and-iron architecture may also be said to have vanished. If the structural details of the Crystal Palace teach us any lesson it is that they are strictly limited in application to the purpose for which that building was erected, and that even for such a purpose their adoption is not unattended by drawbacks.

The Gothic Revival itself was on the whole but little affected by the great event of 1851. Any advantage which may have been derived from the scheme in its supposed encouragement of art manufacture was more than counterbalanced by the abundant opportunities it afforded for the cultivation of bad taste. Crace's furniture, the specimens of stone and wood carving by Myers, Hardman's Mediæval metal-work and stained glass, and Minton's encaustic tiles came in for some admiration, and showed in many instances Pugin's untiring industry in design. But all these objects might have been seen as well elsewhere, and in this department of art at least England found nothing to learn

JEWITT & CO SC.

The University Museum, Oxford.

from the Continent. The specimens of pseudo-Gothic furniture and church fittings which were imported from France and Belgium were with a few exceptions all miserable in design, and the more dangerous in this respect because of the meretricious attractions which many of them presented.

The Great Exhibition came to an end. Not far from the site which it occupied, and in order to pay a national tribute to the memory of the accomplished Prince who originated the scheme, a rich and costly monument is now in course of erection. It may also serve another purpose, and that is to record by its design and decoration how complete and remarkable a change has occurred within the space of a few years in the development of English taste for architecture.

Evidences of that change are scattered far and wide throughout this country, but no single town exhibits them in more regular sequence than Oxford, where, indeed, it would not be difficult to select from the University buildings alone examples illustrating the various phases through which modern Gothic has passed from its earliest revival down to the present time. One of the first-fruits of Mr. Ruskin's teaching is to be found there in the new Museum of Physical Sciences, begun in 1855 under the superintendence of Messrs. Deane and Woodward, and since carried on at intervals. However much opinions may vary as to the general effect of this building, there is no doubt that it exhibits in its details far more originality and grace than were to be found in most contemporary examples of secular Gothic. The principal front consists of two stories with an attic lighted by triangular dormers in the roof. This block is divided in the centre by a tower carried to the height of three stories, and surmounted by a wedge-shaped roof. Under the tower is the main entrance, spanned by an acutely-pointed arch, richly decorated with carving in low relief and voussoirs of dark brown stone and grey marble placed alternately, but at irregular intervals. The first-floor windows partake of an early Italian character. They are divided into two lights by slender marble columns, the arch head above being pierced with circular lights delicately cusped.   The spandrils of the tracery and the arch mouldings which

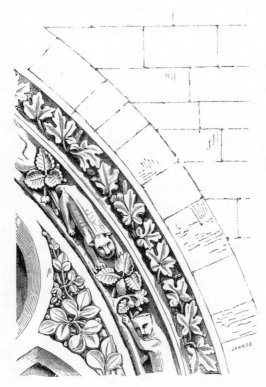

enclose them are filled with relievi of foliage and animals arranged with considerable care and executed with great refinement.

The roof, gay with purple and greyish-green slates symmetrically disposed, contrasts admirably with the rich cream colour of the Bath stone masonry, which in its turn is relieved by marble of various hues introduced in the details above mentioned.   The chromatic effect of the whole seen on a bright sunny day surrounded by natural verdure and with a blue sky overhead, is charming.   The laboratory on the right hand of the principal front is suggestive in its general outline of the well-known Glastonbury kitchen.   This building, together with the residence and offices recently erected on the other side of the Museum, helps to break the external formality of the Museum front and to lend the composition a picturesqueness which is more English than its individual features.

It is, however, in the internal arrangement of the Museum that we trace most distinctly the influence of those principles which the author of 'The Seven Lamps' so earnestly strove to inculcate.   Just as the Pre-Raphaelites—while they existed as a school—aimed at representing the heroic incidents of ordinary life, so those architects who accepted Mr.

Ruskin's guidance endeavoured to realise beauty in their art not by literally reproducing the decorative features of Mediæval work, but by investing with its spirit as far as possible the skill of modern workmanship and the materials of modern use. A large quadrangle had to be roofed with glass and iron—and the difficulty was to do this without limiting the design to the merely structural features of the Crystal Palace or condescending to the vulgar details of a railway terminus. Under these circumstances Messrs. Deane and Woodward did their best to Gothicise their ironwork, and though the attempt displayed great ingenuity it can hardly be called successful. The system of construction adopted may be good of its kind. The system of ornamentation adopted may be good of its kind. But the two are not happily associated. As a rule it is far better to use wrought or beaten metal than cast metal for decoration; but whether in enriching the capital of an iron column the same type of decorative mask should be used as is ordinarily employed for a stone capital may be questioned. In the latter case we know that the carved work represents a portion of its integral strength more or less weakened by the parts cut away. But in the case of an iron capital to which beaten metal is subsequently *attached*, as at the Oxford Museum, we feel that the ornaments of leaves and flowers, however excellent in themselves, are mere additions having no sort of relation to the constructive feature which they adorn and claiming a *raison d'être* of scarcely higher pretensions than the plaster enrichments of a brick cornice.

They appear unnecessary, not because they are simply decorative (a reason which would condemn half the old forms of ornamental iron-

work) but because they are confessedly *applied* decorations to a feature
whose very form is regulated by practical considerations. Objections
of an analogous kind might be raised to the constructive arches formed
of iron *rods* in the same quadrangle. Iron rods have their use as ties
or struts, but the metal requires a different section when it is required
to do service as an arch.

Utilitarians might suggest that the whole of the quadrangle could
have been roofed with half the number of columns employed, and
there can be little doubt that the strictly architectural portion of the
court—viz. the double-storied galleries by which it is surrounded—
would have gained rather than lost in effect by such an arrangement.

These galleries take the form of arcaded cloisters on the ground-
floor level, the arches being pointed and their voussoirs formed of dark
and light stone used alternately. Against the piers which carry them
are placed life-size statues of eminent men of science by Durham,
Armstead, &c., many executed with great vigour but some exhibiting

the almost insuperable difficulty which
the sculptor has to encounter in dealing
with modern costume. The decorative
carving of the capitals is executed with
great care, and consists in the strictly
realistic representation of various types
of plants and tree foliage, many excellently adapted for the purpose, some
hardly so successful. But in these and
other instances we must remember that
the character of these details and the
manner of their execution were tentative.
They represent one of the earliest departures from the beaten track of
architectural design. The result is perhaps not all that could be
wished, but it indicates an association of thought, of ingenuity, and

operative skill which reflects great credit on all concerned in its realisation.

Of the new buildings designed for Christ Church at Oxford by Mr. Deane it is scarcely fair to judge until the carved work with which many of the details are to be enriched has been executed. At present partly owing to their unfinished state, and partly owing to the peculiarities of design in which the architect has indulged, the effect of the work is rather quaint than beautiful. The front facing the Broad Walk is in many respects finely proportioned, and though it must have been no easy matter to give variety to an unbroken elevation of such exceptional length, this has been secured by an ingenious grouping of the windows. The occasional introduction of coloured stone in bands and the *flat* character of the carved foliage which enriches a few capitals and corbels of this *façade* is suggestive of the same influence as that indicated in the design of the Museum, but the details of the latter building exhibit far more refinement.

Mr. Butterfield's additions to Merton College are chiefly remarkable for their studied simplicity. But here, as in almost every work carried out by this architect, one may note his inclination to *oddities*. The corbelling of the chimney shaft on a wall facing the meadow is extremely whimsical, but it has the advantage of setting his seal on the design. No one else would have attempted so bold an experiment.

The tendency to deviate from English types of Gothic was for a long while, and indeed is still, far less marked in ecclesiastical than in domestic architecture, and for obvious reasons.

Ancient examples of the latter class are rare in this country, and those which exist would in the majority of cases be unsuitable for literal reproduction. The character of style in such buildings has always been directly affected by the social requirements and conditions of the period in which they were erected. Days of civil strife necessitated the feudal castle, baronial splendour and hospitality were typified in the Tudor mansion, rural peace and prosperity in the gabled homestead, commercial welfare in the city hall; but habits of life in the present century differ so radically from those of our ancestors that it would scarcely be possible to select whether for town or country, whether for a nobleman's seat or a suburban villa, any authentic model of Mediæval Architecture which in plan and internal arrangements should exactly fulfil our present notions of comfort and convenience. And modifications of plan involve modifications of proportion. The increased height of rooms, the altered distribution of doors and windows, the improved modes of heating and ventilating, and in London the stringent regulations of the Building Act, all present obstacles to a strict revival of national Gothic —in the antiquarian sense of the word—for a modern residence. The departure from early precedent in this respect became almost a necessity, and there was on that account a less urgent plea for the retention of those constructive and ornamental details which are specially characteristic of old English work.

In the case of Ecclesiastical Architecture it was different. The Reformation, it is true, had introduced changes which for a while deprived many features in an English church of their old use or significance, and it is probable that if buildings of any importance had been erected for the purpose of public worship in the days of Puritan rule, they would have retained little or no resemblance to the Mediæval type. But the Puritans confined their zeal to works of destruction, and in course of time, when a reactionary feeling set in and brought about a better state of things, the builders of churches returned to the ancient model. In later times it was still held in respect, though the introduction of Italian Architecture prevented its imitation. But with the modern High Church party faith in the merits of English Gothic rose to the level of a religious creed, and for years those who favoured the re-establishment of Anglican ritual and those who encouraged the revival of national architecture made common cause.

There was nothing in the general plan of a Mediæval church to prevent it from being adopted in its integrity for modern service. That eastern portion of the aisles which had formerly been occupied by chapels dedicated respectively to the Blessed Virgin and the Holy Sacrament was easily made available for the organ on the north side, or additional sittings on the left. With this single exception, everything could and did remain *in statu quo.* The altar retained its old position. The choir stalls were again filled with occupants. The sedilia, the piscina, and even the credence table, served their original purpose : the tower rang out its peal of bells : the pulpit, the font, and entrance porches, were as much needed in the modern English church as they had been five centuries ago. And all these features could be copied, and copied literally, from old examples. There was no need (as in the case of domestic architecture), to alter the internal arrangement of the building in respect of dimensions, proportion, or the admission of light, whilst in all minor details, such as the distribution of seats, the fittings of doors and windows, the roofing and paving of the edifice, the work of our ancestors presented an excellent and all-sufficient model for imitation.

Hence it happened, that when, in consequence of Mr. Ruskin's teaching, a foreign element was introduced in the designs for houses and civic buildings of a Mediæval character, the general aspect of ecclesiastical architecture was for some time scarcely, if at all, affected by the new doctrines of taste.

In 1850 and 1860, however, the list of English architects who devoted themselves more specially to the building and restoration of churches was largely increased. Messrs. E. Christian, J. Clarke, S. S. Teulon, and J. H. Hakewill, were among those who followed, with more or less tendency to individual peculiarities, in the footsteps of Mr. Scott ; while a certain number of younger men, including Messrs. G. E. Street, H. Woodyer, W. White, and G. F. Bodley, showed an early inclination to strike out in a new line for themselves.

In 1853 Mr. Street, whose name was well known at Oxford both as a local member of the profession and as a contributor to the literature of

U

his art, was employed by the bishop of the diocese to prepare designs for the Theological College at Cuddesdon, near Wheatley, a large work, including the usual accommodation for students, a dining hall, common room, oratory, and rooms for a vice-principal. The building was picturesquely planned, and met with favourable criticism at the time, though exception was made to the un-English character of some

J.K.K.R.SC.

of its details. The remodelling of St. Peter's Church at Bournemouth was another of Mr. Street's early achievements, or at least that portion which was finished at the time, for the works have been carried on since at various intervals. The original structure had no pretensions to age or architectural excellence, but it has been gradually transformed into a very interesting example of the Revival. The decorative sculpture of the reredos is an instance of this architect's fertility of invention in the treatment of detail. The accompanying woodcut will serve to show the general character of this feature, though it is far from conveying an adequate idea of the beauty and refinement of the carving.

About the same period Mr. White began the large church dedicated to All Saints at Notting Hill, a work exhibiting great cleverness in design allied with a certain inclination to peculiarities which are not always justified by their effect. Among these may be reckoned the treatment of the chancel roof and sedilia, and, externally, the gable turrets of the north transept. These, however, are but details. By a judicious attention to the proportions of the interior Mr. White has managed to secure for it a great appearance of size. The fenestration of the north aisle, though eccentric, is undeniably picturesque, and the western tower, with its octagonal belfry stage, makes a remarkable and interesting feature in the composition. The chancel of this church has been since decorated with a fine mural painting of the Annunciation by Mr. F. Holiday, an engraving of which forms the frontispiece to this volume. This artist is one of a very few, the style of whose decorative works occupies a middle place between the archaisms of the ultra-mediæval school and the quasi-classical, or more frequently naturalistic treatment of other painters. While completely free from affectations, whether of an archæological or sentimental kind, his designs possess a certain quality of saintly grace which exactly fits them for ecclesiastical decoration, and it is in this field of art that his abilities have found most successful expression.

It is much to be regretted that the revival of modern Gothic Architecture has not been more intimately associated with mural painting, for the adornment not only of our churches but of our private dwelling houses and public institutions. Half, and less than half the money lavished on fashionable upholstery, gilded cornices, and rococo furniture, bought for mere show and luxury and affording no real pleasure to anyone, would pay for a band of figure subjects round many a drawing-room wall. For the price of a single easel-picture (as such works are now valued) many a wealthy man might secure the services of a Marks, a Holiday, or an Albert Moore to enliven every room in his house with pictured allegory or old-world lore.

It happens that the chancel of another church designed by Mr. White, viz. that of Lyndhurst, in Hampshire, is also decorated by an eminent artist, Mr. F. Leighton, R.A., whose mural painting, though it may not accord with the architecture around it, is nevertheless a very fine work of its kind. The church itself exhibits evidence of Mr. White's ingenuity and vigour in design side by side with those eccentricities of form either structural or decorative which distinguish nearly every building that he has erected. How far these eccentricities result from individual caprice, whether they are the consequence of some peculiarity in early studies, or whether they arise from an endeavour to escape from conventionalities in design it is impossible to say, and perhaps Mr. White himself could scarcely explain. If they are to be judged fairly they must be judged on their own merits, and quite apart from the question as to how far they indicate a departure from ancient precedent. When an architect, as in the case of Lyndhurst Church, chooses to introduce a large dormer window in the clerestory, we ought to try and forget that in such a situation the latter feature is an unusual one, and simply ask ourselves first whether it serves its purpose, and secondly whether it helps the composition. If these conditions are fulfilled it is sheer pedantry to raise further objections. Nothing is easier than to design a church which shall be perfectly orthodox in plan and general appearance from an ecclesiological point of view, nothing more difficult than to design one which shall be effective and interesting in an artistic sense. London, for instance, at the present time swarms with churches built within the last twenty years, and models of architectural propriety—correct in the length of their chancels, correct in the height of their naves, correct in the width of their aisles, and fre-

Lyndhurst Parish Church.

W. White, F.S.A., Architect, 1858.

quently (though not so often) correct in the proportion of their towers and spires. But of how many can it be said that they are the work of an artist's hand, or worth entering to examine? The truth is that nineteen out of every twenty are absolutely commonplace, and stand in about the same relation to architectural art as the sickly *genre* pictures of pseudo-cottage life and portraits of gentlemen which crowd the walls of an annual exhibition can claim to the art of painting.

An architect of more than average ability naturally endeavours to rise above this level. He alters proportions which (as Mr. Ruskin has truly pointed out) are infinite in their variety. He modifies the form of constructive features, he devises new combinations of parts, and he invents new types of ornament. If he can do all this and yet retain the *spirit* of old work (on which we cannot hope to improve) he will do well. But if he sets himself recklessly to invert conditions of design which owe their origin to practical reasons, if he changes round for square and square for round merely for the sake of change, if, in short, he will be original at any price, we may be sure that he must fail. Mr. White's work is never of this thoughtless kind, but occasionally it seems to want repose.

The interior of Lyndhurst Church exhibits many peculiarities, and among them is the extremely naturalistic treatment of carved foliage in the capitals. There is no more subtle question of architectural taste than that which is involved in the design of such details. Probably the most noble type of decorative sculpture is that wherein the forms of animal life and of vegetation are found to be *suggested* rather than imitated. But the secret of this abstractive treatment is precisely that which our wood carvers and stone carvers have lost. It belonged to the days of pure Gothic art, and has never been satisfactorily revived. The modern designer, therefore, is compelled to follow one of three courses. He may reproduce line for line and leaf for leaf the grotesque forms and conventionalised foliage of old sculpture, or he may do his best to copy nature literally, or he may omit all representation of natural objects, and content himself with mouldings. In the case of Lyndhurst Church Mr. White took the second course, and if we accept the principle which guided him in this choice, we cannot but admit that the work of its kind is excellent.

The same year in which Lyndhurst Church was begun (1858), found Mr. G. G. Scott employed in the rebuilding of Exeter College Chapel at Oxford. Although this stately building exhibits here and there, especially in its decorative details, evidence that its designer was not uninfluenced by the now rapidly-increasing taste for Continental Gothic there is nothing in the design which suggests a thorough conversion to the new doctrines. For its external effect the Chapel chiefly depends on its lofty proportions, on the varied character of the window tracery, on its massive buttresses, and on the highly ornate treatment of the south porch. In place of the ordinary dripstone over the window arches a hollow moulding is carried round, enriched with carved foliage. The topmost stage of each buttress is provided with a pedestal and canopy for a statue, but at present only a few are executed. The east end of

South Porch of Exeter College Chapel, Oxford.

G. G. Scott, R.A., Architect, 1858.

the building terminates in a semi-octagonal apse, while towards the west and rising from the roof ridge a lofty wooden belfry lends grace and dignity to the design.

It is, however, the interior of the chapel which is most impressive by reason of its elegant proportions, the refinement of its detail, and the sumptuous nature of its embellishments. The groining is particularly well studied, and its *élancé* character gives it an appearance of great strength. The engaged columns from which it springs are supported on richly-sculptured corbels. Both in design and execution these features reach a degree of excellence rarely approached in modern work. The whole of the apse is filled with stained glass by Messrs Clayton and Bell, admirable in design as far as draughtsmanship is concerned, but somewhat crude in colour. The apse wall is arcaded below the windows, each compartment being filled with figures executed in coloured mosaic work on a gold background. A stone screen, consisting of open arches on coupled columns, divides the chapel from

the ante-chapel. The decorative carving of this screen, as indeed throughout the building, is very delicate though perhaps a little too much accentuated here and there.

The Library at Exeter College (also designed by Mr. Scott) was erected a year or two before the chapel. Its principal external features are the mural arcuation of the main story, and the four solid-looking stone gablets which rise from its parapet and enclose windows lighting the library roof. The internal fittings of the building are excellent of their kind and show how easily, in judicious hands, modern furniture may be invested with a Mediæval character without becoming either monumental or inconvenient.

If the evidence of Mr. Scott's professional skill rested on his works at Oxford alone it would be sufficiently established. An architect who thirty years ago could design the Martyr's Memorial—ordinary as its design may now appear—might fairly be expected to play a prominent part in the Gothic Revival. An architect who a dozen years ago could design and carry out such a work as Exeter College Chapel must be accredited with the power of keeping pace with the steadily advancing ability of his contemporaries. It has been said of Mr. Scott's later work that it does not rise above the level of popular appreciation. To this he would probably reply that those examples of architectural design which exhibit greater originality are the productions of men who in many instances differ entirely from each other as to the principles of beauty in their art, and that while such works have been exposed to severe criticism, his own have escaped direct censure.

While Mr. Scott was year by year adding to his reputation by the design of churches such as those at Nottingham, Cirencester, Doncaster, and Halifax, other architects who shared his enthusiasm for Mediæval art were not idle. Salvin was employed to restore or rebuild many an ancient castle—a class of work for which his studies had eminently qualified him. Hardwick was reaping the fruits of his labours at Lincoln's Inn in the form of numerous commissions for Tudor mansions. St. Aidan's Theological College, near Birkenhead, was being executed from the joint design of Messrs. T. Wyatt and D. Brandon. Mr. E. Christian was building churches in Kent. Mr. J. Prichard found favour and a good practice in Wales. The Roman Catholics of the northern counties supplied ample occupation for Messrs. Hadfield and Weightman; while in the west of England—not locally remarkable for the Mediæval sentiment of its population—Mr. H. Woodyer and Mr. J. Norton made many converts to Gothic, and St. Aubyn's Devonport churches were confessed to be models of excellence.

It was lucky that the Revival at this period found able championship, for it had still to incur much opposition. Many architects were still living who had devoted themselves from their earliest youth to the study and practice of Italian architecture, and it was impossible to expect them in middle life to renounce those principles of their art which had guided them to fame and fortune. Some, indeed, willingly conceded the point that for ecclesiastical purposes Gothic might be appropriately adopted; but neither they nor that portion of the public who shared their views could be brought to believe in its general application to domestic buildings and still less to structures of a public and municipal kind.

It was ingeniously argued that to return to the architecture of our forefathers was as absurd as to return to their dress, their literature, and their habits of life; that inasmuch as no one would dream of adopting the orthography of Chaucer's time, so no one could venture to recommend that a house in the nineteenth century should assume the appearance of one erected four centuries ago. To this the Mediæval party retorted with reason that there was more affectation in employing Gothic for churches and Italian for dwelling-houses than there would be in readopting Gothic altogether; that in the best periods of all art, whether Greek or English, one style sufficed for all purposes, whether religious or secular, and that to use one style for a church and another for a dwelling-house was, in the abstract, as absurd as printing our Bibles in black-letter to distinguish them from ordinary books. It was moreover urged that architecture, as an art, is subject to the condition of all arts which in modern life are necessarily deficient in originality, but that English Gothic was a national inheritance, which was more than could be said of pseudo-classic design. With arguments such as these and countless others the Battle of the Styles was carried on by many who forgot, on both sides, that although reason may explain and even justify a taste, it must be possessed before it can be either justified or explained. And possession is nine points of the law.

CHAPTER XVII.

NO one who has watched the progress of modern architecture in this country can fail to be struck with the enormous disadvantage under which it labours, when compared with other arts, in regard to popular interest. Many reasons might be assigned for the apathy and ignorance which it has been its fate to endure from the public. Severed as it was for centuries from association, except in rare instances, with the sister arts of painting and sculpture, people even of reputed taste came gradually to regard it as a useful science, which enabled them to live in comfort—sometimes in luxury—but one that was incapable of appealing to such a sense of beauty or creating such emotions of pleasure as are awakened by the sight of a skilful picture or a noble statue. Nothing in modern days has done more to educate national taste in pictorial art than the establishment of annual exhibitions, but from that advantage architecture is necessarily debarred. The most cleverly tinted drawing, the most perfectly finished model can give at best but a feeble idea of any executed structure. It is a suggestion of the work, not the work itself.

When, therefore, the Royal Academy (which, by the way, was established as an academy of *arts* and not of painting only) annually devoted one of its rooms to the exhibition of architectural designs, it is scarcely to be wondered that they were passed hastily over by people who were deeply interested in the historical pictures and landscape subjects by which they were surrounded. And, as time went on, even this opportunity of drawing public attention to contemporary architecture was curtailed. Crayon portraits and water-colour sketches gradually intruded on the small space conceded to architects, who felt at last that they ought to have an exhibition of their own. In 1852 the experiment was tried under the patronage of Earl de Grey, at that time President of the Institute. It met with great success and laid the foundation for that exhibition which was afterwards annually held in Conduit Street under the management of a committee.

The removal of the Royal Academy to Burlington House, and the spacious accommodation thus secured have since enabled that body to set apart more room for the display of architects' drawings. The Architectual Exhibition as a separate scheme has ceased to exist, but there can be no doubt that in its early days it did good service to the Revival by enabling professional designers to compare their work at a time when there were but few who devoted themselves exclusively to Gothic, and whose example, therefore, had immense influence on younger men.

The formation of an Architectural Museum was another scheme set on foot about the same time and zealously supported by the Mediæval party. Singularly enough, among all the antiquarian collections in London, accessible to the public, there were none which included a good assortment of casts from decorative sculpture, and the few which did exist were almost exclusively taken from classic and Italian examples. The advisability of securing such objects for the inspection and study, not only of young architects, but of art-workmen, became apparent to all who knew how much the success of modern Gothic depends on the spirit and vigour of its details. Every cathedral in England contained examples of such details, but every cathedral was not within reach of the student. Engravings and lithographs of such work were comparatively useless, but a careful cast was, for the sculptor's purpose, as good as the original. A few architects and amateurs united their efforts to supply this deficiency. Mr. Scott procured a fine collection of casts from Ely and Westminster. Mr. B. Ferrey laid Wells under like contribution. Mr. Ruskin imported some exquisite examples from France and Italy. Messrs. Hardwick, Burges,

Cundy, Clarke, Hakewill, and others, presented various specimens, and the Ecclesiological Society added their own collection to the rest. For these objects a humble and somewhat inconvenient repository was found in Cannon Street, Westminster, where they remained until constant additions and donations increased their number to such an extent that it became necessary to remove them to South Kensington. In course of time a building was raised for their reception in Bowling Street, Westminster. The Royal Architectural Museum, as it is now called, has had many friends and supporters, but to none is it more indebted than to Mr. J. Clarke, who for years has acted as its honorary secretary, and to Sir William Tite, who, with his usual liberality, has contributed largely to its support.

It is impossible to say how far the opportunities for study which such a museum as this affords would have affected professional skill in the design of details if it had been established twenty years earlier. The probability is that in such a case the class of examples selected would have been different; but we may at least regard the character of the present collection as an evidence of the phase which architectural taste had entered at the time that collection was made. For, in truth, it has passed during the Revival through many phases. Pugin talked much of the true principles of Gothic art, but he raised many buildings which would scarcely bear the test of modern criticism. Pugin is dead, but the practice of many of his contemporaries has extended to the present time, and in judging of them we must remember that their artistic creed was to a great extent modelled on his principles, and that unless we may be supposed to have reached a climax of perfection, the most advanced designers of the present day will, if they live to be old enough, have to defend their theories against the attacks of a future generation of critics.

It has been the lot of some architects to see many aspects of the Revival, and of those who have steered a safe middle course between old errors and modern heresy, Mr. T. H. Wyatt may be selected as an

Orchardleigh Park, Somersetshire—the Seat of W. Duckworth, Esq.

example. When it is remembered that so long ago as in 1836 this gentleman was entrusted with the restoration and enlargement of Llantarnam Abbey in what was then called the ' castellated ' taste, and that he only recently designed and executed the Italian Gothic residence of Capel Manor, in Kent, for Mr. F. Austen, his experience as a designer may be said to extend over a wide range of time and style. Nor is it limited to the field of domestic architecture. In addition to numerous churches in Wales of a simple but picturesque character, which he has designed, and including that of Glanogwen, near Bangor, he erected several in Wiltshire. Among these may be mentioned one in Savernake Forest, built at the cost of Lord Ailesbury in 1860, and remarkable for the ingenious and effective treatment of the interior, where the easternmost bay of the nave is divided from the aisle on each side by a screen of marble columns and open tracery. The church of Hindon in the same county is of an earlier type, with plain lancet windows and broad masses of wall which give the building the appearance of great stability. Here the *square* stone spire rising from a tower on the south is a novel feature, but well suited to the character of the building.

A small but creditable specimen of Mr. Wyatt's skill is the ' Herbert Memorial ' Church at Bemerton, erected by subscription in 1858, as a tribute of respect to the memory of that accomplished statesman whose blameless life and zealous devotion to the Anglican Church are now a matter of history. There is a quiet rural simplicity about this work which fits it excellently for its purpose. The tower is particularly successful, both in its proportions and fenestration, and only wants a spire to render it a complete and graceful example of its class.

In 1850 Mr. Wyatt and his former partner, Mr. D. Brandon, were employed to design and erect the church of the Holy Trinity, at Haverstock Hill, in which the chancel as well as the nave is provided with aisles. The plan by which this arrangement was secured, and the fact that the clerestory windows were of an earlier date than the rest of the church, incurred the censure of the ' Ecclesiologist,' which at the time and for many years afterwards published criticism based more on notions of orthodoxy than on artistic considerations, and showed little sympathy with works unidentified with ritualistic reform.

It is, however, as the designer of large country mansions, rather than as a church architect, that Mr. Wyatt is chiefly known.   In dealing with them he has generally adhered to the late Tudor type of architecture, to which rural squires of the last generation gave a decided preference, and which certainly presents many advantages as to convenience of plan and distribution of window space.

Carlett Park in Cheshire, the residence of Mr. John Torr, is an example of this class, and was erected in 1860.   In comparing this with one of Mr. Wyatt's first works—Malpass Court, Monmouthshire, built just twenty years earlier—one is struck with the remarkable advance which has been made during that period in the study of Domestic Gothic.   The *aim* of the designer has apparently been the same in both cases ; but the Gothic of 1840 has a thin cold look ; the proportions are formal and the details uninteresting ; while in Carlett Park, and still more in Mr. Duckworth's seat of Orchardleigh, Mr. Wyatt has shown of what artistic treatment the style is capable.

The quasi-Lombardic details of Capel Manor give it a character of its own, in which national traditions find no place.   But the picturesque disposition of its masses, the rich quality and colour of the materials used in its construction, and the elaborate nature of the carved work, combine to render it a most effective structure.   Its owner, Mr. F. Austen, has long been known as an architectural amateur, and it is probable that the general design is a reflex of his own taste no less than that of Mr. Wyatt himself.

Mr. J. L. Pearson's name has been already mentioned among the second group of contemporary architects, whose works have been conspicuous in the Revival, and perhaps there are none which illustrate so accurately as his own, both in domestic and ecclesiastical architecture, its progress and the various influences to which it has been subject, from the days of Pugin down to the present time. Mr. Pearson, like many of his fellow-students, began his professional career with the fixed intention of adhering not only to the principles of Mediæval art but to national characteristics of style. His early churches in York-shire and other parts of England, many of which were erected between 1840 and 1850, exhibit those characteristics in an eminent degree. Treberfydd House in South Wales, which he designed for Mr. Robert Raikes, is thoroughly English in its leading features and general com-position. The plain but well-proportioned mullioned windows, the modest gables, outlined by *thin* coping stones (the early Revivalists made them of clumsy thickness), the battlemented entrance porch and clustered chimney shafts, all indicate an attention to details then rarely given, and though the architect was at first limited to the alteration of an existing house, which must have considerably taxed his abilities, this accident led to a picturesque treatment of the design, which no artist would regret.

Quar Wood, of which an illustration is given, was begun some nine years later, and shows a freer and less conventional distribution of parts. The saddle-back roof and open loggia of the tower suggest the influence of Continental study, which, as time went on, considerably affected Mr. Pearson's taste. It was, however, in his churches that this change became most apparent. Only five years elapsed between the erection of St. Mary's, Dalton Holme, in Yorkshire, and that of Christchurch at Appleton-le-Moors in the same county; but the difference between them in point of style is extraordinary, the former being a pure specimen of Middle Pointed, treated indeed with more originality of detail than the Church of the Holy Trinity at West-minster, which Mr. Pearson had completed in 1852, but still quite northern in its leading features and internal arrangement. Christchurch, on the contrary, is modelled on the earliest and severest type of French

Gothic, with an admixture of details almost Byzantine in character. The tie-beam roof, the rounded apse, with its open arcade and decorative painting, the severe and primitive foliage of the carved capitals, and the square-edged arches which they carry; above all, the reredos, with its incised figure-subjects and quaintly-treated panels, all scholar-like and noble work of its kind, bear evidence of the extraordinary vicissitudes through which modern Gothic has passed in this country during the last twenty years.*

If the art of the Revival had been only methodically progressive—or, more strictly speaking, *retrogressive*—in regard to the chronological order of styles; if it had even consistently assimilated this or that foreign element at a time and by common consent; its development would have been intelligible to posterity. As it is, the future antiquary may well despair of attempting to reduce to a system the complicated changes and counterchanges which have taken place, and which are rendered still more intricate by individual caprice and the accidental circumstances of professional study. We have borrowed in turn from France, Germany, and Italy. We have retraversed whole centuries of time in search of the beautiful. We have adopted one by one our favourite types, and as time rolled on we have one by one discarded them.

Only twelve months after Quar Wood was begun, Mr. J. Prichard of Llandaff, whose ability had secured to him more than provincial repute was called on to remodel the country residence of Mr. John Shirley at Eatington Park in Warwickshire. This is at all times a difficult task, especially when the building to be altered has either no architectural character of its own, or possesses one at variance with the style which it is expected to assume. Mr. Prichard, however, after making

---

* There is a mortuary chapel, with a groined roof, on the north side of the chancel, enriched with mural decoration of figure subjects suggested by Psalm cvii. 23–30, the chapel having been expressly dedicated by the founder of the church (Mrs. Shepherd) to the memory of her husband, who had passed nearly his whole life at sea, beginning as a cabin boy and ending a very wealthy man, largely given to good works. A tomb, with recumbent figures of the founder and her husband, will hereafter be placed in the chapel.

Quar Wood, Gloucestershire. Erected for the Rev. R. W. Hippisley.

J. L. Pearson, F.S.A., Architect, 1857.

sundry alterations of a substantial kind, proceeded to clothe the whole
structure with what Mr. Ruskin would call a new ' wall-veil.' And
perhaps it is not too much to say that it is a wall-veil which Mr. Ruskin
would have approved.   The use of natural colour in construction was
one of the points which had been frequently advocated in ' The Seven
Lamps ' and in ' The Stones of Venice,' where also may be found many

a plea for the introduction of decorative sculpture and many an
argument to prove the superiority of what is there called *surface*
Gothic over *linear* Gothic.   Whether Mr. Prichard was influenced by
this advice, or whether his own course of professional study had led
him to the same conclusions, is a matter of little moment; but no one
who has examined the work at Eatington can doubt that it embodies

x

in its design much of those principles which were at one time identified with Mr. Ruskin's name.

The general plan of the house was, from the condition of things, English in arrangement, but the horizontal bands of colour in the masonry, the character of the arcading and upper windows, and, above all, the square campanile which rises from an internal angle in the building, are all Italian in character. The same may be said of the cornices, parapets, and enriched string-courses, while the carving of the capitals and some other details suggest a French origin. Decorative sculpture is largely employed in panels above the ground-floor windows, and the tympana of arches over those on the main floor are similarly enriched, and this not merely after the rude conventional way in

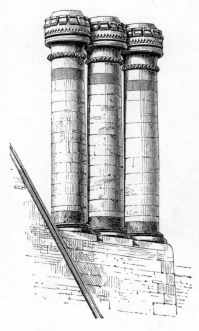

which such work is usually executed, but with figure subjects most artistically designed, and executed with consummate skill.

The main entrance to the house is under a groined porch, which is perhaps the least satisfactory part of the design, owing to the semi-ecclesiastical appearance which it assumes, and the somewhat restless character of the details. But there are features in the building which, for merits of general form, judicious ornament, and refined workmanship are worthy of the highest praise, especially when it is remembered that the adaptation of the style to such a purpose was at the time almost a complete novelty in this country. The whole work exhibits evidence of close and attentive study. Even the chimneys are invested with a picturesque character which is all their own, and none the less admirable for its originality.

Eatington Park—the Seat of E. P. Shirley, Esq.

Whatever may be urged in support of national traditions, there can be little doubt that Italian Gothic lends itself more readily than most styles to the treatment of a *façade* in which the relation of wall space to aperture is restricted by modern requirements. The employment of almost every type of English Gothic except the latest, involves either an anachronism in plan and elevation or a sacrifice of those internal arrangements which rightly or wrongly the modern householder deems necessary to his comfort. That quality of proportion which the art architect endeavours to secure is, however desirable for the effect of his design, frequently obtained by peculiarities of plan which seem inconvenient to the inmates. On the other hand, when an ordinary modern plan is retained and the building is allowed to derive what character it can from the application of old English details, the result is often an unreal and cockneyfied appearance. The peculiar merit of Eatington is that, while preserving the general arrangement of an ordinary country house, its architectural effect is genuine and unstrained. Even the use of sash-windows and plate glass, generally unsatisfactory in association with English Gothic, does not seem out of place here. And it may be safely asserted that for one client who is prepared to give up his plate-glass sashes on artistic grounds, an architect may remonstrate with ninety-nine in vain.

If obstacles to the Revival were represented only by such objections as these, they would speedily have been overcome ; but twenty years ago prejudices of a more general character still lingered against Mediæval architecture. A popular idea existed that it was suitable for churches and almshouses, that it was tolerable for schools and parsonages, that it might with modifications be adopted for a country seat, but that it was utterly unsuited to the requirements of a town house or public building.

These delusions Mr. G. G. Scott, both as an architect and as an author, endeavoured to dissipate.

In London he found an opportunity of showing the public the capabilities of Gothic for street architecture. The block of houses in the Broad Sanctuary at Westminster, which he designed and erected in 1857, was once stupidly likened, in parliamentary debate, to a convent. The sneer, if it had any real significance at all, was intended to convey the notion that houses bore a certain resemblance to conventual buildings of the Middle Ages. Now, whatever faults may be ascribed to the design, this certainly cannot be reckoned one of them. The one pre-eminent fact which asserts itself in this work to any but the shallowest critics is that the design as a whole bears an unmistakably *modern* stamp. The conditions of form maintained throughout are those which not only fulfil the requirements of a London house, but also keep within the intention of the Building Act. And this is the more to be observed because the composition has been palpably and carefully studied with an aim at the picturesque. For instance, in the west wing, the front wall is carried up into stepped gables, while in the east wing it terminates in a battlemented parapet at the foot of the main roof which is lighted by dormers. The distribution of parts in the fenestration and porches of their wings is intentionally unsymmetrical. The introduction of an oriel or rather a group of oriel windows, which forms a feature at the north-east angle, is another well-intentioned violation of the uninteresting uniformity which had hitherto been considered essential to our street architecture.

In 'Belgravia' the entrance porch is a necessary adjunct to every dwelling house. Here we have not only a porch but a bay window above it, by which means additional room is gained on the first floor. The projection of these bays and of the buttress, which at once define and strengthen the party walls, would have been far more conspicuous if the *façade* had not unfortunately faced the north and thus been deprived of that play of shadow which is the essence of architectura effect.

The entrance porch to Dean's Yard forms the central feature in this group, and rises in a square mass flanked by angle turrets above the adjoining roofs. The pointed arch over the main gateway, the groined vault above it, and the general features of this building, if not strikingly original are at least undeniably *correct* in detail, while the carved work is executed with a spirit which was remarkable eighteen years ago.

Not long after these buildings were finished, Mr. Scott, in an able paper read at Doncaster before the Yorkshire Architectural Society, offered the following earnest plea for Domestic Gothic:

I now come, however, to the great hindrance to the perfect success of our Revival, and the great object which we must set before us in all our future efforts. The hindrance referred to is the absurd supposition that Gothic architecture is exclusively and intrinsically ecclesiastical. Every form of architecture may in some sense be said to be religious, for each succeeding style has both arisen and culminated in the temple, and has thence spread itself through all other classes of building. . . . But it is not to be argued from this that our revived style is unsuited to other uses, any more than that those of Egypt and Greece were only applicable to temples. . . . Do our houses need less architectural improvement than our churches? Look at the streets of our towns, look at our workmen's cottages, at the mushroom growth of streets, terraces, and crescents at our watering places, or the villas which disfigure the suburbs of our cities, and the answer will not be long suggesting itself. Do our commercial buildings want no reformation? Compare then our warehouses, &c., with those that remain in the ancient cities of Europe, the one disgracing and disfiguring, the other forming noble ornaments to the towns in which they were erected. . . . To cut the matter short, compare Manchester, Leeds, Birmingham, and Bradford in the height of their glory with Antwerp, Ghent, Bruges, Ypres, or Nuremberg in their decay, and say whether the state of secular architecture among us does or does not stand in need of reformation.

Mr. Scott, we may be sure, spoke with no ordinary zeal on this occasion, for a question was then under discussion which affected not only the prospects of the Revival but his personal interest in that cause, and the final result of which must have placed him as a champion of Gothic architecture in a very difficult and delicate position. The Government had invited English and foreign architects in general competition to submit designs for the new public offices. The competition, like many a similar one, was unfortunately mismanaged. One set of prizes was offered for the best Foreign Office design ; another set of prizes was offered for the War Office design, although both were to be included in one group ; and lest this arrangement should not lead to sufficient confusion, a third premium was offered for a ' block plan' of both. More than two hundred designs were sent in. They were exhibited in Westminster Hall and inspected by thousands. The public journals were deluged with criticism. After much delay and doubt, and the award of some 5,000*l.* in premiums, Mr. Scott was appointed architect to the new buildings. His original design was, as might have been expected, Mediæval, and with some necessary modifications would probably have been executed. But an unexpected difficulty presented itself. The Government under which he had received his appointment went out of office, and Lord Palmerston became Premier.

Lord Palmerston's knowledge of art was never profound, and his taste for architecture now manifested itself after a negative rather than a positive fashion. He may have been unable to explain what style he liked, but he knew very well what style he did *not* like, and that style was Gothic. He attacked Mr. Scott's design in the House and out of it. He called it unsuitable for its purpose, and a frightful structure; compared the building (with singular ingenuity) to a Jesuit college, and the well-known taste of its author to a monomania. A deputation of members of Parliament interested in the adoption of Gothic waited on his lordship at Cambridge House, and expostulated with him, but in vain. He had determined that so far as his influence could prevail no Mediæval design should be executed. He illustrated some of his arguments on this occasion by familiar example.

Everybody who has seen the Speaker's house, says it is most inconvenient in point of arrangement. Lord John Russell dined there at the first dinner which was given in it : I was there also ; and when we got into the Speaker's drawing-room, he said very naturally that it was all very well for our ancestors to fit up rooms and apartments in that way, because they knew no better ; but why should we, who do know better, make buildings so inconsistent with the purposes for which they are intended ?

It had long been a popular objection to Gothic that it involved a dark and gloomy interior.* As this fallacy had been dissipated by the report of a Parliamentary Committee, Lord Palmerston found it advisable to substitute another of a completely opposite kind.

One advantage in point of light which the Gothic style possesses, is that it is light from the time the sun rises ; and the Speaker complains that his windows are so constructed that there cannot be any shutters put to them, and that when he goes to bed at 3 o'clock in the morning (as he probably did to-day) there is the sun pouring full in at his bedroom, and he has no chance of repose except what a green baize curtain can afford him.

This might be truly called a glaring objection to Gothic, yet before the deputation withdrew Lord Palmerston had so far forgotten it as to express his intention of requesting Mr. Scott ' to devise some elevation that shall be in a different style, more cheap, *more light, more cheerful,* and better adapted to the position and purposes of the building.'

Further than this inconsistency could scarcely be carried. The truth is that the Premier had made up his mind and there was no help for it. The Speaker's comfort at dinner, and the Speaker's chance of morning repose were, it is to be hoped, insured, after the domestic revelations above mentioned. How far the consideration of these important points bore upon the question at issue may, after a lapse of years, seem doubtful. But as to Lord Palmerston's opinion there could be no doubt. He was determined that the new Foreign Office should not be Gothic, and he had his way. Mr. Scott stood his ground to the last. He might, indeed, have taken one step which would have

* Lord Palmerston himself is reported to have said in Parliament, ' We all know that our northern climate does not overpower us with an excess of sunshine. Then, for Heaven's sake, let us have buildings whose interior admits, and whose exterior reflects, what light there is.

made him not only a champion but a martyr in the cause of the
Revival : he might have resigned his commission.   Perhaps some of the
younger Gothic architects of the day, who regarded him as their leader,
expected him to take that step.   If there are any who still hold that he
was bound to do so, it is to be hoped that they may never find themselves in a similar predicament.   From an æsthetic point of view it
would have been a grand act.   From a practical point of view it would
have been Quixotic.   Mr. Scott would have been reckoned a hero,
but we should not on that account have secured a Mediæval Foreign
Office.

As it was, the caprice and prejudice of a statesman who had no sort
of claim to connoisseurship were allowed to prevail, and Mr. Scott
was reluctantly compelled to raise a building in a style with which he
had little sympathy, and to which he had probably devoted little
attention.   Under these circumstances, the result may well surprise his
friends and disarm his adversaries by its excellence.

Although the Gothic Revival had thus received a decided check in
London, it met with more encouragement in the provinces.

The Manchester Assize Courts competition attracted more than a
hundred candidates, among whom were many whose names had been
little known before, but who have since become eminent in their profession.   The choice of the judges fell upon Mr. Alfred Waterhouse,
a local architect, who had sent in a Mediæval design, which united
considerable artistic merit with unusual advantages in regard to plan
and internal arrangement.   The original treatment of its individual
features did not indeed indicate evidence of a thorough and consistent
attempt to realise in this building the character of any special phase or
type of Gothic art.   The formal proportions of its principal *façade*,
the outline of its roof, the fenestration of its upper story, and, above
all, the nature of its ornamental details, showed a tendency to depart
from the unities of architectural style.   At the time of this competition
many young architects had devoted themselves with enthusiasm to the

Entrance to Assize Courts, Manchester.

A. Waterhouse, Architect, 1859.

study of Early French Gothic, and had really caught much of the spirit of twelfth century work. Others still clung to national traits, and endeavoured to preserve them in their designs. A few had studied the Mediæval examples in Lombardy and Venice to some profit, while others were allured by the more specious attractions of the Italian Renaissance. Some of these several types were ably represented in the Manchester competition, and perhaps if the decision of the judges had been based on artistic considerations alone, more than one of the candidates would have taken precedence of Mr. Waterhouse, the principle of whose design was confessedly eclectic. But experience has proved that whatever may be accomplished in ecclesiastical or domestic architecture, the special characteristics of individual style can rarely be renewed in their integrity for modern public buildings without some sacrifice of convenience, and that is precisely the requisite which those who have the management of public buildings are bound to secure.

Time has shown that Mr. Waterhouse's plan for the Assize Courts is admirably adapted for its purpose; and, with regard to the artistic merits of the work, it will be time enough to criticise when any better modern structure of its size and style has been raised in this country.

During the interval which elapsed between the selection and execution of his design, Mr. Waterhouse introduced many improvements in the *façade*. The central block, of which the lower portion is devoted to an entrance porch, had terminated above in a fantastically-shaped roof, surmounted by a clock turret. In place of this feature, a lofty gable, pierced with a large wheel window, is now substituted. The upper windows of the principal front had been enriched with ogival hood mouldings. These were omitted in execution, and the window heads gain immensely in effect by the change. In the Southall Street front other modifications were adopted in the plan, which considerably enhanced the general effect. The best view of the building as a composition is at some little distance from the corner formed by the junction of Great Ducie Street and Southall Street, where the principal masses of the building group excellently together.

The aim of the architect seems to have been to secure general symmetry with variety of detail. Thus the principal *façade* is exactly divided by the central block : the wings on either side are lighted by exactly the same number of windows, but the windows themselves vary in their tracery. Perhaps the least satisfactory feature in the design at first sight is the lofty tower, which, rising in the centre from the rear of the building, looks like an Italian campanile, but really serves the purpose of a ventilating shaft. Yet, after the eye has become accustomed to its proportions, there are really no definite faults to find with it but faults of detail, on which it would be hypercritical to enter here. At this stage of his career, and it was a very early stage, Mr. Waterhouse perhaps erred in over-prettifying his work. This tendency may be noticed here and there in the design ; but it never lapses into fussiness or descends to vulgarity.

The interior of the great hall is most successful in its proportions. It has an open timber ' hammer-beam ' roof, and a large pointed window with geometrical tracery, at each end. The doorways leading hence to the corridors and adjoining offices are studied with great care ; and indeed the same may be said of every feature in the hall, from its inlaid pavement to the pendant gasaliers. The Civil Court and the Criminal Court (each capable of holding about 800 people) are respectively to the north-east and south-east of the hall. They are identical in size and arrangement, and are provided with the usual retiring rooms for judges and juries.

The barristers' library is a picturesque and effective apartment, with a roof following the outline of a pointed arch, and divided into panels. The barristers' corridor is lighted by a skylight, supported at intervals by arched ribs cusped and slightly decorated with colour. This, together with many other features in the building, represents with more or less success an attempt to invest modern structural requirements with an artistic character which shall be Mediæval in motive if not in fact. The trying conditions of this union cannot be too constantly kept in view by critics, who, applying an antiquarian test to such works as this at Manchester, proceed to condemn the association of features for which there is no actual precedent in old and genuine Gothic.

Now it is quite certain that if any modern architect were so ingenious as to be able to raise in the nineteenth century a municipal or any other building, which, in its general arrangement and the character of its details thoroughly realised the fashion of the thirteenth or fourteenth century, it would be about as uncomfortable, unhealthy, and inconvenient a structure as could be devised. There must be a compromise. Gothic architecture under its old conditions, and where the ordinary requirements of life are concerned, is impossible. Gothic architecture under modern conditions—improved methods of lighting and ventilating, sanitary considerations, the use of new materials, and habits of ease and luxury—may be, and indeed is, very possible. But it is open to various interpretations, and in judging of its examples we must apply to them a new standard of taste—a standard of no narrow limit to place or time, artistic rather than archæological, founded on necessity rather than on sentiment. Judged by such a standard as this, Mr. Waterhouse's work at Manchester is a decided success.

CHAPTER XVIII.

ATTEMPTS have frequently been made to identify the various phases through which modern Gothic has passed during the last twenty years, with the names of individual architects who are popularly supposed to have formed by their influence and example special schools in the practice of their profession. And, indeed, no more convenient method of classification could be adopted in recording the progress of the Revival if it were one which might be safely relied on. The past history of some arts is capable of this analysis, which materially aids the student in arriving at a knowledge of style, and of those distinct qualities which help to form a style. In our own day it is not unusual for writers to group together for purposes of criticism the names of certain painters whose aim is understood to be uniformly directed, and who incline to the same choice of subjects or to the same class of treatment. But in a description of modern architecture such a course could not be systematically pursued. Here and there it might serve in a general way to indicate the position of such a man as Pugin or Scott, in reference to those who for a while acknowledged him as their leader ; but, as a rule, most architects decline to entertain the notion of having been led at all, except by their own convictions. As pupils, their natural tendency is, of course, to design after the fashion of their masters ; though, even at this stage, a few weeks' study on the Continent, the erection of a new and striking building, or the genial influence of an art clique, may turn the current of their ambition. But when once an architect has entered on practice for himself, his admiration of individual talent undergoes considerable abatement; his great desire is to be original, and one cannot pay him a poorer compliment than by supposing that his designs have been suggested by any previous design, or that he is indebted for a single detail to the invention of his contemporaries.

Now without accepting the conclusion that no modern architect's work could possibly be mistaken for any other than his own, it is easy to see that a young designer is subject to a variety of impressions from various sources, which, acting together, may prevent him from pledging himself to a particular school of art, and, further, that as he gains in experience, his taste, in whatever direction it may have set, will assuredly undergo a change.

During the last fifteen years the current of architectural taste has been turned in more than one direction. Mr. Ruskin's influence sent it rushing for awhile towards North Italy. The Lille Cathedral competition, in which, though open to all the world, the first two prizes were awarded to Englishmen,* naturally drew attention to the merits of French Gothic, while a strong party strove hard to maintain our own national traditions of style.

Of the three schools thus represented, French Gothic was for some years decidedly in the ascendant. It was novel; it appealed by the adventitious aid of sculpture and other decorative details to a popular taste; it admitted of general application, and a work was then being published which promised peculiar advantages for its study. This was M. Viollet-le-Duc's famous 'Dictionnaire raisonné de l'Architecture Française du XIᵉ au XVIᵉ Siècle,' of which it is scarcely too much to say that no more useful or exhaustive treatise could have been written on the subject. In examining this extraordinary contribution to the

---

* The first to Messrs. Clutton and Burges; the second to Mr. Street. In the same competition silver medals were awarded to Messrs. Holden and Son of Manchester, Mr. Brodrick of Leeds, and Messrs. Evans and Pullan; while the designs of Mr. Goldie, Mr. Pedley, and Mr. Robinson were ' honourably mentioned.'

literature of the Revival, it is difficult to say which is most worthy of admiration, the patient research and archæological labour which occupied its author during fourteen years of a busy life, or the artistic taste and skill which enabled him to fill nine quarto volumes with illustrations so various in their range, so ingenious in their character, so attractive in their form, and so delicate in their execution, that they leave nothing to be desired in the form of technical information or artistic record.

In illustrating the constructive details of Mediæval masonry and carpentry, previous authors had been content to supply plans and sections, which explained themselves indeed to the professional reader, but left many a youthful student and amateur in doubt as to their practical significance. M. Viollet-le-Duc not only supplied geometrical drawings of such features, but added perspective sketches, in which the parts to be illustrated are *dissected* in a manner that renders them intelligible to everyone at first sight. The same principle is frequently applied to general views in this admirable work. One looks down upon a church or town hall, partly stripped of its roof or gable, and straightway the whole anatomy of its walls is revealed. The various buildings of an abbey or the ramparts of a fortified town are shown, not only by a plan, but by a bird's-eye view. If the author is describing a piece of timber construction he is not content until he has pulled the whole framework to pieces, and described with his pencil as well as with his pen the nature and purpose of every joint.

Nothing is too abstruse—nothing too insignificant for explanation. Under the heads of '*Voûte*' and '*Arc-boutant*,' the scientific principles of Mediæval groining are made clear. When M. Viollet-le-Duc is dealing with '*Serrurerie*,' he is at the pains to enter into a minute description of ancient locks. The subject of sculpture forms the text for a valuable essay. That on military architecture is of such length and importance that it has been reprinted in a separate volume. The examples of towers and spires, of window tracery, of door-jambs, of parapets and cornices, capitals and bases, not to mention other details,

Entrance to the Digby Mortuary Chapel, Sherborne.
W. Slater, Architect, 1860.

with which these volumes are filled, are innumerable. A more convenient book for reference was never devised for the architectural
student. If he wants a suggestion for the plan of an apse, the construction of a staircase, the shape of a dormer, the decoration of a fireplace, he has but to turn out ' *Chevet*,' ' *Escalier*,' ' *Lucarne*,' or
' *Cheminée*,' and forthwith he finds a dozen models to choose from. If
he wishes to learn something of the history of Mediæval art, he will do
well if he can digest half the information supplied in the first volume
under the head of ' Architecture.' If he seeks to understand its
artistic principles or their practical application, he will scarcely open a
single page that does not enlighten him.

It was not long before the influence of this work became perceptible
in England. Gothic architects began to introduce French details in
their work. Decorative sculpture assumed a different character. The
small and intricately carved foliage of capitals which had hitherto been
in vogue gave place to bolder and simpler forms of leaf ornament.
The round abacus was superseded by the square. In place of compound or clustered pillars, plain cylindrical shafts were employed.
Arch mouldings grew less complex. Crockets and ball-flower enrichments were reduced to a minimum. The plans, the proportions, the
general composition of many a church and private dwelling were
sensibly affected by the change. Artistically considered, the examples
of modern Gothic might be said to approach a more archaic type than
previously. From a constructive point of view they were pronounced,
in the professional slang of the day, more ' muscular.'

After the first few volumes of the ' Dictionnaire raisonné ' had been
published, Mr. R. Norman Shaw, a young architect who had carried
off more than one prize at the Royal Academy, was sent abroad as its
travelling student. He returned from a lengthy tour on the Continent
with a portfolio of interesting sketches, which were afterwards published in the well-known volume which bears his name. It is a significant evidence of the prevailing taste in architecture at this period

that the sketches were all from Mediæval buildings, and that half of them were made in France.

Not long afterwards Mr. W. E. Nesfield made a similar tour, and for a like purpose ; but in his case nine-tenths of the specimens selected for illustration were French, and for the most part French of the earliest types.

To estimate the true value of these works we must remember that they were the first of any importance which represented Continental architecture in a style of drawing at once artistic and accurate enough for professional reference.   The skill, the delicacy of touch, the attention to perspective, and the knowledge of detail which they exhibit, are worthy of all praise.   Comparisons are sometimes made between the ability of modern students and those of the good old times when the taste for classic art was at its zenith.   Whatever else may be said of the Gothic Revival and its tendencies, there can be little doubt that it has encouraged students to *draw*.   In this respect the present generation has a decided advantage.   In our grandfathers' days the artist architect was a rarity, and for one who could then sketch with freedom we have twenty who can do so now.

The introduction of a French element in the Gothic of this period may be exemplified in the Digby Mortuary Chapel at Sherborne (designed by Mr. W. Slater, the partner and professional successor of Mr. Carpenter), where the rich details of the entrance door and the carved tympanum of the arch-head are eminently suggestive of foreign study.   Mr. Slater was associated with Mr. Carpenter in the execution of many buildings, among which may be mentioned the Church of SS. Simon and Jude at Earl's Hilton in Leicestershire, and the Episcopal Chapel of St. Peter in Edinburgh.   After Mr. Carpenter's death, Mr. Slater was commissioned to rebuild Kilmore Cathedral in Ireland, and to erect St. John's Schools, St. Pancras——a plain but excellent example of secular Gothic.   In conjunction with his present partner (the late Mr. Carpenter's son) he has since designed and carried out numerous works, and has been largely employed in restorations.

Baptistery of St. Francis' Church, Notting Hill.

J. F. Bentley, Architect, 1861.

In 1861 Mr. J. F. Bentley added the baptistery, schools, and other buildings to the Roman Catholic Church of St. Francis of Assisi at Notting Hill. The baptistery, as the production of a young architect then little known to fame, was much admired. There is a breadth and simplicity about the design which distinguished it from previous work, as well as from much that was executed at that time. In the character of the capitals, the treatment of the font, and other details, a tendency to depart from English tradition may be noticed, and this is the more remarkable because the architect, like many others, has since retraced his steps, and is now emphatically insular in his taste.

But in no instance was this revolt from national style more marked than in the Church of St. James the Less, erected at Westminster by Mr. Street. Here the whole character of the building, whether we regard its plan, its distinctive features, its external or internal decoration is eminently un-English. Even the materials used in its construction and the mode by which it is lighted were novelties. The detached tower with its picturesquely modelled spire, its belfry stage rich in ornamental brick-work and marble bosses, the semi-circular apse and quasi-transepts, the plate tracery, the dormers inserted in the clerestory, the quaint treatment of the nave arcade, the bold vigour of the carving, the chromatic decoration of the roof—all bear evidence of a thirst for change which Mr. Street could satisfy without danger, but which betrayed many of his contemporaries into intemperance. Even here there is something to regret in the restless notching of edges, the dazzling distribution of stripes, the multiplicity of pattern forms, and exuberance of sculpture detail. But it is all so clever and so facile, so evidently the invention of a man who enjoys his work—and who, full of rich fancies and quaint conceits, is incapable of insipidity, but at any moment if he so chooses can rein himself back from extravagance—that it is impossible but to regard it with pleasure.

If Mr. Street had never designed anything but the campanile of this church—and its Italian character justifies the name—it would be sufficient to proclaim him an artist. In form, proportion of parts, decorative detail, and use of colour, it seems to leave little to be desired. To form a just appreciation of its merits, let the architectural amateur walk down to Garden Street from any part of London, and note as he passes the stereotyped patterns of towers and spires which he will find to right or left of his road. How neat, how respectable, how correct, how eminently uninteresting they are! No one cares to look at them twice. They are all like each other, or so little different that if they changed places any day, by help of Aladdin's lamp, the London world would never find it out. But here, in one of the poorest and meanest quarters of town, hidden away behind dull masses of brick and mortar, this fair tower, when one does see it, is something not to be easily forgotten. It is the fate of more than one noble church in London to be thus obscured. And there is no help for it. The poorest neighbourhoods want them most, and on that account the choice of site does infinite credit to its founders.* But it is to be regretted that so fine a work should be placed where it must be rarely seen by those who could best judge of its artistic excellence.

The rich fertility of this architect's inventive power is only equalled by the sagacious tact which guides its application. He is not only master of many styles, but he can give original expression to every one of them. Where decoration can be afforded, he invests his work with a sumptuous refinement which reveals itself in every detail. Where simplicity is required, he makes simplicity attractive. This faculty of design belongs to that rare order which unites artistic instinct with practical ability. He sees his opportunity at a glance and makes the most of it. Sometimes his originality is manifested in a novel plan, as in the Church of St. Saviour, Eastbourne, where the chancel is joined to the nave by a ' canted ' bay ; sometimes in the clever association of ecclesiastical and domestic architecture, as at Boyne Hill ; sometimes in the design of

* St. James the Less was erected by the Misses Monk in memory of their father, the late Bishop of Gloucester and Canon of Westminster.

Church of S. Philip and S. James, Oxford.

G. E. Street, A.R.A., Architect, 1862.

decorative sculpture, as at Brightwaltham Church, where the carved figures which enrich the altar exactly realise that combination of quaintness and grace which is so characteristic of Mediæval work.

Mr. Street was one of the first architects of the Revival who showed how effective Gothic architecture might be made where it simply depends for effect on artistic proportion. In this respect he brought about a great and useful reformation in the practice of his art. If Pugin and his followers could decorate their walls with carved panels, fill their windows with tracery, crown their buttresses with crocketed pinnacles, and enrich their porches with canopied niches, they made a showy building. But shorn of such details it cut a sorry figure. Now, if Mr. Street were limited to the arrangement of four walls, a roof, a couple of windows, a door, and a chimney shaft, on the distinct understanding that none of these features were to be ornamented in the slightest degree, we may be quite sure that he would group them in such a fashion as to make them picturesque. Nothing can possibly be simpler than his works at Cuddesdon and East Grinstead—the first a college, the latter a convent. They have literally no architectural character beyond what may be secured by stout masonry, a steep roof, and a few dormer windows. But there is a genuine *cachet* on each design which it is impossible to mistake. They are the production of an artist hand.

Perhaps there is no better test of an architect's originality in design than when he has to deal with the design of a very small village church. It must have its sanctuary, its porch, its pulpit, and its belfry, but it must be spanned by a single roof, and the picturesque subdivision of nave and aisles is of course out of the question. How can such a building as this be made to express its purpose, to look interesting, and avoid conventionality? Mr. Street has shown us how to do this in his design for Howesham Church. He gave the chancel an apsidal end, decorated its windows with *escoinson* shafts, cusped the chancel arch, reduced the pulpit to a little quadrant in plan (which was just the thing for a corner), planned a snug little porch with a lean-to roof for the west end, and carried up a picturesque belfry turret by its side. The effect of the whole is charming. Nothing better could have been devised. It is simplicity itself, but simplicity with meaning and effect.

In his larger works Mr. Street is equally successful. Of all the churches which he has built there is scarcely one which is not remarkable for some originality of treatment. And this originality is always secured by legitimate means, without an approach to that license which with the less accomplished designer results in extravagant proportions or *bizarrerie* of detail. It is by slight and temperate departures from ordinary types of form and decoration that this architect frequently ensures a novel grace without startling by oddities of design. Thus in the Church of SS. Philip and James, at Oxford, the tower which rises over the intersection of the nave and transepts is a little broader in plan from north to south than it is from east to west. The division of the clerestory windows does not exactly coincide with the division of the nave arcade. The fenestration of the north transept differs from that of the south. The building is enriched with natural colour, not by covering it over with stripes like a zebra, but by introducing bands of reddish stone at rare intervals and by marking the voussoirs in the same manner. The nave of this church is of unusual width in relation to its aisles, but the easternmost bay of each arcade slopes slightly inwards to meet the piers which carry the central tower. This forms a peculiar and by no means an uninteresting feature. The nave roof, instead of being open timbered and of the ordinary type, is ceiled internally and takes the form of a pointed arch, decorated at intervals with bands of colour. The picturesque grouping of the aisle windows, the rich inlay and carving of the reredos (heightened in effect by contrast with the plain wall lining and simple wood fittings of the chancel), even the iron-work of the screen—are all full of character, and that type of character which if verbally expressed would only be a synonym for artistic grace. Once, and once only, in this building does the architect appear to have drifted

Chancel of St. John's Church, Torquay.

into *random* work, and that is in the design of the circular window which lights the western gable. But even here the result is rather quaint than distasteful. The best view of the exterior is certainly from the east end, where the central tower and spire, rising from the *crux* with an octagonal turret at the south-east corner, form with the chancel and transepts an admirably composed group, in which two architectural features constantly adopted by Mr. Street—viz. the round apse and the louvred belfry windows—are conspicuous.

In one marked particular, church building of the present day differs from that which was carried on formerly, and that is in the gradual manner of its execution. Twenty or thirty years ago, when a church was begun, the great object was to complete it as soon as possible, and to provide accommodation for a certain number of sitters. The money granted or subscribed for this object was applied to the erection of the whole structure, which became simple or ornate in proportion to the amount of funds available. At the present time it is not at all uncommon, when means are limited, to begin by building the chancel, and even to enrich it and decorate it before the rest of the building is complete. This has happened with two of Mr. Street's churches, viz. that of All Saints', Clifton, and St. John's at Torquay, both admirable specimens of his ability. The chancel of All Saints' is decorated internally with stone of three different hues—white, bluish gray, and light red, judiciously apposed in the construction of the piers, &c. With such fair building materials as these but little carved work is necessary, and to a critical eye the perpetual notching of the arch edges throughout this church appears tedious. There is no type of ornamentation more mechanical or less interesting in itself than this notched work; and so much thought and ingenuity have been bestowed on the building that one is impatient of details which exhibit neither, and have, moreover, been woefully hackneyed elsewhere. The chancel screen is an instance of Mr. Street's luxuriant fancy when let free to play with brass and iron, but its elaboration is cleverly concentrated on the upper and lower portions, leaving the centre a plain transparent *grille* of octagonal rods.

It is remarkable that this architect, who was one of the first to set aside home traditions of style in favour of Continental Gothic, should also be among the earliest of his professional contemporaries to return to English models. Among his admirers, who watched with interest the completion of St. James the Less, there was probably not one who foresaw the change which was destined to take place in the spirit of his design. Yet the stately church now rising in Toddington Park, near Winchcomb, is eminently *northern* in the character of its plan and details. We have had a French fashion, and we have had an Italian fashion: but the tide of architectural taste is once more returning to our shores.

It was perhaps when the rage for foreign Gothic was at its height that a building was begun in London, which, from its size, the nature of its construction, and the masterlike skill of its design, deserves especial mention. The Church of St. Peter's, Vauxhall, is not only an excellent example of Mr. Pearson's originality in design, but may be fairly described as one of the most successful instances of modern ecclesiastical architecture in London. The plan and general arrangement of this structure are extremely simple; its most remarkable features being a semicircular apse and triforium at the east end, the bold and unconventional treatment of the west front, and the groined vaulting which roofs the whole of the interior. It is also distinguished by the very early character of its internal details, especially of the carved work, which, where finished (the capitals of the nave piers are still left *en bloc*), has been executed with great spirit and refinement.

The wall of the apse immediately below the triforium is decorated with fresco painting in seven panels or compartments, devoted to the following subjects illustrative of the last incidents in the life of our Lord: The Last Supper, The Agony in the Garden, Christ bearing His Cross to Calvary, The Crucifixion, The Descent from the Cross,

Church of S. Peter, Vauxhall.

J. L. Pearson, F.S.A., Architect, 1863.

The Resurrection, and Christ's subsequent appearance to the Apostles. The figures in each subject are closely grouped and are relieved in alternate panels on a dark blue and Indian red ground. Other tints are employed to represent some of the accessories, but the figures themselves are for the most part left uncoloured, the folds of drapery, &c., being expressed by lines only.

Below this series of pictures the wall is covered to a depth of about eight feet with a diaper pattern in two tints of Indian red separated by a narrow band of white from the lower portion of the wall which is diapered in green to a height of some three feet from the pavement. The altar, which is detached from the wall, is surmounted by an alabaster reredos simple in general form but judiciously enriched with coloured marble and gold Mosaic. The choir stalls are extremely plain in general form, and depend for their effect on the novel introduction of iron grille-work which rises behind them, and forms a canopy overhead. It is impossible to praise too highly the skill and attention which have been bestowed on the design of these screens, and indeed on the whole of the metal-work in this church.

The groined work over the chancel, nave, aisles, and north transept is executed in brick with stone ribs. The nave is divided into five bays by obtusely-pointed arches and columns which are nearly cylindrical in plan, but from which two slender shafts project towards the aisle, apparently for the purpose of carrying the stone ribs of the aisle vaulting.

The windows of this church are simply lancet headed without cusping. At the west end they are arranged in double couples with a circular cusped light over each couple. The large round window filled with plate tracery, which is seen in the centre of the gable outside, lights not the church itself but the roof above the groining. The square bell turret which rises to the right of the gable, and the three bold buttresses which descend to the narthex below are unusual features, and add considerably to the original and picturesque character of the composition.

Such is a brief description of St. Peter's, Vauxhall, a work which must always be regarded with interest, not only on its own account but as marking the extent to which the Revival was for a while influenced by the introduction of a foreign element in Gothic design. The French school found many admirers among the Mediævalists. For accurate knowledge of its details, skilful adaptation of its characteristic features, and intimate acquaintance with its hagiology and iconography, Mr. W. Burges was second to none. Of those who shared his views, and in some cases rivalled his ability, may be mentioned Messrs. E. W. Godwin, G. Goldie, J. P. Seddon, and *at first* (though not latterly) Messrs. W. E. Nesfield, R. N. Shaw, and J. F. Bentley, besides many older practitioners who, like Messrs. G. Somers Clarke and R. J. Withers, found themselves more or less influenced by the prevailing taste.

From these last there were, however, some notable exceptions. Mr. Butterfield, for instance, modified English Gothic after his own fashion, but in his hands, and perhaps from his attachment to its most characteristic features, its tracery, its mouldings, and its wood-work, it never lost its nationality. Among the earliest and most successful followers of Mr. Butterfield's school—the school which has been marked throughout by a steady fidelity to Middle Pointed, which has avoided the extravagances of the Revival, and (except in a few instances) has resisted the influence of Continental study—is Mr. Henry Woodyer. His Church of the Holy Innocents at Highnam, near Gloucester, is an example of pure scholarlike design, which, without pretending to any striking originality in general composition or treatment of detail, reveals itself at first sight as *genuine* work of its class. The tower and spire are exquisitely proportioned. The interior is enriched with mural paintings executed by Mr. T. Gambier Parry, at whose cost the church was erected in 1849.

A smaller but perhaps not less characteristic work of the same architect is that of St. Raphael's College at Bristol, a set of almshouses for the use of retired seamen, commenced in 1853. This modest but eminently picturesque building, with its ample roof of tiles rising from the eaves at an obtuse angle and taking a steeper pitch above, lighted by dormer windows, and its snug wooden cloister extending the whole length of the principal front, is thoroughly English in spirit, and apparently well adapted for its purpose.

In the chapel attached to these buildings may be noticed many details in which, though the influence of Mr. Butterfield's taste can be recognised, there is much to identify the author's own peculiarities of design. The window mullions are slight and acutely chamfered, the cusping is refined and thorny in outline. There is a tendency to concentrate rather than to distribute decorative features noticeable in the elaborate external canopy over the east window and in the picturesque but needlessly complex construction of the wooden belfry; a tendency to naturalism in the carved work, especially in the corbels of the nave arcade, where, in defiance of Mr. Ruskin, running blocks and other ship's tackle are literally represented by way of nautical emblems; a tendency to severity in the reredos, with its repetition of uncusped pointed arches and six-winged angels only relieved from monotony by the varied treatment and exquisite delicacy of the sculptured panels which they enclose; a tendency to simplicity and sober grace in the general proportions of the interior—the open roof with its canted tie-beam, the plain but well-studied chancel fittings and alabaster pulpit—though the purist may take exception to the chamfer decoration of the last mentioned feature.

Two years later Mr. Woodyer was commissioned by Sir Frederic Ouseley to design the Church and College of St. Michael at Tenbury. The former is a steep-roofed and finely-composed building, depending for effect on its general proportions, which are excellent, rather than on any strongly emphasised or highly decorated feature. The chancel, which is apsidal in plan, is lighted by long two-light windows varying in tracery and carefully studied.

In his additions to Eton College, 1857, Mr. Woodyer had necessarily to deal with a late and debased type of Gothic, but he has made the best of his conditions, and perhaps no architect of our day adhering absolutely and conscientiously to the class of sculptured decoration which the style admits could have treated it more effectively than he has done in his entrance gateway to the new buildings, where the mural carved work, though formal in general effect, is exquisitely graceful in design, and where the natural foliage which enriches the panels is soberly conventionalised without losing its vitality.   Sometimes, indeed, he lapses into strange eccentricities of detail, as in the interior of Christchurch, Reading (1858), where the head of the chancel arch is filled with tracery supported by an inner and obtusely-pointed arch springing from below the main impost.   The canopied capitals of the piers which divide the nave from the north aisle are also of a type which it is difficult to accept as agreeable in an artistic sense, whatever authority there may be for their use ; but even here these idiosyncrasies are redeemed by a certain refinement of motive which is all the author's own, and never descend to commonplace extravagance, while every moulding employed exhibits care and purposeful design.

In the Church of St. Paul's, Wokingham (1861), one recognises less individuality of conception, and impartial critics may condemn as an æsthetic error the almost uniform repetition of proportion in the coupled windows which occur immediately under each other in the tower.   But Mr. Woodyer is an artist who works with a fixed purpose, and would probably be prepared to defend this arrangement by his own theories.

The Surrey County Schools (1863) are a large range of three-storied buildings thoroughly English in character, but of such marked originality that it would be difficult to refer them, except as regards their details, to any special period of old domestic architecture.   Among Mr. Woodyer's contemporaries there is probably but one for whose design this work might be mistaken, and that is the leader of his school, Mr. Butterfield.   The wide but low-fronted dormers springing from above the eaves, and carried back at a picturesque angle into the main roof ;

All Saints' Hospital, Eastbourne.

H. Woodyer, *Architect,* 1866.

the square-headed windows of the first floor; the simple but genuinely national treatment of the ornamental brickwork; the quaint bell turret rising just where it is wanted to help the composition; the judicious disposition of the plan, and the dignified repose of the whole building, are all eminently characteristic of the author's taste. The chapel, a long plain building with a round apsidal end and a clerestory lighted by Early Pointed windows, is less emphatically English, but nowise less graceful in its simplicity. It was raised at the expense of Mr. H. W. Peek, M.P.

Another example of Mr. Woodyer's skill in domestic architecture is All Saints' Convalescent Hospital at Eastbourne, a large and plain but effective building, well adapted for its purpose and situation.

The fenestration is light and cheerful, the distribution of parts judicious and none the less interesting, though perhaps somewhat the less convenient, for a picturesque crowding of dormers and chimney shafts in the Sisters' House. The steep gable, and open gallery on the first and ground floor of this wing contribute not a little to its effect, and are repeated, with some slight variations, at the entrance porch.

One special quality in Mr. Woodyer's work is that it is uniformly studied throughout. It is not mere *façade* planning. Those portions of his buildings which are at the rear and seldom seen receive as much attention as the principal front. This is particularly noticeable in the House of Mercy erected by the Clewer Sisterhood at Bovey Tracy in Devonshire—a spacious and well-arranged group of buildings constructed of rough-dressed granite with quoins of Bath stone and tall picturesquely-treated chimney shafts of red brick.

The principal front faces the south, with projecting wings at east and west, the former being the loftier of the two. The difference of ground level gives to the north front a height of four stories, whereof the uppermost is lighted by large triangular dormers on the roof. The chapel attached to the building is of lofty proportions, with a semi-octagonal east end, two sides of which are panelled internally with richly-veined marble, while the reredos and east wall are lined with alabaster, which material is also used for the columns and sides of the lancet window above.   The reredos is divided into seven niches canopied with the acute trefoil-cusped heads which Mr. Woodyer specially affects.   In each niche is the figure of an angel, carved with rare delicacy and refinement.   The open timber roof, west gallery, and wood fittings of the chapel are exceedingly simple but excellent of their kind.

The picturesque and beautiful site of this building, on a hill overlooking the village of Bovey and the wild moorland beyond, lend additional interest to the exterior, which in effect is well suited to the surrounding scenery.   And this may be considered no small merit when we remember that as yet time has done little or nothing to beautify it.   Nor does its general design, being thoroughly original, affect in any absolute degree the traditions of a by-gone style.   But it has caught the spirit without imitating the letter of old English work. It is the design of an architect who has profited by antiquarian study— not that of an antiquary who has tried his hand at architecture.

CHAPTER XIX.

THE Revival had now reached a stage when its supporters found themselves called upon to consider a fresh question regarding its future progress. Their cause had so far prospered as to survive popular prejudice, to be recognised and approved by a considerable section of the artistic public, and to monopolise the services of many accomplished architects. The Classic school was by no means extinct, but it was in a decided minority, and chiefly represented by members of the profession who had been long in practice, and who, having reaped their laurels under a former condition of taste, could well afford to let their younger rivals win renown by following a new and different *régime*.

There was, in short, a truce to the Battle of the Styles, interrupted no doubt by skirmishes here and there, but on the whole well and generously maintained. The only wonder is how this æsthetic warfare could have been so unconscionably prolonged. The waste of time, of energy, and printer's ink, involved by endless discussions on the respective merits of Mediæval and Renaissance architecture during twenty years, can only be realised by those who have studied the current art literature of that period. If anything has been left unsaid on the subject, any argument *pro* or *con* omitted, any plea forgotten, it is certainly not from want of pains or ingenuity on the part of disputants on either side.

The Mediævalists, however, left in possession of their ground, had now to settle some important points among themselves. They were free to follow their favourite taste, but unfortunately that taste could no longer be considered uniform or well defined in its details. The introduction of a foreign element in the Revival of Pointed Architecture found many advocates who were weary of the cold spiritless copies of old work which had long passed muster as good English Gothic. On the other hand, there was a strong party who felt that in resigning the nationality of their art they would yield a point which had long been considered a strong one in its favour. A third, and perhaps more reasonable section, openly admitted that they saw no great harm in culling from Continental architecture such graces as were deficient in our own, or in amalgamating in one style distinct characteristics of design which would probably have been long since universally adopted but for causes which had ceased to exist.

This eclecticism, especially when applied to Mediæval design, has been severely and unfairly condemned by many critics who forget that every art which is not reduced to a state of stagnation must always be subject to external influences, and that the facilities of travel and study which we now enjoy only tend to accomplish more rapidly changes which have been at all times inevitable. The history of architecture in all civilised countries bears evidence of such changes, and whether they are brought about by the sword of a victorious Norman baron or the pencil of an industrious modern architect they will sooner or later come to pass.

There is a conservative order of sentiment which sternly rejects every element of architectural design that is borrowed from abroad. But if this principle had always been maintained in its integrity we should now be building after the fashion of our Saxon forefathers. The stanchest champion of English Gothic will scarcely deny that for the vigorous treatment of certain features—as, for instance, the pier, the buttress, and the entrance porch, as well as for grace of form in sculpturesque detail—French design of the best period realised an excellence which we never attained in this country. On the other hand, there are many qualities in our Middle Pointed and earlier styles which are peculiarly adapted to our climate and national requirements. To unite these distinct characteristics as far as may be possible in our modern Revival seems a very natural and obvious course. To object to such a union seems akin to sheer bigotry. The wholesale importation of a foreign fashion in architecture, such as took place in England under the Stuarts, and such as seemed possible some years ago when the rage for Venetian Gothic was at its height, must be regarded as the result of mere caprice, and cannot be defended on reasonable grounds. But it is quite possible to avoid this extreme without running into the opposite one of excessive insularity.

A similar kind of tolerance may fairly be recommended to those ultra-purists who are alarmed at what they consider an anachronism involved by the use of mouldings and other details belonging to one period of old art, in structures of which the general form is borrowed from another epoch. In such cases the only genuine test which we can apply is one of educated but independent taste. Is the compromise offensive to the eye? Does it represent an incongruity of *form* as well as an inconsistency of date? If so, the designer is indubitably at fault, but if not, there is little harm done. The antiquary may grumble, but the artist will be satisfied.

To this conclusion many architects came some ten or fifteen years ago, and on this principle not a few of their works have since been executed. The concession was not, indeed, universal, and it showed itself in various forms. There were those who, while strictly adhering to the traditions of English art, had no chronological scruples. There were others who thought less of crossing the Channel for a suggestion, than of bridging over a gap between the thirteenth and fifteenth centuries. But between them, the pharisaism of architectural design— the superstitious reverence for limits of time and place which had hitherto prevailed, fell gradually out of favour, and gave place to a bolder and more artistic treatment of Gothic, as we shall presently see.

It has been observed that one unfortunate drawback to the progress of the Revival in England was occasioned by the popular and deep rooted but thoroughly erroneous impression that Gothic architecture is only suitable for buildings of an ecclesiastical character. The origin of this impression is easily explained when we remember not only that most of the richest and most remarkable relics of the Middle Ages which have been preserved in this country are represented by our churches and cathedrals, but that they are, from the very circumstances of their public nature and uninterrupted use, always more accessible and open to inspection than Mediæval structures of a domestic class. The latter are for the most part private property—sometimes country mansions separated by broad acres of park land and plantation from the rest of the world, and sometimes half-ruinous houses standing in the poorest quarters of a country town, or if in a tolerable state of preservation given up to commercial purposes which rob them of half their ancient dignity. Even in places where, as at Chester and Shrewsbury, a few remain intact, they cannot be planned and professionally examined without intruding on the privacy of their inhabitants.

These causes naturally kept the best examples of old secular architecture from the careful study and illustration which they deserved. The perspective views published by Nash and others were interesting from an artistic point of view, but the architect and the antiquary wanted more than this. It was therefore with much pleasure that the lovers of Mediæval art hailed in 1851 the publication of the first volume of a work by Mr. T. Hudson Turner, entitled, ' Some account of Domestic Architecture in England from the Conquest to the end of the Thirteenth Century.' It had long occurred to the author that our national records might be made available for such a history, and no one was better qualified than himself to conduct the search and turn it to practical advantage. For many years of his life he had been gleaning materials from every possible source, literary and pictorial. Mr. R. C. Hussey, an architect, who had undertaken, but subsequently abandoned, a similar task, made over to him the result of his own labours, while

Mr. Twopeny, Mr. Blore, and Mr. Nesbitt placed their sketches at his disposal. It was the intention of the author to extend his history from the thirteenth to the fifteenth century ; but a sad fate interrupted the task. Soon after the completion of the first volume Mr. Hudson Turner died of consumption, and it was left to his friend and able coadjutor, Mr. J. H. Parker, to add the useful and entertaining volumes which have since been published.

It is the special characteristic of this work that it unites in a succinct and compendious form two distinct kinds of information, viz. that which is serviceable to the architect and that which is interesting to the antiquary. The social habits and ordinary life of our Mediæval ancestors are of course intimately associated with their domestic architecture, and indeed it is almost necessary for the explanation of the last to understand the former. Mr. Hudson Turner and Mr. Parker left no channel unexplored to arrive at this information, and the consequence is that these volumes, while furnishing a vast store of technical details, may be read with equal advantage by the student of art or the student of history. The text is profusely illustrated by woodcuts executed by the careful hand of Mr. O. Jewitt, whose knowledge of the subject enabled him also to contribute some valuable notes and suggestions. Plans, sections, and elevations of many a noted hall and mansion, enlarged and accurate studies of doors, windows, roofs, and fireplaces abound throughout the book. Even the minutiæ of furniture and dress receive in turn their proper share of attention. The examples of domestic architecture are for the most part English, but when it served their purpose neither Mr. Turner nor Mr. Parker hesitated to enrich their pages with descriptions and illustrations of Mediæval France.

The truth is that even at this period the taste for French Gothic was steadily gaining ground, and when, a few years afterwards, from causes which have been already mentioned, its special characteristics received closer and more accurate study, many of the younger English architects were naturally attracted towards a style which, in addition to its intrinsic merits, had all the charm of novelty to recommend it.

Among the designs submitted for the Manchester Assize Courts that of Messrs. Nesfield and Shaw found great credit among professional critics for the scholarlike manner in which early French details had been adapted to the requirements of a modern municipal building, and when at a later period Mr. Shaw entered the lists as a candidate in the Bradford Town Hall Competition, his conception of that building was in many respects marked by a similar treatment.

But in both these cases it may be said that the taste of the designers was of too quaint and archaic a fashion to find favour with that section of the British public which is usually represented on a Competition Committee. The quality of such work is too exotic and far-fetched for ordinary appreciation. It stands in the same position towards the world of architectural taste as the inventions of Mr. Burne Jones or Mr. Simeon Solomon occupy in regard to our modern school of painting, and, bating its foreign origin, as the poems of Mr. Morris fill in the field of literature. It is the prettier, more familiar, less recondite art which pleases the ordinary amateur. The admirers of Wordsworth and Longfellow, the admirers of Maclise and Landseer, the admirers of Auber and Verdi, will always have their corresponding representatives among architectural *dilettanti*, to whom the return to earlier types and more subtle conditions of structural grace seems as pedantic and unintelligible as an attempt to imitate the manner of Van Eyck, the versification of Chaucer, or the scientific harmonies of Palestrina's music. It is strange, in these enlightened days, but none the less true, if we may believe those whose acquaintance with art gives weight to their opinion, that the specimens of modern house-building and church-building which receive the greatest meed of praise, which are described at length in public journals, and which all the world runs to see, are, in the majority of cases, but commonplace inventions which owe their popularity to the mere scale on which they are executed, or to the multiplication of ornamental features which an upholsterer might have devised.

Between such work as this and that of the advanced and most exclusive school of modern purists there are of course many ranks creditably and honourably filled by architects whose early studies, whose taste or whose range of practice may prevent their inclining to extremes. It is from such men that we may expect a steady development of the Revival. The morbid love of change, the restless striving after effect and originality of treatment which some years ago characterised the efforts of certain designers, has worked no good for the cause of Gothic art, and may, if renewed at the present stage, threaten its extinction.

It is remarkable that some of the youngest English architects, who at the outset of their professional career seemed pledged to the adoption of foreign Gothic in its earliest form, should have since rendered themselves conspicuous by their devotion to our own national types of Late Pointed work. From French art of the twelfth century to the English ' vernacular ' which prevailed at the close of the sixteenth, is a bold leap, indicating, indeed, the unsettled state of architectural taste at the present day, but also proving the remarkable power possessed by such designers as Mr. Shaw and Mr. Nesfield, who can acquire so speedily and so thoroughly the special characteristics of any style which they may select for imitation.

And this peculiar ability is shown not only in the design of works which from their size and costliness admit of architectural display, but extends to those which not many years ago were considered beyond or rather beneath the range of artistic study. Whether Mr. Nesfield has to deal with a large and important country house, such as that of Combe Abbey, for the Earl of Craven, or with a gate-keeper's lodge, such as that lately erected in the Regent's Park ; whether Mr. Shaw is planning a Thames-side warehouse or a sumptuously appointed mansion like Leyes Wood in Sussex (the seat of Mr. J. W. Temple) ; the result in each case is distinguished by a picturesque management of proportions, a careful modelling of details, and an ingenious use of features which recall in every line the character of ancient work.

In respect of size, originality of design, and artistic treatment of decorative detail, it would be difficult to select a better example of the latest phase into which the Revival has entered than Cloverley Hall, begun in 1862, and recently completed from Mr. Nesfield's design for Mr. J. Pemberton Heywood. To describe a modern building by the general remark that its style can be properly referred to no precise period in the history of styles, would, not many years ago, have been equivalent to pronouncing its condemnation, and even at the present time there are but few designers who can depart from recognised canons of taste without arriving at a result more original than satisfactory. But in this admirable work Mr. Nesfield has succeeded in realising the true spirit of old-world art, without hampering himself by those nice considerations of date and stereotyped conditions of form which in the last generation were sometimes valued more highly than the display of inventive power.

Cloverley Hall is erected on a wooded slope overlooking a lake in one of the most picturesque parts of Shropshire. The nature of the site made it essentially a *hill-side* house, and thus involved an uneven distribution of floor-levels in its internal arrangement. Under ordinary circumstances this condition of things naturally results in an irregularity of elevation more compatible with artistic effect than domestic convenience. But by the ingenious planning of staircases, and a judicious association of rooms *en suite*, this difficulty has been overcome, and the peculiarity of the levels is scarcely noticeable.

The main entrance to the house is from a courtyard on the upper level. It consists of a spacious vestibule panelled throughout in oak. Thence access is obtained under the music gallery to the great hall, about fifty-five feet long and twenty-eight feet high, the general plan of which, with its ample fireplace and large bay window, is not unlike that adopted in the old manor-house at Ockwells in Berkshire. The

PEARSON Sc.

H. E. NESFIELD ARCHITECT

Cloverley Hall, Whitchurch, Shropshire—the Seat of J. P. Heywood, Esq.

W. E. Nesfield, Architect, 1862.

walls are lined to a height of seventeen feet, with small oak panels, the ceiling being trabeated and moulded in the same material. The bay window is of eight lights divided horizontally by five transoms, and filled with stained glass of an heraldic character, executed with great ability by Messrs. Heaton, Butler, and Bayne, by whom the staircase windows, &c., were also painted. The fireplace is of stone enriched with mouldings and crowned with a band of panels containing *rilievi* representing nine of Æsop's fables, carved by Forsyth. Above this, the oak panelling, which reaches to the ceiling, is decorated with carved work of a quaint and intricate pattern.

It is to be observed that the scheme of this pattern, like that of others in the house, is eminently suggestive of a Japanese origin. The introduction of this *motif* in a modern specimen of the Revival may seem anomalous, but it has long been held by the most liberal of the Mediævalists that there are elements in decorative design common to good art of all ages, and certainly in this instance the oriental graft is most fruitful in effect.*

From the great hall a short flight of steps, groined overhead, leads down to the lower hall, which serves as a garden entrance and also communicates with adjoining apartments. This hall is panelled with long amber-coloured tiles, and enriched with a frieze of the same material representing birds, &c., painted on a white ground. A second flight of steps leads *upwards* from the great hall to the dining-room, drawing-room, and library. The ceilings of the latter rooms are executed in plaster, elaborately decorated in low relief. That over the dining-room is of a constructional type, revealing large beams and moulded joists, while a broad plaster frieze, representing hariers in full chase, is carried round the apartment. The fireplaces in these rooms —as indeed throughout the house—are richly carved and panelled.

Externally the house possesses, in addition to the general picturesque-

---

* A pleasant hope is entertained by some modern Gothic architects, who, like Mr. Burges and others, have studied 'the figure' for decorative purposes, that as time goes on the character of Greek sculpture may be revived in association with the Pointed arch.

ness of its composition, many distinctive characteristics of construction and design. The bricks of which the main masses of the wall are built were manufactured expressly for this building on the estate, and are far thinner than is usual. They are laid with a thick mortar joint, resembling the style of work in old houses of the time of Henry VIII. The parapets (about three feet high) are of wood, covered with lead, which is beaten outwards at intervals in the form of large rose-shaped ornaments, quaintly intersecting each other. Above this parapet, on the main front, rise lofty dormers, bearing in their gables sculptured representations of the seasons, carved by Forsyth from designs by Mr. A. Moore. The effect of these figures, which are about two-thirds of life size and are executed in very low relief, is very striking.

The windows throughout the house are large and boldly treated, with stone mullions and square heads, the architect having evidently preferred this simple type of *lintel* construction to a multiplicity of small arches and elaborate fenestration. Indeed, the nature of the whole design, refined and skilful as it is, may be described as the reverse of pretentious. Its graces are of a modest, unobtrusive kind. The work is homely rather than grandiose, and though it bears evidence of widely directed study it certainly derives its chief charm from its unmistakably national character.

It is a special aim of this school to revive, when occasion permits, the distinctive traditions of style which in former days belonged to certain districts of England. Thus at Leyes Wood Mr. Shaw has done his best to introduce in his design the elements of old Sussex architecture. The half timber construction, the tile-weathered walls, lofty chimney shafts, steep roofs, and overhanging gables of this building reflect not only national but local peculiarities.

If we compare a work of this description with the so-called Tudor mansions which were supposed not many years ago to have realised the true spirit of Mediæval design, the extraordinary advance in at least the imitative power of our architects in the present generation becomes apparent. Time was when a few mullioned windows, a battlemented

A Prospect of Leys Wood in Sussex:

| Stable Court | Stables | Entrance Gateway | Lodge & Gardeners House | Kitchen Offices | Servants Room | Butlers Family | Entrance | Library | Drawing Room |

The Seat of James W. Temple, Esq.

R.NORMAN.SHAW, ARCH:. March 1868

parapet, and a judicious sprinkling of buttresses and pinnacles presented even to people of acknowledged taste a fair embodiment of all that was excellent in Gothic art. In point of real fact such features simply parodied the style from which their forms were ostensibly derived. But at Leyes Wood and mansions of a similar kind there is absolutely nothing in external appearance to distinguish the design and workmanship from those of a building executed when this type of architecture was in ordinary use. The irregularity of plan, the random intersection of roofs, the dormer windows half hidden in odd corners, the fenestration introduced at external angles of the house, the open defiance of those principles of symmetry which were once considered essential to grace in the old and academical sense of the word, all promise a complete and thorough change in the aspect of our rural architecture, at least if such work as this becomes popular, of which there is every probability. For with all its quaintness there is nothing in the interior of the house at Leyes Wood incompatible with modern ideas of comfort and convenience.

For instance, it was once assumed that the orthodox ceiling for a Gothic room must be of a *constructional* type, or in other words that it was proper to exhibit the beams and rafters overhead—a picturesque arrangement, indeed, but one to which there were many practical objections. At Leyes Wood the ceilings are of plaster enriched with delicately moulded ornament in low relief. A frieze of the same material is carried round the walls of the principal rooms and decorated at intervals with panels in which *rilievi* of admirably designed foliage are introduced. Again, though 'pattern glazing' is adopted for the upper portions of the windows, the lower halves are filled with plate glass, thus meeting the natural objection which is frequently raised against a Gothic window of the primitive type, viz. that no one can look out of it with comfort. These details are mentioned here, not of course as being peculiar to Leyes Wood, but to illustrate a few out of numberless instances in which the style adopted by Mr. Shaw admits of necessary modification without the slightest sacrifice of artistic effect.

Nor is the application of this style at all limited by the size of the house for which it is adopted. Not far from Leyes Wood is 'Glen Andred,' the country residence of Mr. E. W. Cooke, R.A., also designed by Mr. Shaw, and realising on a smaller scale all the picturesque elements of old Sussex architecture. It is a special evidence of some architects' ability that the character with which their works are invested finds expression in minute details. The wooden architraves, door panels, staircase railings, &c., which were once allowed to take their chance at the contractor's hands, or were only selected from a series of patterns submitted for approval, have of late years become to architects the objects of as much attention as the plan of a room or the proportions of a façade. *De minimis non curat lex* is a maxim which does not apply to the laws of design, and for this attention to small matters we are indebted to the Gothic school, and especially to its youngest representatives.

There is perhaps no feature in the interior of even an ordinary dwelling-house which is capable of more artistic treatment than the fireplace of its most frequented sitting-room, and yet how long it was neglected ! The Englishman's sacred 'hearth,' the Scotchman's 'ain fireside,' the grandsire's 'chimney corner,' have become mere verbal expressions, of which it is difficult to recall the original significance as we stand before those cold, formal slabs of gray or white marble enclosing the sprucely polished but utterly heartless grate of a modern drawing-room.

How picturesque and interesting an object a fireplace may become when designed by an artist's hand Mr. Nesfield has shown in Mr. H. Vallance's house at Farnham Royal, of which the annexed woodcut is an illustration. Features of a somewhat similar kind may be seen at Glen Andred and in Mr. Craik's house at Shortlands, both, for their size and in their respective ways, excellent examples of Mr. Shaw's skill. To draw round such a cosy hearth as this is rarely given to modern gossips.

The reaction in favour of English Gothic was by no means universal, and even at the present time there are many architects whose work is strongly influenced by Continental study. Among those on whom study of French art has had a decided and permanent influence may be mentioned Mr. George Goldie. This gentleman, formerly as a partner of Messrs. Hadfield and Weightman, and subsequently on his own

account, has been chiefly employed in the design of Roman Catholic churches and conventual establishments.

The part which the Church of Rome has taken in the Revival is a peculiar one and not devoid of historical interest. In early days, as we have seen, Dr. Milner was one of the first and most zealous supporters of the Gothic cause, which was afterwards ably advocated by the pen of Carter and sustained by the professional ability (continued through three generations) of the Buckler family, whose name is creditably associated with the works at Costessy Hall, undertaken for a Roman Catholic nobleman (Lord Stafford). The Earl of Shrewsbury, another member of the same Church, found in Pugin an enthusiast whose ecclesiastical zeal was only equalled by his Mediæval sympathies; and at the time that St. Chad's at Birmingham, St. Barnabas' at Nottingham, and St. George's pro-cathedral in London were being raised there is no doubt that the Church of England was far behind its rival in the encouragement of Gothic art. Even at a later period the Roman Catholic churches built by Mr. C. Hansom at Erdington and Liverpool, by Mr. W. Wardell at Brook Green, Clapham, Greenwich, and Poplar, by Mr. Hadfield at Sheffield, Manchester, &c., and the graceful chapel in Farm Street, London, by Mr. J. Scoles, were all model works in their day, and equal, if not in some cases superior, to any similar structures erected for the Establishment. But for all this, the Church of Rome has never been so earnestly or consistently identified with the Revival as the Church of England. It is well known that Pugin's views on ritual and ecclesiastical usage towards the latter end of his life gave offence to many who shared his faith, and after his death there was a reaction in the artistic predilections of the Romish clergy from the influence of which they have never been thoroughly relieved.

This reaction may be ascribed to three principal causes. The first was the Irish immigration, in consequence of which the Roman Catholics were suddenly called on to provide churches for nearly a million of their poorer brethren, and this too in districts which could ill afford the expense. Schools, priests' houses, and convents had to be erected throughout the land, and in nearly every case for the smallest possible amount of money.

The congregation for whose benefit these works were proposed could of course contribute little or nothing towards their cost.

The wealthy Catholics had had their purses drained by subscriptions levied for the richer and more artistic churches of the Revival, and the consequence was that the structures which were now required had to be executed in any style or no style—it mattered little—so long as they were built and occupied.

The second cause which operated adversely to the interests of Gothic —so far as the Church of Rome is concerned—was the introduction into England of certain religious orders of an Italian origin or character. Such were the Redemptorists, the Oratorians, the Passionists, &c., communities through whose influence and taste such works as the Brompton Oratory (which cost no less than 22,000*l.*) and the Passionist Church at Highgate were raised. Even when Gothic was adopted, the unfortunate architect found himself trammelled by specific conditions which too frequently marred the effect of his design. Shallow chancels, naves of disproportionate width, thin piers, and altars planned after an Italian fashion became necessary, and finally, after a fierce controversy, that beautiful feature in church architecture—the rood-screen—was condemned.*

The third obstacle to Roman Catholic encouragement of the Revival was the preference which Cardinal Wiseman entertained for Renaissance art. It is true that for a time and while guided by the advice of such men as the late Mr. Pugin and Dr. Rock, he offered no opposition to Gothic, but his private tastes were directly at variance with Mediævalism, and during the latter part of his life he made no secret of the fact. For some years before he died most of the churches erected under his authority were of a quasi-Italian character, and by no means satisfactory examples of that school.

Since the Cardinal's death there has been manifest evidence of a desire among the Roman Catholics to return to Pointed Architecture

---

* To such an extent was this form of prejudice carried, that at Clapham a rood-screen of very beautiful workmanship, which was in course of completion, is said to have been taken down and destroyed.

for their churches, schools, and convents; but unfortunately the demand for cheap showy buildings has not abated, and the consequence is that in this direction the artistic aspect of the Revival has considerably suffered. There are, however, some notable exceptions. Messrs. Clutton, Hadfield, Goldie, Hansom, Buckler, Willson, and Nicholl have each in their several ways done their best to secure honest and substantial work—and to keep clear of that tawdry superficial style of design which brings discredit on the Gothic cause.

The Roman Catholic Abbey of St. Scholastica at Teignmouth is a very creditable example of Mr. Goldie's skill. Symmetrical in its general plan, broad and massive in its constructive treatment, and pure in its decorative details, it wears an appearance at once of grace and solemnity eminently characteristic of the purpose for which it was erected, and well adapted to its picturesque site, on a hill overlooking the coast of South Devon. The principal front faces the sea and consists of three stories, whereof the second is enriched by mural arcuation, the alternate voussoirs of each arch as well as the engaged shafts on which they are carried being of red sandstone. From this front two wings project southwards. That on the left hand (including some of the reception rooms, &c.) presents a well-proportioned gable on which the arcade is repeated, with a trefoil-headed window above. The right wing is a chapel, from the end of which rises a cleverly treated bell-turret. Between these two wings, which reach a lower level on the site than the intermediate block, a broad terrace walk is formed, intersected in the centre by a flight of steps. Fastidious critics have pointed out that these steps lead to no entrance doorway, that a blank dormer on the left wing is improperly used as a chimney shaft, and that the uppermost windows on the same side are unfortunately close to the eaves; but these are minor faults amply redeemed by more prominent excellences in the work, which without the slightest approach to archaism or pedantry realises some of the most valuable and attractive qualities of Mediæval art.

Abbey of S. Scholastica, Teignmouth.

G. Goldie, Architect, 1863.

The pro-cathedral of St. Mary at Kensington, also designed by Mr. Goldie, is another and later evidence of the favour with which Gothic architecture has been regarded by Roman Catholics during Dr. Manning's Archiepiscopate. The external effect of this church is much marred by the surrounding buildings which hem it in on every side. These, however, will, it is to be hoped, disappear in due time, and allow the fine proportions and rich sculpture of the western porch to be seen to greater advantage than at present.

The interior is remarkable for the height of its nave, which is provided with a clerestory and unpierced triforium. The nave arcade is pointed, but the arch soffits are flat and simply enriched by a single bead moulding at the edge. The shafts are cylindrical, about two feet in diameter, and of polished granite, divided at about half their height by a richly-moulded stone band. The abaci and large boldly undercut foliage of the capitals are decidedly French in character. The carving of these features, as indeed throughout the church, is executed with remarkable vigour, and is a striking contrast to the small frittered style of work which passed for decorative sculpture in Pugin's days, and which in a town church, where dust and soot quickly accumulate, is for obvious reasons unsuitable. The roof, which is ceiled, follows the outline of a trefoil-headed arch—a form not often adopted, but here peculiarly effective. The bays of the south aisle are recessed for altars and lighted by circular windows, each under a pointed arch. The aisle walls are of brick, plastered internally. This fact, together with the pure whiteness of the stone-work, gives the interior a somewhat cold appearance, which will no doubt be removed in time by fresco painting or other chromatic decoration. There are many incidents in the design of this church—such as the corbelling out of the chancel arch—which are very ingenious and original. Every detail throughout the work—even to the novel gas-standards—bears evidence of artistic care, and though purists may regret the rendering of groins in plaster, and the unorthodox position of the organ-loft, it would be manifestly unfair to hold the architect responsible for conditions of arrangement and economy, against which, as we know, professional protests are usually of small avail.

Mr. Goldie may be said to hold a middle place between the old and modern school of design. He had the advantage of starting in his profession when the study of Gothic was considerably widened and relieved from the bondage which some twenty years ago still limited its range to national examples. But it is curious to mark the extraordinary progress which the revived style has made in the hands of another Roman Catholic architect, Mr. M. E. Hadfield, who as a contemporary of Pugin has seen a complete revolution in the principles of Mediæval art, and has managed in spite of old prejudices and early influence to keep pace with the times and hold his own in competition with younger rivals. The Church of St. Marie at Sheffield, opened for service in 1850, was then considered a model of excellence. But if we compare its details with those of any of Mr. Hadfield's more recent works—that of the chapel erected for the Notre-Dame Sisterhood at Liverpool, for example—we shall see how great a change has taken place not only in the absolute forms but in the spirit and character of Gothic since Pugin's days. The apsidal end of this chapel, the plate tracery, the marble shafts from which the groining springs, the *flèche* which rises from the roof ridge, the very weathering of the buttresses, gathered up in masses instead of being tamely distributed throughout their length —all these indicate an advance in architectural taste which augurs well for the future of the Revival, especially when we remember that it is exemplified not only in the works of the rising generation of architects, but in the works of those whose age and experience naturally tend to keep them aloof from the extravagances of a fleeting fashion, and who may be therefore supposed to have remodelled their manner of design under a conviction that such a change is to be justified on artistic grounds.

Regarded broadly, the association of Roman Catholicism with the

Western Doorway of St. Mary's (R. C.) pro-Cathedral Church.

George Goldie, Architect, 1867.

Revival may be attributed more to the accident that many eminent architects, including Pugin, have belonged to that faith than to any supposed sympathy between the Church of Rome and Mediæval art. Gothic architecture is now constantly adopted by Dissenters for their schools and chapels, and it would be as foolish to suppose the perception of its merits limited to a particular sect as it certainly would be bigoted to desire such a limit in any direction. The belief in good art is at least a harmless creed which may be shared in common by many who differ from each other on more important matters. There was a time when the Pointed arch bade fair to become a symbol of extreme views in theological controversy. But that period has long since passed. The application of Mediæval principles to the design of secular buildings has tended to remove many foolish prejudices on this score, and the day may be not far distant when, so far as external appearance is concerned, it will be difficult to distinguish the church from the conventicle.

CHAPTER XX.

URING the last ten years to which this history extends, viz. from 1860 to 1870, the list of Gothic architects has reached an extraordinary length, while the number of buildings partaking more or less of a Mediæval character which have been erected within that period is probably double that of the preceding *decennium*. Nor is the difference of quality in this class of design less remarkable than the increased range of its application. There are architects now in practice, whose professional career dates from more than thirty years ago, who remember what may be called the *pre-Puginesque* aspect of the Revival, and whose works have been marked by a steady improvement in artistic taste from that time to the present. But there are many more who began to design under advantages which were unknown to the previous generation, who have learnt by degrees to distinguish between the faults and merits of Pointed architecture, and who, having studied the style with respect to its local and national characteristics, are enabled to attain an individuality of treatment to which their predecessors could not aspire.

In addition to the architects already mentioned there are several whose work may be recognised by special traits of taste either distinctly personal or represented by that unconscious mannerism which results from the common sympathies and artistic fellowship of a particular clique. To one or other of these classes belong Messrs. Burges, E. W. Godwin, Bodley, Blomfield, Seddon, Brooks, Champneys, and G. G. Scott jun.

It would be difficult, even if it were within the scope of this work, to attempt so much as a general definition of the several qualities of excellence for which these artists' designs are remarkable. Disparity of age, unequal opportunities, differences of professional education or line of practice, would render a comparison, and even an analysis of such qualities, fallacious. Of all, however, it may be said that they have become known to fame, if not exactly as contemporaries, yet at short intervals within the last ten years.

If the extent of an architect's practice were always in proportion to his artistic ability the works of Mr. W. Burges might ere this have been found in every part of England to which the Revival has extended. No student of his time devoted himself more earnestly and sedulously to master the principles of Mediæval design. No member of his profession has striven more persistently and thoroughly to uphold those principles, to advocate their general adoption, and, whenever he has had an opportunity, to give them material expression.

Yet it is only since 1860 that any building of importance has been erected from his design. We have seen that in a competition open to all Europe, after carrying off, in conjunction with Mr. Clutton, the first prize for Lille Cathedral, he and his colleague were unfairly excluded from the honour of erecting it. Mr. Burges has since played a prominent part in more than one public competition, but in one case only has he traversed this always arduous road to fame with anything like substantial success. And even the cathedral church of St. Finbar, Cork, the commission for which he gained in 1863, affords little scope for his ability, not because, for its purpose, the building is a comparatively small one, but because the sum set apart for its cost renders it impossible at present to complete the structure in accordance with the architect's original intention.

Mr. Burges's design may generally be distinguished by two leading and strongly marked characteristics, viz. the tendency towards an early type of French Gothic, and the attention bestowed on figure drawing in decorative sculpture. The various essays which he has written and the lectures which he has delivered contain ample apology, if apology be needed, for both these peculiarities, and if, as seems likely, they hereafter become the peculiarities of a school, it will be mainly due to his influence and example.

Simple and severe as the west front of St. Finbar is, Mr. Burges could not resist the opportunity which it afforded for the exercise of that art which he holds to be the one indispensable attribute of architectural effect. The spandrils of the wheel window, which occupies a central position in the façade, are filled with life size *rilievi* of the four evangelistic symbols carved in the solid masonry of the wall. In the gable above a seated figure of Christ is to occupy a vesica-shaped panel with angels censing on either side. Of these works, executed by Mr. Thomas Nicholls from Mr. Burges's design, it is not too much to say that no finer examples of decorative sculpture have been produced during the Revival. They exactly represent that intermediate condition between natural form and abstract idealism which is the essence of Mediæval and indeed of all noble art, and they possess the further merit of being admirably adapted to their position.

Mr. Burges has done much to dissipate the frivolous extravagance of detail and wilful irregularities of plan which once found favour with those younger architects who for a while mistook license for freedom in design and conceived that the conditions of Gothic art were not thoroughly fulfilled unless one half of an elevation differed from the other and every edge in masonry or woodwork were notched or chamfered.

His own work, careful and scholarlike in its treatment, never condescends to such vagaries. While devoted to the archæological aspect of architecture, and especially to the study of all the decorative arts with which it is allied, he can deal effectively when occasion demands with plain bricks and mortar, tempering his inventive power in such instances to conditions of site and purpose which are generally considered incompatible with artistic design. A model lodging-house for the poor in St. Ann's Court, Soho, and a warehouse in Upper Thames Street, erected between 1864 and 1866, have tested this ability to the full, and with a result which is hopeful for our city lanes and alleys.

One of Mr. Burges's most recent works is the new tower at Cardiff Castle, recently erected for the Marquis of Bute, and perhaps no better subject could have been suggested for the exercise and illustration of his peculiar talents.

A tower in itself is essentially a Mediæval structure, and this one happens to unite all the architectural severity usually associated with such a feature to graces of sculptured and pictorial decoration, which in its internal appointments have given full scope for the designer's luxuriant fancy. The outside of the tower, up to a height of about sixty-five feet from the ground, is a rectangular block of masonry pierced with narrow windows on three sides. At that level each wall is divided into arched panels, whereof the centre is given up to the clock-face and the rest are occupied by life-size figures symbolising the principal planets.

The topmost story of the tower overhangs the substructure, the walls being machicolated or corbelled outwards to the necessary width, and the whole is surmounted by a highly picturesque roof broken into two slopes by a lantern light of trefoil-headed windows. On this apartment, which is appropriated as a summer smoking-room, and on those below, devoted to winter occupation, the architect has lavished his utmost care. Stained glass, mural painting, marble, encaustic tiles, and wood inlay of a rich and delicate description will, when the work is finished, present an appearance of artistic beauty which, since the Middle Ages, has rarely been realised in this country.

As a rule the architect's labour terminates with the structural completion of the building which he is commissioned to design. The interior is given up to upholsterers and decorators, who too frequently are allowed to execute their work independently of his control. It is to this cause that we may attribute the melancholy *bathos* which exists between what we call fine art and industrial art in modern days. We enter a Renaissance palace or a Gothic mansion and find them respectively fitted up in the style of the nineteenth century, which in point of fact is no style at all, but the embodiment of a taste as empirical, as empty, and as fleeting as that which finds expression in a milliner's fashion book.

This goodly tower of Cardiff Castle is an excellent and notable exception to a foolish custom. Its interior, from roof to basement, has been the object of as much care to Mr. Burges as its external aspect, and down to the minutest detail exhibits evidence of thoughtful study.

Knightshayes, near Tiverton, the residence of Mr. J. H. Amory, M.P., is another example of this architect's skill in the field of domestic architecture. A reference to the illustration of this building will show that, though the main front is uniform in its general masses, the entrance doorway is not precisely in the centre. This slight deviation from what is commonly called symmetry in design was no doubt adopted for convenience of internal arrangement, and is an instance of the ease with which a Gothic elevation may accommodate itself to exigencies of plan without sacrifice of artistic effect. In the case of an Italian villa such a license would have been almost impossible.

The class of art to which Knightshayes belongs is of a severer type than that adopted at Eatington, and less emphatically national than that which characterises Leyes Wood. The reddish local stone employed for the masonry is extremely hard, and there is a kind of sympathy between its stern unyielding nature and the robust rather than refined character of the work with which it is associated.

Massive walls, bold gables, stout mullions nearly half the width of the lights which they divide, large and solid looking chimney shafts, corbelled from the walls or riding on the high pitched roofs, are the principal incidents which give this building dignity and effect. Such gentler graces as are imparted into the design by aid of mouldings or decorative sculpture (as in the central dormer) indicate a French origin. The great feature of the interior is a large hall to be used for the re-

Knightshayes, near Tiverton, Devon—the Seat of J. H. Amory, Esq., M.P.

W. Burges, Architect, 1869.

ception of the owner's tenantry.   This is fitted up with a gallery and rostrum at one end, and is eminently picturesque both in plan and proportions.   For this quality of design as well as for a certain vigour of treatment, Knightshayes may be considered a typical example of the Revival.

There is perhaps no better sign of the extent to which architectural taste has been cultivated and refined within the last ten years than the marked and steady increase of simplicity in the design of Gothic—at least among the most accomplished of our Mediæval school.   In the earliest days of the Revival, when architects were content to copy, and while a belief still lingered that the distinctive features of Pointed architecture could be measured out bit by bit and applied to this or that façade under a system as complete, as infallible, and as decorous as that which had been devised for the Five Orders during the late Renaissance, dullness and formality necessarily prevailed.   Then came a reaction. Under the influence first of Pugin and afterwards of Ruskin, architects found themselves suddenly emancipated from the conditions and restrictions which had hampered their efforts, and the result was at first a reckless extravagance of design.   It was delightful to invent new mouldings, to revel in fresh whims of fenestration, to enliven walls with local colour and sculptured ornament, to reverse accepted rules of proportion, to set at defiance those prosy principles of art whose last-born offspring had been respectable insipidity.   Freedom from precedent, freedom from national traditions, freedom from structural and decorative conventionality, these were the watchwords of our youngest and most enthusiastic reformers.   They had their liberty, and like all liberty thus suddenly and lawlessly attained it was wofully misused.   The absurd and barbarous specimens of modern architecture which have been erected in this generation under the general name of Gothic have done more to damage the cause of the Revival than all that has been said or written in disparagement of the style.

As a matter of course educated designers recoiled from this condition of things, and from that time down to the present the best and most scholarlike work has been also the most simple and unobtrusive in its character.

It is probable that Mr. Ruskin's plea for Italian Gothic would have had a more lasting and more favourable influence on our architecture but for the hasty response with which it met and the manner in which it was misinterpreted. Real artists shrank from the adaptation of structural features and the ornamental detail which had been copied *ad nauseam* and had been vulgarised in the copying. A single instance may suffice, by way of illustration. Among those modern architects whose work has always aimed at a refined and elevated standard is Mr. E. W. Godwin. The Town Hall at Northampton, begun in 1861, is an excellent example of his early taste. Its plan is at once simple and ingenious. The conditions of its site admit of only one façade, but that is treated with becoming dignity. Now, it is impossible to examine this front without feeling that at this period the designer was strongly influenced by the then prevalent taste for Italian Gothic and by the principles of design which Mr. Ruskin had lately advocated. The fenestration of the principal story, the sculptured and star-pierced tympana of the windows below, the character of the balconies, inlaid work, and angle shafts of the tower—all suggest an Italian origin.

A few years later the same architect was employed to erect the Town Hall at Congleton, and a marked difference is at once observable in the character of his work. Venetian angle shafts and Italian tracery have become common property, and Mr. Godwin disdains to adopt them. The general outline of the central tower and the open arcade on the street level still indicate a lingering affection for southern art; but a French element predominates in the design, which is simpler and more ascetic in its character. This tendency to shun the minutiæ of decorative detail, to aim at effect by sturdy masses of unbroken wall space, and by artistic proportion of parts, is perhaps the main secret of

Mr. Godwin's artistic power, and has been exemplified to the full in his design for Dromore Castle—lately built for the Earl of Limerick —one of the most picturesque and interesting examples of domestic architecture which has yet graced the Revival.

Definitions are difficult and dangerous things to employ in recording the progress of modern art, but if, by way of classifying the works of modern Gothic architects, it were possible to arrange them for convenience of description in three general divisions or schools, such a classification might not inappropriately take the following form. We should have:

First. The Traditional or Correct School, which aims as far as possible at a literal reproduction of art in the Middle Ages : admitting no compromise, abhorrent of eclecticism, selecting one style for absolute imitation, excluding on the score of taste nothing for which there is authentic precedent, inclining to primitive types, tolerant of obsolete contrivances, and sternly sacrificing all notions of modern comfort which interfere with the conditions of ancient design.

Second. The Adaptational or Artistic School, which holds Mediæval art in high respect, but considers that it may be modified to suit the requirements of the present age : testing the character of every feature and the motive of every composition by abstract and æsthetic principles, rejecting even traditional forms which will not bear that test, and, while preserving the main unities of style, tolerant of occasional license in regard to the use of details.

Third. The Independent or Eclectic School, which is regardless of authority, of local peculiarities, of dates and proprieties of design, so long as it satisfies individual taste : not hesitating to unite in one building the distinctive characteristics of English and foreign Gothic, and using Mediæval architecture as a mere mask to modern work, fond of variety and despising antiquarian considerations, inclined to startling proportions, and not unfrequently to extravagance in decorative features.

Between these three groups of designers there are, of course, intermediate ranks, occupied by men who are pledged to no fixed principles of taste, and who have passed from one extreme to the other as the circumstances of their practice or the fleeting fashions of the day have guided them. There are indeed but few Mediævalists of whom it may be said that they have from first to last pursued one aim unaffected by the strange and conflicting influences which have been brought to bear on the Revival.

Among the most notable examples of secular Gothic which have been raised within the last ten years, the University College of Wales at Aberystwith may be mentioned. It was begun in 1864 by Mr. J. P. Seddon, an architect who was conspicuous at the outset of his career as a zealous supporter of Mr. Ruskin's views, and who, with certain modifications suggested by experience, has apparently adhered to the principle that a free and unfettered adaptation of Mediæval forms to the practical requirements of the day is preferable to that severer and more archaic type of design which is adopted by some of his contemporaries. This building, originally designed for a large hotel, was erected under circumstances which must have considerably taxed the designer's ingenuity and patience. It was the result of a sudden and imperfectly matured scheme—required to be executed without an hour's delay; and leaving little or no time for that forethought which every architect needs for his designs. So hurried was the work in its commencement that its foundations were actually being excavated from a sketch plan before the working drawings had been prepared. The walls arose as if by magic : alterations were proposed and executed while the structure was in progress. Here another story was added : there a new wing was thrown out. Five hundred men were to be kept employed, and the architect had to ' rough out ' his ideas as best he could on paper or by means of models. It would be absurd to expect a building designed and erected under these conditions to bear evidence of careful study, but it is an ill wind that blows no good even to

Part of new Buildings at Balliol College, Oxford.

A. Waterhouse, Architect, 1867.

architectural design. The composition is exceedingly bold and unconventional—qualities which may to some extent have resulted from the necessarily swift conception of the project, and from the piecemeal character of its execution. It would be difficult to identify the building generally with any definite period or local character of ancient art. The nature of its fenestration—an important element in the design—may be called Italian. But in the main outline its lofty tower, its roofs, dormers, and other details, as well as in the type of mouldings employed, the influence of French example is apparent, while the south wing, with its timber framed upper story, might pass for old English work. In spite of these apparently conflicting elements, the whole design is well and harmoniously knit together, and if completed in accordance with Mr. Seddon's intention will form a very effective group.*

The year 1867 found many architects engaged on buildings which either from their site, their size, or their character, represent interesting points in the history of the Revival. The new buildings for Balliol College, Oxford, for example, show that Mr. Waterhouse kept up with the stream of advancing taste without losing that individuality of design which every true artist wishes to retain. A marked improvement is observable in the breadth and vigour with which this work is treated as compared with earlier examples of his skill. It contrasts strangely, indeed, with the old buildings by which it is surrounded, but as a matter of sentiment it may be questioned whether such a contrast is not an advantage when it is explained by a difference of style as well as of date, while as a matter of taste posterity alone will fairly judge between Oxford of the fifteenth and Oxford of the nineteenth century. Is a high pitched roof more picturesque than one raised at an obtuse angle? Is an equilateral arch better than a four centred flat one? Is

---

* In consequence of circumstances on which it is unnecessary to enter here, this building, in an unfinished state, passed out of the hands of its original proprietor and became the property of a committee, to whom the management of the proposed university is entrusted.

such a lintel as Mr. Waterhouse has used for his windows—we need not say the comeliest which might have been devised, but—more comely than the ordinary type of Tudor window-head? Does the building altogether present a richer variety of features, a greater refinement of mouldings, and on the whole more indication of artistic study than if it had been a mere imitation of Brasenose or All Souls? If these questions can be answered in the affirmative—and he must be a bold critic who would answer them otherwise—we may safely leave the rest to the hand of time, whose artistic touch has exercised, perhaps, a more potent influence than we suppose on the opinion of modern amateurs.

Mr. White's name has hitherto been mentioned only in connection with church architecture, and it is with this department of design that it has become most generally associated. But he has also been engaged in the design and erection of many Gothic buildings of a domestic character, among which that of 'Humewood' in Ireland is one of the most notable. It was begun in 1867 for Mr. W. Fitzwilliam Dick, M.P. for Wicklow, and represents for special reasons a combination of Scotch and Irish characteristics in its design. It is built of granite, a material obviously involving a plain massive treatment, in which the lintel must supersede the arch, and delicate mouldings become impossible. To compensate for this deficiency in refinement of detail, the mansion has been most picturesquely grouped with projecting bays, angle turrets, stepped gables, and high pitched roofs, rising above which a square tower, surmounted by a battlemented parapet, gives great dignity to the composition. Though much given to antiquarian research, and especially orthodox in the internal arrangement of his churches, Mr. White has not allowed his acquaintance with Mediæval architecture to affect the character of his plan, which is studied with great attention to modern convenience and requirements, nor has less care been bestowed on the details and fittings whether of a constructional or ornamental character. They exhibit, in many

Humewood, Wicklow, Ireland—the Residence of W. W. Fitzwilliam Dick, Esq., M.P.

W. White, F.S.A., Architect, 1867.

features of the house, evidence of that artistic design by which alone we can hope to revive in these degenerate days the true spirit of ancient handiwork.

There are perhaps few professions, and certainly none within the realm of art, exposed to such unequal chances of that notoriety which should attend success as the profession of architecture. The works of painters and sculptors, whose taste, whose aim, and choice of subject lie widely apart, meet in an exhibition-room on common ground, and appealing though they may to totally opposite classes of admirers, will each in turn command such attention as they deserve.

Not so with the works of architects. One man's practice may take him for years of his life into remote rural parishes, where, except by the squire or parson, his work may long remain unappreciated, while his luckier rival with far less ability may be called on to design a public institution in some populous town, which speedily attracts attention and helps him on the road to fame. There are districts and suburbs in London in which if a new building is raised it stands no more chance of being visited by people of taste than if it had been erected in Kamschatka. What amateur or *dilettante* would ever think of exploring such neighbourhoods as Shoreditch, Hoxton, and Plaistow in search of architectural beauty ? Yet those outlying regions in the far east of London contain some of the largest and most remarkable churches which have been built during the Revival. Mr. James Brooks, by whom they were designed, had no easy task before him. It was required to make these structures the head quarters of mission work in poor and populous localities. There was but little money to spend on them, yet they were to be of ample size and, for obvious reasons, dignified and impressive in their general effect. These conditions are admirably fulfilled. One of the favourite axioms enunciated by Mr. Ruskin is (or was) that there could be no artistic quality in architecture which was not sculpturesque. If this element were wanting, all the rest, he argued, went for nought.

The fallacy of this theory could not be better exemplified in modern design than by a critical examination of these churches. There is scarcely one of them in which decorative carving is a conspicuous feature, and it so happens that where it is intended to be introduced as a mere accessory the work has in several instances been left unfinished.

The buildings may be said therefore to depend for their effect entirely on their plans and proportions, and it must be admitted that the effect in each case is extremely fine. There is much in the character of Mr. Brooks's work which reminds one of Butterfield. An utter absence of conventionality in the treatment of features whose appearance has of late years become stereotyped, a studied simplicity of details which are elsewhere elaborate, a tendency to quaint outlines and unusual subdivision of parts—such are the chief characteristics which distinguish the design of both these architects, who manage to attain originality without condescending to extravagance, and to secure for their works a quiet grace in which there is less of elegance than of dignity.

St. Chad's, Haggerston, one of the group above mentioned, is a lofty church faced internally with brick, and having a round open chancel groined with the same material. The nave piers are of stone, circular in plan and short in proportion to the arches which they carry. These arches are obtusely pointed, and very simple in their mouldings. The aisles, which are low and narrow, could not be provided with windows on account of the adjacent buildings, but four large windows admit ample light from the clerestory on each side of the church. The nave roof is ceiled and polygonal, supported at intervals by semicircular ribs, the prolongation of which, at a tangent drawn towards the clerestory walls, gives them a peculiar and not very satisfactory appearance. A narrow board pierced with quatrefoils does duty as a cornice. The chancel is provided with a stone reredos detached from the wall and enriched with diapered carving, as well as with an inlay of tiles and marble excellent in taste and workmanship. South of the chancel is a chapel intended for daily service, and groined, like the chancel, in brick

Church of St. Chad, Haggerston.

James Brooks, Architect, 1867.

with stone ribs. Externally the western narthex is a striking feature, and the bold fenestration of the north transept tells to advantage; but the real excellence of this work consists in its grand masses of roof and wall planned and proportioned with true artistic ability.

The same may be said of Mr. Brooks's other Haggerston church, St. Columba, which, seen from the Kingsland Road, at its north-west corner, presents an exceedingly picturesque composition, even though the tower is still left incomplete. In this building the floor of the chancel is considerably higher than the floor of the nave, and is crossed by steps raised at broad intervals, and leading up to the altar. The effect of this arrangement lends great dignity and interest to the interior. Here the nave piers are of the ' compound ' type, the aisles are spanned by brick arches, the crux is groined for a central tower, the chancel has a square end, and the nave roof is open timbered. In other respects the general ' motive' of the interior is not unlike that of St. Chad's, though the details are perhaps of a more decorative character.

The Plaistow church (St. Andrew's), which is built of Kentish rag, with freestone dressings, has an arcaded clerestory, lancet windows being introduced in the alternate arches. The roof is of a very simple ' king-post' type, the intermediate rafters being strengthened by semicircular ribs.

In the early days of the Revival the king-post and tie-beam were rarely used—probably from some erroneous impression that they were not legitimately Gothic features. It is curious to note how in this and some other details the artistic conditions of Mediæval design have been widened and modified within the last few years. For example, it was formerly *de rigueur* that the glazing of a pointed window should consist of lozenge-shaped ' quarries,' or in other words that the lines of lead-work should cross each diagonally at an acute angle. In the churches just described, and in many others of recent date, the quarries are nearly square, and are separated from the window jambs by narrow borders of lead-work, arranged in rectangular patterns. It is difficult to say how far such changes as these recommend themselves by their novelty, but at present they certainly seem to infuse a new spirit into features which have long appeared monotonous. The attention which Mr. Brooks bestows on the constructive character of his work is very remarkable. Nothing is more uninteresting than the cold neat look of recently executed masonry. This is in a great measure owing to the uniform finish and flushing of the joints, which admit of no play of light upon the outer edges of each course. In St. Andrew's Church the joints were raked out before the mortar had set, and the result, so far as appearances and effect are concerned, is most satisfactory.*

The Church of the Annunciation at Chislehurst exhibits all the qualities of good proportion and *repose* in its design which distinguish most of this architect's works, coupled, except in one instance, viz. the notching of the wall plates, with greater refinement and beauty of detail. Its fenestration is, however, marked by great peculiarities. The west window consists of a number of round lights associated in triple groups and enclosed by a circle. This arrangement, owing to the judicious distribution of external mouldings, looks well from outside, but is scarcely so well adapted for internal effect. The design of the western doorway is very quaint and original. It has no real porch, but the masonry by which it is enclosed projects slightly from the wall behind, and is carried up in the form of a gable on the arch mouldings. Two other features in this church may be mentioned, if only to indicate the advance which we have made in what may be called the common-sense treatment of Gothic.

There is a flying buttress on the south side of the chancel, where it is required to resist the thrust of the chancel roof. But the plan of the church renders this unnecessary on the north side, where the walls of the sacristy afford sufficient abutment.

There is also a chimney shaft rising from the chancel wall, which,

---

* This method could not be universally adopted without incurring practical objections on which it is unnecessary to enter here.

Church of St. Columba, Haggerston, London.

James Brooks, Architect, 1868.

though by no means an unpicturesque object, is unmistakably designed to carry off smoke and nothing else. Now, if this church had been planned in the early days of the Revival, the architect's aim would have been to secure uniformity, and what was then considered elegance, at a sacrifice of more practical considerations. We should have had two sacristies or two flying buttresses, one on each side of the chancel, and the chimney shaft would have been converted into a decorative feature of some kind terminating perhaps in an open turret or pierced pinnacle— some wretched compromise between use and ornament, but really serving neither one purpose nor the other. Let us be thankful that we have arrived at an age when architectural taste seeks higher objects than to make two sides of a church precisely alike, and when no part of a building which serves its purpose honestly is considered undignified.

There seems to be no reason for supposing that the present struggle for pre-eminence between French and English types of Gothic in this country will terminate for some time to come; and indeed so long as both schools of art find able representatives among our architects, they might be maintained side by side with mutual advantage—the English supplying a standard of sobriety, repose, and refinement, while the French might serve as a model of strength, boldness, and breadth in design. As years roll on a style may arise which shall represent a fusion of these distinct qualities, with additional characteristics marking the epoch of their union, and affording more scope for originality and inventive power than has yet been possible.

Meanwhile it is interesting to note that in proportion as the taste for Continental Gothic gains influence in one direction, a steady reaction propitious to home traditions of style is spreading in another. Countless examples of this influence and this reaction might be quoted; but two will perhaps suffice, each being the work of a well-known architect and recently completed, to illustrate these opposite extremes of contemporary taste.

In the suburbs of London no church has of late deserved or won more notice than that of St. Stephen, erected at Hampstead by Mr. S. S. Teulon.   Its picturesque site, on a slope rapidly inclining from west to east, the novelty of its proportions, and the beauty of the materials used in its construction, present in themselves no small attractions, even to the ordinary observer, but for architects and amateurs it has a deeper interest in the strongly-marked assimilation of an early French character which its design reveals.   The walls are mainly built of fine hard brick ranging in colour from pale gray to Indian red, the admixture of which tints gives them at a little distance a rich stippled texture which is very agreeable.   Stone and granite are also largely employed for the quoins and dressings.   The illustration which is appended to this chapter renders a description of the exterior unnecessary ; but it may be well to explain that the central tower has yet to be finished, and that the west end is provided with a wide porch or narthex, which forms a picturesque feature in the composition.

The interior is sumptuously decorated, especially at the east end, where the apse is groined, and its walls are inlaid with gilt mosaic work. The chancel arch is corbelled out on panelled blocks enriched with sculpture in high relief, illustrating the life and death of St. Stephen. The pillars of the nave arcade are cylindrical, supported on high plinths, and crowned with boldly carved capitals varying in design.   The arches are admirably proportioned to the height and plan of the church, and though fastidious critics may object to the notched and billet-moulded edges of the brickwork introduced, it must be remembered that this mode of decoration has been approved and adopted by some of the leading architects of the Gothic school.   The open-timbered roof over the nave is an excellent example of constructive skill, and we need only compare it with the poor lean-looking specimens of frame-work which shelter some of the early churches of the Revival, to feel that in the design of those features whose effect depends on a judicious combination of art and science we have left the last generation far behind.

To select this building as an example of the extent to which modern

Church of S. Stephen, Hampstead.

S. S. Teulon, Architect, 1869.

Gothic has been, or may be, affected in this country by Continental study would be unfair both to the designer and to some of his contemporaries. In many respects it retains a national character, while certain details—as, for instance, the ornamental brickwork of its interior—can scarcely be referred to any precedent but that of modern fashion. At the same time it represents a sufficiently wide departure from English tradition to be fairly contrasted with works in which respect for that tradition is conspicuous.

The church of St. John, in Tue Brook, a suburb of Liverpool, is an admirable model of the latter class, recently completed from the design of Mr. G. F. Bodley, whose earlier work, St. Michael's, at Brighton, was one of the first to attract attention by its quaint and original character, but who in this instance has returned to that type of Middle Pointed art which reached its highest grace towards the middle of the fourteenth century.

Carefully and ably as the leading elements of that style have been revived by the architect, accurate and refined as the treatment of form throughout the church assuredly is, whether we examine the outline and proportions of its tower and spire, the fashion of its window tracery or the profile of its mouldings, it is probable that these merits would have received respectful rather than enthusiastic admiration, but for one additional element of beauty which pervades the whole building from its primary construction to the last touch of its embellishment. This element is the charm of colour.

The walls are built of red and white sandstone—not arranged in formally alternate courses, nor yet with studied irregularity, but intermixed in such a manner as to relieve the eye by variety without fatiguing it by repetition. For this happily *unconscious* treatment of the material, Nature herself offers the best authority, seeing that the red sandstone is streaked with veins of white and the white with veins of red. Not all the scientific treatises on polychromy could have supplied a better scheme.

Internally, for reasons which will presently appear, this variety of natural tint is avoided, and where the stone is visible its prevailing hue is light Indian red. The seats and wood fittings throughout the church are stained black. This simple chord of colour forms a fitting prelude to the interesting harmonies which follow. Almost the whole of the interior is given up to pictorial decoration. The chancel screen, of a type well known in Yorkshire, is groined out with delicate ribs of wood to support the rood loft above, which is divided into panels enriched with figure subjects and foliage admirably designed and executed. The clerestory is occupied between the windows by mural paintings (executed in *tempera*) of the twelve Apostles, the four Evangelists, &c. A more conventional but still chromatic treatment is reserved for the aisle walls and roof, both of which are, with sound judgment, kept in a light key of colour.

But it is on the space usually occupied by the west window and on the wall above the chancel arch that the artist, Mr. C. E. Kempe, has reserved his greatest care. On the former appears a large and grandly treated painting of the Tree of Jesse in which the figures introduced are nearly life size.

In composition, in delineative power, in judicious choice and association of colour, as well as in attention to the proprieties of costume and other details, this work is worthy of all praise, but it is rivalled, if not surpassed, in excellence by that which is executed on the chancel wall. Among the sacred allegories which have found expression in Christian art there is none more significant or beautiful than that of the Tree of Life as symbolised by the Crucifixion. Mr. Kempe has approached this subject in a manner befitting its dignity and pathos, neither aiming at unnecessary archaism nor adopting a mere pictorial and naturalistic treatment. The design is, in the highest æsthetic sense of the word, *conventional*, but it belongs to that order of conventionalism in which the element of beauty predominates. The Tree of Life is of course the Cross, at the foot of which stand the Virgin Mary and St. John with angels on either side bearing gold censers. These last figures are draped in robes of white and salmon colour, which, relieved on a background of dark olive-green foliage, produce a most lovely combination of tints. Above, the Tree blossoms into fruit representing the Virtues, and the allegory is rendered complete by medallion portraits of the Prophets, and the sacred emblem of the pelican, introduced as decorative adjuncts.

In this truly admirable work the genuine grace of Mediæval art seems at length to have been reached. In the architecture which it decorates no appreciable inferiority, whether of design or execution, to the type selected for imitation, can be discerned. Our too sophisticated age may want the rich instincts of inventive genius, which in days of yore made our streets interesting, our houses loveable and our churches sublime. It may want the simplicity of popular faith, nay, the very social conditions which would render a return to Mediæval principles universally acceptable. But at least we have learnt, or there are those among us who have learnt, in what those principles consist.

That is something to have attained. A more difficult problem, however, still remains to be solved. Is this quaint old-world fashion of structural design which for thirty years past has engaged the attention and bew'tched the fancy of so many practical men—members of a profession which is now no less a business than an art—is this long-lost tradition of the Middle Ages destined, as time rolls on, to reach and influence the taste, not only of our architects and amateurs, but of everyone who builds a house or owns a shop throughout the land? If not, it is to be feared that our neo-Mediævalism will share the fate of the Classic Renaissance, which rising to magnificence in Whitehall has descended to meanness in Baker Street. A style of architecture which cannot accommodate itself to the common requirements of social life, which is beyond the reach of ordinary means, and which is reserved for a special class or for a special purpose, can have no genuine, and therefore no permanent, existence. On the other hand, to drag Gothic down to the level of a cockney villa, to parody its characteristic features in plaster and cast iron, to degrade its fairest details, as the details of Greek and Roman architecture have already been degraded in this country, would be intolerable. The only escape from this dilemma lies in a twofold reform—Architects must learn to sacrifice something of their antiquarian tendencies : the Public must learn to sacrifice something of their conventional taste.

By dint of earnest study and endless experiments, by help of theory and precept, by means of comparison and criticism, the grammar of an ancient art has been mastered. Shall we ever be able to pronounce its language—not in the measured accents of a scholastic exercise, but fluently and familiarly as our mother-tongue ? Will a time ever arrive when, freed from the idle prejudices, the pedantry, the false sentiment, and the vulgarisms which have hampered its utterance and confounded its phraseology, this noble and expressive language shall be used throughout the land, retaining here and there provincial idioms—rising to eloquence in our towns and majestic emphasis in our public buildings, telling of rural beauty in the village homestead, exciting devotion in every church, proclaiming comfort in every home, and stability in every warehouse ? Then and not till then shall we possess—if it be worth possessing—a really national architecture. Then and not till then will the Gothic Revival be complete.

APPENDIX

Selected Examples of Gothic Buildings
erected between 1820 and 1870:
corrected and expanded by J. Mordaunt Crook

Note

Eastlake's comments and stylistic descriptions
have been retained throughout;
the spelling of place names has been modernized;
dates, attributions and references have been altered,
inserted or expanded wherever necessary.

Abbreviations

A.R. *Architectural Review*
B.N. *Building News*
C.L. *Country Life*
Eccles. *Ecclesiologist*
G.M. *Gentleman's Magazine*
I.L.N. *Illustrated London News*
R.I.B.A.Jnl. *Journal of The Royal Institute of British Architects*

1 St Luke, Chelsea, London (Commissioners' church)
   Perpendicular
   1820–24 J. Savage
   1874 chancel decorations by G. Goldie and Child
   1893, 1904 pulpit, altar, etc
The earliest *groined* church of the modern Revival (see p. 141).
   G.M. 1826 pt. i, 201–5. Britton and Pugin, *Public Buildings of London* ii
(1828), 205–18. Pevsner, *London* ii (1952), 87–8. Clarke, *Parish Churches of
London* (1966); 51–2, fig. 33.

2 The Hall, Christ's Hospital, Newgate Street, London
   Tudor
   1825–9 J. Shaw
   Demolished 1902
Foundation stone laid 25 May 1825 by the Duke of York. This was considered a
magnificent work at the time. Portions of the old edifice had fallen into decay,
and it was found necessary to rebuild them (see p. 126).
   W. Trollope, *History of Christ's Hospital* (1834).

3 Costessy Hall, Norfolk
   Tudor
   c. 1809 chapel by Edward Jerningham
   1825 onwards J. C. Buckler
   Largely demolished 1920
Erected for the Earl of Stafford. Built of red and white brick, with stone dressings.
The old mansion (of Queen Mary's time) occupies the site of the intended hall
and principal staircase. The gallery is 109 ft long, with draped panelling of oak
round the walls; drawing-room, 43 × 26 ft, communicating with library of like
dimensions; dining-room, 50 × 30 ft; machicolated and embattled tower, 132 ft
high. The principal apartments and offices are picturesquely arranged round the
fountain court and belfry court, the north side being bounded by a river (see
p. 110).
   G.M. 1830 pt. 1, 541; 1833 pt. i, 543; 1834 pt. ii, 81; 1838 pt. ii, 75. *B.N.*
xvi (1869), 315, 318–19. Pevsner, *N.W. and S. Norfolk* (1962), 125. L.
Bettany (ed.), *Edward Jerningham and his friends* (1919). B. Little, *Catholic
Churches Since 1623* (1963), 53.

4 St Peter, Brighton, Sussex (Commissioners' church)
   Middle Pointed
   1824–8 Sir Charles Barry
   1900–06 chancel by G. Somers Clarke and J. T. Micklethwaite
The principal feature in this church is the quasi-west (really south) tower, which
consists of two separate structures, one inside the other, the space between being
groined over. The inner tower is carried up two stages higher than the outer, with

which it is connected by flying buttresses, and terminates with four octagonal turrets. The main entrance porch is beneath this tower. The nave has an apsidal end. The interior is fitted up with galleries, and is groined throughout in plaster. Although very unorthodox in plan, the building exhibits evidence of study in many of its details.

Pevsner and Nairn, *Sussex* (1965), 435–6, fig. 52b.

5   St Katherine's Hospital, Regent's Park, London
    Tudor
    1826 A. Poynter
    Hospital and chapel now Danish Church
    Master's lodge destroyed in the Second World War
One of the first public works with which the architect's name was associated (see p. 128).

J. Elmes, *Metropolitan Improvements* (1829). Pevsner, *London* ii (1952), 351.

6   National Scots Church, Regent Square, London
    (Scots Presbyterian Church, 1860 onwards)
    Perpendicular
    1824–7 Sir W. Tite
    Demolished
A singular instance of the adoption of Gothic for a London church at this time. Sir W. (then Mr) Tite was also employed, under Mr Laing, to re-erect the church of St Dunstan's-in-the-East.

Builder xvii (1859), 337, 400. *B.N.* ix (1862), 28–9. J. Hair, *Regent Square* (1898). Pevsner, *London* ii (1952), 208.

7   Moreby Hall, Yorkshire
    Tudor
    1828–32 A. Salvin
Erected for Henry Preston, Esq. Built of brick faced with stone (see p. 129).

C.L. xxi (1907), 234–43. Pevsner, *Yorkshire: E. Riding* (1972), 313–14.

8   Mamhead, Devon
    Tudor
    1827–33 A. Salvin
Erected for Sir R. W. Newman, Bt. Built of stone (see p. 130).

G.M. 1830 pt. i, 541. Morris, *Seats* ii, 7. *Views of Devon* (1830), 640–6. Pevsner, *S. Devon* (1952), 202. *C.L.* cxvii (1955), 1366–9, 1428–31. C. Hussey, *English Country Houses: Late Georgian* (1958), 193–205.

9 St Dunstan-in-the-West, Fleet Street, London
   Perpendicular
   1831–3 J. Shaw
   1881 restoration by Fowler and Hill
   The internal plan of this church is octagonal, the sides of the octagon forming a
   series of recessed bays, which are alternately groined and waggon-vaulted; that
   on the north side is used as a quasi-chancel. The clerestory is lighted by eight
   windows filled with stained glass, above which rises a groined dome with a central
   pendant. On the south side is a square tower crowned by an octagon lantern. The
   main entrance to the church is under this tower.
   G.M. 1831 pt. i, 540. Britton and Pugin, *Public Buildings of London*, ed.
   Leeds, i (1838), 187–93. Pevsner, *London* i (1962), 277–8. Clarke, *Parish Churches
   of London* (1966), 48–9, fig. 30.

10 St Peter, Southborough, Kent
   Early English
   1830–31 Decimus Burton
   1883 steeple by E. Christian
   Built of local freestone. Nave, 63 × 40 ft; chancel, 17 × 9 ft; tower 9 ft square.

11 St Peter, Great Yarmouth, Norfolk (Commissioners' church)
   Perpendicular
   1831–3 J. J. Scoles
   Cost £7,600. Nave, aisles, chancel (with oak screen), clerestory, and panelled roof
   with porch and lofty square tower, in five storeys, at west end. Built of white
   Suffolk brick, with Bramley Fall stone dressings. General dimensions, 120 × 60 ft.
   Height of tower, 90 ft; to top of spire, 107 ft. Constructed to accommodate
   1,800 persons.
   Pevsner, *N.E. Norfolk and Norwich* (1962), 147.

12 St Mary, Riverhead, Kent
   Early English
   1831 Decimus Burton
   1882 chancel by Sir A. Blomfield
   Erected for the Trustees. Built of rag-stone.

13 Christ Church, Woburn Square, London (Commissioners' church)
   Perpendicular
   1831–3 L. Vulliamy
   The plan of this church is quasi-cruciform, and the interior is fitted up with
   galleries placed *vis à vis*. The west front has five doorways, of which three are
   real and two are sham. The tower occupies a central position and is surmounted
   by a stone spire. Middle pointed windows, fitted with late tracery. Flat roof of

pseudo-Gothic type. Walls of brick, with stone dressings, piers, etc. There is no chancel.

    Pevsner, *London* ii (1952), 205. Clarke, *Parish Churches of London* (1966), 123, fig. 62.

14   **Westminster Hospital, Broad Sanctuary, London**
    Tudor
    1832–3 W. and C. F. Inwood
    Demolished 1951
A commonplace design, presenting a large front with mullioned windows, central porch, etc. Gothic (such as it is) was probably selected for this building on account of its proximity to the Abbey.

    Jnl. London Soc. no. 379, June 1967, 14–19.

15   **St Peter, Stonyhurst College, Lancashire (R.C.)**
    Perpendicular
    1832–4 J. J. Scoles
    1893 high altar
Erected for the Society of Jesus. Built of stone. Nave (121 × 29 ft), aisles, and transepts; clerestory windows and panelled roofs, with principals carried on corbels. East window filled with stained glass by Miller (see no. 132).

    Orthodox Jnl. 16 May 1835. *Illustrations of Stonyhurst College* (1891). *C.L.* lxxxiv (1938), 60–5, 84–9, 117. Pevsner, *North Lancs.* (1969), 241, 244.

16   **Our Lady's Chapel, St John's Wood, London (R.C.)**
    Early English
    1833–6 J. J. Scoles
    Much altered
This church is remarkable for having been mentioned by Billings in his *History of the Temple Church*, as the best modern work then designed on that model. It is built of brick with stone dressings, and vaulted, but the groins are executed in lath and plaster! The nave piers are formed with a stone core in the centre, and small cast-iron shafts attached. General dimensions, 113 × 43 ft; height, 34 ft.

    Pevsner, *London* ii (1952), 330. B. Little, *Catholic Churches Since 1623* (1963), 76–7.

17   **St Ignatius, Preston, Lancashire (R.C.)**
    Perpendicular
    1834–6 J. J. Scoles
    1858 chancel and outer chapels by J. A. Hansom.
Built of stone. Cruciform plan with tower and spire. Clerestory windows and porch under tower. General dimensions, 96 × 48 ft; height of spire, 112 ft.

    Pevsner, *North Lancs.* (1969), 201.

18   Baynard's Park, Surrey
Tudor
1835–45 J. Rickman and B. Ferrey
Remodelled by Sir M. D. Wyatt
Additions to an old mansion, originally built for Sir George More, but disfigured by modern alterations. Mr Ferrey added the clock-tower, staircase, music-room, offices, etc., and restored the hall to its original design, with oak roof, minstrels' gallery, etc. Rickman had been previously employed, but died during the progress of the works.
G.M. 1837 pt. ii, 175; 1838 pt. ii, 75. Nairn and Pevsner, *Surrey* (1962), 89.

19   St Mary, Goring, Sussex
Decorated
1836–8 Decimus Burton
Erected for David Lyon Esq. Walls of rubble-work (stone and flint) stuccoed externally; roofed with slates; wooden spire covered with copper. Chancel, 35 × 20 ft; nave, 59 × 23 ft; aisles, 46 × 14 ft.
Pevsner and Nairn, *Sussex* (1965), 231.

20   Scotney Castle, Kent
Tudor
1835–43 A. Salvin
Erected for Edward Hussey Esq. Built of stone. This mansion is, for its date, a very creditable specimen of revived Tudor Gothic (see p. 130, ill.).
C.L. xi (1902), 688–92; xlviii (1920), 12–19; cxx (1956), 470–3, 526–9. C. Hussey, *English Country Houses: Late Georgian* (1958), 220–9.

21   St Mary, Liverpool (R.C.)
Decorated
1844–5 A. W. Pugin
1885 moved to Highfield St by Pugin and Pugin
Destroyed in the Second World War; rebuilt 1948–53 by Weightman and Bullen.
An excellent example of a *town* church (see p. 161).
Pevsner, *South Lancs.* (1969), 151–2.

22   Holy Trinity, Eastbourne, Sussex
Early English
1837–9 Decimus Burton
1855 enlarged by B. Ferrey
1861 additions
Built of stone and brick. Nave, 60 × 40 ft; chancel, 14 × 9 ft; tower, 13 ft square.
Pevsner and Nairn, *Sussex* (1955), 487.

23 School for Indigent Blind, St George's Fields, London
   Tudor
   1834–8 J. Newman
   Demolished
Built of white brick, with Park Spring stone dressings. The architect of this building also designed the Roman Catholic church at Finsbury Circus.
Civil Engineer and Architect's Jnl. i (1838), 207–12.

24 St Chad, Birmingham
   [Plate 17]
   Middle Pointed
   1839–41 A. W. Pugin
   1962 Bishop's house demolished
   1967 Screen removed to Holy Trinity, Reading
One of Pugin's most important works (see p. 156).
   G.M. 1841 pt. ii, ·308. Pugin, *Present State of Ecclesiastical Architecture* (1843), 73. *A History of St Chad's Cathedral, 1841–1904* (1904). Pevsner and Wedgwood, *Warwickshire* (1966), 110–12, fig. 53b. J. P. Boland, *St Chad's Cathedral* (Gloucester, 1939).

25 Houses of Parliament, Westminster, London
   Tudor
   1839–60 Sir Charles Barry and A. W. Pugin
The first stone of this great work laid "without ceremony", 5 March 1839 (see p. 175).
   Pevsner, *London* i (1962), 475–87. J. Mordaunt Crook and M. H. Port, *History of the King's Works* (ed. H. M. Colvin) vol. vi (1973).

26 St Matthew, Lister Street, Duddeston, Birmingham
   Early Decorated
   1839–40 W. Thomas
Open timber roof. Tower and spire 125 ft high. This was the first of a series of ten churches erected in this town.
   G.M. 1839 pt. ii, 641. Pevsner and Wedgwood, *Warwickshire* (1966), 131.

27 Queen's College, Bath, Somerset
   Norman
   1839 J. Willson
Erected on Claverton Down. Estimated cost £30,000.

28 St Peter, Leeds, Yorkshire
   Fourteenth century
   1839–41 R. D. Chantrell
   1861 alterations

The same architect designed a church at Middleton, Yorkshire, and the "Poole" Chapel, near Otley.

G.M. 1847 pt. i, 190; 1847 pt. ii, 419. *Eccles.* viii (1848), 132–3. *Builder* xix (1861), 413, 499, 621, 777, 792, 812; xx (1862), 282–3. R. W. Moore, *History of the Parish Church at Leeds* (Leeds, 1877). J. Rusby, *St Peter's at Leeds*, ed. J. G. Simpson (1896). Pevsner, *Yorks., W. Riding* (1959), 310–12. E. Kitson Clark, *Leeds Parish Church* (Leeds, n.d.).

29 Dorset County Hospital, Dorchester
Manorial Gothic
1839–56 B. Ferrey
1862 chapel

This building was erected by degrees. The chapel, forming part of the south wing, in the Second Pointed style, was erected at the expense of N. Williams Esq., then M.P. for Dorchester. Dimensions: centre part, 110 × 30 ft, with projecting porch and wings, 65 × 28 ft; chapel, 65 × 28 ft. Very picturesquely situated.

Murray's *Wilts., Dorset and Somerset* (1869), 191.

30 St Augustine, Flimwell, Kent
Early English
1840 Decimus Burton

Built of local freestone. Nave, 52 × 27 ft; chancel, 12 × 6 ft; tower, 9 ft square.

31 Magdalen College, Oxford: Gateway
[Plate 17]
Temp. Henry VI
1844 A. W. Pugin
1885 Demolished

A pure and graceful example of the architect's skill. See also no. 77.

V.C.H. Oxon. iii (1954), 207. Buckler Drawings, B.M. Add. Ms. 36375 fo. 134–7, 190–1 (1845).

32 St Peter, Fleetwood, Lancashire
Early English
1840–41 Decimus Burton
1880–83 chancel by E. G. Paley and H. J. Austin
1914 chapel added

Erected for Sir H. P. Fleetwood Bt.

Pevsner, *North Lancs.* (1969), 120–1.

33 St John the Baptist, Lean Side, Nottingham (Commissioners' church)
Early English
1843–4 Sir G. G. Scott and W. B. Moffatt

Destroyed in the Second World War
One of the earliest works executed by the architect. Built of Coxbench stone.
Builder i (1843), 504. *G.M.* 1845 pt. i, 86. *A.R.* xcii (1942), 72.

34 Holy Trinity, Trinity Square, Nottingham

Early English
1841–2 H. J. Stevens

A galleried church, with nave, aisles, raised chancel, west tower, and spire; open timbered roof of nine trusses carried on corbels; five triple lancet windows in clerestory; wheel window at east end, with lancet light on each side. Nave, 80 × 54 ft; chancel, 25 × 19 ft; spire, 172 ft high. Cost £10,000.

G.M. 1841, pt. ii, 644–5. *Builder* i (1843), 504. Pevsner, *Notts.* (1951), 138.

35 Martyrs' Memorial, Oxford

Decorated
1841 Sir G. G. Scott

Designed on the model of an "Eleanor" Cross. Divided in three storeys with canopied niches, pinnacles, etc., richly carved. Figures executed by Mr H. Weeks. This monument was greatly admired and attracted much notice at the time of its erection. It is generally admitted to be a most creditable work for its date.

G.M. 1840 pt. ii, 77, 378–82. Scott, *Recollections* (1879), 89–90. *A.R.* cxlii (1967), 251–2.

36 St Giles, Camberwell, London

Early Decorated
1842–4 Sir G. G. Scott and W. B. Moffatt

Built of Sneaton stone, with Caen stone dressings (see p. 221).

Eccles. iv (1845), 89. *G.M.* 1842 pt. ii, 81; 1845 pt. i, 75. *Builder* xviii (1860), 31, 319, 725. Pevsner, *London* ii (1952), 74–5. Clarke, *Parish Churches of London* (1966), 202–3, fig. 156.

37 Clyffe House, Tincleton, Dorset

Manorial Gothic
1841–3 B. Ferrey

Erected for Charles Porcher Esq. Built of Portland and local stones, brick, tiles, etc. General dimensions, 100 × 62 ft, the centre portion and wings slightly projecting from the main front.

Newman and Pevsner, *Dorset* (1972), 423.

38 St James, Nutley, Sussex

Early Pointed
1841–5 R. C. Carpenter
1871 North aisle

This was considered, at the time, one of the most correctly designed churches of the Revival. The plan consisted of a nave and chancel, south aisle and south porch, with a small vestry on the north side of the chancel.

Pevsner and Nairn, *Sussex* (1965), 576.

39 Mount St Bernard, Leicestershire (R.C.)
Early Pointed
1842–4 A. W. Pugin
1870–71; 1934–9 extensions

Erected for the community of English Cistercians. These buildings, which are picturesquely situated, consist of a cloister, church, chapter-house, refectory, dormitory, guest-house, prior's lodgings, etc. The design of the whole is simple to severity, the massive walls of rubble granite, long narrow windows, steep roofs, and gables being thoroughly characteristic of old monastic architecture.

Pugin, *Present State of Ecclesiastical Architecture* (1843), 91. E. S. Purcell, *Life and Letters of Ambrose Phillips de Lisle* 2 vols. (1900). Pevsner, *Leics. and Rutland* (1960), 192–5, fig. 17b.

40 St Mary, Stockton-on-Tees, Co. Durham (R.C.)
Early English
1841–2 A. W. Pugin
c. 1866 and *c.* 1870 additions by M. E. Hadfield

A small but elegantly proportioned church, of which the design is considerably in advance of its date.

Pugin, *Present State of Ecclesiastical Architecture* (1843), pl. viii. Pevsner, *Durham* (1953), 221.

41 Lincoln's Inn, London: Hall and Library
Tudor
1843–5 P. and P. C. Hardwick
1871–3 extended by Sir G. G. Scott

Built of red brick with groins and dressings of Anston stone; wainscot fittings throughout, and open oak roofs over hall and library. Hall, 120 × 45 ft, and 62 ft high; vestibule, 58 × 22 ft; council chamber and drawing-room each 32 × 24 ft; library, 80 × 40 ft and 44 ft high (see p. 211).

Builder i (1843), 39; iii (1845), 521–2, 526. *I.L.N.* vii (1845), 275. *G.M.* 1843 pt. i, 517–18; 1843 pt. ii, 288; 1845 pt. ii, 625–8. Pevsner, *London* i (1962), 295–6.

42 St John, Hildenborough, Kent
Early English
1843–4 E. Christian

Erected by subscription. Built of Kentish rag and local sandstone. Fittings of deal.

G.M. 1843 pt. ii, 289. *R.I.B.A. Jnl.* xviii (1911), 712.

43   St Francis Xavier, Liverpool (R.C.)
     Decorated
       1844–9 J. J. Scoles; 1888 Lady Chapel by E. Kirby
       1853, 1856 and 1877 schools added by Spencer, Clutton and Scoles
     Erected for the Order of Jesuits. Nave, aisles, and chancel. Iron columns used for
     nave arcade. The altars and internal fittings of this church are very rich in sculp-
     tured decoration, and were designed at a later period by Mr S. J. Nicholl, a pupil
     of Scoles (see p. 244).
       Eccles. vii (1843), 34; viii (1848), 262–3; ix (1849), 163–4; xiv (1853), 410,
     414. *Builder* vi (1848), 614; xi (1853), 561. *B.N.* iv (1858), 15. Pevsner,
     South Lancs. (1969), 221.

44   Alton, Staffordshire (R.C.)
     Perpendicular
     A. W. Pugin
       1837–40 additions to Alton Towers, including chapel
       1840–52 St John's Hospital
       1847–52 Alton Castle
     St John's Hospital was erected, for the Earl of Shrewsbury, on a steep rock some
     hundred feet in height. The buildings were planned to surround three sides of a
     quadrangle, but the design was not carried out in its entirety. They include a
     chapel, school, warden's lodgings, cloister, etc., all built of stone; the principal
     roofs, floors, etc. being of English oak. The chapel is richly decorated internally.
       Eccles. ix (1849), 369. Pugin, *Present State of Ecclesiastical Architecture*
     (1843), 88. W. Adam, *The Gem of the Peak* (1843), 247. *A.R.* lxxxvii (1940),
     156–64. *C.L.* iii (1898), 754–7, 788–91; x (1901), 839; cxxvii (1960), 1246–9,
     1304–7, 1454; cxxviii (1960), 1226–9.

45   St Barnabas, Nottingham (R.C.)
     [Plate 17]
     Early English
       1842–4 A. W. Pugin
     A large cruciform church, in which the choir and high altar are surrounded by
     aisles, with a Lady chapel beyond. Beneath the choir is a crypt, of which the
     vaulting is carried on two rows of short columns. The interior is sumptuously
     fitted up with a large rood-loft, and oak screens of open tracery and panelled work
     enclosing the chapels, etc. The choir and sanctuary are paved with encaustic tiles.
       Pugin, *Present State of Ecclesiastical Architecture* (1843), 58. Pevsner, *Notts.*
     (1951), 135–6.

46   St Andrew, Kingsbury, Middlesex
     Third Pointed
       1844–7 C. S. W. Dawkes and Hamilton
     Interior alterations by Street, Burges, Pearson and Butterfield

1933 moved from Wells Street, London

Nave, aisles and chancel, with engaged tower and spire at west end of north aisle. Though late in style and fitted up with galleries, this church was one of the best erected in London at this time. It is carefully designed throughout (see p. 247).

I.L.N. x (1847), 69. *Eccles.* vii (1847), 78–80; xi (1850), 68; xxvii (1866), 316; xxix (1868), 63–4, 218, 372. *Builder* v (1847), 4–5; xxviii (1870), 964, 983. *G.M.* 1847 pt. i, 300; 1847 pt. ii, 66. *Athenaeum* May 1868. *B.N.* xv (1868), 164. Pevsner, *Middlesex* (1951), 120–1.

47 Immaculate Conception, Farm Street, London (R.C.)
Late Decorated
1844–9 J. J. Scoles
Much enlarged

Nave, aisles, and chancel. Richly treated west front with angle turrets, and circular window in gable; lofty arcade and clerestory; polygonal panelled roof; chancel decorated with colour and gilding under direction of Mr Bulmer. Stained glass by Wailes. This church was one of Mr Scoles's most successful works. Nave, 102 × 27 ft; chancel, 27 × 26 ft; aisles, 45 × 13 ft.

Eccles. vii (1847), 206; xvi (1855), 198. *Builder* v (1847), 213; vii (1849), 258. *G.M.* 1847 pt. ii, 417; 1849 pt. ii, 307. Pevsner, *London* i (1962), 450.

48 St Wilfrid, Hulme, Manchester (R.C.)
Early English
1842 A. W. Pugin

The cost of this church, with the priests' house attached to it, did not exceed £5,000 (see p. 160).

Pugin, *Present State of Ecclesiastical Architecture* (1843), pls. iii, vii. Pevsner, *South Lancs.* (1969), 331.

49 Butleigh Court, Somerset
Henry VI
1845 J. C. Buckler
Dismantled

Erected by the Hon. and Very Rev. G. Neville Granville [supposedly with help from Prince Albert]. The hall is entered by a lofty porch. The elevations are varied in design, and embellished with buttresses, turrets, battlements, and other features suited to the style and to their positions. Built of blue lias and Doulting stone. Doors of English oak rich in mouldings and ornaments.

Pevsner, *S. and W. Somerset* (1958), 112. Buckler Drawings, B.M. Add. Ms. 36443 fo. 75–80.

50 **St John the Baptist, Cookham Dean, Berkshire**
Decorated
1844–5 R. C. Carpenter
A small but well studied church. Nave, aisles, chancel, south-west porch, and bell turret. Built to hold 300 persons. Cost, £1,300.
Eccles. iv (1845), 138. Pevsner, *Berks.* (1966), 123.

51 **St Stephen, Rochester Row, Westminster, London**
Decorated
1847–9 B. Ferrey
1967 spire removed
One of the most complete and costly churches erected at this time in London, and one of Mr Ferrey's most successful works. It was founded by the Baroness (then Miss) Burdett Coutts (see p. 247).
I.L.N. xvi (1850), 460. *Eccles.* ix (1849), 331–2; xi (1850), 110–20. *Builder* v (1847), 349–50; viii (1850), 319–20, 547. *G.M.* 1847 pt. i, 537; 1847 pt. ii, 306. Pevsner, *London* i (1962), 460. Clarke, *Parish Churches of London* (1966), 186–7, fig. 144.

52 **St George, Southwark, London (R.C.)**
Decorated
1841–8 A. W. Pugin
Church, bishop's house, convent and school largely rebuilt after the Second World War.
The most important work executed by Pugin in London (see p. 155).
Eccles. ix (1849), 369. *G.M.* 1840 pt. ii, 68; 1844 pt. i, 180–2; 1848 pt. ii, 192–3. *Builder* vi (1848), 335, 439, 449; clxx (1946), 33–5. Pugin, *Present State of Ecclesiastical Architecture* (1843), pls. ii, v, xii. *A.R.* xci (1942), 28. B. Bogan, *The Great Link, a history of St George's Southwark* (1948). Pevsner, *London* ii (1952), 398.

53 **St Thomas, Douglas, Isle of Man**
Early English
1845–50 E. Christian
Erected near the shore. Built of local rubble and black limestone. Internal fittings of deal.
Quiggin's *Guide Through the Isle of Man* (1858), 109–10. Glover's *Guide . . .* (1878), 35–6.

54 **St Augustine's College, Canterbury, Kent**
Early Decorated
1845–50 W. Butterfield
Erected for A. J. B. Beresford-Hope Esq., and a Committee. The first important work undertaken by the architect. Built of Caen stone, flint, and Kentish rag (see p. 225).

I.L.N. xiii (1847), 5. *Eccles.* ix (1849), 1–8. *Builder* iii (1845), 370; iv (1846), 35, 521; vi (1848), 161–2. *G.M.* 1849 pt. ii, 68. R. J. E. Boggis, *St Augustine's College Canterbury* (1907). Newman, *N.E. and E. Kent* (1969), 221–8.

55 St Andrew, Birmingham
Middle Pointed
1844–6 R. C. Carpenter

Built of red sandstone. Nave arcade of five arches; well-proportioned window of four lights at west end; sacristy at south-west of chancel; parapet of tower pierced with trefoils and decorated with ball-flower ornament; octagonal stone spire and gabled spire lights. Dimensions, chancel 38 ft and nave 86 ft. North aisle and engaged tower at west end (see p. 223).

Eccles. iii (1847 ed.), 113, 150; v (1846), 124–5. *Builder* iv (1846), 473, 485. Pevsner and Wedgwood, *Warwicks.* (1966), 130.

56 St Paul, Alnwick, Northumberland
Middle Pointed
1845–7 A. Salvin

Erected for the Duke of Northumberland. The plan consists of a lofty nave, with aisles and clerestory; an aisled chancel; a western tower; north porch, and sacristy on south of chancel; east window of five lights, and flowing tracery. The mouldings of this church are well studied.

Eccles. vi (1846), 153–4. *Builder* iii (1845), 551. *G.M.* 1846 pt. ii, 637. Pevsner, *Northumberland* (1957), 66–7.

57 St Paul, Brighton, Sussex (Commissioners' church)
Early Decorated
1846–8 R. C. Carpenter
Lantern by R. H. Carpenter
1874 additions by G. F. Bodley

A large church, capable of holding 1,200 people. It consists of a nave, two aisles of unequal size, a chancel, and north-east tower. The chancel is of unusually grand proportions for the time at which it was built. It has a seven-light east window, and three windows on the south side of three lights each. Stalls and chancel screen (one of the few sanctioned) of oak and richly carved. No clerestory but lofty nave arcade. Open timbered roof. The windows throughout the church are filled with stained glass by Hardman from designs by A. W. Pugin and Mr Carpenter. Tower only carried up to belfry stage. It was the architect's intention to add a lofty spire of stone.

Eccles. v (1846), 155–6, 203; vii (1847), 153–4; viii (1848), 188–9; ix (1849), 80; x (1850), 204–7; xiii (1852), 60–3; xv (1854), 215–16. H. H. Maughan, *Wagner of Brighton* (1949). Pevsner and Nairn, *Sussex* (1965), 435, 692.

58 **All Saints, North Ferriby, Yorkshire**
Early Decorated
1848 J. L. Pearson
Built on the site of an old church, some portions of which were worked up with present building. Nave of four bays; clerestory lighted by round windows; low aisles; well-developed chancel, with east window of five lights; tower about 54 ft high, surmounted by a lofty broached spire, one of the first which was constructed with an *entasis*. The church is built of local "rubble", with dressings of Mexborough stone.

59 **St James, Weybridge, Surrey**
Decorated
1845–8 J. L. Pearson
1864 enlarged
As originally built this church consisted of a nave and aisles 63 ft long and 50 ft across, with north and south porches. West tower with lofty stone spire, chancel (34 × 17 ft) with vestry on the north side. It has since been enlarged by the addition of a second south aisle to nave. Short aisles have also been added to the chancel. The peculiarity of this structure is the use of chalk for all the pillars, arches, and ashlaring. The chalk was obtained from quarries near Guildford, and is veined with white marble. The effect of this material is very striking.
Nairn and Pevsner, *Surrey* (1962), 432.

60 **St Mary, Burnley, Lancashire (R.C.)**
Very Early Decorated
1846–9 M. E. Hadfield and W. G. Weightman
1860s altar by E. W. Pugin
Built of stone. Spire not completed (see p. 243).
Builder iv (1846), 203. Pevsner, *North Lancs.* (1969), 80.

61 **St Mary, Sheffield, Yorkshire (R.C.)**
English Decorated
1846–50 M. E. Hadfield and W. G. Weightman
The design of this building is, with certain modifications, based on a study of Heckington Church. It is cruciform in plan, with a tower and spire at the south-west end. The chancel is richly fitted up with a reredos, stone and metal parcloses, oak stalls, sedilia, and a handsome rood screen. The nave consists of six bays, lighted by clerestory windows. A mortuary chapel is added to the north side of the north aisle, to which it is open under a double arch, and contains an altar tomb, with a recumbent effigy of the founder. Many of the windows are filled with stained glass of excellent quality. Dimensions: 143 ft long; 90 ft across transepts; tower and spire 195 ft high, built of stone (see p. 243).
Builder v (1847), 41; viii (1850), 448–9. *Eccles.* ix (1849), 163.
Pevsner, *Yorkshire: E. Riding* (1972), 318.

62 St Giles, Cheadle, Staffordshire (R.C.)
[Plate 17]
Early Decorated
1841–7 A. W. Pugin

This church, erected at the expense of the Earl of Shrewsbury, was perhaps the most costly one for its size which Pugin executed. The interior is completely covered with decorative painting. The rood screen is of a very elaborate design. The east window is of five lights. In the walls, on either side, are stone niches richly canopied, and containing statues of the Blessed Virgin and St Giles. Over the altar is placed a stone screen of tabernacle work, with figures of the Apostles. The church has a lofty tower and broached spire at its west end.

Builder iv (1846), 447–8. *G.M.* 1846 pt. ii, 627–31. Pugin, *Present State of Ecclesiastical Architecture* (1843), pls. i, iv, xiii. *Lord Shrewsbury's New Church of St Giles (at Cheadle), in Staffs.* (1846). *I.L.N.* x (1847), 28–9.

63 Landwade Hall, Cambridgeshire
15th century
1847–51 J. C. Buckler

Erected for Alexander Cotton Esq., on the site of an old moated mansion, portions of which were retained and incorporated with the new building. A large embattled tower stood at the inner angle of the front. At the south-west angle, on the edge of the moat, an octagonal turret was added for strength to the ancient wall. The interior is fitted with oak screens, panelled work, carved chimney-pieces, etc. The approach is over a bridge of three arches. Built of red brick, with richly-ornamented chimneys and stone dressings.

Gardner's *History, Gazetteer and Directory of Cambs.* (1851), 389. *G.M.* 1854 pt. ii, 381. Buckler Drawings, B.M. Add. Ms. 3630/45–7.

64 Holy Trinity, Leverstock, Hertfordshire
Middle Pointed
1847–9 R. and J. Brandon

Erected for the Earl of Verulam and other subscribers. Walls of flint, with Caen stone dressings. Nave, 49 × 19 ft; chancel, 26 × 16 ft, with sacristy on north side. Small clerestory; open timbered roof. Cost £1,600.

Eccles. viii (1848), 192, 366. *Builder* vi (1848), 217; vii (1849), 109. Pevsner, *Herts.* (1953), 155.

65 St Matthew, City Road, Islington, London
Early Pointed
1847–8 Sir G. G. Scott
1866 south porch and reredos by G. E. Street
Destroyed in the Second World War

Nave of five bays, with clerestory and aisles; raised chancel, sacristy, and tower at east end of south aisle, with stone spire and angle spirelets; open timbered roof over nave; chancel roof polygonal; east window of five lights.

Eccles. viii (1848), 391–2. *Builder* xxiv (1866), 531.

66   St Philip, Leeds, Yorkshire
       Early English
       1845–7 R. D. Chantrell
      Built for J. G. Marshall Esq. Nave of five bays, with aisles and clerestory; chancel,
      with sacristy on north side; south tower and spire. Walls are of "Bramley Fall"
      stone externally, and Caen stone inside. The church is vaulted with stone through-
      out.
           Eccles. viii (1848), 109–10. *Builder* v (1847), 485, 508.

67   Holy Trinity, Penn Street, Buckinghamshire
       Geometrical Decorated
       1847–9 B. Ferrey
      Built for the Earl Howe on a spot selected by Queen Adelaide, who presented a
      stained-glass window to the church. Materials used in construction were flint,
      Bath stone, and indurated chalk of the neighbourhood. It is 111 ft long, and has
      a lofty central tower and spire.
           Pevsner, *Bucks.* (1960), 223–4.

68   Peckforton Castle, Cheshire
       13th century
       1844–50 A. Salvin
      Erected for J. Tollemache Esq., M.P. Built of stone with interior fittings of oak.
           I.L.N. xviii (1851), 323. Morris, *Seats* iv, 65. *C.L.* cxxxviii (1965), 284–7,
      336–9. Pevsner and Hubbard, *Cheshire* (1971), 300–2.

69   St Barnabas, Pimlico, London
       Early English
       1846–9 T. Cundy and W. Butterfield
       Church, parsonage and schools
      Erected for the Rev. W. J. E. Bennett, later Vicar of Frome (see p. 248).
           Eccles. ix (1849), 331–2; xi (1850), 110–14. *Builder* iv (1846), 298; vii (1849),
      162; viii (1850), 279–80. *G.M.* 1850 pt. ii, 83. Pevsner, *London* i (1962),
      447–8. Clarke, *Parish Churches of London* (1966), 185–6, fig. 145.

70   Treberfydd, Breconshire
       Manorial Gothic
       1848–50 J. L. Pearson
      Erected for Robert Raikes Esq. Mr Pearson was at first employed to make a
      small addition to a square-built modern house, but from time to time further
      alterations were required until at last nearly the whole of the original house was
      pulled down. Unfortunately, however, some of the old arrangements of rooms
      etc., had to be retained, which to some extent interfered with the architect's
      intentions in design. The materials used in the construction were red sandstone

and Bath stone dressings. The garden and grounds were carefully laid out in character with the architecture by Mr Nesfield.

C.L. cxl (1966), 276–9, 322–5.

71 ## Aldermaston Court, Berkshire
Manorial Gothic
1848–51 P. C. Hardwick

Erected for Higford Burr Esq. The first country house on which the architect was engaged. The site is very picturesque. The house stands on a natural terrace overlooking a park filled with oak trees and the valley of the Kennet. The tower is the most conspicuous object, and groups well with the gables and other portions in every direction. The materials used were red brick and Bath stone. Dimensions: 170 × 60 ft, exclusive of stables.

Builder vi (1848), 218. *G.M.* 1843 pt. i, 194. *C.L.* vi (1899), 240–2; xxii (1907), 54–9. Pevsner, *Berks.* (1966), 62.

72 ## St Peter, Chichester, Sussex
Subdeanery Church
"Flowing" Decorated
1848–52 R. C. Carpenter
1881 additions by Dunn and Hansom

This church was built to supply the place of one found in the north transept of the Cathedral, but which was incorporated with the Cathedral when that building was restored. The church is built of Caen stone throughout, with richly-moulded windows on the south side and larger windows at the east end. The nave and chancel are nearly of the same width as the south aisle and chancel aisle, and extend to the same length. A tower was proposed for erection at the west of the south aisle. The nave arcade is of lofty proportions. The details have been worked out with great care and the flowing tracery of the windows is very beautiful.

Eccles. xii (1851), 68. Pevsner and Nairn, *Sussex* (1965), 171.

73 ## St Matthew, Landscove, Devon
Early Decorated
1849–50 J. L. Pearson

The details of this church are very simple. The south aisle has a pointed roof, like the nave, and abuts at the east end of the tower, which is square in plan, and about 40 ft high, with spire 53 ft high. Chancel of full dimensions, and properly stalled. Walls of local stone, with Bath stone dressings.

Pevsner, *S. Devon* (1952), 194.

74 ## Holy Trinity, Clarence Way, Haverstock Hill, London
(Commissioners' church)
Geometrical Pointed.
1849–51 T. H. Wyatt and D. Brandon

Spire destroyed in the Second World War
Nave, aisles, and chancel. Tower and broached spire, with gablets, etc., at west
end. Built of Swansea stone. General dimensions, 133 × 73 ft (see p. 301).

I.L.N. xvii (1850), 312. *Eccles.* xi (1850), 197; xvi (1855), 113. *G.M.* 1850
pt. ii, 461. Pevsner, *London* ii (1952), 362. Clarke, *Parish Churches of London*
(1966), 141.

75   St David, Sketty, nr Swansea, Glamorgan
       Middle Pointed
       1849–52 H. Woodyer
       1889, 1908, 1929 enlarged by T. Glendinning Moxham
Length, 120 ft; spire (of shingled oak), 100 ft high. Walls of limestone, with
Bath stone dressings.
       Eccles. xi (1850), 145. *Builder* viii (1850), 487.

76   St James the Great, Devonport, Devon (Commissioners' church)
       Second Pointed
       1849–51 J. P. St Aubyn
       1861–2 school
Erected for the Rev. A. B. Hutchinson at a cost of £6,288; will hold 1,093
persons. It has a tower and spire on south side, with porch below; nave arcade
of five bays, clustered piers; clerestory has five two-light windows; roofs open
timbered and of good pitch. Built of limestone, with Bath stone dressings. Nave,
80 × 27 ft; aisles, 80 × 15 ft; chancel, 37 × 24 ft; steeple, 125 ft high. The
parsonage house and schools form with the church three sides of a quadrangle,
and are built of the same materials.
       Eccles. xi (1850), 44; xiii (1852), 76; xiv (1853), 208–9; xxii (1861), 200.
Builder ix (1851), 405.

77   Magdalen College, Oxford: Choristers' School
       15th century
       1849–51 J. C. and C. Buckler
       Converted into library
The front towards High Street presents an elevation of five bays divided by
buttresses, and containing a range of square-headed transomed windows. The
north elevation is distinguished by a central porch, with a book-room over,
approached by a turret staircase. The parapet is embattled, and the east and west
walls terminate in gables. Open timbered roof, with arches springing from stone
corbels. Walls of Bladon stone, with Park Spring and Box Hill stone dressings.
General dimensions, 70 × 25 ft.
       G.M. 1844 pt. ii, 75; 1845 pt. ii, 174; 1849 pt. ii, 400. *Builder* ii (1844), 272;
xix (1861), 753; xx (1862), 476. Buckler Drawings, B.M. Add. Ms. 37122
A (2), (1844).

78   Holy Innocents, Highnam, Gloucestershire
      Middle Pointed
      1849–51 H. Woodyer
Lofty tower of three stages, and octagonal spire. Below the belfry stage there is a
deep band of ornamental panelling, with shields, etc. The buttresses, cornice-
mouldings, etc., are well studied. The interior, which is very complete in effect,
includes a lofty chancel with a ceiled roof, rich chancel arch and oak screen, nave
arcade of five bays, clerestory lighted by quatrefoil windows, etc. Length, 130 ft;
spire 200 ft high. Built of grey stone, with Bath stone and Devonshire marbles.
Contains decorative paintings by T. Gambier Parry Esq., at whose expense it was
erected.
      Eccles. xiii (1852), 263–5; xx (1859), 140; xxv (1864), 311–12. Verey, *Glos.*
ii (1970), 269–70.

79   Tortworth Court, Gloucestershire
      Tudor
      1849–52 S. S. Teulon
Built for the Earl of Ducie. The walls are of stone from the estate. Dimensions,
200 × 115 ft.
      Builder xi (1853), 666–7, 702–3. *C.L.* v (1899), 592–6. Verey, *Glos.* ii (1970),
389–90.

80   Holy Trinity, Bessborough Gardens, London
      Early Decorated
      1849–52 J. L. Pearson
      Destroyed in the Second World War
Cruciform plan, with aisles to the nave and chancel. A central tower and spire,
nearly 200 ft high. The tower is open internally to a height of 55 ft, and forms a
lantern, which is groined over. There is a spacious sacristy on the north side. The
chancel is raised on steps and richly paved with encaustic tiles, the altar itself
being placed on a footpace. The organ stands in the north chancel aisle; the east
window is of seven lights. Stone pulpit elaborately carved, and enriched with
black marble shafts.
      Eccles. xii (1851), 231–2; xiii (1852), 409–12. Pevsner, *London* i (1962), 460.

81   St Mary Magdalen, Munster Square, London
      Decorated
      1849–52 R. C. Carpenter
      1883–4 additions by R. H. Carpenter
The plan consists of a nave and chancel with wide south aisle. The north aisle
was proposed to be of the like dimension but was never built. A south-west tower
and spire. The *motif* of this design was the Church of Austin Friars. It has no
clerestory, but nave arcades of great height. The windows are filled with stained
glass, the east window having been designed by Pugin. The west window (by
Clayton and Bell) was filled with stained glass as a memorial to the architect by

his friends. The chancel has mural arcuation, with marble·shafts and richly decorated canopies. This church is one of the few in which the architect was enabled to carry out his views completely without being hindered by pecuniary considerations (see p. 250).

Eccles. x (1850), 353–4, 360; xx (1859), 139. *Builder* xiii (1855), 354–5, 375. *B.N.* iii (1857), 554. Pevsner, *London* ii (1952), 361–2. Clarke, *Parish Churches of London* (1966), 142–3.

82   St Teilo, Merthyr Mawr, Glamorgan
      First Pointed
      1849–51 J. Prichard
Erected for the Rt. Hon. John Nicholl. Built of a local flat bedded stone, with dressings of Sutton stone. Nave, 41 × 22 ft; chancel, 26 × 16 ft 3 in.
Civil Engineer and Architect's Jnl. xxiii (1860), 324. *Builder* vii (1849), 581.

83   All Saints, Margaret Street, London
      [Plate 18]
      Middle Pointed
      1850–59 W. Butterfield
This church, one of the most unique and sumptuously decorated buildings of its class in London, was erected at the cost of Mr Henry Tritton and other subscribers. It was the first important modern structure for which brick was used in a decorative and artistic manner. Stone, granite, marbles, alabaster, and tiles were also employed. The interior is further enriched with inlaid patterns in mastic, and with fresco paintings by the late Mr Dyce R.A. The east and north walls are built against other structures, and were therefore unsuitable for windows (see p. 252).

Eccles. x (1850), 64, 432–3; xviii (1857), 325; xx (1859), 185–9, 301–4. *Builder* viii (1849), 561; xi (1853), 57–8; xvii (1859), 328, 364, 376–7, 392, 437, 472–3. *G.M.* 1859 pt. i, 633–4. Pevsner, *London* ii (1952), 326–7. *Architectural History* viii (1965), 73–87. Clarke, *Parish Churches of London* (1966), 131–4, figs. 103–4.

84   St Matthias, Stoke Newington, London
      Middle Pointed
      1851–3 W. Butterfield
Church, parsonage and school largely rebuilt after the Second World War
A very original and grandly-proportioned work, which attracted much notice on its completion. It is built of common white brick with but little stone dressing. The plan consists of a nave with lofty clerestory; rather low aisles, and a massive gabled tower, which rises over junction of nave with chancel, and is carried on two arches which span the church transversely; the sanctuary is waggon-vaulted in red brick, with stone ribs; the east window is of five cinquefoiled lights with a traceried circle. The church is provided with gas standards, elegantly designed and

wrought. General dimensions, 135 × 45 ft; height to ridge of roof, 70 ft. The parsonage was added a few years later.

Eccles. xi (1850), 142, 208, 233–6. Pevsner, *London* ii (1952), 428. Clarke, *Parish Churches of London* (1966), 169–70, fig. 133.

85 St Stephen, Devonport, Devon
Second Pointed
1850–59 J. P. St Aubyn
1864 parsonage
1870 school
1898 chapel by St Aubyn and Wadling

Erected for the Rev. G. Proctor. The site of this church is bounded on three sides by streets, and the whole area is occupied by a square plan, comprising nave and north aisle, without clerestory; chancel and large east tower. The chancel is fitted up with stalls and *subsellae*. The window tracery is varied, but rather late in style. Built of limestone, with Bath stone dressings. Chancel fittings oak; roof timbers deal. Nave, 66 × 20 ft; aisles, 66 × 16 ft; chancel, 35 × 16 ft; tower and spire, 160 ft high. South aisle unbuilt.

86 St Serf, Burntisland, Scotland
Early Scots Middle Pointed
1850–54 R. C. Carpenter; continued by W. Slater.
Incomplete church demolished 1875

Designed to include a church, schools, parsonage and baptistery. The three latter are complete, and the church is in progress. The style of the house is after the ancient Scottish model, with stepped gables, etc. The baptistery, which forms a distinct building at the west end of the church, is octagonal, and groined with stone. The design of the church is on a grand scale, with nave, aisles, apsidal chancel, and north-west tower and spire. It is to be erected at the cost of the incumbent.

Eccles. xv (1854), 428–9; xvi (1858), 257; xvii (1856), 231. W. Perry, *George Hay Forbes* (1927).

87 Abbey Mere, Plymouth, Devon
Early Decorated
1850 W. Butterfield

Various buildings, including residences, gateway, hall, large printing-rooms, etc., erected for Miss Sellon. Materials used: local stone, with Bath stone dressings (see p. 256).

88 St Peter, Elsted, Sussex
Geometrical Second Pointed
1849–53 B. Ferrey
Demolished 1951

Erected at great cost by the Rev. L. Vernon-Harcourt. Mr Sharpe, the author of *Architectural Parallels*, describes it as one of the best modern churches of its time. It stands on the slope of one of the South Down hills, and is a conspicuous object from the surrounding country. The materials used in construction were local stone and Caen stone, with Minton's tiles for internal decoration. The woodwork is of oak throughout. Nave, 56 × 20 ft; chancel, 36 × 17 ft; aisles, 9 ft wide; tower and spire, 96 ft high.

Pevsner and Nairn, *Sussex* (1965), 218, 355.

89 Westwood Hall, nr Leek, Staffordshire
16th-century Domestic
1850–53 M. E. Hadfield, W. G. Weightman and G. Goldie
A large and important pile of buildings, constructed of red sandstone.

Pevsner, *Staffs.* (1974), 173.

90 St John, Weymouth, Dorset
Decorated
1850–54 T. Talbot Bury
1868 enlarged
Built of rubble, faced, and Bath stone dressings. Nave and aisles, 75 ft long, and 49 ft across; chancel, 30 × 19 ft; tower, 19 ft square, and 140 ft high to top of spire.

Builder viii (1850), 454; xvii (1859), 510; xxvi (1868), 119, 160, 198, 630.

91 Holy Spirit, Cumbrae, Scotland
Early Decorated
1851–9 W. Butterfield
Church and college
Erected for the Hon. G. H. Boyle (later Earl of Glasgow). The buildings are terraced on the side of a hill at several levels. Materials used: local stone, with some Aberdeen granite; mosaic work of tiles, etc.

Eccles. xx (1859), 379–83. *Builder* ix (1851), 533. J. G. Cazenove, *An Account of the Collegiate Church and College in the Isle of Cumbrae* (Edinburgh, 1872).

92 St John, Kenilworth, Warwickshire
Decorated
1851–3 E. Christian
Built of local "rag" and white sandstone. General dimensions, 111 × 48 ft.

93 St John's College, Hurstpierpoint, Sussex
Early 14th century
1851–3 R. C. Carpenter
1861–5 chapel by R. H. Carpenter and W. Slater
The first of the great schools erected by Canon Woodard in connection with the College at Lancing. It accommodates 350 boys. The buildings are planned in two

quadrangles, measuring respectively 118 × 150 ft and 123 × 150 ft. The dormitories accommodate 50 boys each. There is a large dining hall with an open timber roof. The chapel (unfinished as regards the ante-chapel) was designed by Messrs Slater and Carpenter. A flight of fourteen steps leads to the altar. The reredos (partly completed) is of alabaster and marbles richly carved by Forsyth. Walls of the main building are of flint, with Caen stone dressings. Roof of brown tiles.

Eccles. xiv (1853), 264–6; xxii (1861), 349; xxvii (1866), 30–2; xxviii (1867), 95–8. *Builder* ix (1851), 419–20; xi (1853), 455; xix (1861), 668; xxiii (1865), 749–50, 791; xxiv (1866), 341. *I.L.N.* xxii (1853), 516. Pevsner and Nairn, *Sussex* (1965), 542.

94 St Peter's College, Saltley, Birmingham
        14th century
        1847–52 B. Ferrey
Planned as a quadrangle 100 × 82 ft, surrounded by buildings 30 ft wide, with slightly projecting wings, bay-windows, etc. Built of Bath stone and rag stone of the neighbourhood. Cost about £12,000.
        Pevsner and Wedgwood, *Warwicks.* (1966), 201.

95 Christ the King, Gordon Square, London
        (Ex-Catholic Apostolic Church)
        Early English
        1851–5 R. Brandon and J. Ritchie
One of the largest and most imposing churches in England. It contains an area of 20,000 square feet. Its internal length is 212 ft; width from north to south of transepts, 77 ft; width of nave and aisles, 56 ft. Built of Bath stone, with groined chancel and presbytery, etc. Designed to be extended 40 ft westward; the central tower and spire to be carried up 300 ft high.
        Eccles. xv (1854), 83–8. *Builder* xi (1853), 305; xvii (1859), 408–9; ix (1851), 424. J. M. Lickfold, *The Catholic Apostolic Church, Gordon Square, London* (1935). Pevsner, *London* ii (1952), 207–8.

96 St Charles, Danesfield, Buckinghamshire
        Middle Pointed
        1850–51 A. W. Pugin
        Demolished; high altar, reredos and East window transferred to Sacred Heart, Henley-on-Thames
Erected for Mr Scott Murray. This was the last work which Pugin executed.
        Pevsner, *Bucks.* (1960), 204–5.

97 St John, Eton, Buckinghamshire
        Geometrical Pointed
        1852–4 B. Ferrey

Erected for the Provost and Fellows of Eton College. The foundation stone was laid by the Prince Consort, who took much interest in the building. Nave, 101 × 23 ft. Tower and spire, 160 ft high. Built of Bath stone, Kentish rag, and brick.
Eccles. xv (1854), 283–4. Pevsner, *Bucks.* (1960), 388.

98   Eastbury Almshouses, Lambourn, Berkshire
Tudor
1852 T. Talbot Bury

These buildings occupy four sides of a quadrangle, with a cloister on each side, into which the rooms open. The entrance is in the centre, with a tower above. Built of brick, with stone dressings. General dimensions, including principal's house, 90 × 80 ft.
Pevsner, *Berks.* (1966), 165.

99   Christ Church, Forest Hill, London
Decorated
1852–4; 1862; 1885 E. Christian

Erected by subscription. Built of Kentish rag and Box stone dressings. General dimensions, 146 × 60 ft.
Clarke, *Parish Churches of London* (1966), 244.

100   All Saints, Talbot Road, Notting Hill, London
Middle Pointed
1852–61 W. White

A large church treated with much originality. The tower, which is at the west end, has an octagonal belfry stage in stone of varied tints. After the completion of the main fabric it stood unfinished for some years. It then passed into other hands, when the fitting and decorative portions were carried out under the supervision of a civil engineer! (see p. 291).
Builder xiii (1855), 486. Pevsner, *London* ii (1952), 297. Clarke, *Parish Churches of London* (1966), 104–5, figs. 77, 79.

101   St Stephen, Tonbridge, Kent
Early English
1851–62 E. Christian

In a broad parallelogram under a low pitched roof, with no external distinction between nave and chancel. Tower at east end of south side. A group of five lancet lights forms the east window. Roofs open timbered, but ceiled over chancel. Nave arcade of five bays and a half. Plain cylindrical shafts with well-moulded caps and bases. Built of Kentish rag and local limestone. General dimensions, 104 × 66 ft.
Eccles. xiv (1853), 454–5.

102 **Diocesan Training College, Culham, Oxfordshire**
    14th century
    1852–3 J. Clarke
Quadrangle with chapel, principal's and master's house. Calculated to accommodate about 1,000 pupil teachers.
    Eccles. xiv (1853), 149–52; xv (1854), 215. Sherwood and Pevsner, *Oxon.* (1974), 566.

103 **St Stephen, Redditch, Worcestershire**
    Middle Pointed
    1852–61 H. Woodyer
    1893–4 chancel by Temple Moore
Length, 165 ft; width, 96 ft; spire, 148 ft high. Built of local sandstone and Bath stone.
    Eccles. xxix (1868), 245–6. Pevsner, *Worcestershire* (1963), 248.

104 **Christ Church, Bethesda, Carnarvon** (Commissioners' church)
    Early Pointed
    1855–6 T. H. Wyatt
Built of stone. Nave (with clerestory), chancel, and aisles. Tower and broached spire at south-west. One of the many churches erected by Mr Wyatt in Wales.
    Builder xiii (1855), 629; xiv (1856), 596. M. H. Port, *Six Hundred New Churches* (1961), 172–3.

105 **St Peter, Bournemouth, Hampshire**
    Early Middle Pointed
    1853–79 G. E. Street
This work consisted in the remodelling of an inferior modern structure. The plan comprises a nave of five bays with aisles, a groined chancel with aisles, and western tower. The west portion of the north chancel aisle, used as an organ chamber, opens with a single arch to the chancel. The clerestory has two-light windows in each bay. The tower and spire are at the west end, with a small staircase at the north-east angle. The chancel is richly decorated with marble, etc.
    Eccles. xvi (1855), 62, 129; xxii (1861), 195–6; xxvii (1866), 260–2. *Builder* xix (1861), 313; xxviii (1870), 1026–7. *B.N.* x (1863), 887. N. Taylor, *St Peter's, Bournemouth* (1962). Pevsner and Lloyd, *Hants.* (1967), 118–20.

106 **St Mary, Buckland St Mary, Somerset**
    Late Second Pointed
    1853–60 B. Ferrey
Built of flint and Hamden Hill stone. This is one of the first modern churches which contains sculptured figures in niches. The pulpit, chancel screen, etc., are richly decorated.
    Eccles. xxi (1863), 260. *Builder* xiv (1856), 308. Pevsner, *S. and W. Somerset* (1958), 109.

107 **Theological College, Cuddesdon, Oxfordshire**
Early Middle Pointed
1853–4 G. E. Street
College and vicarage, since enlarged
Built for the Bishop (Wilberforce) of Oxford. A simple but picturesque pile of buildings, chiefly depending for effect on artistic proportions. The upper storey is lighted by large dormers with hipped gables. Most of the windows are square-headed, and arranged in long rows with discharging arches above. An octagonal staircase turret, and an open cloister running the whole length of the structure, are conspicuous features in the design. Further additions and a larger chapel are proposed.
Eccles. xiv (1853), 134–5, 456; xv (1854), 238–41. *I.L.N.* xxii (1853), 308. *G.M.* 1859 pt. i, 77. O. Chadwick, *The Founding of Cuddesdon* (1954). Sherwood and Pevsner, *Oxon.* (1974), 563–4.

108 **St Aidan's Theological College, Birkenhead, Cheshire**
Tudor
1850–56 T. H. Wyatt, D. Brandon and H. Cole
A large and important group of buildings, three storeys in height. Built of brick, with stone dressings. The principal fronts have oriel windows, stepped gables, etc. General dimensions, 240 × 190 ft.
Eccles. xi (1850), 45. *Builder* viii (1850), 162–3. Pevsner and Hubbard, *Cheshire* (1971), 98.

109 **St Mary, Dunstall, Burton-on-Trent, Staffordshire**
14th century
1853 H. Clutton
Erected for John Hardy, Esq. A small church, built of Duffield Bank stone, and Hollington stone.
Pevsner, *Staffs.* (1974), 123–4.

110 **St Raphael's College, Bristol**
Middle Pointed
1853–5 H. Woodyer
Almshouse for seamen, erected by the Rev. Robert Miles, Rector of Bingham, Notts. Front of College, 150 ft long (see p. 329).
Pevsner, *N. Somerset and Bristol* (1958), 432.

111 **House of Mercy, Bovey Tracey, Devon**
Middle Pointed
1853–67 H. Woodyer
Orphanage and hospital
Area, including quadrangle, 37,000 sq. ft. Built of red brick and Bath stone. Erected for the Clewer Sisterhood (see p. 331).
Builder xxv (1867), 823.

112 **St John, Bedminster, Bristol**
    13th century
    1853–5 J. Norton
    1865 parsonage
    Gutted in the Second World War
Built of Hanham stone, with Bath stone dressings. Roofed with green slates. General dimensions, 171 × 82 ft.

    Eccles. xvi (1855), 348–51; xvii (1856), 32–3, 185; xxvi (1865), 55. *Builder* xiv (1856), 273; xvii (1859), 541. *B.N.* vii (1861), 10; viii (1862), 379. Pevsner, *N: Somerset and Bristol* (1958), 453.

113 **All Saints, Boyne Hill, Maidenhead, Berkshire**
    Early Middle Pointed
    1854–7; 1865 G. E. Street
    Church, parsonage, schools, almshouses
    1907–11 enlarged by A. E. Street
These buildings occupy three sides of a quadrangle. The walls are of red brick relieved by bands of stone, and the roofs are of red tiles. The church has a clerestoried nave and aisles of four bays, chancel, etc. Piers alternately circular and quatrefoil in plan. In the spandrils of the arcade are circular panels enriched with stone carving. At the back of the stalls rise iron screens very gracefully designed. The chancel is richly decorated with an elaborate reredos. The church has a detached tower and spire.

    Eccles. xv (1854), 429–30; xix (1858), 314–18. *Builder* xv (1857), 725; xviii (1860), 291, 768–9; xxiii (1865), 178, 666; xxiv (1866), 142. A. Savage, *The Parsonage in England* (1964), 141, fig. xxxiv.

114 **St Luke, Marylebone, London** (Commissioners' church)
    Decorated
    1854–5 E. Christian
    Demolished
Erected by subscription as a thank-offering after the cholera year. Built of Kentish rag, with Bath stone dressings. The site of this church was a difficult one to deal with, its breadth from north to south being greater than its length. The plan includes a nave and aisle of three bays, with a shallow sanctuary beyond. The south aisle is fitted up with a gallery containing the organ. The construction of the roof is very peculiar. The entrance porch is on the south side, in Nutford Place, under a square tower, which is surmounted by four massive pinnacles. The arch and mouldings of this porch are enriched with carving designed and executed with great refinement. General dimensions, 100 × 71 ft.

    Eccles. xv (1854), 170; xvii (1856), 424. *Builder* xiv (1856), 246–7. *R.I.B.A. Jnl.* xviii (1911), 717–18.

115   **Lancing College, Sussex**
      Geometrical Pointed
      1854 onwards, school buildings by R. C. Carpenter, W. Slater and M. Ayrton
      1868 onwards, chapel by R. H. Carpenter and S. E. Dykes Bower
      Still in progress. Buildings planned in three quadrangles, of which one and part
      of another are finished. The dining hall (101 × 36 ft) has a lofty open roof, with
      an oak-shingled lantern. On each side are large stone dormers richly treated.
      Below these is a row of two-light windows. The library has an open panelled roof,
      with a series of gabled windows. The chapel has just been begun, and will be on
      a very grand scale. It will consist of nine bays (groined), besides an ante-chapel
      of three bays and the apse. A crypt will extend under its whole length. There will
      be a triforium gallery at the west end, a tower 300 ft high at the south-west angle,
      and an entrance cloister.
          Eccles. xvi (1855), 220–1, 137; xxix (1868), 314. *Builder* xxvi (1868), 602–3,
      944–5; xxiv (1866), 85. *G. M.* 1855 pt. ii, 189. B. Handford, *Lancing College,*
      1848–1948 (Hove, 1948). Pevsner and Nairn, *Sussex* (1965), 256–9, fig. 54.

116   **Jesus College, Oxford**
      Additions
      15th century
      1853–5 J. C. Buckler
      Erected for the Principal and Fellows. The new front presents a straight line of
      building, but the treatment of certain features in the elevation has produced a
      picturesque effect. The gateway tower is in the centre, rising to a considerable
      height, with a square turret at one angle, and embattled parapet. Over the archway
      is an oriel window. The details are refined and well executed. Built of Box Hill
      and Taynton stone.
          V.C.H. Oxon. iii (1954), 276. Sherwood and Pevsner, *Oxon.* (1974), 142.

117   **Clergy Orphan School, Canterbury, Kent**
      Pointed
      1854–5 P. C. Hardwick
      Built of Kentish rag and Bath stone. Frontage, 230 × 170 ft. Consists of chapel
      (64 × 23 ft), school-room (75 × 25 ft), with class-room and residence for the
      master and a matron. Sleeping accommodation is provided for 125 boys. This
      building occupies a high and commanding position to the north-west of Canter-
      bury. Its details are comparatively plain, owing to restrictions as to cost.
          Builder xiii (1855), 162–3. *Eccles.* xv (1854), 166–7.

118   **St John, Deptford, London**
      Pointed
      1854–5 P. C. Hardwick
      Built of Kentish rag. General dimensions, 140 × 70 ft. Design of church well

adapted for hearing, this having been made an important point in the commission. *Builder* xii (1854), 533. Pevsner, *London* ii (1952), 104. Clarke, *Parish Churches of London* (1967), 221.

119 St James, Plymouth
Decorated
1853–4 J. P. St Aubyn
Built for the Rev. J. Bliss. Peculiar in plan, the nave being double, with clerestory and aisles. Built of limestone, with Bath stone dressings; chancel fittings of oak. Double nave, 56 × 22 ft each; aisles, 56 × 14 ft; apsidal chancel, 38 × 20 ft.
Eccles. xiv (1853), 291–2. *Builder* xii (1854), 378–9.

120 St Simon and St Jude, Earl Shilton, Leicestershire
Decorated
1855–7 R. C. Carpenter and W. Slater
Built of rough Mount Sorrel granite, with Ancaster stone dressings. A reconstruction – tower and spire of ancient church retained. Wide gabled aisles and chancel aisles. Nave arcade low in proportion.
Eccles. xvi (1855), 315. Pevsner, *Leics. and Rutland* (1960), 96.

121 St Andrew, Stamford Street, Blackfriars, London
Early Decorated
1855–6 S. S. Teulon
Destroyed in the Second World War
This church (which stands north and south) is short in proportion to its breadth. The plan comprises a clerestoried nave and aisles of four bays. The nave piers are circular. Roof open timbered. The interior is decorated with red and white brick. The reredos consists of seven trefoiled arches, carried on serpentine shafts, with discs of the same material in the spandrils, and a bold cornice above, enriched with a band of encaustic tiles. The chancel is parclosed by screens. The external walls are of brick and ragstone. The tower, which is on the east side of the church, terminates in four gables and a slate spire. Dimensions, 96 × 65 ft.
Eccles. xvii (1856), 72, 422–4. *Builder* xiv (1856), 314–15.

122 University Museum, Oxford
[Plate 25]
Early Pointed
1855–68 Sir T. Deane and B. Woodward
One of the most important modern buildings in Oxford. It cost £60,000. In style it is a free adaptation of Gothic, strongly influenced by Continental study. The principal front consists of a three-storied building, from the centre of which rises a tower. The details of the entrance doorway and of the windows are richly decorated with carving in low relief, very original in design, and executed with great refinement and artistic taste. The contents of the museum are deposited in

a quadrangle, roofed with iron and glass, and surrounded by an open cloister of brick and stone, the shafts of the arcade being of coloured marble. On the right hand of the principal front is the chemical laboratory, resembling in general outline the Glastonbury Abbey kitchen (see p. 283).

Eccles. xix (1858), 243–4. *Builder* xii (1854), 388, 562, 590, 606, 622, 630, 641; xiii (1855), 291–2, 318–19; xvi (1858), 652, 716, 731; xvii (1859), 252–3, 335–6, 401, 408; xviii (1860), 398–9; xx (1862), 476; xxiv (1866), 337. *B.N.* v (1859), 819; vi (1860), 271, 715; viii (1862), 163. *Civil Engineer and Architect's Jnl.* xx (1862), 188–9. H. W. Acland, *The Oxford Museum* (1893 ed.). H. M. and K. D. Vernon, *A History of the Oxford Museum* (1909). *A.R.* cxxxii (1962), 408–16. Sherwood and Pevsner, *Oxon.* (1974), 280–2.

123   **St James, Leyland, nr Preston, Lancashire**
       Decorated
       1854–5 E. Christian
Erected for Mrs Ffarington. Built of local sandstone. General dimensions, 100 × 70 ft.

124   **St George, Doncaster, Yorkshire**
       Early Decorated
       1854–8 Sir G. G. Scott
Built of magnesian limestone. One of the largest and most successful churches which Mr Scott has erected. It is cruciform in plan, with a grandly vaulted central lantern, lofty nave, transepts, and a deep chancel. The spandrils of the nave arcade are enriched with panels enclosing *rilievi*. The capitals, etc., are boldly carved; roofs open timbered; eight-light east window. The south aisle is groined and paved with encaustic tiles. Aisles spanned by stone arches at intervals. Total length, 167 ft; width, 92 ft.

Eccles. xv (1854), 145; xxi (1860), 145–52. *Builder* xii (1854), 549; xiii (1855), 229; xvi (1858), 695, 708–9; xix (1861), 129, 166, 236; xx (1862), 910. *B.N.* v (1859), 693. *I.L.N.* xxii (1853), 220.

125   **Crown Life Assurance Office, New Bridge Street, Blackfriars, London**
       Italian Gothic
       1855 Sir T. Deane and B. Woodward
       Demolished
One of the most original and carefully designed street house-fronts in London, not exactly referable to any particular period of architectural style, but suggestive of early Venetian, or at least of Italian Gothic. It cost £60,000.

B.N. xii (1865), 447.

126 **St Mary, Lanark, Scotland (R.C.)**
Geometrical Pointed
1855–7 G. Goldie and M. E. Hadfield.
1910 burnt; rebuilt by Ashlin and Coleman
Built of local sandstone faced with Glasgow freestone. Finished as to interior with unusual sumptuousness, though as yet not wholly completed. High altar, pulpit, and communion rails richly sculptured, with much use of marble and alabaster. Fine series of stone statues representing the twelve Apostles. All windows filled with stained glass. Chancel decorated in colour. This building is picturesquely situated, and overlooks the valley of the Clyde.
Builder xvii (1859), 796; xviii (1860), 327; xix (1861), 244.

127 **All Saints, Clapham, London**
Second Pointed
1855–8 T. Talbot Bury and G. E. Hering
Built of brick, faced with Kentish rag and Bath stone dressings. Length, 120 ft; width across from aisle to aisle, 63 ft, with transepts extending 15 ft beyond.
Clarke, *Parish Churches of London* (1966), 216.

128 **Our Lady and St Patrick, Bandon, Ireland (R.C.)**
English Decorated
1855–61 W. G. Weightman, M. E. Hadfield and G. Goldie
Built of local sandstone, with limestone dressings. One of the most important R.C. churches in the south of Ireland; finely situated over the town of Bandon. The interior fittings are now in progress. The tower is unfinished.
Civil Engineer and Architect's Jnl. xxi (1858), 252.

129 **Limerick Cathedral (St John), Ireland (R.C.)**
Pointed
1855–63 P. C. Hardwick and W. Slater
This church is in one of the poorest parishes of any city in Ireland; part of it being the celebrated "Garryowen". ["Garryowen" means "John's Garden", a suburb of Limerick in St John's parish, famous in song and verse as a place of noise and revelry.] It was the first attempt to erect an R.C. church in Limerick. It is constructed of limestone. External length, 178 ft; width, 80 ft. Transepts, 125 × 65 ft, with side chapels. The spire has not yet been finished.
Eccles. xxiii (1862), 67. *B.N.* iii (1857), 236–7. M. Lenihan, *Limerick; its History and Antiquities* (1866), 680–3.

130 **St Michael and All Angels, Tenbury, Worcestershire**
Church and college
Middle Pointed
1855–8 H. Woodyer

Founded by Sir Fred. Gore Ouseley Bt., chiefly as a place for education in music. It is built of "old red" sandstone and Bath stone. The college is 160 × 80 ft in plan, the church about 130 × 80 ft (see p. 329).

Eccles. xviii (1857), 219–22. Pevsner, *Worcs.* (1968), 278.

131 **Orchardleigh Park, Somerset**
Manorial Gothic
1856 T. H. Wyatt
Erected for William Duckworth Esq. Built of stone. General dimensions, 150 × 100 ft (see p. 302).

Builder xvi (1858), 306. *C.L.* x (1901), 808–14. Pevsner, *N. Somerset and Bristol* (1958), 241.

132 **Sodality Chapel, Stonyhurst College, Lancashire (R.C.)**
15th century
1856–9 C. A. Buckler; lengthened 1888
Apsidal end. The altar has wreathed columns of alabaster and carved shrine. Reredos of stone and alabaster, with statue and canopy. Sculptured figures of saints and angels by Earp. Windows filled with stained glass by Hardman. Oak traceried panelling round apse. Choir seats and screens of richly carved oak. Roof arched and panelled. The whole tastefully decorated in polychrome.

Illustrations of Stonyhurst College (1891). J. Gerard, *Stonyhurst College, 1592–1894* (1894). *C.L.* lxxxiv (1938), 60–5, 84–9, 117. Pevsner, *North Lancs.* (1969), 243.

133 **Ferney Hall, Shropshire**
Elizabethan
1856–60 J. Norton
Erected for W. Hurt Sitwell Esq. Built of brick, with Bath stone dressings. General dimensions, 167 × 142 ft.

Eccles. xix (1858), 278. Pevsner, *Salop* (1858), 130.

134 **Balliol College, Oxford: Chapel**
Middle Pointed
1856–7 W. Butterfield
1937 interior by Walter Tapper
A refined and well studied work, very characteristic of the architect's style of design (see p. 261).

Eccles. xix (1858), 241–2; xxii (1861), 22. *Builder* xvii (1859), 402; xx (1862), 476; xxiv (1866), 337. *G.M.* 1856 pt. i, 612. Sherwood and Pevsner, *Oxon.* (1974), 101–2.

135 **15 Upper Phillimore Gardens, London**
Italian Gothic
1856 Sir T. Deane and B. Woodward
Much altered

A curious example of a suburban villa residence treated to a certain extent in a Medieval spirit. The front is of red brick, with stepped gables. A picturesque staircase turret is on the right hand of the building, and a Venetian-looking balcony projects from one of the windows. It cost £3,000.

136 **All Souls, Haley Hill, Halifax, Yorkshire**
Middle Pointed
1856–9 Sir G. G. Scott
Erected for Col. Akroyd. Built of stone, marble used for decorative purposes. Cruciform plan, consisting of a clerestoried nave with gabled aisles of five bays, aisled chancel, low transepts, engaged tower, and lofty spire. The clerestory has a continuous arcade. The west door is of five orders, with cinquefoil arcading on each side. The tympanum above this door is filled with sculpture representing our Lord and the Blessed Virgin. The exterior is rich in carved figures. Nave 88 × 54 ft; chancel, 37 × 24 ft.
Eccles. xvii (1856), 186–7, 304; xxi (1860), 84–8, 145–52, 188. *B.N.* vi (1860), 127. *Builder* xvii (1859), 727–9. *G.M.* 1860 pt. i, 243, 391–3. Pevsner, *Yorks., N. Riding* (1959), 234.

137 **Immaculate Conception, Stroud, Gloucestershire (R.C.)**
13th century
1857 C. A. Buckler
Erected for the Dominican Friars. Nave, 80 × 25 ft; north and south aisles, 12 ft wide. North church and baptistery. Built of Rodborough, Box Hill, and Painswick stone. Choir not yet executed.

138 **Pippbrook, Dorking, Surrey**
Middle Pointed
1856 Sir G. G. Scott
Erected for J. Forman Esq., at a cost of £20,000.
Eccles. xix (1858), 171. *Builder* xvi (1858), 32. Nairn and Pevsner, *Surrey* (1962), 168.

139 **Llysdulas, nr Llanwenllwyfo, Anglesey**
Venetian Gothic
1856 Sir T. Deane and B. Woodward
Erected for Lady Dinorben, at a cost of about £6,000.
B.N. iv (1858), 948.

140 **Addington Manor, Buckinghamshire**
Domestic Pointed
1856–7 P. C. Hardwick
Demolished
The first Gothic house erected by the architect without mullions to the windows:

one of the conditions of its design being that large sheets of plate glass should be used. This was accomplished (without sacrificing the general effect) by a careful attention to the mouldings of the window "jambs", and by associating the windows in groups as far as possible. The design of this house, owing to the necessities of its plan, is more symmetrical and formal than other works of the same class executed by Mr Hardwick, who has nevertheless managed to obtain a broken and effective sky-line for the exterior.

Eccles. xvii (1856), 187. *Builder* xiv (1856), 273.

141 Shadwell Court, Norfolk

14th century with Renaissance detail
1856–60 S. S. Teulon

Erected for Sir Robert J. Buxton Bt. Main building, about 190 × 80 ft. Built of various materials, nearly all local, viz. flint, red and white brick, and freestone.

Eccles. xx (1859), 211, 289–90; xxi (1860), 55–6. *Builder* xvi (1858), 571–2; xvii (1859), 322; xviii (1860), 448–9. Pevsner, *N.W. and S. Norfolk* (1962), 307. *C.L.* cxxxvi (1964), 18–21, 98–102.

142 St James, Baldersby, Yorkshire

Early Decorated
1856–68 W. Butterfield
Church, school, vicarage and cottages

Erected for Viscount Downe. Built of local stone externally, with brick and stone internally; two stones of different colours being used.

Builder xv (1857), 583. Pevsner, *Yorks., N. Riding* (1966), 70–1, fig. 59a.

143 New Lodge, Winkfield, Berkshire

English Domestic
1856–9 T. Talbot Bury

Erected for His Excellency S. Van de Weyer, at a cost of £35,000. A large building, occupying three sides of a quadrangle. The principal front is 150 ft long, the others 130 ft each. Built of white Suffolk bricks, with Bath stone dressings. The whole of the internal fittings are of oak, and of a very elaborate kind.

Builder xvii (1859), 322; xviii (1860), 291. Pevsner, *Berks.* (1966), 306.

144 St Leonard, Scorborough, Yorkshire

Early Decorated
1857–9 J. L. Pearson

A small but highly enriched church. The nave and chancel are of the same width and height; the separation being marked internally by coupled marble pillars with double roof principals. A triple lancet window, richly moulded, at east end. The tower, which is of considerable size, is carried up square to the base of the belfry stage, where it becomes octagonal, with lofty angular pinnacles stretching up into the spire, which is 128 ft from the ground. Walls lined with a light grey stone of fine texture; marble of various colours used for internal decoration.

Eccles. xx (1859), 140; xxi (1860), 48–9. *Builder* xx (1862), 343.

145 Holy Trinity, Hastings, Sussex
14th century
1851–9 S. S. Teulon
1892 vestry

This church is cleverly adapted to an awkward site. It has a broad nave and spacious chancel with apsidal end. A square tower over porch in the angle between chancel and north aisle. A perforated and stepped gable rises between the nave and chancel. The exterior is richly decorated with crosses in stone and metal ridge crests, roof gablets, pierced parapets, etc. The tower is elaborately designed. Built of stone. Internal length, 132 ft; width of nave 35 ft; aisle, 25 ft.

Eccles. xvii (1856), 129; xix (1858), 127–8; xx (1859), 69. *Builder* xv (1857), 350–1; xvi (1858), 306. Pevsner and Nairn, *Sussex* (1965), 522.

146 St Peter, Scarborough, Yorkshire (R.C.)
Geometrical Gothic
1857–9 G. Goldie

Unfinished as to internal fittings and tower; apsidal chancel built without windows and intended for fresco decoration. One of the first designed on this plan. A large and picturesque presbytery executed in Domestic Gothic of the same period adjoins. The situation is fine. The church is seen from the South Bay, standing *à cheval* on the isthmus connecting the Castle Rock with Scarborough. It is built of local wall stone, with Whitby ashlaring. The nave and aisles measure 53 × 88 ft. The chancel is 27 × 23 ft. Total length, 115 ft and 50 ft high internally.

Eccles. xx (1859), 192. *Builder* xv (1857), 432; xvi (1858), 559–60; xvii (1859), 322. *Civil Engineer and Architect's Jnl.* xx (1867), 8. Pevsner, *Yorks., N. Riding* (1966), 323.

147 St Peter, Lutton Place, Edinburgh
14th century
1857–67 W. Slater and R. H. Carpenter

Peculiar in plan. Nave columns are of red granite. The cloister and baptistery roofs are decorated with colour. Windows filled with stained glass executed by Clayton and Bell. Oak slatts. Encaustic tiles expressly designed for chancel. Walls of stone.

Eccles. xix (1858), 276; xxvii (1866), 117.

148 Quantock Lodge, Over Stowey, Somerset
Tudor
1857 H. Clutton

Erected for Lord Taunton. A large and well-appointed mansion, built of local stone. Cost, £40,000.

Pevsner, *S. and W. Somerset* (1958), 270.

149 Quarwood, Stow-on-the-Wold, Gloucestershire
Early 14th century
1857 J. L. Pearson
Remodelled
This house (erected for the Rev. R. W. Hippisley) includes, on the ground floor, three reception-rooms, with kitchen and all the usual offices, and two storeys of bedrooms above. A large and steep-roofed tower contains the principal staircase and three storeys of bedrooms. It is built of local stone. The woodwork used is unstained deal (see p. 303).
Verey, *Glos.* i (1970), 425–6.

150 Eton College, Buckinghamshire: New Schools
Tudor
1861–3 H. Woodyer
1876–7 enlarged
These schools will accommodate 400 boys. They are built of brick, with Bath stone dressings. Frontage, 150 ft; depth, 120 ft. The hall and master's house were restored at the same time; and some works were executed in the chapel.
Builder xx (1862), 119. Pevsner, *Bucks.* (1960), 129.

151 Winchester College, Hampshire
Early 15th century
1857–75 W. Butterfield
Rebuilding of tower, and conversion of the modern buildings of "Commoners" into Gothic library and class-rooms. These works were carried out as a "Crimean Memorial", at the expense of Wykhamists, and of the Warden and Fellows. Materials used, brick and stone.
Builder xix (1861), 601. H. W. Llewellyn Smith, *Winchester College* (1926). Pevsner and Lloyd, *Hants.* (1967), 700–4.

152 Wickham Rectory, Berkshire
15th century
1857–9 T. Talbot Bury
Much altered
Erected for the Rev. William Nicholson. Built of red brick, with Bath stone dressings. Each side is about 70 ft long, with three large bay windows; hall, 25 × 17 ft; and angle tower, 95 ft high.
Builder xxvii (1869), 358. *B.N.* xvi (1869), 404. Pevsner, *Berks.* (1966), 266.

153 St Peter, Rochester, Kent
Early Decorated
1858–60 E. Christian
Erected by subscription. Built of brick, with Bath stone dressings. General dimensions, 105 × 62 ft.

154 St Alban, Holborn, London
Early Decorated
1861–2 W. Butterfield
Church and houses
Partly destroyed in the Second World War; rebuilt by Sir Giles and Adrian Scott.
A lofty and well-proportioned church. Erected for the poor of the district by J. G. Hubbard Esq., on a site given by Lord Leigh. Nave divided into five bays, whereof the last one at the west end is carried above the others, and forms externally a large gabled belfry. Aisle walls are decorated with mural arcuation. Chancel enriched with alabaster, and inlaid ornament in mastic. East wall painted in water-glass by Preedy, from cartoons by H. L. Stylman le Strange. Handsome font of coloured marble. Wrought iron screen on south of chancel. Walls of brick and stone (see p. 257).
Eccles. xx (1859), 287; xxii (1861), 317–24; xxiv (1863), 114, 147–8. *Builder* xx (1862), 442–3; xxi (1863), 157. *B.N.* x (1863), 433. G. W. E. Russell, *St Alban the Martyr, London* (1917 ed.). Clarke, *Parish Churches of London* (1966), 84–5, fig. 61.

155 Immaculate Conception, Farm Street, London (R.C.): Sacred Heart Chapel
13th century
1858–9 H. Clutton; see no. 47.
Erected for the Society of Jesus. A very refined and sumptuous work, rich in marble and mosaics. Size, 30 × 15 ft.
Eccles. xxii (1861), 162. *Builder* xviii (1860), 772, 791; xix (1861), 313.

156 Kelham Hall, Nottinghamshire
Modified Venetian Gothic
1858–62 Sir G. G. Scott
Erected for J. H. Manners Sutton Esq., at a cost of £40,000. Built of brick and Ancaster stone. General dimensions, 224 × 120 ft.
Builder xviii (1860), 205; xxi (1863), 237. *B.N.* vii (1861), 542–3. *C.L.* cxli (1967), 1230–3, 1302–5. Morris, *Seats* iv, 43. Pevsner, *Notts.* (1951), 87.

157 Christ Church, Reading, Berkshire
Middle Pointed
1861–2 H. Woodyer
1874 enlarged
Built of blue Pennant and Bath stone. General dimensions, 140 × 62 ft. Spire to be 150 ft high (see p. 330).
Builder xx (1862), 591.

158 Dunster, Williton and Long Ashton, Somerset:
Constabulary Buildings
14th century
1858–60 J. Norton
Erected for the magistrates of each division. Built of local stone, with Bath stone
dressings. General dimensions, 96 × 66 ft.

159 Kilmore Cathedral, Co. Cavan, Ireland
Geometrical Decorated
1857–60 W. Slater
Built of black limestone. 122 ft long × 82 ft wide at transepts. A fine Romanesque
doorway from the old cathedral (the only feature of any interest which remained)
was removed to the new building.
Eccles. xvii (1856), 374; xviii (1857), 254–5; xxi (1860), 19–22; *Builder* xvi
(1858), 306, 343; xviii (1860), 528–9, 548.

160 St Mary, Dalton Holme, Yorkshire
Early Decorated
1858–61 J. L. Pearson
Erected for Lord Hotham. The plan consists of a nave with north and south
transepts (no aisles); a chancel with aisles, one of which, on the south side, is
formed into a monumental chapel. The tower, which is large, and surmounted
by a spire about 200 ft high, stands at the west end of nave; the lowest storey
being groined. The porch (also groined) is on the south side. Built of Steetley
stone, with Kildeny stone for the interior. Nave, 57 × 23 ft; chancel, 37 × 19 ft;
width across transepts, 69 ft.
Eccles. xxiii (1862), 60–1. *R.I.B.A. Jnl.* v (1898), 114.

161 St John, Bemerton, Wiltshire: Herbert Memorial Church
Early Pointed
1858–61 T. H. Wyatt
Erected in memory of Lord Herbert. Nave, aisles, chancel and tower, the fenestration of which is of a very refined design. Spire not complete.
Eccles. xx (1859), 143; xxi (1860), 56. *Builder* xvii (1859), 286; xix (1861),
265–6. Pevsner, *Wilts.* (1963), 96.

162 St Michael, Lyndhurst, Hampshire
Middle Pointed
1858–70 W. White
Erected for the Rev. J. Compton and Committee. Built of brick, with stone
tracery. This church was reduced to nearly half its cost after the first plans and
estimate were prepared. Reredos wall, painted in encaustic colour by F. Leighton,
R.A. Fine stained glass windows by Morris, Marshall & Co. General dimensions,
120 × 50 ft; height to top of spire, 135 ft (see p. 293).
Eccles. xx (1859), 288. *Builder* xvii (1859), 669. Pevsner and Lloyd, *Hants.*
(1967), 326–7, fig. 88

163   **Minley Manor, Hampshire**
       French Gothic
       1858–62 H. Clutton
       Additions 1886–7 by G. Devey; and 1898

Erected by Raikes Currie Esq. A large house built of brick, with stone dressings, after the style of French *châteaux* in the time of Louis XI.

    Eccles. xix (1858), 173. *Builder* xvi (1858), 306; xix (1861), 244. *C.L.* vi (1899), 808–13. Pevsner and Lloyd, *Hants.* (1967), 338.

164   **Walton Hall, Warwickshire**
       Middle Pointed
       1858–62 Sir G. G. Scott

Erected for Sir Charles Mordaunt, at a cost of about £30,000. Built of stone.

    Builder xviii (1860), 560–1. Morris, *Seats* iv, 53. Pevsner and Wedgwood, *Warwicks.* (1966), 440.

165   **Training College, Ripon, Yorkshire**
       Middle Pointed
       1858–9 G. F. Bodley

An important work. The buildings form a quadrangle 155 × 130 ft, with a well-arranged internal cloister. The north and east sides contain the college proper, domestic offices filling up the remainder. The upper storey is chiefly devoted to dormitories. The oratory, 48 × 20 ft, is well placed in the gable over the library and music school, and is lighted by a large east window.

    Eccles. xx (1859), 289.

166   **St Alphonso Liguori, Limerick, Ireland (R.C.)**
       Middle Pointed
       1858–62 P. C. Hardwick
       1865 high altar by G. Goldie

This church was built for the Order of Redemptorists, who devote themselves more especially to preaching. It was therefore essential that the design should combine the qualities of a building in which every part would be well adapted for seeing the preacher, and would also permit the elaborate functions of the R.C. ritual. In both these respects the building is said to be highly satisfactory. External length (with apse), 182 ft; width, 80 ft; height to ridge of roof, 75 ft. It is built of local limestone.

    Builder xxiii (1865), 660–1. M. Lenihan, *Limerick; its History and Antiquities* (1866), 675–8.

167   **Nutfield Priory, Surrey**
       15th century
       1858–9 J. Norton
       c. 1871 remodelled by J. Gibson

Erected for H. E. Gurney Esq. Built of brick, terra cotta, and local ragstone.

    Eccles. xxi (1860), 326. *B.N.* xiv (1867), 104. Nairn and Pevsner, *Surrey* (1962), 328.

168   **Exeter College, Oxford: Chapel, Library and Rector's Lodge**
Early Pointed
1854–60 Sir G. G. Scott

The chapel is of great height, and, being groined, is surrounded by massive buttresses. It is richly decorated, both internally and externally, with ornamental sculpture. The interior, which is finely proportioned, contains a stone screen, with coupled columns and open arches. The decorative sculpture (of corbels to wall-shafts, etc.) is executed with great refinement. The apse windows are filled with glass by Clayton and Bell. Below these the wall is enriched with mosaic work (figures of saints, etc., with gold background). The whole of the chapel, in regard to fittings, decorations, etc., has been carried out on a most sumptuous scale (see p. 295).

Eccles. xvii (1856), 186; xix (1858), 242; xx (1859), 139; xxii (1861), 22–4. *Builder* xii (1854), 417; xvii (1859), 402, 441, 711; xx (1862), 476, 496–7; xxiv (1866), 337; xxvi (1868), 875; xxvii (1869), 1022. *B.N.* v (1859), 1127; viii (1862), 127. *G. M.* 1860 pt. i, 246. *Civil Engineer and Architect's Jnl.* xxi (1858), 275.

169   **Ettington Park, Warwickshire**
First Pointed
1856–63 J. Prichard and J. P. Seddon

A mansion erected for E. P. Shirley, Esq. In this work the architect had to remodel the exterior of an existing house, the internal arrangement of which was left intact. Built of local white lias in thin courses, with quoins and dressings of Campden, Norton, and Wilmcot stones (see p. 306).

Eccles. xx (1859), 193. *Builder* xvii (1859), 322. *B.N.* xvi (1869), 158–60, 576–8. Pevsner and Wedgwood, *Warwicks.* (1966), 289–90, fig. 56a.

170   **St Peter, Daylesford, Gloucestershire**
13th century
1859–60 J. L. Pearson

A small cruciform church, with central tower and spire, built on the site of an older church. The tomb of Warren Hastings abuts against the east wall and limits the length of the chancel, which is in consequence short. The only features in the original structure which could be preserved were the old north and south doorways. These were restored, and suggested the style of the present church.

Eccles. xxi (1860), 48. *Builder* xix (1861), 342; xxi (1863), 393. *B.N.* x (1863), 374–5; xiii (1866), 275. *I.L.N.* xxxviii (1861), 419.

171   **St James, Titsey, Surrey**
13th century (Lancet)
1859–61 J. L. Pearson

A carefully finished work. On the north of the chancel, which is of some length, there is a mortuary chapel groined in stone, the groining being carried on marble shafts. A rich double arcade connects this chapel (in which stands the tomb of the founder) with the sacrarium. The tower stands on the south side of the nave. It is square in plan and about 42 ft high, with a bold staircase turret and an octagonal spire of wood covered with oak shingles.

Eccles. xxi (1860), 49. *Builder* xix (1861), 849. Nairn and Pevsner, *Surrey* (1962), 409.

172 **Chase Cliffe, Crich, Derbyshire**
Tudor
1859–61 B. Ferrey
Erected for the Messrs Hurt, in character with the ancient domestic architecture of the county. The site is most picturesque, overlooking the river Derwent and the hills of Matlock. It is built of Darley Dale and local stone. General dimensions, 90 × 60 ft, with various projecting porches, etc. Stable and kitchen, 50 × 40 ft.

173 **Carlett Park, Eastham, Cheshire**
Elizabethan
1859–60 T. H. Wyatt
c. 1887 chapel by J. Douglas
Erected for John Torr, Esq. Built of brick with stone dressings, mullioned windows, stepped gables, oriels, etc. General dimensions, 120 × 60 ft.

Builder xviii (1860), 344. Pevsner and Hubbard, *Cheshire* (1971), 207.

174 **Arundel Castle, Sussex: Chapel, School and Gateway**
English Perpendicular
1859–65 M. E. Hadfield and G. Goldie
This chapel, gateway, and other works formed part of a general plan for rebuilding the castle designed by Hadfield for the Duke of Norfolk.

Builder xviii (1860), 499. Pevsner and Nairn, *Sussex* (1965), 92–3.

175 **St John, Maindee, Newport, Monmouthshire**
Geometrical Decorated
1859–60 J. Prichard and J. P. Seddon
The plan of this church consists of a nave and south aisle, with tower at south-west angle. The aisle is divided from the nave by an arcade of four bays. There are west and south porches roofed with slabs of stone on moulded ribs. The windows are large, and filled with geometrical tracery. Built of thin Pennant sandstone, with Bath stone dressings. Bands and arch voussoirs of blue limestone. The church will seat 500 persons. It cost about £3,000. The spire, when completed, will be 180 ft high.

Eccles. xx (1859), 208; xxi (1860), 257–8. *Builder* xvii (1859), 267.

176 **St Michael and All Angels, Brighton, Sussex**
Early Pointed
1859–61 G. F. Bodley
1893 enlarged by W. Burges and J. S. Chapple

The plan of this church is extremely simple. It consists of a nave and chancel under one continuous roof, a lofty clerestory, low aisles, and a western narthex, approached by a flight of steps on each side, as the ground falls considerably from east to west. The east window is raised to some height above the chancel floor and filled with plate tracery. The nave arcade is of four bays with unmoulded arches, carried on short round piers with massive capitals carved in low relief. In the west gable is a large wheel window, enclosing seven plain circular lights distributed round a central one which is cusped. The church is built and lined with brick relieved by bands of stone. It contains some fine stained glass by Morris and Co. *Eccles.* xx (1859), 67–8. *Builder* xviii (1860), 141, 645. *B.N.* xi (1864), 695. *Civil Engineer and Architect's Jnl.* xxii (1859), 213. Pevsner and Nairn, *Sussex* (1965), 434, 691–2.

177 **Assize Courts, Manchester**
13th century
1859–64 A. Waterhouse
Courts and Judges' Lodgings
Bombed 1940, and later demolished

Remarkable for a certain admixture of Italian Gothic in details. A very important and well-planned building, the professional commission for which Mr Waterhouse gained in open competition, and thus established his reputation. It is built of Darley Dale stone. The general dimensions of the courts are 256 × 166 ft. Judges' lodgings, 98 × 92 ft. Tower 10 ft square on plan, and 210 ft high (see p. 312).
Eccles. xxi (1860), 178; xxii (1861), 162; xxix (1868), 180. *Builder* xvii (1859), 286, 289, 296, 307, 318, 323, 328–9, 339, 843; xviii (1860), 436; xix (1861), 504; xx (1862), 264, 936; xxi (1863), 143; xxiii (1865), 135–7; lxxi (1896), 380. *B.N.* v (1859), 426–7.

178 **Capel Manor, Horsmonden, Kent**
Italian Gothic
1859–62 T. H. Wyatt
Demolished

Erected for F. Austen Esq. A large and picturesque mansion raised on a terrace which is vaulted underneath with arches open towards the front. The windows of the principal rooms are arranged in groups, divided by slender columns with richly carved capitals, the arches above being decorated with voussoirs of dark and light coloured stone, placed alternately, and panelled tympana. General dimensions, 160 × 85 ft (see p. 302).

179   **Trinity College Cambridge: Whewell's Court**
      Perpendicular
      1859–60; 1866–8 A. Salvin
      1908 additions by W. D. Caröe
Built of brick, faced with stone.
      Eccles. xxiii (1862), 144. *B.N.* vii (1861), 329; viii (1862), 231. Pevsner,
      Cambs. (1954), 149.

180   **St John's School, Middlesbrough, Yorkshire**
      Middle Pointed
      1859–60 J. Norton
      1864–6 church and parsonage
      1883 steeple
Built of brick, with sandstone dressings. Roofed with green slates. General
dimensions, 176 × 69 ft.
      Pevsner, *Yorks., N. Riding* (1966), 249.

181   **St Peter, Croydon, Surrey** (Commissioners' church)
      Decorated
      1849–51 Sir G. G. Scott
Built of flint and Tonbridge stone. Extreme length, 140 ft; extreme width, 72 ft.
Tower and spire, 146 ft high.
      Eccles. xi (1850), 63. *Builder* vii (1849), 454. Nairn and Pevsner, *Surrey*
      (1962), 160.

182   **St James, Castle Hill, Dover, Kent**
      Edward III
      1859–62 T. Talbot Bury
Built of Kentish rag, with Bath stone dressings. Nave, 99 ft long; width across
aisles, 70 ft; chancel, 33 × 23 ft; tower, 20 ft square; height to top of spire,
170 ft.
      Eccles. xxi (1860), 397. *Builder* xviii (1860), 284; xx (1862), 689–90, 697;
      xxii (1864), 746.

183   **St Ann, Stamford Hill, London**
      14th century
      1859–62 T. Talbot Bury
      Demolished
Erected for Fowler Newsam Esq. Built of brick, faced with Kentish rag, and
Bath stone dressings. Length of nave and aisles, 75 ft; breadth across 54 ft; apsidal
chancel, 37 × 23 ft; tower, 18 ft square, and 130 ft high.
      Eccles. xxiv (1863), 166. *Builder* xxi (1863), 343. *I.L.N.* xxxix (1861), 173–4.

184 **Holy Cross, St Helens, Lancashire (R.C.)**
Perpendicular
1860–62 J. J. Scoles
Erected for the Order of Jesuits. The plan consists of a clerestoried nave with
transepts, aisles, chancel, Lady Chapel, sacristy. Built of Rainford stone with red
sandstone dressings. Columns and arches of Billinge and Yorkshire stone. The high
altar is of Caen stone richly sculptured. The windows are filled with stained glass
by Messrs Pilkington. Panelled roof. General dimensions, 164 × 90 ft; height,
41 ft.
Builder xx (1862), 337. Pevsner, *South Lancs.* (1969), 384.

185 **St James, Tunbridge Wells, Kent**
Geometrical Decorated
1860–62 E. Christian
Built of Jackwood sandstone and Wadhurst stone. General dimensions, 118 ×
57 ft.

186 **St Luke, Heywood, Lancashire**
14th century
1859–62 J. Clarke
Designed to seat more than 1,000 persons without galleries.
Eccles. xx (1859), 136. *Builder* xvii (1859), 193; xviii (1860), 385; xix (1861),
414. *B.N.* vii (1861), 391. Pevsner, *South Lancs.* (1969), 122.

187 **Dunster House, Rochdale, Lancashire**
15th century
1854 and 1863 J. Clarke
Demolished 1968
Erected for F. Nield Esq. Built of brick and stone.
Pevsner, *South Lancs.* (1969), 380.

188 **St Stephen, Spitalfields, London**
Early Decorated
1860–62 E. Christian
Demolished
Erected by subscription. Built of brick, with Bath stone dressings. General
dimensions, 118 × 66 ft.
Eccles. xxii (1861), 328–9. *R.I.B.A. Jnl.* xviii (1911), 713, 719.

189 **St John's Schools, St Pancras, London**
Domestic Pointed
1859–61 W. Slater
Parish schools for 1,000 children. The front towards John Street is in three
storeys (devoted respectively to boys, girls and infants). The buildings towards

Kirkman's Court are arranged on three sides of a quadrangle enclosing an open playground. Built of brick with Bath stone dressings. Steep hipped roofs and ranges of mullioned windows.

Eccles. xx (1859), 289.

190 **Battle Abbey, Sussex: The Library**
16th century
1860–61 H. Clutton
Built of local stone. General dimensions, 80 × 24 ft.
C.L. cxl (1966), 822–6, 918–23. Pevsner and Nairn, *Sussex* (1965), 406.

191 **St Paul, Swanley, Kent**
Decorated
1860–63 E. Christian
This church, which is erected on a triangular piece of ground, presents the peculiar feature of an apsidal west end, lighted by a double range of windows (whereof the upper one is arcaded), and fitted up inside with a gallery. The aisles are gabled. The nave piers are circular, raised on high bases. The windows are, for the most part, filled with plate tracery. Built of Kentish rag, with Bath stone dressings. General dimensions, 92 × 29 ft.

192 **St Mary, Haggerston, London**
Decorated
1861–4 J. Brooks
Church and school; reconstruction of Nash's work, 1825–7
Destroyed in the Second World War
In remodelling this church (which was originally erected by Nash in a nondescript style) the architect has introduced a novel feature in the oblique or "canted" bay which connects the nave arcade with the reduced width of chancel. The alterations are executed in brick. Nave, 80 × 40 ft; aisles, 80 × 16 ft.

Eccles. xxiv (1863), 113–14; xxv (1864), 246–7; xxvi (1865), 254; xxviii (1867), 64. *R.I.B.A. Jnl.* xvii (1910), 496, 514.

193 **All Saints, Fleet, Hampshire**
13th century
1861–2 W. Burges
1934; 1958 additions
Erected for C. Lefroy Esq. Built of brick. General dimensions: nave and aisles, 52 × 38 ft; chancel, 30 × 16 ft. The west entrance is enriched with decorative sculpture, representing our Lord and the Evangelistic symbols.

Eccles. xxi (1860), 322. Pevsner and Lloyd, *Hants.* (1967), 234.

194   Probate and Episcopal Registries, Llandaff
       First Pointed
       1860–63
       J. Prichard
The Probate Registry was erected for the First Commissioner of Works; the
Episcopal Registry for Mr Huckwell, registrar. Built of thin Pennant stone, with
Bath stone groins and Bridgend bands. Street frontage of Probate Registry, 70 ft;
of Episcopal Registry, 35 ft.

195   Bishop's Court, Clyst Honiton, Devon
       First Pointed
       1860–64 W. White
This work, executed for John Garratt Esq., consisted in an entire remodelling
and renovation of the ancient Episcopal palace which had been "modernized".
The chapel, founded in 1284, had been injured and desecrated. Mr White has
used seven or eight varieties of stone in construction.
       Eccles. xxiv (1863), 167. Pevsner, *S. Devon* (1852), 82.

196   Hawkleyhurst, Hawkley, Hampshire
       14th century
       1860–61 S. S. Teulon
Erected for James Maberly Esq. Built of local stone and Bath stone. Dimensions
of main building, 63 × 48 ft.
       Builder xix (1861), 31.

197   St Dochau, Llandogo, Monmouthshire
       Geometrical Decorated
       1859–61 J. P. Seddon and J. Prichard
A small church built of sandstone, with Bath stone dressings. It consists of a nave
and aisles under one span of roof, with an arcade of three bays on either side, west
and south porches, chancel and vestry. Stone of various tints is used for the internal
decoration. There is a bell-turret over the west gable. The church cost about
£1,800. General dimensions, 80 × 40 ft.
       Eccles. xx (1859), 71; xxii (1861), 197. *Builder* xix (1861), 599. *Civil Engineer
and Architect's Jnl.* xxvi (1863), 219.

198   St James-the-Less, Thorndike Street, Westminster
       Foreign Early Pointed
       1860–61 G. E. Street
One of the most original and remarkable churches in London. The design is
greatly influenced by Continental study, and partakes especially of an Italian
Gothic character. The nave, about 60 × 23 ft, is separated by an arcade of three
wide arches from its aisles. The chancel, 36 ft long, ends in a semicircular apse,
and is intercepted by gabled transepts. The windows are filled with plate tracery,

and the walls, both externally and internally, are decorated with brickwork arranged in patterns. The most conspicuous feature of the church is the campanile, which stands detached at the north-west angle. The lowest stage of the tower forms a porch connected with the church by a short gallery (see p. 322).

Eccles. xxi (1860), 322; xxii (1861), 317–27, 414. *Builder* xix (1861), 410–11; xx (1862), 186–7; xxi (1863), 237. *I.L.N.* xl (1862), 122. Pevsner, *London* i (1962), 452. Clarke, *Parish Churches of London* (1966), 188–9, fig. 146.

199   Rugby School, Warwickshire
      Early Decorated
      1860–70 W. Butterfield
      Class-rooms and racket courts
Bricks of various colours and stone are used in the construction. The school chapel is to be rebuilt from Mr Butterfield's design, and at the expense of old Rugbeians.
      Pevsner and Wedgwood, *Warwickshire* (1966), 387–90; J. B. H. Simpson, *Rugby* (1967).

200   Shipley Hall, Derbyshire
      Old English
      1860–61 W. E. Nesfield
Erected for A. M. Mundey Esq. An ornamental farm and dairy. General dimensions, 700 × 400 ft. Several lodges and cottages are included in the design. The ceiling of the dairy is enriched with decorative paintings by Mr Albert Moore.

201   All Saints, Denstone, Staffordshire
      Early Middle Pointed
      1860–61 G. E. Street
      Church, schools and parsonage
Erected at the cost of Sir Percival Heywood Bt. Built of stone.
      Eccles. xxi (1860), 256–7, 259. *Builder* xix (1861), 244; xx (1862), 642; xxi (1863), 343. *B.N.* x (1863), 345. Pevsner, *Staffs.* (1974), 113–14.

202   Combe Abbey, Warwickshire
      Early English and 15th century
      1860–66 W. E. Nesfield
      Additions; largely demolished
Seat of the Earl of Craven. Estimated cost, £58,000. The greater part of the lower portion is early Norman work, which has been retained. The east wing, a bridge over the moat, and the offices are entirely new. The frontage is 350 ft; courtyard, 100 ft square; side elevation about 350 ft. Built of native red and white sandstone. English oak used throughout. A portion of the work has still to be finished.
      C.L. xxxvi (1914), 784–840.

203   St Peter, Great Windmill Street, London
       Early Decorated
       1860–61 R. Brandon
       Demolished 1954
Built of Bath stone. The plan comprises a clerestoried nave and aisles of five bays
(with a gallery in the west bay), and a short apsidal chancel. Nave piers circular
with foliaged capitals of an early French type. Braced open timber roof. The
aisle roof rests on a transverse stone arch in each bay. Apse of five bays defined by
an arch springing from corbels. Red Mansfield stone is used for the small shafts.
General dimensions, 100 × 50 ft; height from floor to roof ridge 55 ft. Tower
and spire not executed.
       Eccles. xx (1859), 288; xxii (1861), 327. *Builder* xviii (1860), 440; xix (1861),
560–1, 718–19. *B.N.* vi (1860), 481. *I.L.N.* xxxix (1861), 50, 58. *Survey of
London* xxxi (1963), 45–6.

204   Digby Mortuary Chapel, Sherborne, Dorset
       Early Pointed
       1860–62 W. Slater
This chapel was built in consequence of the Digby family vault having been
closed. It is constructed entirely of stone and marble. The crypt beneath the
chapel is groined. The chapel itself has a barrel vault, marble shafts and carved
capitals, tile mosaic pavement, and stained glass windows. The tympanum of the
western doorway (both inside and out) is decorated with sculpture. The door is of
bronze. Internal dimensions, 54 × 16 ft and 26 ft high. The crypt is 54 × 16 ft,
and 19 ft high (see p. 320).
       Builder xxxii (1874), 196–7.

205   Crewe Hall, Cheshire: Lodges
       Early 17th century
       1860–66 W. E. Nesfield
Erected for Lord Crewe. Constructed of brick and stone. Small but picturesque
and interesting examples of the return to national types of rural architecture.
       Builder xxiv (1866), 36, 135; xxvii (1869), 485–7. *The Architect* ii (1869),
58. *C.L.* xi (1902), 400–9; xxxiii (1913), 634–40. Pevsner and Hubbard,
Cheshire (1971), 194.

206   Hampton-in-Arden, Warwickshire
       Old English
       c. 1860–78 W. E. Nesfield
Cottages (1868), manor house and lodge (1870–73), church and vestry (1878).
Twenty-five cottages erected for Sir Frederick Peel (half timbered and plastered).
Alterations to the Manor House were subsequently carried out by the same
architect. The clock tower is still in progress.
       Pevsner and Wedgwood, *Warwicks.* (1966), 304–5, fig. 56b.

207 **Croxteth Park, Liverpool: Dairy and Lodges**
Early Pointed
1861–70 W. E. Nesfield
Erected for the Earl of Sefton. Built of brick, stone, and marble. Ceiling painted by Mr Albert Moore, who also designed the figures which decorate the fountain. The whole work is admirably conceived, and executed with great refinement and artistic skill.
Pevsner, *South Lancs.* (1969), 217.

208 **Memorial Cross, West Derby, Liverpool**
12th century
1861–70 W. E. Nesfield
Erected for the Earl of Sefton. Sculptured figure of Our Lord under canopy on coupled shafts, elaborately carved by Forsyth.
Pevsner, *South Lancs.* (1969), 258–9.

209 **St Francis of Assisi, Notting Hill, London (R.C.)**
French Gothic, 13th century
1860–63 H. Clutton and J. F. Bentley
Church, baptistery, schools and presbytery.
This work consisted in the erection of a priest's house, schools, baptistery, etc., in connection with the Church of St Francis of Assisi. It is an excellent example of the French Gothic School which then prevailed, though the architect has since altered his style of design (see p. 321).
Eccles. xxv (1864), 151. *B.N.* x (1863), 45. *Civil Engineer and Architect's Jnl.* xxv (1862), 248–9. Pevsner, *London* ii (1952), 298. W. de l'Hôpital, *Westminster Abbey and its Architect* ii (1919), 350, 369, 520, 528, 560, 564, 568, pl. xlvi.

210 **Holy Trinity, Knightsbridge, London**
Early Pointed
1861 R. Brandon and H. M. Eyton
Demolished
This church is not orientated, but stands north and south. It is lofty in proportion to its width and is provided with a wooden clerestory glazed from end to end in square compartments. The main entrance is from the street at the south end which is picturesquely treated and includes a large window filled with geometrical tracery.
Eccles. xxi (1860), 110; xxii (1861), 327–8. *Builder* xviii (1860), 248–9; xix (1861), 244.

211 **St Mary, Greenock, Scotland (R.C.)**
Early Decorated
1861 G. Goldie

One of the largest R.C. churches in Scotland, erected for the Rev. W. Gordon on the Firth of Clyde. Adjoining is a commodious presbytery (in the same style as the church) adapted to domestic requisites. The general character of the church is simple but dignified. Total length, 120 ft; nave and aisles, 60 ft wide; internal height, 60 ft. Built of local stone with Glasgow freestone ashlar and red Dumbarton sandstone in parts.

Eccles. xxii (1861), 163. *Builder* xix (1861), 896–7.

212 St Leonard, Newland, Worcestershire:
Beauchamp Almshouses and Church
Middle Pointed
1861–3 P. C. Hardwick

These buildings, constructed of brick, with stone dressings, form three sides of a quadrangle, open to the south, and consist of apartments for eight families, eight single men, and eight single women (each having their separate offices), residences for the chaplain, matron, and clerk. The chapel has since become the parish church of Newland. General dimensions, 320 × 170 ft. Cost about £60,000.

Eccles. xxv (1864), 322–5; xxvi (1865), 24–5, 47–9. *Builder* xx (1862), 378; xxi (1863), 536; xxii (1864), 605–6. Pevsner, *Worcs.* (1968), 223–4.

213 Christ's College, Brecon
First Pointed
1861–4 J. Prichard and J. P. Seddon

Erected for the Governors of the College. Not quite completed. North and south elevations, each 75 ft long; east and west elevations, 64 ft. Built of native old red sandstone, with Bath stone dressings.

Builder xvii (1859), 322; xxii (1864), 657; xxix (1870), 359. T. Jones and Sir J. R. Bailey, *Brecknock* iii (1911), 185 *et seq.*

214 Town Hall, Northampton
Geometrical
1861–4 E. W. Godwin
1889–92 extended by M. Holding

Frontage, 90 ft; 180 ft deep; height to ridge of roof, 63 ft; height to top of tower, 110 ft (see p. 358).

Eccles. xxiii (1862), 145; xxiv (1863), 166. *Builder* xviii (1860), 806, 826; xxi (1863), 605; xxii (1864), 693. *B.N.* vii (1861), 892–3; x (1863), 749; xii (1865), 83, 795. *I.L.N.* xliv (1864), 520. Pevsner, *Northants.* (1961), 316.

215 Bulstrode, Buckinghamshire
Tudor
1861–70 B. Ferrey

This mansion, erected for the Duke of Somerset, occupies the site of one commenced by the Duke of Portland, from designs by Mr J. Wyatt, and subsequently modified under the supervision of Sir J. Wyattville, but abandoned by the Duke owing to the enormous cost which the completion of the structure would entail. It is built of red brick and Bath stone. The mansion occupies about 140 × 100 ft in plan.

Builder xix (1861), 313, 860–1. Pevsner, *Bucks.* (1960), 77.

216 **Hafodunos, Llangerniew, Denbighshire**
Middle Pointed
1861–6 Sir G. G. Scott
Erected for H. R. Sandback Esq., at a cost of £30,000. It is built of brick.

217 **St John, Burgess Hill, Sussex**
Third Pointed
1861–3 T. Talbot Bury
Built of brick, faced with the same arranged in patterns of varied colour and design. Bath stone dressings. Nave and aisle, 82 × 39 ft; chancel, 30 × 24 ft; transepts, 25 × 24 ft. The tower is 16 ft square, surmounted by a timber-framed spire, covered with bands of different coloured tiles. Its entire length is 104 ft.

Builder xxi (1863), 483. Pevsner and Nairn, *Sussex* (1965), 462.

218 **St Paul, Wokingham, Berkshire**
Late Middle Pointed
1862–4 H. Woodyer
1874 aisles added.
Erected for John Walter Esq., M.P. Lofty nave with clerestory and low aisles. Transepts, chancel, tower and stone spire at north-west angle. General dimensions: length, 135 ft; width, 63 ft; height to top of spire, 150 ft.

Pevsner, *Berks.* (1966), 308.

219 **St Martin, Scarborough, Yorkshire**
Early Pointed
1861–2 G. F. Bodley
An excellent design. The plan shows a nave 94 × 26 ft, a chancel 30 × 23 ft, aisles to the nave, half aisles to the chancel, and a sacristy at the east end of the south chancel aisle. The nave has four bays besides an additional one to the west, which is treated as a narthex, and has the tower engaged at its north end. The speciality of the church is its unusual height; the aisles are low, but the clerestory extremely lofty and well-developed. The piers of the arcade are clustered shafts; the arches are well moulded.

Eccles. xxii (1861), 281. *Builder* xviii (1860), 708; xix (1861), 264. Pevsner, *Yorks., N. Riding* (1966), 322–3, 454, figs. 16a, 16b.

220 **Cloverley Hall, Whitchurch, Shropshire**
Late 16th century
1862–70 W. E. Nesfield
Partly demolished
Erected for J. P. Heywood Esq., of Liverpool, at a cost of £60,000, exclusive of decoration. This large and magnificent mansion is one of the architect's most important works, and is thoroughly characteristic of his taste. It is built of brick, local stone and English oak. General dimensions, inclusive of courtyard and offices, about 450 × 400 ft (see p. 339).
A.R. i (1897), 242–7, 283–7.

221 **St Wilfrid, York (R.C.)**
Geometrical Decorated
1862–4 G. Goldie
One of the most perfectly finished R.C. churches in England. Rich in sculpture, stained glass and fittings. The great western doorway, resembling the *portails* of Continental churches, measures 23 ft across its jambs by 6 ft deep. Carved oak stalls. Built of Whitby sandstone (for ashlar work) and Bradford wall stone. Shafts of Carlisle red sandstone. Length, 110 ft; width, 59 ft; internal height, 62 ft. Cost £15,000.
Eccles. xxiii (1862), 146. *Builder* xx (1862), 343, 699–70; xxii (1864), 170–1. *B.N.* xii (1865), 898, 900–1. *I.L.N.* xlv (1864), 441.

222 **St Thomas, Agar Town, St Pancras, London**
Geometrical
1858 S. S. Teulon
1862–4 rebuilt
Destroyed in the Second World War
Erected for the present Dean of Rochester. A brick building with plate tracery of stone in the windows. Internal length, 122 ft; width of nave, 48 ft.
Eccles. xix (1858), 276–7; xxi (1860), 324. *Builder* xv (1857), 311; xvi (1858), 394–5. Pevsner, *London* ii (1952), 362.

223 **Bestwood Lodge, Nottinghamshire**
14th century
1862–5 S. S. Teulon
Erected for the Duke of St Albans. Built of red brick and Mansfield stone. Plan dimensions about 113 × 100 ft.
Eccles. xxiv (1863), 190–1. *Builder* xxi (1863), 638–9; xxii (1864), 327. *B.N.* xvii (1869), 152–3. Morris, *Seats* iii, 61. Pevsner, *Notts.* (1951), 35.

224 **Manor House, Framingham Pigot, Norfolk**
Late Pointed
1862–4 J. Norton
1895 additions

Erected for George H. Christie Esq. Built of brick, terra cotta, and Ancaster stone. Roofed with green slate. General dimensions, 117 × 104 ft.
Pevsner, *N. W. and S. Norfolk* (1962), 165.

225 Crown Life Office, 188 Fleet Street, London
Italian Gothic
1862–5 Sir T. N. Deane
Demolished
An interesting and well studied example of street architecture. Cost £15,000.
Builder xxiii (1865), 502–3. *B.N.* xiii (1866), 36, 184.

226 Manor House, Brent Knoll, Somerset
Late Pointed
1862–4 J. Norton
Erected for Gabriel S. Poole Esq. Built of limestone, with Bath stone dressings. Roofed with Bridgwater tiles. General dimensions, 100 × 45 ft.
Eccles. xxiii (1862), 66. Pevsner, *S. and W. Somerset* (1958), 94.

227 All Saints, Brightwalton, Berkshire
Early Pointed
1862–3 G. E. Street
Church and school
The plan consists of a nave, chancel and north aisle, with a baptistery under the south-west tower, which is surmounted by a spire. The interior is lofty, and of excellent proportions. The floor is paved with encaustic tiles. The east window, of three lights, is a memorial of P. Wroughton Esq. of Woolley Park. Beneath the window is a reredos of alabaster finely designed and executed (see p. 323).
Eccles. xxiii (1862), 364–5. Pevsner, *Berks.* (1966), 101–2.

228 Chew Manor, Chew Magna, Somerset
Late Pointed
1862–4 J. Norton
House and parsonage
Erected for W. Adlam Esq. Built of local sandstone, with Bath stone dressings. General dimensions, 80 × 75 ft.
Eccles xxiii (1862), 66. Pevsner, *N. Somerset and Bristol* (1958), 159.

229 House of St Barnabas (House of Charity), Soho, London: Chapel
French 14th century
1862–3 J. Clarke
Designed with eastern apse and same north and south, being part of a general scheme for rebuilding the House of Charity. Built of various kinds of stone; walls lined inside with chalk.
Eccles. xxiii (1862), 61; xxv (1864), 118, 276. *Builder* xx (1862), 406–7. Pevsner, *London* i (1962), 596.

230 **Town Hall, Preston, Lancashire**
Domestic Pointed
1862–7 Sir G. G. Scott
Destroyed by fire
One of Mr Scott's most important works. Built of Longridge stone; columns of polished granite; north front, 92 × 74 ft; south front, 92 × 86 ft; music hall, 82 × 55 ft; height of tower, 197 ft.
Builder xx (1862), 620–1; xxv (1867), 746, 785.

231 **St Stephen, Guernsey**
Early Pointed
1862–3 G. F. Bodley
Built to seat 750 persons. In plan it is an exact rectangle subdivided into a nave of 84 × 27 ft, opening by arcades of five into north and south aisles, 12ft broad, and a chancel 28 ft long, with chancel aisles – that to the south being used as an organ chamber and sacristy. The church is built of granite, and the mouldings, etc. are of the simplest kind.
Eccles. xxiv (1863), 129.

232 **Newstead Abbey, Nottinghamshire: Stables**
Geometrical Decorated
1863–5 M. E. Hadfield
Erected on the old site near the Abbey, for F. W. Webb Esq., to accommodate twenty-five horses. Court, 100 × 95 ft. Built of local stone.
Builder xix (1861), 823. *C.L.* iii (1898), 208, 240; x (1901), 799; xlii (1917), 468, 492. Pevsner, *Notts.* (1951), 114–18.

233 **Tyntesfield, Somerset**
Late Pointed
1862–6 J. Nortòn
Additions by H. Woodyer and Sir A. Blomfield
A large and costly mansion, erected for William Gibbs Esq. (through whose munificence several churches have been erected and endowed). Built of local stone, faced with oolite from the Bath quarries, and roofed with Broseley tiles.
Builder xxiv (1866), 99–101. *C.L.* xi (1902), 624–9. Pevsner, *N. Somerset and Bristol* (1958), 348–9, fig. 71b.

234 **Christ Church, Appleton-le-Moors, Yorkshire**
13th century
1863–5 J. L. Pearson
Church, parsonage, school
Treated in the same manner as Scarborough and Daylesford Churches, except that coloured sandstone and limestone are used instead of marble. Clerestory wall

enriched with inlay of geometrical patterns. Semicircular apse lighted by lancet windows, high up in the wall, with detached arcading inside. Tower stands at east of north aisle, and is surmounted by a lofty square spire. Narthex at west end, with sloping stone roof. Gable alcove lighted by large rose window (see p. 303).

Eccles. xxv (1864), 149. *Builder* xxii (1864), 327; xxiv (1866), 636. Pevsner, *Yorks., N. Riding* (1966), 63–4.

235 St Wilfrid, Hayward's Heath, Sussex
Geometrical Pointed
1863–5 G. F. Bodley

A very ably treated work. "The plan consists of a clerestoried nave and aisles, with a chancel, over the western part of which stands a massive quadrangular tower, having a vestry under a lean-to roof on its north side. The tower, which is considerably broader from north to south than from east to west, is an excellent composition, with a large belfry stage, having three contiguous and deeply recessed lights on each face, and a saddle-back roof above a plain parapet."

Eccles. xxv (1864), 49. Pevsner and Nairn, *Sussex* (1965), 529.

236 St Scholastica, Teignmouth, Devon (R.C.): Benedictine Convent
1863 J. Goldie
1864 and 1878 organ gallery and chancel screen by J. A. Hansom

A very extensive monastic establishment, picturesquely situated, and overlooking the sea. The plan includes the usual apartments of a convent, viz.: a refectory, chapter-house, community-room, infirmary, etc.; spacious accommodation for lady pensioners, consisting of class-rooms, refectory and dormitory; conventual church with choir and side chapels, apsidal sanctuary and bell-turret, and chaplain's residence. Chief façade, about 96 ft long; wing, 110 ft long; average height of front, 35 ft. Built of Bath stone and local grey marble, with red sandstone shafts and bands (see p. 348).

Eccles. xxv (1864), 151. *Builder* xxiii (1865), 334–5.

237 St Mary, East Hendred, Berkshire (R.C.)
13th century
1863–5 C. A. Buckler

Erected for C. J. Eyston Esq. and the Rev. T. Luck. The plan consists of a well-proportioned chancel with an oak rood-screen, and a sacristy on south side communicating with the presbytery. The nave opens by three graceful arches into a north aisle. The baptistery is in the south-west angle of the nave enclosed by a screen. An octagonal belfry rises at the angle formed by the nave and sacristy. The church is built of Drayton and Box Hill stone; the presbytery, school and teacher's residence are of red brick, with stone dressings.

Pevsner, *Berks.* (1966), 134.

238   Merton College, Oxford: Additions
       Middle Pointed
       1861–3 W. Butterfield
       1930 much altered by T. Harold Hughes
A simply designed but characteristic work (see p. 287).
       Eccles. xxii (1861), 218–20. *Builder* xix (1861), 440, 552; xx (1862), 863.

239   Melchet Court, Hampshire
       16th century
       1863–8 H. Clutton
       Alterations 1875–9 and 1912–14
A large mansion, erected for the Earl of Ashburton. Built of brick, with stone
dressings.
       C.L. lxviii (1930), 176–83. Pevsner and Lloyd, *Hants.* (1967), 332–3.

240   Infirmary, Leeds
       Venetian Gothic
       1863–8 Sir G. G. Scott
       Much extended
Built of brick and stone. General dimensions, 415 × 315 ft.
       Eccles. xxiv (1863), 166. *Builder* xxi (1863), 343; xxii (1864), 115–17, 151–3.
       B.N. x (1863), 345; xiv (1867), 849. Pevsner, *Yorks., W. Riding* (1959), 316.

241   Albert Memorial, Hyde Park, London
       Italian Gothic
       1863–72 Sir G. G. Scott
A rich and costly work erected by national subscription. Sicilian marble, granite,
mosaic work, enamelled stones, and gun metal with profuse gilding, are used in
its construction and decoration. A colossal statue of the late Prince Consort will
occupy a central position under the canopy, and four groups of sculpture emblematical of the four quarters of the globe, are to be placed at each angle of the base.
Total height of the monument, 175 ft; base about 70 ft square.
       Builder xxi (1863), 361, 370–1; xxv (1867), 588, 590; xxxi (1873), 917–18,
926. *A.R.* cxxxv (1964), 422–8. *C.L.* cxxx (1961), 1514–16. Scott, *The National
Monument to H.R.H. the Prince Consort* (1873). Pevsner, *London* ii (1952),
254–5.

242   Cranleigh School, Surrey (Ex Surrey County Schools)
       Middle and Early Pointed
       1863–70 H. Woodyer
Constructed of red and black bricks, with Bath and red Mansfield stone, coloured
marbles, etc. This building will accommodate 330 boys and a staff of masters.
Frontage, 350 ft; depth, 90 ft; hall, 100 × 30 ft; chapel, 110 × 70 ft.
       Eccles. xxix (1868), 314. *The Architect* ii (1869), 22.

243 **St Paul, Langleybury, Hertfordshire**
Middle Pointed
1863–5 H. Woodyer
Built of squared black flint and Bath stone. Spire of shingled oak. Length, 120 ft; width, 50 ft; nave 40 ft high; height of spire, 130 ft.
Pevsner, *Herts.* (1953), 152.

244 **All Saints, Clifton, Bristol**
Early Middle Pointed
1863 G. E. Street
Destroyed in the Second World War
Built of local stone, Bath and Pennant stone. Works still in progress. At present the chancel, the chancel aisles, vestries, choir and practising room are completed.
B.N. xii (1865), 546–8. *A.R.* xcii (1942), 18. Pevsner, *N. Somerset and Bristol* (1958), 387.

245 **St Peter, Vauxhall, London**
Early 13th century
1863–4 J. L. Pearson
Built of brick and Bath stone. This church is one of the few modern ones that have been groined throughout. All the groining (except the ribs) is in brickwork. The plan consists of a nave and aisles, large chancel with chancel aisles, and an additional large aisle added on the north side of the nave. The interior effect is very striking. The chancel wall decorated with figure subjects. The altar is detached from the east wall, and is rich in material and workmanship. Nave, 78 × 24 ft; chancel, 42 × 23 ft; height of nave to groining, 47 ft. The design includes a tower and spire (220 ft high) to be erected on the north side of the nave.
Eccles. xxii (1861), 56–8; xxv (1864), 272–4. *Builder* xxii (1864), 327; xxiii (1865), 626–7. *B.N.* xii (1865), 581, 715, 755, 847. Pevsner, *London* ii (1952), 272. Clarke, *Parish Churches of London* (1966), 236, figs. 177, 178.

246 **County Hospital, Winchester, Hampshire**
Decorated
1863–8 W. Butterfield
In this building, many modern features, such as sash windows, etc., are introduced. Constructed of brick and Bath stone. Owing to the site of this building (on the side of a hill), it presents one more storey on the south or garden front than on the north or road front.
Builder xix (1861), 813; xx (1862), 701; xxi (1863), 15. Pevsner and Lloyd, *Hants.* (1967), 706.

247 **All Saints, Cambridge**
Early Pointed
1863–4 G. F. Bodley

This church is an example of the architect's design after his return to strictly English types of Gothic, from which in his earlier works he had considerably departed.

Eccles. xii (1861), 124; xxiv (1863), 127–8; *Builder* xxviii (1870), 891. *R.I.B.A. Jnl.* xvii (1910), 311. Pevsner, Cambs. (1954), 174–5.

248 **Town Hall, Congleton, Cheshire**
Geometrical Pointed
1864–6 E. W. Godwin

An excellent example of secular Gothic. Built of local stone and brick. General dimensions: 144 × 71 ft; height to ridge of roof, 54 ft; height to top of tower, 109 ft (see p. 354).

Builder xxii (1864), 528–30. *B.N.* xii (1864), 10–11.

249 **St Anne's Court, Wardour Street, London**
13th century
1864–5 W. Burges
Demolished

Built of brick and-stone. The ground floor of this building is a school-room, and the walls of the rooms above (ten on each floor) are carried on arches. A simple but well-proportioned and judicious design, admirably adapted for its homely purpose. The fenestration of the lowest storey is original and effective. The two central arches of this building, from the ground level to the top storey, are left open and unglazed to light a stone staircase. The result is very picturesque.

Eccles. xxv (1864), 248. *B.N.* xiv (1867), 24, 26. Pevsner, *London* i (1962), 605.

250 **St Richard, Slindon, Sussex (R.C.)**
13th century
1864–5 C. A. Buckler

Erected for the Earl of Newburgh. The plan comprises a nave (62 × 23 ft), chancel and sacristy, north porch and south aisle of four bays. Built of red brick faced with flint and dressings of Box Hill stone. The roof of the school is of oak, the principals being copied from the remains of an ancient structure.

Builder xxiv (1866), 51. Pevsner and Nairn, *Sussex* (1965), 327.

251 **St Mark, New Brompton, Chatham, Kent**
First Pointed
1866 J. P. St Aubyn

Erected for the Rev. R. Willis. Built of brick, with Bath stone dressings. Nave, 85 × 26 ft; aisles, 85 × 13 ft; chancel, 39 × 24 ft. The steeple is not yet erected.

252 **St Augustine, Penarth, Glamorganshire**
Early Decorated
1866 W. Butterfield
Erected for the Baroness Windsor. Built of various local stones.

253 **University Buildings, Aberystwyth (Ex Castle Hotel)**
Geometrical Decorated
1864–5 J. P. Seddon
Rebuilt 1887–8 by Seddon and J. C. Carter
This large and important building was originally commenced as an hotel for T. Savin Esq., but has been since sold to the promoters of the proposed College. It is built of sandstone (yellowish-drab colour), with Combe Down and Bath stone dressings. The frontage is above 440 ft; the average depth, 75 ft. Cost about £100,000. It is still unfinished.
   Eccles. xxvii (1866), 251. *Builder* xxii (1864), 659; xxiii (1865), 851; xlvii (1884), 850; xlviii (1885), 825; xlix (1885), 215, 591, 635; l (1886), 847; li (1886), 226; lii (1887), 169, 335, 863; liv (1888), 299. *B.N.* xiii (1866), 870–1.

254 **St John the Evangelist, Middlesbrough, Yorkshire**
Geometrical
1864–6 J. Norton
Church, school and parsonage
Built of red brick, with Brotton sandstone dressings; roofed with Bangor slates. General dimensions, 140 × 85 ft.
   Eccles. xxi (1860), 114; xxiii (1862), 62–3; xxiv (1863), 188–9; xxvi (1865), 55. *Builder* xxiii (1865), 872–4. A. Savage, *The Parsonage in England* (1964), 136, fig. xxxii. Pevsner, *Yorks., N. Riding* (1966), 249.

255 **Beckett's Bank, Leeds**
Venetian Gothic
1863–7 Sir G. G. Scott
Demolished 1964
Erected for Messrs Beckett and Denison, at a cost of £33,000. Built of brick and stone. Plan dimensions, about 120 × 120 ft.
   Builder xxv (1867), 449–50. Pevsner, *Yorks., W. Riding* (1959), 318.

256 **Clydesdale and North of Scotland Bank, Lombard St, London**
13th century
1864–6 A. Waterhouse
Erected for Messrs Alexander, Cunliffe and Co. Built of Portland stone, with red granite shafts. Lombard Street frontage, 29 ft; Clement's Lane frontage, 63 ft.
   Builder xxii (1864), 770. *B.N.* xii (1864), 613. Pevsner, *London* i (1962), 234.

257   **All Saints, Viney Hill, Gloucestershire**
      Early English
      1865–7 E. Christian
Erected for the Rev. W. H. Bathurst. Built of local red sandstone with deal
fittings. General dimensions, 86 × 60 ft.
      Builder xxv (1867), 317.

258   **St Mary the Virgin, Freeland, Oxfordshire**
      Early 13th and 14th centuries
      1869–71 J. L. Pearson
      Church and parsonage
Erected for the Raikes and Taunton families. The plan of the church consists of
nave and chancel, with *parvise* over. Tower and vestry on north side of chancel,
which is groined in stone, and has an apsidal end and painted walls. A band of
figure subjects, 3 ft high, is carried all round. Below this is a rich diapered pattern,
and above is another band of figures extending to the window jambs. These are
for the most part treated in outline. An alabaster reredos, detached from east wall,
contains a low relief sculpture of the Crucifixion with angels on each side bearing
emblems. There is a metal rood screen. Nave, 44 × 21 ft and 29 ft high; chancel,
33 × 15 ft and 22 ft high. Built of local stone for walls, with Bath stone for
dressings and interior.
      The parsonage is built of brick and mortar, with open timber work. It com-
municates with the church by a corridor on the north side.
      Sherwood and Pevsner, Oxon. (1974), 606–7.

259   **St Mary Magdalene, Tavistock, Devon (R.C.)**
      13th century
      1865–8 H. Clutton
A large church, built of local stone, with Bath stone dressings. Very simple in its
general design, but with many peculiarities of detail. The nave arcade consists of
obtusely pointed arches, slightly stilted, and carried on piers, resembling in plan
the intersection of two cylinders. The chancel walls are arcuated to a height of
about 10 ft from the floor, to a cornice from which a ceiled roof springs. The
nave roof is open timbered, with tie beams. The pulpit is of stone, circular,
enriched with diapered carving, raised on a single marble column, and reached
by a long flight of steps. Externally, the tower, with its louvred windows and square
spire, forms a striking feature. It stands apart from the main body of the church.
      Pevsner, *S. Devon* (1952), 277.

260   **St Michael, Chetwynde, Shropshire**
      Geometrical Decorated
      1865–7 B. Ferrey
Erected for Burton Borough Esq. Built of local stone, Broxby tiles, and Devonshire marbles. Nave and south aisle, 57 × 33 ft; chancel, 31 × 19 ft; tower
and spire of north-east angle, 100 ft high. The Archbishop of Dublin (Dr
Whateley) was formerly rector (see p. 220).
      Pevsner, *Salop.* (1958), 97–8.

261 St Mary, Woburn, Bedfordshire
13th century
1865–8 H. Clutton
1890 spire removed
Finely groined throughout. Beneath the chancel is a crypt (52 × 24 ft) to be used as a family vault for the Dukes of Bedford. Built of Chepsham and Bath stones.
Builder xxvi (1868), 746. Pevsner, *Beds., Hunts. and Peterborough* (1968), 164–5, fig. 101.

262 Most Holy Saviour, Aberdeen Park, Islington, London
Early Middle Pointed
1865–6 W. White
Vestry etc., T. Wallen
Cruciform plan: lofty clerestory and central lantern. Built of red and buff-coloured bricks, with a little stone in the tracery, etc. The interior is decorated with bricks, arranged in patterns. Nave arcade of three bays, two wide and one narrow. Piers of brick moulded at angles, and crowned with capitals of peculiar form. The tower is central, and carried up square to a height of 15 or 20 ft above chancel arch, and then becomes octagonal. The easternmost part of the chancel is groined. Dimensions: 105 × 50 ft, and 55 ft high.
Builder xxiv (1866), 781–2; xxv (1867), 549–51. Pevsner, *London* ii (1952), 229. Clarke, *Parish Churches of London* (1966), 95–6, fig. 66.

263 Notre Dame Training College, Mount Pleasant, Liverpool (R.C.): Chapel and Convent Cloister
Early Pointed
1865–7 M. E. Hadfield and C. Hadfield
Much altered
Erected for the Community of Sisters of Notre-Dame. Built of brick and stone. Vaulted internally. Chapel, 90 × 30 ft and 39 ft high (see p. 350).
Builder xxv (1867), 398. *B.N.* xiv (1867), 578, 580. Pevsner, *South Lancs.* (1969), 185.

264 St David, Neath, Glamorgan
First Pointed
1865–8 J. Norton
Built of local Pennant, with Bath stone dressings, lined with brick. Tiled roof. General dimensions, 156 × 97 ft.
Eccles. xxvi (1865), 51–2. *Builder* xxii (1864), 729; xxiv (1866), 928; xxv (1867), 354–5; xxvi (1868), 431–2.

265   St Saviour, Eastbourne, Sussex
      Early Middle Pointed
      1865–8 G. E. Street
Built of red brick. Eastern part groined in brick and stone. Steeple and decorations
still in progress.
      Builder xxv (1867), 175–6. *B.N.* xix (1870), 45. Pevsner and Nairn, *Sussex*
(1965), 487.

266   Union Society, Cambridge
      13th century
      1865–7 A. Waterhouse
      Altered 1885, 1933–4, 1949
Built of red brick with Casterton stone dressings. General dimensions: 140 × 90
ft; debating room, 60 × 30 ft.
      The Times 31 Oct. 1866, p. 10. Pevsner, *Cambs.* (1954), 172.

267   Emmanuel, Clifton, Bristol
      First Pointed
      1865–9 J. Norton
Built of local sandstone with Bath stone dressings. Roofed with green slates.
General dimensions, 147 × 96 ft.
      Builder xxx (1872), 546–7. Pevsner, *N. Somerset and Bristol* (1958), 389.

268   Cork Cathedral (St Finbar), Ireland
      13th century French
      1865–83 W. Burges
This is one of the architect's most important works. Among the more striking
features of the cathedral is the west front with its three portals and rose window,
round which will be placed emblems of the four Evangelists nobly carved. The
transept door is enriched with sculpture. The cathedral has a triforium gallery.
The design, when completed, will include towers and spires at the west end, and
one over the centre of the crux, where the piers constructed to carry it are 7 ft 6 in.
square. The plan consists of a nave, choir, ambulatory and aisles. Length, 162 ft;
height from floor to roof, 68 ft. Built of limestone, Stourton (for piers), and Bath
stone dressings (see p. 354).
      Eccles. xxiii (1862), 183; xxiv (1863), 164, 213–14; xxix (1868), 180, 312.
Builder xxi (1863), 350–1; xxviii (1870), 995. *B.N.* x (1863), 345, 551.
A.R. cxli (1967), 422–30.

269   Holy Trinity, Fonthill Gifford, Wiltshire
      Early English
      1865–6 T. H. Wyatt
Erected for the Marquess of Westminster. Nave, transepts and apsidal chancel.
Tower and spire at south-east.
      Builder xxii (1864), 327. *B.N.* xi (1864), 234. Pevsner, *Wilts.* (1963), 219.

270 **Hutton Hall, Nr Guisborough, Yorkshire**
Early Domestic
1865–8 A. Waterhouse
Erected for J. W. Pease Esq., M.P. Built of red brick, with Gatherley Moor
stone dressings. General dimensions, 150 × 120 ft; stables, 102 × 100 ft.
Pevsner, *Yorks., N. Riding* (1966), 197. Morris, *Seats* iii, 7.

271 **St Saviour, Hoxton, London**
Early Pointed
J. Brooks
1864–6 church
1873 parsonage
Destroyed in the Second World War
In this church the nave and chancel (which is apsidal) are of the same height,
and covered by one continuous roof, and both are lighted by a series of plain
lancet windows in the clerestory. The lower part of the chancel is enriched by
mural arcuation, the arches being trefoil-headed, and surmounted by gablets.
Open roof over nave with semicircular ribs and tie-beams, ceiled roof over chancel.
The capitals of nave arcade are left uncarved, except those at junction of nave and
chancel, where the character of the carving is excellent.
Eccles. xxx (1864), 245. *Builder* xxiv (1866), 366. *B.N.* xii (1865), 880, 883;
xiii (1866), 563. *R.I.B.A. Jnl.* xvii (1910), 496, 514. Pevsner, *London* ii (1952),
384.

272 **St Salvador, Dundee, Scotland**
Geometrical Middle Pointed
1865–7 G. F. Bodley
1869 school
A very originally designed church. The plan includes a long and broad nave,
with low arcades of seven, and very narrow aisles, a spacious chancel aisled on the
south side, and a western narthex. The church is very lofty, and effectively proportioned. On the east gable of the nave roof there is a picturesque bell turret.
Eccles. xx (1859), 385; xxvi (1865), 252.

273 **Holy Trinity, Bingley, Yorkshire**
Early Pointed French
1866–8 R. Norman Shaw
1880 tower
Church, vicarage, school and cottages
Built of a common but beautifully coloured walling stone. The plan consists of
a nave, aisles, large west porch, chancel, chancel aisles, and vestry. Tower and
spire are to rise over west portion of chancel. All the walls are very substantial,

varying from 3 ft to 7 ft 6 in. in thickness. Rather lofty clerestory. Alabaster and gold mosaic reredos. Organ in black case with polished metal pipes. Oak chancel fittings. Nave, 70 × 29 ft, chancel, 37 × 20 ft; nave, about 50 ft high.

Builder xxiv (1866), 431. Pevsner, *Yorks., W. Riding* (1968), 102–3, 616, fig. 15.

274 **St Michael, Shoreditch, London**
Early Pointed
J. Brooks
1863–5 church
1867 clergy house
1870 school
1870–75 convent hospital; additions by J. D. Sedding

The plan of this church consists of a chancel with transeptal chapels, a nave and aisles, with south porch, and a narthex or west corridor. The windows are filled with plate tracery. Horizontal courses, and patterns of coloured brickwork, are judiciously introduced as a means of decoration. The interior is spacious and lofty.

Eccles. xxiv (1863), 187–8. *Builder* xxv (1867), 812. *B.N.* x (1863), 700; xiii (1866), 644, 781; xxv (1873), 620, 622, 624, 626–7, 629, 631, 646, 652–3; xxix (1875), 596–7; xxx (1876), 372. *R.I.B.A. Jnl.* xvii (1910), 496, 514. H. Muthesius, *Die Neuere Kirchliche Baukunst in England* (Berlin 1901), 40, pls. viii, ix no. 2. Pevsner, *London* ii (1962), 303–4. Clarke, *Parish Churches of London* (1966), 151–2.

275 **International College, Spring Grove, Isleworth, Middlesex**
14th century
1866–9 J. Norton and P. E. Masey

Erected for the International Education Society. Built of brick, with Bath stone dressings. Roofed with green and blue slates. Dimensions of centre and one wing completed 200 × 130 ft.

Builder xxv (1867), 128–9, 549. *I.L.N.* li (1867), 63–4.

276 **All Saints Hospital, Eastbourne, Sussex**
Middle Pointed
1866–70 H. Woodyer

Erected for the Sisterhood of All Saints', Margaret Street, London, and consists of a home and hospital which will contain about 300 inmates. Built of red brick and Bath stone. Length of building, 348 ft, covering an area of 73,000 sq. ft (see p. 331).

Pevsner and Nairn, *Sussex* (1965), 488.

277 New University Club, St James's Street, London
      13th century
      1866–8 A. Waterhouse
      Demolished
The first London club erected of a Medieval character in design, and presenting a marked contrast to the adjacent buildings. Portland stone front. Fire-proof floors, the construction of which is left visible.
      Builder xxvi (1868), 356–7.

278 All Saints, Chigwell Row, Essex
      Geometrical Decorated
      1866–7 J. P. Seddon
      1918–19 chancel rebuilt
Erected for the Rev. T. Lawrence. Church, 130 × 60 ft and 60 ft high; built of Godalming stone, with Bath stone dressings. Parsonage of yellow brick, cost £4,200. Church not finished.
      Builder xxv (1867), 738. Pevsner and Radcliffe, *Essex* (1965), 122–3.

279 Holy Trinity, West Cliff, Folkestone, Kent
      Early English
      1866–9 E. Christian
Erected for the Earl of Radnor.

280 Warehouse, Upper Thames Street, London
      [Plate 20]
      13th century
      1866 W. Burges
      Demolished
One of the very few instances of the successful adaptation of Gothic for commercial purposes at the east end of London. Mr Burges only added the front (18 ft wide), being limited to the floor lines of an existing building. It is constructed of brick, and decorated with a piece of sculpture in bas-relief representing Commerce.
      Eccles. xxvii (1866), 310–11. *Builder* xxiv (1866), 850–1, 876. *B.N.* xiii (1866), 780. Pevsner, *London* i (1962), 268.

281 Heron's Ghyll, Sussex
      Tudor
      1866–7 J. F. Bentley
Additions to the residence of Coventry Patmore Esq., including an entirely new front. The portions principally studied were the drawing-room and dining-room. The former is lighted by a bay window. Built of local sandstone with tiled roofs and oak fittings. Frontage, 98 ft.
      W. de l'Hôpital, *Westminster Cathedral and its Architect* ii (1919), 480–3, 485, 537.

282   University Buildings, Glasgow
       Early Decorated
       1866–71 Sir G. G. Scott
One of Mr Scott's largest and most important works, having cost nearly £300,000.
It is built of Griffnock and Bannockburn stone. The north frontage is 650 ft;
the south frontage, 629 ft; width, 325 ft.
       Builder xxiv (1866), 32, 368–70; xxvii (1869), 357; xxviii (1870), 915, 964–7.
B.N. xvi (1869), 404.

283   St Pancras Station and Hotel, London
       Venetian Gothic
       1866–74 Sir G. G. Scott
A capacious and elaborately detailed structure of brick, stone and iron, the first
instance of the adaptation of Medieval design for such a purpose in London.
       Builder xxiv (1866), 67–8, 340; xxvi (1868), 744. *B.N.* xvi (1869), 136–41,
280–1; xxvi (1874), 437, 554, 558–9. Pevsner, *London* ii (1952), 368–9.
J. Simmons, *St Pancras Station* (1968).

284   Christ Church, Oxford: Meadow Buildings
       1866–70 Sir T. N. Deane
An important block of buildings facing the Broad Walk. The details are very
peculiar and characteristic of the designer's hand, but much of the decorative
carved work is left unfinished, which greatly detracts from the general effect.
The works cost £30,000 (see p. 287).
       Builder xx (1862), 856–7; xxiv (1866), 337, 346–7.

285   St Andrew, Plaistow, Essex
       Early Pointed
       1867–70 J. Brooks
       Church, parsonage and schools
A lofty church built of Kentish rag, with freestone dressings. The nave is divided
into four bays by obliquely pointed arches of wide span. Semicircular apse lighted
by lancet windows. Chancel separated from chancel aisles by arches filled with
tracery. Arcaded clerestory. Total length about 160 ft.
       Builder xxv (1867), 770; xxviii (1870), 632; xxx (1872), 615. *B.N.* xix
(1870), 189, 207, 391. *R.I.B.A. Jnl.* xvii (1910), 514. Pevsner and Radcliffe,
Essex (1965), 315.

286   Clarendon Laboratory, Oxford
       Early Pointed
       1867–70 Sir T. N. Deane
       Altered

A very picturesque and ably designed building treated with great refinement in detail. It can scarcely be referred to any particular style, but bears evidence of a taste for French Gothic of an early date, while a slight Italian element is represented by the use of colour introduced here and there in bands of red Mansfield and a greenish local stone, the main body of the walls being from Bath quarries. The interior of the laboratory is very ingeniously arranged as to the timbers of its roof and floors, which are of good constructive purpose.

Builder xxvi (1868), 875; xxvii (1869), 386–8, 1023.

287 Humewood, Wicklow, Ireland
Baronial Gothic
1867–70 W. White
1873 Additions by J. Brooks

A large mansion erected for W. W. Fitzwilliam Dick Esq., M.P. Every portion of this building, down to the minutest detail of the fittings, was executed from designs carefully worked out by the architect. General dimensions, 160 × 40 ft; tower 80 ft high (see p. 362).

Builder xxvi (1868), 587–9. *R.I.B.A. Trans.* xix (1868–9), 78–88. *C.L.* cxliii (1968), 1212–15, 1282–5, 1686.

288 St Michael, Lowfield Heath, Surrey
13th century
1867 W. Burges

Erected for the Rev. T. Burmingham. This church has a narthex, or porch, extending across its west front. Sculpture is introduced round the west (rose) window representing the four ages, and over the west door (St Michael and the Dragon). The spire is of wood, covered with oak shingle. Nave, 42 × 23 ft; chancel, 25 × 15 ft. Built of local and Bath stone.

Nairn and Pevsner, *Surrey* (1962), 304.

289 Our Lady of Victories, Kensington, London (R.C.)
Geometrically Decorated
1867–9 G. Goldie and Child
Destroyed in the Second World War

This church, though yet wanting much of its internal fittings and decoration, is rich in sculptured detail, which has been carefully designed and executed with refinement. The great internal height of this building gives it a special character. The exterior is, unfortunately, under the disadvantage of being almost hidden from the Hammersmith Road by intervening houses. When these are removed, the fine western doorway and façade will be seen (see p. 349).

Builder xxvi (1868), 332, 507, 511. *The Architect* ii (1869), 116. *A.R.* xci (1942), 16.

290   St Edward, Windsor, Berkshire (R.C.)
    13th century
    1867–8 C. A. Buckler
Erected for the Rev. A. Applegarth. Built of Kentish rag and Box Hill stone.
Nave of five bays, 80 × 24 ft, with aisles 11 ft wide. Clustered columns and
arches of Painswick stone. Clerestory of cusped triangular windows. Open timber
roof, of which the principals rest on engaged shafts. West window of five lights
with geometrical tracery. In the gable above is a canopied niche containing a
figure of St Edward the Confessor. Lady Chapel at east end of south aisle.
    Builder xxv (1867), 398. Pevsner, *Bucks.* (1966), 300.

291   Sligo Cathedral, Ireland (R.C.)
    Norman
    1867 onwards G. Goldie
Remarkable both for size and character. Nave and aisles: western tower with
flanking staircase; turrets, for access to triforia (used for children); transepts; deep
choir; semicircular apsidal sanctuary, with procession aisle and eastern Lady
Chapel; chapter house, and extensive sacristies adjoining. Total internal length,
211 ft; width across transepts, 115 ft; internal height, 61 ft. Built of local blue
limestone, with partial introduction of sandstone from Donegal. Work still in
progress.

292   Keble College, Oxford
    Decorated
    1868–78 W. Butterfield
    1892; 1957 additions
Built of local brick and Bath stone, with mural bands and patterns of different
coloured brick, which constitute the chief decoration of its façades. This treatment
of brickwork is of course a great novelty at Oxford, and has been much criticized.
The details are refined and artistic in design. The buildings at present erected
enclose the greater part of a quadrangle, 243 × 220 ft.
    Builder xxvi (1868), 323; xxvii (1869), 1023; xxviii (1870), 529.

293   St Chad, Haggerston, London
    Early Pointed
    1867–9 J. Brooks
    Church and parsonage
A very lofty church, faced internally with brick. It has a semicircular apse groined
in brick with stone ribs; nave arches of wide span and simply moulded, carried
on short round pillars. Lofty clerestory lighted by four large windows on each
side. The south chapel is vaulted like the chancel and forms an interesting feature
(see p. 364).

Builder xxv (1867), 812. *B.N.* xix (1870), 188; xxx (1876), 194, 199.
R.I.B.A. Jnl. xvii (1910), 498, 514. Pevsner, *London* ii (1952), 382. Clarke,
Parish Churches of London (1966), 152, fig. 118.

294 Bank, Farnham, Surrey
      Old English
      1867–8 R. Norman Shaw
      Much altered
Bank offices, with residence above. Erected for James Knight Esq. An excellent
example of the revival of ancient half-timbered style of work for house-building.
Two large bay windows project from the first floor, and are carried up three
storeys in height, terminating with gable fronts. A stone staircase leads from ground
to first floor. The chimneypieces, grates, and all internal fittings are in character
with the building, and were expressly designed for it. Large chimney-shafts of
cut and rubbed Farnham bricks with carved brick panels.
      Nairn and Pevsner, *Surrey* (1962), 202.

295 Bristol Cathedral: Nave, Porch and Towers
      Middle Pointed
      1867–88 G. E. Street
New nave, north porch and western steeples. Constructed of Doulting stone.
      Eccles. xxviii (1867), 194–201. *Builder* xxiv (1866), 930; xxviii (1870), 390.
The Architect i (1869), 104–5. Pevsner, *N. Somerset and Bristol* (1958), 380.

296 St Columba, Haggerston, London
      Early Pointed
      J. Brooks
      1865–6 school
      1868–9 church
      1873 parsonage
A remarkably original and boldly-conceived design. The east end of this church,
which abuts on the Kingsland Road, forms the sacrarium. The choir is placed
under the central tower, which is groined. The transepts are short and barrel-
vaulted. There are no aisle windows, the clerestory being of lofty proportions.
Built of brick, with stone piers, etc. (see p. 365).
      Eccles. xxvi (1865), 254. *Builder* xxv (1867), 812; xxvii (1869), 984, 987,
1013. *B.N.* xxii (1872), 52; xxiv (1873), 242. *R.I.B.A. Jnl.* xvii (1910), 496,
514. Clarke, *Parish Churches of London* (1966), 152–3, fig. 117.

297 Balliol College, Oxford: Additions
      13th century
      1867–9 A. Waterhouse
New front towards Broad Street, master's house, etc. One of the most important
modern buildings of the university. Great breadth of effect is gained by keeping

windows small, and leaving large masses of wall surface. Central portion, with groined entrance porch below, rises in a tower-like block above the rest. High-pitched roof, covered with Staffordshire tiles and picturesque dormers. Built of Bath stone. General dimensions: Broad Street front, 240 ft; front towards Trinity, 107 ft (see p. 361).

The Architect i (1869), 6. Sherwood and Pevsner, *Oxon.* (1974), 100–1.

298 Easneye, Ware, Hertfordshire

13th century Domestic
1867–9 A. Waterhouse

Erected for T. Fowell Buxton Esq. Built of red brick and terra cotta, with tiled roof. General dimensions: house, 170 × 100 ft; stables, 140 × 115 ft.

Builder xxv (1867), 651. Pevsner, *Herts.* (1952), 263.

299 St Mary's, Farnham Royal, Buckinghamshire

Early Decorated
1867–9 W. E. Nesfield

Nave and aisles erected on the site of an old church, the chancel of which is retained. Built of flint and Bath stone. General dimensions, 60 × 40 ft. This is a small but characteristic specimen of the architect's skill in design. Proportions good; quiet and refined in detail. The work was undertaken mainly through the exertions of H. Vallance Esq., who resides in the neighbourhood, and to whose house Mr Nesfield has made some important additions (see p. 345).

Builder xxvi (1868), 475. *A.R.* ii (1897), 23–5. Pevsner, *Bucks.* (1960), 133.

300 Allerton Priory, Nr Liverpool

13th century Domestic
1867–70 A. Waterhouse

Erected for J. Grant Morris Esq. Built of grey brick, with local red sandstone dressings.

Pevsner, *South Lancs.* (1969), 210.

301 St Thomas of Canterbury, Exton, Rutland (R.C.)

13th century with later details
1868 C. A. Buckler

Erected for the Earl of Gainsborough. Cruciform and apsidal in plan. Built over a vaulted crypt of brick lighted by windows in the plinth of the superstructure. An aisle between the sanctuary and sacristy opens into the north transept; an apse at the end of the same forms the baptistery, over which rises a bell-cote. The Lady Chapel is in the south transept. The building is connected with the mansion by upper and lower tribunes lined with oak panelling.

Morris, *Seats* iv, 5. Pevsner, *Leics. and Rutland* (1960), 298.

302   St Mary of the Angels, Bayswater, London (R.C.)
        Transitional 13th century
        1868–72 additions by J. F. Bentley to work by Meyer *c.* 1857
This work consisted principally in the addition of two chapels and baptistery to church, and an oratory to the adjoining presbytery. The building materials used were stone, brick and grey slates.
        W. de l'Hôpital, *Westminster Cathedral and its Architect* ii (1919), 366, 377, 441–7, 525, 529, 539, 558, fig. 52. Pevsner, *London* ii (1952), 299–300.

303   Roundwyck House, Ebernoe, Sussex
        Late 13th century
        1868 J. L. Pearson
Erected for Captain Penfold. Contains three reception rooms on ground floor, kitchen, offices, etc., with large dairy and farm buildings attached. One storey of bedrooms over. This house is treated in a very picturesque manner, and the local materials used – viz. stone, brick, tiles, and oak timber – are ingeniously inter-mixed in the design. It was at first intended only for a farmhouse, but it afterwards expanded into a small residence in connection with the farm.

304   St Mary, Kings Walden, Hertfordshire
        15th century
        1868–70 W. E. Nesfield and R. Norman Shaw
A new chancel (40 × 18 ft). Erected for C. Cholmely Hale Esq. The nave of this church was restored at the same time. Materials used, flint and "clunch", with English oak for fittings.
        A.R. i (1897), 26–8. Pevsner, *Herts.* (1953), 148–9.

305   Broadlands, Hampshire: Lodges
        Old English Domestic
        1868–70 W. E. Nesfield
Erected for Viscountess Palmerston. The entrance lodge is of half-timbered work, and is very elaborately executed in oak.
        A.R. i (1897), 239–40. *C.L.* liii (1923), 434, 466. Pevsner and Lloyd, *Hants.* (1967), 145.

306   St John, Torquay, Devon
        Early Middle Pointed
        1868–71 G. E. Street
        1884–5 tower by A. E. Street
This church when completed will be one of the architect's most successful works, and certainly one of the most notable which has been erected in Devonshire during the Revival. The chancel is a very spacious one, carefully groined in brick, with stone ribs. It opens by two pointed arches to a north aisle used as the organ

chamber. The side walls of the sanctuary are arcuated and richly panelled. A bas-relief, representing the Crucifixion, occupies the centre of the reredos. The east window of five lights is filled with stained glass, admirable in design and colour (see p. 325).

Eccles. xxiv (1863), 126–7. *Builder* xxviii (1870), 358. *B.N.* xv (1868), 705. R. J. E. Boggis, *St John's Torquay* (Torquay, 1930). Pevsner, *S. Devon* (1952), 293.

307   Huntsham Court, Devon
Tudor

1868–70 B. Ferrey

Erected for C. A. Williams Troyte Esq. The old mansion, replaced by the present building, was entirely dilapidated, and had been much disfigured by modern additions. General dimensions: 106 × 53 ft; office wing, 60 × 30 ft; entrance tower, 18 × 18 ft on plan. Built of Hamden Hill and local stone; roofed with Bridgwater tiles; oak used in ceilings, etc.

Pevsner, *N. Devon* (1952), 104.

308   St John the Baptist, Tue Brook, Liverpool
Middle Pointed

1867–70 G. F. Bodley

Erected at the sole cost of the Rev. J. C. Reade and Mrs Reade. For correctness of design, refined workmanship, and artistic decoration, this church may take foremost rank among examples of the Revival. It is built of red and white sandstone. The interior is sumptuously decorated with mural paintings executed from the design and under the immediate superintendence of Mr E. Kempe M.A. (see p. 369).

Builder xxv (1867), 317. *R.I.B.A. Jnl.* xvii (1910), 333. Pevsner, *South Lancs.* (1969), 248–9.

309   St Andrew, Toddington, Gloucestershire
Middle Pointed

1868–73 G. E. Street

In course of erection for Lord Sudeley. This church is mainly remarkable for having been executed without any restriction as to cost. The architect has not, however, multiplied its merely decorative features, but the walls are very substantial, and the mouldings elaborate. The chancel, chancel aisle, tower and chapel for monuments, are being groined. The nave is to have an oak roof. The masonry is of wrought stone from quarries in the neighbourhood.

Builder xxvii (1869), 357. *B.N.* xviii (1870), 13.

310   St Margaret, Toxteth, Liverpool
      Middle Pointed
      1868–9 G. E. Street
Erected at the expense of Robert Horsfall Esq. A good example of a town church
(to hold 1,000 people), built very cheaply, as far as the exterior is concerned, in
order to reserve means for ensuring an effective interior. The total cost of the
church and clergy home was only £11,000. Materials used, brick and marble.
      Pevsner, *South Lancs.* (1969), 244.

311   St Mary, Carlisle
      Geometrical Pointed
      1868–70 E. Christian
Built of red and white sandstone, with marble columns, etc. General dimensions,
98 × 64 ft.
      Builder xxvi (1868), 475.

312   Leyswood, Sussex
      Old English
      1868–9 R. Norman Shaw
      Largely demolished
Erected for James W. Temple Esq., in the style of ancient Sussex houses. The
buildings are grouped on three sides of an open court, the access to which is by
an entrance porch under a tower. The picturesque assemblage of steep roofs,
abutting on each other in every variety of form, the lofty brick chimney shafts
and the gabled fronts with their quaintly carved barge-boards, tile-weathering,
and mullioned windows, combine to render this mansion one of the most interesting examples of the Revival (see p. 343).
      Builder xxviii (1870), 359. *B.N.* xviii (1870), 370. Pevsner and Nairn,
Sussex (1965), 512.

313   St Luke, Kentish Town, London
      13th century
      1867–9 B. Champneys
Erected for the Rev. C. H. Andrews. The plan is that of a quasi-cruciform church,
the transepts being formed by a continuation of the aisles. The nave is of four
bays, with clerestory, lighted by lancet windows. The chancel is apsidal, lighted
by three windows of plate tracery. The tower stands in piers between apse and
base. Beneath it are the choir stalls. The apse is groined in brick with stone ribs.
The walls are of red Suffolk brick, with stone dressings, columns, etc. General
dimensions, 127 × 60 ft. Height of tower, 115 ft.
      Builder xxvii (1869), 1009; xxviii (1870), 704–7. Pevsner, *London* ii (1952),
360. Clarke, *Parish Churches of London* (1966), 145, fig. 110.

314   St Luke's Parsonage, Kentish Town, London
        Old English
        1868–9 B. Champneys
        Demolished
Erected for the Rev. C. H. Andrews. In design the style is of a mixed character,
being Gothic in general grouping and some details, while certain features, such
as the sash windows, etc., belong to the "Queen Anne" period. General dimensions
about 44 ft square.

315   Dromore Castle, Co. Limerick, Ireland
        Anglo-Irish Geometrical
        1868–70 E. W. Godwin
        Dismantled
Erected for the Earl of Limerick. A well-studied and most successful work, in
the execution of which the architect was consulted on every point from the choice
of site to the design of furniture. It is rich is carved work, stained and painted
glass, ornamental tiles, marble inlay, and decorative painting, a portion of which
was entrusted to Mr H. Marks, A.R.A. General dimensions: banqueting hall,
56 × 30 ft, and 36 ft high; gateway, 23 × 30 ft and 60 ft high; keep tower,
37 × 32 ft and 85 ft high.
    Constructed of local limestone with brick lining.
    Builder xxvii (1869), 358. *B.N.* xiv (1867), 224, 758; xvi (1869), 404, 533.
C.L. cxxxvi (1964), 1274–7.

316   The Annunciation, Chislehurst, Kent
        Early Pointed
        1868–70 J. Brooks
One of the architect's most successful works, remarkable for the quiet dignity of
its composition, and for the careful study of its details. The choir is placed over
open areas left in the foundations, in order to insure a proper effect of sound.
The nave piers are round, with shallow capitals and square abaci, the arches above
being simply chamfered. The arches which enclose the chancel on the north and
south sides are moulded with great refinement (see p. 366).
    R.I.B.A. Jnl. xvii (1910), 504.

317   Cookridge Convalescent Hospital, Leeds
        Old English
        1868–9 R. Norman Shaw
        1893 extended
Erected for J. Metcalfe Smith Esq., as a memorial to his father. To accommodate
100 patients besides matron, servants, etc. A long building with eight wards (the
largest 86 × 24 ft and 20 ft high), a centre building with long wings extending
right and left, kitchens, etc., in the rear. Red brick ground floor with stone mullions,

etc., all weather-tiled above to keep the wards warm and dry. Rooms heated throughout with hot-water apparatus. An excellent work and very characteristic of the architect's taste in design.

B.N. xiv (1867), 854. Pevsner, *Yorks., W. Riding* (1959), 331.

318 Gonville and Caius College, Cambridge: Tree Court
François I
1868–70; 1873 A. Waterhouse

A very important and successful work, but rather too late to be properly included among examples of the Gothic revival. General dimensions: Trinity Street front, 162 ft; Trinity Lane front, 153 ft; tower, 105 ft high. Built of Ancaster and Casterton stone.

Builder xxvii (1869), 358; xxxi (1873), 544, 547. Pevsner, *Cambs.* (1954), 67–8.

319 Sunnydene, Rockhills, Sydenham
Tudor and Jacobean
1868–70 J. F. Bentley

Erected for Richard Sutton Esq. A well-appointed residence, designed with great care, the garden, etc., being laid out in a style corresponding with the date of the architecture. The house is of red brick with stone dressings, and has a tiled roof. The internal fittings are chiefly of wainscot. General dimensions, 110 × 48 ft.

W. de l'Hôpital, *Westminster Cathedral and its Architect* ii (1919), 474–5, 537.

320 Denstone College, Staffordshire
Early Pointed
1868–72 W. Slater and R. H. Carpenter
1879–82 chapel, Carpenter and Ingelow

In connection with St Nicholas's College, Lancing. Planned in the form of the letter H with two quadrangles each open on one side, measuring respectively 200 × 160 ft and 180 × 160 ft. The school will accommodate 400 boys, and includes a chapel, dining-hall, large school-room, class rooms, offices, etc., and eight dormitories for fifty boys each, with residences for masters, etc. The dormitory wings are three storeys high with ranges of lancet windows. The principal school-room is flanked by two lofty water towers terminating in pyramidal roofs. The grand entrance is in the centre under the school-room. Materials used, brick faced with Alton stone. The building stands on the brow of a range of hills overlooking the beautiful valley near Alton Towers.

Builder xxvi (1868), 801–2; xxx (1872), 506–7. Pevsner, *Staffs.* (1974), 114–15.

321 Our Lady of Mount Carmel
and St Joseph, Battersea, London (R.C.): Convent School
13th century
1868–70 C. A. Buckler

Erected for the Hon. Mrs E. Petre and Mrs B. Shea. Built of stock bricks, with white moulded Suffolk bricks for door and window jambs. Arches pointed and segmental. Stepped gables and dormers. Angular chimney shafts, etc.

322 Seacox Heath, Flimwell, Sussex
> 14th century modified
> 1868–71 W. Slater and R. H. Carpenter

Erected for the Rt Hon. G. I. Goschen, M.P. The principal feature in this structure is the hall, 42 ft square in plan and reaching the entire height of the house: open galleries give access to rooms on each floor. The house itself is nearly square, being 90 × 80 ft with a range of office buildings at the north-east angle; height from ground to parapet, 44 ft. Built of local stone.

> *B.N.* xxii (1872), 356–8. Pevsner and Nairn, *Sussex* (1965), 503.

323 St Matthew, Blackmoor, Hampshire
> 13th century
> 1868 A. Waterhouse
> 1869–73; 1882 school and mansion

Erected for Sir Roundell Palmer, Q.C. General dimensions: 120 × 30 ft; tower, 110 ft high. Built of local stone with Bath stone dressings. Open roof of single span, tiled. Internally the walls are of ashlar lined with tiles to a certain height.

> *Builder* xxviii (1870), 358. Pevsner and Lloyd, *Hants.* (1967), 110–11.

324 St John's College, Waterford, Ireland (R.C.)
> Early Pointed
> 1868 G. Goldie

Modified to suit modern requirements. This is the first college erected in Ireland of this character in design (with the exception of part of Maynooth College by A. W. Pugin). The plan includes a spacious library, refectory, cloistered quadrangle, and a large college chapel, besides the usual class and lecture-rooms, etc. The site is remarkably fine, overlooking the town of Waterford and the adjacent mountain ranges. General dimensions: façade, 150 ft long and 57 ft high; quadrangle, 80 × 70 ft. Built of local blue limestone and sandstone.

325 Cardiff Castle: Tower etc.
> 13th century French
> 1868 onwards W. Burges

For the Marquis of Bute. A very carefully designed work, which will include when finished many rich details of sculpture and decorative painting. The tower is 25 ft square on plan, and 130 ft high. It is built of local stone (see p. 355).

> *Builder* xxviii (1870), 359. *B.N.* xviii (1870), 351; xix (1870), 431. *The Architect* xi (1874), 145–50. Morris, *Seats* v, 1. *C.L.* cxxix (1961), 760–3, 822–5, 886–9.

326 **Quy Hall, Stow-cum-Quy, Cambridgeshire**
    Manorial Gothic
    1868–70 W. White
Erected for Clement Francis Esq. Built of thin bricks (red and buff in colour).
General dimensions, 130 × 40 ft.
    Pevsner, *Cambs.* (1954), 375.

327 **Knightshayes Court, Devon**
    13th century
    1869–73 W. Burges
    Altered internally
For J. H. Amory Esq., M.P. A large and important work, executed with great
spirit and a thorough knowledge of detail. Hall, 40 × 24 ft; staircase, 23 × 20
ft; dining-room, 38 × 21 ft. Built of local stone for walling with Ham Hill
dressings. Shafts of Devonshire marble are used for the interior. The hall has an
open timber roof with a minstrels' gallery, etc. The grand staircase is of teak. Iron
window casements are employed (see p. 356).
    B.N. xviii (1870), 351. Pevsner, *N. Devon* (1952), 111. *The Architect* iv
(1870), 10.

328 **St Margaret, Roath, Glamorganshire**
    Early Geometrical
    1869–71 J. Prichard
    1885 Bute chapel
    1919 tower, without spire
Erected at the cost of the Marquess of Bute. The design was adapted to foundations
planned and laid by another architect (Mr Roos). The tower and spire have yet
to be completed. Built of Pennant stone, with dressings of Bath, red limestone, etc.
For the screens, sedilia, pulpit and reredos, the local (Pennarth) alabaster was
chiefly used. Total length internally 82 ft. Across transepts, 69 ft; length of nave,
51 ft.

329 **Powell Almshouses, Fulham, London**
    Geometrical Decorated
    1869–70 J. P. Seddon
A picturesque row of almshouses, two storeys high, intersected by gablets carried
up over first floor windows, which have pointed heads filled with tracery. The
ground floor has bay windows and projecting porches. These are both included
under one line of roof, which runs the whole length of the building. The tower-
like feature with a saddleback roof at one end of the row greatly helps the composition. General dimensions, 200 × 22 ft. Built of York stone with Camden stone
dressings: the roof is covered with Broseley tiles.
    Pevsner, *London* ii (1952), 134.

330   St Peter's Orphanage, Broadstairs, Kent
       Geometrical Decorated
       1869 J. P. Seddon
Erected for the Archbishop of Canterbury and Mrs Tait, at a cost of about
£10,000. The principal elevation is simply but effectively treated. General
dimensions, 130 × 50 ft and 60 ft high. Built of flint with red brick, and Doulting
stone dressings.

331   St Stephen, Hampstead, London
       12th century
       1869 S. S. Teulon
This church, which is built for a congregation of 1,000 persons, has a nave
(90 × 26 ft), aisles, apsidal chancel (groined, with a vaulted crypt below), and
a central tower. These parts, as seen from the road, group admirably together.
The apse is richly decorated with mosaic, and is lighted with lancet windows
filled with plate tracery of varied form. The aisles, which have rather *flat* roofs,
are lighted by square-headed mullioned windows. The intrados of the chancel
arch is corbelled out from panelled blocks richly carved. The open timbered roof
over nave is of excellent design and proportions. The west porch with its long
front and triple archway is very effective. Materials used: brick, stone, granite,
etc. (see p. 368).
    B.N. xiv (1867), 547. *Builder* xxvii (1869), 706–8. Pevsner, *London* ii (1952),
188. Clarke, *Parish Churches of London* (1966), 80, fig. 59.

332   St Michael, Bishop's Stortford, Hertfordshire
       15th century
       1869 J. Clarke
Built of flint and stone. It contains 1,000 sittings, and has no galleries. This work
was to some extent a restoration, but new additions were also made.
    Pevsner, *Herts.* (1952), 62–3, fig. 19.

333   Glenbegh Towers, Co. Kerry, Ireland
       Anglo-Irish Geometrical
       1868–71 E. W. Godwin
       Dismantled
Erected for the Hon. Rowland Winn. Built of local sandstone and brick lining.
General dimensions: 76 × 39 ft, or including courtyards and out-buildings,
131 × 85 ft; height of main roof, 66 ft; of tower, 114 ft.
    D. Harbron, *The Conscious Stone* (1949), 71, 93.

334   Town Hall, Manchester
      [Plate 26]
         13th century
         1868–77 A. Waterhouse
      Built of stone from the neighbourhood of Bradford. General dimensions: Princess
      Street front, 373 ft; Albert Square front, 306 ft; Lloyd Street front, 336 ft;
      height of principal tower, 260 ft from street level.
         Builder xxvi (1868), 317–19; xxviii (1870), 733; lxxxi (1896), 380. *B.N.* xv
      (1868), 314–15; xvi (1869), 11. *The Architect* ii (1869), 54–5. *C.L.* cxli (1967),
      336–9. W. E. A. Axon, *The Town Hall, Manchester* (Manchester, 1878).
      Pevsner, *South Lancs.* (1969), 280–2.

335   The "Bourne" Schools, Farnham, Surrey
         16th century
         1869 B. Champneys
      Erected for the Ven. Archdeacon Allerton. Lower storey of brick; upper "half-
      timbered", with tiles and plaster. Length, 44 ft; breadth, 20 ft; height, 26 ft.

336   Eton College, Buckinghamshire: Tutor's House
         English Domestic
         1869–70 W. White
      Erected for G. G. Mandarin Esq. Built of slate-stone walling with Bath dressings
      and brick lining. Marble shafts and oak fittings. General dimensions, 106 × 84 ft.
         Builder xxix (1871), 585–7.

337   Charterhouse School, Nr Godalming, Surrey
         Middle Pointed
         1869–72 P. C. Hardwick
         1895 hall by Sir A. W. Blomfield
         1922–7 chapel by Sir Giles Gilbert Scott
      Proposed to consist of several separate buildings, each complete in itself, but so
      arranged as to form an architectural group. The centre building, in which a clock
      tower will be the conspicuous feature, is the Gown Boys' house, having on the
      north side the head master's house, and on the south side the chapel and second
      master's house. The school buildings are in the rear of the Gown Boys' house
      with cloisters for access to them from the different houses. General dimensions:
      Head master's house, 80 × 150 ft; frontage of Gown Boys' house, 270 ft. The
      buildings occupy an area of about 350 ft square. Constructed of Bargate stone,
      with Bath stone dressings.
         Builder xxvii (1869), 357–8; xxviii (1870), 566–7; xxx (1872), 984–7. *B.N.*
      xvi (1869), 404. Nairn and Pevsner, *Surrey* (1962), 121–2.

338 **St Mark, Belgrave Gate, Leicester**
    Geometrical Decorated
    1869–70 E. Christian
Erected for W. Perry Herrick Esq. Built of slate-stone walling with Bath dressings and brick lining. Marble shafts and oak fittings. General dimensions, 106 × 84 ft.
    Builder xxviii (1870), 451, 514. *R.I.B.A. Jnl.* xviii (1911), 714–16.

339 **Eaton Hall, Cheshire: Reconstruction**
    13th century
    1867–82 A. Waterhouse
    Largely demolished
This work, undertaken for the Marquis of Westminster, consists of extensive alterations in the main building, such as removing the pointed tracery windows (some of which were of *cast iron*) throughout the entire building, and substituting for the most part square-headed windows; removing old pinnacles and portions of the sham groining and sham buttresses, making the roofs visible internally, etc. Many *additions* are also being carried out, viz. a new library, 90 × 30 ft, with guests' rooms over; a private wing; a chapel with lofty tower; and general re-arrangement of stables. Masonry of Manley stone.
    Builder xxxv (1877), 687; xxxvii (1879), 886–8; xxxix (1880), 699, 700. *B.N.* vi (1859), 751, 755. *C.L.* ii (1897), 182; ix (1901), 496; xlvii (1920), 724. Morris, *Seats* i, 31. Pevsner and Hubbard, *Cheshire* (1971), 207–13.

340 **St Augustine, Queen's Gate, Kensington, London**
    Early Decorated
    1865–76 W. Butterfield
    1928 alterations by Martin Travers
This church when completed will be one of the most original works yet designed by the architect. The treatment of the west end is very peculiar, the elevation presenting a rectangular composition instead of the usual gabled form. It is surmounted by a massive belfry. Spacious nave with bold arcade and lofty clerestory. Cylindrical piers of white and red sandstone in alternate blocks. Walls of stone and brick, arranged in bands and enriched with tiles. Open timbered roof of simple type.
    Bumpus, *London Churches Ancient and Modern* ii [1910], 307–10. Pevsner, *London* ii (1952), 243. Clarke, *Parish Churches of London* (1966), 109–10, fig. 86.

341 **Manor House, Church Preen, Shropshire**
    Shropshire Half-Timbered
    1870–72 R. Norman Shaw
    Largely demolished

For Arthur Sparrow Esq. An extension of a small house which was originally a cell attached to Wenlock Abbey. Constructed of local walling stone, with Longner stone for dressings; weather-tiling, timber, etc.

Builder xxix (1871), 340. Pevsner, *Salop* (1958), 100.

342 St Audrie's, West Quantoxhead, Somerset
Tudor
1870 J. Norton

This work consists in the remodelling and alteration of a mansion for Sir A. Acland Hood, Bt. The new front is dressed with Williton sandstone lined with brick. The roof is covered with Staffordshire tiles. General dimensions, 170 × 150 ft.

Pevsner, *S. and W. Somerset* (1958), 343. *The Architect* viii (1872), 156.

343 Convent of Our Lady, Chichester, Sussex (R.C.)
13th century
1870 C. A. Buckler

Erected for the Carmelite nuns. These buildings are ranged on three sides of a quadrangular cloister. The entrance hall and strangers' rooms occupy the north front. The choir and chapter room are in the east wing; the recreation room, refectory, and offices in the west. The exterior presents a picturesque composition of simple but effective character. Built of brick, with Bosham white moulded bricks for door and window jambs.

BIBLIOGRAPHY

Place of publication: London unless otherwise stated

I Primary

a. Periodicals

Annals of the Fine Arts (1817–20).
Archaeologia (1770–   ).
Archaeological Journal (1845–   ).
Architect (1869–1926); thereafter united with the *Building News*.
Architectural Magazine, ed. J. C. Loudon (1834–8).
Art Journal (1849–1912).
Art Union (1839–48); continued as the *Art Journal*.
Athenaeum (1828–1921).
British Architect (1874–1919).
British Critic (1827–43).
Builder (1843–   ).
Builder's Magazine (1776).
Building News (1855–1926); thereafter united with the *Architect*.
Church Builder (1862–1904).
Civil Engineer and Architect's Journal (1837–67).
Ecclesiologist (Cambridge Camden Society, 1842–68).
Gentleman's Magazine (1731–1868).
Illustrated London News (1843–   ).
Library of the Fine Arts (1831–3).
Repository of Arts (1809–29), published by R. Ackermann.
R.I.B.A. Transactions/Papers/Journal (1842–   ).
St Paul's Ecclesiological Society Transactions (1881–1938).

b. Separate Works

Adam, W., *Vitruvius Scoticus*, 2 vols. (Edinburgh, 1720–40).
Alison, A., *Essays on the Nature and Principles of Taste* (Edinburgh, 1790).
Anderson, R., *Municipal, Commercial and Street Architecture of France and Italy, 12th–15th cs.* (1870–5).
Audsley, W. and G.,
    Cottage, Lodge and Villa Architecture (Glasgow, 1863).
    Polychromatic Decoration (1882).

Ballantine, J., *A Treatise on Painted Glass* (1845).

Barr, J., *Anglican Church Architecture* (Oxford, 1843).

Barry, A., *Life and Works of Sir Charles Barry* (1867).

Bartholemew, A., *Specifications for Practical Architecture* (1841).

Bayley, J., *Four Churches in the Deanery of Buckrose* (n.d.).

Beckford, W., *Vathek* (1786; new ed. 1834).

Benham and Froud, *Illustrations of Medieval Metal Work* [1877].

Bentham, J., *History and Antiquities of Ely* (1771).

Bielefeld, C. F., *Ornaments in every style of design . . . in the improved papier maché* (1840).

Billings, R. W.,
> *Baronial and Ecclesiastical Antiquities of Scotland* (Edinburgh, 1845–52).
> *The Power of Form Applied to Geometrical Tracery* (1851).

[Blackie and Sons], *Villa and Cottage Architecture* (1880).

Blore, E., *Monumental Remains* (1826).

Bloxam, M. H., *Principles of Gothic Architecture* (1882 ed.).

Bowman, H. and Crowther, J. H., *Churches of the Middle Ages*, 2 vols. (1845–53).

Brandon, R. and J. A., *An Analysis of Gothic Architecture* (1849).

Bridgens, R., *Furniture with Candelabra* (1838).

Britton, J.,
> ——*et al.*, *Beauties of England and Wales*, 18 vols. (1801–15).
> *Architectural Antiquities*, 5 vols. (1807–26).
> *Cathedral Antiquities*, 14 vols. (1814–35).

Burke, E., *A Philosophical Enquiry into the Origin of our Ideas on the Sublime and the Beautiful* (1757); ed. J. T. Boulton (1958).

Burges, W.,
> *Art Applied to Industry* (1865).
> *Architectural Drawings* (1870).

Bury, T. Talbot, *Remains of Ecclesiastical Woodwork* (1847).

Cahier, C. and Martin, A. M., *Melanges d'Archéologie*, 10 vols. (Paris, 1847–77).

[Cambridge Camden Society],
> *A Few Words to Church Builders* (1841).
> *Church Enlargement and Church Arrangement* (1842).
> *Twenty Three Reasons for Getting Rid of Church Pues* (1843).
> *A Few Hints on the Practical Study of Ecclesiastical Architecture and Antiquities* (1843 ed.).
> *Hints to Workmen Engaged on Churches* (1844).
> *A Few Words to Church Wardens. i Country Parishes; ii Town Parishes* (1846 ed.).
> *History of Christian Altars* (1847 ed.).
> *Instrumenta Ecclesiastica* (1847; 1856).

Carlyle, T., *Past and Present* (1843); ed. A. M. D. Hughes (1932).

Carter, J.,
> *Ancient Architecture of England*, i (1795–1806), ii (1807–14); ed. J. Britton (1837).
> *Specimens of Ancient Sculpture and Painting*, i (1780–6), ii (1787–94).

Views of Ancient Buildings, 6 vols. (1786–93).

Caumont, Arcisse de, *Abécédaire ou rudiment d'archaeologie*, 3 vols. (1850–62).

Caveler, W., *Select Specimens of Gothic Architecture* (1825).

Chance, Brothers and Co., *Designs for Coloured Ornamental Windows* (Birmingham, 1853).

Charles, R., *The Cabinet Maker* (1868).

Close, F., *The Restoration of Churches is the Restoration of Popery* (Cheltenham, 1844).

Clutton, H., *Domestic Architecture of France* (1853).

Cockerell, C. R., *Iconography of the West Front of Wells Cathedral* (1851).

Colling, J. K.,
    Gothic Ornaments, 2 vols. (1848–53).
    Art Foliage (1865).
    English Medieval Foliage (1874).

Coney, J., *Beauties of Continental Architecture* (1843).

Cotman, J. S. and Turner, H. Dawson, *Architectural Antiquities of Normandy*, 2 vols. (1822).

Cottingham, L. N., *Working Drawings for Gothic Ornaments* (1823).

Cutts, E. L., *Church Furniture and Decoration* (1854).

Dallaway, J.,
    Observations on English Architecture (1806).
    Discourses upon Architecture (1833).

Davie, W. Galsworthy, *Architectural Sketches in France* (1877).

Decker, P., *Gothic Architecture* (1759; reprinted 1968).

Didron, A.,
    Notre-Dame-de-la-Treille (1856).
    Iconographie Chrétienne (Paris, 1843).

Dodsworth, R. and Dugdale, W., *Monasticon Anglicanum*, ed. J. Caley, H. Ellis and Rev. B. Bandinel (1817–30).

Dollman, F. J., *Examples of Ancient Pulpits* (1849).

——and Jobbins, J. R., *Examples of Ancient Domestic Architecture*, 2 vols. (1858–64).

Dresser, C., *Modern Ornamentation* (1886).

[Drummond, H.], *The Principles of Ecclesiastical Buildings and Ornaments* (1851).

Eastlake, C. L., *Hints on Household Taste* (1868; ed. J. Gloag 1970).

Edis, R. W., *Decoration and Furniture of Town Houses* (1881).

Emmett, J. T., *Six Essays* (1891); ed. J. Mordaunt Crook (1972).

Evans, G. G. and Pullan, R. P., *Photographs of Designs for Lille Cathedral* (Wimbourne Minster, 1857).

Evelyn, J., *An Account of Architects and Architecture* (1664); revised ed. (1737).

Fergusson, J., *History of the Modern Styles of Architecture*, ed. R. Kerr (1872).

Ferrey, B., *Recollections of A. W. N. Pugin and his father Augustus Pugin* (1861); ed. C. Wainright (1978).

Freeman, E. A., *Historical and Architectural Sketches* (1876).

Gibbs, J.,
    Gothic Ornament and Furniture (1853).
    English Gothic Architecture (1855).
    Ecclesiastical and Domestic Ornaments (n.d.).

Gilbert, J., *Fragments towards the History of Stained Glass* (n.d.).
Gilpin, W., *Three Essays on Picturesque Beauty* (1794).
Gilpin, W. S., *Practical Hints on Landscape Gardening* (1835).
Gough, R., *Sepulchral Monuments*, 5 vols. (1786–96).
Gray, T., *Works in Prose and Verse*, 4 vols. ed. E. Gosse (1884).
Griffith, W. P., *Ancient Gothic Churches* (1847–52).
Grose, F.,
    Antiquities of England and Wales, 8 vols. (1783–97).
    Antiquities of Scotland, 2 vols. (1789–91).
——and Ledwick, E., *Antiquities of Ireland*, 2 vols. (1791–5).
Hadfield, J., *Ecclesiastical, Castellated and Domestic Architecture of England* (1848).
Halfpenny, J. and W., *Chinese and Gothic Architecture Properly Ornamented* (1752).
Halfpenny, J., *Gothic Ornaments in the Cathedral Church of York* (York, 1795).
Hall, J., *Essay on the origin and principles of Gothic Architecture* (Edinburgh, 1797).
Handbook to the Prince Consort National Memorial (1872).
Harris, J.,
    Victorian Architecture (1860).
    Architecture of the Victorian Age (1862).
Hope, A. J. B. Beresford,
    The Common Sense of Art (1858).
    The English Cathedral of the Nineteenth Century (1861).
Hunt, T. F., *Exemplars of Tudor Architecture* (1830).
Hurd, R., *Letters on Chivalry and Romance* (1762).
Jackson, Sir T. G.,
    Modern Gothic Architecture (1873).
    Gothic Architecture in France, England, and Italy (Cambridge, 1915).
    Recollections, ed. B. H. Jackson (Oxford, 1950).
James, J., *On the Use of Brick in Ecclesiastical Architecture* (1847).
Johnson, R. J., *Specimens of Early French Architecture* (1864).
Jones, O., *Grammar of Ornament* (1856).
Kendall, H. E., *Designs for Schools* (1847).
Kendall, J., *Principles of English Architecture* (1818).
Kerr, R., *The Gentleman's House* (1864); ed. J. Mordaunt Crook (1972).
King, T.,
    Specimens of Furniture [c. 1845].
    The Cabinet Maker's Sketch Book [1847].
King, T. H.,
    The Study Book of Mediéval Architecture and Art, 4 vols. (1858–68).
    Orfèvrerie (Bruges, 1852).
Knight, H. Gally,
    An Architectural Tour in Normandy (1836).
    The Normans in Sicily, 2 vols. (1838).
    Saracenic and Norman Remains (1840).
    Ecclesiastical Art of Italy, 2 vols. (1842–4).

Knight, R. Payne,
  The Landscape (1794).
  An Analytical Inquiry into the Principles of Taste (1805).
Langley, B. and T.,
  Gothic Architecture Improved (1742; reprinted 1967).
  Treasury of Designs (1745; reprinted 1967).
  The Builder's Director (1747).
  The Builder's Journal (1757).
Lewis, M. G., *The Monk* (1795); ed. H. Anderson (Oxford, 1973).
Loudon, J. C., *Encyclopaedia of Cottage, Farm and Villa Architecture* (1867 ed.).
Lugar, R.,
  Architectural Sketches for Cottages, Rural Dwellings and Villas (1805).
  The Country Gentleman's Architect (1807).
Micklethwaite, J. T.,
  Modern Parish Churches (1874).
  The Ornaments of the Rubric (1901 ed.).
Middleton, C., *Decorations of Parks and Gardens* (1800).
[Miller, S.], *An 18th-century Correspondence*, ed. L. Dickens and M. Stanton (1910).
Milner, J.,
  History and Antiquities of Winchester (1798).
  A Dissertation on the Modern Style of Altering Ancient Cathedrals (1798).
  A Treatise on the ecclesiastical architecture of England during the Middle Ages (1811).
Moller, G., *Memorials of German-Gothic Architecture*, ed. W. H. Leeds (1836).
Morris, W.,
  Collected Works, 24 vols. ed. M. Morris (1910–15).
  William Morris, ed. G. D. H. Cole (1934).
  Selected Writings and Designs, ed. A. Briggs (1962).
Mozeley, T., *Reminiscences, chiefly of Oriel College and the Oxford Movement*, 2 vols. (1882).
Murphy, J. C., *Plans, Elevations, Sections and Views of the Church of Batalha* (1795).
National Memorial to H.R.H. the Prince Consort (1873).
Neale, J. M. and Webb, B., *The Symbolism of Churches and Church Ornaments: a Translation of the First Book of the Rationale Divinorum Officiorum by William Durandus* (1845; new ed. 1893).
Neale, J. P.,
  Views of Seats, 11 vols. (1818–29).
  Westminster Abbey (1856).
Nesfield, W. E., *Specimens of Medieval Architecture . . . in France and Italy* (1862)
Nicholson, P. and Tredgold, T.,
  Practical Carpentry, Joinery and Cabinet-Making (1854).
  Practical Cabinet Maker [1826–35].
Ottolini, V. and Gruner, L., *The Terra-Cotta Architecture of North Italy* (1867).
Over, C., *Ornamental Architecture in the Gothic, Chinese and Modern Taste* (1758).
Paley, F. A.,
  Illustrations of Baptismal Fonts (1844).

A Manual of Gothic Mouldings (1877 ed.).

Parker, J. H.,

    An Architectural Tour in the English Provinces of France (1850–6).

    An Introduction to the Study of Gothic Architecture (1849; 17th ed. 1913).

    A.B.C. of Gothic Architecture (Oxford, 1881; 11th ed., 1900).

Petit, J. L., *Remarks on Church Architecture*, 2 vols. (1841).

——and Delmotte, *Architectural Studies in France* (1852).

Poole, G. A., *The Appropriate Character of Church Architecture* (1842).

Price, F., *The Cathedral Church of Salisbury* (1756).

Price, U.,

    An Essay on the Picturesque as compared with the Sublime and the Beautiful, 2 vols. (1794–8); ed. Sir J. D. Lauder (Edinburgh, 1842).

    A Dialogue on the distinct characters of the Picturesque and the Beautiful (Hereford, 1801).

Pugin, A. C.,

    Gothic Furniture (1827).

    Gothic Ornaments (1831).

    Architectural Antiquities of Normandy (1827).

——and Willson, E. J. [and Britton, J.], *Specimens of Gothic Architecture*, 2 vols. (1821–3).

——, Pugin, A. W. and Walker, T. L., *Examples of Gothic Architecture*, 3 vols. (1831–8).

Pugin, A. W.,

    Gothic Furniture of the 15th century (1835).

    Designs for Gold and Silver Smiths (1836).

    Contrasts (1836; introduction by H. R. Hitchcock, Leicester, 1969).

    Timber Houses of the 15th and 16th century (1836).

    Designs for Iron and Brass Work in the Style of the 15th and 16th century (1836).

    The True Principles of Pointed or Christian Architecture (1841; reprinted, Oxford 1969).

    The Present State of Ecclesiastical Architecture in England (1843; reprinted, Oxford 1969).

    An Apology for the Revival of Christian Architecture (1843; reprinted, Oxford 1969).

    Glossary of Ecclesiastical Ornament and Costume (1844).

    Floriated Ornament (1849).

    Chancel Screens and Rood Lofts (1851).

Pugin, E. W. (ed.), *Photographs from Sketches by A. W. N. Pugin* (1865).

Pullan, A. (ed.),

    Architectural Designs of William Burges, 2 vols. (1883–7).

    The House of William Burges [1885].

    The Designs of William Burges [1885].

——and Texier, C., *Byzantine Architecture* (1864).

Radcliffe, Anne,

    The Mysteries of Udolpho, 2 vols. (1794; new ed. 1965).

    The Italian (1797; new ed. 1968).

Repton, H.,
   Sketches and Hints on Landscape Gardening (1795).
   Observations on the Theory and Practice of Landscape Gardening (1803).
   Fragments on the Theory and Practice of Landscape Gardening (1816).
Richardson, C. J.,
   Architectural Remains of the reigns of Elizabeth and James I (1840).
   Studies from Old English Mansions (1841).
   Studies of Ornamental Design (1848).
   Picturesque Designs from Mansions etc. (1870).
Rickman, T., *An attempt to Discriminate the Styles of English Architecture* (1819).
Robinson, P. F.,
   Rural Architecture (1823).
   Ornamental Villas (1827).
   Village Architecture (1830).
   Gate Cottages, Lodges and Park Entrances (1837).
   Ornamental Cottages (1838).
Rock, D.,
   The Church of Our Fathers, 3 vols. (1849–53).
   Hierurgia (1851).
Ruskin, J.,
   Complete Works, 38 vols., ed. E. T. Cook and A. Wedderburn (1903–9).
   Diaries, ed. Joan Evans and J. H. Whitehouse, 3 vols. (1956–9).
Scott, Sir G. G.,
   Remarks on Secular and Domestic Architecture (1858).
   Lectures on Medieval Architecture, 2 vols. (1879).
   Personal and Professional Recollections (1879).
   Gleanings from Westminster Abbey (1861).
Scott, G. G. jnr.,
   An Essay on the History of English Church Architecture (1881).
Scott, Sir W., *Waverley Novels*, 24 vols. (1871 ed.).
Seddon, J. P.,
   Progress in Art and Architecture (1852).
   Rambles in the Rhine Provinces (1868).
Sharpe, E.,
   Architectural Parallels (1848).
   A Treatise on the Rise and Progress of Decorated Window Tracery in England, 2 vols.
      (1849).
   The Seven Periods of English Architecture (1888).
Shaw, H.,
   The Art of Illumination (1866).
   Specimens of Ancient Furniture (1836).
   Examples of Ornamental Metalwork (1836).
   Dresses and Decorations of the Middle Ages (1843).
   Decorative Arts of the Middle Ages (1851).
   Specimens of Tile Pavements (1858).

Shaw, R. Norman,
    Architectural Sketches from the Continent (1858).
    Sketches for Cottages and Other Buildings (1878).
——and Jackson, T. G., *Architecture: a Profession or an Art* (1892).
Shenstone, W.,
    Letters, ed. D. Mallam (1939).
    Letters, ed. M. Williams (Oxford, 1939).
Shoolbred, J. & Co., *Designs of Furniture* (1874).
Smith, B. E., *Designs and Sketches for Furniture* (1875).
Smith, G., *Cabinet Maker and Upholsterer's Guide* (1826).
[Society of Antiquaries],
    Vetusta Monumenta, 6 vols. (1747 onwards).
    Cathedrals, 7 vols. (1798 onwards).
Statz, V. and Ungewitter, G., *The Gothic Model Book* (1858).
Stevenson, J. J., *House Architecture*, 2 vols. (1880).
Stothard, C. A., *Monumental Effigies* (1817).
Street, G. E.,
    Brick and Marble in the Middle Ages: Notes on a Tour in North Italy (1855).
    Some Account of Gothic Architecture in Spain (1869 ed.).
    Christ Church Cathedral, Dublin (1882).
    Unpublished Note Books and Reprinted Papers, ed. G. G. King (1916).
Stukeley, W., *Itinerarium Curiosum* (1776).
Switzer, *Ichnographica Rustica* (1718).
Talbert, B. J., *Gothic Forms Applied to Furniture* (1867).
Thomson, P.,
    The Cabinet Maker's Sketch Book [c. 1853].
    The Cabinet Maker's Assistant (1853).
Twopenny, W., *Specimens of Ancient Woodwork* (1859).
Turner, J. Hudson, *Domestic Architecture in England*, 3 vols. (Oxford, 1851–9).
Vardy, J., *Some Designs of Inigo Jones and William Kent* (1744; reprinted 1966).
Verdier, A. and Cattois, F., *Architecture Civile et Domestique*, 2 vols. (Paris, 1852–7).
Viollet-le-Duc, E. E.,
    Dictionnaire Raisonné de l'architecture français du XIe au XVIe siècle, 10 vols.
      (Paris, 1854–68).
    Entretiens sur l'architecture, 2 vols. (Paris, 1863).
    Dictionnaire Raisonné du Mobilier Français, 6 vols. (Paris, 1872–5).
    How to Build a House, trans. B. Bucknall (1874).
    Habitations Modernes, 2 vols. (Paris, 1875–7).
    Compositions et Dessins (Paris, 1884).
Walpole, H.,
    The Castle of Otranto (1765); ed. W. S. Lewis (1964).
    A Description of . . . Strawberry Hill (1784; reprinted 1965).
    Letters, 39 vols. to date, ed. W. S. Lewis (Oxford and Yale, 1937–   ).
    Strawberry Hill Accounts, ed. P. Toynbee (Oxford, 1927).

Warton, Rev. T., Bentham, Rev. J., Grose, Capt. F. and Milner, Rev. J., *Essays on Gothic Archictecture* (1800); ed. J. Taylor (1808).

Weale, J. (ed.),
Quarterly Papers on Architecture, 4 vols. (1844–5).
Gothic Church Architecture (1857–9).

Webb, B., *Sketches of Continental Ecclesiology* (1848).

Whateley, T., *Observations on Modern Gardening* (1770).

Whewell, W., *Architectural Notes on German Churches* (1842 ed.).

Whittington, G. D., *Ecclesiastical Antiquities of France* (1809).

Willemin, N.-X., *Monuments Français Inédits*, ed. A. A. Pottier, 2 vols. (Paris, 1839).

Willis, B., *Cathedrals of Great Britain* (1742).

Willis, R.,
Remarks on the Architecture of the Middle Ages, especially of Italy (Cambridge, 1835).
English Cathedrals (1842–63; reprinted, 2 vols., 1972).
(ed.), *Fac-Simile of the Sketchbook of Willars de Honecourt*, ed. M. J. B. A. de Lassus and M. J. Quicherat (1859).

Winkles, B., *Cathedral Churches of England and Wales*, 3 vols. (1842).

[Winston, C.],
Ancient Glass Painting, 2 vols. (1847); revised ed. (1867).
The Art of Glass-Painting, ed. J. L. Petit (1865).

Wornum, R. H., *Analysis of Ornament* (1860).

Wren Society, 20 vols. (1924–43).

Wren, C. jnr. and Wren, S. (eds.), *Parentalia* (1750; reprinted 1965).

Wright, W., *Grotesque Architecture* (1767).

Wyatt, M. D., *Metal Work and its Artistic Design* (1852).

Yapp, G. W., *Art Industry* [*c.* 1880].

II   Secondary

a. Unpublished theses

Adams, D., "Alfred Waterhouse in Cambridge" (B.A. Cantab., 1962).

Allibone, Jill, "Anthony Salvin" (Ph.D. London, 1977).

Brackenbury, M., "William Butterfield" (B.A. Cantab., 1950).

Colley, E. D., "Thomas Rickman" (M.A. Manchester, 1962).

Crook, J. Mordaunt, "The Career of Sir Robert Smirke, R.A." (D.Phil. Oxon., 1961)

Dixon, R., "James Brooks" (Ph.D. London, 1976).

Evinson, D., "J. A. Hansom" (M.A. London, 1966).

Frew, J. M., "The Antiquarian Influence, with special reference to James Wyatt" (D.Phil. Oxon, 1976).

Hawkes, H. W., "Sanderson Miller" (B.A. Cantab., 1964).

Jolley, R., "The Work of Edmund Sharpe, 1809–77" (M.A. Liverpool, 1966).

McCarthy, M. J., "Amateur Architects in England, 1740–70" (Ph.D. London, 1972).

Mellor, H. D., "Blore's Country Houses" (M.A. Courtauld, 1975).
Middleton, R., "Viollet-le-Duc and the Gothic Rational Tradition" (Ph.D. Cantab., 1959).
Muthesius, S., "Die Anfänge der Hoch-Viktorianischen Architektur, 1849–58" (Ph.D. Marburg, 1967).
Powell, R. A., "Arthur Beresford Pite, 1861–1934" (Dip.Arch. Cantab., 1966).
Quiney, A., "J. L. Pearson" (Ph.D. London, 1974).
Richardson, D., "Gothic Revival Architecture in Ireland" (Ph.D. Yale, 1970).
Rowan, A., "The Castle Style in British Domestic Architecture in the Eighteenth and early Nineteenth Centuries" (Ph.D. Cantab., 1965).
Spence, T. R., "Philip Webb" (B.A. Cantab., 1974).
Stanton, Phoebe, "Welby Pugin and the Gothic Revival" (Ph.D. London, 1950).
Stewart, D. R., "James Essex" (B.A. Cantab., 1964).
Willis, P., "Charles Bridgeman: Royal Gardener" (Ph.D. Cantab., 1962).

b. Monographs, biographies, etc.

Addison, Agnes, *Romanticism and the Gothic Revival* (Philadelphia, 1938).
Addleshaw, G. W. O. and Etchells, F., *The Architectural Setting of Anglican Worship* (1948).
Alexander, B., *England's Wealthiest Son* [Beckford] (1962).
Allen, B. Sprague, *Tides in English Taste, 1619–1800*, 2 vols. (Cambridge, 1937).
Ames, W., *Prince Albert and Victorian Taste* (1967).
Anson, P. F., *Fashions in Church Furnishings, 1840–1940* (1960).
[Arts Council], *The Romantic Movement: Council of Europe Exhibition Catalogue* (1959).
Aslin, Elizabeth, *Nineteenth Century English Furniture* (1962).
Aubin, R. A., *Topographical Poetry in Eighteenth Century England* (New York, 1936).
Barbier, C. F., *William Gilpin* (Oxford, 1963).
Bate, W. J., *From Classic to Romantic: Premises of Taste in Eighteenth Century England* (Harvard, 1964).
Betjeman, J.,
    Ghastly Good Taste (1933); revised ed. (1970).
    First and Last Loves (1952).
    English Parish Churches, 2 vols. (1967).
Birkhead, Edith, *The Tale of Terror: a Study of the Gothic Romance* (1921).
Blomfield, Sir R., *Richard Norman Shaw* (1940).
Boase, T. S. R., *English Art, 1800–70* (1959).
Bøe, A., *From Gothic Revival to Functional Form* (Oxford, 1957).
Bolton, A. T., *The Architecture of Robert and James Adam, 1758–94*, 2 vols. (1922).
Bradbury, R., *The Romantic Theories of Architecture of the Nineteenth Century in Germany, England and France* (New York, 1934).
[Brighton Museum], *Gothick, 1720–1840* (1975).
Briggs, M. S., *Goths and Vandals* (1952).
Brilioth, Y.,
    The Anglican Revival (1925).

Three Lectures on Evangelicalism and the Oxford Movement (Oxford, 1933).
Brion, M., *Romantic Art* (1960).
Brockman, H. A. N., *The Caliph of Fonthill* (1956).
Brown, A. T., *How Gothic Came Back to Liverpool* (1937).
Bumpus, T. F., *London Churches, Ancient and Modern*, 2 vols. (c. 1910).
Burne-Jones, Georgiana, *Memorials of Edward Burne-Jones*, 2 vols. (1904).
Bury, Shirley, *Copy or Creation: Victorian Treasures from English Churches* (1967).
Butler, A. S. G., *J. F. Bentley* (1961).
Carritt, E. F., *A Calendar of British Taste, 1660–1800* (1949).
Casson, H., *Introduction to Victorian Architecture* (1948).
Chadwick, O.,
    The Mind of the Oxford Movement (1962 ed.).
    The Victorian Church i (1966), ii (1970).
Chandler, Alice, *A Dream of Order: the medieval ideal in 19th c. English literature* (1971).
Chase, Isabel, *Horace Walpole: gardenist* (Princeton, 1943).
Church, R. W., *The Oxford Movement, 1833–45* (1891 ed.).
Clark, H. F., *The English Landscape Garden* (1948).
Clark, Lord,
    The Gothic Revival, an Essay in the History of Taste (1964 ed.).
    Ruskin Today (1964).
Clarke, B. F. L.,
    Church Builders of the Nineteenth Century (1938; revised 1969).
    Anglican Cathedrals outside the British Isles (1958).
    The Building of the Eighteenth Century Church (1963).
    Parish Churches of London (1966).
Clifford, D., *A History of Garden Design* (1962).
Collins, P., *Changing Ideals in Modern Architecture, 1750–1950* (1965).
Colvin, H. M.,
    A Biographical Dictionary of British Architects, 1600–1840 (1978).
    Architectural Drawings in the Library of Worcester College Oxford (Oxford, 1964).
——and Craig, M., *Architectural Drawings in the Library of Elton Hall* (Roxburghe Club, 1964).
——and Harris, J. (eds.), *The Country Seat: Studies presented to Sir John Summerson* (1970).
Cornish, E. W., *History of the English Church in the Nineteenth Century*, 2 vols. (1910).
Cotton, V. E., *Liverpool Cathedral* (1942 ed.).
Crook, J. Mordaunt,
    Victorian Architecture: a Visual Anthology (1971).
    William Burges and the High Victorian Dream (1979).
——and Port, M. H., *The History of the King's Works, vol. VI, 1782–1851*, ed. H. M. Colvin (1973).
Curl, J. S., *Victorian Architecture, Its Practical Aspects* (Newton Abbot, 1973).
Dale, A., *James Wyatt, Architect, 1746–1813* (1936); revised ed. (1956).
Davis, T.,
    The Architecture of John Nash (1960).

    John Nash (1966).
    The Gothick Taste (1975).
Douglas, D. C., *English Scholars, 1660–1730* (1951 ed.).
Downes, K.,
    Hawksmoor (1959).
    Hawksmoor (1969).
    The Architecture of Sir John Vanbrugh (1977).
Dutton, R., *The Victorian Home* (1954).
Evans, Joan,
    John Ruskin (1954).
    A History of the Society of Antiquaries (1956).
Faber, G. C., *Oxford Apostles* (1933).
Fallow, T. M., *Cathedral Churches of Ireland* (1894).
Fawcett, Jane and Pevsner, N. (eds.), *Seven Victorian Architects* (1976).
Ferriday, P.,
    Lord Grimthorpe (1957).
    (ed.), *Victorian Architecture* (1964).
Fiddes, V. and Rowan, A., *David Bryce* (Edinburgh, 1976).
Fleming, J., *Robert Adam and His Circle in Edinburgh and Rome* (1962).
Frankl, P., *The Gothic: Literary Sources and Interpretations through Eight Centuries*
    (Princeton, 1960).
German, G., *The Gothic Revival in Europe and Britain* (1972).
Gibbs-Smith, C. H., *The Great Exhibition of 1851* (1950).
Girouard, M.,
    Robert Smythson and the Architecture of the Elizabethan Era (1966).
    The Victorian Country House (Oxford, 1971).
    Sweetness and Light: the Queen Anne Revival (Oxford, 1977).
Goodhart-Rendel, H. S.,
    Vitruvian Nights (1932).
    English Architecture Since the Regency (1953).
Grigson, G., *The Romantics: an anthology* (1972).
Gwynn, D., *Lord Shrewsbury, Pugin and the Catholic Revival* (1946).
Haferkorn, R., *Gotik und Ruine* (Leipzig, 1924).
Halsted, J. B., *Romanticism: selected documents* (1969).
Harbron, D.,
    Amphion, or the Nineteenth Century (1930).
    The Conscious Stone [E. W. Godwin] (1949).
Harris, J.,
    *Catalogue of British Drawings for Architecture, Decoration, Sculpture and Land-
        scape Gardening, 1550–1900, in American Collections* (New Jersey, 1971).
—— and Crook, J. Mordaunt and Harris, Eileen, *Sir William Chambers* (1970).
Harris, R. W., *Romanticism and the Social Order, 1780–1830* (1969).
Harrison, M. and Waters, B., *Burne-Jones* (1973).
Hazen, A. T., *A Bibliography of Horace Walpole* (Yale, 1948).
Henderson, G., *Gothic* (1967).

Henderson, P., *William Morris* (1966).
Hersey, G. L., *High Victorian Gothic: a study in associationism* (Baltimore, 1972).
Hewitt, O. W., *Strawberry Fair* (1956).
Hipple, W. J., *The Beautiful, the Sublime and the Picturesque in 18th-century British Aesthetic Theory* (Carbondale, 1967).
Hitchcock, H. R.,
    Early Victorian Architecture in Britain, 2 vols. (New Haven, 1954).
    Architecture: Nineteenth and Twentieth Centuries (1958).
    Richardson as a Victorian Architect (Baltimore, 1966).
Holmes, M., *Proud Northern Lady* [Lady Anne Clifford] (1975).
Honour, H., *Chinoiserie* (1961).
l'Hôpital, Winifrede de, *Westminster Cathedral and its Architect*, 2 vols. (1919).
Howell, P., *Victorian Churches* (1968).
Hunt, J. D.,
    The Pre-Raphaelite Imagination (1968).
    The Figure in the Landscape (1977).
Hussey, C.,
    The Picturesque, Studies in a Point of View (1927; reprinted 1967).
    English Country Houses: Early, Mid and Late Georgian, 3 vols. (1954–8).
    English Gardens and Landscapes, 1700–50 (1967).
Inglis, K. S., *The Churches and the Working Classes in Victorian England* (1963).
Inglis-Jones, Elisabeth, *Peacocks in Paradise* (1950).
Jervis, S., *Victorian Furniture* (1968).
Jolley, R., *Edmund Sharpe* (Lancaster, 1977).
Jones, Barbara, *Follies and Grottoes* (1953).
Jordan, R. Furneaux, *Victorian Architecture* (1966).
Jourdain, Margaret, *William Kent* (1948).
Kendrick, T. D., *British Antiquity* (1950).
Ketton-Cremer, R. W., *Horace Walpole* (1940).
Kidson, P., Murray, P. and Thompson, P., *History of English Architecture* (1965).
Kimberlin, H. A., *The Return of Catholicism to Leicester* (1946).
Klingender, J. D., *Art and the Industrial Revolution*, ed. Sir A. Elton (1968).
Knox, Bishop, *History of the Oxford Movement* (1933).
Ladd, H. A., *The Victorian Morality of Art: an Analysis of Ruskin's Aesthetic* (New York, 1932).
Law, H. W. and Irene, *The Book of the Beresford Hopes* (1925).
Lethaby, W. R., *Philip Webb and His Work* (1935).
Lewis, W. S.,
    Collector's Progress (1952).
    Horace Walpole (1961).
Linstrum, D., *Sir Jeffry Wyatville* (Oxford, 1972).
Little, B.,
    James Gibbs (1955).
    Catholic Churches since 1623 (1967).
Lough, H. G., *The Influence of John Mason Neale* (1962).

Lovejoy, A. O., *Essays in the History of Ideas* (1948).

Lucas, F. L., *The Decline and Fall of the Romantic Ideal* (New York, 1936).

Macaulay, J., *The Gothic Revival, 1745–1845* (1975).

Mackail, J. W., *Life of William Morris*, 2 vols. (1899).

Macleod, R., *Style and Society: architectural ideology in Britain, 1835–1914* (1971).

McNutt, D. J., *The 18th c. Gothic Novel: an annotated bibliography of criticism* (1975).

Madsen, S. T., *Restoration and Anti-Restoration* (Oslo, 1976).

Malins, E., *English Landscape and Literature* (1966).

Manwaring, Elizabeth, *Italian Landscape in 18th-century England* (New York, 1925; reprinted 1967).

Maugham, H. Hamilton, *Seven Churches* (Hove, 1947).

Monk, S. H., *The Sublime, a study of critical theories in 18th-century England* (1935: Michigan, 1960).

Muthesius, H.,
   Die Neuere Kircliche Baukunst in England (Berlin, 1902).
   Das Englische Haus, 3 vols. (Berlin, 1904–5).

Muthesius, S., *The High Victorian Movement in Architecture, 1850–70* (1972).

Newsome, D., *The Parting of Friends* (1967).

One Hundred Years of British Architecture, 1851–1951 (R.I.B.A., 1951).

Papworth, W. (ed.), *Dictionary of Architecture* (Architectural Publication Society), 8 vols. (1852–92).

Pevsner, N.,
   (ed.), *The Buildings of England*, 47 vols. (1951 onwards).
   Pioneers of Modern Design (1960 ed.).
   Studies in Art, Architecture and Design, 2 vols. (1968).
   Robert Willis (Northampton, U.S.A., 1969).
   Ruskin and Viollet-le-Duc (1969).
   Some Architectural Writers of the 19th c. (Oxford, 1972).
   (ed.), *The Picturesque Garden* (Washington, 1974).

Piggott, S., *William Stukeley* (1950).

Pilcher, D., *The Regency Style* (1947).

Pollen, Anne, *John Hungerford Pollen* (1912).

Port, M. H.,
   Six Hundred New Churches: a Study of the Church Building Commission, 1818–56 (1961).
   (ed.), *The Houses of Parliament* (1976).

Praz, M. and Fairclough, P., *Three Gothic Novels: Otranto, Vathek, Frankenstein* (1968).

Prince, H., *Parks in England* (1967).

Prior, E. S., *The Cathedral Builders in England* (1905).

Pye, D., *The Nature and Art of Workmanship* (1968).

Quennell, P., *Romantic England: Writing and Poetry, 1717–1851* (1970).

Reilly, P., *An Introduction to Regency Architecture* (1948).

Rickman, T. M., *Notes on the life . . . of Thomas Rickman* (1901).

Roberts, J. F. A., *William Gilpin on Picturesque Beauty* (Cambridge, 1944).

Robson-Scott, W. D., *The Literary Background of the Gothic Revival in Germany* (1965).

Roe, F. W., *The Social Philosophy of Carlyle and Ruskin* (New York, 1921).

Rosenberg, J. D., *The Darkening Glass, a Portrait of Ruskin's Genius* (1963).

Rowan, A., *Garden Buildings* (1968).

[Royal Academy], *Victorian and Edwardian Decorative Art* (1972).

[Royal Institute of British Architects], *Catalogue of the Drawings Collection* (1968 onwards).

Saint, A., *Richard Norman Shaw* (1976).

Sambrook, J., *Pre-Raphaelitism* (Chicago, 1974).

Savage, A., *The Parsonage in England* (1964).

Scott, G., *The Architecture of Humanism* (1914).

Service, A. (ed.), *Edwardian Architecture and its Origins* (1975).

Sewter, A. C., *The Stained Glass of William Morris and his Circle*, 2 vols. (1974–6).

Simmons, J., *St Pancras Station* (1968).

Sirén, O., *China and Gardens of Europe of the Eighteenth Century* (New York, 1950).

Smith, Logan Pearsall, *Four Words, Romantic, Originality, Creative, Genius* (Oxford, 1924).

Stanton, Phoebe,
> *The Gothic Revival, and American Church Architecture, 1840–56* (Baltimore, 1968).
> *Pugin* (1971).

Steegman, J.,
> *The Rule of Taste* (1936).
> *Consort of Taste, 1830–70* (1950).

Stewart, C., *Stones of Manchester* (1956).

Street, A. E., *Memoir of G. E. Street* (1888).

Stroud, Dorothy,
> *Capability Brown* (1950); revised ed. (1975).
> *Humphry Repton* (1962).

Summers, M.,
> *The Gothic Quest* (1938; reprinted 1969).
> *A Gothic Bibliography* (1940; reprinted 1969).

Summerson, Sir J.,
> *John Nash, Architect to George IV* (1935).
> *The Architectural Association, 1847–1947* (1947).
> *Georgian London* (1945; revised ed. 1963).
> *Heavenly Mansions and other Essays on Architecture* (1949; New York, 1963).
> *Architecture in Britain, 1530–1830* (1969 ed.).
> *Victorian Architecture: Four Studies in Evaluation* (New York, 1970).
> *The London Building World of the 1860s* (1973).
> *The Turn of the Century: Architecture in Britain around 1900* (Glasgow, 1976).
> *The Architecture of Victorian London* (Charlottesville, 1976).

Sykes, N., *Church and State in England in the 18th century* (Cambridge, 1934).

Symonds, R. W. and Whineray, B. B., *Victorian Furniture* (1962).

Talmon, J. L., *Romanticism and Revolt* (1976).

Taylor, N., *Monuments of Commerce* (1968).

Thompson, E. P., *William Morris, Romantic to Revolutionary* (1955); revised ed. (1977).

Thompson, P.,
> *The Work of William Morris* (1967).
> *William Butterfield* (1970).
> (ed.), *The High Victorian Cultural Achievement* (Victorian Society, 1967).

Thorlby, A. K. (ed.), *The Romantic Movement* (1966).

Towle, E. A., *John Mason Neale* (1906).

Trappes-Lomax, M., *Pugin, a Medieval Victorian* (1932).

Turnor, R., *19th-century Architecture in Britain* (1950).

Vallance, A., *English Church Screens* (1936).

Varma, D. P., *The Gothic Flame: a History of the Gothic Novel in England* (1957).

[Victoria and Albert Museum],
> *Victorian and Edwardian Decorative Art* (1952).
> *Victorian Church Art* (1971).
> *Marble Halls* (1973).
> *High Victorian Design* (1974).

Weir, R. Schultz, *William Richard Lethaby* (1938).

Westlake, N. H. J., *A History of Design in Painted Glass*, 4 vols. (1881–94).

Whiffen, M., *Stuart and Georgian Churches: the architecture of the Church of England outside London, 1603–1837* (1947–8).

Whistler, L., *The Imagination of Vanbrugh and his Fellow Artists* (1954).

White, J. F., *The Cambridge Movement* (1962).

Whitehouse, J. H. (ed.), *Ruskin's Influence Today* (1945).

Wilson, H., *A Memorial of . . . J. D. Sedding* (1892).

Williams, N. P. and Harris, C., *Northern Catholicism* (1933).

Willis, P. (ed.), *Furor Hortensis* (Edinburgh, 1974).

c. Articles

(Excluding articles reprinted in book form or already cited in the Appendix.)

Acloque, G. and Cornforth, J., "The Eternal Gothic of Eaton", *C.L.* cxlix (1971), 304–7, 360–4.

Adams, M. B., "Architects from George IV to George V", *R.I.B.A. Jnl.* (1912), 598–607, 643–54.

Anson, P. F., "Sir J. N. Comper", *Trans. Scottish Ecclesiological Soc.* (1950).

Aston, Margaret, "English Ruins and English History: The Dissolution and the Sense of the Past", *Jnl. Warburg and Courtauld Institutes* xxvi (1973), 231–55.

Bailey, B., "Racton Tower, Sussex", *C.L.* cxlv (1969), 682.

Bell, C. F., "Thomas Gray and the Fine Arts", *Essays and Studies by Members of the English Assocn.* xxx (1944), 50–81.

Bence-Jones, M., "Shane's Castle, Antrim Castle, Castle Upton", *C.L.* cxlix (1971), 1037–8.

Betjeman, J., "J. N. Comper", *A.R.* lxxxv (1939), 79–82.

Binney, M., "Mapledurham House, Oxon.", *C.L.* cxlix (1971), 1152–6, 1216–19.

Boase, T. S. R., "An Oxford College and the Gothic Revival", *Jnl. Warburg and Courtauld Institutes* xviii (1955), 145–88.

Bond, Sheila, "Henry Emlyn of Windsor", *C.L.* cxxxii (1962), 607–9.

Boynton, L. O. J., "High Victorian Furniture: the example of March and Jones of Leeds", *Jnl. of the Furniture Hist. Soc.* iii (1967), 54–91.

Brandon-Jones, J., "The Work of Philip Webb and Norman Shaw", *Jnl. Architectural Assocn.* lxxi (1955), 9–21.

Bryson, J., "The Balliol That Might Have Been", *C.L.* cxxxiii (1963), 1558–61.

Bury, Shirley, "In Search of Pugin's Church Plate", *Connoisseur* clxv (1967), 29–35.

Butler, A. S. G., "Castle Drogo, Devon", *C.L.* xcviii (1945), 200–3, 244–7.

Chettle, H. F., "Fonthill", *Wilts. Mag.* xlix (1942), 505–12.

Clapham, Sir A., "The Survival of Gothic in 17th-century England", *Archaeological Jnl.* cvi (1952), 4–9.

Clark, H. F.,
    "18th century Elysiums", *Warburg Institute Jnl.* vi (1943), 165–89.
    "Lord Burlington's Bijou, or Sharawaggi at Chiswick", *A.R.* xcv (1944), 125–9.
    "R. Payne Knight and the Picturesque tradition", *Town Planning Rev.* xix (1947), 142–52.
    "The Sense of Beauty in the 18th, 19th and 20th centuries: aesthetic values in English landscape appreciation", *Landscape Architecture* xlvii (1957), 465–9.

Colvin, H. M.,
    "Gothic Survival and Gothick Revival", *A.R.* civ (1948), 91–8.
    "The Origins of the Gothic Revival in England", *Atti Accademia Nazionale dei Lincei,* 1977.

Conant, K., "Horace Walpole and the Gothic Revival", *Old Wedgwood* xii (1945), 62–9.

Cooper, J., "Victorian Furniture", *Apollo* xcv (1972), 115–22.

Cordingley, R. A., "James Wyatt at Durham", *Trans. Ancient Monuments Soc.* iii (1955), 31–55.

Cornforth, J.,
    "A Countess's London Castle", *Country Life Annual* 1970, 138–9.
    "Adare Manor, co. Limerick", *C.L.* cxlv (1969), 1230–4, 1302–6, 1366–9.
    "Dunsany Castle, co. Meath", *C.L.* cxlix (1971), 1296–1300, 1364–7.
    "Auckland Castle, co. Durham", *C.L.* cli (1972), 198–202, 266–70, 334–7.

Crook, J. Mordaunt,
    "The Restoration of the Temple Church: Ecclesiology and Recrimination", *Architectural History* viii (1965), 39–51.
    "John Britton and the Genesis of the Gothic Revival", in *Concerning Architecture Essays . . . presented to Nikolaus Pevsner,* ed. Sir J. Summerson (1968), 98–119.
    "The Pre-Victorian Architect: Professionalism and Patronage", *Architectural History* xii (1969), 62–78.
    "Xanadu by the Black Sea: the Woronzow Palace at Aloupka", *C.L.* cli (1972), 513–17.
    "Patron Extraordinary: John, 3rd. Marquess of Bute", in *Victorian South Wales,* ed. P. Howell (Victorian Society, 1970), 3–22.
    "Thomas Harrison: a Reluctant Goth", *C.L.* cxlix (1971), 876–9, 1539.

"Northumbrian Gothick", *Jnl. Royal Soc. of Arts* cxxi (1973), 271–83.

"Strawberry Hill Revisited", *C.L.* cliii (1973), 1598–1602, 1726–30, 1794–7, 1886.

"Knightshayes, Devon: Burges versus Crace", *National Trust Year Book* i (1975–6), 44–55.

"Italian Influence on Victorian Gothic", *Atti Accademia Nazionale dei Lincei*, 1977.

de Beer, E. S., "Gothic: Origin and Diffusion of the Term", *Jnl. Warburg and Courtauld Institutes* xi (1948), 143–62.

Dodd, D., "Salvin at Dunster Castle", *National Trust Year Book* ii (1976–77), 88–99.

Downes, K., "Vanbrugh Castle, Mince Pie House, etc.", *C.L.* clix (1976), 1406–8.

Edwards, T.,
"The Gothic Revival in Wales", *Wales* winter 1946, 109–15.
"Pugin and his circle", *Blackfriars* xxvii (1946), 209–13.

Ferriday, P.,
"Francis Price", *A.R.* civ (1953), 327–8.
"The Revival: stories ancient and modern", *A.R.* cxxi (1957), 155–7.
"Professor Moore", *A.R.* cxxvii (1960), 271–2.
"The Church Restorers", *A.R.* cxxxvi (1964), 87–95.

Fleming, J.,
"Adam Gothic", *Connoisseur* cxlii (1958), 75–9.
"William Kent at Rousham", *Connoisseur* cliii (1963), 158–65.
"Robert Adam's Castle Style", *C.L.* cxliii (1968), 1356–9, 1443–7.

Floud, P.,
"Victorian Furniture", in *Concise Encyclopaedia of Antiques* iii, ed. L. G. G. Ramsay (1967).
"Furniture", in *Connoisseur Period Guides: Early Victorian* (1958).

Forge, J. W. Lindus, "Kentissime", *A.R.* cvi (1949), 186–9.

French, C., Stroud, Dorothy, *et al.*, "Triangular Follies", *C.L.* cxvi (1954), 1673; cxxiii (1958), 210, 462, 655, 713, 1019; cxxiv (1958), 236.

Gage, G., "Turner and the Picturesque", *Burlington Mag.* cvii (1965), 16–25, 75–81.

Gemmett, R. J., "The Critical Reception of William Beckford's Fonthill", *English Miscellany* xix (1968), 133–51.

Girouard, M.,
"Alscot Park, Warwicks.", *C.L.* cxxiii (1958), 1064–7, 1124–7, 1184–7.
"Red House, Bexleyheath, Kent", *C.L.* cxxvii (1960), 1382–5.
"Bayons Manor, Lincs.", *C.L.* cxxvii (1960), 430–3.
"Abercairney, Perths.", *C.L.* cxxix (1961), 506–9, 584–7.
"Castleward, co. Down", *C.L.* cxxx (1961), 1260–3, 1320–3, 1534.
"Glin Castle, co. Limerick", *C.L.* cxxxv (1964), 446–50, 502–5.
"Dogmersfield Park, Hants", *C.L.* cxxv (1964), 20–2.
"Lismore Castle, co. Waterford", *C.L.* cxxxvi (1964), 336–40, 389–93.
"Birr Castle, co. Offaly", *C.L.* cxxxvii (1965), 410–14, 468–71, 526–9.
"English Art and the Rococo", *C.L.* cxxxix (1966), 58–61, 188–90, 224–7.
"Swiss Cottage, Cahir", *C.L.* cxl (1966), 688–91.

"Elizabethan Architecture and the Gothic Tradition", *Architectural History* vi (1963), 23–39.

"Milton Ernest Hall, Beds.", *C.L.* cxlv (1969), 1042–6.

"Cragside, Northumberland", *C.L.* cxlvi (1969), 1640–3, 1694–7.

"George Devey in Kent", *C.L.* cxlix (1971), 744–7, 812–5.

"Victorian Church Art", *C.L.* cl (1971), 1354–5.

"Tullynally Castle, co. Westmeath", *C.L.* cl (1971), 1780–3, 1834–7.

"Blackmoor House, Hants.", *C.L.* clvi (1974), 554–7.

—— and Baron Porcelli, "Mount Edgcumbe, Cornwall", *C.L.* cxxviii (1960), 1550–3, 1598–1601.

Godfrey, W.,

"The Work of George Devey", *A.R.* xxi (1907), 23–30, 83–8, 293–306.

"George Devey", *R.I.B.A. Jnl.* xiii (1906), 501–25.

Goodhart-Rendel, H. S.,

"English Gothic Architecture of the 19th century", *R.I.B.A. Jnl.* xxxi (1924), 321–30.

"English Architecture, 1834–1934", in *The Growth and Work of the R.I.B.A.*, ed. J. A. Gotch (1934).

"The English Home in the 19th century", *Architect's Jnl.* cviii (1948), 449–50, 469–70.

"Rogue Architects of the Victorian Era", *R.I.B.A. Jnl.* lvi (1949), 251–9.

Gray, W. F., "The Scott Monument and its Architect", *A.R.* xcvi (1944), 26–7.

Gregory-Jones, D., "Towers of Learning", *A.R.* cxxiii (1958), 393–8.

Grigson, G.,

"Vicarage Picturesque", *A.R.* xciv (1943), 107–10.

"Fingal's Cave", *A.R.* civ (1948), 51–4.

Hadfield, M., "The History of the Ha Ha", *C.L.* cxxxii (1963), 1261–2.

Hague, D. B., "Penrhyn Castle", *Trans. Caernarvonshire Hist. Soc.* (1959).

Handley-Read, C.,

"Notes on William Burges's Painted Furniture", *Burlington Mag.* cv (1963), 496–509.

"England, 1830–1901", in *World Furniture*, ed. Helena Hayward (1965).

"Aladdin's Palace in Kensington", *C.L.* cxxxix (1966), 600–4.

"Cork Cathedral", *A.R.* cxii (1967), 422–30.

Harbron, D.,

"J. F. Bentley", *Architect's Jnl.* lxxxix (1939), 159–60.

"Thomas Harris", *A.R.* xcii (1942), 63–6.

"Queen Anne Taste and Aestheticism", *A.R.* xciv (1943), 15–18.

"Edward Godwin", *A.R.* xcviii (1945), 48–52.

Harris, Eileen,

"Thomas Wright", *C.L.* cl (1971), 492–5, 546–50, 612–15.

"Batty Langley: a Tutor to Freemasons", *Burlington Mag.* cxix (1977), 327–35.

Harris, J.,

"Exoticism at Kew", *Apollo* lxxviii (1963), 103–8.

"Pritchard Redivivus", *Architectural History* xi (1968), 17–24.

—— *et al.*, "Waynflete's Tower [Esher Place], Surrey", *C.L.* lxxxvi (1939), 77 and cxxv (1959), 1076–8; *Builder* clv (1938), 1159; *Burlington Mag.* lxxiv (1939), 99; *The Times* 11 Feb. 1939 p. 8.

—— and Alexander, B., "Fonthill, Wilts.", *C.L.* cxl (1966), 1370–4, 1430–4, 1748.

Harrison, M., "Victorian Stained Glass", *Connoisseur* clxxxiii (1973), 194–9, 251–4; clxxxvii (1974), 144.

Haskell, F., "A Monument and its Mysteries", [Albert Memorial], *Revue de l' Art* xxx (1975), 61–76, 104–10.

Heilman, R. B., "Fielding and the first Gothic Revival", *Modern Language Notes* lvii (1942), 671–3.

Hersey, G. L., "J. C. Loudon and Architectural Associationism", *A.R.* cxliv (1968), 89–92.

Hitchcock, H. R.,
"Victorian Monuments of Commerce", *A.R.* cv (1949), 61–74.
"High Victorian Architecture", *Victorian Studies* i (1957), 47–71.
"G. E. Street in the 1850s", *Jnl. Soc. of Architectural Historians* (U.S.A.), xix (1960), 145–72.

Holroyd, J. E., "J. M. Neale", *C.L.* cxl (1966), 1518–19.

Hussey, C.,
"Hartlebury Castle, Worcs.", *C.L.* lxix (1931), 156–62.
"Culzean Castle, Ayrshire", *C.L.* xcviii (1945), 956–9.
"Tong Castle, Salop.", *C.L.* c (1946), 578–81.
"Rousham, Oxon.", *C.L.* xcix (1946), 900–3, 946–9, 1084–7, 1130–3; c (1946), 34, 80, 127, 266, 356.
"Staunton Harold, Leics.", *C.L.* cvii (1950), 516–19.
"18, Stafford Terrace, Kensington", *C.L.* cxi (1952), 996–9.
"Donnington Grove, Berks.", *C.L.* cxxiv (1958), 588–91, 654–7, 714–17.
"Fort Belvedere, Surrey", *C.L.* cxxvi (1959), 898–901, 960–3.
"Endsleigh, Devon", *C.L.* cxxx (1961), 246–9, 296–9.
"R. Payne Knight: a Regency Prophet of Modernism", *C.L. Annual* (1956).

—— and Taylor, G. C., "Royal Lodge, Windsor", *C.L.* lxxxv (1939), 706–12.

Honour, H., "Lee Priory, Kent", *C.L.* cxi (1952), 1665–6.

Ingram, M. E., "John Carr's Contribution to the Gothic Revival", *Georgian Soc. East Yorks*, ii (1947–8), pt. 3, 43–52.

—— and Eden, W. A., "Carr of York and Gothic Taste", *C.L.* cvi (1949), 692, 838, 910.

—— and Johnson, F. F., "Grimston Garth, Yorks", *C.L.* cxii (1952), 1186–8.

Isaacs, J., "Gothick Taste", *R.I.B.A. Jnl.* lix (1952), 336–40.

Jackson-Stops, J.,
"Newstead Abbey, Notts.", *C.L.* clv (1974), 1122–5.
"Plas Newydd, Anglesey", *C.L.* clix (1976), 1686–9; clx (1976), 18–21.
"Tissington Hall, Derbyshire", *C.L.* clx (1976), 214–7.
"Beaufront Castle, Northum.", *C.L.* clix (1976), 286–9, 342–5.

Jordan, R. Furneaux, "Pugin's Clients", *Cornhill Mag.* Autumn 1962.

Jourdain, M., Whiffen, M., Westwood, L. *et al.*, Grottoes and Shell Houses, *C.L.* xcv (1944), 242–3, 385 and ciii (1948), 924–5; *A.R.* ciii (1948), 216–17; *Notes and Queries* clxxxii (1942), 230–1, 333–4; clxxxiii (1942), 27–8, 51, 113–14, 179, 328–9; clxxxiv (1943), 113.

Kirby, H. T., "Bloxam's Principles", *A.R.* ciii (1948), 27–8.

Kliger, S., "The Goths in England: an introduction to the Gothic vogue in 18th-century aesthetic discussion", *Modern Philology* xliii (1945), 107–17.

Lang, S.,
    "The Principles of the Gothic Revival in England", *Jnl. Soc. of Architectural Historians* (U.S.A.), xxv (1966), 240–67.
    "R. Payne Knight and the Idea of Modernity", in *Concerning Architecture: Essays . . . presented to Nikolaus Pevsner*, ed. Sir J. Summerson (1968), 85–97.

Lawson, J. and Waterson, M., "Pritchard at Powis", *National Trust Year Book* i (1975–6), 8–11.

Lees-Milne, J.,
    "19th-century architectural pasticheurs", *Horizon* xi (1945), 411–28.
    "Hartlebury Castle Revisited", *C.L.* cl (1976), 672–5, 740–3.
—— and Gotch, C., "Inverary Castle, Argyllshire", *C.L.* xcv (1944), 342, 516; cxiii (1953), 2060–3. .

Lewis, W. S.,
    "The Genesis of Strawberry Hill", *Metropolitan Museum Studies* v (1934–6), 66–86.
    "H. Walpole, Antiquary", in *Essays Presented to Sir Lewis Namier*, ed. R. Pares and A. J. P. Taylor (1956), 178–203.

McCarthy, M. J.,
    "The Work of Hanbury Tracy, Lord Sudeley, at Hampton Court", *Woolhope Trans.* xxxviii (1964), 71–5.
    "Tracy of Toddington Manor", *Trans. Bristol and Glos. Archaeol. Soc.* lxxxix (1965), 161–74.
    "Sir Roger Newdigate: Drawings for Copt Hall, Essex, and Arbury Hall, Warwicks.", *Architectural Hist.* xvi (1973), 26–36.
    "Horace Walpole, John Chute and Strawberry Hill", *Walpole Soc.* (1977).
    "John Chute: Drawings for The Vyne", *National Trust Year Book* i (1975–6), 70–80.
    "18th c. Cathedral Restoration", *Studies* lxv (1976), 330–43; lxvi (1977), 60–76.

Meeks, C. V. L., "Picturesque Eclecticism", *Art Bulletin* xxxii (1950), 226–35.

Middleton, R. D., "The Abbé de Cordemoy and the Graeco-Gothic Ideal: a Prelude to Romantic Classicism", *Jnl. Warburg and Courtauld Institutes* xxv (1962), 278–320 and xxvi (1963), 90–123.

Morris, Barbara, "The Harborne Room", *Victoria and Albert Museum Bulletin* iv (1968), 82–95.

Mostyn, Elfrida, "Abney Hall, Cheshire", *C.L.* cxxxiii (1963), 846–9, 910–13.

Musgrave, C., "Arbury, Warwicks.", *Connoisseur* clxiii (1966), 1–8.

Nares, G.,
    "Hagley Hall, Worcs.", *C.L.* cxxii (1957), 546–9, 608–11.

"Painshill, Surrey", *C.L.* cxxiii (1958), 18–21, 62–5.

Oswald, A.,

"Radway Grange, Warwicks.", *C.L.* c (1946), 440–3, 486–9.

"Croft Castle, Herefs.", *C.L.* cvii (1950), 1206–10, 1292–6.

"Hawkestone, Salop.", *C.L.* cxxiii (1958), 640–3, 698–701; cxxiv (1958), 18–21, 72–5, 368–71.

"Casewick, Lincs." *C.L.* cxxxvi (1964), 1762–6, 1808–12.

Pace, G. G., "Alfred Bartholemew, a pioneer of functional Gothic", *A.R.* xcii (1942), 99–102.

Pass, A., "Thomas Worthington: Practical Idealist", *A.R.* clv (1974), 268–74.

Pevsner, N.,

"The Picturesque in Architecture", *R.I.B.A. Jnl.* lv (1947), 55–61.

"An 18th-century Improver" [R. Payne Knight], *Listener* xxxvii (1947), 204–5.

"The Other Chambers", *A.R.* ci (1947), 195–8.

"How to judge Victorian Architecture", *Listener* xlv (1951), 91, 137, 177, 217.

"Originality: Goodhart-Rendel's defence of the Victorians", *A.R.* cxv (1954), 367–9.

"Architecture and William Morris", *R.I.B.A. Jnl.* lxiv (1957), 172–5.

"William Whewell and his architectural notes on German Churches", *German Life and Letters* xxii (1968), 39–48.

—— [as P. F. R. Donner], "A Harris Florilegium", *A.R.* xciii (1943), 51–2.

—— and Lang, S., "Sir William Temple and Sharawaggi", *A.R.* cvi (1949), 391–3.

Piper, J.,

"Decrepit Glory" [Hafod], *A.R.* lxxxvii (1940), 207–10.

"St. Marie's Grange", *A.R.* xcviii (1945), 91–3.

Port, M. H., "The New Law Courts Competition 1866–7", *Architectural History* xi (1968), 75–93.

Powell, H. J., "Herefordshire Churches of the Gothic Revival", *Woolhope Trans.* xl (1972)304–11.

Redfern, H., "W. Butterfield and H. Woodyer", *Architect and B.N.* clxxviii (1944), 21–2, 44–5, 58–60; *Builder* clxvi (1944), 295.

Richardson, Sir A., "The Gothic Revival in the Early 18th century", *R.I.B.A. Jnl.* liii (1946), 457–9.

Roberts, H. V. Molesworth, "L. A. Stokes", *A.R.* c (1946), 173–7.

Rose, E., "The Stone Table in the Round Church and the Crisis of the Cambridge Camden Society", *Victorian Studies* x (1967), 119–44.

Rowan, A.,

"Georgian Castles in Ireland", *Bull. of Irish Georgian Soc.* vii (1964), 3–30.

"Taymouth Castle, Perths.", *C. L.* cxxxvi (1964), 912–16, 978–81, 1150, 1289, 1344.

"Ugbrooke Park, Devon", *C.L.* cxlii (1967), 138–41, 203–7, 266–70.

"Eastnor Castle, Herefs.", *C.L.* cxliii (1968), 524–7, 606–9, 668–71.

"Dunninald Angus", *C.L.* cxlvi (1969), 384–7.

"Raby Castle, co. Durham", *C.L.* cxlvi (1969), 78–81, 150–3; cxlvii (1970), 18–21, 66–9, 186–9 *Architectural History* xv (1972), 23–50.

"Killyleagh Castle, co. Down", *C.L.* cxlvii (1970), 690–3, 774–7.

"Robert Adam's Castles", *C.L.* clvi (1974), 354–7, 430–3, 494–7.

"The Adam Castle Style", *Jnl. Royal Soc. of Arts* cxxii (1974), 679–94.

"Batty Langley's Gothic", in *Studies in Memory of David Talbot Rice* (Edinburgh, 1975), 197–215.

"The Castle Style in British Domestic Architecture, 1770–1820", *Atti Accademia Nazionale dei Lincei*, 1977.

Sewter, A. C., "Victorian Stained Glass", *Apollo* lxxvi (1962), 760–5.

Sirr, H., "A. W. Pugin", *R.I.B.A. Jnl.* xxv (1918), 213–26.

Smith, H. Clifford, "Henry Keene", *C.L.* xcvii (1945), 556, 738.

Stanton, Phoebe,

"Pugin at Twenty One", *A.R.* cx (1951), 187–90.

"Some Comments on the Life and Work of A. W. N. Pugin", *R.I.B.A. Jnl.* 3rd ser. lx (1952), 47–54.

"Principles of Design versus Revivalism", *Jnl. Soc. of Architectural Historians* (U.S.A.), xiii (1954), 20.

"Sources of Pugin's *Contrasts*", in *Concerning Architecture: Essays . . . presented to Nikolaus Pevsner*, ed. Sir J. Summerson (1968), 120–39.

Stewart, D. R., "James Essex", *A.R.* cviii (1950), 317–21.

Summerson, Sir J.,

"An Early Modernist: James Wild and his Work", *Architects' Jnl.* lxix (1929), 57–62.

"An Idealist's Achievement: New College, Finchley Road", *Architect and B.N.* cxliii (1935), 338–9 [unsigned].

"James Wyatt", in *From Anne to Victoria*, ed. B. Dobrée (1937).

"Pugin Effigy: a Chistmas Reminiscence", *Architect and B.N.* clxiv (1940), 181–2.

"Blaise Hamlet", *C.L.* lxxxvi (1939), 396–7; *Architect and B.N.* clxxv (1943), 168–9.

"Norman Shaw", *Listener* xxv (1941), 493.

"Pugin at Ramsgate", *A.R.* ciii (1948), 163–6.

"The London Suburban Villa", *A.R.* civ (1948), 63–72.

"Ruskin, Morris and the 'Anti-Scrape' Philosophy", in *Historic Preservation Today* (Williamsburg, 1966).

—— *et al.*, "Gothic", *A.R.* December 1945.

Symondson, A., "Medieval Taste in Victorian Churches", *C.L.* cxli (1967), 1400–3.

Taylor, N.,

"Wagnerian High Church", *A.R.* cxxxvii (1965), 213–17.

"Byzantium in Brighton", *A.R.* cxxxix (1966), 275–7.

—— and Symondson, A., "Burges and Morris at Bingley", *A.R.* cxliv (1968), 35–8.

Temple, H., "Nash at Attingham and High Legh", *A.R.* clx (1976), 96–100; clxii (1977), 133–4.

Thompson, P.,

"All Saints Church, Margaret Street, Reconsidered", *Architectural History* viii (1965), 73–94.

"Butterfield's Australian Churches", *C.L.* cl (1971), 622–4, 686–90.

Thorpe, W. A., "Rococo to Romanticism", *Times Literary Supp.* 24 April 1946, 187.
Till, E., "Capability Brown at Burghley", *C.L.* clviii (1975), 982–5.
Tipping, H. Avray,
    "Belhus, Essex", *C.L.* xlvii (1920), 656–62, 690–6.
    "Strawberry Hill", *C.L.* lvi (1924), 18–25, 56–64.
Verey, D., "Three Churches by G. F. Bodley", *C.L.* cxlix (1971), 1160–2, 1246–9.
Wainright, C.,
    "Davington Priory, Kent", *C.L.* cl (1971), 1650–3, 1716–19.
    "Specimens of Ancient Furniture", *Connoisseur* clxxxvi (1973), 105–13.
    "Gothic, 1720–1840", *Connoisseur* clxxxix (1975), 325–6.
Warren, E., "The Life and Work of G. F. Bodley", *R·I·B·A· Jnl.* xvii (1910), 305–40.
Whiffen, M.,
    "In the Modern Gothic Manner" [Tetbury Church], *A·R·* xcvi (1944), 2–4.
    "Rickman at Cambridge", *A·R·* xcviii (1945), 160.
    "Apollo's Proper Priest" [William Kent], *A·R·* civ (1948), 161–3; *Listener* xxxix
      (1948), 653–4, 705.
—— *et al.*, "Shobdon, Herefs.", *C.L.* xciii (1943), 315–16; cxv (1954), 101.
Walker, J. H., "Belvoir Castle, Leics.", *Trans. Thoroton Soc.* xli (1937), 87–90.
Williamson, R. P. Ross, Hussey, C., Girouard, M., *et al.*, "Alton, Staffs.", *A·R·* lxxxvii
    (1940), 156–64 and lxxxviii (1940), 36; *C.L.* cxxvii (1960), 1246–9, 1304–7 and
    cxxviii (1960), 1226–9; *Dublin Rev.* ccxviii (1946), 73–9.
Willis, P., "Charles Bridgeman", *Listener* lxxii (1964), 1007–9.
Wilson, Francesca, "Ypres at Bethnal Green" [Columbia Market], *A·R·* xcvi (1944),
    130–4.
Winney, J. and H., "The Wings of North Luffenham", *C.L.* cxliii (1968), 1535–6.
Winstone, F. R., "Hartwell Church", *C.L.* lxxxviii (1940), 464.
Wood, A. C. and Hawkes, W., "Sanderson Miller of Radway and his Work at Wroxton",
    Cake and Cockhorse [Banbury], iv, no. 6, 79–110.
Wood, G. Bernard, "Bishopsthorpe, Yorks.", *C.L.* cxxx (1961), 566–8.
Woodbridge, K., "William Kent's Gardening: the Rousham Letters", *Apollo* c (1974),
    282–91.
Wrinch, Ann Martha, "George Kemp and the Scott Monument", *C.L.* cl (1971),
    322–3.
Young, R. A., Winstone, F. R., *et al.*, "Arno's Castle, Bristol", *C.L.* lxxxix (1941), 86;
    ci (1947), 50; civ (1948), 888, 1117; cix (1951), 1880–1; cxxii (1957), 25; *Builder*
    clxxi (1946), 584–8.

2. St John's College, Cambridge: Oriel window in the library (1624)

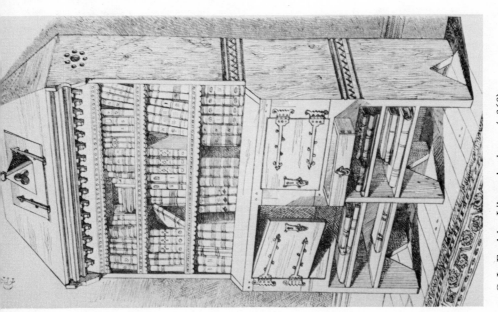

1. C. L. Eastlake: Library book case (1868)

Robert Smythson: Wollaton Hall, Nottinghamshire (1580–8)

Roger Morris: Inverary Castle, Argyllshire (begun 1745)

6. Edward Woodward, John Phillips and George Shakespeare:
Alscot Park, Warwickshire (1750–2; 1762–9)

7. Strawberry Hill: North Front (begun 1749)

Sanderson Miller: Gothick Ruin, Wimpole, Cambridgeshire (1750)

9. Batty Langley:
Gothick Chimneypiece (1742)

10. William Kent: Court of King's Bench, Westminster Hall (1739)

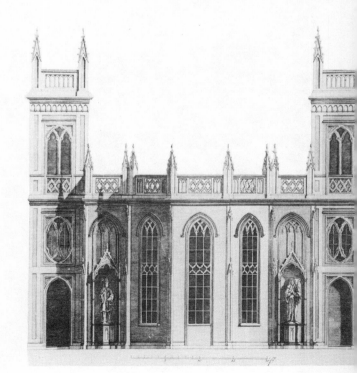

11. J. H. Muntz:
The Gothick Cathedral,
Kew (c. 1758)

Downton Castle, Herefordshire (1772–8)

Robert Adam: Airthrey Castle, Perthshire (1790)

6. Canterbury Cathedral: 'Section of south transept and part of tower;
elevation of north transept and part of tower'

18. William Butterfield: All Saints, Margaret Street, London (1850–9)

21. Philip Webb:
Houses and shops,
91–101 Worship Street,
Finsbury, London (1862–3)

22. Thomas Harris:
Terrace at Harrow, Middlesex,
in 'the Victorian style'
(1860–1)

23. S. S. Teulon:
Elvetham Hall, Hampshire
(1859–60)

24. E. Buckton Lamb:
St Martin, Vicars Road,
St Pancras, London (1866)

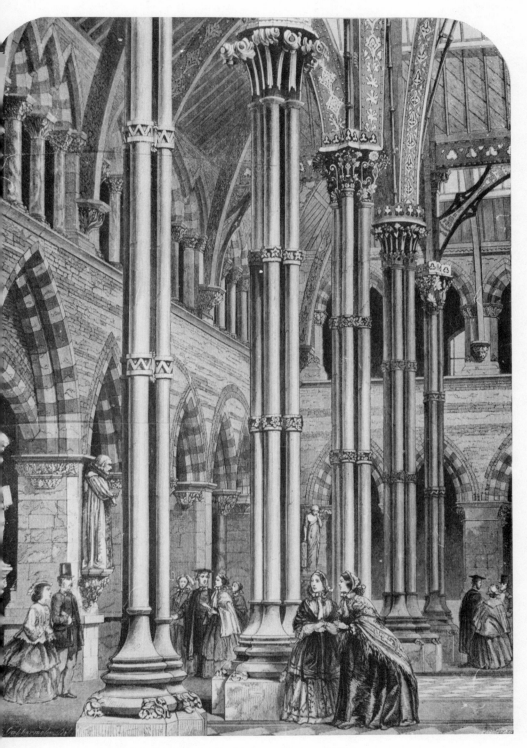

Sir T. Deane and B. Woodward: The Oxford Museum (1855–68)

26. Alfred Waterhouse: Manchester Town Hall (1868–77)

INDEX OF PERSONS AND PLACES

References to Eastlake's text are shown thus: 256 or 290 (plate). References to new material are shown thus: ⟨47⟩. References to numbered entries in the appendix are shown in italic numerals thus: 253. References to plates in the section of new illustrations preceding this index are shown thus: plate 13.